SPECIAL EFFECTS
GAME PROGRAMMING
WITH DIRECTX®

MASON MCCUSKEY

PREMIER PRESS

GAME DEVELOPMENT

Premier

p

Press

Publisher: Stacy L. Hiquet
Marketing Manager: Heather Buzzingham
Managing Editor: Sandy Doell
Series Editor: André LaMothe
Acquisitions Editor: Emi Smith
Project Editor: Heather Talbot
Technical Reviewer: Todd Barron
Copy Editors: Kate Talbot, Jenny Davidson, Mitzi Foster
Interior Layout: Bill Hartman
Cover Design: Mike Tanamachi
Indexer: Sharon Shock
Proofreader: Kim Cofer

NVIDIA and GeForce 3 are registered trademarks of NVIDIA Corporation.

Microsoft, DirectX, Visual C++, Windows 98/Me/2000/XP are registered trademarks of Microsoft Corporation, Inc.

Pyromania is a registered trademark of Visual Concept Entertainment (VCE).

Paint Shop Pro is a registered trademark of Jasc Software.

Bitmap Font Builder is on the CD, courtesy of LMNOPC.

Galaxy is on the CD, courtesy of Diard Software.

The VectorC Compiler is on the CD, courtesy of Codeplay™.

ISBN: 1-931841-06-3

Library of Congress Catalog Card Number: 2001096214

Printed in the United States of America

02 03 04 05 RI 10 9 8 7 6 5 4 3 2

To my wife, Carly

"I fell in love with her courage, her sincerity, and her flaming self-respect... I love her and that's the beginning of everything."
——F. Scott Fitzgerald

Acknowledgments

In no particular order, I'd like to acknowledge the following individuals.

Let me start by saying thank you to André LaMothe, for taking a chance on someone who had never written a book before. Thank you to my technical editor, Todd Barron, and to the staff of Premier Press—Jody, Tracy, Heather, Kate, and Emi—who edited my work, kept the project on track and answered the myriad newbie questions this author had. Without these folks, there would be no book.

Thank you Dave Astle, Ernest Pazera, Kevin Hawkins, John Munsch, Mike Tanczos, John Hattan, and the rest of the GameDev.net staff, for creating a game development site that's actually useful, instead of just self-aggrandizing, and thank you for letting me contribute to its success. You rock, and the stuff you've created proves it.

Thank you Mike Wallace and Leslie Grimm, for creating Robot Odyssey for the Apple II, the game that made me want to be a game programmer.

Thank you Scott Meyers, Steve McConnell, Bjarne Stroustrup, John Vlissides, Erich Gamma, Richard Helm, and Ralph Johnson, for sharing your ideas with the rest of us.

Thanks to my parents for enduring me during my turbulent formative years, and to my brother Donald, for always being up for one last round of multiplayer. Thanks to my parents-in-law, brother-in-law, and sister-in-law, and my extended family members on both sides—y'all always asked about how this book was going, and it always made me happy.

Saving the best for last: thank you Carly, my dearest wife, for sacrificing my companionship so that I could write this book, and for never alluding to that sacrifice. You gave up many a weekend so that I could code and write, and you put up with my geeky chatter and my irritating mood-swings when I found, then fixed, my bugs. Now we can do all those things I said we'd do after the book was done.

About the Author

Mason McCuskey is a software engineer with 7 years of commercial programming experience, and has successfully managed his own game company since 1990. In 2000 his company, Spin Studios, was one of 9 world finalists at the Game Developer's Conference 2nd Annual Independent Games Festival. He has also written dozens of articles for GameDev.net and other Web sites. When not coding, Mason can be found spending time with his wonderful wife Carly, enjoying movies, playing guitar, and loving life in the Pacific Northwest.

CONTENTS AT A GLANCE

Introduction . . . . **xxxviii**

PART 1

THE BASICS ■■■■■■■■■■■■■■■■■■■■■■■■■■■■■1

CHAPTER 1
An Introduction to Windows Programming 3

CHAPTER 2
Advanced Win32 API Programming 43

CHAPTER 3
DirectX 99

CHAPTER 4
3D Math 183

CHAPTER 5
3D Concepts 229

CHAPTER 6
An Introduction to DirectGraphics 267

CHAPTER 7
Lighting 311

CHAPTER 8
Basic Texturing 329

CHAPTER 9
Advanced Texturing 365

CHAPTER 10
Vertex and Pixel Shaders 389

PART 2
2D EFFECTS 425

CHAPTER 11
Fire 427

CHAPTER 12
2D Water 455

CHAPTER 13
Image Feedback 487

CHAPTER 14
Image Warping 505

CHAPTER 15
Clouds 521

CHAPTER 16
Blurs and Other Forms of Image Manipulation 541

CHAPTER 17
Fades, Wipes, and Other Transitions 559

PART 3
3D EFFECTS 583

CHAPTER 18
Rain, Smoke, Magic, and More: The Joy of Particle
Systems 585

CHAPTER 19
Advanced Particle Systems 633

CHAPTER 20
Explosions 681

CHAPTER 21
Guns and Projectiles 721

CHAPTER 22
Lens Flares 749

CHAPTER 23
3D Water 777

CHAPTER 24
Vertex and Pixel Shader Effects 801

CONCLUSION 821

APPENDIX A
Advanced C++ and STL. 823

APPENDIX B
Introduction to DevStudio 875

APPENDIX C
What's On the CD? 891

INDEX 895

CONTENTS

INTRODUCTION XXXVIII

PART 1
THE BASICS 1

CHAPTER 1
AN INTRODUCTION TO WINDOWS
PROGRAMMING 3

Event-Driven Programming 4

Your First Windows Program 5

WinMain(), Not main() 7

Making a Window in Two Not-So-Easy Steps 9

Creating a Window Class 10

Creating a Window 17

Handling Events (Pumpin' Messages) 25

Windows Messages 27

PeekMessage 28

GetMessage 30

TranslateMessage 31

DispatchMessage 31

Fleshing Out WindowProc 32

WM_CLOSE 35

WM_PAINT 36

WM_CHAR 40

Chapter Wrap-Up 40

About the Sample Programs 41

Exercises 41

CHAPTER 2

ADVANCED WIN32 API PROGRAMMING 43

The Windows GDI **44**
  Device Contexts 47
    Getting a Device Context 48
    Releasing a Device Context 48
  A Brief Note about Coordinate Systems in the GDI 49
  Pens, Colors, Brushes, and Shapes 49
    Pens 50
    Brushes 55
    Shapes 56
  Bitmaps 56
    Loading a Bitmap 58
    Creating a Bitmap 59
    Creating a DC 59
    Making the New DC Render to the New Bitmap 60
    Drawing a Bitmap 60
    Deleting the DC and the Bitmap 61
    Making the CGDIBitmap Class 62
    Drawing Nonrectangular Bitmaps 64
  Text and Fonts 65
    Fonts 65
    TextOut 75
    DrawText 76
  Regions and Clipping 77
Error Checking **77**
  GetLastError 78
  MessageBox 80
Using Resources **82**
  Program Icons 85
  Custom Mouse Cursors 86

Making Dialog Boxes **87**

   Making a Dialog Template in the Resource Editor 89

   Modal Dialog Boxes 90

   Modeless Dialog Boxes 91

   Dialog Box Controls 93

Chapter Wrap-Up **95**

About the Sample Programs **96**

Exercises **97**

CHAPTER 3

DirectX 99

What Is DirectX? **100**

Should I Use DirectX? **101**

The Ground Rules for Using DirectX **102**

   What's an Interface? 102

   Always Release Your Interfaces 103

   What's IUnknown? 104

   Other Important COM Stuff 104

      Initializing COM 104

      Uninitializing COM 105

      Checking HRESULT Return Values 105

      Using CLSIDs to Get an Interface 106

   How to Deal with DirectX Enumeration 107

DirectInput **108**

   DirectInput Architecture 109

   Setting Up a Device 110

   Acquiring and Unacquiring Devices 110

   Buffered versus Immediate Data 112

   Reading Immediate Device Data 113

      Reading Keyboard Data 114

      Reading Mouse Data 114

      Reading Joystick Data 115

Reading Buffered Data 116

Action Mapping 118

   How to Use Action Mapping 118

   Setting Up an Action Map 119

   Specifying Your Genre 120

   Setting Up Your Default Game Controls 121

   Enumerating Devices 123

   Reading Devices 125

   Showing Game Controller Configuration to Your User 125

Force Feedback 126

   Enumerating Force Feedback Effects 126

   Creating Effect Objects 126

   Use the Force Editor, Luke! 129

   Playing an Effect Object 130

DirectInput Wrap-Up 131

DirectAudio **132**

How Does Digital Audio Work, Anyway? 132

DirectAudio Architecture 136

Setting Up DirectAudio 137

Playing Sounds and Music 139

   Setting the Search Directory 140

   Loading the File 141

   Downloading the Segment 144

   Playing the Segment 144

Changing Your Sounds Using DirectAudio Effects Filters 146

   Standard Effect Types 146

   Activating an Effect 146

   Removing an Effect 148

   Effects Wrap-Up 148

Audio Scripts 149

   Loading and Initializing an Audio Script 150

   Setting Script Variables and Calling Script Routines 150

   Audio Scripts Wrap-Up 151

DirectAudio Wrap-Up 151

DirectPlay **151**

Why Use DirectPlay? 152

Peer-to-Peer or Client/Server? 152

Using DirectPlay in Seven Easy Steps 154

Setting Up the Callback Function 155

Multiple Threads and DirectPlay Callbacks 156

Selecting a Service Provider 158

Hosting a Game 159

Connecting to a Game 163

Sending Data 166

Receiving Data 168

Important DirectPlay Messages 168

Disconnecting 168

The Joy of Lobbies 168

Using DirectPlay's Voice Features 172

Selecting a Voice Topology 172

Deciding on the Type of Transmission Control 174

The Steps to Using the Voice System 174

Testing the Audio Device 175

DirectPlay Wrap-Up 176

DirectShow **176**

DirectShow Architecture 176

Playing a Video 177

Playing a Video in a Certain Window 178

Playing MP3s 179

DirectShow Wrap-Up 179

Chapter Wrap-Up **179**

About the Sample Programs **180**

Exercises **180**

DirectMusic 180

DirectInput 181

DirectPlay 181

DirectShow 181

CHAPTER 4
3D MATH 183

Welcome to 3D 185
  Is DirectGraphics Left-Handed or Right-Handed? 186
  From Points to Primitives 187
  3D Transformations 188
    Translation 189
    Scaling 190
    Rotation 190
  Local and World Coordinates 191

Vectors 195
  What Is a Vector? 195
    Determining a Vector's Direction 196
    Determining a Vector's Magnitude 197
  Adding and Subtracting Vectors 198
  Scalar Multiplication of Vectors 199
  Normalizing Vectors 199
  The Dot Product of Two Vectors 201
  The Cross Product of Two Vectors 204
  D3DX Vector Helper Functions 205
  Vector Wrap-Up 207

Matrices 208
  What Is a Matrix? 208
  Why Use Matrices? 208
  Matrix Multiplication 209
    Multiplying Two 2×2 Matrices: A Walk-Through 210
    Multiplying Two 3×3 Matrices: A Walk-Through 212
  3D Transformations the Quick and Easy Way 213
    Vectors Are Just Matrices 213
    Three Coordinates, Four Rows: What's Up with w? 213
    Transforming Points Using Matrices 214
    Scaling 214
    Translation 215
    Rotation 216

Identity Matrices 218
Matrix Concatenation (Doing More Than One Thing at Once) 219
Using Matrices in 3D Programs 220
D3DX Matrix Helper Functions 220
Matrix Wrap-Up 222

Quaternions **222**
Why Use Quaternions? 223
What Is a Quaternion? 224
Quaternion Basics 224
The Norm of a Quaternion 224
The Conjugate of a Quaternion 224
The Inverse of a Quaternion 225
Unit Quaternions and Their Inverses 225
Quaternion Multiplication 225
Using Quaternions 226
Quaternion Wrap-Up 226

Chapter Wrap-Up **226**

About the Sample Programs **227**

Exercises **227**

CHAPTER 5
3D CONCEPTS ····························229

3D Models **230**
What Is a Model? 230
The Three Ways Vertices Can Form Triangles 231
Triangle Lists 231
Triangle Strips 232
Triangle Fans 232
Other Primitive Types 232
Okay, Which One Should I Use? 233
Vertex Buffers 233
Index Buffers 234
3D Models Wrap-Up 235

Advanced 3D Model Techniques **236**
  Loading a Model from an X File 236
  Converting a 3D Studio Model to an X File 237
    Basic Usage 238
    Conv3ds Command-Line Arguments 238
  Hierarchical Models and Matrix Stacks 240
    Creating a Matrix Stack 243
    Using a Matrix Stack 243
  Advanced Model Techniques Wrap-Up 245

Cameras and Viewports **246**
  Viewports 246
    Setting the Viewport 247
  Cameras 248
    Projection Modes 250
    Specifying the Camera's Position and Orientation 251
    Specifying the Camera's Projection Mode and Field of View 252
  Cameras and Viewports Wrap-Up 252

The 3D Geometry Pipeline **254**
  World Transformation 254
  View Transformation 255
  Projection Transformation 257
  Clipping and Viewport Scaling 257
  Geometry Pipeline Wrap-Up 257

Depth Buffers **258**
  Why Use a Depth Buffer? 258
  What Is a Depth Buffer? 259
  Z-Buffers and W-Buffers 260
  Rendering Objects on Top of Each Other Using Depth Buffers 261
  Disabling the Depth Buffer and Choosing Its Type 262
  Disabling Depth Buffer Writes 263
  Clearing the Depth Buffer 263
  Changing the Comparison Function 263
  Depth Buffer Wrap-Up 264

Chapter Wrap-Up 265
About the Sample Programs 265
Exercises 265

CHAPTER 6

AN INTRODUCTION TO DIRECTGRAPHICS ...267

DirectGraphics Basics 268
    DirectGraphics Architecture 268
    Device Types 269
    Creating a Device (Setting the Video Mode) 270
    A Quick Lesson about Computer Displays 277
    Finding a Video Mode 280
    Lost Devices 281
    Switching between Devices (Full Screen to Windowed) 283
Your First 3D Program 284
    Flex Those Vertices 284
        Describing Your Vertex Format 285
        Transformed versus Untransformed Vertex Formats 287
        Texture Coordinates in Flexible Vertex Formats 288
        Sample Vertex Formats 289
    Vertex Buffers 290
        Creating a Vertex Buffer 290
        Filling It Up 292
    Setting Up the Matrices 295
    The Seven Steps to Rendering Your Triangle 296
        Clearing the Back Buffer 297
        Beginning the Scene 297
        Setting the Stream 298
        Setting the Vertex Shader 300
        Ending the Scene 300
    Presenting the Screen 301
    First 3D Program Wrap-Up 302

**Fading In, Fading Out, Flashing Color—The
Gamma Controls** 302
    Determining Whether Your 3D Card Supports Gamma Controls 302
    Gamma Ramps 302
    Fading In 304
    Fading Out 305
    Fading to Other Colors 306
    Getting the Gamma Ramp 306
    Setting the Gamma Ramp 307
Chapter Wrap-Up 308
About the Sample Programs 308
Exercises 309

CHAPTER 7

LIGHTING 311

Light in Nature 312
Direct3D Lighting Concepts 313
    Ambient and Direct Lighting 313
    Shading Modes 313
        Flat Shading Mode 314
        Gouraud Shading Mode 314
    Materials 315
Direct3D Light Properties 316
    Diffuse, Specular, and Ambient Color 316
    Position, Range, and Attenuation 316
    Light Direction 317
    Light Type 318
        Point Lights 318
        Spotlights 318
        Directional Lights 320
Direct3D Material Properties 320
    Diffuse Color 320
    Ambient Color 321

Emissive Color 321
Specular Color and Power 321

Programming Direct3D Lights **322**
Setting a Light's Properties 322
Getting a Light's Properties 323
Enabling and Disabling Lights 325

Programming Direct3D Materials **325**
Setting the Current Material 325
Getting the Current Material 327

Chapter Wrap-Up **327**

About the Sample Programs **328**

Exercises **328**

CHAPTER 8

BASIC TEXTURING 329

Basic Texturing Concepts **330**
Textures Are Just Surfaces 330
Texture Management 331
The Fine Art of Knowing When to Texture 331
Tying a Texture to a Vertex 332
To Wrap or Not to Wrap? 334
Texture-Filtering Modes 335
Nearest-Point Sampling 336
Linear Texture Filtering 337
Mipmap Texture Filtering 338
Anisotropic Texture Filtering 339
Texture-Addressing Modes 340
The Wrap Addressing Mode 340
The Mirror Addressing Mode 340
The Clamp Addressing Mode 341
The Border Color Addressing Mode 342
Transparent Textures 344
Transparent Textures through Alpha Blending 345

Transparent Textures through Alpha Testing 345
How Direct3D Blends Textures with Materials 346

Basic Texture Programming **346**
Determining Basic Device Texture Capabilities 347
Setting the Filtering, Addressing, and Wrap Modes 351
Creating a Texture 352
Bare-Bones Texture Creation 352
Creating a Texture Using D3DX 355
Creating a Texture from an Image Using D3DX 355
Extended D3DX Texture Creation Functions 358
Selecting a Texture 361
Mr. Vertex, Meet Mr. Texture 362

Chapter Wrap-Up **362**
About the Sample Programs **362**
Exercises **363**

CHAPTER 9

ADVANCED TEXTURING 365

Multiple Texture Blending **366**
A Tabular Guide to Texturing Terminology 367
Texture Stages 368
Texture Stage Input Arguments 369
Texture Stage Operators 369
A Simple Texture Stage Example 370
A More Complex Example 371
Programming Texture Stages 373

Light Mapping **376**
What Is Light Mapping, and Why Should I Care? 376
Programming Light Mapping 377

Environment Mapping **379**
What Is Environment Mapping, and Why Should I Care? 379
Spherical Environment Mapping 380
Cubic Environment Mapping 381

Other Uses for Multitexturing **382**
  Glow Mapping 382
  Detail Mapping 382
  Color Saturation (a.k.a. Really Bright Objects) 382
Using Effects **383**
  What Are Effect Scripts, and Why Should I Care? 383
  The Process for Using Effects 384
  Creating Effect Files 385
      Variable Declarations 386
      Technique and Pass Blocks 387
  Effects Wrap-Up 387
Chapter Wrap-Up **388**
About the Sample Programs **388**
Exercises **388**

CHAPTER 10

VERTEX AND PIXEL SHADERS 389

Why Shaders? **390**
Vertex Shaders **391**
  Effects You Can Make Using Vertex Shaders 393
  Determining Whether a Device Supports Vertex Shaders 393
  Specifying the Inputs to a Vertex Shader 394
  Vertex Shader Assembly Language 399
      Vertex Shader Registers 399
      Vertex Shader Instructions 401
      Vertex Shader Instruction Modifiers 406
  Creating a Vertex Shader in Your Program 406
  Rendering, Using the Shader 407
  Passing Data to Your Shader, Using Constant Registers 408
  A Simple Vertex Shader Example 409
  A Complex Vertex Shader Example 411
  Vertex Shader Wrap-Up 414

Pixel Shaders 414
   Effects You Can Make Using Pixel Shaders 414
   Pixel Shader Assembly Language 414
      Pixel Shader Registers 414
      Generic Pixel Shader Instructions 415
      Texture-Addressing Instructions 418
      Pixel Shader Modifiers 419
   Creating and Using Pixel Shaders in Your Program 420
   A Simple Pixel Shader Example 420
   Pixel Shader Wrap-Up 422

Chapter Wrap-Up 422

About the Sample Programs 422

Exercises 423

PART 2
2D EFFECTS 425

CHAPTER 11
FIRE 427

How Does It Work? 429

Writing the Code 430
   Creating the Fire Texture 431
   Creating the Fire Color Palette 431
      Palette Files 432
      Grabbing a Palette out of an Image File 434
   Processing the Fire 435
   Putting the Fire on the Texture 436
      Locking the Texture 437
      Filling the Texture 437
      Unlocking the Texture 440
      A Warning about Locking Textures 440

Making the Fire Texture Fill the Viewport 441
   Why Perspective Projections Are Sometimes a Pain 441
   Using Orthogonal Projections to Make a Quad Fill the Screen 442
   Texel/Pixel Alignment in Direct3D 445
Code Wrap-Up 448

Modifying the Fire Effect 448
Cooling Arrays 448
Fuel 449
Color 449

Uses for the Fire Effect 450
Fire Environment Mapping 450
Fire Multitexturing 451

Optimizing the Fire Effect 451
Use the Smallest Possible Texture Dimensions 451
Use Paletted Textures 452

Chapter Wrap-Up 452

About the Sample Programs 453

Exercises 453

CHAPTER 12

2D WATER 455

How Does It Work? 456
The Water Arrays 457
Realistic Water, Using Ray Tracing 460
   Water Bending Light 460
   The Physics Formulas for Bending Light 462
   Calculating the Angle between Surface Normal and a Light Ray 464
   Determining Where the Light Ray Hits 467
   Ray Tracing Wrap-Up 467
Generating Waves 468

Making Bigger Waves 469
Water Effect Wrap-Up 469
Writing the Code **470**
Speeding It Up—Making a Displacement Lookup Table 470
Creating the Image and Water Textures 471
Processing the Water Arrays 472
Animating the Water 473
Rendering the Source Texture onto the Destination 474
Code Wrap-Up 477
Modifying the Water Effect **477**
Wave Speed 477
Wave Lifetime 478
The Dampening Factor 478
The Strength of the Wave 479
Water Currents 479
The Depth of the Water 479
A Better Blending Function 480
Different Ways to Render the Water 481
Uses for the Water Effect **482**
Rain 482
Drippy Mouse Cursors 482
Parallel Waves 482
Boat Wakes 483
Optimizing the Water Effect **483**
Don't Calculate What You Don't Show 484
Reduce the Size of Your Water Array 484
Multithread! 485
Chapter Wrap-Up **485**
About the Sample Programs **486**
Exercises **486**

CHAPTER 13

IMAGE FEEDBACK 487

How Does It Work? 489
Writing the Code 492
   Creating the Textures 493
   Rendering to a Texture 494
   Transforming the Primary Texture onto the Scratch Texture 498
      Render-Copying for Beginners 498
      Transforming as You Render-Copy 500
   Rendering New Image Data onto the Scratch Texture 502
   Blending the Scratch Texture Back onto the Primary Texture 502
Modifying the Image Feedback Effect 503
   Feedback Transformation 503
   Transparency of the Scratch Texture 503
Uses for Image Feedback 503
Chapter Wrap-Up 504
About the Sample Programs 504
Exercises 504

CHAPTER 14

IMAGE WARPING 505

How Does It Work? 507
Writing the Code 508
   One Effect, Two Textures 509
   Setting Up the Vertex Grid 511
      Filling the Vertex Buffer 512
      Filling the Index Buffer 515
Modifying Image Warping 516
   Grid Density 516
   Perturbation Amount 517

Cumulative Versus Non-Cumulative Warps 517
Alpha Blending 517

Uses for Image Warping **518**
Optimizing Image Warping **518**
Chapter Wrap-Up **519**
About the Sample Programs **519**
Exercises **519**

CHAPTER 15

CLOUDS 521

How Does It Work? **522**
Perlin Noise 523
What Is Perlin Noise? 523
Using the 3D Card to Generate Perlin Noise 524
Layering Perlin Noise to Create Clouds 525
Making the Cloud Texture Look Better 528
Square the Combined Texture's Colors 528
Filter the Noise Layers Before You Combine Them 528
Subtract the Texture 528
Animating the Cloud Texture 529
Writing the Code **529**
Creating the Textures 529
It All Starts with a Random Number Generator 530
Making Some Noise 531
Smoothing the Noise Layers 532
Combining the Noise Layers 533
Squaring the Cloud 535
Subtracting 535
Modifying the Cloud Effect **535**
Blending Factors 536
Color Clouds 536

Uses for the Cloud Effect **537**
Slime, Lava, and Plasma 537
Dynamically Generated Landscapes 537

Optimizing the Cloud Effect **538**
Use Fewer Octaves 538
Use Smaller Textures 538
Don't Lock the Textures Very Often (or At All) 538
Minimize the Number of BeginScene/EndScene Calls 539

Chapter Wrap-Up **539**
About the Sample Programs **540**
Exercises **540**

CHAPTER 16

BLURS AND OTHER FORMS OF IMAGE
MANIPULATION **· 541**

How Does It Work? **542**
Talk the Talk 542
What's a Kernel? 543
Some Kernels to Use 544
Blurring 545
Stronger Blurring 545
Sharpening 545
Edge Detection 546

Writing the Code **546**
Class Layout 547
CImageManipulator 548
CImageManipulatorKernel 550

Uses for Image Manipulation **555**
Optimizing Image Manipulation **556**
Use Pixel Shaders 556
Use Lookup Tables 556

Chapter Wrap-Up 556

About the Sample Programs 557

Exercises 557

CHAPTER 17

FADES, WIPES, AND OTHER TRANSITIONS 559

Simple Transitions 560

Fading to Colors Using Alpha Blending 561

Dissolves (Cross Fades) 564

Wipes 566

Directional Wipes 566

Split Wipes 568

Window Blinds 569

Advanced Transitions 569

Melts 569

Fades to Static 572

Crunches 573

Warp-Dissolves 574

Tile Transitions 575

The Secret to It All: Don't Use an Index Buffer 575

Things You Can Do with Tiles 576

Delay Patterns for Tile Transitions 577

Templates to the Rescue 578

Tile Transition Wrap-Up 579

A Class Hierarchy for Transitions 579

Chapter Wrap-Up 580

About the Sample Programs 580

Exercises 581

PART 3
3D EFFECTS 583

CHAPTER 18
RAIN, SMOKE, MAGIC, AND MORE!
THE JOY OF PARTICLE SYSTEMS 585

What Is a Particle System? 586
How Complex Should You Make Your Particle System? 589
Core Particle Properties 591
Core Particle System Properties 591
Writing the Code for a Basic Particle System 593
  CParticle 593
  CParticleEmitter 594
  CRecyclingArray 596
    What Is CRecyclingArray? 596
    Using a Recycling Array 597
    How the CRecyclingArray Works 599
    CRecyclingArray Wrap-Up 601
  Setting Up a Particle System 602
  Point Sprites and a New Vertex Format 603
  Rendering the Particles 604
    Setting Render States 605
    Set Texture and Vertex Buffer Active 608
    Lock the Vertex Buffer 608
    Pump the Particles Into the Vertex Buffer 608
    Push the Vertex Buffer Out to the Graphics Card ... 609
    Cleanup: Push Out the Stragglers 610
    Rendering Wrap-Up 610
  Updating the Particles 611
    Moving and Animating Particles 611
    Creating New Particles 613
  Basic Particle System Code Wrap-Up 614

Making a Particle System Editor 615

    Chindogu and the Question "Why Make an Editor?" 615

    Form Follows Function 616

    Saving and Loading Particle System Properties 616

        Creating the Map 617

        Searching the Map and Setting Properties 618

        Loading Code Wrap-Up 619

    Presenting a GUI 619

        Creating a Tool Window (Really Just a Modeless Dialog) 620

        Message Processing Madness 622

        Pushing Initial Values Into the GUI 623

        Adding Flair—Putting Common Dialog Boxes to Use 624

        GUI Wrap-Up 627

    Editor Wrap-Up 628

Chapter Wrap-Up 629

About the Sample Programs 629

    The Programs 630

    A Camera Class 630

        Camera Basics 630

        Mouselook 631

    The Ground Plane 632

Exercises 632

CHAPTER 19

ADVANCED PARTICLE SYSTEMS 633

Making an Advanced Particle System 635

    Adding Flexibility to the Current System 635

    Events 636

    Event Sequences 637

    Goodbye, GUI 638

    The Birth of a Simple Scripting Language 638

    The Property Shuffle 640

    The Element of Randomness 640

Planning It Out: BNF Grammar 641
    Starting Simple—What's a Number? 642
    Vectors Are Just Numbers 643
    The Other Primitive Data Types 644
    The View from the Top of the Grammar, Down 645
Events 646
Dealing with Fades 647
The Final Keyword 647
Rudimentary Loops: The EventTimer Property 648
The First Steps to Writing the Property File Loader 649
    Dealing with White Space and Comments 649
    Creating the Tokenizer 651
    Determining the Token Type 653
The Beginning of the Actual Loading Code 653
    Handling Errors 654
    The Beginning 654
Processing the Particle System Block 656
    The Beginning 656
    Processing the Particle System's Vector Properties 657
    Processing the Particle System's Event Sequences 661
    Processing the Events of an Event Sequence 662
    Parsing the Time Element of an Event 664
    Using a Factory to Create an Event 664
    Processing the Event Properties and Storing the Event 665
    Loading Code Wrap-Up 666
Using What We Have Loaded 666
Our New Event-Based Update Function 666
Our New Event-Based Render Function 670
Scriptable Particle Systems Wrap-Up 670

Uses for Scriptable Particle Systems 671
Snow 671
Magic Spells 673
Jetstreams and Rockets 675
Faeries 675
Lightning Bugs 677
Other Scripts 677

Optimizing Scriptable Particle Systems 677

Other Potentially Nifty Enhancements 678

Chapter Wrap-Up 679

About the Sample Programs 679

Exercises 679

CHAPTER 20

EXPLOSIONS ••••••••••••••••••••••••••••••••••••••681

Starting Simple: Explosion Sprites 682

Creating the Explosion Textures 683

Creating Sprite and Animation Classes 685

Frame Classes and Animation Classes 685

Creating a Timer Class 687

Keeping Timing and Position Information Separate from the

Animation 688

Deciding which Frame to Display 690

The Problem with CTimer 691

Billboarding 693

Implementing Billboarding 693

Rendering the Explosion 694

Explosion Clusters 696

Dropping in the Particle System Code 698

Adding a Loop Command to Our Particle Sequence 699

Interpreting the Loop Keyword Inside the Particle Script 700

Implementing the Loop Keyword 703

Integrating the Particle System 704

Adding a Shockwave 706

Creating the Shockwave Texture 707

Setting Up the Vertices and Texture Coordinates 707

Rendering the Shockwave 711

Making the Shockwave Fade Out 712

Chapter Wrap-Up 713

About the Sample Programs 714

Skyboxes 714
    Creating the Skybox Images 715
    The Skybox Code 716

Exercises 719

CHAPTER 21

GUNS AND PROJECTILES ■■■■■■■■■■■■■■■■■■■■■■■■721

The Firing Range Framework 722
    The Gun Base Class 722
    Switching Weapons 723
    Positioning and Rendering the Gun Model 727
    Firing the Gun 729

The Machine Gun 730
    Loading the Muzzle Flash Sprite 731
    Firing the Machine Gun 731
    Drawing the Muzzle Flash 733
    Recoil 734

The Plasma Cannon 735
    Bullets and Bullet Arrays 736
    Updating and Rendering Bullets 738
    Firing a Bullet 739
    Plasma Cannon Miscellany and Wrap-Up 740

The Bolt Weapon 741
    The CLaserGun Class 742
    Firing the Laser 743
    Drawing the Laser 744
    Integrating the Particle System 746

Chapter Wrap-Up 747

About the Sample Programs 747

Exercises 748

CHAPTER 22

LENS FLARES 749

What Are Lens Flares? 750
The Concepts 751
   The Flare Spots 751
   Flare without Sun, and Flare Intensities 753
The Lens Flare Object 755
Rendering Lens Flares in 2D 759
   Calculating the Intensity 759
   Calculating Triangle Positions 761
   Rendering the Triangles 763
Rendering Lens Flares in 3D 765
Figuring Out Whether You Should Draw a Lens Flare 768
   Calculating the Ray's Origination and Direction 770
   Performing Ray/Triangle Intersection Tests 771
   Code Wrap-Up 773
The Effect: More Than Just the Lens Flare 773
Chapter Wrap-Up 774
About the Sample Programs 774
Exercises 775

CHAPTER 23

3D WATER 777

The Concepts 778
   Reflection Using Environment Mapping 779
   Refraction 779
The Code 779
   Setting Up the Water Plane 781

Updating the Water 783
  Calculating the New Height Values 785
  Applying the Height Values to the Vertex Grid 786
  Calculating Displacement 788
  Calculating Normals 788
Creating the Environment Map 792
Updating the Environment Map 792
  Splitting the Render Function 792
  The Screen Rendering Method 793
  The Core Rendering Method 794
  The Cube Map Rendering Method 794
Rendering the Water 797
Code Wrap-Up 799

Chapter Wrap-Up **799**

About the Sample Programs **800**

Exercises **800**

CHAPTER 24

VERTEX AND PIXEL SHADER EFFECTS 801

Cartoon Shading **802**
Regular Lighting 802
How Does Cartoon Shading Work? 803
Writing the Cartoon Shading Code 804
Loading the Vertex Shader 805
Setting the Vertex Shader Constants 806
The Cartoon Vertex Shader 807
Texture Stage States for Cartoon Rendering 808
Pumping Out the Triangles 808
Adding Pen Strokes to Cartoon Shading **809**
How Does It Work? 810
Adding Edge Support to the Vertex Shader 811
Adding the Edge Texture to the Texture Stage States 811
Cartoon Rendering Wrap-Up 813

Image Processing Using Pixel Shaders 813

The Framework 814

The Framework's Vertex Shader 815

Why We Want This: The Blur and Sharpen Pixel Shaders 816

Other Cool Pixel Shaders 817

A Simple Black-and-White Shader 817

A Better Black-and-White Shader 818

Inverting an Image 819

Chapter Wrap-Up 819

About the Sample Programs 819

Exercises 820

CONCLUSION 821

APPENDIX A

ADVANCED C++ AND STL 823

APPENDIX B

INTRODUCTION TO DEVSTUDIO 875

APPENDIX C

WHAT'S ON THE CD? 891

INDEX 895

LETTER FROM THE SERIES EDITOR

DirectX and Direct3D are now mature game programming APIs and 90% of the game programming community uses these APIs. This is a good thing, because at this time many game programmers and developers are starting to write quite a bit about these APIs and have a deep and thorough knowledge of these systems. *Special Effects Game Programming with DirectX* is yet another book that I wish I had when I was learning Direct3D. However, learning DirectX/3D is one thing, learning to master it takes months or years of experimenting.

Lucky for both of us, Mason McCuskey is, without a doubt, a master DirectX/3D programmer. I'm very hard to please, my friends can all attest to that. I have very high standards, and I can tell you that Mason and this book have not only exceeded my high standards, but have surprised and delighted me. This book is written in such a friendly and fun manner that Mason's wonderful personality comes through the pages, his love for game programming and discovery make the material fun and interesting to read.

Although this book is more of an advanced book on DirectX/3D special effects, Mason still takes the time to give newcomers a complete foundation on Win32, Math, and DirectX before moving into DirectGraphics, that is, Direct3D basically. This is key since this book is self-contained. Of course, more experienced programmers can just skip to the advanced material, of which there's a lot!

This book is without a doubt a secret weapon, and if you complete and retain this information, you will have cutting-edge knowledge of 3D techniques that leverage DirectX and will amaze your friends and get you lots of dates with hot women (or for our female programmers, hot men). I mean no one has EVER done a book like this, most 3D books show how to use Direct3D, draw polygons, perform lighting, apply texturing, but this book shows how to create fire, smoke, explosions, crazy lighting effects, particle systems, advanced vertex and pixel shaders, and more…. Please flip to the table of contents and just look at all that killer stuff!

I have to admit, I read and edit these books while they are being developed, but I never read the final book since I have already read it in manuscript form, but in this case I can't wait to get my hands on this book just to have a real copy of it—that's how cool this book is. It's the first and the best, in my opinion, on Special FX programming for DirectX and you are going to have a lot of fun with it!

And like all books in my *Premier Press Game Development* series, I want you, the reader, to be able to get something out of the book even if you're not a master C++ programmer, or DirectX guru, so the appendixes cover C++ and the Standard Template Libraries, and if you're rusty or not familiar you will get a jump-start in those areas. So in essence you are getting many books in one: Win32 Programming, DirectX, Direct3D, Math, Special Effects, and C++ Programming.

In conclusion, it has been a pleasure developing this book, and reading the chapters late at night while roller-blading on the empty streets reading some of the coolest stuff I have ever laid my eyes on. I sincerely hope that you get a lot out of this book, and you use the techniques in your next game—or who knows what? These techniques can be used for myriad applications, only your own creativity and vision will limit you….

Sincerely,

André LaMothe
Series Editor

INTRODUCTION

*"'Begin at the beginning,' the king said, very gravely, 'and go
on till you come to the end: then stop.'"*
——*Lewis Carroll, Alice's Adventures in Wonderland*

This is funny—I've written several hundred pages of text, yet it's this one last section—the introduction—that's the most difficult to write.

This book covers writing special effects for 3D games. It's about seeing something cool in a game or demo and wondering, "How on Earth did they do that?". You will be exposed to cool concepts and will learn to apply your knowledge to write awesome programs. Many smart people have written many great books on how to program and create 3D worlds. They've done a good job covering the stuff you need to write impressive 3D applications.

However, games are much more than applications. You're not going to see a pit of bubbling lava in a CAD program, nor are you going to see a menu item in Excel called "Blow up cells A4-A6". Games are a different animal, and this book intends to teach you some of the tricks behind the eye-candy so that not only does no one mistake your games for mere "applications," but also so that your games look as good as they play.

This book is for programmers of all skill levels. I've written some newbie stuff that will bring you up-to-speed if you're new to DirectX or Windows programming. And even if these technologies are old friends, you can still get something out of Part 1, "The Basics," since I've augmented it with a lot of tips and tricks for advanced programmers.

The second and third parts are the jelly inside the donut. Part 2, "2D Effects," describes 2D special effects—effects that rely on your 3D card to work their magic, but that are essentially 2D, such as transitions (fading in/out, cross fading) and image warping. These 2D effects are suitable for any 3D accelerated game, 2D or 3D.

Part 3, "3D Effects," describes 3D effects, tricks designed to simulate the cool stuff as accurately as possible, without killing the frame rate. Explosions, water, lens flare, magic spells, transporters—anything and everything to turn your "app" into a sensory overload that people can't help but spend time playing.

Finally, there's an appendix on C++ and STL (the C++ Standard Template Library). The book uses some advanced C++ features (templates, structured exception handling, std::vectors) that not all programmers are familiar with. So there are a few pages that give you a crash course on these so that you will feel comfortable reading and messing with the sample programs. And I provide an appendix at the end that provides a brief introduction to DevStudio.

That's what the book is. There are also a few things this book isn't. It's not a code dump. I've tried to print only short code segments, not huge listings of entire programs. The best place to teach concepts and algorithms is on paper. The best place to read code and really see how those concepts and algorithms fit together is on the computer, where you can change things, crash things, and fix things, all underneath the comforting umbrella of syntax highlighting and your favorite MP3s. So this book contains code excerpts here and there, but that's it. Most of the excerpts I've snipped down even further so as to draw your attention precisely to where it's needed.

One last thought: there's more to this book than what you hold in your hands. Behind this bundle of pages are a Web site and an author who is ready and willing to answer your questions. That's just how it works—you ask others to help you learn something, and once you learn it, you teach, and give back to the community. I learned the art of game programming primarily through helpful people and books like this one, so I'm grateful that I can now complete the circle and present this knowledge back to you.

Have fun!

Layout of This Book

There are several features of this book with which you are probably already familiar. If your brain is correctly parsing and interpreting this sentence, I'll presume that you already know a lot of standards, including the alphabet, the English language, and the top-to-bottom, left-to-right reading order. Here are some other conventions employed by this book.

Text Formatting

Certain text fonts and styles mean certain things. Here's an overview:

```
This font denotes code.
```

If I use a variable name, such as `m_iWidth`, in a sentence, it will look like that.

NOTE

This is a general note, and contains useful tricks, and procedures.

Sample Program Reference

This box lets you know which sample program on the CD is currently the focus.

CAUTION

This is a warning, and denotes something to watch out for in your code or your algorithms.

HELP REFERENCE

References to DirectX or Win32 help files look like this.

TIP

This is a helpful comment that informs you of an interesting hint about the subject being covered.

This is a sidebar; a small discussion that's a little off-topic but still interesting.

STANDARD CHAPTER SECTIONS

The following sections are part of each chapter:

- **About the Sample Programs**. This section lists all of the sample programs for this chapter, along with a brief description of what each sample program does. For a more detailed discussion of a particular sample program, consult Appendix B.
- **Exercises**. In this section I've listed some things that you should try, to increase your understanding of the topic at hand. Don't feel like you need to do all of these before moving on to the next chapter; they are there simply to guide you should you feel like diving deeper into a particular topic.

Many of the chapters describing the various special effects follow roughly the same progression. I'll start by explaining the concepts behind the effect. After that, I'll begin talking about the code that makes those concepts happen. Next, I'll talk briefly about the uses for the effect—places you can use it now that you know what it is and how it works. Finally, I'll wrap up by talking a little about how to enhance the effect further—different features you may want to add, or different optimization tricks you may want to try.

THE SOURCE CODE

I've employed several conventions to make the source code more readable, portable, and robust. This section enumerates those.

LAYOUT AND CODING STYLE NOTES

Here are a few notes on the layout and coding style of the entire book:

■ The layout of the source code conforms to a 78-column width. This means that I've tried my best to make source code lines a maximum of 78 characters long.

■ The source code printed in this book may differ (insignificantly) from the source code contained on the CD. For example, frequently I've had to play with the white space of the code to make it fit inside the margins of this book. Don't worry; nowhere have I done anything that changes its behavior.

■ Throughout the source code listings, I've clipped out certain parts of code that are unchanged, trivial, or not important. When I remove a large chunk of code, I'll put in a comment, saying "hey, there's some code here but I trimmed it out." This saves trees, and also increases readability, because it frees you to concentrate on the code that is written, rather than get lost in some incidental logic. You should know, however, that what's printed isn't the entirety of what's on the CD—be wary of this if you're keying in code directly from the book.

■ The code itself is written in what many programmers refer to as a "sane subset" of C++. I use some advanced C++ features, such as exceptions, templates, and RTTI. I encourage you to read Appendix A to get up-to-speed on the advanced topics.

■ Generally, the sample programs for a given chapter start simple, and get progressively more difficult. If there is more than one sample program for a chapter, the first program is the simplest demo of the topic at hand, and subsequent examples will build on that simple core.

■ Throughout the book I try to adhere to both the framework and the style of the code for the Microsoft DirectX SDK sample programs. I've employed a fairly standard coding style, complete with Hungarian notation and brackets that line up. I've used spaces, not tabs, to line up brackets, and I've set my tab size to two.

■ I include header files within header files. My philosophy is that every class should be self-contained and ready to go, which means that every class's .h file contains includes for all of the other .h files needed by that class. This means I've also used header file "sentries" to prevent the same header file being included more than once per C++ file. I elected to use the tried-and-true `#define` method instead of using the `#pragma once` directive.

■ I've tried to make the classes as modular and robust as reasonably possible so that you can easily take them and use them in your own programs without many changes. The sample code does not include an abstraction of the DirectX interface—it's written to interface directly with the DirectX API calls and data types. One of the best ways to teach yourself DirectX programming is to write a layer of abstraction: something that takes the functionality of DirectX and wraps it up into a set of classes. The idea here is that you can then easily replace those classes with different ones, to support different graphics APIs (say, OpenGL). Unfortunately, that task is complex enough to warrant a book of its own, so I didn't go there.

■ One of the biggest challenges in writing a book on real-time computer graphics is balancing between code that runs fast and code that's easy to read. The closer to the metal you get, the faster your code runs, and (with few exceptions) the harder it is to read and maintain. When writing the code for this book, I decided to err on the side of readability instead of speed. You can always optimize something once you understand it, and I encourage you to take the algorithms in this book and in the sample code, and optimize them. Go wild—there's many places that can and should be optimized if you're building a professional game. I've highlighted these areas in the text.

Common Code

The sample programs rely on a small base of common code for both Windows programming in general, and Direct3D programming in particular. You'll find this common code living in the Common Code folder on your CD. Table 1 is a quick inventory of what's inside that folder:

Development Environment

I developed the code for this book using Microsoft's Visual C++ compiler, version 6.0. I have not tested it on any other compiler, though my gut says that Visual C++ 5.0 should work as well as the newer compilers. In fact, any Win32 compiler that conforms to the ANSI C++ standard should work for you. Obviously, since the code uses DirectX you're tied to the Windows platform. I developed using version 8.1 of the Microsoft DirectX SDK, under Windows 2000 and Windows XP. I've tested the code on Windows 98 and Windows ME and didn't run into any problems.

Hardware-wise, I developed on a single processor AMD Athlon with a GeForce 3 graphics card and an older TNT card driving a second monitor (multimon is considered by many programmers a must-have for graphics development). I've done rudimentary testing of the code under older hardware, with no real trouble; however, to get the most out of this book you're going to need at least a GeForce 3 (or equivalent). The primary reason is that the GeForce 3 was the first card to support vertex and pixel shaders in hardware. Vertex shaders can run in software emulation with only a slight performance hit, but you're going to hate life if you have to run the pixel shaders in reference mode. Even on the fastest machines you're not going to reach interactive frame rates without dedicated pixel shader hardware.

Table 1 Common Code Contents

Filename	Description
AnimSequence.cpp AnimSequence.h	Header and source code files for an animation sequence class, CAnimSequence. I talk about this in Chapter 20, "Explosions."
Camera.cpp Camera.h	A rudimentary implementation of a moveable camera. I talk about this code at the end of Chapter 18, "Rain, Smoke, Magic, and More: The Joy of Particle Systems."
CommonFuncs.cpp CommonFuncs.h	A collection of useful functions for Win32 programming. These are functions I've written over the years to solve common problems. Because they're very simple, I do not cover them in the book.
D3DHelperFuncs.cpp D3DHelperFuncs.h	Similar to CommonFuncs.h, these files contain useful functions for Direct3D programming. I cover most of these throughout the various sections of the book.
GDIBitmap.cpp GDIBitmap.h	Header and source code for the CGDIBitmap class, a wee class designed to wrap the Win32 bitmap loading and accessing functions. I talk about this class in Chapter 2.
GroundPlane.cpp GroundPlane.h	These files contain an implementation of CGroundPlane, a simple ground-plane class that we use in the 3D effects programs. I give a complete description of this class in Chapter 18.
InputManager.cpp InputManager.h	The CInputManager class defined by these files is a simple wrapper for DirectInput that most of the sample programs use for mouse and keyboard input.
MinMax.h	This header file defines the CMinMax template class. I use CMinMax to store both minimum and maximum values in one convenient container. A complete description of it is given in Appendix A.

Table 1 Continued

Filename	Description
RecyclingArray.h	This header file defines the `CRecyclingArray` template class. `RecyclingArray` makes a static array look like a dynamic array. I provide a complete code rundown in Chapter 18.
RecyclingArrayDyn.h	A close cousin to `RecyclingArray.h`, this header file defines the template class `CRecyclingArrayDyn`. This is a different flavor of `CRecyclingArray`, one that enables you to specify the maximum number of elements at run-time instead of compile-time.
SkyBox.cpp SkyBox.h	These two files define and implement `CSkyBox`, a sky-box class I talk about in Chapter 20.
Sprite.cpp Sprite.h	These files contain `CSprite`, a basic sprite implementation that I talk about in Chapter 20.
Timer.cpp Timer.h	These contain a `CTimer` class, which acts as a virtual stopwatch inside the sample programs. It's primarily used for animation sequences, and makes its debut in Chapter 20.

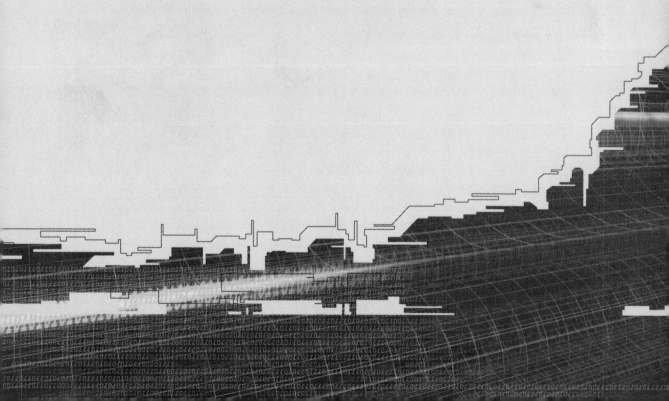

PART 1

THE BASICS

Welcome to the book! As you know, this is the first of three sections. This section is all about getting you up-to-speed on Windows programming, DirectX, and specifically, Direct3D.

Over the course of the next ten chapters you'll be learning several important skills. You'll start by learning the basics of programming within Windows; Windows programming is a different sort of animal, and taming that animal requires some knowledge of event-driven programming. The first two chapters will teach you that.

Next, you'll look at DirectX, and you'll also cover the fundamentals of 3D Math and 3D Concepts. That's Chapters 3, 4, and 5.

The rest of the chapters are all about DirectGraphics, also known as Direct3D, the single most important tool in creating killer visual effects. Chapter 6 introduces you to DirectGraphics; Chapters 7, 8, 9, and 10 are all about specific topics within DirectGraphics. We'll look at lighting, texturing, and shaders (both vertex shaders and pixel shaders).

Also, this is a good time for you to check out Appendix A if your C++ skills need some polish.

Right-o, then. Let's get to it!

CHAPTER 1

AN INTRODUCTION TO WINDOWS PROGRAMMING

"It takes immense genius to represent, simply and sincerely, what we see right in front of us."

—Edmond Duranty

I cannot stress how important this chapter is for those of you who don't already know Windows programming. If you spend some time and learn the basics right now, it will pay off big time when I start talking about advanced topics. Just as you can't expect to learn how to dance without knowing how to walk, you can't expect to learn DirectX special effects without first knowing how to code a basic Windows program.

This chapter teaches you the vital skills you will need. You are going to focus on the traits and quirks that make Windows unique and the paradigms you will have to wrap your brain around to be a successful Windows programmer (and to understand how all the rest of the code in this book works). You will tie everything together by taking a DOS program and moving it step by step into Windows.

With that, let's dive right in.

EVENT-DRIVEN PROGRAMMING

Windows programs, unlike MS-DOS and some UNIX programs, are *event driven*. This means, in a nutshell, that the OS calls a function in your program when certain events occur, for example, when the user clicks a mouse button or presses a key. Your function responds to the event in some way, and with that response, the work of the program is accomplished.

This is a stark contrast to DOS programming, where after the OS invokes your program, it stays out of your way unless you call on it to do something. MS-DOS never calls any function of your program except `main()`. Windows, on the other hand, calls functions other than `main()`. Your program still starts with a call to `main()`—only now it's named `WinMain()` and takes different arguments—but as it runs, Windows also calls certain callback functions in certain situations.

> **TIP**
>
> Just so you know I'm not trying to pull a fast one on you in the very first chapter of the book, there is one way you can get **MS-DOS** to notify you of certain things, and that's by writing interrupt handlers. For example, you use interrupts so that when a device requires immediate attention (say, there's a byte of data coming in through a modem), code is called immediately to handle the situation (say, store the byte in memory or display it on the screen). This, however, doesn't make **DOS** an event-driven language. In DOS, interrupts are the exception to the rule.

A *callback* function is any function the OS calls back when something happens. Imagine that you're at a hotel, and your room doesn't have an alarm clock. You ask the front desk for a wake-up call at 8:00 a.m. Sure enough (if it's a good hotel), at eight the next morning, your phone rings, and you wake up.

In this example, you are a Windows program, and the front desk is acting as the OS. When you place the wakeup call with the front desk, you register a callback with the OS. That is, you tell the OS, "Hey, when this happens, I want to know about it." When the clock strikes eight, the OS takes notice of it and obediently calls back to you.

To extend this analogy further, if you were a DOS program, you wouldn't call the front desk and ask for a wakeup call because DOS doesn't have callback functions (aside from hardware-layer interrupts, explained on the preceding page). Instead, you would call the front desk periodically and ask for the current time. When the front desk person finally says, "Eight o'clock," you would notice and proceed to get up. In this example, the OS would never call you—you would call it.

YOUR FIRST WINDOWS PROGRAM

To illustrate the differences of event-driven programming, I will take a simple DOS program as an example and move it to Windows. Say that you want to write a DOS program that prints a message on the screen, waits until a key is pressed, and then exits. I've taken a screenshot of this program running—you can see it in Figure 1.1.

To make sure that you know what this program does, I've drawn up a flowchart showing, in general, the tasks it will accomplish (see Figure 1.2).

This flowchart basically says that the program starts up, prints a line to the screen, and then enters a loop. Inside this loop, the program asks the system whether a key has been pressed, and if so, it breaks the loop and exits.

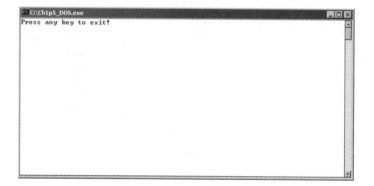

Figure 1.1

The DOS program running inside a console window.

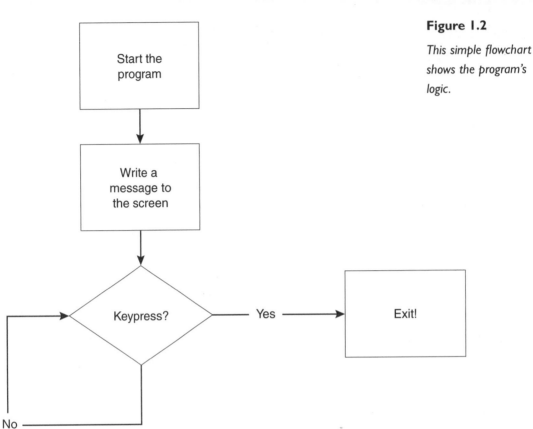

Figure 1.2

This simple flowchart shows the program's logic.

Now that you have the flowchart, you can write some code. After hours of careful calculation, you come up with something similar to this:

```
int main(char argc, char *argv[])
{
  printf("Hello!  Press a key to exit.");
  while (!kbhit()) {
  }
  return(0);
}
```

Now it's time to take that program and move it, step by step, into Windows.

WinMain(), Not main()

The first task is to define your main(). Only, in Windows, it's now named WinMain(), and it takes different arguments from what you're used to. Here's a function prototype:

```
void APIENTRY WinMain(HINSTANCE hInstance,
                      HINSTANCE hPrevInstance,
                      LPSTR     lpCmdLine,
                      int       nCmdShow);
```

Don't worry too much about APIENTRY; it's a macro that turns into _stdcall, which tells the compiler to treat this function's arguments and return value in a way that's compatible with Windows. The bottom line is that you need it for your program to work.

Table 1.1 shows the rest of the parameters.

Now you've seen exactly how WinMain is different from the old main(). Probably the most important things to realize are that you should keep track of your hInstance and that your command line is one big string, not several little strings.

For what it's worth, one thing remains the same between main() and WinMain(): exit codes. The value you return from WinMain() becomes the exit code of your application. You can return any number you want, but you will usually want to follow the standard and return 0 to indicate success and −1 to indicate failure.

You can now write the beginnings of your first Windows program:

```
void APIENTRY WinMain(HINSTANCE hInstance,
                      HINSTANCE hPrevInstance,
                      LPSTR     lpCmdLine,
                      int       nCmdShow)
{
  return(0);
}
```

Note that, if you compiled and ran this program now, everything would work fine, except that nothing would happen. You could say that this program does nothing perfectly. Keep in mind that Windows doesn't "give" you a window when your program starts automatically; it's up to you to create one. At this point, all that happens is that Windows creates a new task, which then immediately exits. You can't even see it.

Table 1.1 The Parameters for WinMain

Parameter	Description
hInstance	The first parameter is an instance handle given to you by Windows. Think of it as an ID card for your program—occasionally, Windows will ask you for your ID, and you will have to give it this value. Internally, Windows uses this to tell your program apart from all the other programs running on the system. When your program starts, it should store the hInstance somewhere so that it can pass back the hInstance to certain Windows functions later.
hPrevInstance	You can ignore this guy. The Win32 SDK documentation tells you that it will always be NULL for a Win32 application. In 16-bit Windows, it used to mean something; it doesn't any longer.
lpCmdLine	This is the new form of the old familiar argc and argv[] variables in the old-style main(). lpCmdLine is a string that contains everything the user specifies on the command line, except your program name. If your EXE is named coolgame, and you launch it on the command line with a few parameters by typing **coolgame /window /fast /nosound**, lpCmdLine will contain /window /fast /nosound.
nCmdShow	This tells you how your program window should be displayed on the screen. When users of your program create a shortcut, they can specify how your program's main window should start. Windows passes their request through this variable. It's up to you to look at this value and then do what it says. For example, if your program is supposed to start up maximized, this value will contain SQ_MAXIMIZED. Of course, you can probably ignore this value for your game because your game will probably start in the same window mode, regardless of what Windows says. It will probably always start up full-screen, or if your game is played in a window, it will have specific window dimensions it will use.

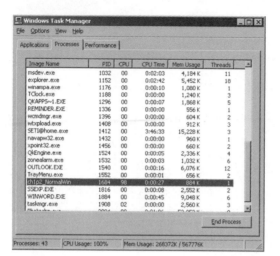

Figure 1.3

Be quick, and you might see your program in the Task Manager.

TIP

If you're really new to Windows, Appendix B contains some instructions on how to compile and run programs using Visual C++, using this as an example. You can find source code for this (and all the code in this book) on the CD-ROM accompanying this book.

TIP

If you're running under Windows NT or 2000 or have access to some sort of Task Manager, you might be able to see your program appear in the task list and then disappear, if you turn up the update speed on your tool. Be quick, and you might see something like Figure 1.3. FYI: You can access the task manager in Windows NT and Windows 2000 by holding down Shift, Ctrl, and Delete, or by right-clicking on your taskbar, but not on a button.

Making a Window in Two Not-So-Easy Steps

Now that you've figured out `WinMain`, it's time to start writing the body of your program. The first thing you must do is to output a line of text, and to output a line of text, you first need somewhere to output it—you need a window. (Yes, you can write text directly onto the desktop or even onto another program's window, but that's not very nice, so I'm not going to talk about it just yet—see the sidebar later in this chapter entitled "Drawing Directly to the Desktop.")

Making a window is a two-step process. First, you register what's called a *window class*. Then, you create a window and link that window to a window class.

Creating a Window Class

Window classes are like character classes in role-playing games. In a role-playing game (RPG), when you create your character, you're usually allowed to choose a character class, such as a thief, wizard, or whatnot. The character class you choose influences your character in several ways—it dictates which skills your character knows, the amount of money your character starts out with, and so on. Each character in an RPG inherits some of its attributes and behavior from its character class.

Similarly, each window in Windows belongs to one, and only one, window class, and the window class influences the window's appearance and behavior. For example, the window class tells Windows which icon appears in the top left of the window.

When you create a window class, you give it a name. When you create a window, you tell it the name of the window class you'd like it to use. That's how windows and window classes are linked together.

The window class was originally made to help out when more than one window or instance of the same application is running. You're not concerned about that here because most games have only one window and only one window class. For now, let the generic explanation suffice, and concentrate on how to register a window class.

The function call to register a window class is RegisterClassEx. Probably everything in

HELP REFERENCE

By the way, assuming that you installed the online help system with Visual C++, you can access help for the RegisterClassEx function by selecting Index from the Help drop-down menu within DevStudio. A new window appears, with tabs on the left side. Click the Index tab, type in **RegisterClassEx**, and select the topmost entry in the list. You are rewarded with detailed online help for RegisterClassEx.

that function name except the last two letters makes sense. The deal with the Ex is that it stands for *Extended*.

Originally, there was only RegisterClass, but as time went on and Windows became more complex, the old RegisterClass function became obsolete. Therefore, Microsoft made a new one and named it RegisterClassEx. The old API function RegisterClass is still around, but it isn't as powerful as the new RegisterClassEx, so you should use the new one.

> **TIP**
>
> As you browse through the DirectX sample programs included with the SDK, you might come across a function named UnregisterClass. Fear not—RegisterClass UnregisterClass simply unregisters the window class you created with RegisterClass. Windows automatically deletes all the window classes you created when your program exits, so you don't need a call to UnregisterClass in your code, although some programmers do, just for the sake of "being clean."

Here's the prototype:

```
ATOM RegisterClassEx(
  CONST WNDCLASSEX *lpwcx  // address of structure with class data
);
```

The good news is that RegisterClassEx takes only one function argument. The bad news is that the one argument is an address of a WNDCLASSEX structure, and the structure contains several variables:

```
typedef struct _WNDCLASSEX {
    UINT     cbSize;
    UINT     style;
    WNDPROC  lpfnWndProc;
    int      cbClsExtra;
    int      cbWndExtra;
    HANDLE   hInstance;
    HICON    hIcon;
    HCURSOR  hCursor;
    HBRUSH   hbrBackground;
    LPCTSTR  lpszMenuName;
    LPCTSTR  lpszClassName;
    HICON    hIconSm;
} WNDCLASSEX;
```

Take a look at Table 1.2, which shows these structure members in detail.

Table 1.2 The WNDCLASSEX Structure Members

Member	Description
cbSize	This one is the easiest to understand. It has no influence on how your window is created; the only thing you must do with cbSize is to set it to the size of the WNDCLASSEX structure. This might seem like a silly thing to do, but it's actually very important because if you don't set this, RegisterClassEx will fail. If you're curious, the reason cbSize exists is so that the RegisterClassEx function can tell what your program thinks the size of the WNDCLASSEX structure is and can, from that information, figure out for which version of the Windows API your program was written. If cbSize is not set correctly, the RegisterClassEx function says to itself, "Well, I have no idea what this guy expects from me," and then proceeds to fail. Always be sure that you set it.
Style	The window's style. You specify style by ORing together the flags for the styles you'd like turned on. There are many available styles, and they're all listed in the help, but the only ones you're going to need are CS_HREDRAW and CS_VRE-DRAW. Together, these two styles tell Windows that you'd like your window *repainted* (redrawn) whenever its width or height is moved or resized.
lpfnWndProc	This is probably the most important element in this structure. This parameter is the address of a WindowProc, which is a callback function in your code. The lpfnWndProc pointer tells Windows which function in your program it should call when an event happens. Don't worry too much yet about the specifics of how this works. I cover those in the "Handlinh Events (Pumping Messages)" section. For now, just know that lpfnWndProc is a pointer to your event-handling function.

Table 1.2 Continued

Member	Description
cbClsExtra, cbWndExtra	These aren't terribly important. They allow you to set up extra storage space in your window and window class so that you have someplace to store custom properties. You will probably always set these to zero because you won't need any custom properties.
hInstance	This is the hInstance you received as a parameter in your WinMain function. This is Windows asking you for your ID— oblige it by providing the hInstance it gave you at the start of your program.
hIcon	This is a handle to a *big icon*. Big icons are 32×32 pixels square. In Windows 3.11, they used to be shown when your application was minimized to an icon. Nowadays, they're displayed in only a few places—for example, on the task-switching window that appears when you press Alt+Tab. To tell Windows the icon it should use for this window class, you need to create an icon in your resource script, give it an ID (usually starting with IDI_), and then put the ID into this variable. Alternatively, you can specify NULL here—if you do that, Windows uses a generic Windows logo as the icon for your application (see Figure 1.4). For more information about resource scripts and custom icons, see the next chapter.
hCursor	This is a handle to a mouse cursor the window should use by default. Usually, you will want to set this to the standard arrow cursor. You do this with the following line of code: `wc.hCursor = LoadCursor(NULL, IDC_ARROW);`

Table 1.2 Continued

Member	Description
	You can also hide the mouse cursor altogether. This is useful if you're running full screen and/or drawing your own mouse cursor. You do this using a strategically placed NULL, like so: `wc.hCursor = NULL;` You can also create custom mouse cursors. I talk about how to do that in the next chapter.
hbrBackground	This contains a handle to something called a *brush*. Brushes tell Windows how to fill an area. For example, if you create a black brush and then draw a rectangle with that black brush, Windows fills the area inside the rectangle black (that is, it "paints" the inside of the rectangle, using the black brush). This variable tells Windows which brush it should use to repaint your window's background automatically. For example, if you put in a white brush here, Windows automatically paints the inside of your window white. You will learn about how to create brushes of specific colors and patterns later, in the GDI brushes section, even though you probably won't need to use one here. Specifying a brush right here can lead to really annoying flickering of your game. If your game is running in a window, and you don't play your cards right, Windows might repaint your window's background at the wrong time, creating an irritating flicker. For now, tell Windows never to repaint your background, by specifying NULL for your hbrBackground.

Table 1.2 Continued

Member	Description
lpszMenuName	You probably won't use this, so set it to NULL. If you want windows of this class to have a menu (you know, the File, Edit, and so on, drop-down menus, shown in Figure 1.5), this is where you specify the resource name of the menu you set up in the resource editor. If not, leave it NULL, and your window will remain menu-less.
lpszClassName	This is the name you'd like to assign to this window class. It is the name you will specify to the CreateWindowEx function to link your new window to this class. In other words, if you created a class with a name of MyCoolWindowClass to tie a window to that class, you'd specify MyCoolWindowClass as the name of the window class you'd like to use when you're creating the window. You don't have to make your class names terribly descriptive, but it helps if they have unique names. A good method is to tack your company name on to your window class names somehow, as in SpinStudiosMainWindow.
hIconSm	This is a handle to a *small icon* (16×16 pixels). Windows displays this icon several places, including the upper-left corner of the window (see Figure 1.6). If you set this to NULL, you get a default Windows logo for a small icon.

Figure 1.4

*The standard-issue
Windows icon.*

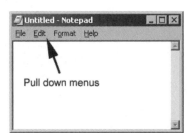

Figure 1.5

*Drop-down menus
in Windows.*

Figure 1.6

*The default small
(16×16) icon in
Windows.*

Wow! Talk about a lot of things to fill in. Take a moment and look at all these at once. The following code illustrates a typical window class creation:

```
// set up and register window class
WNDCLASSEX wc;
memset(&wc, 0, sizeof(wc)); // clear everything, just to be safe.
wc.cbSize = sizeof(wc);
wc.style = CS_HREDRAW | CS_VREDRAW;
wc.lpfnWndProc = WindowProc;
wc.cbClsExtra = 0; // hint: you don't really need these lines,
wc.cbWndExtra = 0; // since we just cleared the struct.
wc.hInstance = g_hInstance;
wc.hIcon = LoadIcon(g_hInstance, "IDI_APP_ICON");
wc.hIconSm = LoadIcon(g_hInstance, "IDI_APP_ICON");
wc.hCursor = LoadCursor(NULL, IDC_ARROW);
wc.hbrBackground = NULL;
wc.lpszMenuName = NULL;
wc.lpszClassName = "SpinStudiosMainWindow";
RegisterClassEx(&wc);
```

Creating a Window

Don't give up now. You're halfway there!

Now you have a window class. The next step is to create a window and link it to that window class. To create a window, you use the surprisingly well-named function CreateWindowEx. CreateWindowEx takes a whole slew of arguments:

> **TIP**
>
> Check out the LoadIcon function used to get handles to hIcon and hIconSm. LoadIcon takes two parameters—your hInstance (ID card) and the name of an icon you created in your resource file. It returns a handle to an icon, which, conveniently enough, is exactly what you need to give to hIcon and hIconSm.

```
HWND CreateWindowEx(
   DWORD dwExStyle,        // extended window style
   LPCTSTR lpClassName,    // pointer to registered class name
   LPCTSTR lpWindowName,   // pointer to window name
   DWORD dwStyle,          // window style
   int x,                  // horizontal position of window
   int y,                  // vertical position of window
   int nWidth,             // window width
   int nHeight,            // window height
   HWND hWndParent,        // handle to parent or owner window
   HMENU hMenu,            // handle to menu or child-window identifier
   HINSTANCE hInstance,    // handle to application instance
   LPVOID lpParam          // pointer to window-creation data
);
```

It's very possible that by now this whole mess seems a little overwhelming. I mean, come on, all you want is to create a window! It might seem simple on the surface, but there are many little details Windows needs to know about before it can create your window, so you must fill in all the arguments here. The good news is that after you understand how CreateWindowEx works, you can wrap the CreateWindowEx and RegisterClassEx functions inside your own window creation function. By wrapping the function, you write it once and then forget about the details of how it works.

And now, Table 1.3 shows the CreateWindowEx parameters.

Those are all the arguments for CreateWindowEx.

Table 1.3 The CreateWindowEx Parameters

Parameter	Description
dwExStyle	This allows you to specify any number of several extended styles you'd like your window to have. (By the way, if you don't know why the first two letters are dw, check out the sidebar on Hungarian notation.) Many cool styles are available, but most of the time you won't need any of them, and you will just set this parameter to 0.
lpClassName	This is a string that tells Windows the name of the window class you'd like your window to use. For example, this is where I would put in SpinStudiosMainWindow to link this window to the window class created in the preceding section.
lpWindowName	This is a string that specifies the name (title) of the window. This is what Windows puts in the title bar of the new window. Usually, you will want to set this to your game's name or a combination of your game and company names.
dwStyle	dwStyle, like its partner in crime, dwExStyle, allows you to specify any number of several window styles. It's through this parameter you tell Windows that you'd like a minimize box, maximize box, thick frame, thin frame, and so on. As you can see in Figure 1.7, many types of windows are available. Here are the most common values for dwStyle: ■ WS_POPUP. Creates a completely blank window (with no menus or anything built in to it) ■ WS_OVERLAPPED. Creates a window with a title bar and a border ■ WS_OVERLAPPEDWINDOW. Creates a "normal" window, with all the controls (min, max, and close)
x, y	These two x and y parameters tell Windows where to place the upper-left corner of the window initially. Keep in mind that screen coordinates are backwards from normal Cartesian coordinates. In Cartesian coordinate systems, positive y means *up*; in screen coordinates, positive y means *down*. Positive x still means *right*.

Table 1.3 Continued

Parameter	Description
	In English, what this means is that (0,0) represents the upper-left corner of the screen, and, assuming that you're running in 1024×768 resolution, (1023,767) represents the lower-right corner of the screen (see Figure 1.8).
nWidth, nHeight	These specify the width and height of your window, in pixels. For your first Windows program, you can just set these to some arbitrary values that give you a nicely sized window. In real life, when you're writing a windowed game, you will probably know exactly how big your window should be (or you will let the user choose a size), so filling these in should be a snap.
hWndParent	This is a handle to the parent of the new window, also known as the *owner* of the new window. If this is your main application window, set this to NULL. A NULL here means that the Windows desktop owns your window, which is correct for top-level application windows.
hMenu	This is a handle to a menu you'd like to appear at the top of this window. If this is NULL, Windows uses the menu handle specified inside the window class—if *that's* NULL, your window doesn't get a menu. Most games don't need drop-down menus because they handle their GUI internally, so most of the time you will want NULL here and NULL in your window class.
hInstance	This hInstance parameter tells Windows which program should be associated with this window. You should pass in here the same hInstance you got in WinMain.
lpParam	lpParam is occasionally used in advanced Win32 application programming and for multiple-document windows. You will more than likely set this to NULL.

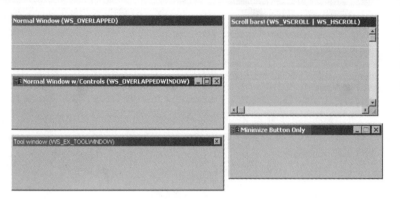

Figure 1.7

A sampling of the window styles available in Windows.

Figure 1.8

The pixel coordinates of a 1024×768 display.

Now, you will wrap up this messy business of window creation by looking at the whole enchilada. Here's some code that registers a window class and creates a window using that class:

```
HWND               hwnd;
WNDCLASSEX         wc;
// set up and register window class
WNDCLASSEX wc;
memset(&wc, 0, sizeof(wc)); // clear everything, just to be safe.
wc.cbSize = sizeof(wc);
wc.style = CS_HREDRAW | CS_VREDRAW;
wc.lpfnWndProc = WindowProc;
wc.cbClsExtra = 0; // hint: you don't really need these lines
wc.cbWndExtra = 0; // because you just cleared the struct.
```

```
wc.hInstance = g_hInstance;
wc.hIcon = LoadIcon(g_hInstance, "IDI_APP_ICON");
wc.hIconSm = LoadIcon(g_hInstance, "IDI_APP_ICON");
wc.hCursor = LoadCursor(NULL, IDC_ARROW);
wc.hbrBackground = NULL;
wc.lpszMenuName = NULL;
wc.lpszClassName = "SpinStudiosMainWindow";
RegisterClassEx(&wc);

// create a window
hwnd = CreateWindowEx(0, "SpinStudiosMainWindow", "My First Window",
        WS_POPUP, 0, 0, xres, yres, NULL, NULL, hInstance, NULL);
if (!hwnd) {
  ::MessageBox(NULL, "CreateWindow failed!",
    "My First Window", MB_ICONSTOP);
}
```

Hungarian Notation

Hungarian notation is a technique you can use to make your code more read-able for yourself and other people. It also helps you read Windows functions because most Microsoft code adheres to Hungarian notation.

It's called *Hungarian notation* because one day while working at Microsoft, an Hungarian programmer named Charles Simonyi had an idea: Make code easier to read by formatting every variable a certain way.

In particular, a variable starts with a few letters that define its type, followed by a verbose name in which each word begins with a capital letter.

There is a small set of "standard" variable prefixes:

c	char
f	float
d	double
b	bool
by	byte
dw	DWORD (unsigned long)
i	Integer
ndx	Array index (for looping, short or long integer)
n	Number (for looping or just general storage)

fn	Function pointer
ui	Unsigned integer
ul	Unsigned long
s, str	String (usually a string class, not a char *)
sz	NULL-terminated, ASCIIZ string
lp	Long pointer
lpstr	Long pointer to a string (char *)
lpcstr	Long pointer to a constant string (const char *)
lpctstr	Long pointer to a constant TCHAR string (const TCHAR *)
msg	Windows message
h	Handle
hwnd	Window handle
hbrsh	Brush handle
hdc	Device context handle

Based on these prefixes, you can make variables such as iPosX (an integer specifying an x position), strPlayerName, ulHitPoints, hInstance, and so on.

You should also use prefixes that make sense for other unlisted variable types. For example, rectDrawingArea would be a good name for a rectangle that specifies your drawing area; sprPlayer would be a good name for a player character sprite. Keep the prefix at three or four characters, and stay consistent throughout your code.

There are a couple additional rules for C++. First, every class name should start with a C, for example, CPlayerCharacter, CGameRules, and so on. Also, member variables of a class should be prefixed with an additional m_, so if CPlayerCharacter had a hit points variable, it would be named m_ulHitPoints.

Global variables are usually noted with a g_, as in g_lpCmdLine.

Some programmers believe the benefits of Hungarian notation to be vast—errors stemming from programmers' forgetting variable types are virtually eliminated, so code readability is improved, and syntax errors are reduced. Other programmers believe Hungarian notation to be the work of the devil. One of the main problems with it, they argue, is that if you change a variable type after writing some code, you must also change the name of the variable. Or, even worse, you may forget or neglect to change the variable name, in which case the Hungarian notation actually obfuscates the true behavior of the code. The only way you will know whether you like it is to try it.

TIP

Notice the `::MessageBox` **line. The** `MessageBox` **Win32 API function is a great way to display critical errors or status to your user. The first parameter is an** `HWND` **that owns your message box (if you pass in** `NULL`**, the desktop will own your message box, as if your message box were an application). The second parameter is the text of your message; the third parameter is the caption of the message box. The last parameter can be one of several message box styles—for example, it's here that you can specify which icon you'd like to display with your message, whether you want Yes and No buttons or just an OK button, and so on.**

If you want to learn more about message boxes right now, you can skip ahead to the next chapter, where there's a whole section on how to use them.

That's all there is to it! Easy, right?

As mentioned earlier, the good news is that you don't need to know every detail of window creation. This section goes into all that detail simply because it's important that, for your first Win32 program, you understand exactly what each line of code does. In reality, you will find that most games create normal windows, so you should be able to cut and paste the code here into a function in your own game and not worry about the specific inner workings of it.

Before you can call this section done, you need to learn about one more function—`ShowWindow`. As its name implies, `ShowWindow` displays a window on the screen. By default, just because you create a window doesn't mean that it appears. You need to make a separate call to `ShowWindow` to get your window to appear.

In the sample programs for this chapter, you will find this function at the very end of the `InitWindow` function. You call `ShowWindow` right after you create your window, to make sure that the window is visible.

Sample Program Reference

If you don't believe me, run the `Ch1p1_HackedWindowProc` **program included with this book.**

`ShowWindow` takes one of several `SW_` constants, which let you specify whether you'd like your window maximized, minimized, and so on. All these constants are listed in the help, but luckily, you don't have to know about them—one of the arguments to your `WinMain` function is named `nCmdShow` and contains the correct constant to pass to `ShowWindow`. You simply pass it this value, whatever that might be.

TIP

Note that even now, you still can't run this program. If you try to put the sample lines into a CPP file and compile it, you're going to get an error because you don't have anywhere for lpfnWndProc to point.

Say that you put on your hacking hat and set lpfnWndProc to NULL in your window class. This gets your program to compile, but what happens when it runs? Well, it crashes. This should tell you that it's probably not okay to have lpfnWndProc set to NULL.

Undeterred by the crash, say that you then define an empty WindowProc, like so:

```
/ our hacked WindowProc function
LRESULT CALLBACK WindowProc(HWND hwnd, UINT uMsg,
                            WPARAM wParam, LPARAM lParam)

{
return(1);
}
```

You make lpfnWndProc point to this hacked WindowProc, and you get things to compile. If you're lucky, when you run your program, you will see the flash of a window appearing and then immediately disappearing (but don't take my word for it—compile and run the Ch1_HackedWindowProc program included on your CD).

This is because, when your program exits, Windows automatically destroys all windows associated with it (that is, all windows that have the same hInstance as the program that just exited). Your program begins, creates a window, ends, and then gets its window destroyed, all in the blink of an eye.

TIP

Alternatively, rather than call ShowWindow, you could use the window style WS_VISIBLE, which automatically shows the window when it's created. Which one you use is up to you, just so long as when all's said and done, your window is shown.

Handling Events (Pumpin' Messages)

At this point, the logical question you're probably asking is, "How do I get my cute little window to stay up?" Because Windows destroys your window when your program exits, the logical answer to that is, "Don't return from `WinMain`."

Say that you put an endless loop inside your `WinMain` function, right after you create your window, like so:

```
while (1) { /* do absolutely nothing! */ }
```

Now your window stays up, but it absolutely refuses to do anything. It won't move, you can't minimize it, and you can't even close it. Obviously, your code is missing something.

What it's missing is called a *message pump*. As hinted before, Windows generates *events* (called *Windows Messages*) when certain things happen. When you tried to close your window by clicking its × button, Windows dutifully generated a close message and put that in your program's message queue.

The problem was that the program never checked its message queue.

Pretend that you go down to your local post office and open a post office box in your name. The post office will put any messages for you inside your post office box, but it's up to you to check it every so often and to do something with any messages you find inside the box. The reason your program wasn't responding to anything is that it was never checking its "post office box" (that is, its message queue). Windows was putting messages in your queue; you just never bothered to retrieve them.

How do you get your program to check its message queue? Easy. You write a message pump. A *message pump* is a chunk of code that periodically checks its message queue. To begin learning how a message pump works, look at a completed message pump. Here's a typical game's message pump:

```
MSG msg;
while (1) {
  if (PeekMessage(&msg, NULL, 0, 0, PM_NOREMOVE)) {
    if (!GetMessage(&msg, NULL, 0, 0)) return msg.wParam;
    TranslateMessage(&msg);
    DispatchMessage(&msg);
  }
}
```

Yes, that looks overwhelming, but, I hope that you can follow the basic structure (check out the flowchart in Figure 1.9).

TIP

Here's another thing to think about. When a program *hangs*, or stops responding, it's because for some reason or another it has become locked in an endless loop and has stopped checking its message queue.

Ever notice how sometimes a hung application will come back from the dead? That is, it will suddenly start responding again? This is the application finally getting around to checking its message queue once again.

Even when applications are dead, Windows still dutifully puts messages into their message queues. If you start clicking around on a hung application, Windows will still put messages in that application's message queue. If that application eventually finishes whatever's causing it to hang, it processes all those messages.

This is why, if you click minimize on a hung application, when the hung application comes back to life, it immediately minimizes. It finally gets around to looking in its message queue, sees the old minimize message, and acts on it.

This is also the reason you can continue typing into a busy application and not lose any letters—each key you press is a separate message that is put into that application's message queue.

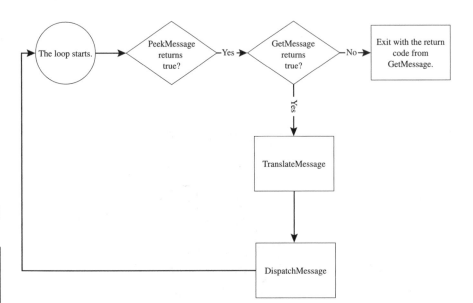

Figure 1.9

A flowchart showing how a message pump works.

You have an endless loop (the `while(1)` business).

Within that loop, you're calling `PeekMessage`.

If `PeekMessage` returns true, you call `GetMessage` and then `TranslateMessage` and `DispatchMessage`, whatever *those* are.

If `GetMessage` returns false, you return from `WinMain` with an exit code defined by `msg.wParam`. (Notice that this is the *only* way you can escape from the endless loop.)

I'm going to spend the next several pages discussing these four functions—`PeekMessage`, `GetMessage`, `TranslateMessage`, and `DispatchMessage`—but first, you should find out what a message is, exactly.

Windows Messages

Windows Messages are one of the ways Windows communicates with your program. These Windows Messages are represented by the `MSG` structure. Take a peek at the inside of the `MSG` structure, and see what each member is for:

```
typedef struct tagMSG {
    HWND    hwnd;     // target of message
    UINT    message;  // type of message
    WPARAM  wParam;   // parameter
    LPARAM  lParam;   // parameter
    DWORD   time;     // time message was received
    POINT   pt;       // cursor position when message was generated
} MSG;
```

First, all messages have a type. The type is a constant, which is prefixed with `WM_`, for *Windows Message*. When a key is pressed down, you get a `WM_KEYDOWN` message. When the mouse moves, you get a `WM_MOUSEDOWN` message, and so on. The `message` member of the `MSG` structure is the message type.

Next, each message can contain parameters. For example, a `WM_KEYDOWN` message contains specific parameters that tell you which key was pressed. These additional parameters live in the two variables `wParam` and `lParam`. `wParam` and `lParam` are 32-bits long each.

HELP REFERENCE

If you're curious, you can use the DevStudio help to get a list of all the available message types. Type **WM_** in the search box on the Index tab, and double-click the `WM_messages` entry at the top of the list. From there, you can browse all the message types.

Yeah, there are quite a few.

Exactly *how* all the parameters are stuffed into these two 32-bit variables depends on the type of message. For example, one message might break the 32 bits into 4 bytes of distinct information, whereas another might use all 32 bits to hold one long integer. If you look at the Windows API documentation for a specific WM_ type, it will tell you how all the parameters are stuffed.

A message also contains a window handle (hwnd), which specifies where the message is supposed to be delivered. For now, just know that this exists; you will learn about it in more detail later, when you get to the section on dispatching messages.

Finally, each message contains two additional tidbits of information: the time when that message was generated and the position of the mouse cursor when that message was generated. You will probably never use these, but you should sleep better at night knowing that they're there if you need them.

So that's a message. Now look at how the four functions PeekMessage, GetMessage, TranslateMessage, and DispatchMessage work together to make a message pump. You will start with PeekMessage.

PeekMessage

PeekMessage is a flexible function that behaves in different ways, depending on what you pass it. It can be used to see quickly whether any messages are waiting, to get a particular message, or to filter messages (if you want to know only about messages of a certain type). To start this explanation of PeekMessage, here is its function prototype:

```
BOOL PeekMessage(
    LPMSG lpMsg,          // pointer to structure for message
    HWND hWnd,            // handle to window
    UINT wMsgFilterMin,   // first message
    UINT wMsgFilterMax,   // last message
    UINT wRemoveMsg       // removal flags
);
```

Table 1.4 shows PeekMessage's parameters.

PeekMessage returns true (nonzero) if a message is waiting and false (zero) if not.

As you can see, PeekMessage is a flexible little guy. However, you're probably going to use him to do only one thing: to see whether there are any messages you'd like to process. Now revisit the PeekMessage line of code in your message pump:

```
if (PeekMessage(&msg, NULL, 0, 0, PM_NOREMOVE)) [
```

Table 1.4 PeekMessage Parameters

Parameter	Description
lpMsg	This is a pointer to an MSG structure that will be filled in with the data of the first message in the queue (or, if you're filtering, the first message that makes it through the filter).
hWnd	This allows you to filter out messages belonging only to a certain window (you pass the handle of the window you're interested in here, if you want to filter). If you put in NULL here, you get messages to all windows—generally speaking, you *always* want to put in NULL, or you might "miss" a message, causing your dialog buttons not to work or other things to break.
wMsgFilterMin, wMsgFilterMax	These are the low and high bounds for the types of messages you want to filter on. All the WM_ message types are really just numbers, so if you only care about a certain range of messages, you can filter everything else out by specifying a range here. Setting both of these to 0 turns off filtering, which is generally what you will want.
wRemoveMsg	This parameter tells PeekMessage whether it should remove the message from your message queue. It can be one of two values: PM_REMOVE or PM_NOREMOVE. PM_REMOVE means that PeekMessage will remove the message it puts in lpMsg from the message queue; PM_NOREMOVE tells PeekMessage to leave the message in the queue.

From what you now know of how `PeekMessage` works, you can see that this line requests any type of message (the two zero parameters) for any window (the `NULL` parameter) and puts it into `msg` without removing it from the queue (the `PM_NOREMOVE`). You can see that the `if` statement is really saying, "If there's a message to process...."

For the second half of that sentence, take a look at `GetMessage`.

GetMessage

The `GetMessage` function is similar to the `PeekMessage` function, but with a couple key differences.

If no messages are in the queue, `GetMessage` waits until there is one. In other words, when you call `GetMessage`, the potential exists that it will wait a long while before returning. Because most games do background animations and whatnot, this is usually a bad thing. Most of the time, you want to be absolutely sure that there's something for `GetMessage` to get before you call it. That's why, in the preceding message pump code, there's a previous call to `PeekMessage`—to make sure that there's a message for `GetMessage` to get.

`GetMessage`'s return value has special significance because it tells your program when it should quit.

Now take a quick look at `GetMessage`'s parameters:

```
BOOL GetMessage(
    LPMSG lpMsg,           // address of structure with message
    HWND hWnd,             // handle of window
    UINT wMsgFilterMin,    // first message
    UINT wMsgFilterMax     // last message
);
```

Looks familiar, doesn't it? In fact, these four parameters are identical to the first four parameters of `PeekMessage`. The only thing missing is the last parameter (the `PM_REMOVE` or `PM_NOREMOVE`). This is because `GetMessage` always removes the message from the message queue—you have no choice in the matter.

Here's an important point. `GetMessage` returns 0 if your application should quit—that is, if your application receives a quit message.

Now the second line of your message pump makes more sense:

```
if (!GetMessage(&msg, NULL, 0, 0)) return msg.wParam;
```

Basically, you just pull the message out of the message queue and put it into `msg`. If you're supposed to quit, you use the message's `wParam` value as your exit code.

If you combine this now-understood line of code with what you know about PeekMessage, you can finally complete your sentence: "If there's a message to process, remove it from the queue and put it in msg. And by the way, if I should quit, do so."

Two down, one to go. TranslateMessage and DispatchMessage come next.

TranslateMessage

Here's the function prototype:

```
BOOL TranslateMessage(
  CONST MSG *lpMsg   // address of structure with message
);
```

TranslateMessage is a very easy function prototype to understand: It takes a pointer to a message and returns either true or false—but what's it doing?

It's translating certain messages into different messages. For example, say that you have both a WM_KEYDOWN message and a WM_KEYUP message in your message queue. What this means is that the user pressed a key. It'd be much more convenient if, instead of having two messages, you had just one message telling you that a key has been pressed.

You're in luck—that's exactly what TranslateMessage does. It sucks out all the WM_KEYDOWN and WM_KEYUP messages from your message queue and converts them into one WM_CHAR message.

What do you do with a message after you translate it? Most of the time, you *dispatch* it, that is, allow Windows to send the message to the window where it's supposed to go. This is where DispatchMessage comes into play.

DispatchMessage

Here's the prototype:

```
LONG DispatchMessage(
  CONST MSG *lpmsg   // pointer to structure with message
);
```

Brace yourself—this is where you tie a lot of loose ends together.

Recall that at the start of this chapter, I talked about callback functions. Also recall that as you went through the process of creating a window class, there was one particular value—lpfnWndProc, the pointer to a window's callback function—that I glossed over.

Here's how that's used. You give the `DispatchMessage` function a message. It looks at the target window of that message, finds the window class of that window, and calls the function that you specified in the `lpfnWndProc` structure member for that window class.

In other words, the `DispatchMessage` function dispatches the message to the appropriate window callback function. The return value of `DispatchMessage` is the exact same return value of the callback function—if your callback function returns 3, `DispatchMessage` returns 3.

Take a breather while I summarize this complex process.

The first thing that happens is that you peek and see whether a message is waiting to be processed. If so, you get the message (which removes it from your message queue). When you have the message, you translate it (to simply which messages are available). You then tell Windows to dispatch the message to the appropriate window. You assume that your main window's callback function looks at the message, acts on it somehow, and returns a number to `DispatchMessage`, which returns that same number. Presto, message processed.

You do this until `GetMessage` returns zero, which means that it's time to quit. When `GetMessage` returns zero, you use the `wParam` value of the message you just got as your return code from `WinMain` (which is your program's exit code).

That's how a message pump works. The cool thing about knowing about message pumps is that you have a base from which to learn how all the other parts of a windowed application or game fit together. If a Windows application is like the Death Star, the message pump is the mechanism at the center that Luke has to destroy. If someone handed you all bazillion lines of code to Microsoft Word tomorrow, you could eventually figure out how the entire application works if you found the message pump.

There's one part you still haven't addressed: how your window's callback function processes a message that was dispatched to it. Next session, please.

Fleshing Out WindowProc

You've learned the intricacies of how to translate and dispatch messages. Now it's time to learn how to use the `WindowProc` function to accomplish work within your application.

I'll begin talking about `WindowProc` by presenting the required function prototype:

```
LRESULT CALLBACK WindowProc(
    HWND hwnd,          // handle to window
    UINT uMsg,          // message identifier
    WPARAM wParam,      // first message parameter
    LPARAM lParam       // second message parameter
);
```

> **TIP**
>
> Realize one thing, before I get started talking about `WindowProc`: You don't have to name it `WindowProc`. The `lpfnWndProc` member of the window class needs to point to a function that has a certain *signature* (that is, it has to have the same number of arguments, argument types, and so on), but it doesn't have to be named `WindowProc`. In fact, most of the time it *shouldn't* be named `WindowProc`—better to name it something that makes sense to you, such as `MainGameWindowProc` or even `GamewindowMessageProcessor`.

Let's start with the return value. `LRESULT` is really just a long; specifically, it's a 32-bit value. It can be anything, but the general convention is to return nonzero if you successfully processed the message and zero if you didn't.

Next, the `CALLBACK` modifier tells Windows that this is a callback function. `CALLBACK` specifies a certain type of calling convention that's required for Windows to call the function properly. The bottom line is that you should have it in there, right before the name of your function.

> **TIP**
>
> Many programmers use static methods of C++ objects as their message-handling callback function. This is perfectly legal because static C++ methods don't have a hidden `this` parameter. For example, you could write code like the following:
>
> ```
> class CMyWindow {
> ...
> public:
>   static LRESULT ProcessMessage(HWND hwnd,
>     UINT hMsg, WPARAM wParam, LPARAM lParam);
> }
>  LRESULT CMyWindow::ProcessMessage(HWND hwnd,
>                         UINT hMsg,
>                         WPARAM wParam, LPARAM lParam)
>  {
>  // message handling goes here
> }
> ```
>
> This is perfectly okay, and if your program is truly object oriented, using static methods as message-handling functions makes a lot of sense.

Now look at the arguments you get, presented in Table 1.5.

You have your target window, message, and message parameters. To get work done, the first thing you do is to make a switch statement for the message ID, something like this:

```
switch(uMsg) {
  case WM_MOUSEMOVE:
    // the mouse has moved! do something!
    return(1); // to show that we've processed this message.
  case WM_CHAR:
    // the user has typed a character! do something!
    return(1); // to show that we've processed this message.
}
```

Table 1.5 Arguments to WindowProc

Parameter	Description
hwnd	This is a handle to a window. Remember, this WindowProc function is linked to a window class, not a specific window. If you have more than one window with the same window class, you need a way to identify them. That's what hwnd does. Usually, you won't have to worry about this situation because you will probably have only one window class and one window using that class. Just know that hwnd refers to the window that got the message.
uMsg	This is the ID of the message (WM_MOUSEMOVE, WM_KEYDOWN, and so on) and the two parameters for that message (wParam and lParam). Bonus points for you if you noticed that all these are contained in the msg you gave to DispatchMessage in your message pump. Your WindowProc function gets everything contained in the MSG structure, except the time and the cursor position (which you don't need anyway).
wParam, lParam	These are the arguments for the message. Their exact value and format vary, depending on which message you receive (that is, which message is in the uMsg parameter).

Of course, WM_MOUSEMOVE and WM_CHAR aren't the only messages you would receive. In fact, if you looked at the WM_ list in the help for DevStudio, you know that there are a *lot* of different messages, and to be a good little window, you have to respond to all the messages somehow. It would be really irritating if you had to make a separate case in your switch statement for each one. Your switch would take up 20 pages of code! How do you cope?

The good news is that Microsoft has provided a Win32 API function named DefWindowProc. You can hand this function the parameters you received (hwnd, uMsg, wParam, and lParam), and it will do something "normal" for that message. In other words, when you call DefWindowProc, you're saying, "I have nothing special I want to do with this message, so, DefWindowProc, I would like you to process this message just as all the other normal windows do." That way, you don't have to worry constantly about correctly processing all the messages—you just handle the ones you're interested in and hand off all the other junk to DefWindowProc.

It's certainly possible to hand off *all* your messages to DefWindowProc. When you do that, you end up with a perfectly normal window. It has nothing in it, but it moves around, sizes, and generally behaves just like all the other windows.

Now, finally, you can come back to your original goal—creating a Windows program that displays a message to the screen (in a window), waits for a key, and then exits. To make this work requires nothing more than paying attention to three key messages—WM_CLOSE, WM_PAINT, and WM_CHAR.

Because WM_CLOSE is the most important, I will talk about that one first.

> ## Sample Program Reference
> If you'd like to see an example of a normal window in action, check out the Ch1p2_NormalWindow sample program.

WM_CLOSE

The WM_CLOSE message is sent to you when the user closes your window (by clicking the × in the upper-right corner, by double-clicking the icon in the upper right, or by any of the other bazillion ways it's possible to close a window).

At this point, you need to learn about an important distinction between WM_CLOSE and WM_QUIT. Your program already processes WM_QUIT—you don't have a case for it in your callback function's switch statement, but you do check the return value from GetMessage, which returns zero if it sees a WM_QUIT. Therefore, when the OS says, "Quit!" you hear it and respond appropriately.

However—and this is a big distinction—just because a user closes a window doesn't mean that the program always exits. For example, the program may continue to run in the system tray, or in "stealth mode" (in other words, without any visible indication that it's running). Windows doesn't assume that *close* means *quit*. It's your responsibility to make sure that your program ends when its main window is closed.

To quit when your window is closed, you need the following case statement inside your switch:

```
case WM_CLOSE:
  PostQuitMessage(0);
  return(0);
```

> **TIP**
>
> In case you're wondering, DefWindowProc doesn't automatically quit when it gets a close message. In fact, it doesn't do *anything* when it gets a close message.

The PostQuitMessage function is a Win32 API call that places a WM_QUIT message inside your message queue. The next time around the infinite loop, GetMessage notices the WM_QUIT message, and you exit properly.

> **TIP**
>
> Windows has two messages, WM_CLOSE and WM_DESTROY, which have very similar uses.
>
> The WM_CLOSE message is sent to tell the window that it should terminate. You can watch for this message and intercept it to keep your window alive. For example, you might want to ask the user whether he or she really wants to close the window. If the answer is no, ignore the close message and keep your window open.
>
> The WM_DESTROY message is sent to tell the window that it *is* terminating and should destroy any objects it has created. There is nothing you can do to keep your window alive at this point.

You might not realize it, but you've just hit a monumental stage in your learning of Windows programming. At this very moment, you have all the knowledge you need to write a program that displays a normal window and exits when that window is closed.

To celebrate this grand occasion, a sample program named Ch1p2_NormalWindow does just that. Take some time now to check it out and make sure that you understand everything in it before you go any further.

WM_PAINT

The WM_PAINT message is sent when your window needs to redraw itself. It might come as a surprise to you to learn that Windows does not automatically keep track of the contents of each window. Programmers who are first learning how to program in Windows sometimes assume that for each window on the screen, Windows keeps, in memory, a bitmap of that entire window. When a window needs to be drawn, Windows takes care of the drawing by copying (and clipping) the bitmap onto the screen.

That isn't how it works—the memory requirements to store the image of each window are much too intense. Instead, when a window needs to be redrawn, Windows sends a message, and it's up to the individual program to process that message and redraw its window's contents. Windows does keep track of *clipping*, that is, making sure that your window draws only in the area the end user can see, but it's up to your program to redraw its contents.

Also, note that this happens when any part of the window needs to be redrawn. If a user drags another window across your program's window, your program is going to get a lot of WM_PAINT messages.

Let's return to the small program you're trying to port to Windows. Your program should respond to the WM_PAINT message by writing into its window a line of text telling the user that he or she can press any key to exit. How do you write a line of text? Here's the code first, followed by a description of it:

```
case WM_PAINT:
{
  PAINTSTRUCT ps;
  BeginPaint(hwnd, &ps);
  char buf[] = "Look Mom!  I can code in Windows!";
  TextOut(ps.hdc, 0, 0, buf, strlen(buf));
  EndPaint(hwnd, &ps);
}
return(0);
```

First of all, you might be asking yourself, "Self, why did he put opening and closing braces, { and }, around the painting code?" The braces are there to get around the compiler complaints about declaring a variable inside a case statement. In C++, you can declare a new scope anywhere you like—you can even nest your braces arbitrarily. In this scenario, you have to declare a PAINTSTRUCT variable, and your alternatives are either to put it inside braces (which makes a new scope block, which, in turn, makes the compiler happy) or to declare it before the switch statement. Because it isn't going to be used anywhere *other* than inside the WM_PAINT case, it makes sense just to declare a new scope.

The first thing you do is to declare a PAINTSTRUCT. Here's the definition of this structure:

```
typedef struct tagPAINTSTRUCT { // ps
    HDC   hdc;
    BOOL  fErase;
    RECT  rcPaint;
    BOOL  fRestore;
    BOOL  fIncUpdate;
    BYTE  rgbReserved[32];
} PAINTSTRUCT;
```

Notice that you don't initialize anything about the PAINTSTRUCT before you use it in a Win32 API call, BeginPaint. There's not even a cbSize you have to fill in! The structure is here only so that Windows can pass *you* information you need to paint your window. You don't have to pass anything to Windows.

Specifically, Table 1.6 shows everything Windows passes you in the PAINTSTRUCT.

Table 1.6 PAINTSTRUCT Members

Member	Description
hdc	hdc is a handle to something called a *device context*. In the next chapter, I talk more about device contexts (or, as they're known to their friends, *DCs*). Internally, the DC helps Windows keep track of exactly where on the screen your painting is going to happen. For now, just realize that you use this device context in the TextOut function a couple lines down.
fErase	This is a flag telling you whether you should erase your entire background or you can get away with leaving most of your window untouched. If this is nonzero (true), you should erase the background. (Note that if you specified NULL as your background brush when you registered your window class, you're *always* responsible for repainting your background.)
rcPaint	This is a rectangle struct that tells you where you're supposed to be painting. Rectangle structs are really easy; they just have four members: top, bottom, left, and right. The upper-left corner of the rectangle is at (left, top); the lower right is at (right, bottom). This rcPaint variable comes in handy if you need to clear the entire window—you just pass the rectangle directly to a function that makes a solid rectangle of a certain color.
fRestore, fIncUpdate, and rgbReserved	These last three variables are off-limits for you. They're reserved for use by the OS—you should not read them or change them in any way. Pretend that they aren't there.

After your call to BeginPaint, you create a constant string, which is what you're going to display. Next, you hand off the hdc you got in the PAINTSTRUCT—along with a coordinate pair, the string you want to display, and its length—to a function named TextOut. TextOut is a Win32 API function that displays a line of text using the given hdc. Because the hdc Windows gave you corresponds to the display area of your window, the end result is that after TextOut returns, your text is displayed inside your window.

Realize that the coordinates you give to TextOut are relative to the position of your window. In other words, (0,0) doesn't mean the top-left corner of the screen. It means the top-left corner of the inside of your *window*. Windows uses these coordinates, along with the hdc you give it, to determine exactly where on the screen to draw. It looks at your hdc, which is tied to a certain window. From there, it figures out where on the screen the top-left corner of that window is, and it adds those coordinates onto what you gave TextOut in order to come up with the final position at which to draw the text.

Drawing Directly to the Desktop

When I began this chapter, I mentioned that it is possible to draw on the desktop, but I put off telling you exactly how to do it. Now that you know about what's going on behind the scenes, the way you draw to the desktop is by getting the desktop's device context (DC). When you have that, you can pass it to TextOut, and you will be able to write text anywhere.

How do you get the desktop's DC? The following line shows you how:

```
HDC dc = GetDC(NULL);
```

After you have that, you can say

```
TextOut(dc, 0, 0, but, strlen(buf));
```

and your text will appear in the top-left corner of the screen (yes, it will clobber the Start button).

An important caveat: Whenever you call GetDC, as you do here to get the desktop DC, you must also call ReleaseDC. This means that when you're done drawing to the desktop, you must call ReleaseDC(NULL). Failure to do this means that you keep getting new DCs but never releasing them, which can eat up all the available resources on your system. That not only will crash your program but can also cause your entire computer to crash.

By the way, forgetting to release something you got is commonly called a *resource leak*.

That's basically all there is to displaying a message. As you can see, it's quite a bit more involved than just a `printf` call or something, but the good news is that it's also much more powerful. To learn more about what you can do with DCs when you're responding to your paint message, check out the next chapter.

> **Sample Program Reference**
>
> The `Ch1p3_WindowPainting` sample program shows you exactly how to paint inside a window.

WM_CHAR

Now you have a window that paints a message on itself. The next and final step in remaking the program you started this chapter with is to exit when a key is pressed.

You will be delighted to know that this is very easy—you watch for a `WM_CHAR` message, and when one comes in, you post a quit message:

```
switch(uMsg) {
  ...
  case WM_CHAR:
    PostQuitMessage(0);
    return(0);
}
```

> **Sample Program Reference**
>
> For your convenience, the entire source code to the Windows version of this little program is included on the CD. It's named `Ch1_PaintWaitAndExit`.

Easy! With that, you've completed the Windows equivalent of your "wait for a key and exit" program.

CHAPTER WRAP-UP

Wow, talk about warp speed! You've gone from zero to a basic Windows program in just a couple dozen pages. Time to recap.

In this chapter, you learned about the differences between event-driven programming (Windows programming) and regular (DOS) programming. You started your journey into Windows by learning about `WinMain`, window handles, and instance handles (`hInst`).

Next, you learned a bit about window classes and windows and then took a peek at how to create a window class, register it, create a window, and link it to a window class. This included a whole bunch of little topics, such as how to set up the default mouse cursor, display a simple message box, and make windows of different styles. (If you didn't play around with the `WS_EX_TOOLWINDOW` style, you should—it's really cool!)

Finally, you took the window you'd created, added a message pump to it, learned about a few messages (WM_CLOSE, WM_PAINT, and WM_CHAR), and wrote code to respond to those messages so that you ended up with a Windows program that displays a message, waits for a keystroke, and then exits.

Not bad for just a few pages, but this is only the tip of the iceberg. In the next chapter, I discuss advanced GDI techniques, which you can use to draw pictures and maybe even write a simple game!

ABOUT THE SAMPLE PROGRAMS

This chapter's sample programs take you on a coding voyage, from a two-line, empty Windows program to full-fledged window message processing:

- **Ch1p1_HackedWindowProc.** This program shows what happens when you try to hack together a WindowProc. Try it out—it won't do much.
- **Ch1p2_NormalWindow.** This program uses DefWindowProc to create a window that behaves normally. It doesn't do a lot, but at least it isn't rude.
- **Ch1p3_WindowPainting.** This program demonstrates how to process the WM_PAINT message.
- **Ch1p4_PaintWaitAndExit.** This is the finished Windows conversion of the DOS program you made in the beginning of the chapter. This program paints a message to the screen, waits for a keystroke, and then exits.
- **Ch1p5_DOS.** This is the console-based (aka DOS-style) program you convert into Windows during the course of this chapter. It displays a message, waits for a keypress, and then exits.

EXERCISES

Want to learn more? Here are a few exercises you can try.

1. Play around with the various window styles. By combining styles in certain ways, you can create some interesting windows—including windows you've probably never seen before.
2. Make a program that creates a new window, in a different style, when its first window is destroyed, or write one that creates multiple windows and draws different messages in each of them. Doing this will teach you more about the usefulness of hwnd.
3. In the Ch1p1_HackedWindowProc program, figure out why it's important for your blank, hacked WindowProc to return 1 and not 0. Why does CreateWindowEx fail if WindowProc always returns 0? (Need a hint? Check the documentation for CreateWindowEx, and specifically, the WM_NCCREATE message.)
4. Make a program that tracks the mouse cursor's position by intercepting the WM_MOUSEMOVE message, or make one that does something when the left mouse button is clicked. (I'm not going to give away the message for that one! You yourself will have to search the docs.)

CHAPTER 2

ADVANCED WIN32 API PROGRAMMING

"Though this be madness, yet there is method in it."
——*William Shakespeare, Hamlet (II.ii.206)*

This chapter is a collection of topics that will move you beyond knowing just the basics. In this chapter, you'll find detailed information on the Windows GDI, resources, message boxes, and other helpful Win32 topics.

THE WINDOWS GDI

One of my favorite games is still Command and Conquer: Red Alert, by Westwood Studios. For those of you who also played that game, this section is *not* about how to win as the Global Defense Initiative. Besides, I never liked playing the GDI. I always played the Brotherhood of Nod and terrorized everyone with those killer Tesla coils.

But I'm getting off topic. This section is all about the Windows graphics device interface (GDI). The *GDI* is a set of API functions that allow you to draw things to the screen (or to the printer, although for most games, that's irrelevant).

Once again, I have some good news and some bad news.

The good news is that Windows really shines when it comes to graphics functions. One of the primary goals since the *beginning* of Windows (I'm talking Windows 1.0 here, folks) has been to make an operating system that is completely WYSIWYG (*What You See Is What You Get*, pronounced "wussy-wig"—yes, like a cowardly hairpiece). Windows needs to be WYSIWYG, even for high-end desktop publishing applications. As a result of this, the text-, shape-, line-, and font-processing functions of Windows are very powerful. Trust me, you're going to find Windows GDI functions to do anything you can possibly imagine.

The GDI can be divided into several functional areas:

- **Pens, brushes, and shapes.** The GDI supplies you with line- and shape-drawing functions. These functions allow you to draw lines, points, and shapes in various outlines and fill colors. You specify the shape's outline using a "pen"; the fill color is specified through a "brush." You create pens and brushes, use them to draw shapes, and then delete them when you're done. There are several functions you can use to draw all sorts of shapes— rectangles, ellipses, and so on. You probably won't end up using these functions extensively for games. Most 2D games are bitmap (or *sprite*) based, and the GDI isn't really suited for 3D.

- **Bitmaps.** The GDI also allows you to manipulate bitmaps. There are functions to facilitate loading and saving bitmaps, as well as to *blit* (copy) them to a certain part of the screen, stretch them, and so on. GDI is comfortable handling all types and formats of bitmaps, from monochrome to true color. If you write a game using the GDI, you will probably make extensive use of the bitmap functions.
- **Fonts and text.** Font and text output are important parts of the GDI, too. To write text in a particular font, you follow the same process as if you were going to draw a shape in a particular color. That is, you first create the font (if this sounds silly, think of it as creating an *instance* of a font), select the font, output your text, and then delete the font when you're done. (Again, you delete the *instance* of the font. This way, you can't delete the font file stored on disk.) The font- and text-drawing functions are useful for all types of games, especially for drawing title screen menus and such.
- **Regions and clipping.** Finally, the GDI's clipping functions ensure that you're drawing only in the areas you want. Clipping allows you to *mask off* an area of the screen (that is, prevent any drawing from occurring on that area). Windows uses clipping to make sure that your drawing stays within your window, but you can also use it to achieve some interesting effects, as you will see.

The bad news (you knew it was coming, right?) is that because these functions are powerful, they're also somewhat slow. For normal applications, such as Microsoft Word, the GDI functions are fast enough, but for a game that needs to keep a high frame rate, they can be too slow.

Take all the knowledge in this section with a grain of salt. You won't have any speed problems with GDI if you're writing a card or puzzle game (or even a turn-based strategy game). However, you shouldn't try to make extensive use of the GDI in the frame-rendering loop of an action or shooter game. It will probably slow you down too much.

Then why spend time learning it at all, right? Well, there might be certain features of your game you can implement in GDI and thus save yourself a "ton" of development time (at the cost of slow run-time performance). Here's a good example of this.

Say that you're writing an RPG, and you'd like the names of the characters to appear in an Olde School, scripty font. Because the names are chosen by your player, you can't code them into the game. This leaves you two choices. First, you can dig up a book on font programming and begin writing a font engine that supports scripty characters. You spend a couple weeks on the basic code and then three-to-four more weeks making it as fast as possible so that you can call it in every frame of your game and still maintain a good frame rate. A month and a half later, you have your player's name in a cool font (assuming that there are no bugs).

That's option one. The advantage there is that you've written a fast font engine. The disadvantage is that it took you a month and a half to do it.

Color Depths

Seems like every operating system has a different way of specifying color depths. Windows uses several strange names for its color depths.

Both 16-color mode and 256-color mode are easy. In these color modes, pixel colors are computed via a color palette. For example, if you ask a pixel what color it is, it'll say, "I'm color #5." You then have to go look in the color palette to determine what RGB value color #5 corresponds to. In 16-color mode, your palette consists of 16 colors. In 256-color mode, it consists of 256 colors.

When you get past 256-color mode, you leave the realm of the color palette. The next available color depth is called "16-bit color." In this color depth, pixels don't reference a color palette. Instead, their RGB values are stored directly.

16-bit, 24-bit, and 32-bit color are all similar. The only difference involves how many bits each pixel gets to store its color information. This varies somewhat from graphics card to graphics card, but in general, in 16-bit mode (also called "HiColor"), each pixel gets five bits for red, five bits for green, and five bits for blue (leaving one bit unused). This means that each pixel can have 32 (two to the fifth power) distinct levels of red, green, and blue.

24-bit and 32-bit modes up the ante even further. In 24-bit mode (aka, "TrueColor"), each pixel gets eight bits for red, eight bits for green, and eight bits for blue. This gives 255 distinct levels of red, green, and blue color. This approaches the limit of what the human eye can detect.

In 32-bit mode, each pixel gets one byte for red, green, and blue, plus a byte for alpha, which represents how transparent each pixel is. Whether or not this extra byte is actually used varies from card to card.

Now say that you use the GDI instead. Because you've read this chapter, you know that it's really easy to whip up some code to write text in a particular font. Say that you use this in your game. The advantage? You code it in five minutes. The disadvantage? It doesn't run fast in the game.

That might or might not be a problem. If you render the name of the character only once and then store it in an off-screen bitmap or something, you might not care whether the GDI's text output functions are slow. If, on the other hand, you absolutely have to write scripty text each frame, you might have to write the font engine.

The point is that you shouldn't immediately ignore the GDI because it's slow. A horrible assumption most beginning game programmers make is that everything has to be as fast as possible.

That isn't true. *Only the things you call every frame have to be fast.* The rest of it just has to work, and you will come out with a much better game if you spend a month and a half working on something cool (say, extra gameplay features or eye candy) rather than on making something unnecessarily fast.

With that, now you will learn how to use the GDI.

Device Contexts

To use the GDI, you first need to know what a device context (DC) is. There are hints about DCs in the last part of the preceding chapter, but here you're going to sink your teeth into them.

In essence, a *DC* is a handle to a drawing surface. Think of it this way: DCs are to drawing surfaces what file handles are to files (see Figure 2.1).

File Handle   File

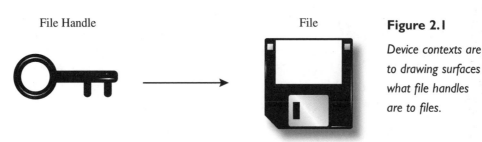

Figure 2.1

Device contexts are to drawing surfaces what file handles are to files.

File handles give you access to files.
DCs give you access to drawing surfaces.

Device Context   Drawing Surface

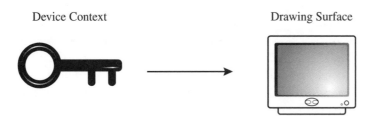

When you want to read or write from a file, you first open that file and retrieve a handle to it. Similarly, when you want to draw to the screen in Windows, you first get a DC for it. Also, just as you must close file handles, you must also "release" DCs when you're done with them.

As said before, Windows internally links your DC to a certain window. From that information, it takes care of clipping your screen output so that if your window is behind another window, and you get a paint update, you don't clobber the other window's contents.

DCs also maintain state; they keep track of the active brush and pen (you will learn about that later), active font, pen position, and a whole slew of other things. This means that if you move the pen position in one DC, you don't move it in another.

> **TIP**
>
> By the way, WYSIWYG is the reason why DCs are a part of Windows. DCs help to abstract screens and printers and make it easier to write WYSIWYG applications.

Additionally, a DC abstracts your drawing surface. For example, if you want to print something, you first get a DC for the printer to which you want to print. You then call GDI functions using that DC just as if you were drawing to the screen.

Stop for a second and think about how useful that is. Your program no longer cares whether it's drawing to a printer or to the screen. In fact, when you have a DC, it's very difficult even to *figure out* whether the DC is to a printer or the screen. Just as when you get a file handle, it's hard to tell whether the file handle is a handle to a file on a disk, CD-ROM, or network connection, and so on.

Now that you know what a DC is, I'll talk about how to get one.

Getting a Device Context

The process for "correctly" getting a DC varies, depending on whether you're responding to a WM_PAINT message.

If you're responding to the paint message, you call the BeginPaint and EndPaint functions and use the DC Windows provides you with in the PAINTSTRUCT.

> **TIP**
>
> There's also a GetDCEx function, but you will probably never use it. The only extra GetDCEx gives you is additional advanced clipping options.

If you need to draw something at any other time or to draw outside your window, you call the Win32 API function GetDC.

Releasing a Device Context

To prevent resource leaks in your program, you must be sure to release the DCs you get.

There are a couple ways to release a DC. If you called BeginPaint, you release your DC by calling EndPaint. Otherwise, you call the ReleaseDC Win32 API function.

Keep in mind that after you release a DC, you can no longer use it to draw anything. You can't, for example, release it and stash the hdc variable for later use.

A Brief Note about Coordinate Systems in the GDI

One other important thing to realize is that the coordinates you supply to the various GDI functions aren't necessarily pixel coordinates. That is, if you say, "GDI, I would like you to draw a dot at (50,50)," you won't necessarily end up with a dot 50 pixels from the left and 50 pixels from the top.

This is because your DC can be set up to use different coordinate spaces. This enables you to zoom in and out easily. (You don't have to worry about properly scaling everything all over your code. You can just set a different coordinate system, and Windows takes care of translating your code's values into actual pixels.) This can be confusing, though.

From a game programming perspective, the only coordinate system you will probably want to use is the screen coordinate system. In this system, one "unit" is 1 pixel, which means that if you say that you'd like a dot at (49,49), it will appear 50 pixels from the left of the screen and 50 from the top (remember, coordinates are zero-based).

The way you tell Windows that you'd like screen coordinates is by calling the `SetMapMode` function with the `MM_TEXT` flag, like so:

`SetMapMode(hdc, MM_TEXT);`

`hdc` is your DC handle.

> **TIP**
>
> Even though it's possible, you probably won't want to use the GDI's coordinate space functionality to spice up your game. The GDI is too slow to be used for real-time scaling and rotating, unless the scene is very simple.
>
> If it's something you'd like to try out, though, look at the help for the `SetMapMode` function.

Pens, Colors, Brushes, and Shapes

The easiest thing to do with a DC is to create shapes. The Windows GDI has numerous functions devoted to drawing shapes of all kinds—rectangles, polygons, circles, you name it.

To draw a shape, you first need two things: a pen and a brush. The pen dictates the line style of the shape, and the brush dictates the fill style. You can set up and use any combination of pens and brushes.

Now you will learn how to create and select pens and brushes. Then you will tie it all together by learning how to use pens and brushes to draw shapes.

Pens

Here's a pen's lifetime, from start to finish.

To create a pen, you decide three basic things: your pen's color, width, and style. When you have these three things, you plug them all in to the Win32 GDI function CreatePen, which gives you back an HPEN, or a handle to a pen.

You then call the Win32 GDI function SelectObject to associate your new pen with a DC (this is like grabbing a real pen in preparation for drawing). Now you can draw shapes using that pen.

When you're done, you call SelectObject again to make your pen inactive (this is like putting down a real pen after you finish drawing). You need to do this because SelectObject won't let you destroy a pen that's *active* (that is, the pen you're currently "holding").

Finally, you destroy the pen you created, so that you don't leak resources.

Don't worry; you will walk through it all.

To begin, look at the CreatePen function:

```
HPEN CreatePen(
   int fnPenStyle,     // pen style
   int nWidth,         // pen width
   COLORREF crColor    // pen color
);
```

As you can see, you have three arguments. The first, fnPenStyle, can be any one of several flags that determine the pen's line-drawing style; these are presented in Table 2.1.

The only pen style you're probably clueless about right now is PS_INSIDEFRAME. It's a strange one, but you probably won't ever use it. It tells Windows how to interpret the coordinates you pass to the GDI shape-drawing functions.

The second parameter CreatePen wants is nWidth, which is the width of the pen. The documentation for CreatePen says that the width should be specified in logical units. As you just learned, because you set the mapping mode to MM_TEXT (via your call to SetMapMode), one logical unit equals one pixel. In other words, nWidth is the pen's width in pixels.

The final parameter, crColor, has a weird type: COLORREF. In essence, COLORREF is a 32-bit integer that specifies a color.

Colors in the Windows GDI are made up of three components: red, green, and blue. These three components represent how strongly the beam of your monitor excites the red, green, and blue phosphor, and therefore, how much light of that color (red, green, or blue) is emitted. You represent each of these components as a number, in the range of 0 to 255, with 0 representing no light of that color and 255 representing the strongest possible light of that color.

Table 2.1 Pen Styles

Style Flag	Description
PS_SOLID	Draws a solid line
PS_DASH	Draws a dashed line
PS_DOT	Draws a dotted line
PS_DASHDOT	Draws a line that alternates between dots and dashes
PS_NULL	Draws nothing (an invisible pen!), useful if you don't want your shapes to have an outline
PS_INSIDEFRAME	A weird pen style, basically the same as PS_SOLID but changes the meaning of the coordinates you pass to the shape-drawing functions

For example, to create a pure red color, you set the red component to 255 and the green and blue components to 0. Similarly, to create a pure green color, you set green to 255 and red and blue to zero. Remember, you're dealing with *light* colors, not *paint* colors. When you combine green and red paints, you get brown, but when you combine green and red lights, you get yellow.

To make sure that you understand this difference, Table 2.2 presents some common colors, along with some component values you can use to make them. Component values are specified as *(red, green, blue)*.

The next question you're probably asking is, "How do I fit these three color components into a single 32-bit value?" The answer to this is bit shifting. A 32-bit value can be divided into four 8-bit values. An 8-bit value, conveniently enough, can store any number between 0 and 255 (see Figure 2.2).

You yourself don't have to shift the bits. Windows defines an RGB macro that takes three color components and hands you back a COLORREF. For example, if you want a red color, you get it using the following line of code:

```
COLORREF redcolor = RGB(255,0,0);
```

Easy! To create a blue solid pen that's 1 pixel thick, you use this code:

```
HPEN bluepen = CreatePen(PS_SOLID, 1, RGB(0,0,255));
```

Presto! You've just created a pen!

Table 2.2   Common Color RGB Values

Color	Component Values (R,G,B)
Black	(0,0,0)
White	(255,255,255)
Red	(255,0,0)
Green	(0,255,0)
Blue	(0,0,255)
Cyan	(0,255,255)
Gray	(128,128,128)
Yellow	(255,255,0)
Purple	(255,0,255)

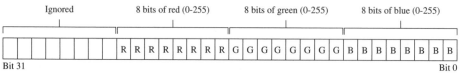

Ignored   8 bits of red (0-255)   8 bits of green (0-255)   8 bits of blue (0-255)

R R R R R R R R G G G G G G G G B B B B B B B B

Bit 31   Bit 0

Figure 2.2

How RGB colors are stored in a single 32-bit value.

If you're curious, you can use a couple additional Windows GDI functions to create a pen. One is named `ExtCreatePen`, which is a little more powerful than the standard `CreatePen` discussed here. `ExtCreatePen` lets you do cool things such as bevel (round) the edges your pen draws.

The other function is named `CreatePenIndirect`. `CreatePenIndirect` takes the exact same arguments as `CreatePen`, except that it takes them in the form of a `LOGPEN` structure. This is a bit like NyQuil. Regardless of whether

CAUTION

Important note: You must remember to destroy any pens you create. You can destroy a pen using the Win32 API function `DeleteObject`, which takes one argument: a handle to your device object (pen, brush, whatever). Failure to delete pens will create a resource leak, which can eventually bring down your whole system (ouch!).

you take it in pill or liquid form, it still works, but some people dislike the taste of liquid NyQuil. To suit people's taste, Microsoft made `CreatePenIndirect`.

Actually, that's not fair. There's a legitimate reason for using `CreatePenIndirect`—when you're loading or saving pens from disk. `CreatePenIndirect` allows you to save the whole structure, then just read that structure in whenever you want, and instantly create a pen.

> **TIP**
>
> As you progress through the sections in this chapter, you will notice a pattern. Most GDI objects (brushes, fonts, and so on) have a `CreateXXXIndirect` function. Keep this in mind. It will prove useful some day.

Now that you have a pen, you need to select it. To select this pen into your device context (which is like the code equivalent of grabbing a real pen in preparation for writing), you call the Win32 GDI function `SelectObject`:

```
HGDIOBJ SelectObject(
  HDC hdc,            // handle to device context
  HGDIOBJ hgdiobj     // handle to object
);
```

You might be surprised to see `HGDIOBJ` instead of `HPEN`. Fear not. `HGDIOBJ` is a generic type that can stand for not only `HPEN` but also `HBRUSH`, `HFONT`, and a few other Hs (which you will learn about in the following sections). If this were C++, `HGDIOBJ` would be a base class, and `HPEN` would be derived from it.

Unfortunately, the GDI isn't C++, which means that you must cast your Hs when you pass them to `SelectObject` and when you assign `SelectObject`'s return value to an H variable. As an example, consider the following code, which creates a blue pen and then selects it:

```
HPEN bluepen = CreatePen(PS_SOLID, 1, RGB(0,0,255));
HPEN oldpen = (HPEN)SelectObject(hdc, (HPEN)bluepen);
```

Notice also, in the preceding code, that you pay attention to the return value of `SelectObject`. This is because you will need this return value later, when you're finished drawing (see Figure 2.3).

At that time, you must select the pen that was active (before you came along), thereby deactivating your pen and enabling you to destroy it. Check out the following code sample:

```
// create the pen
HPEN bluepen = CreatePen(PS_SOLID, 1, RGB(0,0,255));
// select it into our DC
HPEN oldpen = SelectObject(hdc, (HPEN)bluepen);
```

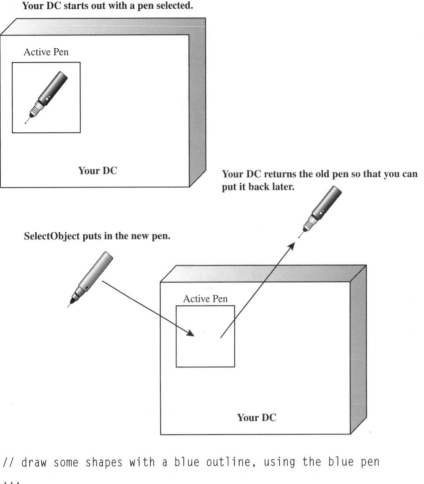

Your DC starts out with a pen selected.

Active Pen

Your DC

SelectObject puts in the new pen.

Your DC returns the old pen so that you can put it back later.

Active Pen

Your DC

Figure 2.3

SelectObject makes a certain pen active for your DC and then returns the pen that was kicked out of the active slot.

```
// draw some shapes with a blue outline, using the blue pen
...
// deselect our pen, and put the old pen back
SelectObject(hdc, (HPEN)oldpen);
// destroy our blue pen
DeleteObject((HPEN)bluepen);
```

You will see this same pattern in virtually any program that uses the GDI. The process of creating, selecting, using, deselecting, and destroying is common, although programs differ on when they create and destroy objects. For example, it's perfectly okay to create your pens and other objects once, at the beginning of your application, and destroy them once, at the end of your application. It's equally acceptable (albeit somewhat slower) to create and destroy your objects every time you enter and leave your paint function, or even every time you draw a shape (really slow!).

Brushes

Brushes are very similar to pens in that they have the same create/select/use/deselect/destroy life cycle. Creating a brush is more complex than creating a pen, however, mainly because you have several Windows GDI functions from which to choose, as shown in Table 2.3.

You're going to focus on `CreateSolidBrush` here because that's the one you will probably use the most.

Here's the prototype for `CreateSolidBrush`:

```
HBRUSH CreateSolidBrush(
  COLORREF crColor    // brush color value
);
```

There's nothing too surprising here. You give it a color; it hands you back a handle to your new brush. For example, the following code creates a yellow brush:

```
HBRUSH yellowbrush = CreateSolidBrush(RGB(255,255,0));
```

After you create a brush, you select it the same way you would a pen:

```
// select it into our DC
HBRUSH oldbrush = SelectObject(hdc, (HBRUSH)yellowbrush);
```

Table 2.3 The GDI Brush Creation Functions

Function Name	Description
CreateSolidBrush	The simplest of all these functions, creates a solid brush of a certain color
CreateHatchBrush	Creates a brush with a certain hatch pattern, for example, diagonal lines, vertical lines, horizontal lines, and so on
CreatePatternBrush	Allows you to specify a bitmap and use that as a fill pattern
CreateDIBPatternBrushPt	Similar to CreatePatternBrush but with slightly different requirements (see the section "Bitmaps" for details)
CreateBrushIndirect	Creates a brush using a structure

Now you can draw your shapes, and they'll all be yellow. When you're done, you deselect and destroy the brush, like so:

```
// deselect our brush, and put the old brush back
SelectObject(hdc, (HBRUSH)oldbrush);
// destroy our yellow brush
DeleteObject((HBRUSH)yellowbrush);
```

Again, use brushes just as you would pens.

Shapes

Now that you know how to create pens and brushes, you can start drawing shapes. The GDI has many shape-drawing functions, and Table 2.4 summarizes the important ones.

As you see, you can do many things.

> ### Sample Program Reference
> The Ch2p1_Shapes sample program shows you how to create pens and brushes and use them to draw shapes.

Bitmaps

The ability to load and display bitmap files is very important to game programming, so it's a good thing that Windows provides a lot of bitmap functions. It's easy to load a BMP file, blit it to the screen, stretch it, perform logical operations on it, and mess with its colors.

However, to understand how all those things work in Windows, you must first take a step back and revisit device contexts—specifically, to figure out how device contexts interact with the drawing surfaces they represent.

The screen is just a big bitmap. At some point, everything is converted into a big grid of pixels, which are then displayed by the hardware and your monitor. Now you will do a little substitution: If you use DCs to draw on the screen, and the screen is a bitmap, you use DCs to draw on the bitmap.

In other words, all device contexts operate on a bitmap, behind the scenes. All DCs have an active bitmap, to which all the DC drawing functions render. Whether this bitmap is the actual screen, a printer, or simply an in-memory array of pixels doesn't matter. They're all considered "canvases."

DCs also remember which color mode they're in, as well as the dimensions of the canvas to which they're drawing.

Table 2.4 GDI Shape-Drawing Functions

Function Name	Description
Chord	Draws a *chord* (the intersection of an ellipse and a line segment)
Ellipse	Draws an ellipse (or circle)
FillRect	Fills in a rectangle with a brush, without drawing the edges with a pen
FrameRect	Draws a border around a rectangle, using a specified brush
InvertRect	Performs a logical NOT operation on an area, effectively inverting its colors
Pie	Draws a pie-shaped *wedge* (the intersection of an ellipse and two radials)
Polygon	Draws a shape consisting of two or more vertices and three or more lines
PolyPolygon	Draws a series of closed polygons
Rectangle	Draws a rectangle
RoundRect	Draws a rectangle with rounded corners

Therefore, creating a bitmap by itself doesn't get you anything. To get anything onto that bitmap, you have to jump through several hoops:

1. Create a bitmap. You can do this by loading a BMP file directly from disk or by creating a new, empty bitmap.
2. Create a DC. Because it's impossible to have a DC that doesn't draw to a bitmap, when you initially create a DC, you also create a 1×1 monochrome bitmap. By default, the new DC is pointed at this little bitmap.
3. Tell the DC you created to draw on the bitmap you created in step 1. This involves a SelectObject call, where you "select in" your bitmap and stash away the handle for the 1×1 mono bitmap.

At this point, you can draw anything you want. For example, you can call the Windows function that blits a section of one DC to another (which, in effect, blits your bitmap), or you can render shapes and such onto your in-memory bitmap.

When you're done with the bitmap, you deselect it from the DC (which means making the 1×1 mono bitmap active). Next, you delete the bitmap you created and then delete the DC you created (which deletes the 1×1 mono bitmap, too).

Yes, it's complicated, but that's the nature of the Windows beast. The easy things are really hard, but the hard things are really easy. Now I will run through each of those steps in detail.

Loading a Bitmap

To create a new bitmap and load a BMP file into it, you call LoadImage, which looks like this:

```
HANDLE LoadImage(
  HINSTANCE hinst,     // handle of the instance containing the image
  LPCTSTR lpszName,    // name or identifier of image
  UINT uType,          // type of image
  int cxDesired,       // desired width
  int cyDesired,       // desired height
  UINT fuLoad          // load flags
);
```

Put your program's instance into hinst, put the filename of the BMP you want to load into lpszName, and put IMAGE_BITMAP into uType (in case you're curious, LoadImage can also load icons and cursors). Leave cxDesired and cyDesired zero, which tells Windows that you want to use the dimensions of the bitmap you're loading. You will want fuLoad to be LR_LOADFROMFILE, which instructs Windows to load the BMP from a file on disk (as opposed to loading from a resource script, which I'll get to later in the "Using Resources" section near the end of this chapter).

Other flags are available for fuLoad, most of which deal with color translation. You probably won't ever need them, but you should check the documentation for the whole set if you're trying to do something unusual.

LoadImage, if all goes well, returns an HBITMAP (a handle to a bitmap), which you eventually give to the SelectObject function to link the DC you're about to create to this bitmap.

Here's an example that loads the ch2p6_trippy.bmp file into a new bitmap:

```
hBitmap = (HBITMAP)LoadImage(
  NULL, "ch2p6_trippy.bmp",
  IMAGE_BITMAP, 0, 0, LR_LOADFROMFILE);
```

Creating a Bitmap

If you want to start with a blank bitmap rather than load a BMP file, you use the
CreateCompatibleBitmap Windows API function. It takes three parameters:

```
HBITMAP CreateCompatibleBitmap(
  HDC hdc,        // handle to device context
  int nWidth,     // width of bitmap, in pixels
  int nHeight     // height of bitmap, in pixels
);
```

CreateCompatibleBitmap creates a bitmap that has the same
color depth as the DC you give it in the hdc parameter.

> **TIP**
>
> You can also use the
> Windows API function
> CreateBitmap, but you
> must know the color
> depth of the bitmap you
> want to create.

Creating a DC

When you have a bitmap, you create a DC. This can be very difficult (if you want to create a DC
for a particular device, color depth, and so on) or very easy (if you just want a DC that's compatible with the screen).

Fortunately, most of the time you will want a DC that's compatible with the screen, which means
that you only need to call CreateCompatibleDC:

```
HDC CreateCompatibleDC(
  HDC hdc   // handle to the device context
);
```

Easy! This guy takes in a DC and returns a DC compatible with the one you gave it. To get a DC
that's compatible with the screen, you first get a DC for your window, pass it to
CreateCompatibleDC, and then release the DC you just got, like so:

```
// get a DC for this window
HDC hdcWindow = GetDC(hwnd);

// create a compatible in-memory device context
hdcBitmap = CreateCompatibleDC(hdcWindow);
// release the DC we obtained
ReleaseDC(hwnd, hdcWindow);
```

That's all there is to it!

Making the New DC Render to the New Bitmap

This is also easy. To make your new DC render to the bitmap you just created, simply call
SelectObject, like so:

```
// select the image into the memory dc
hOldBitmap = (HBITMAP)SelectObject(hdcBitmap,hBitmap);
```

Be sure to save the handle to the little 1×1 mono bitmap that SelectObject returns. You will need
it when you have to delete your bitmap.

Drawing a Bitmap

Finally, you draw your bitmap to the screen. Windows has several functions that can blit a section
of one DC into a particular location on another DC. The two you will use most often are BitBlt
and StretchBlt. BitBlt performs a direct 1:1 copy of the pixels in the source DC to the pixels in
the target DC. StretchBlt can enlarge or shrink the source to fit within the destination rectangle.

Let's start with BitBlt:

```
BOOL BitBlt(
  HDC hdcDest, // handle to destination device context
  int nXDest,  // x-coordinate of destination rectangle's upper-left
               // corner
  int nYDest,  // y-coordinate of destination rectangle's upper-left
               // corner
  int nWidth,  // width of destination rectangle
  int nHeight, // height of destination rectangle
  HDC hdcSrc,  // handle to source device context
  int nXSrc,   // x-coordinate of source rectangle's upper-left
               // corner
  int nYSrc,   // y-coordinate of source rectangle's upper-left
               // corner
  DWORD dwRop  // raster operation code
);
```

It looks complicated, but it isn't. In essence, you put in your destination DC, a destination rectangle on that DC, a source DC, and the upper-left coordinate of the source rectangle. (You can't
specify the size of the source rectangle because it has to be the same size as the destination rectangle.)

The only weirdness is the last parameter, dwRop. dwRop can be any one of several flags that deter-mine how to merge the pixels in the source rectangle with the pixels in the destination. This enables you to do logical operations as you blit. For example, you could AND the bits together.

Occasionally, you will use the logical operations. They're handy when you need to blit things that aren't rectangular, which you will learn about in "Drawing Nonrectangular Bitmaps" later in this chapter. Most of the time, though, you will want to use SRCCOPY here, which simply copies the source pixels onto the destination, overwriting anything that might already be there.

StretchBlt is very similar to BitBlt:

```
BOOL StretchBlt(
  HDC hdcDest,        // handle to destination device context
  int nXOriginDest,  // x-coordinate of upper-left corner of dest. rectangle
  int nYOriginDest,  // y-coordinate of upper-left corner of dest. rectangle
  int nWidthDest,     // width of destination rectangle
  int nHeightDest,    // height of destination rectangle
  HDC hdcSrc,         // handle to source device context
  int nXOriginSrc,   // x-coordinate of upper-left corner of source rectangle
  int nYOriginSrc,   // y-coordinate of upper-left corner of source rectangle
  int nWidthSrc,      // width of source rectangle
  int nHeightSrc,     // height of source rectangle
  DWORD dwRop         // raster operation code
);
```

As you can see, the only difference is that StretchBlt allows you to specify two rectangle sizes, one for source and one for destination. If the source rectangle is smaller than the destination rectangle, the source image will be stretched. Conversely, if the source rectangle is larger, it will be shrunk to fit in the destination.

CAUTION

StretchBlt is wicked slow, and it doesn't do anything to smooth the "jaggies" that can occur when bitmaps are scaled (that is, it doesn't use bilinear interpolation or anything like that). For these reasons, it's probably not suited to do any sort of real game animation.

Deleting the DC and the Bitmap

The final step in dealing with bitmaps is deleting them. Fortunately, this, too, is nothing horrible:

```
// de-select the bitmap from our in-memory DC
SelectObject(hDCBitmap, hOldBitmap);
// delete the bitmap
```

```
DeleteObject(hBitmap);
// delete our in-memory DC
DeleteDC(hDCBitmap);
```

Sample Program Reference

The Ch2p6_Bitmaps program illustrates the process of loading, drawing, and destroying a bitmap.

As you can see, you select the little 1×1 mono bitmap into the DC, which frees up your big bitmap so that you can delete it. You then call DeleteObject to delete the bitmap and DeleteDC to delete the DC.

Making the CGDIBitmap Class

Now that you know the details of how to load and draw bitmaps, you are ready to become extraordinary by creating a class that helps you out. The class you create should hide the details of what it takes to create and destroy bitmaps. Name this class CGDIBitmap, following the Hungarian notation practice of prefixing class names with a *C*.

The easiest way to create clean and beautiful C++ classes is to ask yourself, before you begin coding, what you'd like the class to do. The old adage says that C++ classes should do one thing, but do it very well. The one thing your CGDIBitmap class should do is to hide the details of creating and destroying a bitmap.

To do this, you have to ask, "What information is absolutely necessary to create or load a bitmap?" Well, if you're loading a bitmap, you obviously need the filename. If you're creating a bitmap, the only thing you need is the device context you should use in your call to CreateCompatibleDC—the DC you want your bitmap to be compatible with, in other words.

Your class will store the HDC of the in-memory DC and the HBITMAP of your new bitmap, as well as the old (1×1 mono) bitmap.

Given that, you can define your class's interface:

```
class CGDIBitmap
{
public:
  CGDIBitmap();
  virtual ~CGDIBitmap();
  void Load(HDC hdcCompatible, LPCTSTR lpszFilename);
  void CreateBlank(HDC hdcCompatible, int width, int height);
private:
  HDC m_hdcBitmap;      // handle of DC for our bitmap
  HBITMAP m_hBitmap;    // handle to our bitmap
  HBITMAP m_hOldBitmap; // handle to the 1x1 mono bitmap
```

```
    int m_iWidth;          // width of our bitmap, in pixels
    int m_iHeight;         // height of our bitmap, in pixels
};
```

As you can see, you have two main methods: one that loads a BMP file from disk and one that creates a new, blank bitmap.

You need something else, though. To blit, you have to know your bitmap's HDC. This gives you two options. You can expose your class's HDC, or your class can insist on doing the blit itself. In the latter case, you make your own BitBlt class method, which takes, among other things, the handle of the blit's destination.

Both approaches are equally valid, but just exposing the HDC makes more sense. It allows CGDIBitmap to work with any Windows bitmap function, and it stays true to your class goals. After all, you're not trying to make CGDIBitmap completely hide the way Windows bitmap functions work. You're just trying to hide the work of creating and destroying a bitmap.

Now, expose the HDC. While you're at it, expose the width and height of your bitmap, too, because you will need those when you call StretchBlt:

```
class CGDIBitmap
{
public:
    ...
    // properties
    int GetWidth(void) const { return(m_iWidth); }
    int GetHeight(void) const { return(m_iHeight); }
    HDC GetBitmapDC(void) const { return(m_hdcBitmap); }
    ...
};
```

TIP

Rather than create an explicit GetBitmapDC function, you can create an implicit conversion operator that converts a CGDIBitmap into an HDC (by simply returning the HDC of the CGDIBitmap). That enables you to pass a CGDIBitmap in place of an HDC anywhere in your code, which is pretty slick (but potentially confusing to someone who doesn't know your code).

Drawing Nonrectangular Bitmaps

All this is great if all your bitmaps happen to be rectangular. If you try to BitBlt a circle, though, you end up with a circle in a box because BitBlt doesn't know which colors are *transparent* (that is, should not be copied onto the destination DC). There's no way to tell it, either.

The only choice you have is to use some logical operations in conjunction with a mask. The *mask* is a 1-bit (black or white) bitmap that has the same dimensions as the nonrectangular bitmap you're trying to draw. Any pixel in your original bitmap that you don't want copied to the destination should be white in your bitmap mask (and black in your original bitmap). Any pixel you *do* want drawn should be black on the mask. For example, if I had a small 5×5 bitmap of a small ball (see Figure 2.4), I'd make a mask that looks like Figure 2.5, where only the pixels that are part of the actual ball are black.

Figure 2.4

A magnified bitmap image of a small ball. Ideally, you'd blit only the gray pixels, not the black ones.

Figure 2.5

The corresponding mask for the small ball. Pixels you don't want are white, and pixels you do want are black.

Using your mask, you draw nonrectangular bitmaps by doing the following:

1. Blit your mask down, using a logical AND operation. (For BitBlt, this is SRCAND.) This causes the black pixels of your mask bitmap to kill any colors underneath them (so that you end up with a black hole where your bitmap goes). The white pixels of your mask leave the corresponding destination pixels unchanged.

> **Sample Program Reference**
>
> The Ch2p7_TransBitmaps program illustrates how to do this (and shows the CGDIBitmap class in action, too!). Be sure to check it out.

2. Blit your original bitmap using a logical OR operation. (For BitBlt, this is SRCPAINT.) Because the transparent parts of your original bitmap are black, they don't change any of the colors on the destination DC. The nonblack pixels in your bitmap are copied exactly to the destination because AND-blitting the mask in step 1 eliminates any color that used to be there.

Text and Fonts

The Windows GDI has several functions for rendering text in a certain color or font. It has several *more* functions that allow you to select a font, determine which fonts are available, and measure different aspects of a font—for example, to determine how wide or how tall a character is in a certain font. When all is said and done, there are roughly 40 functions.

As you might have guessed, though, you're going to use only a few of those functions. Next, take a look at the most useful functions for fonts and text.

Fonts

You use a font the same way you use brushes and pens. You create an instance of that font, select it, draw text in that font, deselect it, and delete it. When your font is selected, any text you write (regardless of how you write it) will be in that font.

Specifying a Font Directly

If you know exactly which font you want to use, you can call upon the power of the CreateFont function:

```
HFONT CreateFont(
    int nHeight,              // logical height of font
    int nWidth,              // logical average character width
    int nEscapement,         // angle of escapement
    int nOrientation,        // base-line orientation angle
    int fnWeight,            // font weight
    DWORD fdwItalic,         // italic attribute flag
    DWORD fdwUnderline,      // underline attribute flag
    DWORD fdwStrikeOut,      // strikeout attribute flag
    DWORD fdwCharSet,        // character set identifier
    DWORD fdwOutputPrecision,  // output precision
    DWORD fdwClipPrecision,  // clipping precision
    DWORD fdwQuality,        // output quality
    DWORD fdwPitchAndFamily,  // pitch and family
    LPCTSTR lpszFace         // pointer to typeface name string
);
```

Brace yourself. As you can see in Table 2.5, this function takes more arguments than CreateWindowEx!

CreateFont returns a handle to the font if successful and NULL if something goes wrong.

Table 2.5 The CreateFont Parameters

Parameter	Description
nHeight	The desired height of the font you'd like to create. This parameter is specified in logical units, which in your MM_TEXT mapping mode are pixels.
	If this parameter is zero, you get a default height value.
	If it's less than zero, you're telling Windows how tall you'd like the characters in the font. (Windows takes an absolute value, so −50 here means *character height of 50*.)
	If it's greater than zero, you're telling Windows how tall you'd like the *cell* of the font, which is slightly different than specifying how tall the characters should be.
	Most of the time, you want to specify height in terms of characters, so remember to negate this value.
nWidth	The desired average width of the font. The word *average* is important because in most fonts, the width of the letters is different. For example, in this book's font, the W and M characters are huge, but the I is skinny.
	Again, if this is zero, Windows chooses a suitable width proportional to the font's height.
nEscapement	The angle between the x-axis of the device and the line on which the text is written. You can use this value to write text that slopes, but most of the time you want your text to be perfectly straight horizontally, so put a zero in here.
nOrientation	Similar to nEscapement, only now you're sloping each letter instead of the whole line of text. In other words, you can have text written in a straight line but with each letter leaning forward or backward. Again, most of the time you want characters that stand up straight, so a zero here will do the job.

Table 2.5 Continued

Parameter	Description
fnWeight	The weight of the font, from 1 to 1000. Higher numbers mean bolder text; 400 is normal, and 700 is considered bold. (**This is bold text.**)
	You can use many constants here, such as FW_NORMAL and FW_BOLD.
	If you put a zero here, Windows uses a sensible default weight.
fdwItalic	If this is set to true, Windows makes your font italic (slanting forward, *like so*).
fdwUnderline	If true, Windows underlines your font.
fdwStrikeOut	If true, Windows *strikes through* your font (draws a line through the middle, ~~like this~~.)
fdwCharSet	The character set of this font. You probably want the ANSI character set, so put ANSI_CHARSET in here. Other flags are available for different character sets, so check out the help.
fdwOutputPrecision	Use this parameter to tell Windows how stringent you are about your parameters, that is, how closely the real width and height must match what you've specified here.
	Realistically, this is where you tell Windows whether you're willing to accept TrueType fonts, raster fonts, or both. Most of the time, you want a TrueType font because that's what 99 percent of all fonts out there are, so put OUT_TT_PRECIS in here. Other available flags are listed in the documentation.
fdwClipPrecision	Use this parameter to specify the clipping precision for the font (that is, what to do with characters that are partially outside the drawing area).

Table 2.5 Continued

Parameter	Description
	Usually, you set this to CLIP_DEFAULT_PRECIS to enable default behavior. Other available flags are listed in the documentation.
fdQuality	The quality of output you're striving for. There are basically two values: low (DRAFT_QUALITY) and high (PROOF_QUALITY). If you're in low-quality mode, and you're using a raster font in a size for which there are no bitmaps, Windows stretches the closest available size, giving you blocky text but text of the appropriate size. If you're in high-quality mode, Windows won't stretch raster fonts, so they'll look good but won't necessarily be in the size you requested. That's all fine and great, but normally you will be using TrueType fonts, and because TrueType fonts scale to any size perfectly, this parameter is a moot point. Put PROOF_QUALITY here.
fdwPitchAndFamily	This poor parameter is actually overloaded with two parameters. Its bits are split so that the two low-order bits contain one parameter and the four high-order bits contain one parameter. The two low-order bits specify the pitch of the font. You have three options here: DEFAULT_PITCH, VARIABLE_PITCH, and FIXED_PITCH. Usually, you use the DEFAULT_PITCH value. The four high-order bits contain a flag that specifies which font family you'd like to use. You can specify several families. The flags you can use are listed in the documentation. Also, there's a FF_DONTCARE flag, if you don't care about selecting a particular family. To set both these parameters, you OR them together, like so: DEFAULT_PITCH | FF_DONTCARE.

Table 2.5 Continued

Parameter	Description
lpszFace	The name of the font you want to use, that is, Courier or Times New Roman. It can be up to 32 characters in length.
	If this is NULL or empty, Windows uses the first font that matches all the other criteria you've specified. Otherwise, it uses the font name you specify here.

It looks worse than it is. Most arguments you can leave at their default values. For example, here's code to create a 50-pixel high, Times New Roman font:

```
// create a 50-pixel tall Times New Roman font!
HFONT fontTimesNewRoman = CreateFont(
  -25, // height (negative means use character heights
  0, // width (0 means use default)
  0, // escapement (0 means none)
  0, // orientation (0 means none)
  FW_NORMAL, // "boldness" of font
  false, // italic? true or false
  false, // underline? true or false
  false, // strikeout? true or false
  ANSI_CHARSET, // desired character set
  OUT_TT_PRECIS, // output precision - use TrueType only
  CLIP_DEFAULT_PRECIS, // clip precision - use default
  PROOF_QUALITY, // proof quality
  DEFAULT_PITCH | FF_DONTCARE, // pitch and family
  "Times New Roman" // name of font face desired
);
```

To make things easier, you can wrap this function up in your own function, which may take only the font size and name.

Asking the User to Select a Font

If you need to ask the user to choose a font, you will be happy to learn that it's very easy to open a Choose a Font dialog box. This is probably more useful for normal applications than for games, but it's helpful to know that such a mechanism exists. If you tried to write your own Font dialog, you would quickly go insane. Stay sane! Use the `ChooseFont` function, which displays a Windows default Font dialog box (see Figure 2.6).

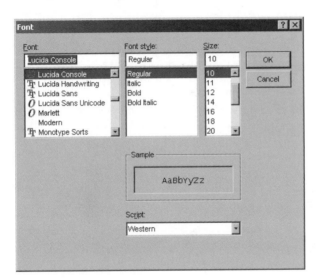

Figure 2.6

The standard-issue Windows Font dialog box.

`ChooseFont` takes only one argument, but (surprise!) it's a structure that contains a whole bunch of things you can set. Take a look at the structure:

```
typedef struct {     // cf
    DWORD          lStructSize;
    HWND           hwndOwner;
    HDC            hDC;
    LPLOGFONT      lpLogFont;
    INT            iPointSize;
    DWORD          Flags;
    DWORD          rgbColors;
    LPARAM         lCustData;
    LPCFHOOKPROC   lpfnHook;
    LPCTSTR        lpTemplateName;
    HINSTANCE      hInstance;
    LPTSTR         lpszStyle;
    WORD           nFontType;
    INT            nSizeMin;
    INT            nSizeMax;
} CHOOSEFONT;
```

Table 2.6 shows a breakdown of what everything in that structure means.

Table 2.6 The CHOOSEFONT Structure Members

Member	Description
lStructSize	The length of the structure, in bytes. This is similar to the cbSize member you saw when you were learning about RegisterClassEx in Chapter 1, "An Introduction to Windows Programming."
hwndOwner	A handle to the window that will own the Choose a Font dialog box. Normally, you'd want this to be the handle of the window you created for your application, but it can also be NULL if you want the dialog owned by the desktop.
hDC	This is used only if you've used the Flags member to specify that you want to list printer fonts (that is, you've chosen CF_PRINTER-FONTS or CF_BOTH).
	If you aren't going to specify these flags (and you usually won't), you can set this to NULL.
lpLogFont	When you first call ChooseFont, you can make a certain font be selected initially, when the dialog box first opens. To do this, fill in a LOGFONT structure with the details of the font you'd like selected, and specify the CF_INITTOLOGFONTSTRUCT flag in the Flags member.
	You might think that if you didn't want any fonts selected initially, you could set this to NULL. You probably shouldn't do that because this member has another purpose: When the user clicks the OK button, the details of the font he or she has chosen are put here. Therefore, it's best to make this point to an empty LOG-FONT structure if you don't care about selecting a font initially.
iPointSize	When the user clicks the OK button, Windows puts the font size he or she has chosen into this variable. The size is specified in units of 1/10 of a point, so 720 means a 72-point font. If your coordinate system is set to MM_TEXT, a 72-point font is a 72-pixel font.

Table 2.6 Continued

Member	Description
Flags	Here you specify flags that determine exactly how Windows displays the dialog box. You can use these flags to set limits on what the user can choose, and you can provide some initial settings.
rgbColors	If the CF_EFFECTS flag is set in Flags, this member specifies the text color. Set it before you call ChooseFont to specify an initial color value; check it when ChooseFont returns to determine which color the user has chosen.
lCustData, hInstance, lpfnHook, lpTemplateName	These members can be used to augment or override how the font dialog appears. Basically, you specify a template in lpTemplateName and a callback function in lpfnHook, to which you can pass data contained in lCustData. Normally you won't want to change the appearance of the dialog box, so you just set all these guys to NULL. Note that if you are interested in changing the dialog box's appearance, you also have to specify a few flags in the Flags member. Check the docs for the full details.
lpszStyle	Another in/out value. Before you call ChooseFont, set this up with the name of the style you'd like initially selected in the style combo box. When ChooseFont returns, this will contain the name of the style the user has chosen. If you want to use this, remember to set the CF_USESTYLE flag in the Flags member, also.
nFontType	When ChooseFont returns, this will be filled in with the type of the font. Valid values here are any combination of several flags, all listed in the help.
nSizeMin and nSizeMax	If you've specified the CF_LIMITSIZE flag in Flags, these two parameters tell Windows the minimum and maximum font size the user can choose.

Here are the flags you can specify inside the Flags parameter:

- CF_TTONLY. If you specify this flag, the dialog box will list TrueType fonts only.
- CF_EFFECTS. If you specify this flag, the dialog box will display settings that allow the user to add special effects to the font, such as strikethrough and colors.
- CF_LIMITSIZE. If you specify this flag, Windows won't let the user choose any font size that's less than nSizeMin or greater than nSizeMax. (nSizeMin and nSizeMax are members of this structure, explained in Table 2.6.)

You can see all the flags in the docs, but those are three of the more useful ones. Also, here are the flags you'll most often run into for the nFontType parameter:

- BOLD_FONTTYPE. The user selected a bold font.
- ITALIC_FONTTYPE. The user selected an italic font.

As you can see, most of the members of this structure are concerned with two things: first, specifying an initial value that is displayed in the dialog box and, second, returning the value the user chose. This is a common pattern used by several of the other default Windows dialog boxes.

> **TIP**
>
> By the way, Windows provides default dialog boxes for color selection, file selection, find/replace, and print—in case you need them.

Setting the Text Color, Background, and Alignment

There's more to writing cool text than picking a cool font. You also want to set the text's color, background, and alignment (left/center/right justified). Fortunately, Windows provides functions that do all these things, as Table 2.7 shows.

All these functions return the previously set value, so you can squirrel it away somewhere and restore it later. It's good programming practice to do this, but not always required.

> **Sample Program Reference**
>
> That's all you need to know to use these guys. For an example of them in action, check out the Ch2p2_Text program.

Selecting, Using, and Deleting Your Font

One way or another, you end up with a font chosen. The next step in the process is to select this font into your DC. This can be accomplished with SelectObject, like so:

```
HFONT oldfont = (HFONT)SelectObject(hdc, myfont);
```

Table 2.7 The GDI Functions for Controlling Text Color

Function	Description
SetTextColor	Takes as parameters an HDC and a color. All text rendered after the call will be in the color specified. The preceding color is returned to you (so you can set it back when you're done).
SetBkColor	Just like SetTextColor, only it sets the background color of the text.
SetBkMode	Allows you to specify whether you'd like the background of your text to be opaque or transparent. If you set it opaque, the text will have a tight box of "background" around it; if it's transparent, only the letters will be drawn. This takes two parameters: an HDC and a flag parameter that can be either OPAQUE or TRANSPARENT.
SetTextAlign	Allows you to specify the alignment (horizontal and vertical) you'd like your text to have. It takes two parameters: an HDC and a flags variable. Several flags are available, but here are the most interesting ones: TA_CENTER. Center-justifies text TA_LEFT. Left-justifies text TA_RIGHT. Right-justifies text

You still need to follow the same pattern of stashing the font that used to be selected, so that you can eventually reselect it. This frees up your font so that you can delete it, just as with pens and brushes.

After you select a font, you write some text. To do that, you can use several functions, shown in Table 2.8.

I don't need to go into detail about how all these work because most of the time your text output is through two functions: TextOut and DrawText. You're going to concentrate on those two, starting with the TextOut function.

Table 2.8 The GDI Functions for Text Output

Function	Description
TextOut	The simplest (and therefore least powerful) text-rendering function. Give it an (x,y) coordinate and some text, and it will draw that text.
PolyTextOut	This allows you to batch up several TextOut calls by specifying several sets of coordinates and output strings. This is better than calling TextOut repeatedly because you only deal with the overhead of calling PolyTextOut once for several strings.
TabbedTextOut	Like TextOut, only you can also specify an array of tab stops you'd like the text to use.
ExtTextOut	An extended TextOut function. Does everything that TextOut does, but also allows you to specify a clipping rectangle, outside of which no text should be drawn, and some intracharacter-spacing parameters.
DrawText	Powerful text output. Draws formatted text in a rectangle you specify. This function does all sorts of useful things, such as automatic line and word wrapping and automatic placement of an ellipsis (…) on text that doesn't fit a rectangle.
DrawTextEx	The mother of all text-drawing functions! This does everything DrawText does and also allows you to control the margins and tab stops of the text you're outputting.

TextOut

TextOut has very simple function parameters:

```
BOOL TextOut(
  HDC hdc,            // handle to device context
  int nXStart,        // x-coordinate of starting position
  int nYStart,        // y-coordinate of starting position
  LPCTSTR lpString,   // pointer to string
  int cbString        // number of characters in string
);
```

To use TextOut, put your device context handle in the first parameter, the coordinates of where you'd like to draw the text in parameters two and three, and the text and its length in the final two parameters.

TIP

A couple TextOut tips: When you're writing constant strings, you might be tempted to put the constant string directly inside the TextOut function twice: once for the actual text and once again to get the size of that text, like so:

```
TextOut(hdc, 0, 0, "Hi Mom!", strlen("Hi Mom!"));
```

Resist with all your might the temptation to do this! Inevitably, you will want to change that constant string and will forget to change it in both places, which will cause you all sorts of headaches later ("Ack! How come not all my text is drawing?!")

Instead, put the constant string in a pointer and use that:

```
const char *strHiMom = "Hi Mom!";
TextOut(hdc, 0, 0, strHiMom, strlen(strHiMom));
```

Also, don't use sizeof(strHiMom). TextOut wants the number of characters in the string, not including the NULL terminator. Doing a sizeof includes the NULL, and you end up with a funny box on the end of your text.

DrawText

The DrawText function is a little more complicated than TextOut:

```
int DrawText(
  HDC hDC,            // handle to device context
  LPCTSTR lpString,   // pointer to string to draw
  int nCount,         // string length, in characters
  LPRECT lpRect,      // pointer to struct with formatting dimensions
  UINT uFormat        // text-drawing flags
);
```

You still have the text and its length, just as in TextOut, but instead of just an (x,y) coordinate pair, you have a rectangle. Also, you have a place where you can specify some flags.

You can specify many flags. Most flags tell DrawText to do something special, such as add an ellipsis (...) to the text if it doesn't fit the rectangle, or they tell DrawText how to measure and align the text it's drawing. The docs do a great job of explaining all the flags, but two flags, DT_CALCRECT and DT_WORDBREAK, demand a detailed examination.

You use DT_WORDBREAK to wrap lines of text automatically at word boundaries. When you specify DT_WORDBREAK in the uFormat parameter, DrawText, when it reaches the end of a line, makes sure that the last word is not cut in half and continued on the next line. This is handy because writing your own text-wrapping function is irritating.

DT_CALCRECT is especially useful because it allows you to measure how much space the outputted text will take up. When you specify DT_CALCRECT in the uFormat parameter, DrawText doesn't draw any text. Instead, if the text is only one line, DrawText calculates the width of the text (which you can use to set the right edge of your rectangle). If the text is multiline, DrawText calculates the height of all the lines (which you can use to set the bottom of your rectangle).

Most of the time, drawing line-wrapped text is a two-part process. First, you call DrawText with DT_CALCRECT specified and calculate how much space you will need. Then, you call DrawText again, to do the actual text output.

Regions and Clipping

Windows clippers are slow but powerful. You probably can't sustain a decent frame rate with them, but if you need to use them occasionally to do some ornery clipping task, they're powerful enough to get the job done.

You can also combine regions to form more complex shapes (see Figure 2.7).

You do this by using the CombineRgn function, which takes as input a destination region, two source regions, and a combine mode (AND, OR, XOR, and so on). If you need to fill a region, use the FillRgn function, which fills a region using a specified brush. (You don't even have to call SelectObject to select the brush!)

> **NOTE**
> For an example of regions, check out the Ch2p8_Regions program on the CD.

After you select a region into a DC, all subsequent drawing operations are clipped to that region until you deselect it.

ERROR CHECKING

Until now, I've glossed over error handling, which isn't a good habit to form. The truth is, the vast majority of Windows API functions let you know, through their return values, whether they've succeeded or failed. How specifically they do that varies from function to function, but you can do some standard things to figure out why a Windows function fails.

Figure 2.7

Creating complex regions by combining simple regions.

You can take basic region shapes . . .
and combine them using logical operations to form more complex regions

Logical OR   **Logical AND**   **Logical XOR**

GetLastError

The first question you're likely to ask when something fails is simply, Why? If you're lucky, you can figure out the reason by looking at the function's return value, but sometimes that isn't enough.

You use the GetLastError function to retrieve additional information about the last error you encountered. This is like the old C global variable errno, only it's for Windows API calls.

GetLastError takes no parameters and returns the last error code as a DWORD.

You can use this DWORD to analyze the problem yourself, or you can use another function that converts the code from GetLastError into an error message. This magic function is named FormatMessage and looks like this:

```
DWORD FormatMessage(
  DWORD dwFlags,        // source and processing options
  LPCVOID lpSource,     // pointer to message source
  DWORD dwMessageId,    // requested message identifier
  DWORD dwLanguageId,   // language identifier for requested message
  LPTSTR lpBuffer,      // pointer to message buffer
  DWORD nSize,          // maximum size of message buffer
  va_list *Arguments    // pointer to array of message inserts
);
```

What Is Clipping?

In case you're unfamiliar with the term, *clipping* is the fine art of making sure that all art is restricted to a certain area of the screen. Clipping is what ensures that drawings in one window don't leak into another window, and that everything stays inside its borders. Essentially, when you say "Windows, I'd like a pixel drawn at (x,y) inside my current window," Windows checks to make sure the point (x,y) falls within the window area you've set up. If it does, no problem; otherwise, it refuses to draw the pixel. So, for example, if you have a 50 by 50 pixel window with the upper-left corner positioned at (10,10), the only pixels you can play with are those that fall between (10,10) and (60,60), which is the area of your window. All other pixels are considered "clipped," or out-of-bounds.

A *region* is just another GDI object, which means that it has the same create/select/use/deselect/destroy life cycle as all the other GDI objects (pens, brushes, and so on). To create a region, you can use any one of several functions, shown in Table 2.9.

Table 2.9 The GDI Region/Clipping Functions

Function	Description
CCreateEllipticRgn	Creates an elliptical region.
CreatePolygonRgn	Creates a polygonal region. You give it an array of points, and it creates a region from those.
CreateRectRgn	Creates a rectangular region.
CreateRoundRectRgn	Creates a rounded-rectangle region. A *rounded rectangle* is a rectangle with slightly rounded corners.

You could look at all the parameters FormatMessage takes, but that wouldn't be worthwhile. The bottom line is that you want a function that calls GetLastError and then turns the error code into a formatted message. Here you go:

```
void ConvertLastErrorToString(LPSTR szDest, int nMaxStrLen)
{
  LPVOID lpMsgBuf;
  FormatMessage(
    FORMAT_MESSAGE_ALLOCATE_BUFFER |
    FORMAT_MESSAGE_FROM_SYSTEM |
    FORMAT_MESSAGE_IGNORE_INSERTS,
    NULL,
    GetLastError(),
    MAKELANGID(LANG_NEUTRAL, SUBLANG_DEFAULT), // Default language
    (LPTSTR) &lpMsgBuf,
    0,
    NULL
  );
  strncpy(szDest, reinterpret_cast<char *>(lpMsgBuf), nMaxStrLen);
  LocalFree( lpMsgBuf );
}
```

That's all you need to know. The basic process is to call FormatMessage and let it allocate a message buffer and then to copy the error message out of the buffer and to wherever the caller wanted it. Finally, you free the memory FormatMessage allocated for you.

Sample Program Reference

ConvertLastErrorToString is just one of many nifty Windows helper functions contained in CommonFunc.cpp, inside the Common Code directory on your CD-ROM.

FormatMessage takes flags that determine in which language to output the error and all sorts of other options, which you can see in the docs.

MessageBox

You have an error string. Now, how do you get it to the user's eyes?

The MessageBox function does a great job of this. MessageBox takes a string and displays it in a little dialog box, shown in Figure 2.8.

Figure 2.8

The MessageBox function displays a dialog box containing a message.

Here are `MessageBox`'s parameters. Table 2.10 gives details about these guys:

```
int MessageBox(
  HWND hWnd,              // handle of owner window
  LPCTSTR lpText,         // address of text in message box
  LPCTSTR lpCaption,      // address of title of message box
  UINT uType              // style of message box
);
```

Table 2.10 The MessageBox Parameters

Parameter	Description
hWnd	The window handle of the window that owns this message box. If you pass in NULL here, the message box will be owned by the desktop.
lpText	The text you'd like to display in the message box.
lpCaption	The caption of the message box. (This appears in the title bar of the message box.)
uType	The message box's style. This can be any number of several flags, all of which are listed in the help. You use these flags to specify which kinds of buttons should be displayed, which icon should be displayed, and which button should be selected by default.

Here are a few of the more interesting flags for the `uType` parameter:

MB_OK	The message box contains a single button labeled OK.
MB_OKCANCEL	The message box contains OK and Cancel buttons. The function returns either IDOK or IDCANCEL, depending on which button was pressed.
MB_YESNO	The message box contains Yes and No buttons. The function returns IDYES or IDNO.

MB_ICONWARNING	The icon is an exclamation point (see Figure 2.9).
MB_ICONSTOP	The icon is a stop sign (refer to Figure 2.9).
MB_ICONINFORMATION	The icon is an *i* in a circle (refer to Figure 2.9).
MB_ICONQUESTION	The icon is a question mark (refer to Figure 2.9).

 MB_ICONWARNING

 MB_ICONSTOP

 MB_ICONINFORMATION

(?) MB_ICONQUESTION

Figure 2.9

A collection of message box icons and their associated flags.

Sample Program Reference

That's all there is to it! The Ch2p9_MessageBoxes program included on your CD demonstrates how to create messages.

USING RESOURCES

Before I begin talking about how to use resources, I should define what a resource is.

Basically, a *resource* is anything your program needs to run that isn't code. For games, resources are bitmaps, and images (for your background, characters, and so on), as well as sound effects, and music. For normal Windows applications, resources also include icons, cursors, dialogs, and menus. You might have specific resources for your application as well (such as level maps, office assistants, URLs, whatever).

Windows has a set of API functions you can use to collect these resources and eventually store them directly into your EXE (see Figure 2.10).

This is a boon for two reasons. It keeps things all in one place and makes it harder for people to go in and muck with things they shouldn't. Obviously, Windows also has functions that allow you to get at resources contained within your application. (Apple programmers will recognize this as Microsoft's answer to Mac OS's two-pronged data fork/resource fork paradigm.)

TIP

You can't store resources in a static library (lib). You can store them only in an EXE or a DLL. You can share resources between two EXEs by putting the resources in a *resource-only DLL*—that is, by making a DLL that contains only resources, no code.

Figure 2.10

Storing resources directly in your EXE.

Every resource has a *resource ID*, which can be either a string or an integer (most of the time, it's an integer). You use this resource ID to tell Windows which resource you want to use. Resource IDs are unique only within a given program. They're not globally unique. That is, different programs can potentially use the same resource IDs.

> **TIP**
>
> By the way, you can name your resource IDs anything you like, but there is a standard to naming resources, a bit like Hungarian notation. Table 2.11 shows some resource types and their associated prefixes.

Because working directly with integers is somewhat clumsy, most people create a `resource.h` header file, which defines constants that map to integers. DevStudio automatically creates a `resource.h` header when you add your resources. For more information on this, see Appendix A.

Windows has focused on supporting several basic resource types:

- **Dialogs and menus.** Dialog boxes and menus are saved into the resource script as text blocks. Basically, the text tells Windows which dialog controls go where and how to label the menus. Conceptually, it's similar to how Web pages are stored as HTML. You don't store the actual pixels of the Web page; you store a description of it and let the Web browser re-create it. Similarly, you don't store the actual image of the dialog; you store a description of it and let Windows re-create it.

- **Bitmaps, icons, and cursors.** These are stored in separate files that the resource script references (similar to how <IMG> tags work in HTML—every pixel of these is stored directly in your compiled EXE).
- **String tables.** It might seem weird to store strings in resources, but there's a good reason for it. If you store all your error messages and such in the resource script, you can support different languages by swapping the resource script in and out. Also, the strings don't have to remain in memory if they're in the script. They can just be loaded as needed.

> **TIP**
>
> Although it's possible for you to store your game resources (images, sound effects, music) as custom resources in the resource script, it's probably not a viable solution because you might want finer control over how things are stored. For example, you might want to optimize the order in which things are stored, implement compression, or encrypt the data.
>
> For that reason, many professional games have their own code to handle resource packs.

Table 2.11 Standard Prefixes for Resource Types

Resource Type	Standard Prefix
Dialog	IDD_
Dialog control (button, and so on)	IDC_
Menu	IDM_
Icon	IDI_
Bitmap	IDB_
String	IDS_
Accelerator	IDA_
Cursors	IDC_ is standard, but I use IDP_ (for *pointer*) so that I can tell the difference between a control and a cursor.

■ **Keyboard accelerator tables.** These are basically maps that tell Windows what should happen when certain key combinations are pressed (for example, it's here that you link Ctrl+C with your Copy to Clipboard command). These aren't terribly useful for game programming, but they're important to know about nonetheless.

All other resources types are considered *custom resources*. This means that about the only thing Windows can do with them is to pack them into your EXE file and then extract them as a string of bytes when you ask for them.

For now, you're going to concentrate on how to create and store "normal Windows application" stuff in the resource scripts.

Program Icons

You will probably want to give your game a cool icon that appears in Windows Explorer. To do this, you first create your icon in DevStudio (see Appendix A if you don't know exactly how to do this). You make two icons: a *big* icon, which is 32×32 pixels, and a *small* icon, 16×16 pixels. You should probably use only 16 colors when creating your icon.

After you create your icons, make a note of their resource IDs. For the sake of this example, assume that you've named them IDI_APP_SMALL and IDI_APP_BIG.

Finally, to make your icon appear in the Windows Explorer (and while your game is running), you hook up the icon to your window class. To do this, you load up the big and small icons and then put their handles (HICONs) into the appropriate members of the structure you use when registering a window class:

> **TIP**
>
> Normally, you set up the hIcon members so that they point to icons that are the correct size. hIconSm should point to a small icon that's 16×16 pixels, and hIcon should point to one that's 32×32. If you set hIconSm to a 32×32 icon, Windows automatically shrinks it to 16×16. Conversely, if you point hIcon to a 16×16 icon, Windows enlarges it.
>
> It's perfectly okay to create one big 32×32 icon, specify it for both hIcon and hIconSm, and let Windows automatically shrink it for your small icon.

```
// set up and register window class
WNDCLASSEX wc;
...
wc.hIcon = LoadIcon(g_hInstance,
  MAKEINTRESOURCE(IDI_APP_ICON_BIG));
```

```
wc.hIconSm = LoadIcon(g_hInstance,
  MAKEINTRESOURCE(IDI_APP_ICON_SMALL);
...
RegisterClassEx(&wc);

// create a window
...
```

In this example, assume that your icon resource IDs are IDI_APP_ICON_BIG and IDI_APP_ICON_SMALL.

You're probably wondering about the MAKEINTRESOURCE. MAKEINTRESOURCE is a macro defined by Windows that takes an integer and converts it to a value compatible with the resource management functions.

If you look at the function prototype for LoadIcon, you see that the second parameter is a string, not an integer. This is because it's possible to give resources string names instead of IDs. The reasons for doing this are varied, but usually the standard is to use integer IDs (defined in the resource.h header file).

The LoadIcon function, along with most of the other resource management functions, can take either a string or an integer, but because the Win32 API is strictly C, Microsoft couldn't make a C++ overloaded function. Instead, Microsoft decided to make the second parameter a pointer and differentiate between string IDs and integer IDs by looking at the low-order word of the pointer. If the high-order word of its second parameter is zero, LoadIcon assumes that it's not a pointer to a string but is, instead, an integer ID (specified in the low-order word).

The MAKEINTRESOURCE macro makes all this confusion easier for Windows programmers. The macro simply takes what you give it and converts it into a pointer whose high-order word is zero and low-order word is your integer ID.

Sample Program Reference

The Ch2p3_AppIcon sample program demonstrates how to create custom icons and mouse cursors.

The bottom line is that if you're using integers as your resource IDs, you have to use the MAKEINTRESOURCE macro. Otherwise, things don't work correctly.

Custom Mouse Cursors

Many games replace the standard mouse cursor arrow with a custom mouse cursor because having custom mouse cursors often makes games a little more entertaining. It's also surprisingly easy:

```
// Set up and register window class
WNDCLASSEX wc;
...
wc.hCursor = LoadCursor(hinst, MAKEINTRESOURCE(IDC_SMILE));
```

As you see, all you need to do is set the default cursor for your window class to be a custom cursor you've created.

That works great if the mouse cursor never has to change. If it does have to change, this becomes more complex because you must intercept and handle the WM_SETCURSOR message.

Windows sends you a more or less continuous stream of WM_SETCUR- SOR messages. All you have to do is intercept those messages, quickly decide what your cursor should be, set the cursor, using a call to the SetCursor API function, and then return zero.

The DefWindowProc function han- dles WM_SETCURSOR messages for your

> **TIP**
>
> If you make a custom cursor, don't forget to set its hotspot. The hotspot is an offset that Windows uses to figure out to which exact pixel the mouse cursor is pointing.
>
> For a default arrow pointer, the hotspot is at (0,0), but if you make an arrow pointing right and down- ward, you will probably want your hotspot to be (31,31) so that people point with the arrowhead and not the tail.
>
> You can make a hotspot using DevStudio by clicking the Set Hotspot button in your toolbar. You'll find the button immediately to the right of the label telling you the location of the current hotspot.

main window by setting the cursor to whatever you specified when you registered your window's class. That's why the LoadCursor line works—because, by default, you don't handle the WM_SETCUR- SOR message, so DefWindowProc catches it.

MAKING DIALOG BOXES

You've learned the depths of Windows messaging and have written your own callback functions. You've taken a long look at how the GDI works and have used it to draw shapes, text, bitmaps, and regions of all sorts. You've even learned how to make nonsquare windows and custom mouse cursors.

Yet, you still don't know how to open a dialog that asks users to enter their name. Embarrassing! Let's fix that right now.

First, you should learn some terminology. Dialog boxes can be categorized into two types: those that force you to answer them before you can do anything else and those that stay up even while you're doing other things. For example, in most word processing programs, you can edit documents while the Find and Replace dialog box is open.

Dialogs that force you to answer them, such as the one in Figure 2.11, are called *modal dialogs* (pronounced with a long *O*, like "mode-all," not like "model" airplanes). Those that stay up but let you do other things, as shown in Figure 2.12, are called *modeless dialogs*.

Figure 2.11

A modal dialog box.

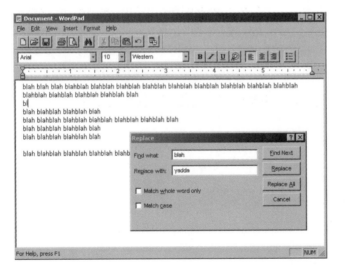

Figure 2.12

A modeless dialog box.

A modal dialog is slightly easier to deal with than a modeless one because you must explicitly create, show, and destroy modeless dialogs. With modal dialogs, Windows hides some of these details.

Dialog boxes are just windows. As such, they have their own window handle and message handler callback function and can respond to messages, as you learned in the first chapter. Dialog box windows usually have a standard appearance (that is, no upper-left icon, no

Minimize/Maximize buttons) that sets them apart from other types of windows, but it's entirely possible to make a dialog box that looks like a tool window or a main window. The main difference between a dialog box and a normal window is how you create one; dialogs are usually created through dialog templates.

Dialog boxes contain check boxes, edit boxes, buttons, and all sorts of other things, which are collectively referred to as *controls*. These dialog box controls are also windows, which use built-in window classes that alter their appearance. For example, a button is nothing more than a window that is linked to the BUTTON window class; an edit box is just a window that belongs to the EDIT window class. Each control in a dialog box has its own HWND, and you communicate with the controls by sending messages to them.

There are a few steps to creating a dialog box:

1. Create your dialog template in the resource editor. A *dialog template* specifies the layout of your dialog box—which buttons you have, where they go, what their labels are, and so on. This is where you can let your artistic skills go wild.
2. Write the code that creates and shows the dialog box. This is similar to creating and showing a window.
3. Write the dialog box's message handler. A dialog box is just another window, and all windows have message handler callbacks. The dialog box handler, DialogProc, is slightly different from a normal WindowProc, but the concepts are the same.

Now let's examine each of those steps in detail.

Making a Dialog Template in the Resource Editor

If you have a lot of free time, you can create a dialog box using nothing more than a text editor. You follow the rules of resource scripting and eventually come up with something like this:

```
IDD_NAMEDLG DIALOG DISCARDABLE  0, 0, 186, 73
STYLE DS_MODALFRAME | WS_POPUP | WS_CAPTION | WS_SYSMENU
CAPTION "Enter your name"
FONT 8, "MS Sans Serif"
BEGIN
    DEFPUSHBUTTON    "OK",IDOK,129,52,50,14
    PUSHBUTTON       "Cancel",IDCANCEL,73,52,50,14
    LTEXT            "What is your name?",IDC_STATIC,13,14,64,8
    EDITTEXT         IDC_NAME,13,28,160,14,ES_AUTOHSCROLL
END
```

That chunk of text gives you a dialog similar to the one in Figure 2.13.

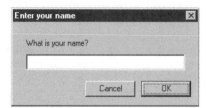

Figure 2.13

A simple What Is Your Name? dialog box.

There's a much easier way, though, and that's to set up your controls graphically, using a resource editor, such as the one supplied inside DevStudio, and let it handle the minutia of generating the resource script.

Detailed directions on how to work with DevStudio's resource editor to place and set up controls are given in Appendix A.

You should have two main goals when you make a dialog in the resource editor:

- Lay out the controls in a way that makes sense and is intuitive for your end user.
- Assign an ID to each control you're going to be manipulating. The control ID is your way of getting at a specific control in code, so you need one for every control you create (don't forget that you also need an ID for the dialog itself!).

After you lay out your dialog and assign IDs to everything, you're ready to write the code to display the dialog.

Modal Dialog Boxes

Creating and showing a modal dialog box is very easy:

1. Design the dialog template.
2. Write the dialog's message handler callback function.
3. Call DialogBox to show your dialog.
4. Call EndDialog when you want the dialog to go away.

Writing the dialog's callback function is no big deal; the DialogProc function is basically the same as the WindowProc function. The only new thing you need to learn is how to call the DialogBox macro (yep, it's a macro cleverly disguised as a function).

DialogBox looks like this:

```
int DialogBox(
  HINSTANCE hInstance,    // handle to application instance
  LPCTSTR lpTemplate,     // identifies dialog box template
  HWND hWndParent,        // handle to owner window
  DLGPROC lpDialogFunc    // pointer to dialog box procedure
);
```

All the parameters here are easy. hInstance is just Windows asking for your ID. lpTemplate is the resource ID of the dialog template you created in the resource editor (that is, IDD_MYCOOLDIALOG). hWndParent is the handle of the window that owns this dialog (usually, the main window you created at the beginning of the program).

> **TIP**
>
> It's possible to have a dialog box as the main window of your application. In that case, you'd set hWndParent to NULL here.

lpDialogFunc is a pointer to the dialog's message-handling function, which is basically the same as WindowProc. I'll talk about this further in the next section.

DialogBox doesn't return until the dialog has been dismissed. This is why it can be used only to create modal dialog boxes. It's possible still to do stuff while the dialog box is displayed, but you have to make your application multithreaded and then spawn a separate thread. This is tricky, but it can be done.

In your dialog's message-handling function, you should watch for and respond to the WM_COMMAND message because that's what Windows sends when a button has been clicked. You figure out which button's been clicked by looking in the parameters for WM_COMMAND. Usually, when a certain button has been clicked (OK or Cancel), you want to hide the dialog.

You do this by calling EndDialog. EndDialog takes two parameters: the handle of the dialog box window you want to kill and a return code. This return code is passed back through the guts of Windows and eventually

> **Sample Program Reference**
>
> You can compile and run the Ch2p4_Dialog sample program to see a modal dialog box in action.

comes out as the return value for DialogBox. In this way, you can communicate which button was clicked to whatever section of code originally opened your dialog.

Modeless Dialog Boxes

Modeless dialog boxes are trickier than modal ones because you yourself have to do most of the heavy lifting. In particular, here's what you do to implement a modeless dialog box properly:

1. Design the dialog template.
2. Write code that creates and shows the modeless dialog.
3. Enhance your main application message pump so that it also dispatches messages to your modeless dialog.
4. Write the message handler for the dialog.
5. Call DestroyWindow when you want the dialog to go away.

The code that creates and shows modeless dialogs is different from the code that creates and shows modal dialog boxes. For a modeless dialog box, you have to call CreateDialog. CreateDialog takes the same parameters as DialogBox, but it returns the window handle of the new dialog.

For example, the following code creates a dialog box window:

```
HWND hwndDialog = CreateDialog(g_hInst,
  MAKEINTRESOURCE(IDD_MYCOOLDIALOG),
  hwnd, DialogProc);
```

Also, remember that for the dialog to appear, you must either call ShowWindow or set the visible flag in the window styles. You do this in the resource editor. In DevStudio, open the properties for the dialog box by right-clicking the dialog and selecting Properties, and go to the More Styles tab—see Figure 2.14.

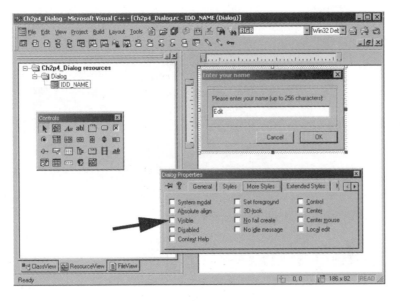

Figure 2.14

Setting the visible flag from within DevStudio.

If you opt to use ShowWindow, you will usually just use the SW_SHOW flag, like this:

```
ShowWindow(hwndDialog, SW_SHOW);
```

This gets your dialog box on the screen, but to get your dialog to respond to mouse clicks and such, you must enhance your program's message pump.

To process the dialog's messages, you need a couple additional functions. I'll spoil the surprise and let you see the whole message pump first, and then I'll explain the new functions:

```
if (PeekMessage(&msg, 0, 0, 0, PM_NOREMOVE))
{
  int result = GetMessage(&msg, 0, 0, 0);
  if (!result) return(msg.wParam);
  if (!IsWindow(g_hwndDlg) || !IsDialogMessage(g_hwndDlg, &msg)) {
    TranslateMessage(&msg);
    DispatchMessage(&msg);
  }
}
```

The first new function, IsWindow, simply answers the question, Is this handle actually a window? You use it to determine whether your modeless dialog box is created; if not, there's no sense trying to dispatch messages to it.

If it is created, you call the IsDialogMessage function, which is a bad name for the function. It does tell you whether the message you pass it is destined for the given dialog handle, but if so, it just goes right ahead and dispatches the message. It should be named something like IsDialogMessageAndIfSoDispatch, although I can see why Microsoft went with just IsDialogMessage.

At any rate, you now know what the new if code block in your message pump does. It says, "If the modeless dialog window is valid, and the message is targeted for the dialog, process the message. Otherwise, translate and dispatch the message as usual." The logic is funny and somewhat hard to follow because it's negating things and ORing them together, but it makes sense, if you think about it, and is relatively concise.

The final unplaced piece in this modeless dialog puzzle is how to make the modeless dialog go away. That, fortunately, is easy: You just call DestroyWindow and give it the dialog box's window handle. Presto, no more dialog box.

> **Sample Program Reference**
> Check out the Ch2p5_ModelessDialog sample program if you want to see real-life modeless dialogs in their native habitat.

Yes, modeless dialogs are more of a bother than modal ones, but they're still straightforward, when you understand the basic concepts.

Dialog Box Controls

Of course, the whole point to this dialog box business is to obtain and present information, and to do that requires knowledge of how dialog box controls work.

In general, you communicate with controls by sending messages to them and receiving messages from them. Two functions in Windows allow you to stuff a message into a window's message queue. These two functions are PostMessage and SendMessage. I'm only going to show the PostMessage function prototype because both functions are very similar:

```
BOOL PostMessage(
  HWND hWnd,       // handle of destination window
  UINT Msg,        // message to post
  WPARAM wParam,   // first message parameter
  LPARAM lParam    // second message parameter
);
```

PostMessage simply takes your message, puts it in the target window's queue, and returns success or failure. SendMessage, on the other hand, calls the target window's message handler directly, so your message is acted on immediately. SendMessage won't return until the message has been processed, and SendMessage's return code is the return value of the message handler function.

Table 2.12 briefly outlines how you can interact programmatically with various types of controls by sending specific messages.

Table 2.12 Controls and Common Interactions

Control	Interaction
Push buttons	You simulate a button click by sending your own WM_COMMAND message to a certain window.
Edit boxes	You retrieve the text in an edit box by using the Windows API call GetWindowCaption, and you set the text by using SetWindowCaption. (By the way, you can also use those two functions to change the title of your window at run time.)
	To put the cursor in an edit box, use the SetFocus API call.
	To select a certain range of characters, send the text box an EM_SETSEL message, with wParam set to the index of the first character you want selected and lParam set to the last index of the character you want selected.
Check boxes and radio buttons	You use CheckDlgButton to check a check box or select a radio button, and you use IsDlgButtonChecked to determine whether a check box or radio button is set.

Table 2.12 Continued

Control	Interaction
List boxes	You use the `LB_ADDSTRING` and `LB_DELETESTRING` messages to add and delete strings from a list box. `LB_RESETCONTENT` deletes all messages from a list box.
	Use the `LB_GETCURSEL` and `LB_SETCURSEL` messages to get and set the current selection.
	If you want to list files with a list box, you can quickly populate a list box with files by using the `DlgDirList` function, and you can figure out what the user has selected by using the `DlgDirSelectEx` function.
Combo Boxes	A combo box is a combination of an edit box and a list box. `CB_GETCURSEL` and `CB_SETCURSEL` get and set the combo box's list box selection, respectively, and `CB_INSERTSTRING` and `CB_DELETESTRING` add and remove strings, respectively. `CB_RESETCONTENT` removes all strings from the list.

A couple other quick tips for using dialog controls:

- The Windows API call `SetFocus` sets the focus to any control you like.
- You send a `WM_SETFONT` message to any control to tell it which font to use.
- You change the color of your controls by watching for the `WM_CTCOLOR...` messages in your dialog message handler. Windows sends these messages to your dialog when a particular object is about to be drawn. By catching these messages and responding to them, you can set your controls' text and background colors.

CHAPTER WRAP-UP

Sometimes I wish that smart people would hurry up and invent the device in *The Matrix* that downloads knowledge directly into a human brain. Oh, the fun! I'd take the entire MSDN online documentation, put it on a little mini-CD, and attach it to the back of this book. Then you could go home, jack in, download the MSDN docs into your skull, and you'd know everything there is to know about Win32 programming.

Alas, until that device exists, you must stick with the tried-and-true, paper-and-ink method of conveying knowledge, and paper-and-ink just isn't compact enough for me to explain every nook and cranny of the Win32 API.

You now know the important stuff about using Win32 to program games. You've learned about using pens and brushes in conjunction with the GDI to draw shapes. You've seen how to load and draw bitmaps and how to write text in various fonts and colors. You've learned how to open modal and modeless dialogs, interface with dialog controls, and use resource scripts. You've learned about error handling, about how to take a cryptic error code and convert it to a descriptive error message.

You might think that you've covered most of the API, but in reality you've only scratched the surface. You can learn much more about Win32, and I encourage you to learn it in the future, but right now you need to get moving. On to the next chapter!

ABOUT THE SAMPLE PROGRAMS

This chapter's examples build on the examples from the preceding chapter, adding a few minor enhancements. First, the window name used by CreateWindow has been moved into a global variable. This helps to eliminate code duplication because now you can easily use the same variable as your caption in MessageBox.

Second, two new global variables have been introduced, which track the width and height of the window. At startup, they're initialized to a certain value and are used by CreateWindow. After the window is created, the WindowProc function watches for the WM_SIZE message, which it gets when the size of the window has changed. When it gets this message, WindowProc notes the new size in the global variables. In this way, you always know exactly how big your window is, which is useful in window painting. Some programs use additional global variables to stash window handles and such.

As you will eventually learn, there are cleaner ways of dealing with global data (namely, put it in a singleton object!). For now, so that I don't obfuscate the technique I'm supposed to be teaching, I just use raw global data.

Those are the global enhancements. Here's what each program does:

- **Ch2p1_Shapes.** This program demonstrates how to use the Windows GDI to draw shapes. It paints its window by drawing random shapes out of random pens and brushes.
- **Ch2p2_Text.** This program shows how to use GDI's text functions. It paints various text effects, from colored text, to different fonts, to centered and word-wrapped text.
- **Ch2p3_AppIcon.** This program shows how to set up a custom icon for your program and a custom mouse cursor. When you move your mouse cursor over this program's window,

your cursor turns into a smiley face. Also, note that this program has a custom icon in Windows Explorer and in its upper-left system menu.

- **Ch2p4_Dialog.** This program shows how to display and interpret a dialog. It asks for a string of text from the user (via a dialog box) and then draws that text in random colors all over the window.

- **Ch2p5_ModelessDialog.** This demonstrates how to deal with a modeless dialog. It also shows how to communicate between windows and how to write a message pump for multiple-windowed programs. It does the same thing as Ch2p4_Dialog, only the dialog box stays up, enabling you to change your inputted text and redraw.

- **Ch2p6_Bitmaps.** This demonstrates how to load a bitmap and display it. It loads a trippy BMP file and then displays it inside its window.

- **Ch2p7_TransBitmaps.** This program builds on Ch2p6_Bitmaps in two ways. First, it uses the CGDIBitmap class to hide all the details of creating bitmaps and DCs. CGDIBitmap allows you to automatically create bitmaps and bitmap DCs as if they were one object—and you get automatic deletion, to boot!

  TransBitmaps also shows how to draw nonrectangular bitmaps using masks. It starts with the same background as the preceding program, but now you can press a key to draw a purple ball at a random location. As you draw more balls, you will see that they overlap correctly.

- **Ch2p8_Regions.** This program shows how to use regions. It does the same thing as Ch2p6_Bitmaps, only it sets up an elliptical region before drawing the bitmap, so you get an elliptical trippy shape that fills the window. This program also introduces CommonFunc.h/cpp, which is a file full of handy Windows functions, such as CenterWindow, which automatically centers a window on the screen. Check it out.

- **Ch2p9_MessageBoxes.** This program shows how to display message boxes in a wide variety of icons and styles. It also demonstrates how to make a *console-style* application, that is, a Windows application that behaves like a DOS program. Notice that the main() function is DOS style.

EXERCISES

1. Write an application that allows you to create a color by selecting red, green, and blue components.

2. Put your C++ skills to the test! Create a set of classes that abstract away all this HDC, HPEN, HBRUSH, and so on, nonsense. Your C++ classes should present an intuitive, object-based approach to dealing with pens, brushes, shapes, text, and every other GDI primitive. After you write these classes, see how Microsoft tackled the same problem, by checking out the CDC, CBrush, CPen, and the other GDI wrapper objects in the Microsoft Foundation Classes (MFC).

3. Figure out exactly how the resources are stored in Windows EXEs. Hint: Check out the RESOURCEHEADER structure in the docs.

4. Write a class, CGDIMaskBitmap, that expands on CGDIBitmap by automatically keeping track of both a bitmap and its associated mask. Hint: Make each CGDIMaskBitmap contain two CGDIBitmaps—one for the image and one for the image mask.

CHAPTER 3

DirectX

"The nice thing about standards is that there are so many of them to choose from."
——Andrew S. Tanenbaum

This chapter introduces you to the wonderful world of DirectX programming. I have two goals for this chapter: first, to show you the features of DirectX so that you can more intelligently decide whether it should be a part of your game. Contrary to what you might have heard, programmers have created some very good equivalents and alternatives for most of the DirectX API, and in some situations your best bet is to use one of these alternatives rather than bind yourself to the Win32 platform. In this chapter, I discuss these situations.

In general, however, most games are not concerned with being cross-platform and therefore probably use at least one of the DirectX components, which brings me to the second goal: to whet your appetite and show you how to do basic DirectX tasks. Nothing fancy, just the fundamentals to get you on your way.

Let's get started.

What Is DirectX?

Microsoft created the first version of DirectX, the Game SDK, to lure game developers away from MS-DOS and into Windows. Before DirectX, Windows had very limited capabilities when it came to accessing graphics and sound hardware directly, and what it did have was usually too slow to be used in a game. Microsoft realized that most games need direct hardware access to run fast and created DirectX so that Windows programmers could access hardware directly. That's why Microsoft eventually renamed the Game SDK *DirectX*.

DirectX has a second benefit as well: It makes different hardware look the same to the programmer. Which kind of chipset is on your graphics card or which vendor made it does not matter. All cards look the same when viewed through DirectX. DirectX achieves this device independence by using drivers, which basically take DirectX commands and convert them into the appropriate proprietary hardware commands.

> **TIP**
>
> Microsoft has a thing about the letter *X*—to Microsoft, it means *something* or *anything*. You see this all over the company. Sixteen-bit versions of Windows used device drivers named *VxDs*, which stands for *Virtual "Something" Device*. There's also *X-Box*, which, if you follow Microsoft's way of thinking, could be interpreted as a box that does anything.

DirectX is divided into several parts:

- **DirectGraphics.** This part of DirectX takes care of drawing graphics to the screen. In previous versions of DirectX, there were separate components for 2D graphics (called *DirectDraw*) and 3D graphics (called *Direct3D*). With DirectX 8, these components have been combined into DirectGraphics.

> **NOTE**
>
> I do not cover anything about DirectGraphics in this chapter. You will start learning Direct3D in the next chapter.

- **DirectAudio.** This part of DirectX is all about making music and sound effects. You use it to play sound effects and audio tracks that sound as though they're coming from any point in 3D space, complete with special filtering effects.
- **DirectPlay.** This is, in a word, networking. This component allows you to create multi-player games easily that work over the Internet, modem, LAN, serial line, and so on. It also provides functionality for real-time voice communications in multiplayer games.
- **DirectInput.** This provides access to keyboards, mice, joysticks, and other input devices. DirectInput also provides a means to control force feedback devices.
- **DirectShow.** This provides video and multimedia playback capabilities.

You will concentrate mostly on DirectGraphics in this book, but the other components are important enough to spend some time on. For the rest of DirectX, I'm going to show how to do some of the most common tasks and where to go for additional examples.

SHOULD I USE DIRECTX?

The first question to ask yourself is simply, "Should I use DirectX?" If you're planning on making your application *cross-platform*—that is, if you want to release your game for two different OSes, say, Windows and Macintosh—you need to think carefully about using any of the DirectX features.

Keep in mind this handy rule: The cost of using a DirectX feature is reimplementing that feature on platforms that don't have it. For example, if you decide that you're going to use DirectMusic to make your game's soundtrack change at run time, you face the following decision when you port to another OS: Drop the feature—that is, make a soundtrack that doesn't change—or code the Macintosh equivalent of DirectMusic (or, at least, the parts of DirectMusic that you need).

Keep in mind, also, that there are cross-platform equivalents to DirectX out there. For example, OpenGL (the *Open Graphics Library*) is a good cross-platform equivalent to DirectGraphics. OpenAL (the *Open Audio Library*) is gaining momentum as a cross-platform equivalent to DirectAudio. Good old Berkeley Sockets are a good cross-platform alternative to DirectPlay, although you still need to code support for IPX, modem, and serial communication if you want those.

The point is that DirectX is just another API. Like all APIs, you must evaluate it carefully against the needs of your application.

The Ground Rules for Using DirectX

DirectX is implemented using COM, Microsoft's Component Object Model. I'm not going to get into the details of how COM works. It's useful knowledge to have, but it isn't necessary. Instead, I am going to talk about what COM requires from your program: how to play nicely with the DirectX components and, in general, with COM.

I will start with this sentence: *Everything in DirectX is accessed through a COM interface.*

What's an Interface?

You can think of an *interface* as a pointer to a C++ class that doesn't have member variables (it has only functions). That's not the precise definition of an interface, but it's close enough for your work here.

You get interfaces by calling specific DirectX API functions, similar to the way you get handles when you call certain Windows API functions. In fact, an interface can be regarded as a C++ version of a handle. The difference between an interface and a handle is that you can call methods of an interface, whereas a handle is basically a void pointer that you give to global functions to tell them on what to operate.

Conceptually, if you were using a handle, you could write something like this:

```
HANDLE hSomething = CreateAHandle(params); // get a handle
OperateOnHandle(hSomething, params); // tell it to do something
```

You see this pattern all over the GDI. For example, when you create a device context and then select something into it, you say

```
HDC hDC = GetDC(hWnd); // get a handle
SelectObject(hDC, hBrush); // tell it to do something
```

You first create a handle, hDC, and then you tell that handle to do something (in this case, make hBrush the active brush). You pass two arguments to SelectObject. The first argument tells SelectObject which DC you'd like to mess with, and the second argument tells SelectObject what you'd like to do to that DC.

Now, imagine that the Windows GDI is in C++. (It isn't, but just pretend.) You could write something like this:

```
CDeviceContext *dc = GetDC(hWnd);
dc->SelectObject(hBrush);
```

The difference there is that the SelectObject member function doesn't take two parameters. It needs only one because it knows that you're operating on dc, because you're calling it through the dc object. In other words, the SelectObject implementation would use the this pointer, which would be dc, in place of the old hDC parameter.

It's for this reason that I like to think of an interface as a C++ version of a handle.

> **NOTE**
>
> Interfaces are different enough from classes to warrant their own letter in Hungarian notation. Hungarian notation denotes interfaces by an *I* in front of their name, whereas classes have a *C*.

Always Release Your Interfaces

There is one golden rule when it comes to using interfaces: *Release what you create.* If I could, I would distribute with this book a little wooden plaque with *Release What You Create* written in olde style "scripty" letters on it. It's that important.

Failing to release what you create can lead to resource leaks. All resource leaks are bad, but when you're dealing with DirectX, they can be catastrophic. If you leak an interface that, in turn, causes you to leak some precious graphics card or sound card memory, your game can be brought to its knees in no time. Always remember to release your interfaces when you're done with them.

To *release* an interface, you simply call its Release member:

```
m_iDirectGraphics->Release();
```

> **TIP**
>
> You can use a technique called a *smart pointer* to make sure that you always delete your interfaces properly. Basically, the smart pointer wraps an interface pointer and releases it during its constructor. It also uses reference counting to make sure that it doesn't inadvertently release something that's being used.
>
> There are many smart pointer implementations, for example, the CComPtr implementation in **ATL**, and it's not too difficult to roll your own. Check them out. They're useful tools.

One last rule about releasing interfaces: Before you release an interface, you must first make sure that all other interfaces you created using that interface are also released. Say that I have an interface X that has a method that returns another interface, Y. I must release Y before I release X. Otherwise, I'll "pull the rug out from under" interface Y, because it might indirectly rely on an X object that's already been freed.

TIP

Remember that, just like a handle, an interface pointer becomes invalid after you release it. It's always a good idea to play it safe and set your interface pointers to NULL after you release them. In several DirectX sample files, you will find SAFE_RELEASE macros that do just that. You can find the SAFE_RELEASE macro inside dxutil.h.

What's IUnknown?

Occasionally, you run into DirectX methods that take an IUnknown* as a parameter. DirectMusic has many of these methods.

In essence, an IUnknown* is a pointer to an unknown interface. Without diving into a dozen-page discussion on COM, suffice it to say that all COM interfaces are derived from a base interface, IUnknown.

This means that, when you see an IUnknown* parameter, you should realize that you can put any sort of interface pointer there.

Other Important COM Stuff

All programs that use COM must call two functions that initialize and uninitialize the COM layer. Because DirectX is COM, your program will also have to call these two functions.

Initializing COM

Before you make any COM calls, you first call CoInitializeEx. This function initializes the COM layer so that your application can use COM. (Yes, there is a normal CoInitialize, but the online help file says that new applications should use CoInitializeEx instead.)

CoInitializeEx looks like this:

```
HRESULT CoInitializeEx(
  void * pvReserved,  //Reserved
  DWORD dwCoInit      //COINIT value
);
```

Table 3.1 shows the parameters this function takes.

Table 3.1 The CoInitializeEx Parameters

Parameter	Description
pvReserved	Reserved, must be set to NULL.
dwCoInit	A flag that tells Windows the concurrency model you'd like to use.

You can choose from the following models for the dwCoInit parameter:

- **COINIT_APARTMENTTHREADED.** Use this if you're a single-threaded application (see the sidebar on threads) or if all your COM calls will be made from only one thread. Most of the time, this is the value you go with.
- **COINIT_MULTITHREADED.** Use this if you plan on making COM calls from multiple threads in your application.

Additionally, the following flags can be optionally OR'd in:

- **COINIT_DISABLE_OLE1DDE.** Disables DDE for OLE1 support. This is a somewhat esoteric option, so you should not have to worry about it.
- **COINIT_SPEED_OVER_MEMORY.** Tells COM to trade memory for speed, usually a good idea for game programming.

You need to call CoInitializeEx only once for your application. If you call it more than once, all calls but the first return S_FALSE. Note, however, that you must call CoUninitialize for each CoInitializeEx call you made; that is, the inits and uninits must be balanced.

Uninitializing COM

Easy. Just call CoUninitialize, and you're done. CoUninitialize takes no parameters and returns nothing.

Checking HRESULT Return Values

The correct way to determine whether a DirectX COM call failed or succeeded is to use the SUC-CEEDED or FAILED macros. For example, if you were checking to see whether the CheckDeviceFormat method of IDirect3D8 succeeded, you'd write something like the following:

```
HRESULT hr = CheckDeviceFormat(/*parameters go here!*/);
if (SUCCEEDED(hr)) {
  /* do something */
}
```

If you wanted to save keystrokes, you'd write

```
if (SUCCEEDED(CheckDeviceFormat(/*blah*/))) {
  /* do something */
}
```

> ## CAUTION
>
> It is *not* a good idea to check a method's return code explicitly
> against S_OK to see whether it went okay. Even though most methods
> return S_OK to indicate success, some methods return other codes to
> indicate "success but nothing happened" or "success but just barely"
> or something. Play it safe—always use the macros.

Using CLSIDs to Get an Interface

The first step to using a DirectX component is to get its top-level interface. This is the one interface that creates all the other interfaces. For example, in DirectInput, you call the `DirectInput8Create` function to give you an `IDirectInput8` interface, which you use to do all your other DirectInput tasks.

Unfortunately, not all DirectX components have a handy create function that returns their top-level interface. In these situations, you must talk to the COM API directly and ask it to give you a specific interface of a specific COM object (COM objects can contain more than one interface).

The way you do this is by calling `CoCreateInstance`. `CoCreateInstance` takes a class ID (CLSID) that identifies the COM object and an interface ID (IID) that defines the specific interface you want within that COM object. This is what `CoCreateInstance` looks like:

```
STDAPI CoCreateInstance(
   REFCLSID rclsid,      //Class identifier (CLSID) of the object
   LPUNKNOWN pUnkOuter,  //Pointer to whether object is or isn't part
                         // of an aggregate
   DWORD dwClsContext,   //Context for running executable code
   REFIID riid,          //Reference to the identifier of the interface
   LPVOID * ppv          //Address of output variable that receives
                         // the interface pointer requested in riid
);
```

Table 3.2 shows the parameters `CoCreateInstance` takes.

Note that you can get at all top-level DirectX interfaces this way, even the ones that have helper functions to create the interface for you.

Table 3.2 The CoCreateInstance Parameters

Parameter	Description
rclsid	Specifies the CLSID of the object you want to create. Microsoft defines CLSIDs in the DirectX header files, and they all start with CLSID_ (for example, CLSID_DirectMusicLoader).
pUnkOuter	Put NULL here to indicate that you are not creating the object as part of an aggregate.
dwClsContext	The context in which your code is running. Put CLSCTX_INPROC here to specify that you're running in the same process as the COM object.
riid	Specifies the IID of the class's interface you want to use. Microsoft defines IIDs in the DirectX header files, and they all start with IID_ (for example, IID_IDirectMusicLoader8).
ppv	The address of a pointer that will be filled with the new interface, if the call succeeds.

CAUTION

You should *not* try to get interfaces that aren't top-level; instead, you should use the methods of the top-level interface. For example, you should use the CreateTexture method (or one of its variants) to get an IDirect3DTexture8 interface. *Don't* try to get an IDirect3DTexture8 interface by calling CoCreateInstance.

How to Deal with DirectX Enumeration

Many functions in DirectX provide your application with a list of items, such as video modes and joystick devices. The process that DirectX uses to *enumerate* (list) these devices is always the same, even though what's being listed differs. Here are some general tips on how to work with DirectX to enumerate things.

The DirectX enumeration functions have a parameter that's a pointer to a callback function. The idea is that you write a function that DirectX will call once for every object in the list. DirectX calls your function so that you can look at the information it's presenting to you and either store it in your own list (which might be an array, an STL vector, or whatever) or act on it directly.

For example, say that you're enumerating video modes and your program is running on a system with 15 available video modes. When you call the DirectGraphics function that enumerates video modes, you pass it the address of a callback function. DirectGraphics calls that callback function 15 times, each time passing it different values that indicate information about a particular video mode. You probably want your callback function to store that information in an array or vector of available video modes. When all video modes have passed through your callback function, the DirectX method returns.

The DirectX enumeration functions allow your application to pass one 32-bit value "through" DirectX and to your callback function, when DirectX calls the callback function. Microsoft put this functionality in so that you can easily pass, say, a pointer to a class or the address of an array to your callback function, eliminating the need to rely on global variables.

DirectX expects your callback function to return a certain code. These vary from function to function, but generally your callback function can return one code to continue the enumeration process or another code to stop the enumeration (in case you run out of memory or find whatever you're looking for).

In summary, here are the usual steps for enumeration objects and storing them in an array:

1. Clear your array, and set your array size to zero.
2. Call the DirectX enumeration method, passing to it the address of your callback function. Pass the address of your array (or a pointer to your array class) as the application-defined data.
3. DirectX calls your callback function once for each item in the enumeration. Your callback function uses the 32-bit application-defined data to get to your array, or array class. Your callback function then adds the current item to your array.
4. The DirectX method returns after all objects have been enumerated.

DIRECTINPUT

DirectInput gives your game an interface to your users' keyboard, mouse, and joysticks. Now you're probably saying to yourself, "But Windows already *has* an interface to keyboards, mice, and joysticks!" You're right. The standard Win32 API provides many ways to read the devices, and for many simple games (card games, puzzles, and the

> **TIP**
>
> By the way, Microsoft defines a *joystick* as anything that isn't a mouse or keyboard.

like), these methods are completely adequate. For action games and 3D games, however, the Win32 methods just don't cut it—you need to use DirectInput. DirectInput sits directly atop the device drivers for all the input devices and is therefore much more flexible than the Win32 API.

DirectInput Architecture

Figure 3.1 shows the interfaces that make up DirectInput.

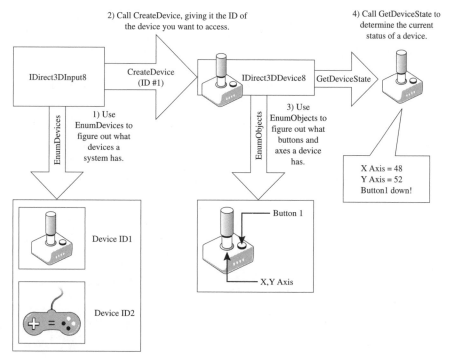

Figure 3.1

The main DirectInput interfaces and how they relate.

To do anything at all with DirectInput, you first need to create a DirectInput object by calling `DirectInput8Create`. After you create that, you can ask DirectInput to enumerate all *attached* devices, that is, give you a list of all available devices. Each device has a device ID and information such as its name, type, and so on. Presumably, you'd present this information to the user in your game's controller configuration screen so that the user could choose a device.

You gain access to a particular device by calling the CreateDevice method of IDirectInput8, which creates a DirectInput device object (IDirectInputDevice8) for the device ID you specify.

To figure out what sort of control gizmos (control axes, sliders, buttons, and the like) a device has, you call the EnumObjects method of IDirectInputDevice8. Each control on the device has an ID, along with information such as the type of control, the control's name (for example, *x-axis* or *Right Shift*), whether it can deal with force feedback effects, and the like.

That's how you access everything. Now you will learn how to set up, acquire, and read from a device.

Setting Up a Device

When you have your device object and know which controls it has, you set it up. For example, you tell DirectInput the ranges of the axes of a joystick you like.

The most important part of setting up a device is setting the device's *data format*, that is, how the device passes its state back to you. To set the device's data format, call the SetDataFormat method of IDirectInputDevice8. This method takes one parameter, which is technically a pointer to a DIDATAFORMAT structure. Fortunately, you have to worry about the DIDATAFORMAT structure only if you want to create a custom data format. Most of the time, you pass in one of the predefined global variables, shown in Table 3.3.

After you set up the device object, you have to acquire it—more about that in the next section.

Acquiring and Unacquiring Devices

To read any data out of a DirectInput device, that device must first be *acquired*. You can set up the device, but you can't read from it unless it's acquired. Similarly, after you acquire a device, you can't set it up unless you first unacquire it. In other words, the one and only thing you can do to an acquired device is read from it.

When you acquire a device, you gain access to read it. One advantage of using the acquire/unacquire mechanism is that the device itself knows that, when it's been acquired by some program, it has to deal with only that one program until it's unacquired. This is a good thing because without it, whenever a program requests data from a device, that device would have to spend time ensuring that its configuration is appropriate for that program.

Say that your user is playing your action game and is holding down the Shift key to swing his sword, fire his weapon, whatever. Now, say that the user tasks out (via Alt+Tab or whatever) while still holding the Shift key. He does some other stuff and in the process releases the Shift key. The problem is that without the acquire/unacquire mechanism, when the user comes back to your game, your game still thinks that the Shift key is down (because nobody told it otherwise), which is incorrect.

Table 3.3 The Global Variables for DIDATAFORMAT

Variable Name	Description
c_dfDIKeyboard	Use this variable if the device you're setting up is a keyboard. This makes the device return its state as an array of 256 bytes, one byte for each key (and some extras!).
c_dfDIMouse	Use this if the device you're setting up is a mouse. This makes the device return its state inside a DIMOUSESTATE structure.
c_dfDIMouse2	Just like c_dfDIMouse, only the device returns its state inside a DIMOUSESTATE2 structure. The DIMOUSESTATE2 structure has 8 bytes for button states, and the DIMOUSESTATE structure has only 4.
c_dfDIJoystick	Use this if you're setting up a joystick. This makes the device return its state inside a DIJOYSTATE structure.
c_dfDIJoystick2	Just like c_dfDIJoystick, only the device returns its state inside a DIJOYSTATE2 structure. DIJOYSTATE2 has many more members to support advanced joysticks.

With the acquire/unacquire mechanism in place, when the user comes back into your game, your game cannot read from the keyboard. It gets an error saying that the keyboard is no longer acquired. At this point, your game realizes that something happened and reacquires the device and requeries it so that it is again in sync with what is happening.

Fortunately, acquiring and unacquiring a device is really easy. Just call the Acquire and Unacquire methods of your IDirectInputDevice8 interface. Both these functions take no parameters and return an HRESULT indicating success or failure.

The best time to check whether you need to acquire or unacquire anything is when you get a WM_ACTIVATE message, which means that your window has become either active or inactive. If you're using DirectGraphics, you're probably already on the lookout for this message because, when you get it, you should also restore your DirectGraphics surfaces.

Also, you need to check your HRESULTs when you're reading data from a device, because you can occasionally get a DIERR_NOTACQUIRED error, which means that the device is no longer acquired by you for some reason. To fix this, simply call Acquire and then try to read the data again.

Buffered versus Immediate Data

DirectInput supports two ways to read devices (see Figure 3.2): by reading the device state directly (immediate data) or by letting DirectInput buffer the device changes for you (buffered data).

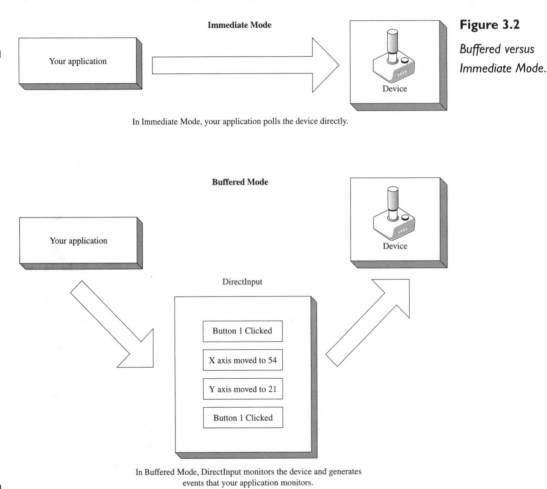

Figure 3.2

Buffered versus Immediate Mode.

In Immediate Mode, your application polls the device directly.

In Buffered Mode, DirectInput monitors the device and generates events that your application monitors.

Immediate data is simply a snapshot of a device. For example, you use the GetDeviceState method of IDirectInputDevice8 to query the current *state* of the keyboard—exactly which keys are pressed and not pressed at the moment. That's immediate data. This is the simplest way to access the device, but it's also a lot of work. Your application must constantly monitor the device and interpret changes in its state. For example, your application must be able to realize that, if it calls GetDeviceState once and a key is up, calls GetDeviceState again and the key is down, and calls

`GetDeviceState` a third time and the key is up again, well, that's a keypress. Furthermore, if a key or button is pressed and released in between calls to `GetDeviceState`, you will never know about it.

Buffered data is more akin to the way Windows messages work. When something happens to a device (say, a key is pressed), DirectInput generates an event and places that event into a buffer. Your game then reads from that buffer. DirectInput takes care of the details of what constitutes a keypress or button click, and it never misses an action by the user.

You set up buffered data by calling the `SetProperty` method of the device you want to buffer. `SetProperty` takes a structure named `DIPROPDWORD`. Most members in `DIPROPDWORD` are just sizes or can be left as zero. The only two that matter are `diph.dwHow`, which should be set to `DIPH_DEVICE`, and `dwData`, which should be set to the size of the buffer you want.

For example, the following code sets up a buffer that can hold 32 events:

```
DIPROPDWORD dipdw;
dipdw.diph.dwSize       = sizeof(DIPROPDWORD);
dipdw.diph.dwHeaderSize = sizeof(DIPROPHEADER);
dipdw.diph.dwObj        = 0;
dipdw.diph.dwHow        = DIPH_DEVICE;
dipdw.dwData            = 32;

HRESULT hr = pDevice->SetProperty(DIPROP_BUFFERSIZE, &dipdw.diph);
```

You can use buffered or immediate data or a combination of the two for your game. Generally, you use buffered data for buttons and immediate data for other things, such as determining where a device axis is.

Reading Immediate Device Data

To get a snapshot of a device's current state, call the `GetDeviceState` method of the `IDirectInputDevice8` interface. (Remember, this works only if you have previously acquired and set up the device.) `GetDeviceState` needs two parameters: an address to a memory region and the size of that memory region.

What exactly `GetDeviceState` puts into that memory region (and, therefore, how big you should make it) depends on the device format you set for the device. For example, if you've set the device format to `c_dfDIKeyboard`, the `GetDeviceState` method is expecting you to pass in an array of 256 bytes, so you'd put 256 in the first parameter and the address of the array itself in the second parameter. If you've set the device format to `c_dfDIJoystick`, the `GetDeviceState` method is expecting you to pass in a `DIJOYSTATE` structure, so you'd set the first parameter to `sizeof(DIJOYSTATE)` and the second parameter to the address of the structure.

Reading Keyboard Data

If you've set the device format to c_dfDIKeyboard, GetDeviceState populates the 256-byte array, using one byte for each key. If the high order bit of the byte is on, the key is pressed. DirectX defines a whole bunch of keyboard device constants that you use to check whether a specific key is down. For example, if you wanted to know the state of the down arrow, you'd use DIK_DOWN as your array indexer:

HELP REFERENCE

For the full list of keyboard device constants, look in the DirectX 8 SDK help under DirectInput\DirectInput C/C++ Reference\Device Contexts\Keyboard Device Constants, or browse the DirectInput header files.

You will find constants for mice and for joysticks in the same place.

```
BYTE diKeys[256];
if (FAILED(lpdiKeyboard->GetDeviceState(256, diKeys))) { /*error!*/ }
if (diKeys[DIK_DOWN] & 0x80) { /*down arrow hit!*/ }
```

Reading Mouse Data

If you've set the device format to c_dfDIMouse, GetDeviceState is expecting a DIMOUSESTATE structure. Table 3.4 illustrates how to interpret the contents of the DIMOUSESTATE structure.

The DIMOUSESTATE2 structure is interpreted the same way, only it has eight buttons instead of four.

Table 3.4 The DIMOUSESTATE Structure Members

Member	Description
lX	The x-axis of the mouse cursor.
lY	The y-axis of the mouse cursor.
lZ	The z-axis of the mouse cursor. This is typically a mouse wheel.
rgbButtons[4]	The state of up to four mouse buttons. If the high order bit is set for any of these bytes, that button is depressed.

Reading Joystick Data

Reading the joystick is also straightforward, assuming that you've set the device format to c_dfDIJoystick or c_dfDIJoystick2. Table 3.5 shows the contents of the DIJOYSTATE structure (also see Figure 3.3).

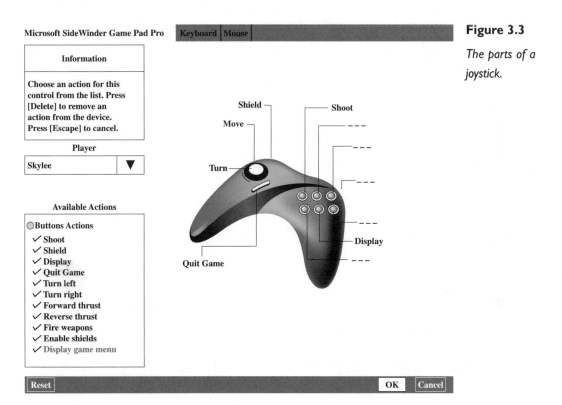

Figure 3.3

The parts of a joystick.

The DIJOYSTATE2 structure is for joysticks with extended capabilities. It has a few more members that you can look at to determine the amount of velocity, acceleration, torque, and other forces for a particular axis. Most of the time, however, the standard issue DIJOYSTATE structure will suit your needs.

Table 3.5 The DIJOYSTATE Structure Members

Member	Description
lX, lY, lZ	The x-, y-, and z-axes of the joystick. The x-axis is usually left/right movement, and the y-axis is up/down. The z-axis is usually the throttle control.
lRx, lRy, lRz	The x-, y-, and z-axes rotation. The z-axis rotation can also be called the *rudder*.
rglSlider[2]	These are the positions of up to two additional sliders present on the joystick. You use the GetObjectInfo method of the IDirectInputDevice8 interface to determine exactly what these are.
rgdwPOV[4]	The positions of up to four directional controls, like POV hats. The position is indicated in hundredths of a degree from North.
rgbButtons[32]	The state of up to 32 joystick buttons. The high order bit of a byte is set if that button is down and is clear if it's up (or doesn't exist).

Reading Buffered Data

To read buffered data, call the GetDeviceData method. (Remember, you must have already set up your buffer via a call to SetProperty.)

Here's what GetDeviceData looks like:

```
HRESULT GetDeviceData(
  DWORD cbObjectData,
  LPDIDEVICEOBJECTDATA rgdod,
  LPDWORD pdwInOut,
  DWORD dwFlags
);
```

Table 3.6 explains the parameters for GetDeviceData.

After you call GetDeviceData, your DIDEVICEOBJECTDATA array might contain some events (or it might be empty—be sure to check pdwInOut to see whether you need to do anything).

Table 3.6 The GetDeviceData Parameters

Parameter	Description
cbObjectData	This should be set to the size of the DIDEVICEOBJECTDATA structure, in bytes. Just set this to sizeof(DIDEVICEOBJECTDATA).
rgdod	This specifies where you want the buffered data to be put. It's an array of DIDEVICEOBJECTDATA structures.
pdwInOut	When you call the function, set this to the number of elements in the rgdod array. When the call returns, this is the number of elements obtained.
dwFlags	Only one flag can be specified here, DIGDD_PEEK, which tells DirectInput that it shouldn't remove items from the buffer. Normally, you want the items removed after you read them, so set this to zero.

Let's look at the DIDEVICEOBJECTDATA structure:

```
typedef struct DIDEVICEOBJECTDATA {
    DWORD     dwOfs;
    DWORD     dwData;
    DWORD     dwTimeStamp;
    DWORD     dwSequence;
    UINT_PTR  uAppData;
} DIDEVICEOBJECTDATA, *LPDIDEVICEOBJECTDATA;
```

Table 3.7 explains the members of this structure.

As you see, working with buffered data is just as easy as working with immediate data. You just have to do a little extra setup in the beginning to create your buffer.

Sample Program Reference

The Mouse DirectInput sample program shows in detail how to read buffered and immediate data. You can find it at (SDK Root)\samples\Multimedia\DirectInput\Mouse.

Table 3.7 The DIDEVICEOBJECTDATA Structure Members

Member	Description
dwOfs	The specific control or button that has been pressed or changed.
dwData	The new state of the axis or button.
dwTimeStamp	The system time at which the input event was generated, in milliseconds.
dwSequence	The sequence number for this event (you can compare sequence numbers between two events to see which was generated first).
uAppData	Application-defined data. This is used for action mapping; ignore it if you're not using action mapping.

Action Mapping

One of the neat new things Microsoft provides in DirectX is action mapping. Action mapping helps you to escape the low-level details of configuring axes and buttons and instead concentrate on the controls your game needs. For example, using action mapping, you can tell DirectInput what your game actions are (that is, "move," "fire," "use item"), and DirectInput will take care of all the details of mapping those actions to keys or joystick buttons or whatever.

Using action mapping, you can give DirectInput additional information about your game so that it can more accurately select appropriate controls for your actions. For example, you can tell DirectInput that you are a racing game, and DirectInput will automatically know that you'd prefer to use a steering wheel joystick. This is a Good Thing because you no longer have to bother with trying to figure out the best set of controls for your game.

How to Use Action Mapping

Here's an overview of how to use action mapping:

1. Set up your *action map*, the set of actions that need to be mapped to devices.
2. Specify your genre.
3. Assign the actions in your action map to default controls.
4. Enumerate the devices that best fit the action map you've set up.

5. For each player in your game, select a device, and configure that device to use your action map.
6. Read the devices by polling each device, and then watch the buffer for any events.

Here's each of those steps in more detail.

Setting Up an Action Map

An action map is nothing more than a list of 32-bit values that your program uses to identify an action. Most games use integers to identify their actions. For example, they use an action map like the following:

```
enum {
  ACTION_SHIELDS = 1,
  ACTION_FIRE = 2,
  ...
}
```

These IDs are eventually passed back to you from DirectInput when events occur. DirectInput sends you a message when an action occurs. In effect, the action map tells DirectInput what you'd like that message to be. If you use an enum here, there will be a switch statement somewhere in your code that looks at an action received from DirectInput and switches based on these type values.

It's easy enough to create action maps that are strictly buttons, but dealing with an axis movement action, such as car steering, is more involved. The problem is that you don't know whether the user will steer the car using one axis control (say, the x-axis on a joystick) or two button controls (say, the left and right arrows on the keyboard).

Because you don't know, you have to be able to handle both situations. This means that you need three actions for car steering (and every other axis movement in your game).

> **TIP**
>
> The IDs don't have to be integers. They can be any 32-bit value, including function pointers, pointers to classes, and so on. This enables you to take a more object-oriented view of actions. For example, you can make your action map a set of pointers to action classes, all derived from a common base class, say, CAction. Then, when you receive an action from DirectInput, you can simply cast it to CAction * and call a virtual ProcessInput method or something.

The first action is for a joystick. When you receive a DirectInput message of this action type, you look at the position of the axis associated with the action (provided by DirectInput), and from that, you determine whether the user is steering left or right. DirectInput sends you a message that says, "Steering: The steering axis is at –1003," and you know from that message that the user is pushing the joystick left (because negative x-axis is to the left).

The second and third actions are needed for keyboard control, or actually any button control. It's possible that the user has a joystick with two buttons right next to each other, and she might decide that the best way to control your car is to use these two buttons as her steering controls. You need to create two actions, one for steering left and one for steering right. When your program

> **TIP**
>
> It's possible for all three actions to be mapped. Players can use as many devices as they like, so most players map the two button actions to keys and the axis action to a joystick. This way, they can switch back and forth between keyboard and joystick control without having to reconfigure anything.

receives these action messages, it can adjust the car's steering by a certain amount. In other words, DirectInput will send you a message that says "Steer Left!," and your program will move the steering wheel left a bit.

Given that, you can create a simple action map for an Asteroids clone:

```
enum {
  ACTION_BTN_SHIELDS = 1,
  ACTION_BTN_FIRE,
  ACTION_BTN_THRUSTERS,
  ACTION_AXIS_ROTATE,
  ACTION_BTN_ROTATE_LEFT,
  ACTION_BTN_ROTATE_RIGHT,
}
```

Note that you've used three actions for the ship's rotation: ACTION_AXIS_ROTATE, which is the joystick control, and ACTION_BTN_ROTATE_LEFT and ACTION_BTN_ROTATE_RIGHT, which are the two keyboard (button) controls.

Specifying Your Genre

Action mapping works on the principle that every game can be put into a genre. Just as we have genres of comedy, drama, and documentary for film, we now have video game genres, such as driving, flying, 3D shooter, platform, and the like. DirectInput uses this genre information to create a set of virtual controls for your game.

These virtual controls allow you to bind actions at a high level of abstraction. Again imagine that you're creating a driving game and need actions for steering and shifting. Knowing no better way, you write code that binds those actions to a joystick axis and buttons, say, the x-axis for steering and two joystick buttons for shifting up and down.

By specifying a genre, however, you can bind your actions to virtual controls, which DirectInput then maps to actual controls, based on information about the controller hardware and the player's preferences. For example, if you defined your genre as DIVIRTUAL_DRIVING_RACE (the racing game genre), you could specify that your steering action be bound to the steering control and let DirectInput take care of figuring out what exactly a steering control is. On a hardcore gaming system that actually has a steering wheel controller, DirectInput would say to itself, "Oh, okay, this game wants a steering wheel, and this system has one, so let's make the steering wheel control use the steering wheel device." On a system with just a normal joystick, DirectInput might say, "Well, this game wants a steering wheel, but the best I can do is the x-axis on this normal joystick."

The point is that by defining a genre, you gain virtual controls. By mapping your actions to those virtual controls whenever possible, you give DirectInput more information and freedom, so it can make intelligent decisions about where to map your actions.

Note that there isn't really any code going on in this step—you're just deciding on a genre. You will specify that genre later when you start to enumerate and select devices.

Setting Up Your Default Game Controls

Now you have two things that you need to tie together. In one hand, you have a list of all your game's actions. In the other hand, you have a set of real controls and a set of virtual controls as defined by your genre. It's time to map your actions to default controls.

You do this using the DIACTION structure, described in Table 3.8. Take a peek at it:

```
typedef struct _DIACTION {
    UINT_PTR    uAppData;
    DWORD       dwSemantic;
    DWORD       dwFlags;
    union {
        LPCSTR  lptszActionName;
        UINT    uResIdString;
    };
    GUID        guidInstance;
    DWORD       dwObjID;
    DWORD       dwHow;
} DIACTION, *LPDIACTION;
```

Table 3.8 The DIACTION Structure Members

Member	Description
uAppData	The 32-bit value you want returned with any messages triggered by this action. This is the value from your action map, that is, ACTION_BTN_SHIELDS.
dwSemantic	The control to which you want to bind the action by default. This can be any of the virtual control IDs defined by your genre or an ID of a certain key on the keyboard or button on the mouse.
dwFlags	Flags you can use to specify additional information. For example, put DIA_APPFIXED in here if you want to prevent the user from mapping this action to a different control.
lptszActionName, uResIdString	This is the name of the action, specified as either a string or a resource ID. This name is displayed to the user as the name of the action, that is, "Activate Shields," "Fire!," and so on.
guidInstance	If you want to tie this action to a specific device, put that device's GUID here. Normally, you set this to GUID_NULL.
dwObjID	The control identifier. Normally, you leave this as zero.
dwHow	You don't need this when you're setting up default controls, so leave it as zero.

You might be wondering about how to set the dwSemantic member for a certain key, say, F5. To do this, you have to use a keyboard-mapping constant, in this case, DIKEYBOARD_F5. Similarly, to map an action to a certain mouse button, you use a mouse-mapping constant, say, DIMOUSE_BUTTON0. You can also map controls to DirectPlay voice channels.

Now that you have your actions bound to controls, you can start the enumeration process.

HELP REFERENCE

There is a list of keyboard-mapping constants you can use to map actions to a specific key. You can find the full list in your documentation, under DirectInput\DirectInput C/C++ Reference\Action Mapping Constants.

TIP

Because your default game controls are probably hard-coded anyway, there's no reason why you can't use some C "shorthand" to create an array of DIACTION structures. Check out the following code, which creates an array of DIACTIONs that's totally set up and ready to go:

```
DIACTION rgActions[]=
{
  {ACTION_AXIS_STEER, DIAXIS_DRIVINGR_STEER,0,"Steer",},
  {ACTION_AXIS_ACCEL, DIAXIS_DRIVINGR_ACCELERATE, 0,"Accelerate", },
  {ACTION_AXIS_BRAKE, DIAXIS_DRIVINGR_BRAKE,0,"Brake",),
  ...
};
```

That's a slick way to specify default controls—most of the Microsoft sample programs use it.

Enumerating Devices

Enumerating devices starts with calling the EnumDevicesBySemantics method of the IDirectInput8 interface. Table 3.9 explains this method, which looks like this:

```
HRESULT EnumDevicesBySemantics(
  LPCTSTR ptszUserName,
  LPDIACTIONFORMAT lpdiActionFormat,
  LPDIENUMDEVICESBYSEMANTICSCB lpCallback,
  LPVOID pvRef,
  DWORD dwFlags
);
```

Your callback function should do the following:

■ **Build the action map**. It should take the given action map, along with the device at which it's currently looking, and ask DirectInput to build an action map for the device. You do this by calling the BuildActionMap method of IDirectInputDevice8. This is like asking DirectInput, "Dear Mr. DirectInput, if you had to bind these controls to this device, how would you do it, and why?"

Table 3.9 The EnumDevicesBySemantics Parameters

Parameter	Description
ptszUserName	If you're writing a game that supports more than one player on the same computer, pass in the name of the player you're configuring here. DirectInput will display this name so that players know which controls go to which users.
	If your game supports only one local player, set this to NULL, which tells DirectInput to use the login ID of the user currently logged in to the system.
lpdiActionFormat	This is your action map. It's a structure that contains the set of action and control pairings you created in the preceding section, as well as information such as your game's genre and the friendly name of the action map.
lpCallback	A pointer to the callback function you'd like to use to enumerate the devices.
pvRef	You get one 32-bit value that you can pass to the callback function (the preceding parameter). This is useful in C++, where you can put a class pointer here or a this pointer.
dwFlags	Flags you can use to specify which devices should be enumerated. For example, you use the DIEDBSFL_FORCEFEEDBACK flag to specify that only devices that support force feedback should be enumerated.

■ **Look at the action map that DirectInput built**. At this point, you can see DirectInput's answer to your question: where the controls are mapped to, why they are mapped there, and whether there were any errors while trying to figure out where a control goes. The dwSemantic member inside each function in the structure you passed to BuildActionMap now contains a new value—where the control is mapped to—and the dwHow member contains the reason DirectInput put the control where it did.

- **Override DirectInput's action map setup, if necessary**. Usually, you won't want to do this—DirectInput is normally right about where things go—but if you absolutely, positively need something changed, you can change it now by modifying the action map.
- **Bind the action map to the device**. When everything is as you like it, you bind the action map to the device, which creates the binding between actions and physical controls. Call the SetActionMap method to do this.

Reading Devices

When you have your action maps set for a device, you can read from that device as if it were a normal, buffered data device. First, poll everything. Then, look in your buffer (using GetDeviceData).

The DIDEVICEOBJECTDATA structures you get from GetDeviceData will have their uAppData member filled in with your action type (that is, ACTION_BTN_SHIELDS), and the dwData member will contain the state of the control (high bit set if a button is down or the value of an axis, and so on).

Showing Game Controller Configuration to Your User

DirectInput comes with built-in support for displaying dialogs that show users what their game controls are and allow them to change those controls. This is great because writing your own version of these dialogs is a pain. Now you can do your entire control configuration by calling a DirectInput API. As an added bonus, your users will see a picture of their game controller, along with callouts to show which buttons do what.

> ### Sample Program Reference
>
> The DirectInput sample program MultiMapper demonstrates everything you need to know about action mapping. It's available in (SDK Root)\samples\Multimedia\DirectInput\MultiMapper.

To display the dialog, call the ConfigureDevices method of IDirectInput8. ConfigureDevices takes, among other things, a DICONFIGUREDEVICESPARAMS structure in which you can specify all sorts of information about the dialog—the color set, whether the dialog is view-only or the user can edit the controls, and so on.

That's it for action mapping!

Force Feedback

Force feedback is a powerful tool for enhancing realism in games. DirectInput provides extensive support for force feedback, and this section explains the basics.

Here's the general process you'd follow to use force feedback:

1. After you find a device you want to use, enumerate the force feedback effects available on that device.
2. You create effect objects, using the effects you've enumerated. If you were painting a picture, the effects you enumerate in step 1 would be your color palette, and your finished painting would be an effect object. In other words, you combine the effects you get from step 1 with an envelope, amplitude, and a few other parameters to create effect objects.
   You create effect objects using the CreateEffect method. CreateEffect takes several parameters, which you can specify at run time, or you can read from a file, using the EnumEffectsInFile method. When CreateEffect succeeds, it gives you a new IDirectInputEffect interface for the new effect.
3. You play the effect. There are many ways to do this, but the easiest is to call the Start method of IDirectInputEffect.
4. You clean up. Release the IDirectInputEffect interface(s) you created.

Now take a look at each of those steps in more detail.

Enumerating Force Feedback Effects

Enumerating force feedback effects is similar to enumerating anything else. You call a DirectInput method, which calls back to a function you specify once for each effect.

Calling the EnumEffects member of the IDirectInputDevice8 interface starts the enumeration process. Through the callback function you write for EnumEffects, you learn which effects a device supports, as well as any constraints on the effects. Table 3.10 lists the available effect types.

As you enumerate each available effect, pay close attention to the things passed to you by DirectInput. It's possible that certain effects are missing or are restricted in their use for a certain device.

Creating Effect Objects

When you know which effects are available, you can create effect objects using those effects.

To create an effect object, call the CreateEffect method of IDirectInputDevice8. CreateEffect takes three parameters, shown in Table 3.11:

```
HRESULT CreateEffect(
  REFGUID rguid,
  LPCDIEFFECT lpeff,
  LPDIRECTINPUTEFFECT *ppdeff,
  LPUNKNOWN punkOuter
);
```

To use one of the predefined effects, you need to supply one of the following GUIDs in the first parameter to CreateEffect:

- GUID_ConstantForce. A constant force effect
- GUID_RampForce. A ramp force effect
- GUID_Square. A square wave force effect
- GUID_Sine. A sine wave force effect
- GUID_Triangle. A triangle wave force effect
- GUID_SawtoothUp. An upward sawtooth force effect
- GUID_SawtoothDown. A downward sawtooth force effect
- GUID_Spring. A spring force effect
- GUID_Damper. A damper effect
- GUID_Inertia. An inertia effect
- GUID_Friction. A friction effect

Table 3.10 The Effect Types

Force	Description
Constant force	A constant force of a certain amount. If you were to graph this, it would be a perfectly straight horizontal line (see Figure 3.4).
Ramp force	A force that starts at one value and moves linearly to a second value. If you were to graph this, it would be a sloped line (see Figure 3.4).
Periodic force	A pulsating force of a certain waveform type. If you were to graph this, it would appear as a sine wave, square wave, triangle wave, or sawtooth wave (see Figure 3.4).

Table 3.10 Continued

Force	Description
Conditional force	A force that occurs based on sensor values within the device. There are four main conditional forces: friction, damper, inertia, and spring, all of which use the joystick's position to create an effect (see Figure 3.4).
Custom and device-defined forces	You can create custom forces, or certain devices may ship with unique forces that aren't defined by DirectInput.

Table 3.11 The CreateEffect Parameters

Parameter	Description
rguid	Each effect object you create is based on one of the predefined effects listed in the preceding section (constant force, ramp force, and so on) This parameter is a GUID that corresponds to the effect type you're using in your effect object.
lpeff	This is a pointer to a DIEFFECT structure that describes in detail the parameters of the effect object. It contains information such as whether the effect object is triggered by a joystick button, the axis on which the effect object works, and so on. For a full description of this structure, refer to the DirectInput documentation.
ppdeff	The address of a pointer that will receive the new IDirectInputEffect interface created for this effect.
pUnkOuter	Unused and reserved; set this to NULL.

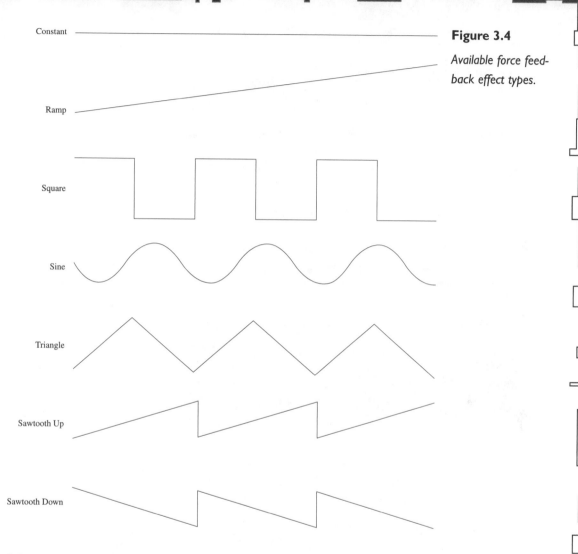

Figure 3.4

Available force feedback effect types.

Use the Force Editor, Luke!

The DIEFFECT structure is complex. Fortunately, however, Microsoft provides a nifty editor that allows you to create effect objects, preview them, and save them to a file for use in your games.

HELP REFERENCE

The Force Editor is available as part of the DirectX SDK and can be found at (SDK Root)\bin\dxutils\fedit.exe. See Figure 3.5 for a screenshot of it in action.

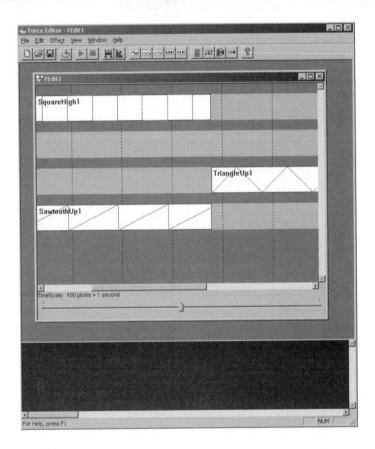

Figure 3.5

The Force Editor is your friend.

To load effects that you've created with the Force Editor, you use the EnumEffectsInFile method of the IDirectInputDevice8 interface. This is a standard method that uses a callback function—it calls back to this function for each effect in the given file.

Normally, the callback function you write takes the parameters passed to it by DirectInput and creates an effect. DirectInput supplies the populated DIEFFECT structure, so it's easy to have your callback function hand off this structure to CreateEffect and squirrel away the new effect interface pointer it creates.

Playing an Effect Object

To make the joystick wiggle, you "play" an effect object, sort of like how you play a sound effect. This is very easy. Just call the Start method of the IDirectInputEffect interface you want to play.

Start looks like this (see Table 3.12):

```
HRESULT Start(
  DWORD dwIterations,
  DWORD dwFlags
);
```

Table 3.12 The Start Parameters

Parameter	Description
dwIterations	The number of times to play the effect. You can specify INFINITE here to play the effect continuously.
dwFlags	Only two flags are available, DIES_SOLO and DIES_NODOWNLOAD.

Here are the flags available for you to pass to the Start method:

- **DIES_SOLO.** Specifying this flag means that you want the effect to be played *solo*; that is, all other effects that are playing are stopped.
- **DIES_NODOWNLOAD.** Tells DirectInput not to download the effect automatically into the device. Normally, you don't use this unless you yourself are managing effect object downloads.

When an effect is playing, you use the Stop method to stop it. With that, you know the basics for using force feedback in DirectInput.

DirectInput Wrap-Up

That's DirectInput in a nutshell. You can keep your sanity by remembering the principles of object-oriented programming (OOP) when writing your DirectInput code. DirectInput is a great example of OOP because everything you're dealing with in

Sample Program Reference

You will want to start analyzing DirectInput hands-on by looking at the DirectInput sample programs.

The three, surprisingly well-named sample programs Keyboard, Joystick, and Mouse show how to use DirectInput to read the keyboard, joystick, and mouse.

The Scrawl example shows all sorts of important yet easily overlooked things—capturing the focus of a device, presenting context menus, and so on.

Look at the FFConst example to see force feedback code in action.

code corresponds to tangible objects. Devices, buttons on devices, force feedback effects—they're all real things you can touch.

DIRECTAUDIO

In previous versions of DirectX, there are two separate components: DirectSound, which you use to play sound effects, and DirectMusic, which you use to play music. In Direct8, Microsoft merges these two components to create DirectAudio.

In DirectAudio, DirectMusic sits above DirectSound and tells it what to do. However, you can still access DirectSound and use it directly without having to instantiate any DirectMusic objects. There are actually two ways to play a sound: through DirectMusic or DirectSound.

Microsoft recommends that you play sounds through DirectMusic because doing so frees you from having to parse the wave file and stream it into the buffer as needed. DirectMusic knows what a WAV file is, and it knows how to load it. DirectSound does not, so you have to use your own functions (or the functions supplied by Microsoft in the DirectSound utility library, DSUtil) to load and prepare WAVs for DirectSound.

> **NOTE**
> If you need to know how to work DirectSound, consult the DirectX SDK. A good place to start is DirectX 8.0\DirectX Audio\Using DirectX Audio\Wave Playback in DirectSound.

This section shows you how to do things from a DirectMusic perspective.

How Does Digital Audio Work, Anyway?

If you're not familiar with how your computer records and plays back digital sound, here are the basics.

A sound wave, like any other sort of wave, can be measured by recording its amplitude periodically. Math nuts (or at least those of you who have taken calculus) will quickly recognize this procedure as being very similar to the concept behind taking an integral.

If you don't know what an integral is, to see how the computer converts a sound wave into a sequence of bytes, find a piece of graph paper and draw a squiggly line on it, as shown in Figure 3.6.

The squiggly line is your sound wave. One way to measure the shape of that line is to start at the leftmost column of grid squares and note how many *whole* lines (no fractions or decimals) down from the top you have to move until you intersect a part of the squiggly line. (You can also count the number of lines up from the bottom. Same difference.) Jot down this measurement, repeat this procedure for every column, and you will construct a series of numbers that make up a

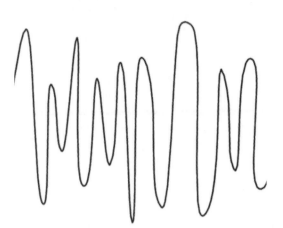

Figure 3.6

*A squiggly line repre-
senting a sound wave.*

rough approximation of the shape of your squiggly line (see Figure 3.7). This is how the computer "records" sound.

Now, grab a blank sheet of graph paper. To reconstruct your squiggly line on this new sheet, start
with the first number in your series, move that many lines down the page, and then draw a portion of the line in that square. Because you have no information about what the shape of the line
is *within* the grid square, between the left and right vertical lines, the best you can do is to draw a
flat line across the whole grid square. This means that some of the curves of your original sound
will be lost, as shown in Figure 3.8.

Repeat this process for each number in your series, and you wind up with a blocky but mostly
accurate representation of your original squiggly line, as shown in Figure 3.9.

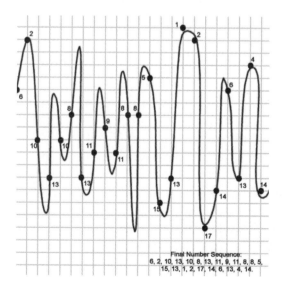

Figure 3.7

*The numbers of
your squiggly line.*

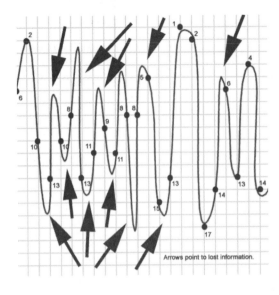

Figure 3.8

Information inside each square is lost.

Arrows point to lost information.

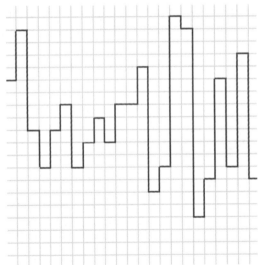

Figure 3.9

The reconstructed sound.

That's how the computer stores and plays back sounds. When you tell it to record a sound, it periodically notes the amplitude of the sound wave coming from the microphone. How often it does this is known as the *sampling rate*. For example, CD-quality audio has a sampling rate of about 44,000Hz, which means that the computer makes 44,000 measurements every second. Taking fewer measurements (samples) per second means that you save memory because you don't have as many numbers, but it also means that you lose sound quality because your reconstruction of the sound wave isn't as accurate as the original (see Figure 3.10). For that reason, you can think of the sampling rate as the width of your grid squares on your graph paper.

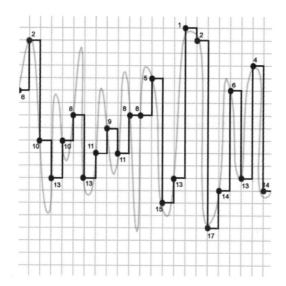

Figure 3.10

*The reconstructed
sound isn't an exact
image of the original,
but it's close.*

There's more to sound quality than just sampling rates, however. Back to the graph paper. You could have measured the sound wave more accurately had your grid square *heights* been smaller, that is, had there been twice as many rows of squares on the page.

The accuracy to which the computer measures the height of the sound wave is called the *sample quality*. For example, *8-bit quality* means that the computer uses 8 bits (1 byte) to measure the height of the sound wave, which means that it records numbers from 0 to 255. *Sixteen-bit quality* means that the computer uses 16 bits (2 bytes, or the numbers 0 to 65535) to record the height of the sound wave. As you can see, 16-bit is better than 8-bit because with 16-bit, the computer has a much bigger range of numbers, which enables it to measure the sound wave much more precisely. Of course, 16-bit sounds also consume twice as much memory as 8-bit sounds.

If that's still confusing to you, imagine that you want to know how tall your friend is. If he could give you an answer only to the nearest foot, the number he would give you would be small (between 0 and 8), but it wouldn't be accurate. If he could answer to the nearest inch instead, that would be much more accurate, but the number range would be larger (between 0 and 96).

Now, return to the computer. Figure out how many bytes you'd need to record one second of CD-quality, stereo audio. *CD-quality* means a 44KHz sample rate and a 16-bit sample quality, and because the sound is stereo, you need to record both the left and right channels. Each 16-bit sample takes 2 bytes, and you're doing that 44,000 times per second, which means that you need 88,000 bytes (88k) for one second. That's just one channel, so to record both channels for stereo sound, you need 88,000 * 2, or 176,000 bytes. Think about that for a minute. That's 176,000 bytes, or about 176k, for *one second* of CD-quality audio. To store a typical 3-minute song would take 176,000 * 60 seconds per minute * 3 minutes, or 31,680,000 bytes—approximately 31 megabytes! Digital audio isn't cheap!

MP3s have killer compression algorithms. That's why an MP3 file is usually only 3–4 megabytes. However, an MP3 is *lossy*—the compression loses some information. That's why, to a keen ear, MP3s sound muffled when played through a really high-quality audio system. Some of the high-frequency information is lost in the compression.

DirectAudio Architecture

Before you dive into code, you need to know a few things about the DirectAudio architecture.

First things first. The whole point to DirectAudio is to move a sequence of bytes from somewhere inside the computer out to your sound card and eventually to your speakers. DirectSound deals with the low-level details of moving this chunk of memory out to the sound card, and it refers to this chunk of memory as a *primary buffer*. I like to think of a primary buffer as a big conveyor belt. I put sounds on the belt, and the primary buffer carries them out to the sound card.

Additionally, DirectSound can create *secondary buffers*, which are chunks of memory (system RAM or sound card RAM) that contain sounds. At the most basic DirectSound level, to play a sound, you load it from disk into a secondary buffer. Then you mix the secondary buffer with the primary buffer, which causes your sound to play (mixed in with whatever other secondary buffers you have mixed onto the primary buffer).

DirectMusic sits atop this DirectSound layer and generally frees you from having to deal with the details of mixing a secondary buffer onto the primary one.

At the highest level of DirectMusic sits an object called a DirectMusic *performance*. Keep in mind that when I use the word *performance* in DirectMusic, it refers to a musical performance, a set of songs. The DirectMusic performance object has *nothing* to do with measuring the system performance—CPU use, and so on. You use the performance object to do basically everything you want DirectMusic to do—play songs, play sound effects, and so on.

In DirectMusic, you play these songs and sound effects using an *audio path*. An audio path is similar to a DirectSound buffer but on a higher level. An audio path is a path your sound or music takes to get to the outside world. This often means that an audio path is really just a secondary DirectSound buffer.

When you initialize DirectMusic, it sets up a default audio path, which is what you will use most of the time. However, you might need to create additional audio paths that have special

> **TIP**
>
> Remember that the audio paths you create have DirectSound secondary buffers under their hoods. You can also take an audio path, reach in and grab its DirectSound buffer, and then change that buffer's properties directly. This, for example, is how you get effects to work, as you will see in the "Changing Your Sounds Using DirectAudio Effects Filters" section.

traits. For example, you might want to create an audio path that has an echo filter applied to it. Play the sound on this echo audio path, and it comes out echoed; play it on the default audio path, and no echo is applied. Creating multiple audio paths is important if you want, say, the sound effects inside a cave to be echoed, but you don't want to echo the background music.

Setting Up DirectAudio

Before you can begin making noise, you must do the following:

1. **Initialize COM**. This isn't specific to DirectAudio. You must initialize COM before you can use any of the DirectX components.
2. **Create an IDirectMusicPerformance8 interface**. This is the top-level interface for DirectAudio. Create one using a call to CoCreateInstance with CLSID_DirectMusicPerformance and IID_IDirectMusicPerformance8. You need only one of these for your entire application.
3. **Create an IDirectMusicLoader8 interface**. The DirectMusic loader interface loads files and caches the loaded data. You need only one loader for your entire application.
4. **Call InitAudio to set up your audio system**. When you have both your interfaces, you must call the InitAudio method of IDirectMusicPerformance8. This sets up your default audio path in preparation for playing sound.

In essence, you need two interfaces, IDirectMusicPerformance8 and IDirectMusicLoader8, before you can do anything interesting with DirectAudio.

Of particular interest is step 4, the call to InitAudio. InitAudio looks like this (see Table 3.13):

```
HRESULT InitAudio(
  IDirectMusic** ppDirectMusic,
  IDirectSound** ppDirectSound,
  HWND hWnd,
  DWORD dwDefaultPathType,
  DWORD dwPChannelCount,
  DWORD dwFlags,
  DMUS_AUDIOPARAMS *pParams
);
```

The options for dwDefaultPathType are as follows:

- **DMUS_APATH_DYNAMIC_3D**. One bus to a 3D buffer
- **DMUS_APATH_DYNAMIC_MONO**. One bus to a mono buffer
- **DMUS_APATH_SHARED_STEREOPLUSREVERB**. An ordinary music setup, with stereo outputs and reverb
- **DMUS_APATH_DYNAMIC_STEREO**. Two buses to a stereo buffer

Table 3.13 The InitAudio Parameters

Parameter	Description
ppDirectMusic	This parameter has multiple meanings, depending on what you pass into it:
	If you pass in the address of a valid IDirectMusic pointer, you tell DirectAudio to use the IDirectMusic interface you're giving it.
	If you pass in NULL here, you tell this method that it must create a DirectMusic interface and use it. You don't care about it, and you don't want to know about it.
	If you pass in the address of an IDirectMusic pointer, but the pointer whose address you're passing is NULL, you tell this method that it should create a DirectMusic interface and put the interface pointer into this pointer.
	Usually, you go with the second or third option. Very rarely will you have a DirectMusic interface you want to use. Most of the time, the third option is your best bet because you get back the interface this method creates.
ppDirectSound	Essentially, this has the same type of behavior as ppDirectMusic, only with a DirectSound interface instead of a DirectMusic interface.
	Usually, your best bet is to pass in the address of a DirectSound pointer, but make the pointer point to NULL so that this method will create a DirectSound interface and hand it back to you.
hWnd	Your application's top-level window handle, or NULL if you want this method to use the current foreground window's handle. You're better off passing your window handle here. Using the current foreground window when your application is initializing is a risky process because you can't be sure that you're *in* the foreground at that point.

Table 3.13 Continued

Parameter	Description
dwDefaultPathType	This tells DirectAudio the type of audio path you would like to create.
dwPChannelCount	The number of performance channels to allocate to the audio path. Usually, 64 channels work just fine.
dwFlags	Flags that specify the kind of features you want your audio path to have.
pParams	A DMUS_AUDIOPARAMS structure that specifies additional parameters for the synthesizer. Usually, you leave this as NULL, which tells DirectAudio to use the default parameters.

You will typically go with DMUS_APATH_SHARED_STEREOPLUSREVERB here. For a detailed description of the other available audio paths, see the DirectX SDK help.

The following is a list of flags specifying the features of your audio path:

- **DMUS_AUDIOF_3D**. 3D buffers
- **DMUS_AUDIOF_ALL**. All features
- **DMUS_AUDIOF_BUFFERS**. Multiple buffers
- **DMUS_AUDIOF_ENVIRON**. Environmental modeling
- **DMUS_AUDIOF_EAX**. EAX effects
- **DMUS_AUDIOF_STREAMING**. Streaming wave files

Usually you don't need any of those flags, but I listed them just in case.

Playing Sounds and Music

When you have your performance and loader interfaces, you can use them to play sounds and music. DirectMusic supports three main audio types:

- **MIDI files**. MIDI is an acronym for *Musical Instrument Digital Interface*. MIDI files are very small but don't guarantee that the song will sound the same on all systems. This is because sound cards implement the standard set of MIDI instruments differently.

- **DirectMusic segment files**. These are like MIDI files on steroids, and they form the foundation of dynamic music. You can embed variations into these files so that they never sound the same twice. You create them using the DirectMusic Producer.
- **WAV files**. A standard digital audio file (wave file).

> **TIP**
> DirectAudio doesn't directly support MP3 files, but you can use DirectShow to play them. See the DirectShow section for more information.

DirectMusic refers to all three of these file types as *segments*. It treats all segments the same way, regardless of what they contain. This means that the process you go through to play a MIDI file is exactly the same as what you'd do to play a wave or DirectMusic segment file. Here's the process:

1. **Set the search directory**. If the file you're loading depends on other files, as some DirectMusic segment files do, you must tell the loader interface where it can find those other files. To do this, call the SetSearchDirectory method of the IDirectMusicLoader8 interface. If you're sure that the file you're using is self-contained, you can skip this step.
2. **Load the file**. To do this, call the GetObject method of IDirectMusicLoader8. Note that the loader caches some elements of your segments, so GetObject may or may not result in an actual disk read. When GetObject succeeds, it gives you the interface to the object you request, usually a IDirectMusicSegment8 interface.
3. **Download the file**. Call the Download member of the IDirectMusicSegment8 interface you got in step 2. Download puts all the data needed to play the segment into the sound card. This can mean downloading a *DLS band* (a set of instrument sounds) or, in the case of WAV files, downloading the raw sound data itself.
4. **Play the segment**. Call the PlaySegment or PlaySegmentEx methods of the performance object (not the segment object) to start the file playing.

That's the general process. Now look at each of those steps in detail.

Setting the Search Directory

To set the search directory for your application, call the SetSearchDirectory method of the IDirectMusicLoader8 interface. SetSearchDirectory looks like this (see Table 3.14):

```
HRESULT SetSearchDirectory(
  REFGUID rguidClass,
  WCHAR* pwszPath,
  BOOL fClear
);
```

Table 3.14 The SetSearchDirectory Parameters

Parameter	Description
rguidClass	This specifies the class of objects for which you want to set the search directory. Most of the time, you set this to GUID_DirectMusicAllTypes, which tells DirectMusic that you're setting the search directory for everything.
pwszPath	The file path of the directory you want to set as the search directory.
fClear	If you set this to TRUE, DirectAudio clears all previous information about where to find this class of object. Usually, you do this.

Loading the File

When you have your search directory set, you call the GetObject method of IDirectMusicLoader8 to load the file. GetObject looks like this (see Table 3.15):

```
HRESULT GetObject(
  LPDMUS_OBJECTDESC pDesc,
  REFIID riid,
  LPVOID FAR * ppv
);
```

As you see, there isn't a lot going on with the parameters of this function. Look at the DMUS_OBJECTDESC structure, which describes the object you're loading (see Table 3.16):

```
typedef struct _DMUS_OBJECTDESC {
    DWORD        dwSize;
    DWORD        dwValidData;
    GUID         guidObject;
    GUID         guidClass;
    FILETIME     ftDate;
    DMUS_VERSION vVersion;
    WCHAR        wszName[DMUS_MAX_NAME];
    WCHAR        wszCategory[DMUS_MAX_CATEGORY];
    WCHAR        wszFileName[DMUS_MAX_FILENAME];
    LONGLONG     llMemLength;
    LPBYTE       pbMemData;
    IStream      *pStream
} DMUS_OBJECTDESC, *LPDMUS_OBJECTDESC;
```

Table 3.15 The GetObject Parameters

Parameter	Description
pDesc	The address of a `DMUS_OBJECTDESC` structure, which tells DirectAudio the object you want to load.
riid	An interface ID that describes the type of object you want to load, as well as the type of interface you will eventually get back from this function when it succeeds. Generally, the interface ID is simply `IID_` and the interface name. For example, the interface ID of `IDirectMusicTrack8` is `IID_IDirectMusicTrack8`. Usually, you put `IID_IDirectMusicSegment8` here because you're loading a segment from disk.
ppv	When the function succeeds, this is where it puts the interface of the object it loaded.

Table 3.16 The DMUS_OBJECTDESC Structure Members

Member	Description
dwSize	The size of the structure, in bytes.
dwValidData	A set of flags that tell DirectAudio which other members of this structure you've filled up with valid data.
guidObject	A unique identifier for this object. Because you specified only `DMUS_OBJ_FILENAME` or `DMUS_OBJ_FULLPATH`, you leave this blank when loading a file.
guidClass	A unique identifier for the class of the object. Because you specified only `DMUS_OBJ_FILENAME` or `DMUS_OBJ_FULLPATH`, you leave this blank when loading a file.

Table 3.16 Continued

Member	Description
ftDate	The date the object was last edited. Because you specified only DMUS_OBJ_FILENAME or DMUS_OBJ_FULLPATH, you leave this blank when loading a file.
vVersion	A DMUS_VERSION structure that contains version information. Because you specified only DMUS_OBJ_FILENAME or DMUS_OBJ_FULLPATH, you leave this blank when loading a file.
wszName	The name of the object. Because you specified only DMUS_OBJ_FILE-NAME or DMUS_OBJ_FULLPATH, you leave this blank when loading a file.
wszCategory	The category of the object. Because you specified only DMUS_OBJ_FILENAME or DMUS_OBJ_FULLPATH, you leave this blank when loading a file.
wszFileName	The file path for the object. If DMUS_OBJ_FILENAME is set, you put only a filename here, with no path information, because DirectAudio will search for it in the directories you specified by calling SetSearchDirectory. On the other hand, if DMUS_OBJ_FULLPATH is set, you need a full path here because DirectAudio won't search.
llMemLength	The size of the data in memory. Because you specified only DMUS_OBJ_FILENAME or DMUS_OBJ_FULLPATH, you leave this blank when loading a file.
pbMemData	The data in memory. Because you specified only DMUS_OBJ_FILENAME or DMUS_OBJ_FULLPATH, you leave this blank when loading a file.
pStream	The address of a custom stream interface (IStream) that DirectAudio can use to load the object into memory. Because you specified only DMUS_OBJ_FILENAME or DMUS_OBJ_FULLPATH, you leave this blank when loading a file.

This structure looks complex, but all you usually have to do is set `DMUS_OBJ_FILENAME` in the `dwValidData` flags and then put a filename into `wszFileName`.

The following are the flags for the `dwValidData` parameter:

- **DMUS_OBJ_CATEGORY**. You filled in `wszCategory`.
- **DMUS_OBJ_CLASS**. You filled in `guidClass`.
- **DMUS_OBJ_DATE**. You filled in `ftDate`.
- **DMUS_OBJ_FILENAME**. You filled in `wszFileName`.
- **DMUS_OBJ_FULLPATH**. You filled in `wszFileName` with a full path. DirectAudio will not search the directory you've set by calling `SetSearchDirectory`.
- **DMUS_OBJ_LOADED**. The object is currently loaded in memory.
- **DMUS_OBJ_MEMORY**. The object is in memory; you filled in `llMemLength` and `pbMemData`.
- **DMUS_OBJ_NAME**. You filled in `wszName`.
- **DMUS_OBJ_OBJECT**. You filled in `guidObject`.
- **DMUS_OBJ_STREAM**. You filled in `pStream`.
- **DMUS_OBJ_URL**. Not currently supported. Eventually, this will mean that the `wszFileName` member actually contains a URL.
- **DMUS_OBJ_VERSION**. You filled in `vVersion`.

Typically, you set either `DMUS_OBJ_FILENAME` or `DMUS_OBJ_FULLPATH` if you're loading an object from a file on disk.

Downloading the Segment

After you load the object and get its interface, the next step is to call its `Download` method to download it into your sound card.

`Download` looks like this:

```
HRESULT Download(
    IUnknown *pAudioPath
);
```

Put your `IDirectMusicPerformance8` interface into `pAudioPath`, and you're all set!

Playing the Segment

After you download the segment, you play it by calling `PlaySegmentEx`:

```
HRESULT PlaySegmentEx(
    IUnknown* pSource,
    WCHAR *pwzSegmentName,
```

```
    IUnknown* pTransition,
    DWORD dwFlags,
    __int64 i64StartTime,
    IDirectMusicSegmentState** ppSegmentState,
    IUnknown* pFrom,
    IUnknown* pAudioPath
);
```

Table 3.17 shows the parameters of PlaySegmentEx.

And that's how you play a sound!

> **TIP**
>
> DirectAudio also provides a PlaySegment method that has slightly less flexibility than PlaySegmentEx. Check out the help file if you're interested in this.

Table 3.17 The PlaySegmentEx Parameters

Parameter	Description
pSource	The address of the interface of the object you want to play. This is the address of the segment interface (IDirectMusicSegment8) you just loaded and downloaded.
pwzSegmentName	Not currently implemented, so set this to NULL. Looks as though you will eventually be able to play segments by name.
pTransition	If you want to play a segment as a transition into the segment you specified in pSource, put its interface here. Otherwise, leave this NULL.
dwFlags	A set of flags that tell DirectAudio the specifics of how it should play the file. For example, the DMUS_SEGF_BEAT flag tells DirectAudio to start playing the segment on a beat boundary (at the end of a measure).
i64StartTime	The performance time at which you want to begin playing the object. Usually, you put zero here.
ppSegmentState	If you would like to receive an IDirectMusicSegmentState interface that you can use to monitor the segment as it's playing, put the address of a pointer for it here. Otherwise, set this to NULL. Most of the time, you leave this as NULL.

Table 3.17 Continued

Parameter	Description
pFrom	If you would like to stop a particular segment when this one starts playing, put the interface of the segment you would like to stop here. Otherwise, set this to NULL.
	Most of the time, you leave this as NULL.
pAudioPath	If you want to play this segment on a particular audio path, put the interface for that audio path here. Otherwise, set this to NULL.
	Most of the time, you leave this as NULL.

Changing Your Sounds Using DirectAudio Effects Filters

In addition to playing sounds and music for you, DirectAudio gives you awesome power over the output of the final sound. You can use DirectAudio effects filters to distort your sound in all sorts of weird ways.

Standard Effect Types

Table 3.18 shows the standard effects that ship with DirectX. Microsoft refers to these effects as *DMOs* (*DirectX Media Objects*).

In addition to these, the user might have installed some custom effects on his or her system. You can also use these custom effects (whatever they are) to change your DirectAudio sounds.

Activating an Effect

The effects hook up to DirectSound buffers, which means that the hardest part of activating an effect is digging through the DirectMusic layer to fish out a DirectSound buffer. The following describes how to activate an effect.

Choose an audio path to which you'd like to apply the effect. You can apply the effect to your default path (generally not a good idea), or you can make a new audiopath and apply the effect to that.

Table 3.18 The Standard DMOs

Effect Name	Effect Interface/ Params Struct	Description
Chorus	IDirectSoundFXChorus8 DSFXChorus	Echoes the original sound with a slight delay and modulation, creating a voice-doubling effect.
Compression	IDirectSoundFXCompressor8 DSFXCompressor	Reduces the fluctuation of a signal above a certain amplitude.
Distortion	IDirectSoundFXDistortion8 DSFXDistortion	Adds harmonics to a signal so that the waveform becomes cut off (clipped), distorting the sound.
Echo	IDirectSoundFXEcho8 DSFXEcho	The entire sound repeats after a delay, resulting in an echo effect.
Environmental reverberation	IDirectSoundFXI3DL2Reverb8 DSFXI3DL2Reverb	Uses the I3DL2 standard for environmental reverberation to create realistic sound environments by modeling direct paths and early/late reflections.
Flange	IDirectSoundFXFlanger8 DSFXFlanger	Like an echo but has a much shorter delay and varies over time, creating a *flange* effect, or sweeping sound.
Gargle	IDirectSoundFXGargle8 DSFXGargle	Modulates the amplitude of a signal, creating a gargle.
Parametric equalizer	IDirectSoundFXParamEq8 DSFXParamEq	A parametric equalizer, allowing you to mess with the amplitude of different sound frequencies of a signal.
Waves reverberation	IDirectSoundFXWavesReverb8 DSFXWavesReverb	For use with music, this effect uses the Waves MaxxVerb technology, which reverberates the music.

If you're making an effect on the *default* audio path, call the GetDefaultAudioPath method of IDirectMusicPerformance8 to get an audio path interface (IDirectMusicAudioPath8) for the default audio path you set up in the call to InitAudio.

Before effects can be put on an audio path, that audio path must be disabled, so you disable your default audio path by calling the Activate method of IDirectMusicAudioPath8 and specifying FALSE (to deactivate it).

If you're making a *new* audio path for the effect, call the CreateStandardAudioPath method of IDirectMusicPerformance8 to create your new audio path and give you back a new IDirectMusicAudioPath8 interface.

By this point, one way or another, you have an IDirectMusicAudioPath8 interface. The next step is to call the GetObjectInPath method of IDirectMusicAudioPath8 to grab the IDirectSoundBuffer8 interface of the path (specify the IID_IDirectSoundBuffer8 interface ID in your call).

You now have an IDirectSoundBuffer8 interface. Call the SetFX method of this interface to set up your effect(s); SetFX also allows you to set up several effects simultaneously. Supply SetFX with an array of DSEFFECTDESC structures; inside each DSEFFECTDESC structure is the GUID of an effect you want to set up. If you're creating several effects simultaneously, they get chained together in the order you specify them in the array you pass to SetFX.

To adjust the parameters of the effect you just activated, you need an interface into your effect; for example, for the flange effect, you need a IDirectSoundFXFlanger8 interface. To get this interface, call the GetObjectInPath method of IDirectSoundBuffer8.

When you have your effect interface, you set its parameters by calling the SetAllParameters method. Most effects have this method.

Don't forget to activate your audio path when you're done, by calling Activate!

Removing an Effect

To remove an effect that's already on an audio path, all you need to do is call SetFX and put in 0 and NULL for the number of effects and effects array address parameters (dwEffectsCount and pDSFXDesc). Doing so removes all effects from the audio path.

> **CAUTION**
>
> **You must deactivate your audio path before you call SetFX.**

Effects Wrap-Up

After you get past the initial confusion of audio paths and buffers and all that, you will find that the effects in DirectAudio are very powerful. They work a lot like guitar pedals, only without all the

> **HELP REFERENCE**
>
> **For more information on effects, check out the DirectX SDK help at DirectX 8.0\DirectX Audio\Using DirectX Audio\Using Effects.**

messy wires. You string effects together in code to create an effects chain, and anything you play through that effects chain comes out, well, "effected" in some way or another.

Audio Scripts

One last handy feature you should know about before I wrap up this section—DirectAudio allows you to use a subset of the Visual Basic programming language to create audio scripts, which you call from your game code to play sound effects.

But why bother? You already know how to play sounds in code. Why should you spend time making a script interface for them? In two words, the answer is *turnaround time*.

Imagine that you're a sound guy. Your game designer comes to you one day and says, "Hey, we need some grunting sounds for the monsters in our game." You say, "Of course!," and some time later you email them five grunt sounds. The coders take these grunting sounds and add code to the game that plays a random grunt every so often for each monster:

```
void CMonster::Grunt(void)
{
  // play a random grunting sound
  switch(RandomNumber(5)) {
    case 0:  PlaySound("Grunt.wav"); break;
    case 1:  PlaySound("BigGrunt.wav"); break;
    case 2:  PlaySound("LittleGrunt.wav"); break;
    case 3:  PlaySound("SqueakyGrunt.wav"); break;
    case 4:  default: PlaySound("MadGrunt.wav"); break;
  }
}
```

So far so good—no need for audio scripts. The coders give you a new build of the game with your sounds included, and you delight in hearing them in action.

You wake up the next day, though, and say to yourself, "You know, that SqueakyGrunt shouldn't be used for the Crystal Dragon boss." You email the coders the next day and say, "Hey, only use the BigGrunt for the Crystal Dragon boss."

They do as you say and give you a new build the next day—and that's when you realize that the Crystal Dragon still sounds dumb because dragons don't grunt. They roar. You make a new Roar.wav file and send it in an email to the coders, telling them to use this sound effect for the dragon.

They do as you say and give you a new build the next day—and that's when you realize that virtually *no* monsters in your game should use the SqueakyGrunt. You email the coders, and they take out the SqueakyGrunt. The next day, when running the new build, you realize something else and ask for another code change and build to test out. The pattern continues like this until one day, one coder, sick of doing minor code changes and rebuilds of the game every day, goes postal, charges down to your office, and rips off your head for making so many changes.

Now, imagine that your coders used audio scripts. By using audio scripts, they could write their Grunt function like this:

```
void CMonster::Grunt(void)
{
  // Tell the audio script what type of monster we are
  m_pMonsterScript->SetVariableVariant("MonsterType", m_strType, ...);
  // Call the "Grunt" routine of the audio script to play the correct
  // grunt sound.
  m_pMonsterScript->CallRoutine("Grunt", ...);
}
```

With this mechanism in place, when you, the sound guy, needed to mess with how a monster grunts, you could just open the audio script in DirectMusic Producer, change the Grunt function, and rerun the game. You could do this as many times as you liked, and you wouldn't have to wait for the coders to rebuild the game. Best of all, there would be no postal coders, and your head would still be attached to your body.

Loading and Initializing an Audio Script

In essence, to use a script, you call the LoadObjectFromFile method of your loader interface (IDirectMusicLoader8). This method hands you back an IDirectMusicScript8 interface. You then call the Init method of this interface, and you're good to go.

Setting Script Variables and Calling Script Routines

To use a script, you set the variables the script needs first and then call a script routine that examines those variables and does something.

To set the variables, you use the SetVariableNumber, SetVariableObject, and SetVariableVariant methods of your script interface, IDirectMusicScript8. You can also use the GetVariableNumber, GetVariableObject, and GetVariableVariant methods to get the values of your variables.

To run a script routine, call the CallRoutine method. This method takes the name of the function inside the audio script you want to call and hands you back any errors that occur.

Audio Scripts Wrap-Up

In a nutshell, that's how audio scripts work. If you're working on a game all by yourself, you might find their use limited, but I guarantee that in a team or large team environment, they're worth their weight in gold.

> **HELP REFERENCE**
>
> For more information on audio scripts, check out the DirectX SDK help at DirectX 8.0\DirectX Audio\Using DirectX Audio\Using Audio Scripts.

> **TIP**
>
> Even if you detest Visual Basic, if you're working on a big project with many people, you owe it to yourself to consider implementing a scripting language for your game's characters and enemies. You can use your scripting language for all sorts of things besides audio scripting—Artificial Intelligence, cinematic sequences, and so on.

DirectAudio Wrap-Up

One of the most powerful tools in DirectAudio is the DirectMusic producer, which allows you to create dynamic soundtracks for your game and save them as DirectMusic segments (which you just learned how to play back). Using these dynamic soundtracks, you can accomplish virtually anything you want—music that strengthens as the character enters combat, turns spooky when an enemy is about to jump out, and so on. You can even create musical themes that play when the character picks up a certain weapon or powerup.

Additionally, the power of DLS guarantees that your music will sound the same on all systems. Gone are the days of writing a killer MIDI file only to hear it slaughtered by a primitive sound card's FM synthesis of MIDI instruments. DLS allows you to embed digitized instrument sounds into your songs, similar to how the MOD or S3M music formats of yesteryear worked.

Spend some time playing with it, and I'm sure that you will agree that DirectAudio is a powerful component.

DIRECTPLAY

I've always thought that DirectPlay should have been named *DirectNetworking* because that's what it's really about. DirectPlay is what you use to add multiplayer support to your applications. DirectPlay allows you to connect two or more computers and send data between them—the core technique necessary for networked multiplayer gaming.

In addition, DirectPlay provides support for real-time voice chat over the Internet. Gone are the days of having to madly type out a message in the heat of battle. Now, using DirectPlay technology and certain types of hardware, players can speak directly to each other. I don't have to tell you how exhilarating this is, or how much it could add to your game.

Why Use DirectPlay?

Depending on the type of game you're creating, you might want to use DirectPlay or forego it completely and just use the Win32 TCP/IP API functions.

The main advantage to using DirectPlay is that it abstracts away the differences in several communication protocols. Using DirectPlay, you can write one set of code that supports TCP/IP, IPX, serial, and modem communication and any other weird protocol (as long as there's a driver for it). Without DirectPlay, you have to code support for all of these separately.

On the other hand, the main disadvantage to using DirectPlay is that it binds you to the Windows platform. For most games, this isn't a problem because other DirectX components have already bound you to Windows. It doesn't make sense to avoid DirectPlay because you want to maintain cross-platform compatibility when, say, your game's graphics uses DirectGraphics, its sound uses DirectAudio, and so on. On the other hand, if you're using OpenGL for graphics and you have a good cross-platform sound library, it makes a lot of sense to write your multiplayer code using only TCP/IP so that it's cross-platform as well.

However, don't write off DirectPlay as meaningless until you know exactly what it does. I think that you will be surprised to find out how much work DirectPlay does for you.

Peer-to-Peer or Client/Server?

DirectPlay supports two network topologies: peer-to-peer and client/server. If you're unfamiliar with these terms, *client/server* means that there is a central server to which all game clients connect (see Figure 3.11).

Clients never communicate directly with one another; all messages pass through the server. For example, when a player moves, that player's client computer sends a message to the server. The server then relays this message to all other clients.

In a *peer-to-peer* topology, there is no central server. The clients communicate directly with one another, and each client makes sure that all the other clients know about anything that happens (see Figure 3.12).

When a player moves in a peer-to-peer environment, that player's computer sends out several messages, one to each of the other clients, letting them know that the player has moved.

TIP

The majority of games today use a client/server topology; only a few use peer-to-peer.

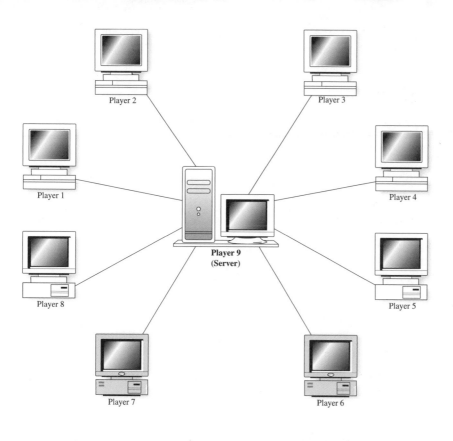

Figure 3.11

Client/server architecture.

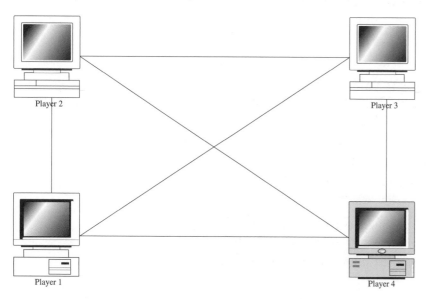

Figure 3.12

Peer-to-peer architecture.

Depending on your decision, you must create a particular interface. For peer-to-peer, you create an `IDirectPlay8Peer` interface. For a client/server topology, you create an `IDirectPlay8Server` interface if you're running as a server or an `IDirectPlay8Client` interface if you're running as a client.

Using DirectPlay in Seven Easy Steps

It's no coincidence that most of the games that use DirectPlay have a very similar process for selecting and joining a multiplayer game. You will find your use of DirectPlay much more straightforward if you follow this same basic process:

Put a multiplayer option on your title screen or main menu. Also, take this opportunity to create your DirectPlay interface.

When the player clicks it, that's your cue to enumerate all the available DirectPlay service providers. When you finish enumerating, show the list to your player, and let him select one.

After he selects one, you should ask whether he would like to join or host a game. If you're using a client/server model, his answer will dictate whether you create a client or server DirectPlay interface. Create the appropriate interface; then call `Initialize` and give it the address of your DirectPlay message-handling callback function.

Present additional configuration dialogs depending on whether the user is joining or hosting a game.

If he is hosting a game, all you need to do is prompt for the name of the game and the name of his player. Set this information using the `SetPeerInfo` or `SetClientInfo` methods, depending on whether you're in a peer-to-peer topology or you're a client. For more information, see the section on hosting.

If he is joining a game, you must enumerate the available games by calling the `EnumHosts` method of your peer-to-peer or client interface (note that the server interface doesn't have this method). Present the list of hosts to the user, and let him select one; then call `Connect`. For more information, see the section on connecting.

When the user is hosting or connecting, your game should move to a staging screen where the players can chat, wait for others to connect, and set up game options before the game begins. At this point, your game should be sending and receiving its own messages to communicate changes in game setup to everyone who is connected. It should also be processing the `DPN_MSGID_INDICATE_CONNECT` and `DPN_MSGID_CREATEPLAYER` messages.

As the players play your game, you send messages by calling the `Send` method (if you're a client) or the `SendTo` method (if you're a server or in a peer-to-peer topology). You receive messages by watching for the `DPN_MSGID_RECEIVE` message.

When you're finished, call the `Close` method, which kills the connection you opened by calling `Host` or `Connect`.

These steps are illustrated in detail in the following sections.

Setting Up the Callback Function

DirectPlay communicates with your game by using a callback function (surprise!). This callback function is responsible for receiving DirectPlay messages (similar to Windows messages) and acting on those messages.

Your callback function should take three parameters and return an `HRESULT`, as shown here and in Table 3.19:

```
HRESULT WINAPI DirectPlayMessageHandler(
  PVOID pvUserContext,
  DWORD dwMessageType,
  PVOID pMsgBuffer
);
```

Table 3.19 The DirectPlayMessageHandler Parameters

Parameter	Description
pvUserContext	A pointer to an application-defined structure. You can communicate with yourself through the callback by putting the data you want to pass in a structure and handing that structure's address to DirectPlay during your call to `Initialize`. DirectPlay, in turn, passes that address to your callback function here, allowing your callback to access what you originally put into the structure, for example, a class's `this` pointer.
dwMessageType	The message ID. If this were a callback to handle a Windows message, this parameter could be `WM_CREATE`, `WM_DESTROY`, and so on. All the DirectPlay messages start with `DPN_MSGID`; consult the SDK help for the full list of them.
pMsgBuffer	This is where the rest of the information regarding the message is stored. This is a pointer to different things, based on the `dwMessageType` value.

Usually, your callback function returns S_OK to indicate success, but, depending on the messages you get, you might need to return certain message-specific values. See the help for more information.

Multiple Threads and DirectPlay Callbacks

DirectPlay callbacks differ from other Windows callbacks in that DirectPlay callbacks have to be thread-safe. DirectPlay is a *multithreaded* component, meaning that it uses threads to process more than one thing at a time (if you're not familiar with this, see the next sidebar). This means that your callback function must expect that a thread can enter it at any time, even while another thread is already inside it. If your game itself isn't multithreaded, you can use a critical section to ensure that only one thread is in your callback function at any one time.

The following code shows an example of a critical section. In this code, you're using a critical section to guarantee that only one thread at a time can execute the code that deals with a DPN_MSDID_CREATE_PLAYER (create player) message:

```
CRITICAL_SECTION g_csPlayerContext; // a global object
void InitSystem(void)
{
  // you must call InitializeCriticalSection once, when your
  // app sets up.
  InitializeCriticalSection(&g_csPlayerContext);
}
HRESULT WINAPI DirectPlayMessageHandler( PVOID pvUserContext,
                                         DWORD dwMessageId,
                                         PVOID pMsgBuffer )
```

```
{
    switch( dwMessageId )
    {
        case DPN_MSGID_CREATE_PLAYER:
        {
            EnterCriticalSection( &g_csPlayerContext );
            //callback is now locked
            //perform operation on player data
            LeaveCriticalSection( &g_csPlayerContext );
        }
    }
}
```

Notice the two calls EnterCriticalSection and LeaveCriticalSection. Any code in between these two calls is guaranteed to have only one thread in it. The g_csPlayerContext is the place in memory where the OS keeps track of whether there's a thread in the critical section.

> **TIP**
>
> Even though it's possible for more than one thread to try to enter your callback function at any time, DirectPlay guarantees that you won't start receiving a second message for a certain player until you've processed the first message. In other words, the messages are serialized on a per-player basis.

Threads!

Windows is a multitasking environment. This means that you can run more than one application and that all applications are executed "simultaneously." I put *simultaneously* in quotes because unless you're on a multiprocessor system, nothing's really happening simultaneously. Instead, the operating system is switching back and forth between different things very quickly, creating the illusion of simultaneous processing.

To illustrate this, imagine for a moment that you're a making a meal. If you have only one pan, it's going to take a long time for you to make the meal because you must constantly sit and wait for something. However, if you have several pans, the meal preparation goes much quicker because while one pan is heating water to a boil, another pan is being used for sautéing something, and a third pan is simmering the sauce.

In this example, as the cook, you're the CPU. The pans are the applications. They demand a little attention every once in a while, but they very rarely require your concentration for any length of time. You create the illusion of doing several things at once by carefully dividing your attention between the pans, juggling the tasks so that nothing is left unattended.

To extend this analogy, having two cooks would be like having a dual processor CPU. Now two things really are happening simultaneously, and the end result is that the two cooks can handle many more pans than just one can alone.

That's how the CPU handles multitasking. It switches between tasks periodically, only it's so fast that things seem to be happening at once. In a way, your computer is like an Iron Chef.

Your computer can multitask within an application as well. For example, Microsoft Word is spell checking my work in the background as I type this. It's doing two things at once, and it's using the same mechanism, quickly switching between both tasks. (By the way, the amount of time the CPU spends working on any one thing is called a *time slice*.)

Now I can finally define a thread. A *thread* is a thread of execution inside an application. For example, Microsoft Word is using (at least) two threads, one that's responding to my keystrokes and another that's spell checking what I type. An application can have many threads, and it's common for some types of applications to have dozens, if not hundreds, of them. For example, most Web servers use one thread for each Web page they have to send out. This means that in a heavily loaded server hundreds of threads can be running at once.

Threads can be executing the same code at the same time. Each thread contains a number that tells the CPU where in the code the thread is; as the thread runs, the number is updated. When the CPU has to divert attention to another thread, it uses this number (called the *instruction pointer*) as a bookmark to determine where to pick up. Each thread also contains its own stack (for storing variables passed to functions and whatnot), as well as a unique ID number.

To see an example of threads, check out the `Ch3p2_Threads` sample program on your CD.

Selecting a Service Provider

In most games, when players decide that they want to play multiplayer, the first dialog of the game asks them to choose a service provider (TCP/IP, IPX, modem, or serial connection). To display this list of service providers, your game must enumerate them.

To enumerate the available service providers, call `EnumServiceProviders` (both `IDirectPlay8Client` and `IDirectPlay8Peer` define this method).

`EnumServiceProviders` is different from the other `Enum` functions because it doesn't use a callback function. Instead, it uses an array to contain your information. It looks like this:

```
HRESULT EnumServiceProviders(
const GUID *const pguidServiceProvider,
const GUID *const pguidApplication,
const DPN_SERVICE_PROVIDER_INFO *const pSPInfoBuffer,
DWORD *const pcbEnumData,
DWORD *const pcReturned
constDWORD dwFlags,
);
```

Table 3.20 shows you the parameters it takes.

If your array is too small to hold the entire list of available service providers, this method returns `DPNERR_BUFFERTOOSMALL`, and the value stored in `pcbEnumData` tells you how big an array you need.

This array/array size method of passing information appears in a few Win32 API calls, so it's no surprise to see the same pattern used here. The best way to deal with this pattern is to call `EnumServiceProviders` once with a zero-length array. This causes the method to error out (with a return code of `DPNERR_BUFFERTOOSMALL`) and return the array size it needs in the `pcbEnumData` variable. You use this method to set up an array of the correct size, and then you call the method again to get the data. It's a roundabout way to get your information, but it's failsafe.

The `DPN_SERVICE_PROVIDER_INFO` structure contains information about a certain service provider. The most important member of that structure is `Guid`, which stores the ID of the service provider. After your user chooses a service provider, you need to note the `GUID` of its choice because you will eventually pass that `GUID` back to DirectPlay to select a specific service provider.

Hosting a Game

Assuming that you have an `IDirectPlay8Server` or `IDirectPlay8Peer` interface, hosting a game requires only two steps. First, you set up your player name and other information by calling the `SetPeerInfo` method (if you have an `IDirectPlay8Peer` interface) or the `SetServerInfo` method (if you have an `IDirectPlay8Server` interface).

After you set up your player information, call `Host` to start hosting the game. Both `IDirectPlay8Peer::Host` and `IDirectPlay8Server::Host` have the same function signature:

Table 3.20 The EnumServiceProviders Parameters

Parameter	Description
pguidServiceProvider	Specifies whether to enumerate all service providers or subdevices for a particular service provider.
	If you want to enumerate all available service providers, set this to NULL.
	If you want to enumerate the subdevices for a certain service provider (for example, if you want to know which physical modems can be used with the modem service provider), put the GUID of that service provider here.
	Most of the time, you want this NULL.
pguidApplication	Similar to the preceding parameter, you can use this to specify whether to enumerate service providers for all applications or a certain application. Put the GUID of the application you're interested in here, or leave this NULL to enumerate all service providers.
	Most of the time, you want this to be the GUID of your application.
pSPInfoBuffer	Points to an array of DPN_SERVICE_PROVIDER_INFO structures. DirectPlay fills in this array with information about valid service providers.
pcbEnumData	Points to a DWORD. DirectPlay fills in this DWORD with a number that specifies how big your array should be to capture all information properly.
pcReturned	Points to a DWORD. When this call completes, DirectPlay puts the number of structures it filled in successfully here.
dwFlags	Only one flag is available: DPNENUMSERVICEPROVIDERS_ALL. When you specify this flag, DirectPlay enumerates all available service providers, even those that aren't properly set up. It's like asking DirectPlay for the set of *potential* service providers.

```
HRESULT Host(
const DPN_APPLICATION_DESC *const pdnAppDesc,
IDirectPlay8Address **const prgpDeviceInfo,
const DWORD cDeviceInfo,
const DPN_SECURITY_DESC *const pdpSecurity,
const DPN_SECURITY_CREDENTIALS *const pdpCredentials,
VOID *const pvPlayerContext,
const DWORD dwFlags
);
```

Table 3.21 explains the parameters.

The Host method creates and connects you to the game network. When you call Host, your game should move to its staging screen, where your player can wait for others to connect, set game options, and so on.

What's a DirectPlay Address?

With DirectPlay comes the concept of *DirectPlay addresses*. A DirectPlay address is a text string that looks like a URL, only instead of containing information to access a resource on the Internet, it contains all the parameters necessary to connect to a certain place.

All DirectPlay addresses contain a GUID of a service provider. Additionally, DirectPlay addresses can contain service provider–specific information. For example, if a DirectPlay address contained the modem service provider, the service provider–specific information would include the phone number, baud rate, stop bits, and so on. If the service provider was TCP/IP, the service provider–specific information would be the IP address and port to which you connect.

Again, there's no slick wrapper function for creating a DirectPlay address, so you must call CoCreateInstance directly, specifying CLSID_DirectPlayAddress. Then you call the methods of the IDirectPlay8Address interface you get back to set up the specific address parameters.

Also, remember to call Release on the address when you're done with it!

Table 3.21 The Host Parameters

Parameter	Description
pdnAppDesc	This is a pointer to a DPN_APPLICATION_DESC structure, which contains additional parameters you must set up to host a game (for example, the name of the game, the maximum number of players, the password if it's a private game, and so on). Most of the values you put in this structure should come from player input. Your game should give your player options to set the game name and maximum players, make it password-protected, and so on.
prgpDeviceInfo	This parameter points to an array of IDirectPlay8Address objects specifying the service providers and parameters you want to host on (see the preceding sidebar).
cDeviceInfo	This specifies the number of addresses you put in prgpDeviceInfo.
pdpSecurity, pdpCredentials	These two parameters are reserved for use by DirectPlay; set them to NULL.
pvPlayerContext	An optional parameter that specifies the context value of the host player. You can use this to pass additional information to your DirectPlay message-handling callback. This is the value that DirectPlay passes in conjunction with the DPN_MSGID_CREATE_PLAYER message. Most of the time, you set this to NULL.
dwFlags	Only one flag can be specified, but it's an important one. If you specify the DPNHOST_OKTOQUERYFORADDRESSING flag here, DirectPlay presents a dialog box to your users, allowing them to set up the specifics of the network service provider. Usually, you specify the flag unless you're sure that you have everything DirectPlay needs inside the addresses you pass it.

Connecting to a Game

Connecting to a game is more complex than hosting one because you must first enumerate and display all the active games so that your players can select the one to which they want to connect.

To enumerate all the active games, call the EnumHosts method of IDirectPlay8Peer or IDirectPlay8Client.

EnumHosts works by pumping messages into your callback function. When you call EnumHosts, the method immediately returns, but then, as hosts are found, your DirectPlay message-processing callback function receives DPN_MSGID_ENUM_HOSTS_RESPONSE messages. The parameters of this message contain DirectPlay addresses (IDirectPlay8Address interfaces) for each host that is found.

You continue to receive DPN_MSGID_ENUM_HOSTS_RESPONSE messages until DirectPlay's internal time limits are reached (you can override these time limits, but Microsoft does not recommend it). You can cancel the operation at any time by calling the CancelAsyncOperation method.

Here are the specific parameters for EnumHosts (see Table 3.22):

```
HRESULT EnumHosts(
PDPN_APPLICATION_DESC const pApplicationDesc,
IDirectPlay8Address *const pdpaddrHost,
IDirectPlay8Address *const pdpaddrDeviceInfo,
PVOID const pvUserEnumData,
const DWORD dwUserEnumDataSize,
const DWORD dwEnumCount,
const DWORD dwRetryInterval,
const DWORD dwTimeOut,
PVOID const pvUserContext,
HANDLE *const pAsyncHandle,
const DWORD dwFlags
);
```

Following are the three flags you can set for the dwFlags parameter:

- **DPNENUMHOSTS_SYNC.** Specifying this flag causes the enumeration to be performed synchronously. In other words, this call does not return until you receive all the host response messages.
- **DPENUMHOSTS_OKTOQUERYFORADDRESSING.** If you specify this flag, you give DirectPlay permission to display a dialog box that asks the user for information about how he or she wants to connect (assuming that you haven't given DirectPlay everything it needs).
- **DPENUMHOSTS_NOBROADCASTFALLBACK.** If you're using a service provider that supports broadcasting, this flag forces DirectPlay not to use broadcasting.

Table 3.22 The EnumHosts Parameters

Parameter	Description
pApplicationDesc	This is a pointer to a DPN_APPLICATION_DESC structure, which you can use to restrict the search for hosts. For example, to tell DirectPlay to enumerate only hosts for your application (as opposed to all DirectPlay hosts, regardless of the game they're hosting), you would put your application's GUID into this structure. Most of the time, you do just that. Also, remember to set the dwSize member of the structure to the correct value, sizeof(DPN_APPLICATION_DESC).
pdpaddrHost	This specifies the address of the computer that is hosting the application. If you specify NULL here, DirectPlay creates an address using the pdpaddrDeviceInfo parameter. Most of the time, you specify NULL here.
pdpaddrDeviceInfo	This is a pointer to an IDirectPlay8Address object that specifies the local settings to use when enumerating. This is where you tell DirectPlay that it should look for hosts on the TCP/IP service and not the serial service. Any additional service provider–specific settings have to be set in this address object as well. For example, if you were using a modem service provider, you'd need to set the baud rate, stop bits, and so on.
pvUserEnumData	A pointer to a block of data that is sent across the network to each host that is enumerated. This allows you to send game-specific information to the hosts during the enumeration process. Most of the time, you won't need to send anything specific, so you can leave this set to NULL.
pvUserEnumDataSize	The amount of data contained in the pvUserEnumData parameter. Again, usually you're not sending anything specific, so you can put zero here.

Table 3.22 Continued

Parameter	Description
dwEnumCount	This value specifies how many times you want to send the enumeration data, that is, how many times your application will yell, "Hey, is anyone out there?"
	Usually, you put zero here, which tells DirectPlay to use a sensible default value. However, you can also specify INFINITE, in which case the enumeration does not stop until you cancel it with a call to CancelAsyncOperation.
dwRetryInterval	This parameter specifies how many milliseconds to wait in between sending enumeration data. In other words, it tells DirectPlay how long to wait before again yelling, "Hey, is anyone out there?"
	Again, you probably want to set this to zero, telling DirectPlay to use a sensible default value.
dwTimeOut	This parameter specifies the number of milliseconds DirectPlay will wait after sending enumeration data the last time.
	Same old, same old—you probably want to set this to zero, which makes DirectPlay use a sensible default value. You can also set it to INFINITE to make DirectPlay listen until you stop it (with a call to CancelAsyncOperation).
pvUserContext	You use this parameter to show you which host responses came from which enumerations. DirectPlay passes this value back to you in the DPN_MSGID_ENUM_HOSTS_RESPONSE messages so that you can tell which enumeration call generated the host response. It's like tagging your luggage at the airport.
	If you're doing only one enumeration at a time, you don't need to use this value, so most of the time you will probably just set it to NULL.
pAsyncHandle	When this method returns, this pointer contains a DPNHANDLE that represents this operation. This is the handle you should specify in your call to CancelAsyncOperation to kill this enumeration process.
dwFlags	You can set any of the three flags mentioned previously.

Usually, you specify the DPENUMHOSTS_OKTOQUERYFORADDRESSING flag here.

Eventually, your user selects a host that you've enumerated, and you must connect to that host. Before you connect, you must set your player name and other information by calling SetClientInfo (in a client/server topology) or SetPeerInfo (in a peer-to-peer topology).

After you do that, call Connect to connect to a game. Connect looks suspiciously similar to Host, so there's no need to cover it again here. Keep in mind, however, that when calling Connect, you're not setting game options. DirectPlay pays attention to a few fields inside the DPN_APPLICATION_DESC structure: the GUID and instance of your application, the password, and the flags. In this context, the password you specify either grants or denies you access to the game—if it matches what the host has set, you're in.

The Connect method returns immediately by default; when the connection process completes (either successfully or unsuccessfully), your application receives a DPN_MSGID_CONNECT_COMPLETE message.

Sending Data

When you're connected, you can send data to other computers by calling the SendTo method (if you're the server in a client/server topology or if you're in a peer-to-peer topology) or by calling the Send method (if you're a client in a client/server topology).

Send and SendTo take exactly the same parameters, with one exception: The SendTo command has an additional parameter that allows you to specify to whom a message goes. (The Send command always sends to the server in a client/server world.)

Here's a detailed look at SendTo (see Table 3.23):

```
HRESULT SendTo(
const DPNID dpnid,
const DPN_BUFFER_DESC *const pBufferDesc,
const DWORD cBufferDesc,
const DWORD dwTimeOut,
void *const pvAsyncContext,
DPNHANDLE *const phAsyncHandle,
const DWORD dwFlags
);
```

CAUTION

Be sure that you request guaranteed delivery only on truly important messages. A message whose delivery must be guaranteed takes much longer to send and process than a normal message.

When the send completes, your DirectPlay message-handling callback function receives a DPN_MSGID_SEND_COMPLETE message. You can use this message, in conjunction with the pvAsyncContext parameter, to learn when a specific message actually crosses the wire.

Table 3.23 The SendTo Parameters

Parameter	Description
dpnid	The ID of the player or group to whom you want to send. Set this to DPNID_ALL_PLAYERS_GROUP to send to all the players in the game.
pBufferDesc	A pointer to a DPN_BUFFER_DESC structure that describes the data you want to send. DPN_BUFFER_DESC contains a pointer to the actual data, as well as a DWORD that specifies the size of the data.
cBufferDesc	In future versions of DirectPlay, it will be possible to specify an array of DPN_BUFFER_DESC structures in pBufferDesc, instead of just one. When that glorious day arrives, this parameter will specify the number of structures in the array pointed to by pBufferDesc. For now, however, you can send only one structure, so this parameter must be set to one.
dwTimeOut	The number of milliseconds to wait for the message to be sent. If DirectPlay can't send within this amount of time, it won't send at all. If you want DirectPlay to send, regardless of how long it takes, set this to zero (usually, this what you do).
pvAsyncContext	A pointer to a user context value. DirectPlay gives back this value inside the parameters for the DPN_MSGID_SEND_COMPLETE message. You put in an ID number or something here so that you can differentiate this message from others when you get the "send complete!" message.
phAsyncHandle	When this method returns, this points to a valid DPNHANDLE that corresponds to this operation. You can use this handle in a call to CancelAsyncOperation to abort the send.
dwFlags	There are several flags you can set to control how DirectPlay sends messages. The two flags you use most often are DPNSEND_GUARANTEED, which guarantees that the message will arrive at its destination, and DPNSEND_PRIORITY_HIGH, which marks a message as high priority (meaning that it will be sent before messages with normal or low priority).

Receiving Data

When a message arrives for your game, its DirectPlay message-handling callback function receives a `DPN_MSGID_RECEIVE` message. It also gets the corresponding `DPNMSG_RECEIVE` structure, which looks like this:

```
typedef struct {
    DWORD       dwSize;
    DPNID       dpnidSender;
    PVOID       pvPlayerContext;
    PBYTE       pReceiveData;
    DWORD       dwReceiveDataSize;
    DPNHANDLE   hBufferHandle;
} DPNMSG_RECEIVE, *PDPNMSG_RECEIVE;
```

Table 3.24 contains a description of all those members.

Important DirectPlay Messages

There are several types of messages in DirectPlay—not as many as in Win32 but enough to be confusing. To help clear the confusion, Table 3.25 contains a list of the most important messages, showing when they occur and what you should do with them.

Disconnecting

This is easy. To disconnect from a game, call the `Close` method. The only parameter this method takes is a flag value, which DirectPlay does not currently use (you can set it to zero).

When you call `Close`, it's over. You can't send or receive any more messages until you call `Connect` or `Host` again.

The Joy of Lobbies

If you've ever played on The Zone gaming network or any other online gaming sites, you've probably experienced the strange sensation of having a game launch without your starting it. Usually, this occurs after you hook up with and meet your fellow players. When everything is set up, one person usually says, "Go!," and all the other players' computers automatically launch the game.

Table 3.24 DPNMSG_RECEIVE Structure Members

Member	Description
dwSize	This is the size of the structure, in bytes.
dpnidSender	This is the ID of the player that sent the message.
pvPlayerContext	This is the player context value (that your game can optionally set up and tie to a player) of the player that sent the message.
pReceiveData	The actual data of the message. Note that DirectPlay deletes this buffer after your callback function returns, so if you need it later, you must copy it into a safe place.
	Alternatively, you can tell DirectPlay that you will take ownership of the buffer by returning DPNSUCCESS_PENDING from your callback function. When you do this, you own the buffer. When you're done with the buffer, you must call ReturnBuffer to free the buffer.
dwReceiveDataSize	The size of the data in pReceiveData.
hBufferHandle	The handle of the buffer in pReceiveData. If you return DPNSUCCESS_PENDING, this is the value you pass to ReturnBuffer to delete this buffer.

Table 3.25 Common DirectPlay Messages and What to Do with Them

Message Type	Occurs When	What to Do
DPN_MSGID_CONNECT_COMPLETE	A connection call has completed (successfully or not).	Look at the hResultCode to see whether the connection completed successfully.

Table 3.25 Continued

Message Type	Occurs When	What to Do
DPN_MSGID_CREATE_PLAYER	A player joins the game.	Look at his name and ID, and construct the appropriate game objects for him (give him a spaceship to fly, car to drive, gun to shoot, whatever).
DPN_MSGID_DESTROY_PLAYER	A player quits the game.	Destroy any game objects associated with him, and tell the other players that he is gone.
DPN_MSGID_ENUM_HOSTS_QUERY	Your server or host has received a message from a computer that is enumerating available connections.	Fill in the DPN_APPLICATION_DESC structure to effectively say, "Hey! I'm a host! I'm right here!"
DPN_MSGID_ENUM_HOSTS_RESPONSE	A host has responded to your client's enumeration request.	Jot down the host details provided in the message, and add the host to the list of known hosts you're displaying to the user.
DPN_MSGID_INDICATE_CONNECT	A player wants to join the game you're hosting.	Return S_OK from your callback function to let him in or any other return value to reject him. You can also leave him a message by setting the pvReplyData parameter of the message.

Table 3.25 Continued

Message Type	Occurs When	What to Do
DPN_MSGID_RECEIVE	Your computer gets a message from the network message data.	Read the message data contained in the pReceiveData parameter of the message, and act on that data.
DPN_MSGID_SEND_COMPLETE	A message you sent out with a call to end or SendTo finally goes out to the network.	Nothing, really, unless it's a specific or important message. Usually, though, it's just good to know.
DPN_MSGID_TERMINATE_SESSION	The host of the game has terminated the session.	Display a message to the user, and if you're nice, bring him back to a place where he can choose another game to which he can connect.

DirectPlay refers to this process as *lobby launching*. A *lobby* is a program that connects to the Internet and allows you to chat with other players, form rooms, and set up the game (similar to a hotel lobby). When everything's set, one player (usually, the host or the person who originally set up the room) clicks a button, and the lobby program launches the game and automatically tells it the connection parameters (usually, to which IP address to connect). This saves you the trouble of having to write down the IP of the server, launch the game, select Multiplayer, type in the IP you wrote down, and so on.

DirectPlay has a nifty feature: By conforming to a certain interface, your game can be launched from an online DirectPlay lobby. A game that conforms to the DirectPlay lobby interface is called a *lobbyable* game. Making your game lobbyable is a great feature to have, but because it probably isn't on the top of your to-do list, I am going to cover it briefly here. I encourage you to look at the samples included with the SDK for a deeper understanding of how lobbyable games work.

Using DirectPlay's Voice Features

One of the most exciting new things in DirectPlay 8 is its capability to send and receive voice communications. Your game can capitalize on these features to provide your players with real-time voice chat over the Internet—or however you're connecting through your game. (The usefulness of real-time voice chat over a serial cable is debatable. Who knows, though, maybe the serial cable runs through a wall or something.)

Also, you can combine DirectPlay voice features with DirectAudio 3D sound effects so that when someone behind you speaks in your 3D world, his or her voice sounds as if it's coming from behind you.

DirectPlay's voice features run "on top of" the normal DirectPlay networking mechanism. In other words, they call Send and SendTo just as your application does. This means that the first step in using voice features is setting up and connecting to a DirectPlay game session, which you learned to do in previous sections.

Selecting a Voice Topology

You also need to decide on a voice topology. Just as normal DirectPlay works in client/server or peer-to-peer topologies, the voice features of DirectPlay work with certain topologies. DirectPlay supports three voice topologies:

- **Peer-to-peer.** Similar to a normal peer-to-peer DirectPlay topology. Each client sends voice data to every other client, as shown in Figure 3.13. Each client is responsible for mixing all the incoming voices.
- **Forwarding server.** Similar to a normal client/server DirectPlay topology. Each client sends voice data to a central server. The server then takes care of sending the voice data to all the other clients (see Figure 3.14). Each client is still responsible for mixing all the incoming voices.
- **Mixing server.** Similar to the forwarding server topology, only in this topology, the server takes care of mixing the data as it comes in (see Figure 3.15). The clients don't mix their data directly. Instead, the mixing server sends them a premixed stream that they play directly.

Usually, the forwarding server is your best bet, with the mixing server a close second (depending on whether you want your clients to do the mixing). Peer-to-peer generates a lot of traffic, so be wary of using it.

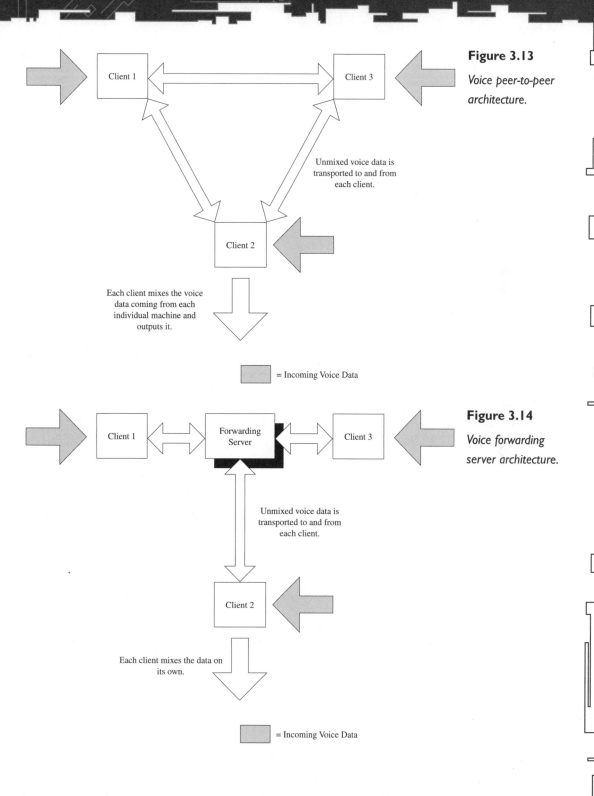

Figure 3.13

Voice peer-to-peer architecture.

Unmixed voice data is transported to and from each client.

Each client mixes the voice data coming from each individual machine and outputs it.

= Incoming Voice Data

Figure 3.14

Voice forwarding server architecture.

Unmixed voice data is transported to and from each client.

Each client mixes the data on its own.

= Incoming Voice Data

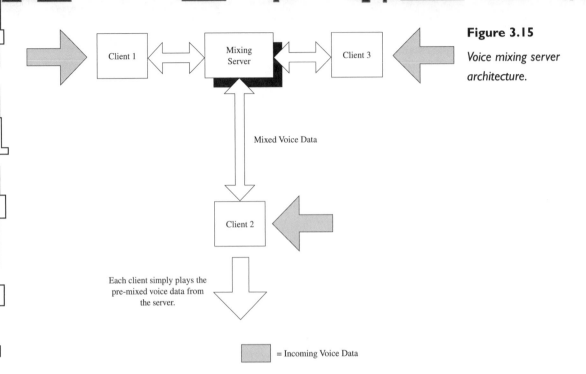

Figure 3.15

Voice mixing server architecture.

Deciding on the Type of Transmission Control

You also need to decide which type of transmission control your game will use. There are two types of transmission control from which to choose:

- **Voice activation.** DirectPlay Voice keeps an eye on the microphone's input level; when a player speaks, the voice system automatically starts recording. The advantage here is that it allows for hands-free communication. The disadvantage is that background noise can inadvertently be detected and sent as voice data.
- **Push-to-talk.** Players must press a button when they want to speak, like using a two-way radio. The advantage is that there's no chance of inadvertently sending background noise. The disadvantage is that the voice system is no longer hands-free.

Which method is best for you depends on your game design, but I would recommend letting users decide which method they prefer, by providing an option in a configuration dialog box somewhere.

The Steps to Using the Voice System

Here's an outline of the steps your application must take to set up and use the DirectPlay voice system.

1. Create an `IDirectPlay8VoiceClient` or `IDirectPlay8VoiceServer` interface by calling `CoCreateInstance` with a class ID of `CLSID_DirectPlayVoiceServer`.
2. Call `Initialize` to set up your voice callback function and other parameters.
3. If you're a voice client, call `Connect` to connect to a voice session. In truth, this method doesn't really "connect" anywhere (because by this point you're already connected to a DirectPlay session). Instead, this method just sets up client and audio parameters in preparation for voice communication.

> **TIP**
>
> Note that if you're a DirectPlay Voice server, you don't need to connect.

You can link your voice to a 3D sound at this point by calling the `Create3DsoundBuffer` method.

That's it! You're set up, and your players are talking. When you're finished, you should call `Disconnect` to disconnect yourself from the voice session.

Testing the Audio Device

DirectPlay Voice contains one additional interface you should know about: `IDirectPlayVoiceTest`. This interface has only one method, `CheckAudioSetup`. When you call this method, DirectPlay presents a wizard dialog box to the user, guiding him or her through the process of setting up the audio hardware, making sure that the volume is correct, and so on.

The best way to integrate this feature into your game is by making a button in your audio configuration labeled *Setup Voice Hardware...* or something to that effect. Write code that calls this method to display the wizard when that button is clicked.

Sample Program Reference

As always, if you want to dive deeper into DirectPlay or DirectPlay Voice, there are some great sample programs you can pick apart to guide you. The ChatPeer SDK example illustrates very simple peer-to-peer communication and is a great place to start learning about DirectPlay hands-on. Maze is an interesting application, too. Check it out to see how DirectPlay fits into your game.

For voice, check out the DirectConnect and DirectClientServer, which show simple examples of connecting to a voice session and using a client/server topology.

The SDK lists other sample programs in DirectX 8 (C++)\DirectPlay\DirectPlay C++ Samples.

DirectPlay Wrap-Up

That's the end of your whirlwind DirectPlay tour. The new messaging concepts sound a little tough written down here. When you start writing a DirectPlay program, however, you will see that DirectPlay has an intuitive structure.

DIRECTSHOW

Last but not least, you have DirectShow. This component facilitates playback (*streaming*) of full-motion video (FMV) and high-quality audio. If you made an introductory movie for your game, DirectShow could play it back for you. It can do all sorts of other things, too, such as record video, but you're not going to get into that here because it's not terribly useful for most games.

DirectShow Architecture

The DirectShow architecture resembles an assembly line.

The workers on the assembly line correspond to DirectShow filters. A *DirectShow filter* takes a data stream as input, performs a single operation on that data stream, and then streams out the results. For example, a filter can take as input an MPEG stream, decompress it, and output uncompressed video data.

DirectShow works by typing multiple filters together. That is, the output of one filter becomes the input for another filter. This forms the assembly line (or, in DirectShow terminology, a *filter graph*) that can eventually go from a file on disk to a video stream displayed on your monitor.

DirectShow also contains a component, the filter graph manager, that manages all these filters. For example, you can tell the filter graph manager, "Run!" and it will take care of the details of starting up the whole assembly line and getting data moving through it. Additionally, you can use the filter graph manager to build a sequence of filters automatically that play a certain video file (see Figure 3.16).

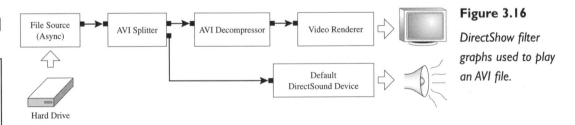

Figure 3.16

DirectShow filter graphs used to play an AVI file.

Thanks to the filter graph manager, your program's process for using DirectShow becomes straightforward. You create an interface to the filter graph manager by calling `CoCreateInstance` with a class ID of `CLSID_FilterGraph` and an interface ID of `IID_IGraphBuilder`.

After you get the filter graph manager, you use it to create a filter graph. The easiest way to do this is to hand it a filename, and it will automatically construct a filter graph for you. If you're a DirectShow expert, you can then go in by hand and tweak the filter graph.

When the filter graph is all set up, you call methods of the filter graph manager to start and stop the video. You also need to watch for events the filter graph manager throws back at you, for example, when playback reaches the end of the video.

Playing a Video

Let's cut to the chase—here's the code to play a video:

```
#include <dshow.h>
void main(void)
{
    IGraphBuilder *pGraph;
    IMediaControl *pMediaControl;
    IMediaEvent   *pEvent;
    CoInitialize(NULL);

    // Create the filter graph manager and query for interfaces.
    CoCreateInstance(CLSID_FilterGraph, NULL, CLSCTX_INPROC_SERVER,
                     IID_IGraphBuilder, (void **)&pGraph);
    pGraph->QueryInterface(IID_IMediaControl, (void **)&pMediaControl);
    pGraph->QueryInterface(IID_IMediaEvent, (void **)&pEvent);
    // Build the graph. IMPORTANT: Change string to a file on your system.
    pGraph->RenderFile(L"C:\\Hello_World.avi", NULL);
    // Run the graph.
    pMediaControl->Run();
    // Wait for completion.
    long evCode;
    pEvent->WaitForCompletion(INFINITE, &evCode);
    // Clean up.
    pMediaControl->Release();
    pEvent->Release();
    pGraph->Release();
    CoUninitialize();
}
```

The program starts by calling CoCreateInstance to get the IGraphBuilder interface. When it has that interface, it uses it to obtain two more interfaces: an IMediaControl interface, which it eventually uses to start playback on the video stream, and an IMediaEvent interface, which it uses to know when the stream has completed.

Next, the call to the RenderFile method of IGraphBuilder sets up the filter graph (the DirectShow "assembly line") needed to decode the given file and display it on the screen.

The Run method of the IMediaControl interface sets the whole thing in motion. At this point, the video starts playing to the screen. The program uses the WaitForCompletion method to wait until the video is done playing (WaitForCompletion does not return until the video is done). Then it simply releases all its interfaces and cleans up its mess.

That's all there is to playing a video—simple, especially when compared to reading the file yourself and writing your own decoding functions! Try it yourself by looking at the PlayWnd sample program included with the DirectX SDK.

> **TIP**
>
> Notice the *L* in front of the filename in the call to RenderFile. You need this because the RenderFile method takes only wide-character strings. This is subtle, but it's also very important.

Playing a Video in a Certain Window

Now that you know how to play a video, you can learn how to display it inside any window you want.

The key to doing this is the IVideoWindow interface, which you query from the IGraphBuilder interface, like so:

```
IGraphBuilder    *pGraph = NULL;
IVideoWindow     *pVidWin = NULL;
// Create the filter graph manager.
CoCreateInstance(CLSID_FilterGraph, NULL, CLSCTX_INPROC,
  IID_IGraphBuilder, (void **)&pGraph);
// query for the IvideoWindow interface
pGraph->QueryInterface(IID_IVideoWindow, (void **)&pVidWin);
```

When you have the IVideoWindow interface, you must tell it your window handle and size and set its window properties, like so:

```
//Set the video window.
pVidWin->put_Owner((OAHWND)g_hwnd);
pVidWin->put_WindowStyle(WS_CHILD | WS_CLIPSIBLINGS);
```

```
RECT grc;
GetClientRect(g_hwnd, &grc);
pVidWin->SetWindowPosition(0, 0, grc.right, grc.bottom);
```

The two methods `put_Owner` and `put_WindowStyle` set the owner and the window style of the window in which the video plays. You need to set the `WS_CHILD` and `WS_CLIPSIBLINGS` flags so that the window is properly rendered within your window.

The `SetWindowPosition` method tells DirectShow where it should render the window. In the preceding code, you set this to the size and position of your global window, which makes DirectShow render inside your global window.

At this point, you can call `Run` and start the video playing within your window.

Playing MP3s

You can use DirectShow to play MP3 files as background music for your game. To play them, go through all the steps you would use to play a video, but rather than load an AVI or MPG file, you load an MP3 file. Nothing to it!

Note that this method of playing MP3s streams the MP3 off disk. That is, DirectShow doesn't load the whole thing into RAM at startup; it reads it off the disk as needed.

DirectShow Wrap-Up

DirectShow is a very complex component. Fortunately, DirectShow also makes doing common things very easy, so there's rarely, if ever, a need to dive deep under the hood and figure out, say, how all these filters connect together. Most of the time, all you have to do is call `RenderFile` and `Run` to display full-stream video or MP3 files on your computer.

CHAPTER WRAP-UP

Understanding the features available in DirectX will help you in 3D game programming. Even if you decide not to use any other DirectX components, knowing the functionality they contain gives you a good starting place for determining the sort of support for sound, input, and networking you'd like in your title.

This chapter concludes the section on general Windows game programming. From here on, everything I talk about is for 3D programming. You will start with the essential concepts and math for 3D, apply those to your first 3D scene, and spend the rest of this part of the book looking at textures, lighting, and generally how to improve the quality of your scenes.

About the Sample Programs

The sample programs for this chapter use the utility libraries provided by DirectX. The source code for these utility libraries is located in the following files:

- **dxutil.cpp**. General DirectX utility functions
- **dmutil.cpp**. DirectMusic utility functions
- **dsutil.cpp**. DirectSound utility functions
- **diutil.cpp**. DirectInput utility functions
- **d3dutil.cpp**. DirectGraphics utility functions

I encourage you to look at the contents of these files (the DirectX SDK installation puts them in samples\Multimedia\Common\src) to see what kind of utility functions Microsoft has already written for you. For example, inside dmutil.cpp you can find code for classes that encapsulate the DirectMusic interfaces and make common DirectMusic tasks much easier.

Here's what each sample program does:

- **Ch3p1_PlayAudio**. Demonstrates how to use DirectMusic to play a DirectMusic segment, MIDI, or wave (WAV) file.
- **Ch3p2_Threads**. Shows you the very basics of multithreading—how you get your applications to do two things at once. (This program goes with the sidebar on threads in the DirectPlay section.)

Exercises

I've included several different exercises for this chapter, each designed to teach you more about programming the DirectX components.

DirectMusic

1. Write a command-line MIDI, WAV, or DirectMusic segment player. The program should take as command-line parameters the filenames of files to play, play those files in order, and then exit.
2. Create a small program that lets you run a sound through different DirectAudio effects.

DirectInput

1. Write a program that allows the user to control the value of two variables (X and Y) using the keyboard, joystick, or mouse. This will show you how to set up the basics of DirectInput without having to bother with doing any graphics.
2. Enhance the program in exercise 1 to support action mapping.

DirectPlay

1. Write a simple client-server or peer-to-peer chat program. This will show you the essentials of using DirectPlay without making you worry about how to move properly or animate your game characters based on DirectPlay messages. Your chat program should send DirectPlay messages for every line (or character!) of text your chatters type.

DirectShow

1. Write a command-line MP3 player. The program should take as command-line parameters the filenames of MP3s to play, play those files in order, and then exit.

CHAPTER 4

3D MATH

"The Universe is a grand book which cannot be read until one first learns to comprehend the language and become familiar with the characters in which it is composed. It is written in the language of mathematics."

—Galileo

I learned the fine art of game programming the same way you're doing now—I read a lot of books, wrote many programs, made a bunch of mistakes, and learned from each one. I believe that this is the best way to learn most things, provided that what you're learning allows you to make mistakes without hurting yourself and/or someone else. I'm sure that I speak for everyone else on the planet when I say please do not try to learn how to control a nuclear reactor by making a bunch of mistakes.

I have a very hard time learning by conventional methods, that is, by watching others do something or by listening to them rattle on about it. It is for this reason that I learned virtually all my higher math skills not in a classroom but in the pages of game programming and computer graphics books.

Therefore, I can easily say that you will not understand this chapter if you just read it. Make no mistake—what's in this chapter is complex math. Most people on this planet will live their entire lives without even *attempting* this. If math were magic, you'd need to be a high-level mage even to look at this chapter without your brain exploding—and the only way to become a high-level mage is by constantly using math magic to slay small math monsters, grabbing a handful of XP for each mathematical Red Slime you destroy.

One other point, this time without the silly RPG comparison. In this chapter, I've tried to strike a balance between showing you how math works and how you can use math without knowing how it works. I find the mathematics of 3D programming incredibly interesting, and I could easily fill up hundreds of pages explaining how a given technique works. On the other hand, I also realize that not many people would want to read those hundreds of pages. Many people want to skip the details of how or why a particular technique works and just concentrate on the math as a tool, learning when to use it and what it does. I also know from personal experience that it's easier to learn how something works when you know why you're learning it and when to use it.

For every technique I show you, I start by explaining what it is and why you need to know it. From there, I go into more detail on some techniques, and others I mention only briefly. For each section, I implore you to study the examples, do your own exercises, and make your own mistakes. Do this, and enlightenment your way will surely come.

WELCOME TO 3D

I'll start teaching 3D by doing a quick review of 2D. Any point on a 2D plane can be represented using 2D Cartesian coordinate systems. You have an x-axis, which runs horizontally, and a y-axis, which runs vertically (or more precisely, perpendicular to the x-axis). The origin of the coordinate system is in the center, at (0,0); positive x goes out to the right, and positive y goes up, as shown in Figure 4.1.

3D throws another axis into the mix. The z-axis runs perpendicular to both the x-axis and y-axis in 3D space; it is the "depth" of 3D. Take a piece of paper and draw an x-axis and a y-axis on it; then poke a pencil straight through the paper. The pencil is the z-axis (see Figure 4.2).

> **NOTE**
>
> Note that this is different from screen coordinates, where the origin is in the upper-left corner and positive y goes down.

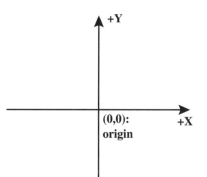

Figure 4.1

The 2D Cartesian coordinate system.

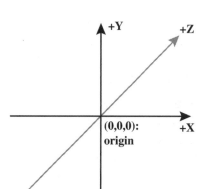

Figure 4.2

The z-axis in 3D runs perpendicular to the x-axis and y-axis. It is the "depth" of 3D.

There is no standard about whether the point of the pencil is positive or negative z. That depends on whether you're using a left-handed or right-handed coordinate system.

Is DirectGraphics Left-Handed or Right-Handed?

In a right-handed coordinate system, positive z points toward you (in other words, positive z is the eraser end of the pencil). In a left-handed system, positive z points away from you (it's the pencil point).

These are called *left-handed* and *right-handed* systems because you can use your thumb to determine the direction of the z-axis. The process is very simple. Take your left hand (as an example) and orient it so that your fingers are pointing to your right (that is, your fingers are pointing in the positive x direction) and your palm is facing up (that is, your palm points in the direction of positive y). Your thumb now points away from you, which is why the z-axis points away from you in a left-handed coordinate system. If you use your right hand (again, keeping your palm up and fingers to your left—this basically means that you bend your wrist at a 90-degree angle, like a waiter carrying a tray), your thumb points toward you (if

> **TIP**
>
> DirectGraphics uses a left-handed coordinate system, so from now on, when you see the words *positive z-axis*, remember that they mean *away from you* or *into the scene*.

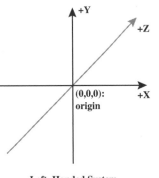

Left–Handed System

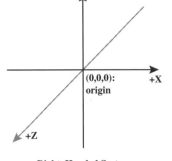

Right–Handed System

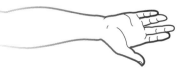

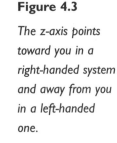

Figure 4.3

The z-axis points toward you in a right-handed system and away from you in a left-handed one.

you're human). The z-axis points toward you in a right-handed coordinate system. See Figure 4.3 for a picture of this.

Regardless of how the z-axis runs, the important thing is that any point in 3D space can be represented by an x-value, a y-value, and a z-value. The point (0,0,0) is at the center of the 3D space, whereas the point (5,10,15) is 5 units to the left, 10 units up, and 15 units deep—or away from you (in a left-handed system!).

> **TIP**
>
> OpenGL, a popular alternative to DirectGraphics, uses a right-handed coordinate system. If you're porting an application from OpenGL to DirectX, the Direct3D utility library, D3DX, provides functions that help you switch from right to left.

From Points to Primitives

Now you know how to locate any point in 3D space using 3D coordinate triplets. (By the way, points in 3D space are also called *vertices*.) However, points in space are just that—points in space. You need *objects*, not just points, to create a 3D game.

As you might have already guessed, all 3D objects are created from points.

You need at least three vertices in space to create a polygon (a triangle). You can use more. For example, you can use four vertices to create a rectangle (or quad, slang for *quadrilateral*), but you can't use less because that would be like trying to build a table with two legs.

Now, instead of dealing with just vertices, you're dealing with triangles or quads. You can use groups of triangles or quads to create 3D objects, or *models*. For example, you can take six quads (or 12 triangles), carefully arrange them in space, and create a hollow cube. This is the essence of how all 3D games work and the reason that triangles and quads are also called *3D primitives*. They're the primitive 3D objects from which 3D models are created.

> **TIP**
>
> When you create a triangle from three points, make sure that you specify the points in a clockwise order. Otherwise, your triangle can be incorrectly *culled* (clipped out of existence) because DirectX thinks you're looking at its backside.

This realization is a little like biting into a chocolate bunny on Easter only to find (to your horror!) that it's hollow inside. All 3D models are hollow. In fact, your computer's 3D graphics hardware doesn't even have a *notion* of solid or hollow—it just draws 3D primitives where you tell it. It's up to your program to make sure that the 3D primitives rendered to the screen give the illusion of solid objects, corridors, people, and everything else in your world.

This concept is important enough for me to inflict another example on you. Take a peek at Figure 4.4.

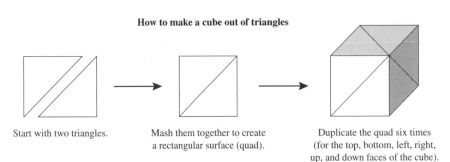

How to make a cube out of triangles

Start with two triangles.

Mash them together to create a rectangular surface (quad).

Duplicate the quad six times (for the top, bottom, left, right, up, and down faces of the cube).

Figure 4.4

Constructing a cube from a set of 3D primitives (triangles).

It shows one way to create a 3D cube from a set of 3D primitives (triangles, in this case, because most 3D games work in triangles, not quads). Here's a quick walk-through of the process.

You start by creating three points, which all have the same z coordinate; that is, they're all exactly the same depth away from you. These three points form a right triangle. Next, you create three more points that specify another, upside-down right triangle. Now you have two right triangles, which you push together to create a square. This is the front of your cube. Finally, you create five more faces (using 10 more triangles)—one face each for the left, right, back, top, and bottom sides of the cube.

When all is said and done, you have taken six faces, 12 triangles, and 36 points and arranged them in space to create the appearance of a cube.

TIP

By the way, the reason triangles make such good primitives is that all three points of a triangle are guaranteed to be on the same plane. If you have more than three points, you can create a situation in which one point is floating above the other three, which makes some 3D calculations difficult.

3D Transformations

Now that you have a cube to play with, I'm sure that you're dying to know how to move it around.

In graphics lingo, moving an object around is known as *transforming* it because you're transforming the vertices that compose the model. There are three basic types of transformations:

- **Translation.** This is what normal people refer to as *movement*. A translation transformation involves adding or subtracting a fixed amount from a vertex, which, in effect, moves it. For example, if you have a point at (3,6,9), you translate that point to (4,8,12) by adding 1 to the x component, 2 to the y component, and 3 to the z component. Do this for all the vertices in a model, and you can move the model.
- **Rotation.** You can rotate an object around any of the three axes. Rotating an object around an axis is like sticking a needle through it and then spinning it on that needle.

For example, rotating about the x-axis means that you push an imaginary needle through your object horizontally and then spin it. Rotating about the y-axis means pushing a needle through the object vertically and then spinning. Rotating about the z-axis means pushing a needle into the front of an object, having it come out the back, and then spinning it (see Figure 4.5).

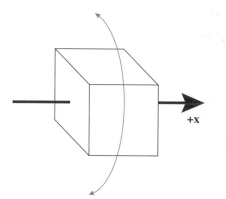

Figure 4.5

Rotation about an axis means pushing a needle parallel to that axis through the object and then spinning the object on the needle.

+x

- **Scaling.** This means changing the size of an object, by multiplying each vertex by a fixed amount. There are two scaling types: uniform and non-uniform.
  When something is scaled *uniformly*, the proportions of the object remain intact—the whole object just gets bigger or smaller. For example, if you have a cube that's 5 units wide, 5 tall, and 5 high (5×5×5), and you scale it up to 10 units wide, 10 tall, and 10 high (10×10×10), you are using uniform scaling.
  Non-uniform scaling means that the proportions don't stay the same. If you took your 5×5×5 cube and stretched it into a 3D rectangle 10 units wide, 7 units tall, and 5 units high, you'd be scaling it non-uniformly.

Mathematicians have, of course, deduced formulas that do all these things. You will start with the translation formula because it's the easiest to understand.

Translation

Given an x, a y, and a z coordinate, here are the formulas to translate that coordinate to a new position:

$$x_{new} = x_{old} + d_x$$

$$y_{new} = y_{old} + d_y$$

$$z_{new} = z_{old} + d_z$$

d represents the distance that you want to move the point in the x, y, or z direction. These formulas just say, "Take your old coordinate, add on a distance, and that equals your new coordinate." Nothing to it!

Scaling

Now look at scaling. Here are the formulas to scale a point:

$$x_{new} = s_x(x_{old})$$

$$y_{new} = s_y(y_{old})$$

$$z_{new} = s_z(z_{old})$$

Here, *s* represents the scale factor that you want to apply to the point in the x, y, or z direction. The scaling formula just multiplies the point by the scaling factor, which is a *scalar* (a math term for a single numeric value). To scale uniformly, all three components of s should be equal; that is, you should multiply x, y, and z by the same amount.

Rotation

Now, the hairiest of all three equations: rotation. Rotation is divided into three sets of formulas, depending on whether you want to rotate around the x-axis, y-axis, or z-axis, as shown in Table 4.1.

All these formulas assume that theta (θ) is the angle by which you want to rotate.

Table 4.1 Rotation Formulas

To Rotate around This Axis	Use These Formulas
x-axis	$y_{new} = y_{old} \cos(\theta) - z_{old} \sin(\theta)$ $z_{new} = y_{old} \sin(\theta) + z_{old} \cos(\theta)$
y-axis	$x_{new} = x_{old} \cos(\theta) - z_{old} \sin(\theta)$ $z_{new} = x_{old} \sin(\theta) + z_{old} \cos(\theta)$
z-axis	$x_{new} = x_{old} \cos(\theta) - y_{old} \sin(\theta)$ $y_{new} = x_{old} \sin(\theta) + y_{old} \cos(\theta)$

These formulas are complicated, so I will break them down step by step, using z-axis rotation as an example. To figure out the new x coordinate, given an old x coordinate and an angle, you multiply the old x coordinate by the sine of the angle and then subtract the sine of the angle multiplied by the old y coordinate. To get the new y coordinate, you take the old x coordinate, multiply it by the sine of the angle, and add to that the y coordinate multiplied by the cosine of the angle.

> **TIP**
>
> Note that you have only two rotation formulas for each axis, not three, even though you have three coordinates. This is because when you're rotating something, you're guaranteed that at least one coordinate (the one corresponding to the axis around which you're rotating) will stay the same. In other words, if I'm spinning something around on the x-axis, the x coordinates will not change. It helps to visualize why this is true.

The reason these formulas work, in a word, is trigonometry. Beginning graphics programmers don't need to know exactly how they work, although I will try to entice you into looking at their proofs by saying that it's a fascinating exercise in math.

At the very least, however, you should run through the math a couple times with sample coordinates so that you see for yourself that it works. An easy test is to try to rotate something by 90 or 180 degrees ($pi/2$ or pi radians—see the following sidebar). You should get the same numbers you started with, only switched around or with different signs.

Local and World Coordinates

Real-life computer graphics uses more than one coordinate system. To explain why, I need to show you a problem in the rotation formula first.

The problem with the rotation formula is that when you rotate something, the formula rotates the object around the center of the universe, not around the center of the object. Imagine that you have a cube that's centered on the point (20,20,0), as shown in Figure 4.7.

One would expect the rotation formula to rotate the cube in place, but it doesn't. If you rotate the cube 180 degrees (or pi radians) using the formula, it ends up at the point (–20,–20,0). In other words, the cube moves (work the numbers if you don't believe me). The cube is seemingly attached to a metal pipe whose other end is at (0,0,0), and when you rotate using the formula, you're spinning the cube around on the pipe! What's up with that!?!

If the rotation formula were sold in a box at Fry's, the fine print on the back of the box would say something like *WARNING: This formula does not work on objects whose center is not at (0,0,0).* The rotation formula as written here assumes that your model's center is at (0,0,0), which it clearly cannot be if it's off somewhere in your 3D world.

What's a Radian, Anyway?

Most of us are familiar with using degrees to measure angles, but in computer graphics, *radians* are often used instead.

In essence, instead of 360 degrees in a circle, you now have 2*pi (or roughly 6.28) radians. A span of 180 degrees is a distance of *pi* radians, 90 is *pi/2* radians, and a distance of 270 degrees is *pi+(pi/2)* radians. 45 degrees is *pi/4*, and so on.

In the radian system, you still move clockwise, with one small difference—0 radians points east, not north, as usually assumed in degrees. This means that south in radians, or 180 degrees, is really *pi/2* radians, west is *pi* radians, and north is *pi+(pi/2)* radians (see Figure 4.6).

It's different, but it's nothing more than another way of measuring angles. Computer graphics uses the radian system because it's cleaner mathematically. After all, 360 is a totally arbitrary number, whereas 2*pi has mathematical significance. It's like using yards instead of meters—having 72 inches in a yard is completely arbitrary and more cumbersome to work with than having 100 centimeters in a meter.

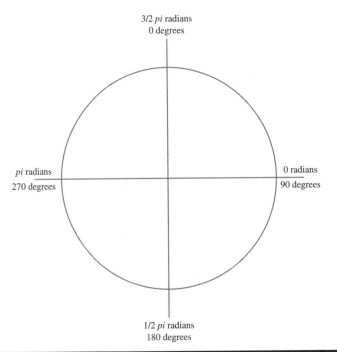

3/2 *pi* radians
0 degrees

pi radians
270 degrees

0 radians
90 degrees

1/2 *pi* radians
180 degrees

Figure 4.6

Radian directions and their degree equivalents.

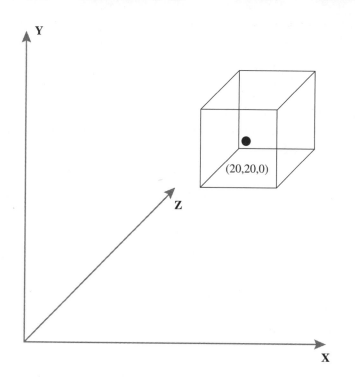

Figure 4.7

A cube centered on the point (20,20,0).

To combat this problem, 3D graphics programmers use two coordinate systems—the *model* (or *local*) coordinate system and the *world* coordinate system. Every model has two sets of coordinates. The set of local coordinates specifies the location of the points on the model relative to the model's center (or local origin). The world coordinates of the model specify the model's location in 3D space relative to the world origin. This is illustrated in Figure 4.8.

This is a hard concept to understand at first. To illustrate it, you can be an example. Imagine that the exact center of your chest is the origin of your local coordinate system. Given that, you can say that your head is roughly 1 or 2 feet above the origin of your local coordinate system (depending on how tall you are, of course). Say that you're tall, so your head is 2 feet up from the center of your chest. This means that a point representing your head can be placed at $(0,2,0)$. Similarly, because your feet are below your chest and slightly off to the left or right of it, the two coordinate points for your feet can be placed at $(-1,-3,0)$ and $(1,-3,0)$. If you're having trouble visualizing the coordinates, check out Figure 4.9.

Here's the important part. No matter where you go on the planet, the local coordinates for your feet and head remain the same. Your head is always 2 feet up from your local origin (the center of your chest), and your feet are always 3 feet down and 1 foot to the left or right. In other words,

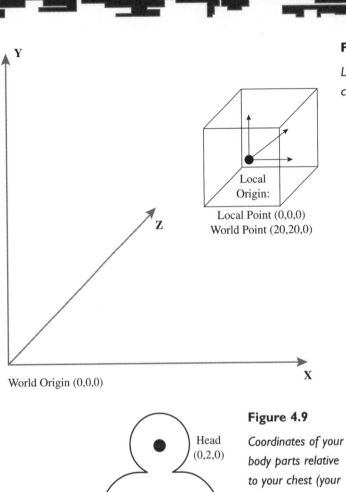

Figure 4.8

Local and world coordinate systems.

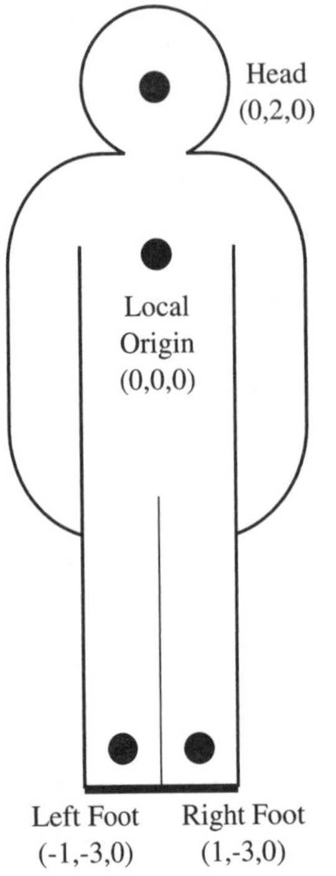

Y

Local Origin:
Local Point (0,0,0)
World Point (20,20,0)

Z

X

World Origin (0,0,0)

Figure 4.9

Coordinates of your body parts relative to your chest (your local origin).

Head
(0,2,0)

Local
Origin
(0,0,0)

Left Foot   Right Foot
(-1,-3,0)   (1,-3,0)

the three coordinates—(0,2,0) for your head and (–1,–3,0) and (1,–3,0) for your feet—are said to be relative to your local origin. They're in *local space*.

To convert local coordinates to world coordinates (*world space*), you simply add the two. Imagine that I mark a dot 7 feet to the left of you and declare that space as the origin of the world coordinate system. Because you're standing 7 feet to the right of the dot and the center of your chest is probably about 3 feet off the ground, your local origin is at world coordinate (7,3,0). Given that, you can figure out where your head and feet are in world space by adding your world coordinate to all your local coordinates—your head becomes (7, 5, 0), and your feet become (6, 0, 0) and (8,0,0). Again, check out Figure 4.9.

Local (or *model*) space allows you to track 3D objects using just one point: the center of the model. If I give you 36 local coordinates for a cube and tell you that the cube's local origin is at world coordinates (5,10,15), it's easy for you to extrapolate the world coordinates for all 36 local coordinates of the cube. You convert the cube's local coordinates to world coordinates by adding 5 to each x value, 10 to each y value, and 15 to each z value.

VECTORS

Now that you know how to represent a point in 3D space, you can learn about vectors. Vectors are used extensively in 3D graphics and in the physics that makes your game objects behave realistically. They're good tools to have in your 3D graphics toolbox, and you will need them when you get to matrices later. I will start with a simple definition.

What Is a Vector?

A vector is a magnitude and a direction.

That's all. Now, what does that mean?

Say that you're zooming down the highway in a car. Because a vector is both a magnitude and a direction, you could use a vector to describe both the speed of your car and its direction. For example, you could say that you're heading south at 30MPH, or if you're in the car for the express purpose of killing yourself, as well as a few innocent motorists, your vector might be east at 120MPH. The point is that a vector is both a magnitude (your MPH) and a direction.

In 3D graphics, a vector is three numbers, which specify x, y, and z coordinates. From this information, you can deduce a vector's direction and magnitude.

Determining a Vector's Direction

You can use arrows to convey both magnitude and direction graphically, if you say that the length of an arrow can be interpreted as its magnitude. As an example, Figure 4.10 shows two vectors, both with the same direction but one whose magnitude is twice that of the other.

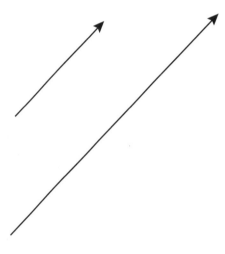

Figure 4.10

Two vectors, both with the same direction but different magnitudes.

It makes sense that vectors are represented geometrically as arrows because arrows display both magnitude and direction intuitively.

Now, to get down to the details. A 3D vector is just like a 3D coordinate in that it has an x, a y, and a z component. The difference is that a 3D coordinate defines a point in space, but a 3D vector defines a direction and magnitude. In other words, the x, y, and z components of a vector represent the point where the arrowhead goes. The tail of the arrowhead is always at (0,0,0).

For example, a free vector of (1,2,0) means that the arrowhead of your vector is at (1,2,0). Because the tail of a free vector is always at (0,0,0), you end up with an arrow pointing up and to the right (see Figure 4.11).

TIP

A vector whose tail is at (0,0,0) is called a *free vector*. It's perfectly okay for you also to use vectors whose tails aren't always at the origin. Of course, you have to have two sets of coordinates (one for the head, one for the tail), but everything will still work.

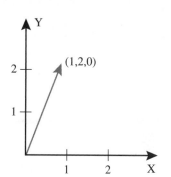

Figure 4.11

A free vector has its tail at the origin.

Determining a Vector's Magnitude

Okay, you know which direction a vector points. How do you know the magnitude? You use the distance formula:

$$d = \sqrt{x^2 + y^2 + z^2}$$

In the formula above, x, y, and z represent the vector's x, y, and z components.

The distance formula is an application of the Pythagorean theorem. If you're interested in how it works, I encourage you to look up the proof for the formula and learn it. However, this is one of those times when, as a beginning 3D graphics programmer, you don't really care how it works. You just care that it *does* work.

To make sure that it does work, plug a vector into it whose distance you already know, say, a vector of (10,0,0). Unless the fundamental laws of mathematics have changed behind your back, the distance formula should tell you that this vector has magnitude 10.

$$d = \sqrt{x^2 + y^2 + z^2}$$

Plug in your vector's elements:

$$d = \sqrt{(10)^2 + (0)^2 + (0)^2} = \sqrt{100} = 10$$

Woo-hoo, it works! You should also try it with vectors that aren't parallel to any of the axes, because that's more interesting than just squaring zeros.

Now you know how to extrapolate magnitude from a vector. Next, you start to appreciate the power of vectors, by learning how to add, subtract, and multiply them.

Adding and Subtracting Vectors

To add a vector graphically, all you have to do is put the tail of one vector on the head of another vector. The second vector then points to the head of the vector you'd get by adding the two vectors together.

It's much easier to show graphically than explain in words, so check out Figure 4.12. You are adding two vectors here, A and B, and the sum of them is vector C.

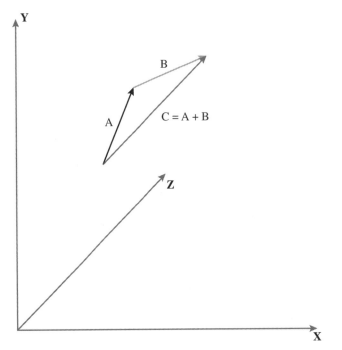

Figure 4.12

Adding vectors.

To add vectors numerically, all you have to do is add their components. If you have a vector A, (5,8,13), and add it to a vector B, (–3,2,10), you end up with a vector of (2,10,23) because you add the x values (5+(–3)=2), y values (8+2=10), and z values (13+10=23) together. Cake!

To subtract a vector, you just negate all the components of the second vector before adding it to the first. In the preceding example, you would negate B's values, giving you (5,8,13)+(3,–2,–10), or (8,6,3), as the result of your subtraction. Again, this can be represented graphically by reversing the second arrow before you add it (see Figure 4.13).

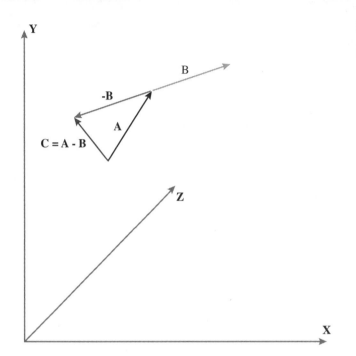

Figure 4.13

Subtracting vectors.

Scalar Multiplication of Vectors

Scalar multiplication of vectors means simply multiplying the vector by a single number. If you have a vector A, (6,8,5), and want to multiply it by 3, you find the result of your scalar multiplication by multiplying each component of the vector (x, y, and z) by the number (the scalar) 3. Therefore, 3A=(18,24,15) or ((6*3), (8*3), (5*3)).

Graphically, this elongates your arrow without changing its direction. It's like adding A to itself three times—you get a vector that has three times the magnitude of A but points in the same direction (see Figure 4.14).

Normalizing Vectors

Mathematics terminology defines a *unit vector* as a vector whose magnitude is 1:

$$\sqrt{x^2 + y^2 + z^2} = 1$$

TIP

People sometimes refer to unit vectors as *normalized vectors*. The two terms are interchangeable.

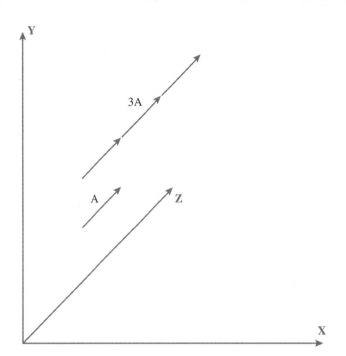

Figure 4.14

*Scalar multiplication
of a vector.*

If you know that something's a unit vector, you can eliminate many complex (and therefore time-consuming) steps from certain processes.

To make a unit vector out of any old vector, you scale it so that its magnitude is 1 but its direction remains unchanged. Math heads refer to this as *normalizing* the vector.

To normalize a vector, you use the following equation:

> **CAUTION**
>
> A normalized vector is *not* the same as a normal vector. A *normal vector* is the result of the cross product of two vectors, which I'll get to in a moment. A *normalized vector* is simply a vector with magnitude 1.
>
> Watch your terms carefully.

$$N = \frac{V}{|V|}$$

This means that to normalize a vector, you divide each of its components by the magnitude of the vector.

To see whether this works, normalize the vector (5,5,0), which, as you can tell from the coordinates, points northeast. You know that, to be pointing in the same direction after the normalization, the vector's x and y components must be equal, and the z component must still be 0.

Here goes:

$$N = \frac{V}{|V|}$$

$$N_x = \frac{V_x}{\sqrt{V_x^2 + V_y^2 + V_z^2}}; \; N_y = \frac{V_y}{\sqrt{V_x^2 + V_y^2 + V_z^2}}; \; N_z = \frac{V_z}{\sqrt{V_x^2 + V_y^2 + V_z^2}}$$

$$N_x = \frac{5}{\sqrt{5^2 + 5^2 + 0^2}}; \; N_y = \frac{5}{\sqrt{5^2 + 5^2 + 0^2}}; \; N_z = \frac{0}{\sqrt{5^2 + 5^2 + 0^2}};$$

$$N_x = \frac{5}{\sqrt{50}}; \; N_y = \frac{5}{\sqrt{50}}; \; N_z = \frac{0}{\sqrt{50}};$$

$$N_x \approx 0.707; \; N_y \approx 0.707; \; N_z = 0;$$

As you can see, you end up with a vector $(0.707, 0.707, 0)$, which certainly does point in the same direction as $(5,5,0)$. Now see whether $(0.707, 0.707, 0)$ really has a magnitude of 1:

$$\sqrt{x^2 + y^2 + z^2} = 1$$

$$\sqrt{(0.707)^2 + (0.707)^2 + 0^2} = 1$$

$$\sqrt{0.49985 + 0.49985} = 1$$

$$\sqrt{0.9997} = 1$$

$$0.9998 = 1$$

Darn close! Of course, the reason it isn't *exactly* 1 is that I rounded off the square root of 50 to only three decimal places. The math is working perfectly; I'm just not accurate enough for it.

The Dot Product of Two Vectors

We care about dot products because they give us the angle between two vectors, which you need for performing lighting calculations, clipping, and other important functions.

The dot product is a scalar (single number), which you obtain by multiplying the components of each vector and then summing the results of those multiplications. For example, if you have two vectors, U and V, you calculate the dot product using the following equation:

$$U \cdot V = U_x V_x + U_y V_y + U_z V_z$$

This isn't terribly useful as it stands, but there's also another equation that defines a dot product:

$$U \cdot V = |U||V|\cos\theta$$

That equation says that the cross product is equal to the magnitude of U times the magnitude of V times the cosine of the angle between the two vectors (called *theta*).

But wait! You don't *know* the angle! That's what you're trying to find out! To glean something useful from these two equations, you first need to combine them by setting them equal to each other:

$$U_x V_x + U_y V_y + U_z V_z = |U||V|\cos\theta$$

Now you can use algebra to solve for theta. Divide both sides of the equation by the magnitude of U times the magnitude of V:

$$\frac{U_x V_x + U_y V_y + U_z V_z}{|U||V|} = \cos\theta$$

Then take the arccosine of both sides of the equation to get theta:

$$\cos^{-1}\left(\frac{U_x V_x + U_y V_y + U_z V_z}{|U||V|}\right) = \theta$$

This new equation tells you that you can figure out the angle between any two vectors by multiplying their components, adding the results of those multiplications together, dividing by the product of their magnitudes, and finally calculating the arccosine of that division.

As an example, take the dot product of the two unit vectors (1,0,0) and (0,1,0), shown in Figure 4.15.

> **TIP**
>
> Recall that a unit vector is a vector whose magnitude is 1. This means that if you're taking the dot product of two unit vectors, you don't need to bother with dividing by their magnitudes. That whole bottom part drops out of the equation—a great thing because floating-point division is very slow. This is one of the reasons unit vectors are so special.

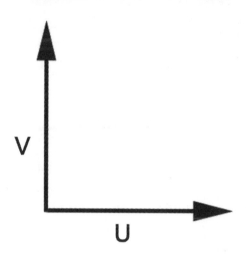

Figure 4.15

Testing out the dot product using two perpendicular vectors.

These two vectors point in the direction of the positive x and y axes. Because you know that those axes are perpendicular, you expect to find that the angle between these two vectors is 90 degrees, or *pi/2* radians.

Here's the number crunching:

$$U = (1,0,0)$$

$$V = (0,1,0)$$

$$\theta = \cos^{-1}\left(\frac{U_x V_x + U_y V_y + U_z V_z}{|U||V|}\right)$$

$$\theta = \cos^{-1}\left(\frac{(1)(0) + (0)(1) + (0)(0)}{(1)(1)}\right)$$

$$\theta = \cos^{-1}\left(\frac{0}{1}\right) = \cos^{-1}(0) \approx \frac{\pi}{2} \approx 1.5707$$

It works! You wind up with exactly what you expect—*pi/2* radians.

The Cross Product of Two Vectors

Taking a cross product of two vectors gives you a third vector that's perpendicular to both original vectors. This new vector is called a *normal.* If you were standing on the plane defined by two vectors, the normal vector would point up.

3D graphics uses the cross product of two vectors in several places. First, the normal tells DirectGraphics which way a polygon is facing, which is important for DirectGraphics to figure out how to light the polygon properly. The surface normal also tells DirectGraphics which polygons it doesn't need to render (that is, which polygons can be culled).

TIP

If you want to irritate people with math humor, next time they ask you, "What's up?" you say, "The normal vector of the plane you're currently standing on."

That's one of my favorite math jokes because it's *so awful.*

Given two vectors, A and B, the cross product C (A×B=C) is defined as

$$C_x = A_y B_z - A_z B_y$$

$$C_y = A_z B_x - A_x B_z$$

$$C_z = A_x B_y - A_y B_x$$

The magnitude of the normal vector is given by the following equation:

$$|A \times B| = |A||B|\sin\theta$$

where theta is the angle between the two original vectors, A and B. Note that because you have the vector's three components (you figure them out by taking the cross product), you could use the magnitude formula (the square root of the sum of the vector's components, squared) and figure out the magnitude that way. Either way, you get the same answer—the advantage to this equation is that you don't have to figure out Cx, Cy, and Cz to get the magnitude. It's a shortcut.

TIP

You can use your right hand to determine the direction a normal vector points. Curl the fingers of your right hand from **A** to **B**—your thumb points in the direction of the normal. Mathematicians call this the *right hand rule.*

Now plug some numbers into the system and see whether it does what it's supposed to. Again, you play with the x-axis and y-axis because multiplying all those zeros makes doing the arithmetic easy.

If you cross a unit vector pointing parallel to the positive x-axis with a vector pointing parallel to the positive y-axis, you should get a normal vector that's parallel to the positive z-axis.

Here goes nothing:

$$A = (1,0,0)$$

$$B = (0,1,0)$$

$$C_x = A_y B_z - A_z B_y = (0)(0) - (0)(1) = 0$$

$$C_y = A_z B_x - A_x B_z = (0)(0) - (1)(0) = 0$$

$$C_z = A_x B_y - A_y B_x = (1)(1) - (0)(0) = 1$$

Just what you expect—all is still right with the universe.

CAUTION

Vector cross products are not commutative. In other words, A×B doesn't equal B×A—one's normal points in the opposite direction from the other. You can visualize this by using the right hand rule. Curl your fingers from A to B, and notice that your thumb points in the opposite direction than if you curled them from B to A.

Be careful about the order in which you cross vectors.

D3DX Vector Helper Functions

D3DX, a utility library supplied by Microsoft as part of the DirectX SDK, provides several functions that do vector math. I'm not going to talk about all of them here, but I do want to mention them briefly so that you don't spend time developing math code that is already written.

Table 4.2 shows the vector helper functions supplied by D3DX. Note that there are separate

TIP

Additionally, in C++, the D3DVECTOR2, D3DVECTOR3, and D3DVECTOR4 classes have overloaded operators for the most common operations (adding, subtracting, multiplying, and dividing, as well as the equivalence operator, ==). Check out the SDK help or the D3DX.h header file to see exactly what these classes support.

Table 4.2 D3DX Vector Functions

Function	Description
D3DXVec2Add, D3DXVec3Add, D3DXVec4Add	Adds two vectors.
D3DXVec2BaryCentric, D3DXVec3BaryCentric, D3DXVec4BaryCentric	Returns a point in Barycentric coordinates, using the specified vectors.
D3DXVec2CatmullRom, D3DXVec3CatmullRom D3DXVec4CatmullRom	Performs a Catmull-Rom interpolation, using the specified vectors.
D3DXVec2CCW	Returns the z component by taking the cross product of two 2D vectors.
D3DXVec2Dot, D3DXVec3Dot, D3DXVec4Dot	Calculates the dot product of two vectors.
D3DXVec2Hermite, D3DXVec3Hermite, D3DXVec4Hermite	Performs a Hermite spline interpolation, using the specified vectors.
D3DXVec2Length, D3DXVec3Length, D3DXVec4Length	Returns the length of a vector.
D3DXVec2LengthSq, D3DXVec3LengthSq, D3DXVec4LengthSq	Returns the square of a vector's length. This is faster than the normal length function because it doesn't have to calculate a square root.
D3DXVec2Lerp, D3DXVec3Lerp, D3DXVec4Lerp	Performs a linear interpolation between two vectors.
D3DXVec2Maximize, D3DXVec3Maximize, D3DXVec4Maximize	Returns a vector made up of the largest components of two vectors.

Table 4.2 Continued

Function	Description
D3DXVec2Minimize, D3DXVec3Minimize, D3DXVec4Minimize	Returns a vector made up of the smallest components of two vectors.
D3DXVec2Normalize, D3DXVec3Normalize, D3DXVec4Normalize	Returns the normalized version of a vector.
D3DXVec2Scale, D3DXVec3Scale, D3DXVec4Scale	Scales a vector.
D3DXVec2Subtract, D3DXVec3Subtract, D3DXVec4Subtract	Subtracts one vector from another.
D3DXVec2Transform, D3DXVec3Transform, D3DXVec4Transform	Transforms a given vector by a given matrix.
D3DXVec2TransformCoord, D3DXVec3TransformCoord	Transforms a given vector by a given matrix and projects the result back to w=1.
D3DXVec2TransformNormal, D3DXVec3TransformNormal	Transforms a vector normal by the given matrix.

functions for 2D, 3D, and 4D vectors, prefixed with D3DXVec2, D3DXVec3, and D3DXVec4, respectively.

As you can see, D3DX provides more or less the same functionality for 2D, 3D, and 4D vectors.

Using these functions saves you the time and effort of writing math code.

Vector Wrap-Up

Congratulations, you now know the basics of vector math! Such knowledge will prove incredibly useful when you begin to write 3D programs.

Practice your vector math skills until you feel comfortable doing all the math just covered. Such knowledge will help you in debugging.

MATRICES

Don't worry. This math chapter is almost over!

Before you move back into the cozy world of programming, you have to spend time on matrices because they are used all over the place in 3D graphics. Without at least a rudimentary understanding of matrices and matrix math, you will be totally lost when you try to decipher any 3D graphics code. If this subject is new to you, be sure to read this section carefully.

I will start with a simple definition.

What Is a Matrix?

A matrix can be formally defined like this:

If *m* and *n* are positive integers, then an *m×n* (read "m by n") matrix is a rectangular array in which each entry is a number.

That's how math defines it. You can think of a matrix as simply a 2D array of numbers. Here are some examples of matrices:

$$\begin{bmatrix} 1 & 5 & 8 & 65 \\ 87 & 2 & \cos(1.5) & 0 \\ 13 & \sin(2) & 4 & 1 \\ 9 & 55 & 59 & -14 \end{bmatrix} \quad \begin{bmatrix} 6 & 3 \\ 0 & 7 \end{bmatrix} \quad \begin{bmatrix} 4 & -9 & 0 \end{bmatrix} \quad \begin{bmatrix} 3 \\ 9 \\ 0 \end{bmatrix}$$

The first matrix is 4×4, the second is 2×2, the third is 3×1, and the fourth is 1×3. The numbers inside these matrices don't mean anything. I threw them in there so that you can get used to how a matrix looks. Each number in the matrix is called an *element*.

A couple additional definitions: If the matrix has the same number of rows as columns, it is said to be *square* and of an *order* that is the dimension of the matrix. For example, the 4×4 matrix is a square matrix of order 4. Most of the time, you will be using square matrices of order 4 in 3D graphics programming.

Why Use Matrices?

3D graphics programming uses matrices for the following reasons:

- **Translation, rotation, and scaling can all be accomplished using the same formula.** If you are working without matrices, you need to rely on the three equations you looked at earlier to perform 3D transformations. With matrices, transformations become much simpler—all three equations can be represented using simple matrix multiplication. This is awesome because it allows you to concentrate on doing just one thing—multiplying matrices. If you make a speedy matrix multiplier, you get speedy translation, speedy rotation, and speedy scaling. As the RISC architecture has proven, the simpler the basic building blocks are, the easier it is to make them really, *really* fast in hardware.
- **You can combine operations and calculate the results simultaneously.** Say that you want to rotate and then translate a point in 3D space. Without matrices, you'd have to run through two equations. First, you'd use the rotation equation; then, you'd plug the results of that equation into your translation equation. With matrices, however, you can set up one matrix that does both operations at once—run your original point through the rotation/translation matrix, and it comes out both rotated and translated.
  Now, imagine that you have 1,000 3D points you need to rotate and then translate. Would you rather do 1,000 rotations, followed by 1,000 translations, or would you rather start with a rotation matrix, do one concatenation to get a combination translation/rotation matrix, and then do 1,000 matrix multiplies? That's 1,001 steps instead of 2,000 steps. You've basically cut the steps in half to solve the problem. If game programming were basketball, that'd be a slam-dunk that breaks the glass of the backboard.
- **Matrix equations are easier to read than conventional equations.** When you understand the basics of matrix math, you find it much easier to write operations as matrices than as equations. I know that you don't believe me yet. I didn't believe it either, but it is true.

Hopefully, that's enough to sell you. The next question is, "How do they work?" To answer that, take one point in 3D space and see how you can transform that point using matrix multiplication.

Matrix Multiplication

3D graphics programming uses matrix math extensively, but multiplying especially, so knowing how to multiply two matrices is one of the most important skills you can have as a 3D graphics programmer. I realize that many people (including me) have a tendency to skip the "mathy" details of something and think, "Well, I don't need to know *how* it works, so long as it *does* work."

In many cases, that's true, but *this isn't one of them.* You can do yourself a big favor by studying this section until you know how matrix multiplication works. Matrices form the foundation of 3D programming because of how you multiply a matrix. Be smart, and learn it now. Besides, it's interesting to see how matrices work.

Enough of this idle chitchat! Time to break out the pencils and learn some math.

First, here's the formal definition of matrix multiplication. If you're like me, this will probably be as clear as thick mud. Don't worry. I will translate it into English later.

Let A be an m×n matrix and B be an n×p matrix. Then, the product of A and B is the m×p matrix C, whose (i,j)th entry is given by

$$C_{ij} = \sum_{k=1}^{n} X_{ik}Y_{kj} \text{ for } i = 1..m \text{ and } j = 1..p.$$

The product XY is defined only if the number of columns of X is the same as the number of rows of Y.

XY and YX might not both be defined. If they both exist, they are not necessarily equal and, in fact, might not even be of the same size.

It's not as bad as it looks. For starters, the thing that looks like a mean thrasher E is called a *sigma*. It's basically a for loop; in the formula, it means, `for (k=1; k <= n; k++)` and the stuff to the left of the sigma is what goes inside the for loop. The $X_{ik}Y_{kj}$ tells you to multiply elements of the X matrix by elements of the Y matrix. In particular, you're supposed to take the element at (i,k) in the X matrix and multiply it by the element at (k,j) in the Y matrix.

Multiplying Two 2×2 Matrices: A Walk-Through

Take this new formula for a quick test drive by trying to multiply two 2×2 matrices:

$$\begin{bmatrix} 10 & 20 \\ 30 & 40 \end{bmatrix} \times \begin{bmatrix} 50 & 60 \\ 70 & 80 \end{bmatrix} = \begin{bmatrix} ? & ? \\ ? & ? \end{bmatrix}$$

Start with the upper left. Looking again at the handy formula

$$C_{ij} = \sum_{k=1}^{n} X_{ik}Y_{kj}$$

you replace i and j with 1 because you want to know the value at position (1,1) (the upper left) in your matrix. That gives you:

$$C_{1,1} = \sum_{k=1}^{2} X_{1,k}Y_{k,1}$$

In words, you should loop k from 1 to 2, multiplying the value at (1,k) in the first matrix with the value at (k,1) in the second matrix. You then increment k, start with the result from the multiplication, and add to it the result of the next multiplication.

If you write it all out, you have

$$C_{1,1} = (X_{1,1}Y_{1,1}) + (X_{1,2}Y_{2,1})$$

Now it's just a matter of plugging in the numbers and doing the math:

$$C_{1,1} = ((10)(50)) + ((30)(60))$$

which gives your final result:

$$C_{1,1} = (500) + (1800) = 2300$$

The upper-left question mark in your matrix evaluates to 2300. So far, so good.

To answer the upper-right question mark, you plug in (2,1) for (i,j) in the original formula, which gives you

$$C_{2,1} = \sum_{k=1}^{2} X_{2,k}Y_{k,1}$$

Expanding that out, you get

$$C_{2,1} = (X_{2,1}Y_{1,1}) + (X_{2,2}Y_{2,1})$$

Plug in the elements:

$$C_{2,1} = ((20)(50)) + ((40)(60)) = (1000) + (2400) = 3400$$

The bottom-left and bottom-right elements can be found the same way:

$$C_{1,2} = \sum_{k=1}^{2} X_{1,k}Y_{k,2} = (X_{1,1}Y_{1,2}) + (X_{1,2}Y_{2,2}) = ((10)(70)) + ((30)(80)) = (700) + (2400) = 3100$$

$$C_{2,2} = \sum_{k=1}^{2} X_{2,k}Y_{k,2} = (X_{2,1}Y_{1,2}) + (X_{2,2}Y_{2,2}) = ((20)(70)) + ((40)(80)) = (1400) + (3200) = 4600$$

The final solution is

$$\begin{bmatrix} 10 & 20 \\ 30 & 40 \end{bmatrix} \times \begin{bmatrix} 50 & 60 \\ 70 & 80 \end{bmatrix} = \begin{bmatrix} 2300 & 3400 \\ 3100 & 4600 \end{bmatrix}$$

Multiplying Two 3×3 Matrices: A Walk-Through

Now multiply two 3×3 matrices:

$$\begin{bmatrix} 911 & 921 & 931 \\ 912 & 922 & 932 \\ 913 & 923 & 933 \end{bmatrix} \times \begin{bmatrix} 811 & 821 & 831 \\ 812 & 822 & 832 \\ 813 & 823 & 833 \end{bmatrix} = \begin{bmatrix} ? & ? & ? \\ ? & ? & ? \\ ? & ? & ? \end{bmatrix}$$

As you can see, I've picked numbers that reflect the row and column they're in so that you can more easily track the elements as you work it out.

Start with the upper-left, (1,1) element. Substituting (1,1) for (i,j) in the original formula gives you

$$C_{1,1} = \sum_{k=1}^{3} X_{1,k} Y_{k,1}$$

which expands into

$$C_{1,1} = (X_{1,1}Y_{1,1}) + (X_{1,2}Y_{2,1}) + (X_{1,3}Y_{3,1})$$

Plugging the elements into that gives you

$$C_{1,1} = ((911)(811)) + ((912)(821)) + ((913)(831)) = (738821) + (748752) + (758703) = 2246276$$

Here are the rest of the equations. I'll let you do the math from here.

$$C_{1,2} = \sum_{k=1}^{3} X_{1,k} Y_{k,2} = (X_{1,1}Y_{1,2}) + (X_{1,2}Y_{2,2}) + (X_{1,3}Y_{3,2})$$

$$C_{1,3} = \sum_{k=1}^{3} X_{1,k} Y_{k,3} = (X_{1,1}Y_{1,3}) + (X_{1,2}Y_{2,3}) + (X_{1,3}Y_{3,3})$$

$$C_{2,1} = \sum_{k=1}^{3} X_{2,k} Y_{k,1} = (X_{2,1}Y_{1,1}) + (X_{2,2}Y_{2,1}) + (X_{2,3}Y_{3,1})$$

$$C_{2,2} = \sum_{k=1}^{3} X_{2,k} Y_{k,2} = (X_{2,1}Y_{1,2}) + (X_{2,2}Y_{2,2}) + (X_{2,3}Y_{3,2})$$

In essence, what you're doing is, for each element, multiplying the row of that element in the first matrix with the column of that element in the second matrix and then adding everything together.

I hope that you survived the math and have arrived at this line of text grasping the process required to multiply two matrices. Again, I encourage you to spend time working the numbers of various matrices until you intuitively grasp the pattern.

Now you will learn why matrix multiplication is useful.

> **CAUTION**
>
> Matrix multiplication isn't commutative—A multiplied by B is not always equal to B multiplied by A. For this reason, you must be very careful when determining who multiplies whom.

3D Transformations the Quick and Easy Way

The beauty of matrices is that they can be used to translate, rotate, and scale 3D coordinates very easily.

Vectors Are Just Matrices

The core fact that makes the whole thing work is this: A vector is just a matrix with four columns and one row—one column for each x, y, and z value of the vector and a fourth column that's set to 1. This fourth column, also known as *w*, is used in the projection phase of rendering a scene, where the graphics code converts a 3D vector to a position on a 2D screen.

For example, if you have a vector (3,2,–5), you can represent that using a 4×1 matrix:

$$\begin{bmatrix} 3 \\ 2 \\ -5 \\ 1 \end{bmatrix}$$

Three Coordinates, Four Rows: What's Up with w?

You would think that you'd need only three rows because you're using only three coordinates: x, y, and z. However, you also need a fourth row. I don't have enough space to go deep into the math behind this, but the bottom line is that *translations* (simple movements from one place to another) would not work correctly if it were not for this fourth item, known as *w*. If you were working in 2D space, you'd need three rows: x, y, and w.

I encourage you to read more on your own about this little quirk. For now, though, just understand that you need this fourth element and that you should always set it equal to 1.

Transforming Points Using Matrices

You can multiply vectors together with matrices. Multiplying a vector and a matrix is just like multiplying two matrices, except that one matrix is 1×4.

To transform a point using matrices, all you do is plug the point into a 1×4 matrix and then multiply that matrix by another matrix, depending on the type of transformation you want to do.

Scaling

Take a scaling transformation as an example. Here's the matrix you'd multiply your vectors by to scale them:

$$\begin{bmatrix} sx & 0 & 0 & 0 \\ 0 & sy & 0 & 0 \\ 0 & 0 & sz & 0 \\ 0 & 0 & 0 & 1 \end{bmatrix}$$

where *sz*, *sy*, and *sx* are the scale factors for each axis.

You will work through the numbers so that you see exactly how this works. Say that you have a vector (2,4,6) and want to scale it by factors of 10, 100, and 1000 in the x, y, and z directions. You know already that you should end up with a vector (20,400,6000), but follow the process of matrix multiplication and see what you get.

First, you set up your two matrices. You know that your answer will be a 1×4 matrix because of the definition of matrix multiplication:

$$\begin{bmatrix} 2 \\ 4 \\ 6 \\ 1 \end{bmatrix} \begin{bmatrix} 10 & 0 & 0 & 0 \\ 0 & 100 & 0 & 0 \\ 0 & 0 & 1000 & 0 \\ 0 & 0 & 0 & 1 \end{bmatrix} = \begin{bmatrix} ? \\ ? \\ ? \\ ? \end{bmatrix}$$

Now it's just a matter of crunching the numbers. Here's the original matrix multiplication formula:

$$C_{ij} = \sum_{k=1}^{n} X_{ik} Y_{kj}$$

Applying that for the (1,1) position and expanding out the sigma gives you

$$C_{1,1} = \sum_{k=1}^{4} X_{1k} Y_{k1} = (X_{1,1} Y_{1,1}) + (X_{1,2} Y_{2,1}) + (X_{1,3} Y_{3,1}) + (X_{1,4} Y_{4,1}) = ((2)(10)) + ((4)(0)) + ((6)(0)) + ((1)(0))$$

which just reduces to 20 because all those multiplications by zeros drop out. So far so good—your new x value is 20.

Here are the rest of the formulas:

$$C_{1,2} = \sum_{k=1}^{4} X_{1k} Y_{k2} = (X_{1,1} Y_{1,2}) + (X_{1,2} Y_{2,2}) + (X_{1,3} Y_{3,2}) + (X_{1,4} Y_{4,2}) = ((2)(0)) + ((4)(100)) + ((6)(0)) + ((1)(0)) = 400$$

$$C_{1,3} = \sum_{k=1}^{4} X_{1k} Y_{k3} = (X_{1,1} Y_{1,3}) + (X_{1,2} Y_{2,3}) + (X_{1,3} Y_{3,3}) + (X_{1,4} Y_{4,3}) = ((2)(0)) + ((4)(0)) + ((6)(1000)) + ((1)(0)) = 6000$$

$$C_{1,4} = \sum_{k=1}^{4} X_{1k} Y_{k4} = (X_{1,1} Y_{1,4}) + (X_{1,2} Y_{2,4}) + (X_{1,3} Y_{3,4}) + (X_{1,4} Y_{4,4}) = ((2)(0)) + ((4)(0)) + ((6)(0)) + ((1)(1)) = 1$$

Fascinating, isn't it! Can you see how all the zeros drop out and make it so that you're really just multiplying each coordinate by its scale factor?

Translation

Translating a point using matrix multiplication is also easy. Just use this matrix:

$$\begin{bmatrix} 1 & 0 & 0 & 0 \\ 0 & 1 & 0 & 0 \\ 0 & 0 & 1 & 0 \\ tx & ty & tz & 1 \end{bmatrix}$$

where tx, ty, and tz are the translation amounts. Notice that all the variables live within the fourth row—the row you added (the w) to make the translations work. Now you will see how.

Again, use your formula. Say that you want to translate a vector (5,10,15) by (–10,–100,1000), which should give you (–5,–90,1015). First, you set up the matrices:

$$\begin{bmatrix} 5 \\ 10 \\ 15 \\ 1 \end{bmatrix} \begin{bmatrix} 1 & 0 & 0 & 0 \\ 0 & 1 & 0 & 0 \\ 0 & 0 & 1 & 0 \\ -10 & -100 & 1000 & 1 \end{bmatrix} = \begin{bmatrix} ? \\ ? \\ ? \\ ? \end{bmatrix}$$

Using the matrix multiplication formula, you get the following:

$$C_{1,1} = \sum_{k=1}^{4} X_{1k}Y_{k1} = (X_{1,1}Y_{1,1}) + (X_{1,2}Y_{2,1}) + (X_{1,3}Y_{3,1}) + (X_{1,4}Y_{4,1}) = ((5)(1)) + ((10)(0)) + ((15)(0)) + ((1)(-10)) = -5$$

$$C_{1,2} = \sum_{k=1}^{4} X_{1k}Y_{k2} = (X_{1,1}Y_{1,2}) + (X_{1,2}Y_{2,2}) + (X_{1,3}Y_{3,2}) + (X_{1,4}Y_{4,2}) = ((5)(0)) + ((10)(1)) + ((15)(0)) + ((1)(-100)) = -90$$

$$C_{1,3} = \sum_{k=1}^{4} X_{1k}Y_{k3} = (X_{1,1}Y_{1,3}) + (X_{1,2}Y_{2,3}) + (X_{1,3}Y_{3,3}) + (X_{1,4}Y_{4,3}) = ((5)(0)) + ((10)(0)) + ((15)(1)) + ((1)(1000)) = 1015$$

$$C_{1,4} = \sum_{k=1}^{4} X_{1k}Y_{k4} = (X_{1,1}Y_{1,4}) + (X_{1,2}Y_{2,4}) + (X_{1,3}Y_{3,4}) + (X_{1,4}Y_{4,4}) = ((5)(0)) + ((10)(0)) + ((15)(0)) + ((1)(1)) = 1$$

TIP

Notice that the number I at the bottom of your vector plays an important part in the translation process. Basically, the I allows you to add the translation values without multiplying them by your original coordinates. This is the primary reason w is so important.

Rotation

And now, the final segment in translating by matrix multiplication: rotating a point. Just as there are three rotation equations, there are three rotation matrices, depending on the axis around which you want to rotate. Table 4.3 lists those rotation matrices.

Rather than use sample numbers to see how these formulas work, take it to the next level: Prove that multiplying a vector by the matrix that rotates around the z-axis is the same as the rotation equations you learned about at the start of the chapter.

Table 4.3 Matrix Rotation Formulas

To Rotate around This Axis Use This Matrix

$$\begin{bmatrix} 1 & 0 & 0 & 0 \\ 0 & \cos(\theta) & \sin(\theta) & 0 \\ 0 & -\sin(\theta) & \cos(\theta) & 0 \\ 0 & 0 & 0 & 1 \end{bmatrix}$$

x-axis

$$\begin{bmatrix} \cos(\theta) & 0 & -\sin(\theta) & 0 \\ 0 & 1 & 0 & 0 \\ \sin(\theta) & 0 & \cos(\theta) & 0 \\ 0 & 0 & 0 & 1 \end{bmatrix}$$

y-axis

$$\begin{bmatrix} \cos(\theta) & \sin(\theta) & 0 & 0 \\ -\sin(\theta) & \cos(\theta) & 0 & 0 \\ 0 & 0 & 1 & 0 \\ 0 & 0 & 0 & 1 \end{bmatrix}$$

z-axis

Here are the two rotation equations:

$$x_{new} = x_{old} \cos(\theta) - y_{old} \sin(\theta)$$

$$y_{new} = x_{old} \sin(\theta) + y_{old} \cos(\theta)$$

Now see whether you can get to those by using a matrix multiplication. You set up your multiplication like this:

$$\begin{bmatrix} x_{old} \\ y_{old} \\ z_{old} \\ 1 \end{bmatrix} \begin{bmatrix} \cos(\theta) & \sin(\theta) & 0 & 0 \\ -\sin(\theta) & \cos(\theta) & 0 & 0 \\ 0 & 0 & 1 & 0 \\ 0 & 0 & 0 & 1 \end{bmatrix} = \begin{bmatrix} x_{new} \\ y_{new} \\ z_{new} \\ 1 \end{bmatrix}$$

From the matrix multiplication formula, you have

$$x_{new} = \sum_{k=1}^{4} X_{1k} Y_{k1} = (X_{1,1}Y_{1,1}) + (X_{1,2}Y_{2,1}) + (X_{1,3}Y_{3,1}) + (X_{1,4}Y_{4,1})$$

Putting in the elements gives you

$$x_{new} = ((x_{old})\cos(\theta)) + ((y_{old})-\sin(\theta)) + ((z_{old})(0)) + ((1)(0))$$

When you reduce this by eliminating the zeros, you get exactly what you'd expect:

$$x_{new} = (x_{old})\cos(\theta) - (y_{old})\sin(\theta)$$

which is exactly the same as the original formula! That makes sense! You can extrapolate the new y formula the same way:

$$y_{new} = \sum_{k=1}^{4} X_{1k} Y_{k2} = (X_{1,1}Y_{1,2}) + (X_{1,2}Y_{2,2}) + (X_{1,3}Y_{3,2}) + (X_{1,4}Y_{4,2})$$

$$y_{new} = ((x_{old})\cos(\theta)) + ((y_{old}) - \sin(\theta)) + ((z_{old})(0)) + ((1)(0))$$

$$y_{new} = x_{old}\cos(\theta) - y_{old}\sin(\theta)$$

Again, you're right back where you started.

As you can see, transforming a point using matrix multiplication is just like transforming a point using the traditional equations. The only difference using matrices is that you follow the exact same process regardless of the type of translation you're doing. Rotate, scale, and translate all use the same multiply-and-add process, and that's one of the things that makes matrices so powerful.

Identity Matrices

In normal multiplication, if you multiply by 1, you always get what you started with (I hope that this doesn't come as a shock to anyone).

There is an equivalent in matrix multiplication, and it's called the *identity matrix*. An identity matrix is a square matrix that has its top-left to bottom-right diagonal filled with 1s and the rest of its elements filled with 0s:

$$\begin{bmatrix} 1 & 0 & 0 & 0 \\ 0 & 1 & 0 & 0 \\ 0 & 0 & 1 & 0 \\ 0 & 0 & 0 & 1 \end{bmatrix}$$

If you multiply the identity matrix by any other matrix, you get that matrix back, unchanged—just like multiplying by 1.

TIP

The identity matrix is the same thing as the scaling matrix, with *sx*, *sy*, and *sz* all set to 1. Scaling something by 1x (or 100 percent) doesn't do anything to an object. The identity matrix is also a translation matrix that moves 0 units in the x, y, and z directions. Moving something 0 units is also a clever way to do nothing. And yes, the identity matrix is also equivalent to a rotation matrix where theta equals 0.

CAUTION

You can't start with an empty (all-zero) matrix. If you work the numbers, you will see that an all-zero matrix wreaks havoc on your coordinates. You should usually start with an identity matrix instead of an all-zero matrix.

In 3D programming, identity matrices are used as a base from which you create other matrices. Notice that all the transformation matrices you learned about in the preceding section are based on the identity matrix.

For example, to create a translation matrix, you start with an identity matrix and then add the appropriate elements in the appropriate rows and columns to turn that identity matrix into a translation matrix.

Matrix Concatenation (Doing More Than One Thing at Once)

To get a matrix to do more than one thing at once, you *concatenate* it with another matrix. If you've ever seen the movie *The Fly*, matrix concatenation is like combining Dr. Brendle with the housefly—you end up with Brendlefly, a combination of Dr. Brendle and the fly, a creature possessing the benefits of both human and fly. Fortunately, matrix concatenation does not lead to all the icky consequences poor Dr. Brendle had to endure.

To concatenate two matrices, just multiply them.

Using Matrices in 3D Programs

As you've seen, all 3D transformations can be accomplished using two matrices. One matrix stores the original x, y, and z values of your existing vertex. You multiply the first matrix by the second matrix, and the result of that multiplication is your new x, y, and z values. Like magic!

Matrices are very powerful because they allow you to set up what I like to think of as a mathematical assembly line for transforming 3D models.

For example, say that you want to rotate a 3D model. You first create a rotation matrix, which contains the parameters of your rotation. Next, you loop through all the vertices in your model. For each vertex, you set up a matrix containing the original x, y, and z values of that vertex. Then you multiply that matrix by your rotation matrix, which gives you the new x, y, and z values for that vertex. Then you move on to the next vertex. That's the assembly line.

The *really* important fact to keep in mind is that the assembly line remains the same, no matter what you're doing to a model. For example, if you wanted to scale the model rather than rotate it, you'd simply replace your rotation matrix with a translation matrix—you'd still run all the points through the assembly line just as you did before. If you wanted to scale *and* rotate, you'd set up a combination rotation/scaling matrix and then run your points through it just once. Your rotation/scaling matrix would perform both operations simultaneously.

For this reason, I like to think of transformation matrices as plug-ins you can use in the assembly line.

D3DX Matrix Helper Functions

It wouldn't be nice of Microsoft to give you all these D3DX functions for vectors and not provide any for working with matrices. D3DX also includes several functions designed to ease the pain of matrix math.

Table 4.4 shows the functions available.

Learn to use these functions, rather than waste time writing your own.

> **TIP**
>
> Additionally, in C++, the D3DXMATRIX class has overloaded operators for the most common operations (adding, subtracting, multiplying, and dividing, as well as the equivalence operator, ==). Check out the SDK help or the D3DX.h header file to see exactly what it supports.

Table 4.4 D3DX Matrix Functions

Function	Description
D3DXMatrixAffineTransformation	Builds an affine transformation matrix
D3DXMatrixDeterminant	Calculates the determinant of a matrix
D3DXMatrixIdentity	Creates an identity matrix
D3DXMatrixInverse	Calculates the inverse of a matrix
D3DXMatrixIsIdentity	Determines whether a matrix is an identity matrix
D3DXMatrixLookAtRH, D3DXMatrixLookAtLH	Builds a right- or left-handed look at a matrix, for setting up your view (camera) matrix to look at a point
D3DXMatrixMultiply	Determines the product of two matrices
D3DXMatrixOrthoRH, D3DXMatrixOrthoLH	Builds a right- or left-handed orthogonal projection matrix
D3DXMatrixOrthoOffCenterRH, D3DXMatrixOrthoOffCenterLH	Builds a customized right- or left-handed orthogonal projection matrix
D3DXMatrixPerspectiveRH, D3DXMatrixPerspectiveLH	Builds a right- or left-handed perspective projection matrix
D3DXMatrixPerspecitveFovRH, D3DXMatrixPerspecitveFovLH	Builds a right- or left-handed perspective projection matrix based on a field of view (Fov)
D3DXMatrixPerspectiveOffCenterRH, D3DXMatrixPerspectiveOffCenterLH	Builds a customized right- or left-handed perspective projection matrix
D3DXMatrixReflect	Builds a matrix that reflects the coordinate system about a plane
D3DXMatrixRotationAxis	Builds a matrix that performs a rotation around an arbitrary axis
D3DXMatrixRotationQuaternion	Builds a rotation matrix from a quaternion

Table 4.4 Continued

Function	Description
D3DXMatrixRotationX, D3DXMatrixRotationY, D3DXMatrixRotationZ	Builds a matrix that rotates around the x-, y-, or z-axis
D3DXMatrixYawPitchRoll	Builds a "yaw, pitch, and roll" matrix that rotates around the x, y, and z axes simultaneously
D3DXMatrixScale	Builds a matrix that scales along the x, y, and z axes
D3DXMatrixShadow	Builds a matrix that flattens geometry onto a plane, useful for making shadows
D3DXMatrixTransformation	Builds a transformation matrix
D3DXMatrixTranslation	Builds a translation matrix
D3DXMatrixTranspose	Calculates the transpose of a matrix

Matrix Wrap-Up

I've said it before, and I'll say it again. The single most important thing you can learn about matrices is how to multiply them. You can ride the coattails of the D3DX matrix helper functions for most other things, but knowing how to multiply is essential. If you grasp how matrices are multiplied, you will find it much easier to learn most of the other concepts—not only the matrix concepts but also 3D concepts in general.

At any rate, you now have the matrix basics you need as a 3D graphics programmer. You've glimpsed the inner sanctum of mathematical wizardry. If the inner sanctum of mathematical wizardry were a dog, its bark would be worse than its bite.

QUATERNIONS

You've conquered vectors and matrices. Now you have only one topic left: quaternions. My first advice before you even get started is simply, "Don't be afraid." The mathematics behind quaternions uses all sorts of fancy vocabulary that can seem very intimidating to someone who's not a college math professor. Yet, at their core, quaternions are very simple, even elegant.

Why Use Quaternions?

Quaternions buy you arbitrary axis rotation. You already know how to rotate a model by a certain angle around the x-, y-, or z-axis. In other words, you know how to poke a needle mathematically through a model and spin it on that needle, provided that you push the needle straight in from the left, straight up from the bottom, or straight through from the front (that is, the needle is always parallel to the x-, y-, or z-axis).

However, what if you want to push the needle through the model at an angle? Imagine that you have a cube model and want to poke a needle diagonally through it so that the needle enters and leaves the cube at opposite corners. Then you want to spin the cube on that needle. In other words, you want to rotate the cube around an arbitrary axis—not the x-, y-, or z-axis, but any axis you can dream up.

You could certainly try to accomplish this by combining rotations around the x-, y-, or z-axis. It's easy to come up with a matrix that rotates a model to an angle. The hard part is animating (or *interpolating*) that rotation so that instead of it happening at once, it happens over the course of a few frames of animation. If you tried to do this using rotation only around the x-, y-, or z-axis, you'd quickly run into a problem known as *gimbal lock*.

Gimbal lock causes one or more of your rotation steps to have no effect because of the order in which you perform the rotations. For example, you're rotating an object x degrees around the x-axis, 90 degrees around the y-axis, and z degrees around the z-axis. When you go to do the rotation, you find that the x rotation works fine, the y rotation works fine, but the z rotation doesn't because when you rotate 90 degrees on the y-axis, the z-axis *becomes parallel to* the x-axis.

Quaternions to the rescue! Using quaternions, you can define any vector as your axis of rotation (your needle). You can define starting and ending rotation angles on that axis, and you can plug all these things into a formula, along with a time value. The formula will return to you the precise orientation you need, from which you can construct a rotation matrix.

> **TIP**
>
> When I was learning this, I found it difficult to visualize 3D rotations. Something I found helpful was to make a physical model of the x, y, and z axes out of three different-colored straws. After all, this is 3D space, and 2D drawings on a piece of paper can go only so far.

In other (math) words, you have a parametric equation for rotation around an arbitrary axis. This allows the enemy jets in your combat flight sim to roll realistically, the turrets in your RTS to pivot and seek to their targets smoothly, and so on. Smooth rotation is a great tool to have in your 3D toolbox.

There are other merits to these magical mathematical creatures, but, hopefully, I've already convinced you that quaternions are worth studying. Now you will learn how they work.

What Is a Quaternion?

The word *quaternion* means simply *a group of four*. If you're into etymology, the word *quaternion* shares its Latin roots with *quarter, quartet,* and *quadruple.*

Quaternions are a four-dimensional extension to complex numbers. Don't panic. All this means is that a quaternion, defined mathematically, is a group of four real numbers (floats). Three of the four numbers (x, y, and z) define a vector, and the fourth number (w) is a scalar.

The precise mathematical definition of a quaternion says that the components of the vector (x, y, and z) are actually coefficients of imaginary numbers. Don't worry about this for now.

Mathematicians write quaternions using brackets. For example, [0,(1,2,3)] defines a quaternion whose scalar component is 0 and whose vector is (1,2,3).

Quaternion Basics

Here are a few additional basics you need to know about quaternions. You will be using these later when you use quaternions to do rotations.

The Norm of a Quaternion

A quaternion's norm is similar to a vector's magnitude. It can be calculated by summing the squares of all four quaternion components:

$$N(q) = w^2 + x^2 + y^2 + z^2$$

The Conjugate of a Quaternion

The conjugate of a quaternion is simply the opposite of the quaternion. To calculate the conjugate, take the original quaternion, and negate each of the vector components (but not the scalar w), as shown:

$$q* = [w,-v]$$

where w and v are the scalar and vector components of the original quaternion.

The Inverse of a Quaternion

To calculate the inverse of a quaternion, take the conjugate of the original, and divide it by the norm of the original:

$$q^{-1} = \frac{q*}{N(q)}$$

Unit Quaternions and Their Inverses

Let's pause for a minute and consider what happens when you take the inverse of a quaternion that has a norm of 1. (By the way, such a quaternion is called a *unit quaternion*, similar to what you call vectors with magnitude 1 unit vectors.)

Look at the preceding equation. When you plug a unit quaternion into that baby, the bottom $N(q)$ part drops out of the picture (because you know that the norm is 1), and you're left with

$$q^{-1} = q*$$

A shortcut! You've just proven that the inverse of a unit quaternion is the same as its conjugate.

Quaternion Multiplication

Quaternion multiplication is somewhat hairy. Given two quaternions, a and b, their product is a quaternion c, defined like this:

$$c_w = a_w b_w - a_x b_x - a_y b_y - a_z b_z$$

$$c_x = a_w b_x + a_x b_w + a_y b_z - a_z b_y$$

$$c_y = a_w b_y - a_x b_z + a_y b_w + a_z b_x$$

$$c_z = a_w b_z + a_x b_y - a_y b_x + a_z b_w$$

TIP

Mathematicians have deduced many ways to multiply two quaternions quickly. Those four lines probably aren't the fastest way to multiply two quaternions, but I find those formulas the easiest to understand.

Using Quaternions

The most common way to use a quaternion is to create one and then use it to create an affine transformation matrix. The math behind this is complex, but without going into all the messy details, all you do is plug in a rotation quaternion, along with a few other parameters, and churn some numbers, and you wind up with a matrix you can use.

Here's an example of that in code:

```
// Set the view matrix
D3DXQUATERNION qR;
D3DXQuaternionRotationYawPitchRoll(&qR, m_fYaw, m_fPitch, m_fRoll);
D3DXMatrixAffineTransformation(&m_matOrientation, 1.25f, NULL, &qR, &m_vPosition );
D3DXMatrixInverse( &m_matView, NULL, &m_matOrientation );
```

Here you can see that you begin by creating a quaternion, qR, by supplying the yaw, pitch, and roll that you want (m_fYaw, m_fPitch, and m_fRoll). You then pass this to the D3DX utility function that does an affine transformation. This function hands back an orientation matrix (m_matOrientation) that you invert to arrive at the view matrix.

Quaternion Wrap-Up

If you'd like to visit some of the math behind quaternions, I encourage you to do so. It's not necessary to understand what's going on behind the scenes if you're using quaternions only for simple solutions (like what you've seen here). However, if you're going to be doing more advanced 3D programming, you owe it to yourself to check them out.

CHAPTER WRAP-UP

How did you do? Did you survive okay?

I promise that the rest of the chapters in the book contain very little math. I realize that most people just beginning 3D programming don't want to spend time learning the math. However, you need a fundamental knowledge of vectors and matrices before you can learn how to program 3D applications.

That said, if you're making beginner-level 3D programs, you probably won't have to *code* much of the math. The DirectX utility libraries do a great job of hiding the math behind useful functions, so it's conceivable that you will never need to write your own matrix multiplication or vector normalization code.

ABOUT THE SAMPLE PROGRAMS

No global enhancements to the coding style for this section. Here's what the program does:

■ **Ch4p1_MatrixMult.** This program demonstrates how to multiply two matrices.

EXERCISES

1. Optimize the matrix multiplication code in the sample program. It can be optimized significantly.
2. Write a program that takes a vector as input, computes the magnitude of a vector given its distance, and then generates a normalized vector.
3. Write a program that generates two random 4×4 matrices and multiplies them. However, don't have it display the results immediately—use this program to generate practice matrices that you can multiply together. Have the program wait until you press a key or something before it spits out the answer, so that you can check the answer you arrived at by hand against the machine-generated answer. (Hint: Make sure that your code works before using this program as an answer key!)

CHAPTER 5

3D CONCEPTS

"Act in haste and repent at leisure;
code too soon and debug forever."
—Raymond Kennington

In the preceding chapter, you learned the math behind generating 3D images. In this chapter, I build on that math foundation and show you the *programming* concepts to get that math working for you. I cover 3D models in intricate detail because 3D models are indispensable for making 3D games. You are going to look at the geometry pipeline—the process your system goes through to take 3D coordinates and put them on the screen. You're also going to learn about depth buffers, which ensure that objects that are behind other objects don't appear on the screen.

This chapter, like the preceding, is more concept than code because you must always have concept before code. I promise, you will get to the code in the next chapter, but for now, be patient, learn the concepts first, and you will find the code much easier to understand.

3D MODELS

3D models form the foundation of most 3D programs. Most games use models to represent virtually everything in the game world—your character, the weapons and items he or she can pick up, the projectiles from those weapons, the enemies, you name it. It makes sense that your understanding in detail how 3D models work will help you make excellent 3D games.

What Is a Model?

Simply put, a *model* is a collection of vertices, with some additional properties for each vertex (the corresponding texture coordinate for that vertex, the vertex's normal, and the like). You specify the x, y, and z components of a model vertex relative to the model's local origin; in other words,

---

TIP

You can use several commercial, shareware, or freeware tools to create models. One of the best commercial 3D editors out there is 3D Studio Max. Many commercial game artists use 3D Studio Max to create the models for their games. Unfortunately, 3D Studio Max carries a very high price tag (last I checked, it was $3,000), so you might want to turn to the Internet and search for freeware modeling tools. One good one is MilkShape 3D, which has a slightly more reasonable price ($20). Check it out at http://www.swissquake.ch/chumbalum-soft/ms3d1x/index.html.

the vertices are in local or model space. Models can contain additional information, depending on how you use them, but that's the basic idea.

All the model information is stored in a model file. Each 3D editor has a different file format; several model file formats exist today, just as several image file formats (GIF, JPG, BMP, and the like) exist. DirectGraphics supports the X file format, and it also provides a utility program, Conv3ds, that converts a 3DS (*3D Studio* model file) to an X file.

Unfortunately, for all other formats, you yourself must write the code to read them.

The Three Ways Vertices Can Form Triangles

As you learned in the preceding chapter, you construct everything in your 3D world from vertices. Vertices form triangles, triangles form surfaces, and surfaces form your hollow models.

To render your model properly, Direct3D must interpret the vertices you give it and must form those vertices into triangles. It can do this in three ways: triangle lists, triangle strips, and triangle fans. Direct3D calls these *primitive types*.

Here is a look at each primitive type in more detail.

Triangle Lists

You will start with triangle lists because they have the honor of being both the easiest to understand and the most widely used.

When you feed Direct3D a triangle list, you feed it each and every vertex of each and every triangle in that list. Each triangle has three vertices, so if you had a 30-triangle model, you'd feed 90 vertices into Direct3D. Figure 5.1 shows the triangle list concept in action.

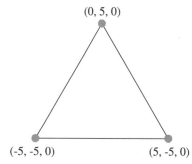

(0, 5, 0)

(-5, -5, 0)   (5, -5, 0)

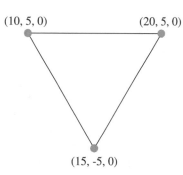

(10, 5, 0)   (20, 5, 0)

(15, -5, 0)

Figure 5.1

In a triangle list, each vertex of each triangle is specified.

Triangle Strips

Using triangle lists, you end up with a lot of duplicated vertices. For example, if I'm using two triangles to define a quad, I duplicate two of the four vertices because the two triangles share a common diagonal.

The more vertices you use, the more memory you use, and that's not a good thing. Ideally, you like to have no vertices duplicated, so Direct3D allows you to feed it triangle strips, as shown in Figure 5.2.

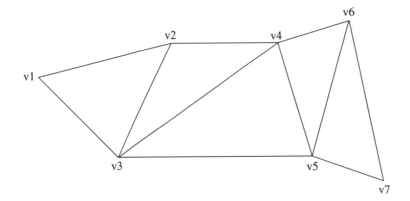

Figure 5.2

In a triangle strip, each triangle uses two vertices from the last triangle.

In a triangle strip, the first three vertices define a triangle. Direct3D forms the *next* triangle by using the last two vertices of the first triangle and one new vertex. Direct3D forms the third triangle using the last two vertices of the second triangle and one new vertex. In essence, every triangle shares two of its vertices with the preceding triangle.

Triangle Fans

Direct3D can also interpret your list of vertices as a triangle fan: a chain of triangles, all linked together, forming an oriental fan shape, as in Figure 5.3.

In this mode, you send Direct3D the vertex at the base of the fan, followed by all the vertices on the top of the fan, and it's smart enough to know that the end vertex for one triangle is the start vertex for another. Essentially, each triangle in the fan has the same base vertex and one vertex it shares with its fan neighbor.

Other Primitive Types

Direct3D supports three other primitive types: point lists, line lists, and line strips. You can use these types for rendering points or lines, instead of triangles. In practice, you will find them useful only rarely, so I won't spend time talking about them here.

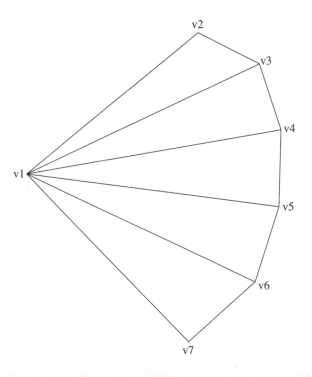

Figure 5.3

In a triangle fan, each triangle uses the base vertex and one vertex from the preceding triangle.

HELP REFERENCE

For more information on these types, as well as a more detailed explanation of the three triangle primitive types, check out the DirectX SDK at DirectX 8.0\DirectX Graphics\Using DirectX Graphics\Direct3D Device\Device-Supported Primitive Types.

Okay, Which One Should I Use?

The method you use depends largely on the model in question. In general, however, you use triangle lists.

TIP

3D cards that can perform T&L (*transformation and lighting*) in hardware—for example, the GeForce-based cards—*love* triangle lists.

Vertex Buffers

Now that you know how you can assemble your list of vertices, the next question on your mind is probably, "After I assemble a list of vertices, where do I put them?" In a vertex buffer!

A vertex buffer contains all the vertices of your model. It has nothing to do with triangle lists, strips, or fans—it's just a chunk of memory containing an array of vertex structures. Each vertex structure contains, among other things, an x, y, and z coordinate. That's all. For example, if your model had 100 vertices, and each vertex structure was 16 bytes, you'd need a 1,600-byte vertex buffer.

You can store your vertex buffers in system memory (slow, but there's lots of it) or in graphics memory (fast, but there's very little of it), or you can let Direct3D manage where the vertex buffer lives, moving it into and out of graphics memory as needed.

In the next chapter, you will get to the code used to create and fill a vertex buffer. For now, make sure that you understand what a vertex buffer is.

Index Buffers

Direct3D can interpret your vertex data three ways, allowing you to conserve memory usage by not having to specify duplicate vertices. You can also save more memory in certain situations by using an index buffer.

Index buffers are closely related to vertex buffers in that they're both chunks of memory that you fill up to make Direct3D render a model. Vertex buffers contain the vertex data, and index buffers contain indices into the vertex buffer. These indices can be repeated, saving you from having to specify two vertices with the same coordinates.

Take, for example, a simple quad made of two triangles. Say that you want to represent this quad using a triangle list and an index buffer (disregard for a moment that you could use a triangle strip, also).

Again, you really have only four unique vertices; the two triangles share two of the vertices. Say that you put the four vertices into the vertex buffer in the following order: The upper-left vertex is index 0 (remember, index counts start at zero, not one), the upper-right is index 1, the lower-right is index 2, and the lower-left is last at index 3.

Now, you create your index buffer. Because you have two triangles, you need six entries in the buffer. The first triangle consists of the upper-right vertex, the lower-right vertex, and the upper-left vertex, so the first three indices in your index buffer are 1, 2, 0. The second triangle uses the upper-left, lower-right, and lower-left vertices, so the next three indices in your buffer are 0, 2, 3. Your final index buffer contains 1, 2, 0, 0, 2, 3.

When you want to render this quad, you point Direct3D at both the vertex and index buffers, and it uses the index buffer as offsets into the vertex buffer to assemble the triangles for your model.

Note that you can use index buffers in conjunction with any primitive type, except one—point lists. It is completely okay to use an index buffer with a triangle fan or strip.

I'm not going to spend time covering in detail the code necessary to use index buffers because the process for using them is virtually identical to the process for using vertex buffers. As you will see in the next chapter, you create, lock, fill, and unlock a vertex buffer. You do the same with an index buffer.

You create an index buffer by calling the `CreateIndexBuffer` method of `IDirect3DDevice8`. This gives you back an `IDirect3DIndexBuffer8` interface to your new index buffer.

To get data into the buffer, you call the `Lock` method of `IDirect3DIndexBuffer8`, which tells Direct3D that you're going to be accessing the contents of your index buffer. The `Lock` method returns a pointer to the memory of the index buffer.

Use this pointer to fill up the buffer with the indices you want. This process can be nothing more than a `memcpy` call, or it can be complex.

Unlock the buffer by calling its `Unlock` method, which tells Direct3D that you're done messing with the contents of the buffer.

To use the index buffer to render a model, bind it to Direct3D using the `SetIndices` method of `IDirect3DDevice8`. This is the equivalent of calling `SetStreamSource` to bind a vertex buffer.

Render your model using the `DrawIndexedPrimitive` method of `IDirect3DDevice8`. `DrawIndexedPrimitive` uses the index buffer and vertex buffer you set by calling `SetIndices` and `SetStreamSource`.

CAUTION

Don't forget to Release your index buffer after you're done with it!

3D Models Wrap-Up

At this point, you should be familiar with the basics of how models work. There's still a big hole in your knowledge—namely, how to load models from a file—which is addressed in the "Advanced 3D Model Techniques" section. For now, delight in the fact that you know how models are represented using primitives and how they're stored in RAM using vertex and index buffers.

HELP REFERENCE

For more information on vertex buffers, see the DirectX help at DirectX 8.0\DirectX Graphics\Using DirectX Graphics\Vertex Buffers.

The DirectX help also has more information on index buffers at DirectX 8.0\DirectX Graphics\Using DirectX Graphics\Index Buffers.

Advanced 3D Model Techniques

In this section, I crank it up a notch. Here you will find information on hard-core model programming.

Note that you don't have to learn all of this now. In fact, if you're reading this book sequentially, it might be better to skip this section and come back to it after you write your first 3D program and have a grasp of texturing basics.

Loading a Model from an X File

To load a model from an X file (Microsoft's file format for storing models), you need to do two basic things:

1. Call the `D3DXLoadMeshFromX` function to load the vertex data into a vertex buffer.
2. `D3DXLoadMeshFromX` will tell you all the textures the model needs. You usually load all of these by using the `D3DXCreateTextureFromFile` function.

`D3DLoadMeshFromX` looks like this (see Table 5.1):

```
HRESULT D3DXLoadMeshFromX(
    LPSTR pFilename,
    DWORD Options,
    LPDIRECT3DDEVICE8 pDevice,
    LPD3DXBUFFER* ppAdjacency,
    LPD3DXBUFFER* ppMaterials,
    PDWORD pNumMaterials,
    LPD3DXMESH* ppMesh
);
```

> **TIP**
>
> You won't find a detailed description of `D3DXCreateTextureFromFile` here. That is covered in Chapter 8, "Basic Texturing."

The following are the most common options you can specify in the `Options` parameter:

- **D3DXMESH_MANAGED.** Tells Direct3D to manage moving the mesh into and out of graphics memory as appropriate. In other words, it loads the mesh into the `D3DPOOL_MANAGED` pool.
- **D3DXMESH_SYSTEMMEM.** Puts the mesh into system memory.
- **D3DXMESH_WRITEONLY.** Tells D3DX that you will never be reading the mesh's data.

Table 5.1 The D3DXLoadMeshFromX Parameters

Parameter	Description
pFilename	The filename from which you want to load.
Options	A set of flags that specify various loading options. The full list is given in the help.
tthpDevice	A pointer to the device on which you eventually render the mesh.
ppAdjacency	When this function returns, it gives you an ID3DXBuffer interface in this parameter that contains an array of DWORDs specifying the three neighbors for each face in the mesh. (You need this when generating progressive meshes.)
ppMaterials	When this function returns, it gives you an ID3DXBuffer interface in this parameter that contains an array of D3DXMATERIAL structures telling you the textures and materials the model uses.
pNumMaterials	Specifies the number of materials in the D3DXMATERIAL array at ppMaterials.
ppMesh	When this function returns, it puts a ID3DXMesh interface here, which you can use to render the mesh.

Converting a 3D Studio Model to an X File

3D Studio Max is one of the most popular 3D editing packages out there, and as a result, the 3DS file format has come dangerously close to becoming a standard way to save models. Direct3D includes a utility, Conv3ds.exe, that converts 3D Studio 3DS files to X files.

NOTE

This section probably won't make a lot of sense to you unless you have some experience with 3DS files.

Now you are going to learn how to use Conv3ds.exe to convert your models. You can find the Conv3ds program inside your DirectX SDK folder, under the bin\DXUtils\XFiles directory.

Basic Usage

If you're not doing anything fancy, the easiest way to convert a 3DS file into an X file is to run Conv3ds.exe like this:

```
CONV3DS FILE.3DS
```

Assuming that FILE.3DS is the name of your 3DS file, that command outputs FILE.X, the X file equivalent of your 3DS file. It doesn't get much easier than that!

Conv3ds Command-Line Arguments

Occasionally, you need to use the command-line arguments in Table 5.2 to change the behavior of Conv3ds.

> **TIP**
>
> Keep in mind that Conv3ds command-line arguments are case-sensitive!

Table 5.2 The Conv3ds Command-Line Arguments

Argument	Effect
-A	Tells Conv3ds that you want to create an animation set.
-m	Makes an X file that contains a single mesh made from all the objects in the 3DS file. In other words, if you have more than one model in your 3DS file, this clumps all of them together into one big model.
-T	Wraps all the objects and frame hierarchies into a single, top-level frame. The top-level frame goes into the X file. All the other frames and meshes are put in x3ds_filename, without the .3DS extension.
	Note that this option has no effect if you also specify the -m option.
-s	Scales the model by multiplying all the vertices by a certain value, which you specify immediately after the s.

Table 5.2 Continued

Argument	Effect
	For example, the following command scales FILE.3DS by 10x, making objects 10 times bigger: CONV3DS -s10 FILE.3DS. The following command scales FILE.3DS by 0.1, making all objects 10 percent of their original size: CONV3DS -s0.1 FILE.3DS.
-r	Reverses the winding order of the faces in the model. If your X file looks inside-out inside your program, specify this option to correct it. Also, note that you need this option if you are converting from 3DS files exported using Lightwave.
-v	Turns on verbose mode. You have four verbosity levels from which to choose, by specifying a number between 0 and 3 immediately after the v: v0 means *verbose mode off*. v1 prints general information about what it's doing and warnings. v2 prints detailed information about the objects being saved and included in the conversion process. v: means *very verbose*. Use this to debug.
-e	Changes the extension for texture-mapped files. You specify the extension, in quotes, immediately after the e.
	For example, the following command changes the extension for texture-mapped files to .ppm: Conv3ds -e"ppm" file.3ds. If there's a texture named brick.gif inside file.3ds, it will be brick.ppm inside file.x. Conv3ds does not touch the texture map file itself.
-x	Produces a text X file instead of a binary one.
-X	Includes the X file templates inside the X file.
-t	Specifies that the X file produced should not contain texture information.
-N	Specifies that the X file produced should not contain normal vector information. The normals are generated when you load the file.
-c	Specifies that the X file produced should not contain texture coordinates.

Table 5.2 Continued

Argument	Effect
-f	Specifies that the X file produced should not contain a frame transformation matrix.
-z, -Z	You can use these flags to add or subtract an amount from the alpha face color values. The little z specifies the amount to add or subtract (use negative numbers), and the big Z specifies which value the alpha must be under to begin with to get the addition or subtraction.
	For example, this command adds 0.1 to all alphas under 0.2: CONV3DS -z0.1 -Z0.2 file.3ds. This command subtracts 0.2 from all alpha values: CONV3DS -z"-0.2" -Z1 file.3ds. Notice the quotes on the negative number. Also notice that this works because there's no way an alpha value can be greater than 1.0.
-o	Allows you to specify an output name for the X file produced.
-h	Tells Conv3ds not to try to resolve any hierarchy information that might be in the 3DS file.

Hierarchical Models and Matrix Stacks

Most 3D games have complex models that represent the player and enemies in the 3D world. For these models to appear realistic, they must pivot at the places you'd expect them to—the elbows, legs, wrists, and the like.

To accomplish this, game programmers use what they call *hierarchical models*. A hierarchical model contains a complex figure broken down into simple objects. For example, game programmers might break down a humanoid model into a torso, two upper arms, two lower arms, two upper legs, two lower legs, two hands, two feet, ten fingers, and ten toes. They might then arrange these parts into a tree, like the one in Figure 5.4, with the torso at the top, the arms and leg segments as children of the torso, and finally, the fingers and toes as child nodes of the lower arms and legs.

This hierarchy shows which things derive their position, in part, from other things. For example, because you've set up the hand and finger models as children to the lower arm model, what

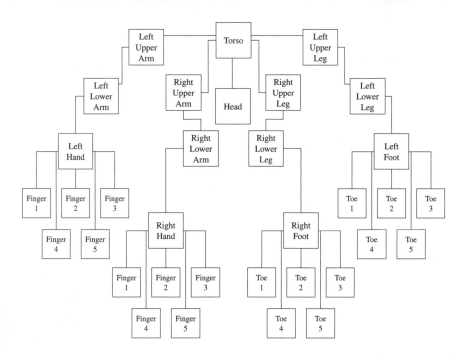

Figure 5.4

A tree of a humanoid hierarchical model.

you're saying is that the positions of the hand and finger models depend, in part, on the position of the lower arm. The hand and fingers can also have their own positions, but these positions should be relative to the lower arm. If you move or rotate the lower arm, the hand and fingers should also move because they're connected through the hierarchy.

Saying the same thing, only this time using 3D programming terminology, the transformation matrices for the hand and fingers are based, in part, on the matrix for the lower arm. If you change the transformation matrix for the lower arm to generate realistic results, you must also change the transformation matrices for the hand and fingers so that they move with the arm.

This means that you can start with your world transformation matrix for your model and draw the torso, because it's the top level of the tree. To draw all the other limbs, though, you combine the matrix with a new matrix, which contains the limb's position and orientation relative to the torso. To draw the fingers or toes of your model, you combine the limb's matrix with the individual finger/toe matrices.

As you can see, a lot of multiplication is going on. Basically, what you're doing is performing a depth-first traversal of the hierarchy tree, multiplying a matrix every time you move down toward the leaf nodes.

One of the best ways to keep track of all those matrices is to use a *matrix stack*. When you're about to descend down into a child node to render a new part, you push the results of your matrix multiplication onto the stack. Remember, you're multiplying the parent's matrix by the child's, which means that you're multiplying the top of the stack by the child's matrix and then pushing the result of that multiplication onto the stack. You use the matrix at the top of the stack as you pump the vertices for that body part into Direct3D. When you're done with that part and moving back to the parent node, you pop the matrix off the stack so that the new top of the stack represents the matrix needed for the parent node you're about to go back up into.

Well, that's about as clear as a brick is round. Let's eliminate any confusion by walking through the process of rendering the torso and an arm. You might want to grab a pencil (not pen) and paper (or write in the margins!) and keep track of the contents of the stack as you go along.

Initially, the matrix stack is empty. You start at the torso. When you enter the torso node, you push the torso's transformation matrix onto the stack. You render the torso. Now you need to descend into the upper arm node, so you multiply the current top of the matrix (the torso matrix) by the matrix for the upper arm, and you push the results of that multiplication onto the stack. Now your stack has two entries: On top is the combination torso/upper arm matrix, and on bottom is the torso matrix.

You render the upper arm. When you're done, you need to travel down into the lower arm node, so you multiply the top of the matrix by the lower arm's matrix and push the results of that multiplication onto the stack. Now your stack has three entries: On top is your combination torso/upper arm/lower arm matrix, followed by your torso/upper arm matrix, with the torso matrix on bottom.

Next comes the hand. Again, as you descend to the hand node, you multiply and push the matrix onto the stack. The top of your stack is now the torso/upper arm/lower arm/hand matrix. After you finish rendering the hand, you need to move down into the first finger node, so you multiply and push another matrix onto the stack. The top of the stack is now the torso/upper arm/lower arm/hand/finger1 matrix. See the pattern?

After you render the finger, you need to move back *up* to the hand node to continue your traversal. On your way up, you pop the stack, removing the torso/upper arm/lower arm/hand/finger1 matrix and leaving the torso/upper arm/lower arm/hand matrix on top. Notice that, thanks to the matrix stack, you don't have to recalculate anything before you draw the second finger. Your matrix stack has the appropriate matrix ready and waiting for you on top.

When you move down into the second finger node, you multiply and push, putting a torso/upper arm/lower arm/hand/finger2 matrix onto the stack. When you're done rendering the second finger, you pop this on the way back up to the hand node, so that once again, by the time you're back at the hand node, you have a torso/upper arm/lower arm/hand matrix ready to be multiplied with the next child node (the third finger).

This process continues until you've rendered the whole model.

See how, when using a matrix stack, the process of rendering a hierarchical model becomes simple and elegant? All you do is push and multiply on your way down and pop on your way up. For that little effort, you're always guaranteed to have the correct matrix on the top of the stack! Clever, isn't it?

Now, the only thing left to do is learn how to program a matrix stack. Even though it probably would be trivial to program your own, you don't have to—the Direct3D utilities module, D3DX, provides one for you.

Creating a Matrix Stack

To create a matrix stack, call the D3DXCreateMatrixStack function. This function gives you an ID3DXMatrixStack interface.

D3DXCreateMatrixStack looks like this (see Table 5.3):

```
HRESULT D3DXCreateMatrixStack(
  DWORD Flags,
  ID3DXMatrixStack** ppStack
);
```

Using a Matrix Stack

After you create a matrix stack, you use the methods shown in Table 5.4 to manipulate it.

Refer to the DirectX SDK if you need more detailed explanations of any of these functions. You use MultMatrix, Push, and Pop the most when rendering hierarchical models.

CAUTION

Don't forget to release the matrix stack interface after you're done with it! Failure to do so results in resource leaks!

Table 5.3 The D3DXCreateMatrixStack Parameters

Parameter	Description
Flags	Not used; set this to zero.
ppStack	The address of the pointer that will receive the ID3DXMatrixStack interface.

Table 5.4 The Matrix Stack Methods

Method	Description
GetTop	Returns a pointer to the *current* matrix (the one at the top of the stack).
LoadIdentity	Sets the current matrix equal to the 4×4 identity matrix.
LoadMatrix	Replaces the current matrix with a supplied matrix. Does *not* push the matrix onto the stack.
Pop	Decrements the stack pointer, effectively replacing the current matrix with the matrix below it in the stack. If the stack is empty, this method does nothing. If only one matrix is in the stack, this method clears the stack.
Push	Duplicates the current matrix, pushing a copy of it onto the stack.
MultMatrix	Right-multiplies the current matrix by a given matrix. After this call, the current matrix is the result of the multiplication. This is equivalent to doing the following: `m_stack[m_currentPos] = m_stack[m_currentPos] * <given matrix>;`.
MultMatrixLocal	Left-multiplies the current matrix by a given matrix. After this call, the current matrix is the result of the multiplication. This is equivalent to doing the following: `m_stack[m_currentPos] = <given matrix> * m_stack[m_currentPos];`.
	Remember that matrix multiplication, unlike regular multiplication, is order-dependent. A×B does not always equal B×A!
RotateAxis	Right-multiplies the current matrix by a rotation angle calculated from the given axis and angle of rotation.
RotateAxisLocal	Left-multiplies the current matrix by a rotation angle calculated from the given axis and angle of rotation.

Table 5.4 Continued

Method	Description
RotateYawPitchRoll	Right-multiplies the current matrix by a rotation angle calculated from the given rotations around the x-axis, y-axis, and z-axis.
RotateYawPitchRollLocal	Left-multiplies the current matrix by a rotation angle calculated from the given rotations around the x-axis, y-axis, and z-axis.
Scale	Right-multiplies the current matrix by a rotation angle calculated from the given x, y, and z scale factors.
ScaleLocal	Left-multiplies the current matrix by a rotation angle calculated from the given x, y, and z scale factors.
Translate	Right-multiplies the current matrix by a rotation angle calculated from the given x, y, and z translations.
TranslateLocal	Left-multiplies the current matrix by a rotation angle calculated from the given x, y, and z translations.

Advanced Model Techniques Wrap-Up

The X file format has been around since DirectX 2.0, and every DirectX release since then has piled on functionality, making the X files of today very powerful creatures indeed.

I'd also like you to note that even though it was extremely painful, I went through all the sections on X files without making any jokes regarding Mulder, Scully, or The Cigarette-Smoking Man.

HELP REFERENCE

For more information on X files, look at DirectX 8.0\DirectX Graphics\Advanced Topics in DirectX Graphics\X Files. The DirectX SDK also ships with several sample X files with which you can play.

CAMERAS AND VIEWPORTS

3D worlds would be boring if you couldn't move a camera through them. Just like the movies, most good 3D games start with the notion of a camera.

This section takes a look at the techniques you need to know to set up your camera properly and move it around.

TIP

This is way off topic, but if you're curious, you can, in fact, make a movie without using a camera. In 1955, a man by the name of Norman McLaren made a short movie called *Blinkity Blank* by scratching images directly onto the film with a razor blade. Other film pioneers have done similar experiments using different techniques.

Viewports

Let's knock this out of the way right now—cameras and viewports are totally different things. A *viewport* defines the destination of your 3D rendering, whereas a *camera* represents a position and orientation in your 3D world that you want to render.

A viewport defines a destination rectangle into which Direct3D renders your scene. Viewports also allow you to define the range of z-values you want in the final scene. Really, a viewport is a 3D box; it has width, height, and depth.

In Direct3D, you specify the viewport's rectangle using four variables: X, Y, Width, and Height. Direct3D assumes that the X and Y values represent the screen coordinates relative to the top-left corner of the rendering surface and that Width and Height represent the width and height of the viewport. For example, x/y values of (50,50), along with width and height values of 100×100, would put the upper-left corner of the viewport rectangle 50 pixels to the right and 50 pixels down from the upper-left of the rendering surface and make it 100 pixels square, as shown in Figure 5.5.

A viewport has two additional variables, MinZ and MaxZ, which tell Direct3D the minimum and maximum z-values of the rendered scene. You will see more precisely how these values come into play when you get to the section on the 3D geometry pipeline, but for now just realize that most of the time you set MinZ to 0.0 and MaxZ to 1.0.

Note that most 3D games fill the entire screen with a 3D scene, so the viewports of most 3D games have x/y values of (0,0) and width and height values equal to the width and height of the backbuffer. However, if you want a status area, a border, or something around your scene, you can adjust the viewport to accommodate those.

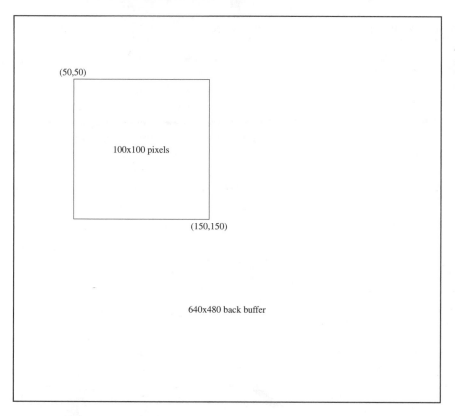

Figure 5.5

A viewport spanning from (50,50) to (150,150).

Setting the Viewport

In Direct3D, to set the viewport, call the SetViewport method of IDirect3DDevice8. SetViewport looks like this:

```
HRESULT SetViewport(
  CONST D3DVIEWPORT8* pViewport
);
```

Basically, it wants a D3DVIEWPORT8 structure, which looks like this (see Table 5.5):

```
typedef struct _D3DVIEWPORT8 {
    DWORD       X;
    DWORD       Y;
    DWORD       Width;
    DWORD       Height;
    float       MinZ;
    float       MaxZ;
} D3DVIEWPORT8;
```

Table 5.5 The D3DVIEWPORT8 Structure Members

Member	Description
X	The x coordinate, in pixels, of the upper-left corner of the viewport. Usually, this is zero.
Y	The y coordinate, in pixels, of the upper-left corner of the viewport. Usually zero.
Width	The width of the viewport. Usually, this is equal to the width of the backbuffer.
Height	The height of the viewport. Usually equal to the height of the backbuffer.
MinZ	The minimum z-value of the viewport's clip volume. Usually 0.0.
MaxZ	The maximum z-value of the viewport's clip volume. Usually 1.0.

You can set MinZ and MaxZ to values other than 0.0 or 1.0 to achieve special effects. For example, if you're rendering a heads-up display onto a previously rendered scene, you probably want both MinZ and MaxZ to be 0.0, which guarantees that Direct3D will put the scene you're rendering on top of everything else.

HELP REFERENCE

For more information on viewports, see the DirectX help at DirectX 8.0\DirectX Graphics\Understanding DirectX Graphics\Direct3D Rendering Pipeline\Fixed Function Vertex and Pixel Processing\Viewports and Clipping.

Cameras

I'll start the camera discussion by defining the characteristics a camera has. Cameras in Direct3D are similar to, but not exactly equal to, camcorders, with the primary difference being that one is for sale at Fry's and the other is simply a mental construct designed to simplify how you think about 3D scenes.

When you refer to a *camera* in 3D graphics programming, what you're talking about is ultimately a combination of the view matrix and the projection matrix. The view matrix is like the position and orientation of the camera. As you will learn in the 3D geometry pipeline section, the view matrix transforms your world coordinates so that they form a scene as viewed from a certain position and orientation in 3D space.

The projection matrix determines the camera's field of view, along with the nearest and farthest point a camera can see (see the next sidebar if you don't know what *field of view* means). The projection matrix takes the 3D points in your 3D world and converts them to 2D points on the screen. In other words, it "projects" the 3D world onto a 2D plane (your viewport).

As you see in Figure 5.6, the field of view, along with the near and far clipping planes, defines a *view frustum*, a pyramid with a flat top instead of a point. The finished 3D scene contains only the objects inside this frustum—all other objects are not visible. Some objects might have to be clipped, if they're partially inside the frustum.

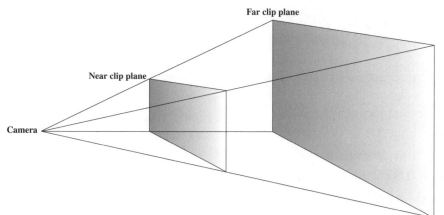

Figure 5.6

The near and far clipping planes, together with the field of view value, define the view frustum.

What's a Field of View?

The best way to define *field of view* is to use an example. Fix your eyes on something so that what you're looking at is right in the center of your vision. Now note the farthest things to the left and right of that point that you can see without moving your eyes or head. The angle between the leftmost thing and the rightmost thing is your field of view.

In other words, field of view is an angle that determines the width of a line of sight (see Figure 5.7).

Larger fields of view typically produce a "fisheye" effect, and smaller fields of view produce a "zooming" effect.

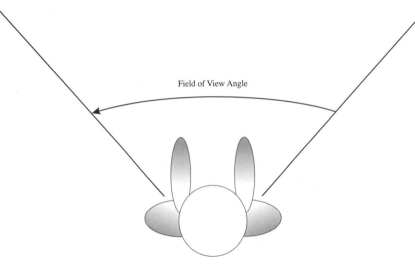

Figure 5.7

A field of view is an angle showing how far to the left and right you can see.

Field of View Angle

Direct3D does not include functions that support the notion of cameras. There's no SetCamera function. Instead, you must specify your camera by specifying view and transformation matrices. You create your matrices and then tell Direct3D about them by calling the SetTransform method of IDirect3DDevice8.

Projection Modes

Just as there are different ways to project the round Earth onto a rectangular piece of paper in map making, Direct3D supports different ways to project the 3D scene onto a rectangular rendering surface.

The most common projection is the *perspective projection*. When you use this projection, Direct3D creates the illusion of 3D by making objects in the distance appear smaller than objects up close (see Figure 5.8).

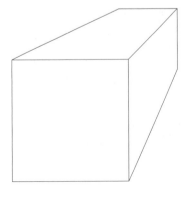

Figure 5.8

An example of perspective projection.

The second most common projection is an *orthogonal projection*, in which distant objects are not rendered smaller than near objects. Orthogonal projections don't scale the size of the objects they render, which makes them useful when you want to stop Direct3D from shrinking far away objects and enlarging near objects. For example, when you're using Direct3D to write a 2D game, you may still want to use z values to determine the drawing order, but you may not necessarily want the size of the sprite to change (though you would like Direct3D to take care of making sure that near objects still appear on top of distant ones).

You're going to concentrate on perspective projections because the vast majority of 3D games use them.

Specifying the Camera's Position and Orientation

To place the camera at a certain point in your 3D world and orient it to look at another 3D point, use the D3DX helper function D3DXMatrixLookAtLH. It looks like this (see Table 5.6):

```
D3DXMATRIX* D3DXMatrixLookAtLH(
  D3DXMATRIX* pOut,
  CONST D3DXVECTOR3* pEye,
  CONST D3DXVECTOR3* pAt,
  CONST D3DXVECTOR3* pUp
);
```

Table 5.6 The D3DXMatrixLookAtLH Parameters

Parameter	Description
pOut	The view matrix the function creates is placed here.
pEye	The position of the camera in 3D space.
pAt	The point in 3D space at which the camera is looking.
pUp	A normalized vector that points straight up in the current world. D3DX needs this value to calculate the rotation for the camera properly.
	Usually, you want this to be (0,1,0), but if you want to rotate the camera, you can put a different value here.

There are two ways the D3DXMatrixLookAtLH function gives you back the matrix it calculates: It returns the matrix, and it puts the matrix in pOut. Microsoft coded it this way so that you can use the function directly inside the SetTransform function, as shown here:

```
D3DXMATRIX matView;

g_pd3dDevice->SetTransform( D3DTS_VIEW,
  D3DXMatrixLookAtLH( &matView,
    &D3DXVECTOR3( 0.0f, 3.0f,-5.0f ),
    &D3DXVECTOR3( 0.0f, 0.0f, 0.0f ),
    &D3DXVECTOR3( 0.0f, 1.0f, 0.0f )));
```

> **TIP**
>
> The LH on the end of the function name stands for *left-handed,* as in left-handed coordinate system. D3DX also includes a D3DXMatrixLookAtRH, which you use if you're in a right-handed coordinate system (if, say, you're porting from OpenGL).

This code puts the camera at (0,3,–5) looking at the origin.

Specifying the Camera's Projection Mode and Field of View

D3DX includes several functions you can use to set the projection mode of the camera. Table 5.7 lists them.

All these functions work identically to how D3DXMatrixLookAtLH works. They take a pOut parameter and a few other parameters and return the calculated matrix in pOut and as a return value.

You can use them in code like this:

```
D3DXMATRIX matProj;
D3DXMatrixPerspectiveFovLH( &matProj, D3DX_PI/4, 1.0f, 1.0f, 100.0f );
g_pd3dDevice->SetTransform( D3DTS_PROJECTION, &matProj );
```

or you can do something slick like the following:

```
D3DXMATRIX matProj;
g_pd3dDevice->SetTransform( D3DTS_PROJECTION,
  D3DXMatrixPerspectiveFovLH(
    &matProj, D3DX_PI/4, 1.0f, 1.0f, 100.0f )));
```

> **TIP**
>
> As you see in the code, *pi*/4, or 45 degrees, is a good default value for the field of view.

Cameras and Viewports Wrap-Up

Using D3DX makes managing the camera a snap. I didn't go into the matrix math behind the D3DX functions because, as a beginner, you don't need to know it. Later, when you're trying to

Table 5.7 The D3DX Projection and Field of View Functions

Function	Description
D3DXMatrixPerspectiveLH D3DXMatrixPerspectiveRH	Sets up a left- and right-handed projection matrix. You specify the width and height of the near plane of the viewing frustum, and D3DX calculates the rest.
D3DXMatrixPerspectiveOffCenterLH D3DXMatrixPerspectiveOffCenterRH	Sets up a left- and right-handed projection matrix. You yourself specify all the values for the viewing frustum.
D3DXMatrixPerspectiveFovLH D3DXMatrixPerspectiveFovRH	Sets up a left- and right- handed projection matrix. You specify the field of view, aspect ratio, and z-values of the near and far planes, and D3DX calculates the rest.
D3DXMatrixOrthoLH D3DXMatrixOrthoRH	Sets up a left- and right-handed orthogonal projection matrix. You specify the width and height values and the minimum and maximum z-values for the volume, and D3DX calculates the rest.
D3DXMatrixOrthoOffCenterLH D3DXMatrixOrthoOffCenterRH	Sets up a left- or right-handed orthogonal projection matrix. You yourself specify all the values for the volume.

do something wild, you might need to build your own custom view or transformation matrix, but in general, you can sit back and let D3DX do all the work.

HELP REFERENCE

For more information on view and projection matrices, including the math working behind the scenes, see the DirectX help at DirectX 8.0\DirectX Graphics\Understanding DirectX Graphics\Direct3D Rendering Pipeline\Fixed Function Vertex and Pixel Processing\ Transformation and Lighting Engine\The Projection Transformation.

THE 3D GEOMETRY PIPELINE

Flip through the pages of any good book about 3D programming, and eventually you will find the infamous pipeline figure. This figure graphically explains the process your 3D card goes through to convert model vertices into screen vertices. The reason all the 3D books have this information is simple: It's the core of 3D graphics programming.

In this book, you can find the requisite drawing in Figure 5.9.

Going into the pipe are model-space vertices. Coming out the end of the pipe are screen vertices, which are actually direct pixel coordinates, ready for rasterization. Take a look at each of the steps in between.

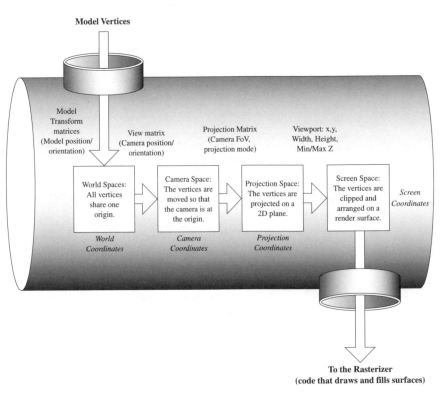

Figure 5.9

The 3D geometry pipeline.

World Transformation

Recall from the beginning of this chapter that 3D graphics programming uses several coordinate systems. A typical 3D application has several local coordinate systems (one local coordinate system for each 3D model). The origin of each of those local coordinate systems is usually at the center of that particular 3D model. In addition, a typical 3D application has one world coordinate system, whose origin is literally the center of the game universe.

The first order of business is to take all the model's local coordinates and transform them into world coordinates so that they all share a single world origin.

When you think about it, converting local vertices on a model to world vertices is the same as applying a transformation to them. Because you know that matrices really shine when it comes to applying transformations, it makes good sense to use a matrix to convert your local coordinates to world coordinates.

In the world transformation step, the system multiplies each model's vertex by a matrix that rotates it, scales it, and translates it to a specific position in the world. Of course, each model has a separate matrix. After you do this for all the models in your scene, there is no longer any notion of model space. You're now just dealing with vertices located in world space.

For example, say that you have a cube you want to be at world position (20,40,60), scaled 2x, and rotated 45 degrees (or *pi*/4 radians) around the x-axis.

To place this model in your world, you first create the 45-degree rotation matrix you need. Then you concatenate that matrix with a matrix that scales your cube to 2x. Finally, you concatenate that resulting matrix again, this time with one that translates your cube to (20,40,60). You end up with a matrix that, when plugged into the vertex processing assembly line, rotates, scales, and moves the vertices of your cube, effectively converting them from local coordinate space into world space. Cool!

The matrix you plug into the assembly line to place your model in the world is called the *world transformation* matrix. It's named this because it's the matrix that transforms local coordinates into world coordinates.

To see where world transformation matrices fit into the grand scheme of things, assume that you have a C++ class that represents a 3D model in your game. Obviously, you want to have class members that represent the position, scaling, and rotation of your model. When the time comes to place your model into the world, your code will look at those class members and create from them a world transformation matrix.

View Transformation

Until now, I've left out an important piece of the 3D puzzle—the position of the viewer of the scene, or, as some people like to think of it, the position of the camera.

This might come as a surprise to you, but your 3D graphics hardware has no notion of a camera. It's not as though you can hand your 3D card all your world vertices and then say, "Now draw what this would look like if I were standing over here." Your 3D hardware simply renders the vertices you give it, which means that the viewer of your scene is hard-coded to be at (0,0,0), looking down the positive z-axis into the screen.

Simply transforming all your model vertices into world vertices isn't enough. You need to transform them one more time to account for where the viewer of the world is.

Fortunately, this is very easy. All it takes is another pass through your vertex-processing assembly line. This is because what you're really doing is transforming your whole world so that the camera position is shifted to the world origin (0,0,0), and is right side up. This is the second step in the pipeline.

For example, say that you have a teapot floating in space at position (12,14,76). Now imagine that you put a camera at (12,14,75), looking in a positive z direction. What you'd expect the camera to see would be an up-close-and-personal image of your teapot. After all, the camera is only one unit in front of the teapot and is looking right at it.

Unfortunately, your graphics hardware can render scenes only as seen from (0,0,0). To deal with this, you just move everything in the world by (–12,–14,–75), which works because now the camera's at (0,0,0) and that makes your graphics hardware happy. The cube also is moved (–12,–14,–75), so it ends up at position (0,0,1), which is also correct—still one unit in front of the camera. When you render this scene, you will see an up-close-and-personal image of the cube, which is As It Should Be.

In other words, everything is relative. It doesn't matter where exactly your camera is located. What matters is where it's located *relative to all the other objects in the scene.* You care only about keeping those relative distances intact—in this case, keeping the cube exactly one unit in front of the camera.

That's how cameras work. The next time you play Quake, you will know that it's an illusion. Even though it seems as though you're moving through the world, in reality, you're standing still, and the world is moving around you.

The view transformation matrix is simply the matrix that takes each vertex and translates it so that the camera is at (0,0,0) and facing straight up (positive y-axis). In the preceding example, your view matrix would need to move everything –12 units on the x-axis, –14 on the y-axis, and –75 on the z-axis. If the camera were rotated, you'd also have to compensate for that by *unrotating* it around each axis (that is, rotating it an equal amount in the opposite direction).

Most view matrices are concatenations of four matrices: one matrix that translates the objects and three rotation matrices that rotate the world so that the camera's x, y, and z axes are pointing correctly—that is, positive x-axis pointing left, positive y-axis pointing up, and positive z-axis pointing into the scene (remember, this is a left-handed coordinate system!).

Projection Transformation

After you do view transformation, you have a set of vertices that graphics programmers consider to be in *view space*. They're all set up. The only problem is that they're still 3D, and your screen is 2D. Projection transformation takes all the 3D coordinates and projects them onto a 2D plane (the monitor), at which point they're said to be in *projection space* (some graphics books also call it *post-perspective homogeneous space*). It converts the coordinates by (surprise!) using a matrix called the *projection transformation matrix*.

You set up the projection transformation matrix to set up the camera's field-of-view and viewing frustum.

Clipping and Viewport Scaling

After the vertices come through projection transformation, Direct3D looks at each one and discards the ones that aren't visible on the screen (this is called *clipping*). Direct3D might have to do more work than just removing a vertex. If the vertex it removed is part of a surface that *is* on the screen, Direct3D might have to do some additional work with that vertex so that the surface on-screen appears to have a vertex off-screen.

At this point, it also looks at the MinZ and MaxZ values you specified when you set up your viewport, and it scales the z-values of all the vertices so that they fit within your range.

Geometry Pipeline Wrap-Up

After the vertices come through the clipping and viewport scaling process, they're sent to the rasterizer, which takes the vertex data and begins drawing the pixels of the scene.

The geometry pipeline is a complicated little beast, but it provides a lot of flexibility for different 3D applications. It's amazing to think that all those steps happen for thousands of vertices, hundreds of times per second, though. You've just read three pages on something that happens in a few milliseconds!

> **HELP REFERENCE**
>
> For more information on the geometry pipeline, see the DirectX help at DirectX 8.0\DirectX Graphics\Understanding DirectX Graphics\Direct3D Rendering Pipeline\Fixed Function Vertex and Pixel Processing\Transformation and Lighting Engine.

DEPTH BUFFERS

You know about models, cameras, and the geometry pipeline, but there's still one important concept you need to know: depth buffers. Depth buffers are a crucial element of 3D programming, so you're going to spend a lot of time learning what they are, how they work, and so on. Here you go.

Why Use a Depth Buffer?

One of the most difficult aspects of rendering a 3D scene is determining which polygons are covered up (or *occluded*) by other polygons closer to the viewer. For example, if I have a 10×10 quad centered at (0,0,1) and a 5×5 quad centered at (0,0,2), I shouldn't see the little quad because the big quad is occluding it. Similarly, if the positions were reversed, I should be able to see the outline of the big quad behind the little quad.

Throughout the years, many algorithms have been created to address this problem. For example, the Painter's Algorithm says, "Start at the back, and draw everything in order from farthest away to closest." In other words, this means rendering the scene as a painter would paint a picture, by first drawing the objects in the background and then drawing over it with the objects in the foreground (see Figure 5.10).

At first thought, this sounds like a great solution, but consider the infamous case of three overlapping polygons (see Figure 5.11).

> **TIP**
>
> In the future, a few graphics card companies might introduce better alternatives than plain old depth buffering. A few technologies on the horizon look quite promising.
>
> Constant technology changes and upgrades are just part of the fun of being a game developer.

Figure 5.10

The Painter's Algorithm: Draw the far-away objects first. Then draw nearer things over them.

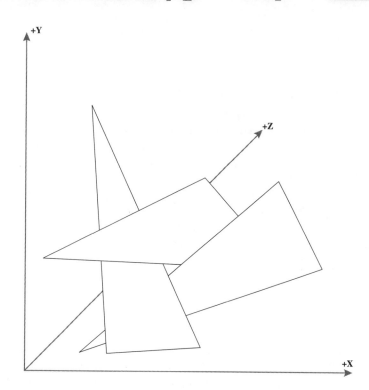

Figure 5.11

A case that breaks the Painter's Algorithm.

In this scenario, all the polygons overlap each other to some extent, so no matter which polygon the system chooses to render first, the scene will be incorrect. As you see, to render this scene properly, you can't simply ask yourself, "Which vertex is closer to the viewer?" You must ask this on a per-pixel basis: "Is the pixel I'm about to render closer to the viewer?"

Depth buffers allow you to occlude things on a per-pixel level.

What Is a Depth Buffer?

A *depth buffer* is a 2D array of numbers that has the same dimensions as your final scene. If I'm rendering a 640×480 image, my depth buffer must be 640×480. The 3D graphics hardware stores the depth buffer in its RAM.

When you first start a scene, you clear the depth buffer by setting every array element to its highest possible value. Then, for each pixel you want to render, you compare the pixel's z-value (or, in the case of w-buffers, the pixel's w-value) to the corresponding number in the depth buffer. If the pixel's z-value is lower than the number in the depth buffer, you plot the pixel and store its z-value in the depth buffer. If the pixel's z-value is greater than the number in the depth buffer, you don't render the pixel.

Essentially, as you render the scene, the depth buffer keeps track of the lowest z-value. The only way you can put a pixel on the screen (and overwrite what's there already) is by having a z-value lower than the current lowest z-value for that point.

For example, say that I have three points, all at the same (x,y) screen coordinates. The three points have the following properties: The first is a blue point at coordinates (50,50,0.75), the second is a red point at (50,50,0.25), and the third is a green point at (50,50,0.10). Just by looking at their z-values, you know that the green point is closest to the viewer, so it should occlude the red and blue points. Now walk through the algorithm so that you understand what's happening.

Say that you clear the screen to black and you clear the z-buffer to 1.0. Next, you render the red pixel. Before putting the pixel on the screen, you check the (50,50) array element of the z-buffer, which is currently 1.0. Because the point's z-value is less than that currently in the z-buffer, you render the red pixel and put its z-value of (0.75) into the z-buffer.

Now you render the green pixel. Again, you look at element (50,50) of your z-buffer, which is currently 0.75. The green pixel's z-value of 0.10 is less than the value in the z-buffer, so you render the pixel and put 0.10 into the z-buffer.

Finally, you turn your attention to the blue pixel. Now element (50,50) of your z-buffer is 0.10. Your blue pixel's z-value is 0.75, which is *greater* than the value in the z-buffer, so you can't render the pixel (leaving the green one still there), and you leave the z-buffer unchanged.

Presto! The end result is that the green pixel ends up on top. Notice how the z-buffer tracks the frontmost pixel as each point is rendered. That's how a depth buffer works!

> **TIP**
>
> Note that one way you can speed up your rendering is to render things from front to back. This is backwards from the way you'd expect, but it works because the things you render up front get the z-buffer's values low early. By the time you get to the objects in the back, the z-buffer is blocking virtually all the pixels from being drawn.

Z-Buffers and W-Buffers

Direct3D supports two types of depth buffers: z-buffers and w-buffers. Z-buffers use the interpolated z-values of the point, and w-buffers use the interpolated w-values.

Direct3D supports both types because each type has distinct advantages and disadvantages. This is because, in most scenes, the vertices aren't distributed evenly all over the range of possible z-values or w-values. For example, if you're rendering an outside landscape, 98 percent of your polygons will fall within the first 2 percent of the z-buffer's numeric range (typically 0.0 to 1.0, with 1.0 being farthest away). In other words, the vast majority of polygons will be crammed up toward the 0.0 end of the z-buffer, with only a few off in the higher numbers.

This in itself wouldn't be that bad, but remember also that most of the time you have only 16 bits to represent a floating-point number, which means that your accuracy is limited. For a z-buffer to work unconditionally, you need to know that 0.00005 is closer than 0.00007. However, you might not have enough bits to represent that level of precision, which means that your scene might not be rendered correctly.

To minimize the chance of this happening, use z-buffers when your near and far clipping planes are relatively close to each other. Use w-buffers when you're rendering outdoor areas or other areas where your near and far clipping planes are very far apart. Z-buffers work best when objects are bunched up close to the viewer; w-buffers work best when objects are far away or spread far apart.

TIP

Virtually all the cards out there today support z-buffering in hardware, but w-buffering isn't nearly as widely supported. You might not have a choice. If w-buffering isn't supported, go with z-buffering because it's better than nothing!

The following code snippet checks for a w-buffer and enables it. If it can't use a w-buffer, it falls back to using a z-buffer.

```
D3DPRIMCAPS* pdpc = &m_pDeviceInfo->ddDeviceDesc.dpcTriCaps;
if(pdpc->dwRasterCaps & D3DPRASTERCAPS_WBUFFER != 0) {
  // card supports a w-buffer!  Use it!
  m_pd3dDevice->SetRenderState(D3DRS_ZENABLE, D3DZB_USEW );
}
else {
  // nope, sorry, no w-buffer.  Use a z-buffer.
  m_pd3dDevice->SetRenderState(D3DRS_ZENABLE, TRUE );
}
```

If you're confused about the SetRenderState calls, don't worry—all will be made clear in a couple sections. See the section "Disabling the Depth Buffer and Choosing Its Type" for more information.

Rendering Objects on Top of Each Other Using Depth Buffers

It's common to render two polygons directly on top of each other. 3D programmers often do this, for example, when they're rendering shadows onto a wall. They render the wall first and then come back to do the shadow.

Unfortunately, the depth buffer can mess up things in this situation. When you come back to render the shadow, because the shadow has exactly the same z coordinate as the wall, the z-buffer can prevent some or all of it from being drawn.

To correct this problem, Direct3D allows you to put a *z-bias* onto certain vertices. Direct3D subtracts your z-bias from the points before checking them against the z-buffer, which means that you can use the z-bias to make sure that things render on top of each other.

The z-bias can be anywhere from 0 to 16. Note that this isn't the actual amount Direct3D subtracts from the coordinates; it's a relative figure. The higher the z-bias, the closer the object. For example, objects with a z-bias of 14 are on top of objects with a z-bias of 10.

The z-bias is just another rendering state, so to set it, call the `SetRenderState` method of `IDirect3DDevice8`. Put `D3DRS_ZBIAS` into the `State` parameter and a value from 0 to 16 into the value parameter.

The z-bias you set remains active until you set a new one. To use it, you should set it to zero, render all the bottom vertices, set it up a bit (say, to 5), and then render all the top vertices.

Disabling the Depth Buffer and Choosing Its Type

In certain situations, you want to disable the z-buffer when you draw a set of vertices. In effect, this says to Direct3D, "I don't care whether these vertices are supposed to be occluded. I want them drawn, no matter what!"

To enable or disable the z-buffer, set the `D3DRS_ZENABLE` render state to one of the values shown in Table 5.8.

Table 5.8 The D3DRS_ZENABLE Render State Values

Value	Meaning
D3DZB_TRUE	Use a z-buffer as the depth buffer.
D3DZB_USEW	Use a w-buffer as the depth buffer.
D3DZB_FALSE	Don't use a depth buffer.

Disabling Depth Buffer Writes

You can also prevent Direct3D from writing to the depth buffer by setting the D3DRS_ZWRITEENABLE value to zero. Not allowing Direct3D to write to the depth buffer is useful when you're creating certain special effects. When you render a set of vertices with depth buffer writing off, you're effectively telling Direct3D that those vertices do not occlude anything. They do not exist, as far as the depth buffer is concerned.

Clearing the Depth Buffer

To clear the depth buffer, make sure that you've included the D3DCLEAR_ZBUFFER flag in your call to the Clear method of IDirect3DDevice8. Clear also allows you to specify the number to which you want the depth buffer cleared. Here's a quick line of code that clears the depth buffer:

```
m_pd3dDevice->Clear( 0L, NULL, D3DCLEAR_ZBUFFER, 0x000000, 1.0f, 0L );
```

In the preceding code, you can see me passing in the D3DCLEAR_ZBUFFER flag, instructing Direct3D to clear the depth buffer.

Changing the Comparison Function

If you want to mess with things, Direct3D allows you to change the function it uses to compare the value in the depth buffer to the pixel's z-value or w-value. This enables you to make some really weird scenes. For example, you can reverse things so that distant objects occlude nearer ones, creating a bizarre, twisted reality.

The D3DRS_ZFUNC render state controls which comparison function Direct3D uses. You can set this render state, via a call to SetRenderState, to any of the values shown in Table 5.9. (Keep in mind that if the test succeeds, Direct3D draws the pixel and updates the depth buffer; if the test fails, it doesn't draw the pixel or update the depth buffer.)

> **TIP**
>
> Note that some of these values don't make sense. For example, if the test always fails, Direct3D will not render anything, resulting in a pretty boring scene. The funny values are here because Direct3D also uses this set of D3DCMP_ values for things such as the alpha function and the stencil function, where D3DCMP_NEVER and D3DCMP_ALWAYS make more sense.

Table 5.9 The D3DRS_ZFUNC Render State Values

Value	Meaning
D3DCMP_NEVER	The test never succeeds.
D3DCMP_LESS	The test succeeds if the pixel's value is less than the value currently in the depth buffer. This is the default, "normal" operation.
D3DCMP_EQUAL	The test succeeds if the pixel value and the depth buffer value are equal.
D3DCMP_NOTEQUAL	The test succeeds if the pixel value and the depth buffer value are not equal.
D3DCMP_LESSEQUAL	The test succeeds if the pixel value is less than or equal to the depth buffer value.
D3DCMP_GREATER	The test succeeds if the pixel value is greater than the value currently in the depth buffer.
D3DCMP_GREATEREQUAL	The test succeeds if the pixel value is greater than or equal to the value currently in the depth buffer.
D3DCMP_ALWAYS	The test always succeeds.

Depth Buffer Wrap-Up

3D graphics programmers have it easy today, thanks to depth buffers. Without them, you have to manually make sure that your polygons render in the correct order to prevent artifacts. Yuck!

HELP REFERENCE

For more information on depth buffers, see the DirectX help at DirectX 8.0\DirectX Graphics\Using DirectX Graphics\Depth Buffers.

CHAPTER WRAP-UP

This chapter teaches all the important topics that don't fit anywhere else in the book. Now that you have seen some of the basic 3D concepts, such as loading models from X files; setting up the world, view, and projection matrices; and using depth buffers, you can move on to the more advanced techniques.

ABOUT THE SAMPLE PROGRAMS

No real global enhancements have been made to the sample program coding style for this chapter. Here's what the program does:

- **Ch5p1_XFileLoader.** This program demonstrates how to load and display an X file.

EXERCISES

1. Build an X file for a cube model by hand. If you need help, the full solution is given in the DirectX help under DirectX 8.0\DirectX Graphics\Advanced Topics in DirectX Graphics\X Files.
2. Write a program that "breaks" the z-buffers and w-buffers. To do this, write code that crunches a whole bunch of polygons at the front or back of a scene, right next to each other.
3. Modify the sample program you wrote in exercise 2 to see the kinds of effects you can produce by changing the z-buffer comparison function.
4. If you're not sure what a field of view is, edit the sample program (Ch5p1_XFileLoader) so that the field of view becomes smaller or larger each frame of animation, and watch the effect.
5. If you're not comfortable with how the D3DX matrix stack works, you can certainly write your own. In doing so, you will probably realize why Microsoft designed the D3DX matrix stack the way it did.

CHAPTER 6

An Introduction to DirectGraphics

"Mighty is Geometry. When joined with art, resistless."

—*Euripides*

F inally, after two chapters of concepts, this chapter is all about coding. Now that you know the essential 3D concepts and 3D math skills, it's time to put them to use by making your first 3D program!

This chapter is a walk-through. You're going to take a look at every step of the process to render a single triangle to the screen—everything from setting the screen mode to setting up your matrices and vertex buffers and rendering your scene.

DIRECTGRAPHICS BASICS

Before you start with 3D, you must first learn the ground rules for working with DirectGraphics: how to set up the screen, choose a color depth, and generally get things ready to go.

DirectGraphics Architecture

If DirectGraphics were an invading armada of alien craft, the `IDirect3D8` interface would be the mother ship. It's the interface that all the other DirectGraphics interfaces come from.

To get an `IDirect3D8` interface, use the `Direct3DCreate8` function. This function takes one argument, which should always be set to `D3D_SDK_VERSION`. This ensures that your header files are in sync with the version of DirectX on your system. `Direct3DCreate8` returns a pointer to an `IDirect3D8` interface (or `NULL` if something goes wrong).

Each computer system can have one or more *devices*. A device represents the hardware that drives a monitor, specifically, the hardware rasterizer, along with the transformation and lighting (T&L) hardware, if the device supports T&L hardware.

Look at Figure 6.1 to see a sample of various device, video card, and monitor setups. Most of the time, users have a single video card, which means that they have a reference device and a HAL device (if it's a 3D card). If users have a *dual head* video card, they have two reference devices and two HAL devices, one device of each type for each monitor. If users have an old 2D-only card but have augmented their system with a 3D-only card, they have two devices, and their HAL device runs on the 3D-only card. It's possible that two devices drive the same monitor.

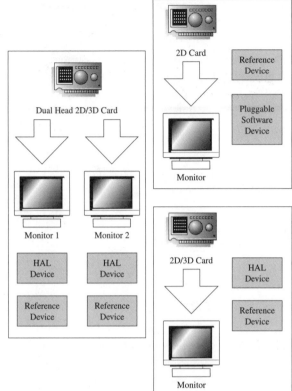
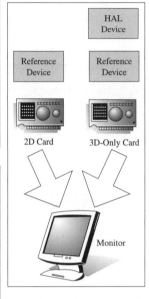

Figure 6.1

The relationships between devices, monitors, and video cards.

Each device has an ID, which you use when you tell DirectGraphics to give you an interface to a specific device. You use the IDirect3D8 primarily to create device interfaces (IDirect3DDevice8 interfaces) for a given device ID. You then use the methods of the IDirect3DDevice8 interface to display 3D scenes.

> **TIP**
>
> Direct3D also defines a special device ID, D3DADAPTER_DEFAULT, that you can use to identify the *default device*, which is the primary monitor on a multimonitor system.

Device Types

Each device in DirectGraphics can be one of the following types:

- **HAL device.** *HAL* stands for *Hardware Abstraction Layer*. A HAL device is, in essence, a 3D card. HAL devices have hardware-accelerated rasterization and shading and can have hardware-accelerated vertex processing.
- **Reference device.** This device is implemented completely in software. Unlike a software device, Microsoft guarantees that a reference device supports every Direct3D feature. These features are implemented totally in software, however, so they're accurate but

really, *really* slow. For this reason, reference devices are typically used by software developers to test features that will eventually be implemented in hardware.

- **Pluggable software device.** These devices are implemented completely in software but are not guaranteed to implement every Direct3D feature. They are used in computers without 3D hardware, where software must emulate 3D card features. Obviously, software devices are slower than HAL devices, but they're also faster than reference devices because they're more focused on speed instead of accuracy. They also take advantage of any processor-specific instructions (such as MMX on Intel chips or 3D-Now! on AMD chips).

You must specify the device type you want to use when you create a device. Usually, you care most about the HAL devices because they are what give you access to 3D acceleration.

Creating a Device (Setting the Video Mode)

When you create a device, Direct3D takes care of everything automatically. It changes the screen resolution to the dimensions you specified, creates as many back buffers as you tell it to, and does whatever else it needs to so that you're ready to render a 3D scene (the only thing it doesn't do is set up a depth buffer, which I'll talk about later).

> **TIP**
>
> This is a big change from previous versions of DirectX, which require you to set up all that. I'm sure you will agree that this new one-call setup is much better.

It's important to note that most games don't hard-code in the device to use, as the sample program does. Instead, most games allow the user to select a desired device, along with a desired screen resolution, color mode, and the like, for that device. DirectX supplies functions that allow you to list (or *enumerate*) all available display modes for a given device.

> **Sample Program Reference**
>
> The Ch6p1_CreateDevice sample program on your CD demonstrates how to create a particular device (a windowed mode default device).

For now, you're going to run through the process of creating a device. The next section builds on this process and shows you how to prompt users for their desired device and then create that device.

To create a 3D device, call the CreateDevice method of IDirect3D8:

```
HRESULT CreateDevice(
  UINT Adapter,
  D3DDEVTYPE DeviceType,
```

```
  HWND   hFocusWindow,
  DWORD BehaviorFlags,
  D3DPRESENT_PARAMETERS* pPresentationParameters,
  IDirect3DDevice8** ppReturnedDeviceInterface
);
```

Table 6.1 shows all the parameters.

The following are the values you can specify for the DeviceType parameter:

- **D3DDEVTYPE_HAL.** Specifies a device type of Hardware Abstraction Layer. Use this if you want your device to use the HAL (and therefore take advantage of any 3D acceleration provided by your hardware). This is the most common setting.
- **D3DDEVTYPE_REF.** Specifies that you'd like to use the reference rasterizer device type. This means that all Direct3D features are implemented in software, which is really slow, but useful if you're trying to test a feature your 3D card doesn't have. For example, if your 3D card doesn't support shaders, you can use the reference rasterizer to see how your shader code will look on the screen. It's time-consuming, but it gets the job done.
- **D3DDEVTYPE_SW.** A pluggable software device type. Use this if you're writing your own, customized software renderer.

Also look at the pPresentationParameters struct:

```
typedef struct _D3DPRESENT_PARAMETERS_ {
    UINT BackBufferWidth;
    UINT BackBufferHeight;
    D3DFORMAT BackBufferFormat;
    UINT BackBufferCount;
    D3DMULTISAMPLE_TYPE MultiSampleType;
    D3DSWAPEFFECT SwapEffect;
    HWND hDeviceWindow;
    BOOL Windowed;
    BOOL EnableAutoDepthStencil;
    D3DFORMAT AutoDepthStencilFormat;
    DWORD Flags;

    UINT FullScreen_RefreshRateInHz;
    UINT FullScreen_PresentationInterval;
} D3DPRESENT_PARAMETERS;
```

Table 6.2 shows a rundown of everything in this structure.

Table 6.1 The CreateDevice Parameters

Parameter	Description
Adapter	This integer specifies the number of the adapter for which you want to create a device. Usually, you specify D3DADAPTER_DEFAULT here, which gives you the primary display adapter.
DeviceType	This specifies the type of device you'd like to create. It can be one of several values (see the preceding bulleted list).
hFocusWindow	This specifies the window handle to which your Direct3D device corresponds. Usually, this is the window handle of your application's main window, but if you are using Direct3D in a child window (for example, a modeless dialog box), you put that window handle here.
BehaviorFlags	This allows you to specify some global behaviors for this device. Most of the behavior flags you won't ever use. The only significant ones are D3DCREATE_HARDWARE_VERTEXPROCESSING, D3DCREATE_MIXED_VERTEXPROCESSING, and D3DCREATE_SOFTWARE_VERTEXPROCESSING. You use one of these three flags to tell Direct3D whether you'd like to use hardware only, software only, or a combination of the two for your vertex processing.
pPresentationParameters	This is the address of a structure that specifies the presentation parameters you'd like to use for this device (screen width, height, number of back buffers, and the like). I'll talk more about this soon.
ppReturnedDeviceInterface	This specifies the address of a pointer that will contain your new IDirect3Ddevice interface, if everything goes well.

Table 6.2 The D3DPRESENT_PARAMETERS Structure Members

Member	Description
BackBufferWidth, BackBufferHeight	The desired width and height of your back buffer. If your app is running in full screen mode, these must correspond to a display resolution that your hardware can handle. For example, 640×480 is probably okay, but 326×267 isn't. (To figure out which display resolutions your hardware supports, use the EnumAdapterModes function of IDirect3D8.) If your application is running in a window, these values can be anything you want (up to the maximum size your hardware can support). If you put in a zero for either of these values, Direct3D will use the corresponding dimension of your window. For example, if your window is 450 pixels wide, passing zero as BackBufferWidth means that you'd like a back buffer that's also 450 pixels wide.
BackBufferFormat	The desired color format of your back buffer. This is where you specify not only the color depth—8-bit indexed (256-color) or 16-, 24-, 32-bit color—but also how the RGB color components will be crammed into the color bits. For example, in 16-bit color modes, some hardware uses a 5-6-5 format, meaning that there are 5 bits of red information, 6 bits of green, and 5 of blue. There are dozens of possible values here but not a good default value.

Table 6.2 Continued

Member	Description
	If you are running in full screen mode, you can choose any color mode that's supported by the hardware. You can use the CheckDeviceType method of IDirect3D8 to determine whether a card supports a given color format. That function will return DD_OK if the card supports it and DDERR_NOTAVAILABLE if it doesn't.
	If you are in windowed mode, you don't have a choice here. You must use the same color format as the desktop. The GetCurrentDisplayMode function tells you which mode the desktop is currently using; simply pass that information in here.
BackBufferCount	The number of back buffers you'd like. This can be 0, 1, 2, or 3.
	Usually, one back buffer does just fine, unless you'd like triple buffering (or more!)
	An important note: If you ask for too many back buffers, the CreateDevice method fails but puts the maximum number of back buffers the card supports into this value. Microsoft did things this way so that you can immediately call the function again and have it succeed (but with fewer back buffers).
MultiSampleType	Multisampling is a technique you can use to achieve motion blur, *anti-aliasing* (smoothing of rough edges), and a few other effects.
	If you want to use any of these effects, this is where you specify the number of samples you'd like, by using the enumerated types D3DMULTISAMPLE_2_SAMPLES through D3DMULTISAMPLE_16_SAMPLES.
	Usually, you don't need to do any multisampling, so just set this to D3DMULTISAMPLE_NONE.

Table 6.2 Continued

Member	Description
SwapEffect	This can be any one of several flags and specifies exactly what happens when you "flip" your back buffers to the front buffer (see the sidebar on computer displays).
	Most games use D3DSWAPEFFECT_DISCARD.
HDeviceWindow	This specifies the window where rendering will occur. Unless you're writing a multiple monitor application, put your main window handle in here.
Windowed	This is a Boolean value that specifies whether you are running in a window. Set it to true for windowed mode and false for full screen.
EnableAutoDepthStencil	Set this to true if you would like DirectX to manage your depth buffers automatically (more about these later).
	Most of the time, you won't want DirectX to do this, so set this to false.
AutoDepthStencilFormat	If you set EnableAutoDepthStencil to true, this is where you'd specify the format of your depth buffers.
Flags	Currently, you can specify only one flag here: D3DPRESENTFLAG_LOCKABLE_BACKBUFFER. You have to use this if you need to lock your back buffer. If you don't (as is most often the case), just put 0 here.
FullScreen_RefreshRateInHz	This specifies how often the display adapter refreshes the screen. The *Hz* means *per second*, so this is the number of times per second the adapter refreshes (that is, *75Hz* means 75 updates per second).

Table 6.2 Continued

Member	Description
	If you are in full screen mode, you can choose any rate your hardware supports. You can also specify D3DPRESENT_RATE_UNLIMITED to tell Direct3D to refresh as quickly as it can.
	If you are in windowed mode, you must put 0 here because the refresh rates of windowed applications are governed by the refresh rate of the desktop.
	Most of the time, you use the D3DPRESENT_RATE_DEFAULT value, which allows Direct3D to choose a suitable rate. This works well for both full screen and windowed games.
FullScreen_PresentationInterval	This specifies how quickly Direct3D presents your back buffer when you tell it to.
	If you're in windowed mode, you must set this to D3DPRESENT_INTERVAL_DEFAULT.
	Most of the time, D3DPRESENT_INTERVAL_DEFAULT is your best choice.

For the FullScreen_PresentationInterval parameter, you have the following choices in full screen mode:

- **D3DPRESENT_INTERVAL_IMMEDIATE.** Direct3D presents your back buffer immediately when you ask it to. It does not attempt to wait for vertical retrace.
- **D3DPRESENT_INTERVAL_ONE.** Direct3D waits for a vertical retrace period before presenting your new back buffer. Waiting for vertical retrace helps reduce shearing or tearing effects.
- **D3DPRESENT_INTERVAL_TWO, D3DPRESENT_INTERVAL_THREE, and D3DPRESENT_INTERVAL_FOUR.** Direct3D lets each frame of your game stay on the screen for two, three, or four vertical refresh periods.

If you're in windowed mode, you must set FullScreen_PresentationInterval to D3DPRESENT_INTERVAL_DEFAULT. Most of the time, this is your best choice.

As you can see, Direct3D offers you a lot of flexibility in deciding what kind of device to create.

Sample Program Reference

The Ch5p1_CreateDevice sample program demonstrates how to fill in the structure and properly call CreateDevice.

TIP

Most of these values can be safely set to their default values, and Microsoft made most of these default enumerations equate to a zero value. Therefore, you can easily zero the entire structure (using a quick call to the Windows API function ZeroMemory) and then just set the options that you need, like so:

```
// get desktop mode
D3DDISPLAYMODE d3ddm;
g_pD3D->GetAdapterDisplayMode(D3DADAPTER_DEFAULT, &d3ddm);

// create windowed device with that mode
D3DPRESENT_PARAMETERS d3dpp;
ZeroMemory( &d3dpp, sizeof(d3dpp) );
d3dpp.Windowed = TRUE;
d3dpp.SwapEffect = D3DSWAPEFFECT_DISCARD;
d3dpp.BackBufferFormat = d3ddm.Format;
```

You will see this "feature" used in many Direct3D sample applications provided with the DirectX SDK.

A Quick Lesson about Computer Displays

In case you're unfamiliar with the back buffer and vertical retrace, here's a crash course in the basics of how 3D hardware operates.

The screen is just a big region of memory. If you're in 640×480 mode, with 32-bit color, you use 4 bytes per pixel (1 for red, green, and blue values and 1 byte for extra information, which I'll talk about later), so the screen takes up about (4*640*480), or 1,228,800 bytes (about 1.2MB), of video memory. This chunk of memory is known as the *front buffer* because the contents of this memory are what's displayed to the user.

The display surface of your monitor is coated with three kinds of phosphors, which, when hit with the monitor's electron gun, emit light in three colors. The red phosphor emits red light, the green phosphor emits green light, and the blue phosphor emits blue light. (Each phosphor has slightly different chemical compositions, which give the phosphor its color.)

To present an image, your monitor starts at the upper-left corner, and your graphics card tells it how long to keep the gun on each of the red, green, and blue phosphors. An RGB value of (0,0,0) means that the gun doesn't hit any phosphors, which makes the pixel black. An RGB value of (0,0,255) means that the gun skips over the red and green phosphors but stays on the blue phosphor as long as possible, producing the brightest possible blue color. RGB (255,255,0) energizes the red and green phosphors as much as possible, producing the brightest possible yellow color.

After the gun hits all three RGB phosphors for that pixel, it moves 1 pixel to the right, and the process continues. When the gun gets to the rightmost pixel, it moves down one line and starts back at the left side of the screen (see Figure 6.2).

It progresses like this, left to right and top to bottom, until it finally finishes with the lower-right pixel. At that point, it moves back up to the top-left corner of the screen and prepares to start the whole process over again. It takes a few moments to move back, though. The time period when the gun is moving back to top-left and preparing to start over is known as the *vertical retrace period*. Note that at this time no pixels are being drawn—no phosphor is being excited.

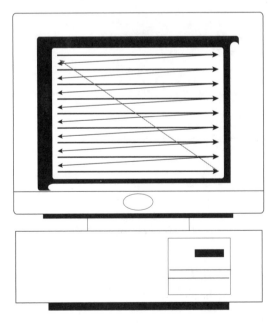

Figure 6.2

The path of your monitor's electron gun.

The number of times per second the gun refreshes the screen is called the *refresh rate*. This number is set by your graphics card and is usually somewhere between 60 and 85Hz. *Hz* is an abbreviation for *Hertz*, which means *per second*. In other words, the screen is being refreshed anywhere from 60 to 85 times per second.

That's how front buffer memory is rendered to the screen. Contrary to what you might think, however, most games don't draw directly to the front buffer. Doing so leads to an annoying flickering animation because you're messing with the buffer as the electron gun is trying to draw it. Instead, most games draw everything onto a *back buffer*, which is simply another chunk of memory (with the exact same dimensions as the front buffer) that *isn't* displayed on the screen. When they're finished drawing to the back buffer, they "present" the back buffer to the screen. This technique is called *double buffering*, and it's been in common use for many years (see Figure 6.3).

How exactly DirectGraphics goes about presenting your back buffer is an implementation detail you don't need to worry about. Depending on your graphics mode and 3D card, it might have to copy the back buffer memory onto the front buffer memory, or it can just tell your graphics card, "Hey, instead of drawing that chunk of memory to the screen, draw this chunk." (In other words,

Initially, your program displays the front buffer while rendering the next frame on the back buffer.

Front Buffer

Back Buffer

Figure 6.3

Double buffering in action.

When you're ready, you flip the front and back buffers. Ideally, the flip occurs while the monitor is in vertical retrace, so the animation is crisp.

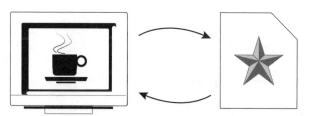

When the flip completes, what used to be on the front buffer is now on the back buffer, and vice versa. However, if you don't need the contents of the front buffer, DirectGraphics just gives you a new back buffer instead, which is sometimes faster.

DirectGraphics can tell your video card what range of memory it should treat as pixel data.) Regardless of how this is done, eventually the contents of the back buffer are presented to the front buffer.

The best time to present the back buffer is when the monitor is in *vertical retrace* (when the gun's moving back to the upper-left and no pixels are being drawn). If you present the back buffer at any other time, you end up with the top part of the screen displaying the old front buffer and the bottom part drawn using the newly presented buffer, which creates an unpleasant tearing effect. DirectGraphics has options you can use to tell it to present the back buffer only during a vertical retrace period.

You can have more than one back buffer, which is better because it allows your application to do less waiting. If you've told DirectGraphics to wait for the vertical retrace, and you have only one back buffer, when your program finishes rendering a frame of animation on the back buffer, it has to wait until the back buffer is presented before it can start rendering the next frame on a new back buffer. If you have two back buffers, however, when your program finishes rendering one back buffer, it can immediately begin drawing the next frame of animation on the second back buffer, while the first back buffer is waiting for the monitor to go into vertical retrace. This means that your game is never waiting for anything and therefore has more time to render cool effects! Having two back buffers is known as *triple buffering*. DirectGraphics calls the entire set of front and back buffers a *swap chain*.

DirectGraphics also includes options you can use to specify whether you care about the contents of the front buffer. Generally speaking, you shouldn't care about what's on the front buffer. Most of the time you re-render your entire screen on the back buffer, so there's no need to worry about what used to be on the screen. In this case, you can tell DirectGraphics to discard the front buffer, which helps make your application run faster.

Finding a Video Mode

Now that you've gone through the process of creating a device, look at how to enumerate (list) all the devices on the system.

Each Direct3D device supports one or more video modes. DirectGraphics defines a video mode as a combination of resolution, color depth, and refresh rate, so 800×600×16 at 65Hz is a differ-ent video mode than 800×600×16 at 85Hz.

To list all the available devices and video modes, follow this process:

1. Call the GetAdapterCount method of IDirect3D8 to determine the number of adapters on the system. Usually, the system has only one, unless multiple video cards are installed, or one video card supports dual monitors.

2. Loop from zero to the number of adapters. For each adapter, you do the following:

    2.1 Get its identifier by calling the `GetAdapterIdentifier` method of `IDirect3D8`. You will need this identifier later, when you tell DirectGraphics what adapter to use.

    2.2 Get the number of video modes the adapter supports by calling the `GetAdapterModeCount` method of the `IDirect3D8` interface.

    2.3 Loop from zero to the number of video modes. Call the `EnumAdapterModes` of `IDirect3D8`. Pass it the device ID and the index of your loop, and it will give you back a display mode. Evaluate this display mode to see whether it meets the needs of your application. If it does, stash this display mode in a *vector* (dynamic array) so that you can display it in a list to the user later.

3. You now have a list of adapters, and for each adapter, you have a list of the video modes it supports. Now all you have to do is decide on a video mode or, alternatively, present the entire list to the user and let him or her decide.

Most games display the list using two distinct list boxes. The first list box displays the available adapters. When the user selects an adapter, the second list box displays a list of all the video modes that adapter supports (see Figure 6.4).

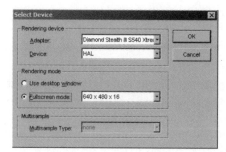

Figure 6.4

A typical GUI allowing the user to choose an adapter and a video mode.

I suppose that you could also use different GUI mechanisms, a tree view, perhaps, although I've never seen this done.

Lost Devices

DirectGraphics must be able to share the system's video card among multiple applications. After all, your user can, at any time, press Alt+Tab and switch to another application, which might need to use the same graphics card you're using.

This in itself isn't a problem, except that if you're a normal game, you have stuffed the graphics card memory full of textures and sprites to render your game and have set up the card with states and options for your game. Not only that, but the other DirectGraphics program probably wants to do the same thing. When the user switches programs, there's a good chance that upon returning to you, your graphics card will be filled with textures and options from another application.

> **TIP**
>
> If you've done any programming in previous versions of DirectX, you're probably familiar with lost surfaces. Lost devices are the DirectX 8 equivalent of lost surfaces in DirectX 7 and below.

This is what's known as a *lost device*. Essentially, it's a device that's had its data or state clobbered somehow. You can't do anything normal with lost devices; DirectGraphics prohibits you from using them to do rendering of any sort. The only thing you can do to a lost device is to *reset* it, which sets it back to a known state. After you do that, you can begin the process of reloading the textures and reconfiguring the card.

DirectGraphics is somewhat passive-aggressive about not letting you render to a lost device. When you call most DirectGraphics functions, they do *not* return an error code, even though they know that they're not doing what you asked them to. They pretend that everything's working, but they don't do anything. Only a handful of functions tell the truth by returning a D3DERR_DEVICELOST error code.

Microsoft implemented DirectGraphics this way so that you don't have to check for a lost device error code every single time you call a DirectGraphics function. The process of rendering a frame for your application can be very complex, and it's usually better if you just push through all that code, rather than constantly be on the lookout for lost devices. After all, if a device is lost, you can't Present anything anyway, so no one will see the half-drawn (or in some cases, completely undrawn) frame.

> **TIP**
>
> Six IDirect3DDevice8 methods can return D3DERR_DEVICELOST. Three of these methods—Present, TestCooperativeLevel, and Reset—are used when reclaiming a lost device.
>
> The three other IDirect3DDevice8 methods that can possibly return a D3DERR_DEVICELOST error code are UpdateTexture, CopyRects, and GetFrontBuffer. Microsoft made these methods "truthful" because if you're calling them, you're probably loading or saving a surface to or from disk. If the device is lost, you probably would not do whatever you're doing. An example of this would be a function that takes a screenshot by grabbing the pixels on the front buffer and writing them to disk. You wouldn't continue writing the screenshot file if you knew the device is lost (and the pixels on the front buffer are therefore garbage).

The best time to check for lost devices is when you call Present. Present is one of the few truthful DirectGraphics functions and returns a D3DERR_DEVICELOST error if you've lost the device.

Here are the steps you must take to reclaim a lost device:

1. Release all video memory you previously allocated. This means graphics memory only. You don't free up anything in the `D3DPOOL_MANAGED` or `D3DPOOL_SYSTEMMEM` memory classes. You do, however, release the following:
   - Any swap chains you created through the `CreateAdditionalSwapChain` method of `IDirect3DDevice8`
   - Any target-rendering surfaces you created through the `CreateRenderTarget` method of `IDirect3DDevice8`
   - Any depth stencil resources you created through the `CreateDepthStencilSurface` method of `IDirect3DDevice8`
   - Anything else in the `D3DPOOL_DEFAULT` memory class

2. Query the device to see whether you can reset it yet. There's a good chance you can't. For example, your full-screen game might still be in the background while the user is working on something else.

3. To see whether the device can be reset, call the `TestCooperativeLevel` method. If it returns `D3DERR_DEVICENOTRESET`, you can reset the device. If it returns `D3DERR_DEVICELOST`, you can't reset the device yet. (By the way, if it returns `D3D_OK`, the card is good to go—it isn't lost and doesn't need to be reset.)

4. If you can't reset the device, your application should wait and try not to use many CPU cycles, because the user is doing other things.

5. When you can, call the `Reset` method of `IDirect3DDevice8`, which resets the device to an initial state. `Reset` fails if you haven't freed all the memory you allocated, as described in step 1.

6. Set up the card again. The easiest way to do this is to call the same function you called when your game first started, to set the resolution, swap chain, depth buffer, and the like.

7. Re-create and/or reload anything you had to free in step 1.

Yes, I know, it's a big pain, but it's a necessary evil. Fortunately, it's not as big a pain as in previous versions of DirectX. In DirectX 8, you need to check for a lost device only when you call `Present`. In older versions, you have to check the return value of practically every method to make sure that things are still okay.

Switching between Devices (Full Screen to Windowed)

If you want, you can give users the option to switch devices as the game is running. For example, they could press pause and select a new video mode, or they could press Alt+Enter to switch from windowed to full screen.

Dealing with this situation is no different from dealing with a lost device. When users ask for a mode switch, you do everything you would do if the device were lost.

You start by freeing up your memory. You have to free everything because you're going to eventually release the device interface. After you free the memory, release the original device, create the new one, and set it up as if it were lost. Finally, reload all the stuff you had to free up.

The only difference here is that instead of calling Reset, as you would for a lost device, you are releasing one device and creating another.

YOUR FIRST 3D PROGRAM

Now that you know everything about how devices and video modes work, it's time to put them to use. This section explains the process for getting a simple 3D scene up and running. Figure 6.5 shows the final scene.

Figure 6.5

A screenshot of your first 3D scene!

Flex Those Vertices

The core of a 3D game is the vertex. All the glorious 3D worlds, all the astounding explosion and water effects, they all start with vertices. It's very important that you intimately understand the details of working with vertices. Pay careful attention to this section.

When it comes to vertices, different applications care about vastly different things. A 2D game that uses Direct3D simply to render 2D scenes does not care about model space and world space; it prefers to hand Direct3D screen coordinates. Conversely, a program that renders a complex 3D world wants to hand Direct3D all sorts of information about a vertex, not only its position in world space but also its normal (for lighting calculations), material, color, and the like.

It would be mean of Direct3D to force the simple 2D application to deal with more than it wants, and it would be silly to dumb down the vertex information and make the complex 3D application calculate things. The only good solution is to let each application decide how much vertex information it's going to give to Direct3D.

Cue heroic music, and enter flexible vertex formats from stage left. The flexible vertex format capabilities of Direct3D enable you, the application using Direct3D, to dictate what information is contained in a vertex.

Describing Your Vertex Format

You describe your vertex structure using a combination of several *flexible vertex format flags*, which tell Direct3D what your structure looks like. Note that you don't have any freedom about the *order* of the information inside your vertex structure; you must conform to Direct3D's order definition. No big deal because sane 3D programmers don't care what the order of the information inside a given vertex is as long as it's documented and adhered to (which it is).

Table 6.3 shows the order to which your vertex structure must adhere.

Table 6.3 Vertex Structure Members and Associated Flags

Vertex Attribute	Data Type	Flag(s) to Tell Direct3D It's There	Description
Position	3 floats (x,y,z)	D3DFVF_XYZ (untransformed) D3DFVF_XYZRHW (transformed)	The position of the vertex either in model space (if untransformed) or screen space (if transformed).
RHW-transformed vertices only	1 float	If you specify D3DFVF_XYZRHW, you must have an RHW float value at this point in your structure.	The w coordinate is used in the 3D pipeline to project your vertices onto the screen properly.
Blending weight data 1 through blending weight data 5	1–5 floats*	D3DFVF_XYZB1 through D3DFVF_XYZB5, depending on how many you want	Weighting (beta) values to use for multimatrix vertex-blending operations.
Vertex normal (untransformed vertices only)	3 floats (x,y,z)	D3DFVF_NORMAL	The vertex's normal. Note that transformed vertices can't have normals.

Table 6.3 Continued

Vertex Attribute	Data Type	Flag(s) to Tell Direct3D It's There	Description
Vertex point size	1 float	D3DFVF_PSIZE	The point size of the vertex. For transformed vertices, this is specified in pixels; for untransformed vertices, it's in camera space units.
Diffuse color	DWORD (RGBA)	D3DFVF_DIFFUSE	The diffuse color of the vertex, in RGBA format (1 byte each for red, green, blue, and alpha values).
Specular color	DWORD (RGBA)	D3DFVF_SPECULAR	The specular color of the vertex. The same RGBA format as for diffuse color.
Texture coordinate set 1 through texture coordinate set 5	(1, 2, 3, or 4 floats)	D3DFVF_TXT0 through D3DFVF_TXT8 D3DFVF_TEXCOORDSIZE2(n), D3DFVF_TEXCOORDSIZE3(n), or D3DFVF_TEXCOORDSIZE4(n)	Tells Direct3D how many sets the vertex contains. Tells Direct3D how many coordinates there are for each set using D3DFVF_TEXCOORDSIZE1(n), where n is the set ID (1–8).

* The last float can be an integer if you specify D3DFVF_LASTBETA_UBYTE4.

Each vertex can be linked with as many as eight texture coordinate sets. Each texture coordinate set can be 1–4 floats, allowing for 1D, 2D, 3D, or 4D (!!!) textures.

Usually, you use 2D textures and only one coordinate set, unless you're doing multitexturing, which I talk about in Chapter 9, "Advanced Texturing."

TIP

A cool trick is to wrap up all these flexible vertex flags into one #define, like so:

```
// Your custom FVF describes your custom vertex structure:
#define MYCUSTOMVERTEX (D3DFVF_XYZRHW|D3DFVF_DIFFUSE)
```

Then, simply use `MYCUSTOMVERTEX` **wherever Direct3D needs your vertex format, for example, in your call to** `CreateVertexBuffer`:

```
g_pd3dDevice->CreateVertexBuffer(
  3*sizeof(CUSTOMVERTEX), 0,
  MYCUSTOMVERTEX, D3DPOOL_DEFAULT, &g_pVB );
```

This trick makes everybody happy. Direct3D is happy because it gets the flags it needs for your vertex format, and you're happy because you save a few keystrokes. If you need to change the vertex format later, you have to edit only one line of code.

Transformed versus Untransformed Vertex Formats

Your application can use either transformed or untransformed vertices. Most 3D games use untransformed and unlit vertices. Direct3D uses its pipeline to transform the vertices from model space into screen space and to light the vertices based on their normals. Direct3D calls these vertices *untransformed* because when you pump them into Direct3D, they haven't been transformed into screen coordinates.

You can also choose to use transformed vertices, in which case Direct3D does no processing on your vertex data. It assumes that you have already put vertex data into screen space, so all it does is rasterize the triangles those vertices specify. With transformed vertices, your application must manually process, light, and clip the vertices, if necessary.

TIP

In case you're curious, many 2D applications use transformed vertices, so they can use the 3D hardware only to "blit" things to the screen. In other words, they don't care about model, world, or view space. They just want a textured triangle to appear at a certain position on the screen.

Direct3D deduces whether your vertices are transformed or untransformed by looking at the D3DFVF_ flags you give it. If you specify D3DFVF_XYZ, D3DFVF_XYZBn, or D3DFVF_NORMAL in your vertex format, Direct3D assumes that you're using untransformed and unlit vertices. The presence of these flags causes Direct3D to transform and light your vertices.

If you specify D3DFVF_XYZRHW, you tell Direct3D that you're using transformed vertices. In other words, you tell it that you will be doing your own transformations to get the vertices to screen space and that all it should do is render triangles.

Texture Coordinates in Flexible Vertex Formats

The last column of Table 6.3 needs a little explaining. If you don't know the basics of texturing, though, now is probably not a good time to read the following paragraphs. Learn the basics by reading the Chapters 8 and 9, and then hop back here. Otherwise, this will make little to no sense.

Direct3D is especially flexible when it comes to texture coordinates. It allows you to specify any-where between zero and eight texture coordinate sets for each vertex. This means that your ver-tex can be linked to as many as eight textures.

Each texture can have between one and four dimensions. Most of the time, textures are 2D, so you have two coordinates, usually referred to as u and v. Occasionally, though, you need a 3D or 1D texture. The 4D texture, like a Unicorn or a Crystal Dragon, exists only in the wild imaginations of game programmers everywhere. You will probably never see or use one, but it's there just in case.

To tell Direct3D about your textures, you use a flag, which specifies the number of texture coordinate sets you have, and a macro, which specifies how many dimensions each texture coordinate set has.

> **TIP**
>
> You will learn a more practical reason for using four sets of texture coordinates when you get to Chapter 10, "Vertex and Pixel Shaders."

The D3DFVF_TXT0 through D3DFVF_TXT8 flags tell Direct3D how many sets you have. For example, if you were using two textures per vertex, you'd use the D3DFVF_TXT2 flag.

You use the D3DFVF_TEXCOORDSIZE1(n) through D3DFVF_TEXCOORDSIZE4 to tell Direct3D how many dimensions compose each texture coordinate set. The parameters are backwards from what you'd expect. You'd expect to specify the coordinate set first, followed by the number of dimen-sions, but what you actually do is specify the number of dimensions first, followed by the ID of the texture set (1–8).

Say that you have two texture sets. The first texture set is 1D, and the second is 3D. You'd use D3DFVF_TEXCOORDSIZE1(0) | D3DFVF_TXTCOORDSIZE3(1). The first part of the Boolean OR tells

Direct3D that texture set index 0 (your first texture set) is 1D (has a texture coordinate size of 1); the second half tells Direct3D that texture set index 1 (the second texture set) is 3D (has a texture coordinate size of 3).

It's a weird thing to understand at first. Just be careful that you don't flip-flop the set ID with the number of dimensions—dimensions first, set ID last.

Sample Vertex Formats

This whole flexible vertex format business is a lot to take in at one time, especially if you're new to 3D programming. To help ease the pain, the following are common vertex formats, along with their associated FVF flags.

Here is a basic untransformed, unlit vertex structure with two texture coordinates:

```
typedef struct _UNLITVERTEX
{
  float x, y, z;      // position
  float nx, ny, nz;   // normal
  DWORD Diffuse;      // diffuse color
  float tu1, tv1;     // texture coords
  float tu2, tv2;
} UNLITVERTEX, *LPUNLITVERTEX;
```

Here are the corresponding flags for that structure:

```
        D3DFVF_XYZ |
        D3DFVF_NORMAL |   D3DFVF_DIFFUSE |
        D3DFVF_TXT2 |
        D3DFVF_TEXCOORDSIZE2(0) |
        D3DFVF_TEXCOORDSIZE2(1)
```

This is a simple untransformed, unlit vertex structure with no texture information but a color and a normal for Gouraud shading:

```
typedef struct
{
  float x, y, z;      // position
  float nx, ny, nz;   // normal
  DWORD Diffuse;      // diffuse color
} UNLITGOURAUDVERTEX;
```

This structure requires the following flags:

```
D3DFVF_XYZ |
D3DFVF_NORMAL | D3DFVF_DIFFUSE
```

The following is a very simple transformed vertex structure with one texture coordinate. A 2D game might use something like this:

```
typedef struct
{
  float x, y, z;      // scrn position
  float rhw;          // rhw
  float tu1, tv1;     // texture coords
} UNLITGOURAUDVERTEX;
```

The flags for this structure are as follows:

```
D3DFVF_XYZRHW |
D3DFVF_TXT1 |
D3DFVF_TEXCOORDSIZE2(0)
```

Vertex Buffers

Vertex buffer is a fancy term for a chunk of system memory (or graphics memory) that contains your vertex data. Usually, you have one vertex buffer for each model. All the model's vertices are stored in the vertex buffer (see Figure 6.6).

Vertex buffers are useful because they allow you to reuse transformed geometry. You perform the vertex calculations once and then use those results as many times as you like.

Creating a Vertex Buffer

Because vertex buffers are accessed through the IDirect3DVertexBuffer8 interface, creating a vertex buffer also means creating an IDirect3DVertexBuffer8 interface. To accomplish this, use the CreateVertexBuffer method of IDirect3DDevice8 (see Table 6.4):

```
HRESULT CreateVertexBuffer(
  UINT Length,
  DWORD Usage,
  DWORD FVF,
  D3DPOOL Pool,
  IDirect3DVertexBuffer8** ppVertexBuffer
);
```

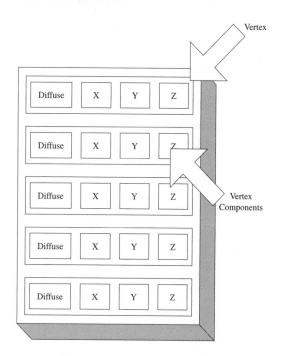

Figure 6.6

You store your model's vertices in the vertex buffer.

Table 6.4 The CreateVertexBuffer Parameters

Parameter	Description
Length	This specifies the size of the vertex buffer, in bytes. Usually, you set this to the size of your custom vertex structure, multiplied by the number of vertices to store. For example, to store four vertices, you could say sizeof(MYCUSTOMVERTEX)*4.
Usage	This set of flags indicates what the vertex buffer will be used for.
FVF	This set of flexible vertex flags describes the format of the vertex structures stored in this buffer. Be slick! Use your #defined set of flags here!
Pool	This specifies the memory pool in which Direct3D should store the vertex buffer.
ppVertexBuffer	This specifies an address of a pointer that will contain the new IDirect3DVertexBuffer8 interface.

The Usage parameter flags include

- **D3DUSAGE_DONOTCLIP.** Specifies that the vertex buffer content will never require clipping.
- **D3DUSAGE_DYNAMIC.** If this flag is specified, Direct3D usually places the vertex buffer in AGP memory.
- **D3DUSAGE_RTPATCHES.** Indicates that the vertex buffer will be used for drawing high order primitives.
- **D3DUSAGE_NPATCHES.** Indicates that the vertex buffer will be used for drawing N patches.
- **D3DUSAGE_POINTS.** Indicates that the vertex buffer will be used for drawing point sprites or indexed point lists.
- **D3DUSAGE_SOFTWAREPROCESSING.** Specifies that the vertices in the buffer will be processed in software.
- **D3DUSAGE_WRITEONLY.** Specifies that your program will never read from the vertex buffer (if Direct3D knows this, it can make optimizations about where in memory to place your vertex buffer). Note that if you try to read from a buffer that has D3DUSAGE_WRITEONLY, the read will fail.

The Pool parameters include

- **D3DPOOL_DEFAULT.** Tells Direct3D to choose the best possible location for this vertex buffer. It can be in graphics or system memory, depending on the amount of free memory and the specified usage of the vertex buffer.
- **D3DPOOL_MANAGED.** Tells Direct3D to manage whether this vertex buffer is in system or graphics memory. Direct3D moves things in the managed memory pool in or out of graphics memory as needed.
- **D3DPOOL_SYSTEMMEM.** Tells Direct3D to put the vertex buffer in system memory (normal RAM).

Usually, you use the D3DPOOL_MANAGED, for a variety of reasons but most notably because it frees you from having to deal with devices being lost. Direct3D automatically "rescues" resources that it manages when a device is lost. For more information, see the section on losing devices.

CreateVertexBuffer returns D3D_OK if all goes well.

> **TIP**
>
> **If you're using more than one device simultaneously, note that vertex buffers are valid only for the device that created them.**

Filling It Up

After you create a vertex buffer, you usually load it with vertex data. For your sample program, you want to load your new vertex buffer with the vertices that specify the triangle you're trying to render.

Filling a vertex buffer is a three-step process:

1. Lock the vertex buffer by calling the Lock method of IDirect3DVertexBuffer8. Locking a vertex buffer tells Direct3D not to move it around in memory or do any other strange things, because you're currently working with its contents.
2. Lock returns a pointer to a chunk of memory. Load your vertices into this memory using memcpy.
3. Unlock the vertex buffer by calling the Unlock method, which tells Direct3D that you're finished manipulating the vertex buffer's contents.

Look at the Lock method first (see Table 6.5):

```
HRESULT Lock(
  UINT OffsetToLock,
  UINT SizeToLock,
  BYTE** ppbData,
  DWORD Flags
);
```

Table 6.5 The Lock Parameters

Parameter	Description
OffsetToLock	This specifies the offset into the vertex data, in bytes, at which you want to start the lock. This is useful if you're modifying a certain section of a vertex buffer, but most of the time you specify zero here because you want to lock the whole thing.
SizeToLock	The number of bytes you want to lock. Usually, you specify zero here as well, which tells Direct3D to lock the entire buffer.
ppbData	The address of a pointer that will contain the current vertex data when the call returns.
Flags	These clue Direct3D in about what you're doing:

Here are the flags you can use for the Flags parameter:

- **D3DLOCK_DISCARD.** Tells Direct3D that you will be overwriting the *entire* contents of this buffer. If Direct3D knows this, it can just allocate new memory (and then delete the original vertex memory when you unlock) without having to copy anything, rather than bother with preserving the actual vertex buffer memory.
- **D3DLOCK_NOOVERWRITE.** Use this if you're only going to append vertex data to the buffer. This flag tells Direct3D that you won't touch any vertex that has already been used in a drawing call since the start of the frame, or the last lock without this flag. If Direct3D knows this, it can take measures to speed things up.
- **D3DLOCK_NOSYSLOCK.** Use this if you're going to be holding the lock for a long time. Specifying this flag makes the lock process slower but allows the system to do other things (for example, update the mouse cursor) while you have the buffer locked.
- **D3DLOCK_READONLY.** Lets Direct3D know that you will only be reading from the vertex buffer, not changing its contents. This allows Direct3D to make some optimizations so that things go as quickly as possible. Note that this flag cannot be used in combination with the D3DLOCK_DISCARD flag nor on a vertex buffer created with the D3DUSAGE_WRITEONLY flag.

Lock returns D3D_OK if everything goes okay.

TIP

Try to use as many D3DLOCK flags as you can because specifying these flags helps speed up your application.

CAUTION

Many a 3D programmer hath been slain by the "I forgot to unlock my vertex buffer" dragon. Tread wisely. Always make sure that you unlock something when you're done with it.

Also, always make sure that the Lock method is successful—in other words, that you have valid memory in the first place—before changing the vertex buffer contents.

The Unlock method is much simpler; it takes no arguments. Just call it, and the vertex buffer is unlocked. It also returns D3D_OK if everything goes okay.

To be totally sure that you understand the process, here is some code that creates a three-vertex buffer and fills it with data:

```
CUSTOMVERTEX g_Vertices[] = {
    { 150.0f,  50.0f, 0.5f, 1.0f, 0xffff0000, }, // x, y, z, rhw, color
    { 250.0f, 250.0f, 0.5f, 1.0f, 0xff00ff00, },
    {  50.0f, 250.0f, 0.5f, 1.0f, 0xff00ffff, },
};
```

```
// Create the vertex buffer.
if(FAILED(g_pd3dDevice->CreateVertexBuffer(3*sizeof(CUSTOMVERTEX),
  0, D3DFVF_CUSTOMVERTEX, D3DPOOL_DEFAULT, &g_pVB))) return E_FAIL;

VOID* pVertices = NULL;

// lock the VB
if(FAILED(g_pVB->Lock(0, sizeof(g_Vertices), (BYTE**)&pVertices, 0)))
  return E_FAIL;

// copy the data
memcpy(pVertices, g_Vertices, sizeof(g_Vertices));

// unlock the VB
g_pVB->Unlock();
```

Setting Up the Matrices

Before you can render a frame of your scene, you have to set up the world, view, and projection matrices. Keep in mind that when you're rendering a real 3D scene (more complex than just one triangle!), you have many world transformation matrices—one for each model in your world.

CAUTION

When you call SetTransform to change the world or view matrices, Direct3D must go through many calculations because it attaches several internal structures to these matrices. It's expensive to call SetTransform to set the world or view matrix thousands of times per frame.

One way you can minimize this speed hit is by concatenating your world and view matrices together and then passing the concatenated matrix as a world matrix and passing an identity matrix for the view matrix. That way, your view matrix always stays the same, reducing the number of times you have to call SetTransform. You keep the real world and view matrices in memory, and when one needs to change, you change it, reconcatenate, and call SetTransform again.

Of course, this makes things harder to read and understand, and that's why I, along with Microsoft, have chosen *not* to implement this optimization in any of the sample programs.

(Remember, the world transformation matrices tell Direct3D how to take a model's vertices and convert them to world vertices.) You still have only one view and projection matrix.

To set a matrix, call the `SetTransform` method of the `IDirect3DDevice8` interface:

```
HRESULT SetTransform(
  D3DTRANSFORMSTATETYPE State,
  CONST D3DMATRIX* pMatrix
);
```

Table 6.6 lists the parameters for `SetTransform`.

The most common values for the `State` parameter are

- **D3DTS_VIEW.** Tells DirectGraphics that you're setting the view matrix.
- **D3DTS_PROJECTION.** Tells DirectGraphics that you're setting the projection matrix.
- **D3DTS_WORLD.** Tells DirectGraphics that you're setting the world matrix.

Table 6.6 The SetTransform Parameters

Parameter	Description
State	Specifies which matrix you're setting—view, world, projection, and so on.
pMatrix	A pointer to the matrix you'd like to use for the given state.

The Seven Steps to Rendering Your Triangle

At long last, now that you have the matrices set up, you can finally render your triangle! Here's the process:

1. Clear your back buffer by calling the `Clear` method of `IDirect3DDevice8`.
2. Call `BeginScene` to indicate to Direct3D that you're starting commands to render a scene.
3. Set the source of the data stream to the address of the vertex buffer you want to render. This is accomplished via a call to the `SetStreamSource` method of `IDirect3DDevice8`.
4. Set the vertex shader by calling `SetVertexShader`. This tells Direct3D what data your custom vertices contain.

5. Call `DrawPrimitive` to render the vertices using the data stream and vertex shader you set up in steps 3 and 4.

6. Call `EndScene` to let Direct3D know that you've finished issuing commands to draw the scene and that it should now begin the rasterization process.

7. Present the back buffer by calling `Present`.

Now, take a look at each of those steps in detail.

Clearing the Back Buffer

The `Clear` method of `IDirect3DDevice8` clears the screen (or a series of rectangles on the screen), along with the depth buffer and the stencil buffer. `Clear` takes a few parameters (see Table 6.7):

```
HRESULT Clear(
  DWORD Count,
  CONST D3DRECT* pRects,
  DWORD Flags,
  D3DCOLOR Color,
  float Z,
  DWORD Stencil
);
```

At least one of the following flags must be used for the `Flags` parameter:

- **D3DCLEAR_STENCIL.** Tells Direct3D to clear the stencil buffer to the value in the `Stencil` parameter.
- **D3DCLEAR_TARGET.** Tells Direct3D to clear the render target to the color in the `Color` parameter.
- **D3DCLEAR_ZBUFFER.** Tells Direct3D to clear the depth buffer to the value in the `Z` parameter.

> **CAUTION**
>
> Be careful about which flags you specify. If you try to make `Clear` wipe out a stencil buffer or a depth buffer that doesn't exist, the method will fail.

Most of the time, you use `D3DCLEAR_TARGET`, along with the `Color` parameter, to tell Direct3D to clear the screen to a certain color. Occasionally, you also combine `D3DCLEAR_TARGET` with `D3DCLEAR_ZBUFFER` or `D3DCLEAR_STENCIL` to wipe the Z and stencil buffers.

Beginning the Scene

You begin the process of rendering the scene by calling the `BeginScene` method of `IDirect3DDevice8`. This method takes no parameters. It simply tells Direct3D that you are now going to send it vertex data, state changes, and the like, for drawing your scene.

> **CAUTION**
>
> Always remember to call `EndScene` after you call `BeginScene`. Otherwise, things will not work.

Table 6.7 The Clear Parameters

Parameter	Description
Count	If you want to clear only certain areas of the screen, this specifies the number of rectangles in the pRects array. Put zero here to clear the whole screen.
pRects	This is a pointer to an array of D3DRECT structures that tell Direct3D which areas of the screen you want to clear. Specify NULL here to clear the entire viewport rectangle.
Flags	The flags indicate which surfaces should be cleared.
Color	This specifies the color you want to clear to. Direct3D wants a 32-bit value that contains RGBA (red, green, blue, and alpha) information. You can use the D3DCOLOR_XRGB macro to specify a color with an alpha value of 0xFF. Usually, you set this to D3DCOLOR_XRGB(0,0,0) to create a black background.
Z	This specifies the new value that the depth buffer should contain. Valid values are anywhere between 0.0 and 1.0, with 0.0 being closest to the viewer and 1.0 being the farthest away. If you choose to use depth buffers, you usually clear them to 1.0.
Stencil	This specifies the integer value to store in each stencil-buffer entry. This can be anywhere between 0 and the maximum value the stencil buffer can hold. Usually, you set this to zero.

Setting the Stream

The IDirect3DDevice8 method SetStreamSource allows you to attach a vertex buffer to one of several input streams. DirectGraphics uses these input streams when you call DrawPrimitive (see Figure 6.7).

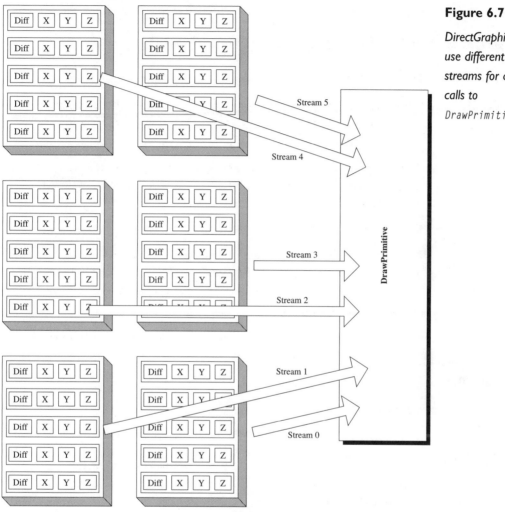

Figure 6.7

DirectGraphics can use different input streams for different calls to `DrawPrimitive`.

Generally, unless you're writing your own vertex shaders or doing other advanced programming, you attach your vertex buffer to stream zero:

```
HRESULT SetStreamSource(
  UINT StreamNumber,
  IDirect3DVertexBuffer8* pStreamData,
  UINT Stride
);
```

Table 6.8 shows the parameters SetStreamSource takes.

Table 6.8 The SetStreamSource Parameters

Parameter	Description
StreamNumber	Specifies the data stream to which you'd like to attach the vertex buffer. This can be anywhere from zero to the maximum number of streams, one, but generally you set it to zero.
pStreamData	This is a pointer to an IDirect3DVertexBuffer8 interface that tells Direct3D the vertex buffer you'd like bound to the stream.
Stride	This tells Direct3D the size of each vertex in the vertex buffer. You must make sure that this size value is the same as the size of your custom vertex structure, that is, sizeof(MYCUSTOMVERTEX).

Setting the Vertex Shader

Next, you call the SetVertexShader method of IDirect3DDevice8:

```
HRESULT SetVertexShader(
  DWORD Handle
);
```

The Handle parameter can be one of two things: a handle to a custom vertex shader you've created or, if you'd like to use the default vertex shader, an FVF code, that is, a combination of flexible vertex format flags.

Most of the time, you specify your #defined vertex FVF flags here.

Ending the Scene

When you're finished with all your DrawPrimitive calls, you call EndScene to tell Direct3D that you're done. At this point, Direct3D and the 3D hardware work their magic to render your scene onto the back buffer.

TIP

Even though it's possible, you should try to avoid having more than one BeginScene/EndScene block for each frame of animation. At the very least, it's a speed hit, and certain cards have trouble coping with applications that use two or more blocks for each frame of animation.

Presenting the Screen

After you call EndScene, the next step is to present your back buffer to the screen. You do this by calling the Present method of IDirect3DDevice8 (see Table 6.9):

```
HRESULT Present(
  CONST RECT* pSourceRect,
  CONST RECT* pDestRect,
  HWND hDestWindowOverride,
  CONST RGNDATA* pDirtyRegion
);
```

You virtually always specify NULL for these parameters.

Table 6.9 The Present Parameters

Parameter	Description
pSourceRect	This specifies the area of the screen you want to present. This is valid only if your swap chain was created with D3DSWAPEFFECT_COPY or D3DSWAPEFFECT_COPY_VSYNC. That is, it makes sense to specify a source rectangle only if your present technique involves copying a section of memory from somewhere into screen memory.
pDestRect	Same situation. This is valid only for D3DSWAPEFFECT_COPY and D3DSWAPEFFECT_COPY_VSYNC, in which case, it specifies the destination rectangle of the presentation, in client coordinates.
hDestWindowOverride	You can override the target for the presentation by specifying a new window handle here. Otherwise, specify NULL, and Direct3D will present to the window you gave it when creating the device.
pDirtyRegion	This is currently not used and should always be set to NULL.

First 3D Program Wrap-Up

You've just walked through the process a typical 3D game goes through to set up and render its scenes. Granted, you weren't rendering a very complex scene—you had only one triangle—but the process remains the same regardless of how complex your scene is. Most of the time, the only variation is that you do more between BeginScene and EndScene.

> ### Sample Program Reference
> The Ch6p2_FirstScene program contains all the code talked about here.

FADING IN, FADING OUT, FLASHING COLOR—THE GAMMA CONTROLS

Because this is a book on special effects, I couldn't let this chapter go by without explaining how to do a fade in and fade out. No, they're not the most "special" of effects, but they are useful and very easy to accomplish, thanks to the DirectGraphics gamma controls. Here's your first special effect!

Every swap chain you create has three gamma controls attached to it, which allow you to amplify or reduce the red, green, and blue components of the front buffer. This enables you to "tint" the image without changing the pixels themselves. For example, when your player's character takes a hit, you could flash the screen red, Quake-style. Think of the gamma controls as filters that are applied to the image as it hits the screen.

Determining Whether Your 3D Card Supports Gamma Controls

First things first. To determine whether the device you're running on supports gamma controls, you call the GetDeviceCaps method of the IDirect3DDevice8 interface. Perform a Boolean AND on the Caps2 member using the values D3DCAPS2_FULLSCREENGAMMA and D3DCAPS2_CANCALIBRATEGAMMA to see whether the device supports gamma controls. Most cards nowadays support gamma controls, but you can never be too careful.

Gamma Ramps

The gamma controls work using gamma ramps. DirectGraphics supplies three gamma ramps, one each for the red, green, and blue intensity of the swap chain. An individual gamma ramp is nothing more than a 256-byte array of WORDs that tell DirectGraphics how to map incoming color intensities to outgoing ones. The array index correlates to the incoming color intensity; the value of the WORD at that index tells DirectGraphics the outbound color intensity (see Figure 6.8).

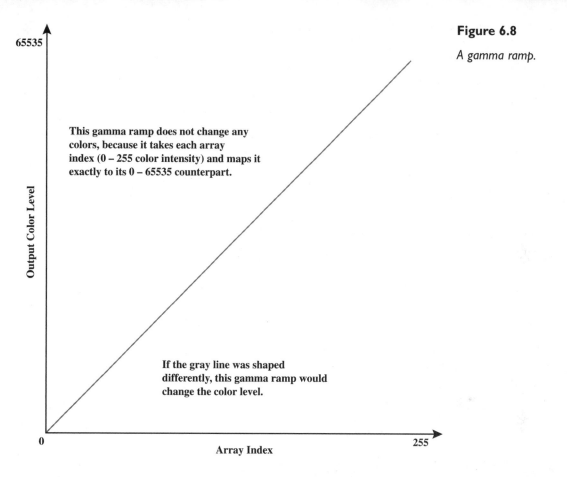

Figure 6.8

A gamma ramp.

65535

This gamma ramp does not change any
colors, because it takes each array
index (0 – 255 color intensity) and maps it
exactly to its 0 – 65535 counterpart.

Output Color Level

If the gray line was shaped
differently, this gamma ramp would
change the color level.

0

Array Index

255

For each pixel in the frame buffer, DirectGraphics takes that incoming pixel's red, green, and blue intensities and converts them to a value between 0 and 255, with 255 being the brightest possible intensity. It then uses those values as indices into the red, green, and blue gamma ramp arrays and looks at the WORDs in those arrays to determine what the incoming intensities change to. It takes the value of the WORDs (which can be anywhere from 0 to 65535) and converts them back into color intensities, which it displays on the screen.

Take a look at the example in Figure 6.9. You have a pixel whose color is RGB value (5,50,125). In this case, DirectGraphics looks at the WORD at position [5] in the red ramp, [50] in the green ramp, and [125] in the blue ramp. You've set up your gamma ramps so that element [5] in the red ramp contains 2570, [50] in the green ramp contains 25700, and [125] in the blue ramp contains 64250. This means that after DirectGraphics looks up the new values in the gamma ramp, your color becomes (2570, 25700, 64250). Remember, this is on a 0–65535 scale now because the gamma ramp is made of WORDs.

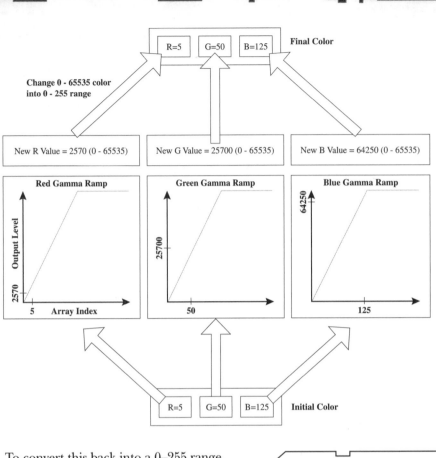

Figure 6.9

How DirectGraphics uses the gamma ramps to adjust a pixel's color.

To convert this back into a 0–255 range, divide each color component by 65,535 and multiply by 255. Converting (2570, 25700, 64250) back to the 0–255 range yields (10, 100, 250), which means that your color will come out on the screen twice as bright as it started. By changing the numbers in the gamma ramp array, you can brighten, darken, or tint the screen.

TIP

It seems counterintuitive to have the range of gamma ramp output be 0 to 65535, instead of just 0 to 255. However, having the larger range enables you to perform very slow fade ins and fade outs while still using integers (you will see what I mean in a second).

Fading In

To fade in, you make all the values of all the gamma ramps start at 0. This makes the screen totally black because every color is converted to (0,0,0). Then, you render the image into which you want to fade and present it to the front buffer (again, it isn't displayed because your ramps are all 0).

Then, slowly add 1 to each array element in each gamma ramp until that element's value is equal to its index (see Figure 6.10). When all the array values are equal to their indices, no colors are changed—a pixel of color (10,20,30) ends up on the screen as (10,20,30). At that point, you've faded in.

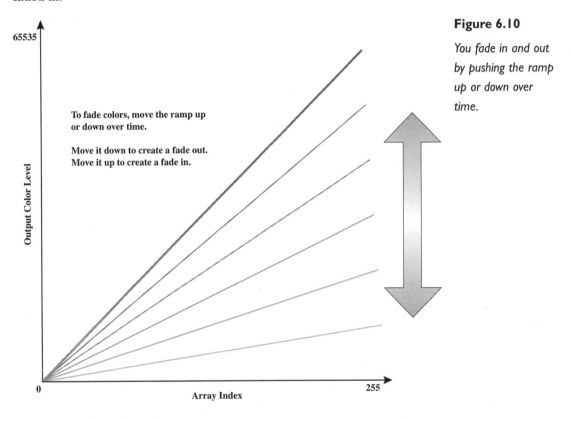

Figure 6.10

You fade in and out by pushing the ramp up or down over time.

To fade colors, move the ramp up or down over time.

Move it down to create a fade out.
Move it up to create a fade in.

Fading Out

Fading out is just like fading in, only you subtract 1 rather than add. For faster fades, you add or subtract 2 or 3, instead of 1 (refer to Figure 6.10).

TIP

For very slow fades, you might have to represent your gamma ramp levels as floats. To send them to DirectGraphics, make a copy of the float gamma array. Then convert the copy to WORD values, and pass *those* to DirectGraphics (not your original float array—that always stays floating point). This method enables you to specify steps less than 1 to achieve very subtle fades.

Fading to Other Colors

To fade to another color, go through the same process, only instead of adding or subtracting 1, add whatever values are necessary to interpolate between original color and destination color.

For example, if you wanted to fade to red, you'd add to the red ramp and subtract from the blue and green ramps. To fade to any arbitrary color, for each component of the color, first figure out how you want the gamma ramps to be when you're finished fading. Then, for each element of each gamma ramp array, determine the *delta* (difference) between what the value of the element is now and what you want it to be. Divide that value by the number of times you are going to set the gamma ramp. This gives you a "step" value for each element, which you will probably store as a floating-point number because it's possible that you will need a value between 0 and 1. For example, if the element has to go from 25 to 35 over 20 ramp sets, that's a delta of 10 over 20 iterations, which means that you add only 0.5 to it each time.

You also store an array of float values as your actual gamma ramps and convert them to integers (round them) right before you call the DirectGraphics routine—rather than try to add, say, 0.3 to an integer and then wonder why the integer doesn't ever change (answer: It keeps getting rounded down).

Getting the Gamma Ramp

The `IDirect3DDevice8` interface has two methods, `GetGammaRamp` and `SetGammaRamp`, which allow you to manipulate the gamma controls.

Look at `GetGammaRamp` first:

```
void GetGammaRamp(
  D3DGAMMARAMP* pRamp
);
```

> **TIP**
>
> This is a change from DirectX 7, where the gamma has its own separate interface.

`pRamp` is a pointer to a `D3DGAMMARAMP` structure, which looks like this:

```
typedef struct _D3DGAMMARAMP {
    WORD red  [256];
    WORD green[256];
    WORD blue [256];
} D3DGAMMARAMP;
```

This structure represents all three gamma ramps. When the call to `GetGammaRamp` returns, the structure contains the current values of the three ramps.

CAUTION

Occasionally, DirectX exhibits some strange behavior when getting the gamma ramp. Depending on the version of DirectX and the graphics card driver, occasionally you get gamma values in the range of 0–255 instead of 0–65535. For a surprising number of graphics cards, this is a known bug.

To work around this bug, after you call GetGammaRamp, you examine the set of values you get back. If there are no values above 255, it's a safe bet that DirectX has given you 8-bit values, which you then convert into their 16-bit counterparts.

Also, even though you pass them 16 bits of information, some graphics cards look at only the top or bottom 8 bits to set the gamma ramp. To make sure that your gamma ramps are set up on all graphics cards correctly, be clever. Use 8-bit precision for your gamma ramps. When you fill in the 16-bit array for SetGammaRamp, set the high byte to the same value as the low byte. For example, make your gamma values numbers like 0×3131, 0×9B9B, and 0×8585. That way, regardless of which byte the card decides to look at, it will get the correct value (at the cost of reduced precision, of course).

Dealing with card quirks and DirectX "features" like this one is just part of the fun of being a graphics programmer.

Setting the Gamma Ramp

To change the gamma ramp, call SetGammaRamp, which looks like this (see Table 6.10):

```
void SetGammaRamp(
  DWORD Flags,
  CONST D3DGAMMARAMP* pRamp
);
```

TIP

One last thing. Keep in mind that setting gamma controls might have no effect if you're running in windowed mode, because you don't have exclusive access to the display.

Table 6.10 The SetGammaRamp Parameters

Parameter	Description
Flags	Two flags allow you to control whether the gamma ramp is calibrated before it is applied. Calibration makes the display more consistent, but it's a slow process. Generally, you use it only when you're setting the ramp once and leaving it there for a while, not when you're animating the ramp to achieve fades.
	Use the D3DSGR_CALIBRATE flag here to tell DirectGraphics to calibrate the ramp. Specify D3DSGR_NO_CALIBRATION if you don't want calibration.
pRamp	This is the address of a D3DGAMMARAMP containing the new gamma ramps.

CHAPTER WRAP-UP

I hope that this chapter ties together the preceding chapters. When you're first learning 3D, it's incredibly difficult to get over the first leap and understand everything that's going on in a simple 3D program. I hope that you now understand all the basic concepts and also know how to implement those concepts in code.

From here, I spend the remainder of this part of the book showing you how to enhance the quality of your 3D renders. You will be learning about lighting techniques and then moving on to texturing.

Trust me, though, if you understand the concepts presented in the preceding three chapters, the hardest part is already over.

ABOUT THE SAMPLE PROGRAMS

This chapter introduces no new global enhancements to the coding style.

Here's what each program does:

- **Ch6p1_CreateDevice.** This program demonstrates how to create a Direct3D device.
- **Ch6p2_FirstScene.** Your first 3D scene! This program demonstrates everything talked about in this chapter: creating a device, creating and filling a vertex buffer, and rendering a scene using that buffer.

EXERCISES

Now that you know the basics, you should put them to use by creating your own 3D application. Don't just go for one triangle, though—that's boring! See whether you can write code that does the following things:

1. Uses a triangle strip or fan or uses the line or point primitive types.
2. Uses multiple primitives instead of just one.
3. Animates the camera instead of the object.
4. Uses an index buffer.
5. Loads an X file from disk and displays it.

CHAPTER 7

LIGHTING

*Cosmo: "[I] learned that everything in this world—
including money—operates not on reality…"
Martin Bishop: "But the perception of reality."*
——*From the movie* Sneakers

In recent years, game programmers have put a huge emphasis on upgrading the quality of the lighting in their games. Accurate light brings a whole new level of realism to games, and often it's the difference between a great game and a bad one.

This chapter shows you how to use Direct3D's lighting capabilities to add that extra oomph to your scenes.

I'll start with a description of natural light.

LIGHT IN NATURE

In real life, light bounces off things. In fact, light bounces off everything, and every time it bounces, some light is absorbed by the surface it hits, and some light is scattered in random directions. Some light eventually bounces its way into our eyes and causes the cones and rods on our retinas to send electrical impulses through our optic nerve and into our brain.

It's possible to calculate all those light bounces and render truly photo-realistic images. We already know the math behind it. We can take each pixel on the screen and use math to trace, in reverse, the path of a light ray. This is called *ray tracing*, and it's a very fascinating field.

Unfortunately, the equations to do this are very complex, which means that a computer must spend much time doing the math. Right now, there's simply not enough power to trace rays and still maintain a decent frame rate. On the fastest consumer computer you can buy, you're lucky to get a frame every 30 seconds. That's a far cry from the minimum 20–30 frames *per second* you need for real-time games. Maybe in the future that will change. I hope that one day I can boot up my Pentium XXX machine

TIP

As you dive deeper and deeper into graphics programming for games, you will realize that this same pattern applies everywhere. The foundation of most game graphics-programming techniques can be found in graphics research, but most graphics research papers are not concerned with generating results in real time. These techniques usually require minutes or hours to render a scene.

A large part of being a game graphics programmer is knowing how to take a research technique and optimize or even fake it so that a slightly less perfect (but still really neat) real-time version can be used in your game.

and play a nice round of ray-traced DOOM XXVI, but for now, real-time ray tracing just isn't going to happen.

Therefore, we have to make compromises and rely on techniques that run fast enough for real-time simulation and generate close, but not perfect, results.

DIRECT3D LIGHTING CONCEPTS

Direct3D's lighting is based on vertices. Direct3D knows where each vertex in your scene is located, as well as where each light is located. It can quickly calculate how much light will bounce off that vertex. It can do this for all vertices forming a surface and then use all those vertex calculations to brighten or darken the color of that surface, creating the illusion of light. It doesn't actually calculate the path of the light rays, so it misses things like shadows and reflections, but the overall effect is good.

Ambient and Direct Lighting

In Direct3D, there are two main kinds of light: ambient and direct.

Ambient light is light in a scene that's "just there." It's light that has been scattered and bounced around so much that you can't tell where it came from. Direct3D doesn't perform any calculations with ambient light. It just uses ambient light to give all the objects in your scene at least a little color. Ambient light is used to establish the minimum amount of light that falls on something. It has no direction or source, but it does have a color and an intensity (brightness), which you can control. Direct3D combines ambient light with the ambient color of the surface's material to determine what color the surface should be when no light is hitting it.

Direct3D, on the other hand, does perform calculations for *direct lighting*. Direct lighting has more than just color and intensity. It also has a source position, direction, falloff value, and so on. Direct3D uses direct light—along with the "material" assigned to a vertex—to brighten or highlight that surface, creating an illusion of light.

The two light types are completely independent of each other. Even though direct light contributes to the ambient light level in nature, in Direct3D, it does not. The ambient light level is one thing, and all the direct lights are another.

Shading Modes

To light a surface, Direct3D takes all the lighting calculations for a surface's vertices and combines them according to a shading mode.

There are only two shading modes: flat and Gouraud.

Flat Shading Mode

In the flat shading mode, Direct3D uses only the first vertex of a surface to determine the color and lighting for that surface. This doesn't make for a very realistic scene because each surface is one flat color, but it is relatively fast to calculate.

For an example of the flat shading mode in action, check out Figure 7.1.

Figure 7.1

The flat shading mode in action.

Gouraud Shading Mode

In this shading mode, Direct3D uses all the vertices of a surface and linearly interpolates between the values for each vertex when it renders the surface. If you're unfamiliar with linear interpolation, check out Figure 7.2.

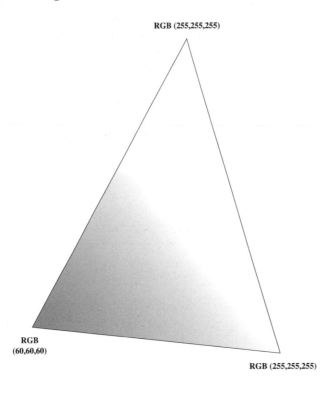

RGB (255,255,255)

RGB (60,60,60)

RGB (255,255,255)

Figure 7.2

Interpolation *means fading from one color to another.*

This triangle has three different vertices. One of the vertices is black, and the other two are white. When Direct3D renders this surface, the result is a fade (or gradient) from black to white. If the three vertices were three colors, the surface would fade between all three of them.

Gouraud shading makes for a much more realistic scene because it blends the edges between the surfaces, making each individual surface much less pronounced. For an example of what Gouraud shading looks like, see Figure 7.3.

Figure 7.3

The Gouraud shading mode in action.

NOTE

You can achieve sharp edges in the Gouraud shading mode by duplicating vertices. Make two different vertex normals to create a sharp lighting edge. For more information, see the DirectX SDK, at DirectX 8.0\DirectX Graphics\Introduction to DirectX Graphics\Getting Started with DirectX Graphics\Shading Techniques\Face and Vertex Normal Vectors.

TIP

Even if you choose not to use Direct3D lighting, you still need to choose a shading mode because shading modes also dictate how to handle vertices that are different colors, transparencies, and so on. For example, even with lighting turned off, if you have three vertices, one red, one green, and one blue, you won't see a color fade unless you enable Gouraud shading.

Materials

Materials comprise the second half of the Direct3D lighting system. Direct3D allows you to assign materials to vertices and, therefore, to the surface your vertices create. Each material contains properties that influence the way light interacts with it. For example, you can set up a shiny or dull surface or even a surface that seems to emit light.

You're going to spend the first part of this chapter learning about the properties of lights and materials. You will get to the code necessary to create lights and materials after you've learned about the properties at your disposal.

DIRECT3D LIGHT PROPERTIES

A direct light in Direct3D has several properties, which allow you to create realistic real-time scenes.

Diffuse, Specular, and Ambient Color

The most obvious property of a light is its color. All Direct3D lights possess three color properties: ambient, diffuse, and specular. Each color property has a red, green, and blue component. Each component can be within the range of 0.0 to 1.0, with 1.0 representing brightness and 0 representing darkness.

A light's diffuse color is the most important of the three colors because it tells Direct3D the actual color of the light. To create a white light, set the diffuse color to (1.0, 1.0, 1.0).

TIP

Note that Direct3D doesn't force you to stay within 0.0 and 1.0 for light color values. You can create lights that have a very bright color (and wash out all the other lights) by specifying color component values way above 1.0.

You can also create *dark lights*, one of my favorite things in 3D programming. Dark lights have *negative* component values, which means that they literally suck light out of a scene rather than add light to it. How cool is *that?*

Position, Range, and Attenuation

Direct3D lights can also have position, range, and attenuation properties, depending on their type. A light's *position* is simply a 3D world coordinate.

Together, the light range and light attenuation property allow you to specify the range of the light and how the brightness of the light changes, based on how far away from it something is. For example, you can create a light that has a short range but maintains its brightness, or you can create a light with a long range but with its brightness decreasing dramatically the farther away from it you get.

The light *range* specifies the maximum distance over which the light still has an effect. Any vertices outside the light's range do not receive light.

The *attenuation* property governs the amount of light a vertex gets when it's within the light's range. Attenuation in Direct3D consists of three floating-point numbers, aptly named Attenuation0, Attenuation1, and Attenuation2.

Direct3D calculates the attenuation using the following attenuation formula (D is the distance from the light to the vertex):

$$A = \frac{1}{Attenuation0 + (D * Attenuation1) + (D^2 * Attenuation2)}$$

No matter what numbers you run through this equation, the light attenuation value (A) always comes out between 0.0 and 1.0. Note that you can't ever make it hit 0.0, but you can come very close if you plug in really big numbers for Attenuation0, Attenuation1, and Attenuation2.

Direct3D multiplies each of the light's three color components by the calculated attenuation value. By adjusting the three attenuation properties, you specify how fast the light fades as distance from it increases, as shown in Table 7.1.

Of course, you can use all sorts of attenuation values besides the three examples listed here.

Light Direction

Light *direction* specifies in what direction the simulated light rays travel. Direct3D expresses light direction as a free vector but uses only the direction component of the vector, not the vector's magnitude. For example, a direction vector of (0,0,1) means that the light is traveling straight

Table 7.1 Attenuation Properties

Attenuation Value	Result
Attenuation0 = 1.0 Attenuation1 = 0.0 Attenuation2 = 0.0	These three values create a *sharp* light, that is, a light whose brightness doesn't decrease with distance. Any point within the light's range is fully lit. If you push Attenuation0 up higher than 1.0, you reduce the brightness of the light.
Attenuation0 = 0.0 Attenuation1 = 1.0 Attenuation2 = 0.0	This creates a *normal* light source. The brightness of the light decreases linearly as the distance from the light increases.
Attenuation0 = 0.0 Attenuation1 = 0.0 Attenuation2 = 1.0	This creates a brightness that decreases exponentially as the distance from the light increases. These values work well for spotlights because they create a tight, focused beam of light.

down the positive z-axis (into your monitor), regardless of where in world space the light is positioned.

Light Type

The most important characteristic of a light is its type. Direct3D supports three main types of lights: point lights, spotlights, and directional lights.

Point Lights

A *point* light is like a light bulb suspended in space. It has a position but no direction. It radiates light equally in all directions. See Figure 7.4 for an example of this.

Figure 7.4

A point light.

Spotlights

Spotlights have a position, as well as a direction in which they emit light. Additionally, spotlights have two cones of light: an inner cone and an outer cone. The *inner cone* is the bright part of the spotlight, and the *outer cone* represents the

> **TIP**
>
> Most programmers set the Falloff value to 1. This is because it's very difficult to see the effects of the Falloff value anyway and causes more work for Direct3D if Falloff isn't 1.

dimmer outer edges of the spotlight. Spotlights have three properties that deal with inner and outer cones, as outlined in Table 7.2 (see Figure 7.5).

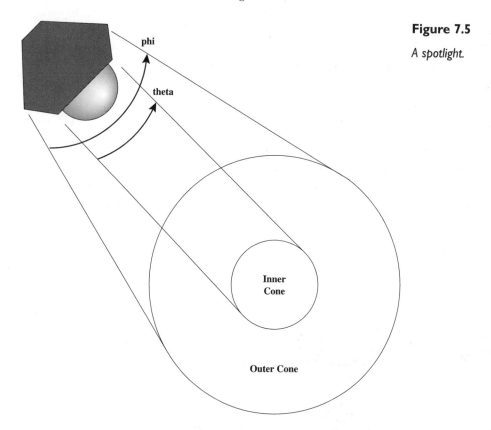

Figure 7.5

A spotlight.

Table 7.2 Spotlight Properties

Property	Description
Phi	This specifies the angle of the outer cone.
Theta	This is the angle of the inner cone.
Falloff	This is a number that represents how light intensity decreases between the outer edge of the inner cone and the inner edge of the outer cone. It tells Direct3D how sharply defined you want the edge between the inner and outer cones to be.

Spotlights are the most computationally expensive of all lights in Direct3D, primarily because they have a falloff property. For this reason, make sure that all the spotlights in your world really need to be there. That is, make sure that there's no way you can replace them with point or directional lights and still achieve the same effect. Also make sure that you're using a Falloff value other than 1 because you really need to. Most of the time you don't.

> **TIP**
>
> It's very difficult to get spotlights to look right. Direct3D calculates the lighting values on a per-vertex basis, which means that to see the halo of light generated by a spotlight, you need either a very big light or a lot of vertices concentrated in a small area.
>
> If you want to get that circular halo of light in your application, try using light mapping instead of spotlights. Chapter 9, "Advanced Texturing," teaches all you need to know about light mapping.

Directional Lights

Directional lights have a direction property but no position. All light generated by a directional light in a scene travels in the same direction. A good real-life example of a directional light is the sun. Because the sun is so far away, all its rays hit the Earth at essentially the same angle, which means to anyone on the surface that the sun is basically a directional light (even though we know that it's more akin to a positional light, very far away).

> **TIP**
>
> Check your device's capabilities to verify that it supports directional lights. Most cards do, but you can never tell with older cards.

Directional lights are the easiest lights to use, computationally.

DIRECT3D MATERIAL PROPERTIES

Materials work like GDI brushes or pens. You set them active and then push vertices into Direct3D. As you push in the vertices, they're assigned to the active material.

A Direct3D *material* is basically a set of four colors: diffuse, ambient, emissive, and specular.

Diffuse Color

Diffuse color has the most effect on your vertices because it specifies how the material reflects diffuse (direct) light in a scene. This parameter tells Direct3D what colors the object reflects when hit with light. In essence, this determines the color of the object under direct light.

Say that you set up a model using only one material and specify a diffuse color of RGB (255,0,0) for that material. This means that the object reflects only red light. When hit with a white light, the object appears red because the only light it reflects is red light. When hit with a red light, the object also appears red. When hit with a blue or green light, however, the object appears black because there's no red within the blue or green light to reflect.

The intensity of the reflected light depends on the angle between the light ray and the vertex normal. The intensity is strongest when the light rays are parallel to the vertex's normal, in other words, when the light is shining directly onto the surface (the surface and the incoming light rays are perpendicular). The intensity is weakest when the light rays are parallel to the surface, because it's impossible for them to bounce off the surface when they're parallel to it.

Ambient Color

The *ambient* color property determines a material's color when no direct light is hitting it. Usually, you set this equal to the diffuse color because the color of most objects is the same when hit by ambient light and when hit by diffuse light. However, you can create some weird-looking materials by specifying an ambient color that's different from your diffuse color.

Ambient color always has the same intensity because it is assumed that the ambient light is coming from all directions.

Emissive Color

You use *emissive* color to create the illusion of materials that glow. They don't actually glow— Direct3D doesn't perform lighting calculations using them as a light source—but they can be used in scenes to create the appearance of a glowing object, without requiring additional light processing (because they aren't a light source).

For example, you can create a material that emits a white color and use it to simulate an overhead fluorescent light in your scene. It won't actually light up anything. You have to compensate for that by, say, assigning a bright ambient color to the objects in your scene, but in certain situations it can be a clever trick.

Specular Color and Power

Last but not least, you use the *specular* color of a material to make an object shiny. Most of the time, you set the specular color to white to achieve realistic highlights, but you can set it to other colors to create the illusion of colored lights hitting your object.

Another property, specular power, goes hand-in-hand with specular color. The *power* property of a material determines how sharp the highlights on that material appear. A power of zero tells

Direct3D that an object has no highlights, and a power of 10 creates very definite highlights (see Figure 7.6).

Figure 7.6

Different specular powers create more highlights or fewer highlights.

Specular Power = 10   Specular Power = 0

PROGRAMMING DIRECT3D LIGHTS

To program Direct3D lights, you need to know about only three methods of the IDirect3DDevice8 interface: SetLight, which sets up the properties for a light, LightEnable, which turns a light on or off, and GetLight, which retrieves the properties for a light.

Each video card supports a different number of maximum lights. Most video cards allow you to have eight lights. You find the exact number allowed by examining the MaxActiveLights member of the D3DCAPS8 structure returned to you after a call to the GetCaps method of IDirect3DDevice8.

Each light is referenced by an index. For example, you say to Direct3D, "Set light #3's color to (0.0,1.0,0.0)," or "Give me the properties for light #6." You turn lights on or off by specifying their index, that is, saying to Direct3D, "Turn on light #2." When you want to use a light, you load up the properties for it into an index you choose. When you're done using the light, you disable it (turn it off). There's no concept of allocating or releasing lights. They're just always there.

Setting a Light's Properties

You set a light's properties by calling SetLight, which looks like this (see Table 7.3):

```
HRESULT SetLight(
  DWORD Index,
  CONST D3DLIGHT8* pLight
);
```

Table 7.3 The SetLight Parameters

Parameter	Description
Index	Specifies the index of the light whose properties you want to set.
Plight	A pointer to a D3DLIGHT8 structure that tells Direct3D the properties you want the light to have.

Now look at the D3DLIGHT8 structure because that's where all the interesting attributes live (see Table 7.4):

```
typedef struct _D3DLIGHT8 {
    D3DLIGHTTYPE    Type;
    D3DCOLORVALUE   Diffuse;
    D3DCOLORVALUE   Specular;
    D3DCOLORVALUE   Ambient;
    D3DVECTOR       Position;
    D3DVECTOR       Direction;
    float           Range;
    float           Falloff;
    float           Attenuation0;
    float           Attenuation1;
    float           Attenuation2;
    float           Theta;
    float           Phi;
} D3DLIGHT8;
```

Setting up a light is as easy as populating the D3DLIGHT8 structure and then calling SetLight. Nothing to it!

Getting a Light's Properties

To retrieve the current properties of a light, use the GetLight method. GetLight takes the same two parameters as SetLight: a light index and a pointer to a structure. When GetLight returns, the structure you pointed it at is filled with the current properties of the light about which you asked.

Table 7.4 The **D3DLIGHT8** Structure Members

Member	Description
Type	Specifies the type of light. This can be `D3DLIGHT_POINT`, `D3DLIGHT_SPOT`, or `D3DLIGHT_DIRECTIONAL` for point lights, spotlights, and directional lights, respectively.
Diffuse	Specifies the diffuse color emitted by a light. You use the `D3DCOLORVALUE` structure to store information about a light's color. `D3DCOLORVALUE` has four components: red, green, blue, and alpha. Direct3D ignores the alpha value for a light, so just set it to 1.0.
Specular	Specifies the specular color emitted by a light.
Ambient	Specifies the ambient color emitted by a light.
Position	A `D3DVECTOR` that specifies a light's position in world space. A `D3DVECTOR` contains three floats: x, y, and z. This has no effect on directional lights.
Direction	A `D3DVECTOR` that specifies the direction the light is pointing. This direction doesn't depend on the light's position. A direction of (0,0,1) creates a light that points into the monitor (positive z-axis), regardless of where in world space that light is positioned. This has no effect on point lights because they radiate light in all directions.
Range	Specifies a light's range, that is, the maximum distance an object can be from the light and still be lit by that light. This has no effect on directional lights. Because they have no position, the range of directional lights is infinite.
Falloff	Specifies the falloff between the inner and outer cones of a spotlight. For more information, see the section on spotlights. This has no effect on directional or point lights.
Attenuation0, Attenuation1, Attenuation2	Use these parameters to control how quickly a light's brightness decreases with distance. See the section on attenuation for a detailed description of these values.

Table 7.4 Continued

Member	Description
Theta	Specifies the angle, in radians, of the spotlight's inner cone. For more information, see the section on spotlights. This has no effect on directional or point lights.
Phi	Specifies the angle, in radians, of the spotlight's outer cone. Obviously, this should be greater than or equal to Theta. For more information, see the section on spotlights. This has no effect on directional or point lights.

Enabling and Disabling Lights

This is even easier than setting a light's properties. Simply call the LightEnable method of IDirect3DDevice8, specifying the light's index and a Boolean indicating whether you want that light enabled or disabled.

If you try to turn on a light before setting its properties, Direct3D assigns the default light properties, shown in Table 7.5.

TIP

Note that this effectively creates an invisible light because the range and other key parameters are set to zero. You have to modify these properties before you can see the light in your scene.

PROGRAMMING DIRECT3D MATERIALS

Coding materials requires nothing more than two methods of IDirect3DDevice8: SetMaterial, which sets the current material, and GetMaterial, which returns the current material.

Setting the Current Material

Every vertex you pump into Direct3D via methods such as DrawPrimitive has the current material applied to it. You can change the current material at any time. If you're using more than one material in your scene (hey, who isn't?), the best tactic is to set your first material, pump in all the vertices that use that material, then switch to the second material, pump in all the vertices of that

Table 7.5 The Default Light Properties

Property	Description
Type	D3DLIGHT_DIRECTIONAL
Diffuse	RGBA (1.0, 1.0, 1.0, 1.0)
Specular	RGBA (0.0, 0.0, 0.0, 0.0)
Ambient	RGBA (0.0, 0.0, 0.0, 0.0)
Position	(0,0,0)
Direction	(0,0,1)
Range	0
Falloff	0
Attenuation0, Attenuation1, Attenuation2	0, 0, 0
Theta	0
Phi	0

material, and so on. For best performance, you should try to minimize the number of times you call SetMaterial.

SetMaterial looks like this:

```
HRESULT SetMaterial(
    CONST D3DMATERIAL8* pMaterial
);
```

All you need to do is pass it a pointer to a structure that contains the material properties you want. The D3DMATERIAL8 structure looks like this:

```
typedef struct _D3DMATERIAL8 {
    D3DCOLORVALUE    Diffuse;
    D3DCOLORVALUE    Ambient;
    D3DCOLORVALUE    Specular;
```

```
    D3DCOLORVALUE    Emissive;
    float            Power;
} D3DMATERIAL8;
```

As you can see, it consists of four colors and a float that specifies the power of the diffuse color (see the Direct3D material properties section if these terms are new to you).

By the way, if you don't set a material before you begin pumping vertices, the vertices are assigned a default material consisting of the properties shown in Table 7.6.

These properties create a matte white material that looks a little like a cross between cement and whipped cream.

Table 7.6 The Default Material Properties

Property	Default Value
Diffuse color	RGBA(1.0, 1.0, 1.0, 0.0)
Ambient color	RGBA(0.0, 0.0, 0.0, 0.0)
Emissive color	RGBA(0.0, 0.0, 0.0, 0.0)
Specular color	RGBA(0.0, 0.0, 0.0, 0.0)
Specular power	0

Getting the Current Material

The counterpart to SetMaterial is (drum roll!) GetMaterial. It also takes only one argument, a pointer to a material structure. When the call returns, this structure is filled with the properties of the active material.

CHAPTER WRAP-UP

Not much to this chapter really. That's probably a good thing because the preceding couple chapters were brutal.

I suppose that I could have fattened up this chapter by going into more detail about the lighting equations Direct3D uses, but I decided that even though the math behind light is fascinating, it's not worth killing trees over. You probably won't need to step through or hand-verify the lighting calculations the way you would for matrix or vector manipulation.

You should at least spend some time getting to know Direct3D lights and materials. If you understand how lights and materials (and soon textures) all interact to determine the

> **NOTE**
>
> If you're curious, you can find a detailed description of the math behind the scenes in your SDK documentation at DirectX Graphics\Understand DirectX Graphics\Direct3D Rendering Pipeline\Fixed Function Vertex and Pixel Processing\Transformation and Lighting Engine\Mathematics of Direct3D Lighting.

final color(s) of a surface, your debugging sessions will go more smoothly.

ABOUT THE SAMPLE PROGRAMS

Only one sample program this chapter:

- **Ch7p1_SimpleLight.** This program demonstrates simple lighting techniques.

EXERCISES

1. Take an example from any of the previous chapters (the simple triangle program is a good choice), and add lighting and material code to it.
2. Experiment with the way light and materials interact. For example, what happens when you shine a blue light on a white material? A blue light on a red material? On a blue material? Develop an understanding of the differences between light color and material color.
3. Create a dark light and see what sorts of interesting effects you can create with it. Create a really bright light, a material that has a bright emissive color, and so on, and see what effects those enable.

CHAPTER 8

BASIC TEXTURING

"Greetings, Starfighter. You have been recruited by the Star League to defend the frontier against Xur and the Ko-Dan Armada...."
—From the movie The Last Starfighter

Textures are by far the single most important technique for creating realistic scenes. At its simplest, the technique of texturing renders a surface based on a bitmap image instead of a flat color, as if you had painted the bitmap onto the surface.

From that basic idea, computer graphics has expanded to include techniques such as *multiple texturing* (putting several partially transparent textures onto a bitmap at once), *bump mapping* (using textures, combined with light calculations, to simulate little bumps, as on a golf ball or dungeon wall), *environment mapping* (making an object appear to be chrome, that is, to reflect its surroundings), and *volumetric* (3D) *textures*.

> **TIP**
>
> One of my favorite 1980s sci-fi movies is *The Last Starfighter*, a cheesy "guy from a trailer park gets recruited by aliens and saves the universe" picture. If you rent it, pay careful attention to the spaceship scenes. Look closely, and you will see that the majority of the spaceships have no textures—they're just flat polygons. Apparently, that was state of the art back in 1984.
>
> If you ever doubt that technology moves at near light speed, take *The Last Starfighter* and put it next to any film made today (say, anything made by Pixar), and see how much advanced texturing techniques improve the quality of the graphics.

This chapter and the next will make you a texturing monster. Careful study of these two chapters will give you the mad texturing skills you need to make a game that doesn't look like it's from an early 1980's sci-fi movie.

BASIC TEXTURING CONCEPTS

This chapter follows the same pattern as the previous chapters in that the first part is all about explaining texturing concepts and the second part is all about how to code those concepts in Direct3D.

Textures Are Just Surfaces

Direct3D stores textures as surfaces. This means that anything you can get into a surface, you can use as a texture. You can load it from a bitmap (Direct3D provides utility functions that allow you to create a texture straight from a BMP file), or you yourself can generate the pixel data (for example, using a fractal algorithm). This also means that you specify the pixel format you'd like when you're creating textures, just as you specify a pixel format for the back buffer.

Most of the time, you want your textures to be the same format as your back buffer, but in a few scenarios you want them to differ—for example, if you want to save graphics memory by using paletted textures.

CAUTION

There's one important caveat involving texture surfaces. Usually, their width and height must be powers of 2. This means that 2×2, 4×4, 8×8, 16×16, 32×32, and so on, textures are okay, but 3×5, 17×84, and so on, are not. Be sure to check the device's capabilities before you try to create a texture that doesn't have power-of-2 dimensions.

Texture Management

Texture management involves deciding which textures reside in graphics memory (and can therefore be used without a speed hit) and which must be relegated to system memory. For simple programs, you might luck out and find that all your textures can fit within 8MB or 16MB of graphics memory; most cards on the market have at least this much RAM. Most of the time, however, you end up with more textures than you can fit in memory, and you must manage which ones get the privilege of living onboard the graphics card.

Direct3D can help you out. It provides support for managing textures. When you create a texture, you specify in which memory pool Direct3D should place it. Most of the time, you choose D3DPOOL_MANAGED, which tells Direct3D that it should manage the texture for optimum performance by moving it in and out of graphics memory when needed.

The Fine Art of Knowing When to Texture

For hundreds of years, a common architectural trick has involved taking a flat side of a building and painting a picture on it that makes it appear to be not flat. The paintings can be anything from a simple bevel here and there to a full-fledged illusion of an arch, a dome, or another feature, all made possible by the careful use of perspective, contrast, and light. The trick works because the people who look at the buildings do so from far below and/or far away, so their eyes can't tell that the scene has no depth.

Good game developers know when they must create a vertex and when they can fake the appearance of a curve or edge by applying a carefully made texture.

Say that you want to create a brick wall. The wrong way to do it is to make a brick out of eight vertices and then duplicate that brick hundreds of times to form a wall that's made out of thousands of vertices. The right way to do it is to create six vertices for the entire wall and use a brick texture to give the illusion that the wall is more than just a flat rectangle.

Game developers also use this technique when designing their character faces. Look closely at the facial features of game characters, and you will notice very few actual vertices—maybe a couple for the nose and ears, sometimes cheeks, but hardly any for things such as lips, eyebrows, and eye sockets (unless, of course, you're playing a game that has progressive mesh optimizations, where the computer puts more vertices into the model when you get close to it).

Obviously, you must find the right balance between vertices and textures. Too many vertices, and your game runs too slow. Not enough vertices, and your graphics quality goes down. Also, the number of textures you need usually goes up, which makes juggling graphics memory harder. Creating models with just the right number of vertices and textures is the mark of an experienced game artist. Keep this in mind as you texture and create models.

Tying a Texture to a Vertex

After you load a texture into a memory pool, the next logical step is to tie it to a surface of a 3D model. The way you do this is through the model's vertices.

Recall that when you create a flexible vertex format (FVF), one of the properties you can include in your vertex is a texture coordinate. This texture coordinate tells Direct3D what texel should be placed at that vertex. (For a 2D texture, this texture coordinate is made up of two components, a u-value and v-value, which correspond to the x-value and y-value in 2D space.) This information, combined with the texture coordinates for other vertices, tells Direct3D how your texture fits onto the surface.

Direct3D considers the entire width of the texture to be a 1.0 texture coordinate unit wide, and the entire height of the texture to be a 1.0 texture coordinate unit tall. In other words, regardless of the texture's

> **TIP**
>
> One other thing: 3D programmers don't refer to the individual dots of a texture as *pixels*. They instead call them *texels*. Just as *pixel* is short for *picture element*, *texel* is short for *texture element*.

resolution, a (u,v) coordinate of (1.0,1.0) always represents the lower-right corner, and a (u,v) coordinate of (0.5,0.5) always represents the center of the texture. If the texture was 100×100 pixels, (u,v) coordinates of (0.5,0.75) would represent the pixel at (50,75). If the texture was 200×200, the same (u,v) coordinates of (0.5,0.75) would represent the pixel at (100,150). Another way to think of it, using percents, (u,v) coordinates of (0.5,0.75) mean 50 percent of the texture's width in from the left side and 75 percent of the texture's height down from the top.

Take another example. Say that you have four vertices representing a 10×10 square (or *quad*), as shown in Figure 8.1.

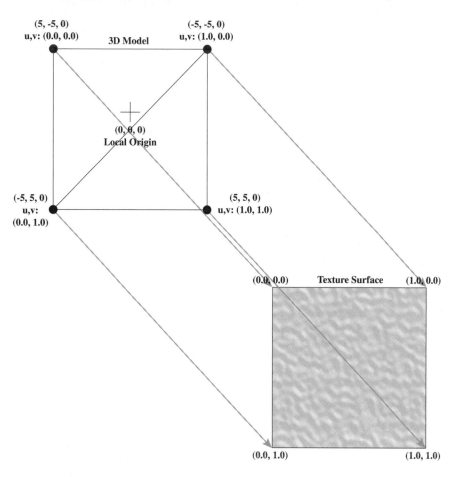

Figure 8.1

Texturing a simple quad.

Your local-space vertex coordinates are $(-5,-5,0),(5,-5,0),(5,5,0),(-5,5,0)$, which center the quad on its origin. You have a 256×256 texel texture you would like to use as the texture for your quad. To do this, you set the (u,v) coordinates for your $(-5,-5,0)$ vertex to be $(0.0,0.0)$, which basically pins the upper-left corner of your texture to the upper-left vertex in your model. Assuming that you want the entire texture to be rendered onto the quad, the (u,v) coordinates for the other three vertices need to be $(1.0,0.0)$ for the upper-right corner, $(1.0,1.0)$ for the lower-right corner, and $(0.0, 1.0)$ for the lower-left corner.

Now, Direct3D runs your model through the geometry pipeline and deduces that your quad's four vertices need to be rendered at screen positions

> **TIP**
>
> As you will soon learn, that example oversimplifies the process, but those are the basic concepts. The important thing to remember is that the (u,v) coordinates of a vertex tell Direct3D where to pin down the texture to that vertex.

(76,54), (204,54), (204,182), and (76,182). Direct3D multiplies your (u,v) coordinates by the width and height of the texture to arrive at the exact texel coordinates that correspond to your vertex coordinates. It then figures out how to stretch or, in this case, shrink the texture so that the texture fits on the surface. Because the quad is 128×128 pixels, but the texture is 256×256 texels, Direct3D skips every other texel so that the texture fits, and you end up with a 50-percent reduced view of your texture (see Figure 8.2).

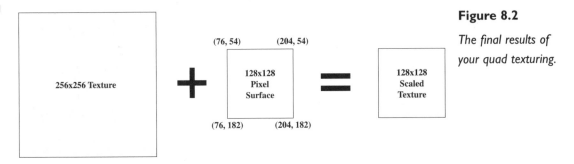

Figure 8.2

The final results of your quad texturing.

To Wrap or Not to Wrap?

For each texture, you decide whether Direct3D can wrap it. Here is another example, to illustrate why you need to do this.

Say that you have the same 10×10 quad, only now your texture coordinates are (0.8,0.8), (0.1,0.8), (0.1,0.1), and (0.8,0.1) clockwise from the upper left. In other words, you're not using the whole texture, just a segment of it, as shown in Figure 8.3.

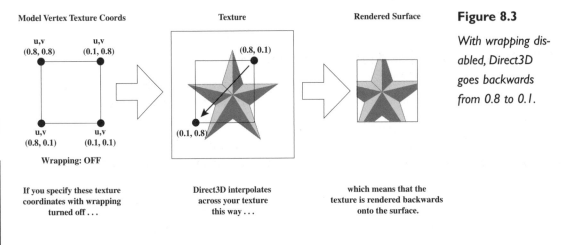

Figure 8.3

With wrapping disabled, Direct3D goes backwards from 0.8 to 0.1.

Direct3D has two ways to get from (0.8) to (0.1). It can start at (0.8) and subtract its way to (0.1), passing through (0.5), or it can start at (0.8) and *add* its way to (0.1) by wrapping around the edge of the texture. Just like when you're trying to go from New York to London, you have two choices: to fly East over the Atlantic or fly West and go around the world (see Figure 8.4).

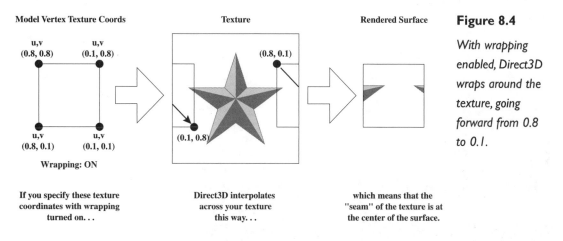

Model Vertex Texture Coords

u,v
(0.8, 0.8)   u,v
(0.1, 0.8)

u,v
(0.8, 0.1)   u,v
(0.1, 0.1)

Wrapping: ON

Texture

(0.8, 0.1)

(0.1, 0.8)

Rendered Surface

Figure 8.4

With wrapping enabled, Direct3D wraps around the texture, going forward from 0.8 to 0.1.

If you specify these texture coordinates with wrapping turned on. . .

Direct3D interpolates across your texture this way. . .

which means that the "seam" of the texture is at the center of the surface.

You control which way Direct3D goes by specifying whether it's allowed to wrap around the edge of the texture. If wrapping is enabled, you tell Direct3D that it can go through the texture's borders. If wrapping is disabled, Direct3D can't go across the borders.

Most of the time, you don't want it to wrap, but in certain situations you need your texture to wrap. For example, if you're texturing all four sides of a pillar using just one texture, you need to allow wrapping, or Direct3D will interpolate across the entire texture when it renders the last side of the pillar.

Texture-Filtering Modes

One of the most basic problems to solve when it comes to texturing involves how exact the computer is when taking a bitmap of a certain dimension (say, 256×256) and mapping it to a surface that's bigger or smaller (say, 73×56 or 372×434 pixels).

Texture-filtering modes determine how Direct3D deals with this problem. Direct3D supports several types of texture-filtering modes: linear filtering, mipmap filtering, anisotropic filtering, and no filtering (also known as *nearest-point sampling.*)

You will start with that last one.

Nearest-Point Sampling

Nearest-point sampling, synonymous with *no filtering*, means that for each pixel in the surface, Direct3D rounds off the math and uses the closest corresponding texel. Usually, you don't want this because it leads to the infamous chunky graphics look of early '90s 3D games, such as DOOM or Wolfenstein 3D (see Figure 8.5).

Figure 8.5

The chunky graphics of early 3D games, caused by a lack of texture filtering.

If you try to apply an 8×8 texture to a 32×32 surface, each texel is going to take up 4×4 surface pixels, and the result will be a 400-percent magnified version of the texture. Blocky, yuck!

Of course, the advantage here is that nearest-point sampling is quick, and if you know that your texture dimensions exactly match your surface dimensions, nearest-point sampling makes sense.

NOTE

If you map a very small texture onto a very large surface using nearest-point sampling, you can run into weird artifacts (graphical bugs) that create mysterious diagonal seams in your surface. For an explanation of why this occurs and what you can do about it, consult the SDK documentation at DirectX Graphics\Using DirectX Graphics\Textures\Texture Filtering\Nearest Point Sampling. You will also find a much more technical description of how nearest-point sampling works.

Linear Texture Filtering

Linear filtering is a step up from nearest-point sampling. When using this method, Direct3D calculates a weighted average between the nearest four texels adjacent to the calculated texel. Because the average is weighted, this creates a smooth blending effect. Small textures rendered to big surfaces appear out of focus but less blocky than with nearest-point sampling (see Figure 8.6).

Original Texture Image

The same texture, enlarged with linear texture filtering.

Without linear filtering, the enlargement looks "blocky."

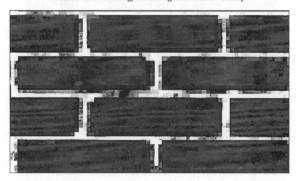

Figure 8.6

Linear texture filtering results in images that are fuzzy instead of blocky.

Specifically, the type of linear filtering Direct3D supports is *bilinear filtering*. You've probably seen this word on the back of old 3D card boxes from the days when it was a buzzword. What it means is that several pixel colors are combined to create the final image.

Resource-wise, linear texture filtering is a good compromise between nearest-point sampling and mipmap texture filtering (or *mipmapping*). Linear texture filtering requires a medium amount of CPU power.

Mipmap Texture Filtering

Mipmap texture filtering hogs memory but allows for quick and highly realistic texture rendering. In essence, the technique of mipmapping involves using several bitmaps of varying sizes as one texture. Direct3D uses high-resolution bitmaps for objects close to the viewer and low-resolution bitmaps for objects far away. This enables you to filter and tweak the low-resolution bitmaps manually so that they become highly accurate counterparts to your high-resolution textures (see Figure 8.7).

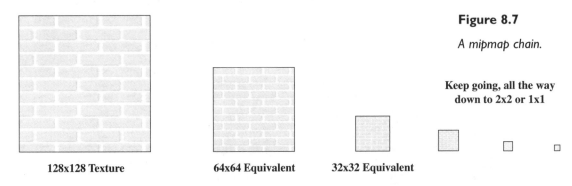

Figure 8.7

A mipmap chain.

Keep going, all the way down to 2x2 or 1x1

128x128 Texture   **64x64 Equivalent**   **32x32 Equivalent**

3D graphics programmers call this set of low- and high-resolution texture images a *mipmap chain*.

Direct3D uses two mipmaps in your chain and blends between them, based on the viewer's distance from the object. It does this so that you don't notice a texture *pop* when one mipmap image replaces another one. Believe it or not, this is faster than using one big texture, because traversing over big textures frequently results in cache misses for the CPU and graphics adapter. 3D programmers refer to this technique as *trilinear filtering*. It's bilinear filtering and mipmapping, combined.

Each bitmap in a mipmap chain must be smaller than the one before it by exactly one power of 2. If your highest-resolution image is 512×512, your smaller images must be 256×256, 128×128, 64×64, 32×32, 16×16, and so on. You specify a mipmap chain in terms of its maximum image and the number of images in it, which means that you can't skip a resolution level. For example, in a mipmap chain with three images, the largest of which is 256×256, Direct3D assumes that the three image dimensions are 256×256, 128×128, and 64×64. You can't have a chain of 256×256, 64×64, and 16×16 images.

> **TIP**
>
> Mipmapping gets its name from *MIP,* an acronym for the Latin phrase *multum in parvo,* or *many things in a small place.* This fits because mipmapping is all about filtering and compressing many pixels from a high-resolution texture (many things) into one pixel (a small place) in a lower-resolution texture.

You can use mipmapping in conjunction with nearest-point sampling or linear filtering. Direct3D uses one of those two modes when it needs to stretch or shrink a mipmap slightly. You have to see for yourself which technique works best for the mipmaps in your game.

By the way, if you use mipmapping, you get to the individual mipmap levels of your texture by calling the GetSurfaceLevel method of IDirect3DTexture8.

Anisotropic Texture Filtering

Like mipmapping, you use anisotropic texture filtering in conjunction with either linear filtering or nearest-point sampling.

To explain anisotropic filtering, I'll start with the word itself, *anisotropic*. *An* means *not*, *iso* means *equal*, and *tropic* means *shape*, so *anisotropic* literally means *a shape that's not equal*. Anisotropic filtering compensates for the distortion that occurs when you're viewing a surface that is at an angle to the plane of the screen. The *not equal shape* to which anisotropic filtering refers is the pixel projection from the screen onto that angled surface.

Imagine that each pixel on your monitor is a little light beam that shines into your scene. Now imagine that your scene consists of a single quad, parallel to your screen, as in Figure 8.8.

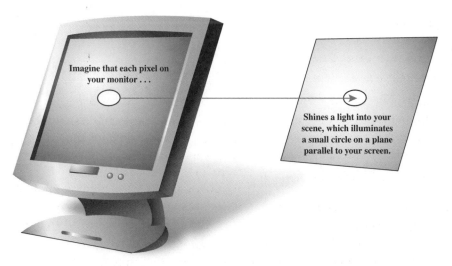

Figure 8.8

A quad parallel to the monitor, lit up by an imaginary beam of light from a pixel.

Imagine that each pixel on your monitor . . .

Shines a light into your scene, which illuminates a small circle on a plane parallel to your screen.

A pixel light beam, when it hits the quad, creates a small circle of illumination. Ideally, the texels that the circle illuminates are the texels the computer should use to determine the final pixel color.

All is fine so far, but consider what happens when you rotate the quad on its y-axis. The circle of light becomes an ellipse as the angle of the quad to the screen changes. Now, all of a sudden, an elliptical area of texels determines the final pixel color.

With anisotropic filtering turned off, the computer does not use the lit ellipse; it always uses a circle (an equal shape). With anisotropic filtering on, the computer correctly models the ellipse of texels, resulting in better image quality at the price of speed (it has to deal with more texels).

The bottom line is that you should turn on anisotropic filtering if the card on which you're running supports it.

Texture-Addressing Modes

As you learned in the beginning of this chapter, you tell Direct3D where on a surface to place a texture by specifying (u,v) texture coordinates for each vertex. Direct3D uses these (u,v) coordinates to determine the texture point (in texture space) that corresponds to the vertex.

Usually, (u,v) coordinates are between 0.0 and 1.0, but they don't have to be. The active texture-addressing mode tells Direct3D what to do when a (u,v) coordinate falls outside this range.

You can choose from four addressing modes: wrap, mirror, clamp, and border color.

The Wrap Addressing Mode

When the wrap addressing mode is active, Direct3D tiles the texture, and every tile has an exact dimension of 1×1 (u,v) coordinate. In other words, the seams of the tiles are at 0.0, 1.0, 2.0, 3.0, and so on (see Figure 8.9).

If you created a square primitive and set the four (u,v) coordinates to (0.0,0.0), (3.0,0.0), (3.0,3.0), and (0.0, 3.0), that surface would have a 3×3 tiled image of your texture on it.

This is obviously most useful for real-life tiles, such as a bathroom floor. Your texture can just be an image of one tile, and Direct3D will take care of applying the pattern across the floor.

The Mirror Addressing Mode

Mirror addressing is very similar to wrap addressing in that your texture repeats itself every 1.0 coordinates. The difference is that each tile is a mirror of its adjacent tiles (see Figure 8.10).

You find this addressing mode useful when you need to tile something but can't spend time ensuring that the seams of the tiles match up so that no edges are visible. A common situation like this involves making grass, desert, or rock textures for landscaping.

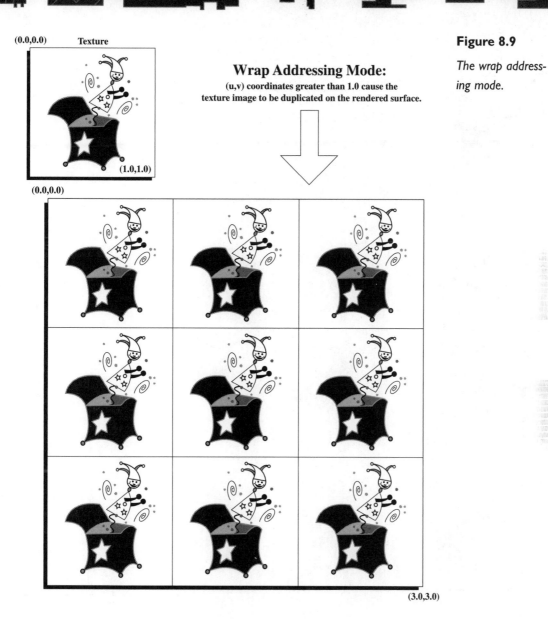

(0.0,0.0) Texture

(1.0,1.0)

Wrap Addressing Mode:
(u,v) coordinates greater than 1.0 cause the
texture image to be duplicated on the rendered surface.

(0.0,0.0)

(3.0,3.0)

Figure 8.9

*The wrap address-
ing mode.*

The Clamp Addressing Mode

In clamp addressing, Direct3D does not tile your image. Instead, it treats any u or v coordinate above 1.0 as if it were 1.0, in effect duplicating the last row and column of your texture across any coordinates greater than 1.0 (see Figure 8.11).

Clamp addressing is good when you know that your (u,v) coordinates won't greatly exceed 1.0, although they can slightly.

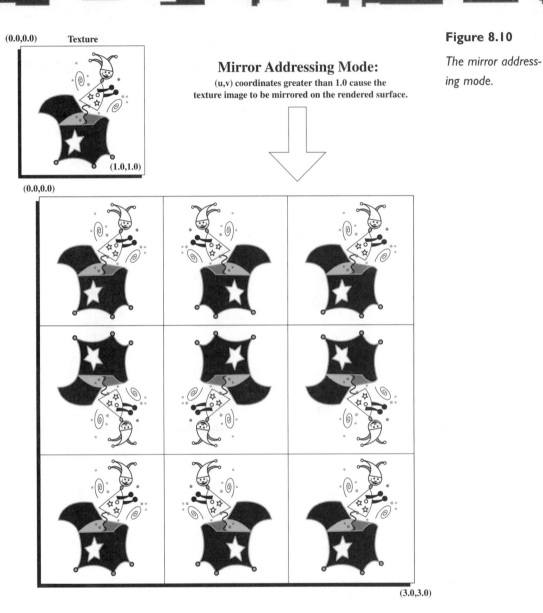

(0.0,0.0) Texture

(1.0,1.0)

Mirror Addressing Mode:
(u,v) coordinates greater than 1.0 cause the
texture image to be mirrored on the rendered surface.

Figure 8.10

The mirror addressing mode.

(0.0,0.0)

(3.0,3.0)

The Border Color Addressing Mode

Border color addressing is similar to clamp addressing, but rather than use the last row and column for any coordinates greater than 1.0, Direct3D uses a solid color you specify (see Figure 8.12).

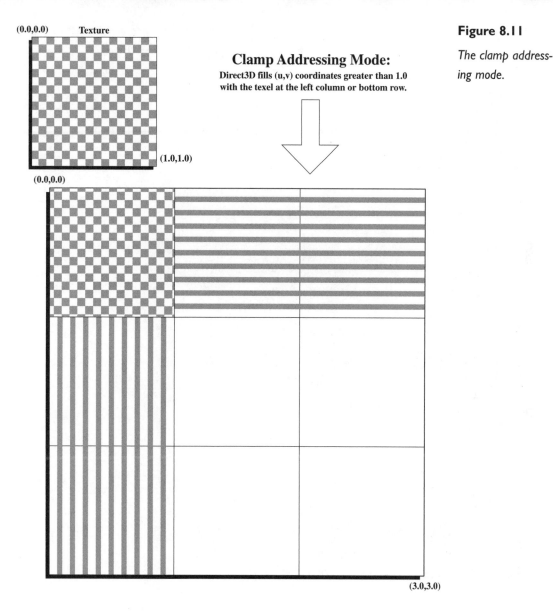

(0.0,0.0)   Texture

(1.0,1.0)

Clamp Addressing Mode:

Direct3D fills (u,v) coordinates greater than 1.0
with the texel at the left column or bottom row.

(0.0,0.0)

(3.0,3.0)

Figure 8.11

*The clamp address-
ing mode.*

This is especially useful if your border color is transparent. If you made a texture of an old wood-
en sign and made the border color *transparent* (having a 0.0 alpha component), you could apply
the texture to any rectangular surface and sleep well, knowing that the sign texture wouldn't tile,
clamp, or mirror itself across the surface. It would just appear in a corner.

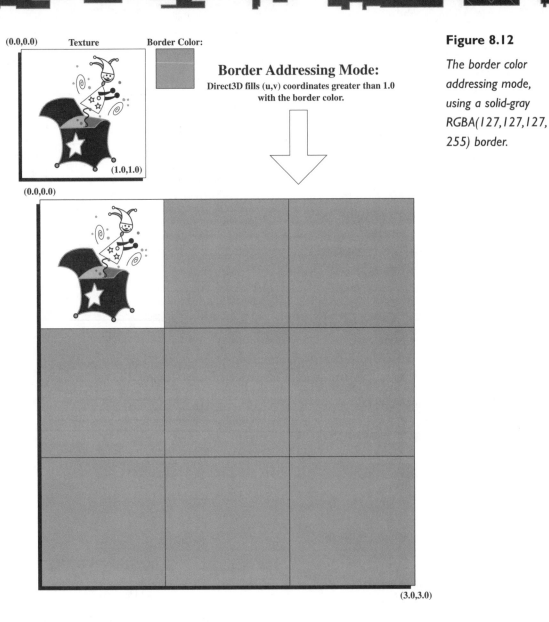

Figure 8.12

The border color addressing mode, using a solid-gray RGBA(127,127,127, 255) border.

Transparent Textures

As you might have already noted, texel colors have four components: the normal red, green, and blue values and an *alpha* value. The alpha value represents the degree of transparency the texel has. An alpha value of 0 means that the texel is completely transparent, and an alpha value of 255 represents complete *opacity* (solidness). An alpha value of 127 represents 50 percent transparency, so if you put a 50 percent red texel, say, RGBA(255,0,0,127), on top of a blue pixel, RGB(0,0,255), you'd end up with a purple pixel RGB(127,0,127).

Say that you're making a simple 2D game using Direct3D. You have a texture of a ball, a person, or another nonrectangular shape. Obviously, for things to look right, you need parts of this texture to be transparent.

Normally, in a 2D paradigm, you'd use color keying; you'd specify a certain color as transparent, and your 2D hardware would make sure that any sprite pixels of that color are not drawn.

> ### TIP
>
> **Texels aren't the only place to store alpha values. You can also store alpha values in the vertex color. This means that you must tell Direct3D which alpha values (vertex or texel) you'd like it to pay attention to. Essentially, you do this by manipulating the texture stage state variables. You will learn in detail about that in the next chapter, "Advanced Texturing."**

If you're a 2D programmer learning Direct3D, you might be a little shocked to hear that Direct3D does not support color keying. Instead, it provides you with two much better alternatives: alpha blending and alpha testing.

Transparent Textures through Alpha Blending

One way to achieve transparent textures is simply to make the alpha component of certain texels 0. If you enable alpha blending, any texels with an alpha component of 0 are not drawn.

The advantage to using this method is that you can also use other alpha values between 0 and 255 to represent partial transparency. Using semitransparent texels, you can create feathering and anti-aliasing effects.

The disadvantage is that this method is slower than alpha testing.

Transparent Textures through Alpha Testing

A second way to achieve transparent textures is to use Direct3D's alpha-testing capabilities. Think back to Chapter 5, "3D Concepts." Remember depth buffers, and specifically, how you change the depth buffer's comparison function by changing a few key render states? Alpha testing works exactly like the depth buffer comparison function, only instead of comparing values in the depth buffer, you're comparing the alpha value of a texel to a *reference* alpha value that you specify.

When alpha testing is enabled, Direct3D compares the alpha value of each of your texels with a reference alpha value you specify. Depending on which comparison function you tell it to use (greater than, less than, or equal to), Direct3D accepts or rejects the texel. If a texel is rejected, it is not drawn to the screen, giving you transparency.

Direct3D includes three render states used to control alpha testing:

- **D3DRS_ALPHATESTENABLE.** Set this render state to TRUE to enable alpha testing and to FALSE to disable it.
- **D3DRS_ALPHAFUNC.** This render state controls the logic that Direct3D uses to accept or reject a pixel. Set this render state to any of the D3DCMPFUNC values (the same set of values you learned about for the depth buffer). The default compare function is D3DCMP_ALWAYS, which accepts all alpha values.
- **D3DRS_ALPHAREF.** This is the alpha value against which Direct3D should compare your texel's alpha. Valid values are from 0 to 255.

Of course, you set all of these using the SetRenderState method of IDirect3DDevice8.

It's generally better to use alpha testing than alpha blending for simple transparency. *Simple transparency* means that your texels are either completely transparent or completely opaque. Alpha testing is generally faster, and it allows you to store only 1 bit of alpha information in your texture.

How Direct3D Blends Textures with Materials

In Chapter 7, "Lighting," you learned that Direct3D pairs each vertex with a material. The properties of the material, along with the light calculations, determine the final color of that vertex, and the surface is colored by *blending* (interpolating between) the colors of each vertex.

Now, with texturing thrown into the loop, you have two sets of color information. There's the color you calculated from the lighting and material properties, and there are the colors of the texture you're applying. You use a texture stage state to tell Direct3D where to get the final color value. In the next chapter, you will learn more about texture stage states.

BASIC TEXTURE PROGRAMMING

Okay, enough with the theory. Time to put it to use and learn how to write some Direct3D texturing code.

Here's the most common process you go through when using textures:

1. Make sure that the device you're running on supports the texture operations you need.
2. Load the texture from disk, or, if you're using an algorithm to generate the texture, generate the texels manually. Either way, you eventually end up with a new IDirect3DTexture8 interface.

3. Make sure that each of your model's vertices contains a (u,v) texture coordinate that tells Direct3D which texel corresponds to that vertex.

4. In your rendering code, select a texture for a surface, and then pump the vertices that use this texture into Direct3D. Select a different texture, pump those vertices in, and repeat until everything is textured. Repeat for each frame of your game.

5. Release the texture interface when you're done with it.

The following sections describe in detail how to accomplish these steps, along with some other common texturing procedures.

Determining Basic Device Texture Capabilities

The first thing you do before you start texturing everything is see what sort of features the device you're running on supports. In previous versions of Direct3D, this was a royal pain, but now it's more straightforward.

To figure out how smart the 3D card is, call the GetDeviceCaps method of IDirect3DDevice8. It fills in a D3DCAPS8 structure you supply with flags and numbers telling you what the card is capable of. Pay particular attention to the two members TextureCaps and TextureFilterCaps. Table 8.1 describes the basic flags against which you can AND these values to determine card capabilities.

> **TIP**
>
> Table 8.1 is not the full set of flags. I've listed only the flags that correspond to the basic texturing concepts you know about now. You will add more flags when you get to the advanced concepts, next chapter.

The TextureCaps flag tells you general information about the device's texturing capabilities. Table 8.1 presents the flags you should watch.

The TextureFilterCaps variable tells you what sort of texture filtering the device can perform for texture magnification (flags that start with D3DPTFILTERCAPS_MAG), texture shrinking (flags that start with D3DPTFILTERCAPS_MIN), and mipmapping (flags that start with D3DPTFILTERCAPS_MIP). Table 8.2 shows the most common flags to check.

The TextureAddressCaps variable tells you what sort of texture addressing the device can perform. Table 8.3 shows these flags.

Direct3D also provides a few important numbers in various members of the D3DCAPS8 structure, summarized in Table 8.4.

Direct3D has a few DevCaps flags that pertain to texturing, too, listed in Table 8.5.

Table 8.1 TextureCaps Flags

Flag	Meaning If TextureCaps & <Flag> != 0
D3DPTEXTURECAPS_ALPHA	This device supports alpha values in textures.
D3DPTEXTURECAPS_ALPHAPALETTE	This device draws alpha values from texture palettes.
D3DPTEXTURECAPS_MIPMAP	This device supports mipmapped textures.
D3DPTEXTURECAPS_NONPOW2CONDITIONAL	This card works with texture dimensions that are not powers of 2, provided that you use the clamp addressing mode, don't mipmap, and don't allow texture wrapping.
D3DPTEXTURECAPS_PERSPECTIVE	This card performs perspective-correct texturing.
D3DPTEXTURECAPS_POW2	All textures must have dimensions that are powers of 2.
D3DPTEXTURECAPS_SQUAREONLY	This card supports only square textures.
D3DPTEXTURECAPS_TEXREPEATNOTSCALEDBYSIZE	This card does not scale the texture indices based on the texture size prior to interpolation.

Table 8.2 TextureFilterCaps Flags

Flag	Corresponding Filter Type Supported If TextureFilterCaps & <flag> != 0
D3DPTFILTERCAPS_MAGFAFLATCUBIC	D3DTEXF_FLATCUBIC
D3DPTFILTERCAPS_MAGFANISOTROPIC, D3DPTFILTERCAPS_MINFANISOTROPIC	D3DTEXF_ANISOTROPIC
D3DPTFILTERCAPS_MAGFGAUSSIANCUBIC	D3DTEXF_GAUSSIANCUBIC
D3DPTFILTERCAPS_MAGFLINEAR, D3DPTFILTERCAPS_MINFLINEAR, D3DPTFILTERCAPS_MIPFLINEAR	D3DTEXF_LINEAR
D3DPTFILTERCAPS_MAGFPOINT, D3DPTFILTERCAPS_MINFPOINT, D3DPTFILTERCAPS_MIPFPOINT	D3DTEXF_POINT

Table 8.3 TextureAddressCaps Flags

Flag	Address Type Supported If TextureAddressCaps & <flag> != 0
D3DPTADDRESSCAPS_BORDER	Border.
D3DPTADDRESSCAPS_CLAMP	Clamp.
D3DPTADDRESSCAPS_INDEPENDENTUV	This flag means that you can set the addressing modes for the u and v coordinates separately.
D3DPTADDRESSCAPS_MIRROR	Mirror.
D3DPTADDRESSCAPS_MIRRORONCE	Mirror once.
D3DPTADDRESSCAPS_WRAP	Wrap.

Table 8.4 D3DCAPS8 Members to Watch

Member Variable	Description
MaxTextureWidth, MaxTextureHeight	Tells you the maximum texture dimensions supported by the card.
MaxTextureRepeat	Tells you the maximum number of times a texture can be wrapped (that is, the highest available value for your (u,v) coordinates).
MaxTextureAspectRatio	Tells you the maximum texture aspect ratio supported by the hardware (usually a power of 2).
MaxAnisotropy	Tells you the maximum anisotropic value supported by the device.

Table 8.5 DevCaps Flags

Flag	Meaning If DevCaps & <flag> != 0
D3DDEVCAPS_TEXTURENONLOCALVIDMEM	The device textures from nonlocal video memory.
D3DDEVCAPS_TEXTURESYSTEMMEMORY	The device textures from system memory.
D3DDEVCAPS_TEXTUREVIDEOMEMORY	The device textures from video memory.

As you see, Direct3D supplies you with a lot of information about a device's capabilities. Normally, you don't check every single little thing, but you should pay attention to the big stuff, such as the maximum texture sizes, so that you can tell up front whether something's not going to work and can compensate for that (or maybe just issue an error message and exit gracefully).

Setting the Filtering, Addressing, and Wrap Modes

Setting these parameters (or *states*) requires a call to SetTextureStageState, which looks like this (see Table 8.6):

```
HRESULT SetTextureStageState(
  DWORD Stage,
  D3DTEXTURESTAGESTATETYPE Type,
  DWORD Value
);
```

> **NOTE**
>
> The states and values listed here are a subset of what's available. The SDK contains the full list of texture states at DirectX 8.0\DirectX Graphics\Direct3D C/C++ Reference\Enumerated Types\D3DTEXTURESTAGESTATETYPE.

Direct3D supports many state types, including the following:

- **D3DTSS_MAGFILTER.** The filter you'd like to use for magnifying textures. You can use one of the following values: D3DTEXF_NONE, D3DTEXF_POINT, D3DTEXF_LINEAR, D3DTEXTF_ANISOTROPIC, D3DTEXTF_FLATCUBIC, or D3DTEXTF_GAUSSIANCUBIC.
- **D3DTSS_MINFILTER.** The filter you'd like to use for minifying the textures. This takes the same values as D3DTSS_MAGFILTER.
- **D3DTSS_MIPFILTER.** The filter to use between mipmap levels (the same values as D3DTSS_MAGFILTER).

Table 8.6 The SetTextureStageState Parameters

Parameter	Description
Stage	Specifies the texture stage that you want to set the state of. For this chapter, put a 0 here, which tells Direct3D to use stage zero. You use the other stages (one through seven) when you're multi-texturing, a technique I describe in detail in the next chapter.
Type	Specifies the state type you want to set.
Value	The value you want to set for this state. The values from which you can choose depend on what you put in Type.

- **D3DTSS_BORDERCOLOR.** A D3DCOLOR value that tells Direct3D what color the texels outside (1.0,1.0) should be when you're using the border filtering mode.
- **D3DTSS_ADDRESSU.** Selects the texture-addressing mode for the u coordinate. Valid values are D3DTADDRESS_WRAP, D3DTADDRESS_MIRROR, D3DTADDRESS_CLAMP, D3DTADDRESS_BORDER, or D3DTADDRESS_MIRRORONCE.
- **D3DTSS_ADDRESSV.** Selects the texture-addressing mode for the v coordinate (the same values as D3DTSS_MAGFILTER).
- **D3DTSS_ADDRESSW.** Selects the texture-addressing mode for the w coordinate. The w coordinate is used in 3D textures; it's the equivalent of the z coordinate. This takes the same values as D3DTSS_MAGFILTER.

Creating a Texture

As part of the DirectX SDK, Microsoft includes a Direct3D utility library, D3DX, that makes short work of the most common tasks, including texture creation. You're going to learn the bare-bones way to create a texture first and then learn the D3DX helper functions.

Bare-Bones Texture Creation

To create a texture without using any helper functions in D3DX, call the CreateTexture method of IDirect3DDevice8 (see Table 8.7):

```
HRESULT CreateTexture(
  UINT  Width,
  UINT  Height,
  UINT  Levels,
  DWORD Usage,
  D3DFORMAT Format,
  D3DPOOL Pool,
  IDirect3DTexture8** ppTexture
);
```

These flags specify how you use the Usage parameter:

- **D3DUSAGE_DEPTHSTENCIL.** Tells Direct3D that you will be using this surface as a depth stencil. If you create a texture using this flag, your usual next step is to pass it as the pNewZStencil parameter of the SetRenderTarget method.
- **D3DUSAGE_RENDERTARGET.** Tells Direct3D that you will be using this texture as a render target (later you will be instructing Direct3D to render a scene onto this texture). If you create a texture using this flag, your usual next step is to pass it as the pRenderTarget parameter of the SetRenderTarget method. Keep in mind that render target textures need to be put in the D3DPOOL_DEFAULT pool.

Table 8.7 The CreateTexture Parameters

Parameter	Description
Width	Specifies the width of the texture. Note that usually this has to be a power of 2.
Height	Specifies the height of the texture. Note that usually this has to be a power of 2.
Levels	Tells Direct3D whether it should create mipmap levels for this texture.
	If this parameter is 0, and you're running on hardware that supports mipmapping, Direct3D generates all texture levels down to 1×1 pixels. You use the GetLevelCount method of your texture to see how many levels Direct3D will generate for a certain texture dimension. You get to each texture level individually by calling the GetSurfaceLevel method.
	If you set this parameter to anything other than 0, Direct3D creates only one texture level.
Usage	Flags that specify how you will be using this texture (see the list preceding this table).
Format	Specifies the format of the new texture. You use one of the D3DFORMAT enumerations here, for example, D3DFMT_R8G8B8 or D3DFMT_R5G6B5.
	There's no way to make different mipmap levels of the same texture have different formats. All levels must have the same format.
Pool	Specifies into what class of memory the texture should go. You can choose one of D3DPOOL_DEFAULT, D3DPOOL_MANAGED, or D3DPOOL_SYSTEMMEM. Usually, you go with D3DPOOL_MANAGED.
ppTexture	If all goes well, Direct3D puts your new IDirect3DTexture8 interface here.

Quick and Painless Power-of-2 Math

The binary number system loves powers of 2. This means that bitmask operations make power-of-2 operations (on positive numbers) a snap. For example, here's a function that returns whether a given number is a power of 2:

```
inline bool IsPowerOf2(int n) { return (!(n & (n - 1))); }
```

To see how that works, simulate it by hand. Use the number *4* as an example:

```
4 = 100b
4-1 = 3 = 011b
100b & 011b = 000b, !000b = true
```

If you have a power of 2, when you subtract 1 from it, you basically invert all the bits below the leftmost set bit. Performing a logical AND on any bit and its inverse always produces 0.

Now take the number *5*, which, last time I checked, isn't a power of 2:

```
5 = 101b
5-1 = 4 = 100b
100b & 101b = 100b, !100b = false
```

In this scenario, you end up with at least one set bit in both the original number n and in n-1; that set bit gets through the logical AND operation and causes the function to return false.

Slick, isn't it. Hungry for more? Here's a GetLowestPowerOf2 function that returns the lowest power of 2 greater than or equal to a given number:

```
inline int GetLowestPowerOf2(int n)
{
  int lowest = 1;
  while(lowest < n) lowest <<= 1;
  return lowest;
}
```

Simple yet elegant. All you do is start with 1 and shift it left 1 bit until it's bigger or equal to your given number.

By exploiting the fact that computers are binary machines, you can quickly and easily calculate powers of 2.

Note that if you plan to use either of the Usage flags, you should check whether the device supports what you're trying to do. Call the CheckDeviceFormat of IDirect3D8.

That's the bare bones function. It gives you a new texture that you then load up with your texel data.

Unless you're doing something special, you usually *don't* use the bare-bones function. Instead, you use one of the D3DX helper functions that greatly simplify the process of loading images from files into textures.

> **TIP**
>
> Remember, there's no shame in using a utility function if it saves you work. Resist the temptation to rewrite your own versions of the D3DX functions (unless, of course, they lack something you need).

Creating a Texture Using D3DX

The D3DX function that creates a texture has a surprisingly good name: D3DXCreateTexture. D3DXCreateTexture takes the exact same parameters as CreateTexture and an additional parameter: the device interface you want to use to create the texture. Remember, D3DX functions exist separate from the methods of the DirectX interfaces, so most of the time they ask for an interface.

> **TIP**
>
> Why use D3DXCreateTexture instead of CreateTexture? Because D3DXCreateTexture checks your request against the capabilities of the device and adjusts your request to fit the device's capabilities, if needed. This means that arguments that don't work in calls to CreateTexture can work when calling D3DXCreateTexture, so less error-code checking and hassle for you.

Creating a Texture from an Image Using D3DX

A team of clever programmers made Direct3D. They realized that the one thing most 3D programmers want to do is load an image from somewhere and use it as a texture, so they created a whole set of D3DX functions to do just that.

D3DX includes six (count them, *six!*) functions that put an image into a texture. Use Table 8.8 to determine which one is right for you.

> **TIP**
>
> The D3DX image-loading functions support BMP, TGA, PNG, JPG, DIB, PPM, and DDS files. Use caution deciding in which image format you're going to store your textures. For example, the JPG (JPEG) image format is *lossy*, which means that your texture can lose detail. PNG, TGA, or BMP files are usually your best bets.

Table 8.8 The D3DX Texture Creation Functions

Image Location	Functions Available
Disk	D3DCreateTextureFromFile
	D3DCreateTextureFromFileEx
Resource	D3DCreateTextureFromResource
	D3DCreateTextureFromResourceEx
Memory	D3DCreateTextureFromFileInMemory
	D3DCreateTextureFromFileInMemoryEx

TIP

The function names in Table 8.8 aren't really names of functions. Internally, the Direct3D header files #define those strings and map them to one of two disk or resource functions, depending on whether you're using Unicode or ANSI strings. For example, D3DcreateTextureFromFile is #define'd to either D3DcreateTextureFromFileA or D3DcreateTextureFromFileW, depending on whether you've #define'd UNICODE.

Don't try to call the A or W versions of the functions directly. It's much better to play nice and use the macros.

In essence, you have two things to decide:

- **The location from which the image should be loaded.** D3DX supports loading from files on disk, resources inside your resource script, or files loaded byte for byte into memory. The memory function is the most useful because it allows you to store your images any way you want. The only requirement is that the block of memory you give to the D3DX function must be identical to what it would read off a file on disk.

- **Whether you want the normal function or the superpowerful extended (Ex) function.** The extended functions allow you to specify explicitly the parameters that D3DX eventually sends to the CreateTexture call. For example, you can specify the memory pool, surface format, and so on.

Look at the basic D3DX texture-loading functions first (see Table 8.9):

```
HRESULT D3DXCreateTextureFromFileA(
  LPDIRECT3DDEVICE8 pDevice,
  LPCSTR pSrcFile,
  LPDIRECT3DTEXTURE8 *ppTexture
);
```

There is nothing out of the ordinary here. In fact, it's so simple, it's a bit like magic—just give it a filename and a device interface, and you get back a texture. If something goes wrong, the function returns D3DERR_NOTAVAILABLE (the device is lost), D3DERR_OUTOFVIDEOMEMORY, D3DERR_INVALIDCALL, D3DERR_INVALIDDATA, or E_OUTOFMEMORY. Keep in mind that the D3DX functions don't pretend to work if a device is lost—they tell the truth.

Now look at the memory loader:

```
HRESULT D3DXCreateTextureFromFileInMemory(
  LPDIRECT3DDEVICE8 pDevice,
  LPCVOID pSrcData,
  UINT SrcData,
  LPDIRECT3DTEXTURE8 *ppTexture
);
```

Table 8.9 The D3DXCreateTextureFromFileA Parameters

Parameter	Description
pDevice	Specifies the IDirect3DDevice8 interface you want D3DX to use to create the texture. It's the device on which you're creating the texture.
pSrcFile	A string containing the filename from which you want to load. Note that this can be either ANSI or Unicode (refer to the preceding Tip).
ppTexture	If the call succeeds, this is where D3DX puts the pointer to the new IDirect3DTexture8 interface.

No need for a parameter table here. The only difference between this function and D3DXCreateTextureFromFile is that instead of the filename parameter, you have a void pointer and an integer that tells D3DX how big the block of memory is (the number of bytes used in memory by the file).

Finally, here's the resource loader:

```
HRESULT D3DXCreateTextureFromResource(
  LPDIRECT3DDEVICE8 pDevice,
  HMODULE hSrcModule,
  LPCSTR pSrcResource,
  LPDIRECT3DTEXTURE8 *ppTexture
);
```

I'm not going to kill more trees and make a parameter table here, either. Instead of asking for a file or memory chunk, this function asks for the handle of the module containing the resource script (usually, you put NULL here, which D3DX interprets as the module handle for the EXE currently running), along with a string specifying the resource from which to create the texture.

Extended D3DX Texture Creation Functions

The extended D3DX texture creation functions give you greater control over how D3DX loads and filters images and how it creates and sets up texture interfaces.

As an example, look at D3DXCreateTextureFromFileEx. The other extended functions (D3DXCreateTextureFromFileInMemoryEx and D3DXCreateTextureFromResourceEx) have more or less the same parameters, differing only where you'd expect them to (see Table 8.10):

```
HRESULT D3DXCreateTextureFromFileEx(
  LPDIRECT3DDEVICE8 pDevice,
  LPCSTR pSrcFile,
  UINT Width,
  UINT Height,
  UINT MipLevels,
  DWORD Usage,
  D3DFORMAT Format,
  D3DPOOL Pool,
  DWORD Filter,
  DWORD MipFilter,
  D3DCOLOR ColorKey,
  D3DXIMAGE_INFO *pSrcInfo,
  PALETTEENTRY *pPalette,
  LPDIRECT3DTEXTURE8 *ppTexture
);
```

Table 8.10 The D3DXCreateTextureFromFileEx Parameters

Parameter	Description
pDevice	Specifies the IDirect3DDevice8 interface you want D3DX to use to create the texture. You're creating the texture on this device.
pSrcFile	A string containing the filename from which you want to load. This can be either ANSI or Unicode (refer to the preceding Tip).
Width	The width of the texture, in pixels. Specify 0 or D3DX_DEFAULT here, and D3DX will take this dimension from the file.
Height	The height of the texture, in pixels. Specify 0 or D3DX_DEFAULT here, and D3DX will take this dimension from the file.
MipLevels	The number of mipmap levels you'd like to create. Specify 0 or D3DX_DEFAULT here, and D3DX will create a complete mipmap chain.
Usage	The only flag allowed here is your buddy D3DUSAGE_RENDERTARGET, which tells Direct3D that you will be using this texture as a render target (see Table 8.7 for a more detailed description of this flag).
Format	Specifies the format of the texture surface. Direct3D requires a member of the D3DFORMAT enumerated type here, for example, D3DFMT_R8G8B8.
Pool	Specifies the memory pool in which D3DX should put the texture. Your choices are D3DPOOL_DEFAULT, D3DPOOL_SYSTEMMEM, or the most common, D3DPOOL_MANAGED.
Filter	A combination of one or more flags that specifies how to filter the image size with the texture size. If you're loading a small image onto a large texture, or vice versa, this is the method D3DX uses to stretch or shrink your image.
	Consult the DirectX help for the full list of these values. Most of the time, you specify D3DX_DEFAULT, which maps to a combination of D3DX_FILTER_TRIANGLE (the slowest but most accurate filter) and D3DX_FILTER_DITHER (which tells D3DX to dither the image).

Table 8.10 Continued

Parameter	Description
MipFilter	Similar to `Filter`, `MipFilter` is a combination of one or more flags that specifies what filter to use when generating the mipmaps of the image (if applicable).
	Again, the DirectX help contains the full list of possible flags. `D3DX_DEFAULT` is your best bet here as well, corresponding to `D3DX_FILTER_BOX`, a filter that works best when the dimensions of the destination are half those of the source (like when you're mipmapping!).
ColorKey	The color key for this image. D3DX replaces this color with transparent black.
	Don't forget the alpha! Microsoft made this parameter a `D3DCOLOR`, which contains an alpha component. This means that it's entirely legal (although somewhat bizarre) to specify a nonopaque color key. Usually, however, your color keys are opaque (they have an alpha component of `0xFF`).
pSrcInfo	Give D3DX a pointer to a `D3DXIMAGE_INFO` structure here, and it will populate that structure, telling you the size of the image, color depth, surface format, and number of mipmap levels generated. If you don't care about these, pass in `NULL` here.
pPalette	Similar to `pSrcInfo`. If you give D3DX a `PALETTEENTRY` structure here, it populates it with the 256-color palette of the image, if applicable. The `PALETTEENTRY` structure hails from the land of general Windows programming. It's not DirectX-specific, so you have to look in the Windows SDK help file for information about it. In essence, it's just an array of 256 colors.
ppTexture	If the call succeeds, this is where D3DX puts the pointer to the new `IDirect3DTexture8` interface.

As you see, a typical extended D3DX texture creation function has many more parameters, which means much finer control.

When writing a serious 3D application, you will probably find yourself using the extended texture creation functions more than the basic ones because the extended functions let you specify color keys and filtering algorithms.

Selecting a Texture

Whew! Finally, through whatever function, you've loaded a texture and created a texture interface. The next step is to use that texture in a scene!

Using a texture is similar to using a Win32 GDI brush or pen. You specify which texture is active by putting its interface into a *stage*, or *active slot*, just as you'd select a Win32 GDI brush or pen.

When you give a vertex to Direct3D, it is tied to whatever texture is currently active. In a typical frame, you set the active texture, send a few vertices to Direct3D, switch the active texture, send a few more, and so on, until your scene is drawn.

You make a texture active by calling the SetTexture method of IDirect3DDevice8 (see Table 8.11):

> **TIP**
>
> Actually, Direct3D has eight active texture slots, or *texture stages*. You will be using only texture stage zero in this chapter. The other seven texture stages are used to achieve single-pass multitexturing, which I talk about in the next chapter.

```
HRESULT SetTexture(
  DWORD Stage,
  IDirect3DBaseTexture8 *pTexture
);
```

Table 8.11 The SetTexture Parameters

Parameter	Description
Stage	Specifies the texture stage you want to set. You use this for single-pass, multiple texture blending. For now, put 0 here.
pTexture	A pointer to the texture interface you want to make active for this stage. Don't be confused by the IDirect3DBaseTexture8 pointer. The IDirect3DTexture8 interface derives from IDirect3DBaseTexture8, so all is well. For mipmaps or other complex textures, this should be the top-level surface.

Direct3D uses reference counting to keep track of whether it's using a texture. When you set a texture stage, Direct3D increments the count of the texture you activated and decrements the count of the texture that was bumped out of the active slot (the texture that used to be active).

> **CAUTION**
>
> Make sure that when a texture stage is no longer needed, you set its texture to NULL (you call SetTexture(#, NULL). Failure to do this causes a memory leak. By the time you're done rendering, all texture stages should be NULL.

Mr. Vertex, Meet Mr. Texture

The final piece to the texturing puzzle involves binding a vertex to a certain (u,v) coordinate on a texture. This is easy. Make sure that your FVF has space for (u,v) coordinates, and then fill in those spaces with the (u,v) coordinate that corresponds to that vertex.

Keep in mind that your (u,v) coordinates are usually between 0.0 and 1.0, but not always. If you're using certain texture-wrapping modes, it's okay to go outside that range.

CHAPTER WRAP-UP

Texturing is tough, and you were introduced to a lot of new concepts this chapter.

The first 3D games had no texturing. The next batch of 3D games (which include early id games such as Wolfenstein 3D and DOOM) had very primitive texturing capabilities. When 3D accelerators hit the PC scene, they blew the doors open for more advanced texturing features, such as texture filtering, alpha blending, and so on. Since then, every new batch of graphics cards has thrown even more texturing features onto the pile, and it doesn't look as though textures are going to be getting any less complex any time soon. Of course, it's all good because it makes for eye-popping graphics. Most of the special effects you're going to learn about in the later parts of this book are really just texture tricks.

Taken all at once, it can be overwhelming, so my advice to you is the same as in previous chapters. Take your time, experiment, and make sure that you're comfortable with this chapter before you dive into the next.

ABOUT THE SAMPLE PROGRAMS

This chapter introduces no new coding style enhancements. You have enough to worry about with just the new texturing concepts! Here's what the program does:

■ Ch8p1_BasicTexture. This program demonstrates the most basic method of texturing.

EXERCISES

Only three exercises this chapter, but they're big ones:

1. Figure out the core texturing code, that is, the code that does the math to fit an arbitrarily sized bitmap into an arbitrarily sized rectangle. It's tough, so here's a hint: Don't loop through all the texels and try to figure out where each one goes in the destination rectangle. Reverse it—loop through all the points in the destination rectangle, and figure out what texel belongs at each point.

2. Experiment with the different alpha settings for your textures so that you can see for yourself what sorts of effects you can create with alpha blending. In the third part of this book, you're going to be spending a lot of time with alpha blending.

3. Use quads, along with textures, to simulate sprites and make a sprite-based game. Direct3D provides support for this, called *Point Sprites*, which you will learn about later. The exercise of writing your own sprite-based game using quads and textures will make learning about Point Sprites wicked easy. Besides, haven't you always wished for the excuse to remake a classic platform game?

CHAPTER 9

ADVANCED TEXTURING

Carl: "Hey, that's not easy, what I just did!"
——from the movie Sneakers

In the preceding chapter, you learned the basics of how to use textures to enhance the realism of a scene. You now continue this brave odyssey with some advanced texturing techniques you can use to make some very sweet eye candy.

MULTIPLE TEXTURE BLENDING

Multiple texture blending is a very complex and very important topic. In fact, given the amount of time you're going to spend on it, I could have easily titled this chapter "Multiple Texture Blending, with a Little Bit of Other Stuff." Brace yourselves.

In the preceding chapter, you learned that a 3D card can take a bitmap and use it to texture a surface. That's only half the story—Direct3D, along with virtually all the graphics cards out there today, can take *multiple* bitmaps and blend them together to texture a surface (see Figure 9.1).

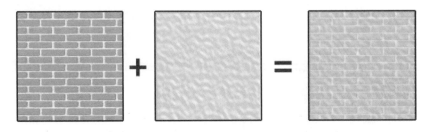

Figure 9.1

Multitexturing *means taking multiple textures and blending them together.*

3D graphics programmers refer to this as *multitexturing*, and it's a good tool for achieving nifty effects. Say that you're making an FPS game in which players run around and nuke one another with rocket launchers. Of course, you have textures for all the walls in your arena, but if you want to get fancier, you can also create crater or scorch mark textures and use multitexturing to blend those textures onto walls where rockets hit, creating battle scars in the arena.

CAUTION

I make that seem too simple. You also have to deal with the z-buffer to make sure that your geometry doesn't try to *clip* itself—that the first set of wall vertices doesn't inadvertently hide the second set. You do this using the z-bias render state, explained in Chapter 5, "3D Concepts."

Even if your card doesn't support texture blending, you can achieve the same results by just pumping all the geometry in twice. Set the wall texture active, push the wall vertices in once, set the scorch mark texture active, and then pump the wall vertices into Direct3D again. You render the same geometry repeatedly, with different textures.

The huge disadvantage to this method, called *multiple-pass texture blending,* is that you're doubling the amount of triangles in the scene. Unfortunately, that's the sacrifice you sometimes make to achieve the same effects on an older 3D card.

> **TIP**
>
> **You can use effects to make Direct3D choose the appropriate technique: single-pass multiple texture blending on cards that support it or slower multipass blending on old cards that don't. For more information, see the section "Using Effects."**

A Tabular Guide to Texturing Terminology

Keep in mind that there is a difference between multiple texture blending and multitexturing. Table 9.1 will set you straight.

Table 9.1 Texturing Terminology

Phrase	Meaning
Multiple texture blending, single-pass multitexturing	The process of combining multiple textures in a single rendering pass by using several texture stages instead of just texture stage zero.
Multiple-pass texture blending, multipass texture blending	You use two or more rendering passes to blend textures. You set one texture active, pump all your geometry in, set the second texture active, and pump the same geometry in again—or you render the whole scene once and then come back for the second pass.
Multitexturing	A generic term that means either multiple texture blending or multipass texture blending. Nowadays *multitexturing* generally means multiple texture blending, but some holdouts still consider it to mean multiple rendering passes.

Texture Stages

In Direct3D, you multitexture by using more than one texture stage. A *texture stage* has one purpose, to take two colors (and by *colors*, I mean RGB and alpha values) and blend them together. You specify the two color inputs, along with two operators (one for the RGB components of the color and one for the alpha component), which together determine how the texture stage combines those two input colors into a single output color (see Figure 9.2).

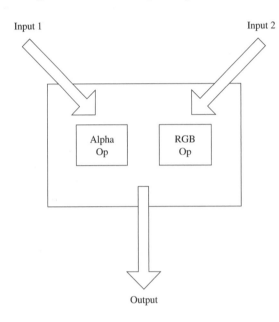

Input 1   Input 2

Alpha Op   RGB Op

Output

Figure 9.2

A texture stage consists of two inputs, two operators (one for RGB and one for alpha), and one output.

It might seem weird to have two operators. Normally, you tend to think of colors as RGBA components that can't be divided. Normally, you expect texture stages to have two inputs but only one operator that dictates what to do with those two inputs.

In practice, however, it's very useful to treat the color separate from the alpha. Specifically, it's very common to leave the color component unchanged but vary the alpha somehow, say, by interpolating it based on vertex alpha information. Also, you might want the color operator to add the two colors together and the alpha

CAUTION

A word of warning: Different video cards have very different multitexturing capabilities. Some cards allow only certain operators in certain texture stages, and hardly any cards are powerful enough to use all eight texture stages.

Be certain that you check the device caps before doing any hard-core multitexturing. You can also use effects, explained later in this chapter, to help ease the pain of all these card differences.

operator to apply a constant alpha (transparency factor). The final output color contains the results of both the color and alpha operations. In this case, it would be the two input colors added together and paired with a constant alpha value.

As you see, this is complex. By looking at the arguments and operators Direct3D supports and working through examples using those operators, all will become clear to you.

Texture Stage Input Arguments

The input colors into the texture stage can come from any of the following:

- **Bitmaps**. This is the most common case. Usually, one of your texture stage input colors comes from a bitmap (texture). (You spent the preceding chapter learning how to load and play with bitmaps.)
- **Lighting**. Recall that Direct3D can calculate a color for a surface (or, in the case of Gouraud shading, a smooth blend or interpolation of color) based on light and material information you supply. You can use the color it calculates as an input to a texture stage.
- **Constant**. This is the easiest case to explain. You can pass any color and/or alpha constant into a texture stage as an input.
- **Output of another texture stage.** Yep, you can chain these babies together by making, say, the output of stage zero one of the inputs for stage one. You will learn more about this in a few paragraphs.

Texture Stage Operators

When you have your inputs, you can perform the following operations on them:

- **Math**. You add or multiply (modulate) the two inputs, or you subtract one input from the other. Direct3D also includes many variations that enable you to manipulate the results of the math. For example, you can bit-shift the result of the modulation.
- **Select**. This is a simple pass-through operator. You tell Direct3D that the output of this texture stage should be either the first or second input, unchanged (you simply select one input to be the output).
- **Alpha blending**. You blend the two inputs using a constant alpha value or an interpolated alpha value coming from the vertex or texture. For example, you could choose a constant alpha of 0.5, which would blend the two inputs equally, or you could choose constant alphas of 0.25 or 0.75 to "sway" the blend in favor of the first or second input. Direct3D includes several alpha-blending operators, which use different formulas to blend the two inputs using an alpha parameter. You will learn about all these formulas when you get to the section on programming texture states.
- **Bump map**. You use a bump map operator to create the illusion of a rough surface by using another texture. You will learn the details of this later.

■ **Disabled**. The final operator isn't really an operator, but it deserves special mention. When you set a texture stage operation to disabled, you're telling Direct3D that the chain stops at the texture stage before the disabled one. If you set texture stage six to disabled, Direct3D uses the output of texture stage five as the final color. If you disable texture stage zero, you disable texture mapping altogether.

Don't worry if all of this seems overwhelming. Like the Force, the power of texture stages is vast, and it takes some time to appreciate fully all the things you can do. You will spend the next few pages deciphering this stuff, and you will also be using various combinations of inputs and arguments when you implement some of the effects in the second and third parts of this book. You will get to see a few combinations in action then as well.

A Simple Texture Stage Example

I'll pause at this point and use a simple example to illustrate how all of this works. Say that you have a wall texture, and you want to tint it slightly red (maybe the wall is red hot). To do this, you use texture stage zero only. You make the first input of texture stage zero your wall texture and then make the second input a constant RGB value of (255,0,0), which is bright red.

Now you choose an operator. What you want to do is blend the texture with your vertex's constant red color, so you need an alpha-blending operator. You choose an operator named D3DTOP_BLENDDIFFUSEALPHA, which tells Direct3D to blend the two inputs based on the alpha values contained in your vertices (see Figure 9.3).

For example, if your vertices have 0.5 for the alpha component of their diffuse color, Direct3D gives you an output that's blended equally with each input. Plugging in 0.75 or 0.25 sways the blend in one direction or another, like using a cross-fader on an audio- or a video-mixing device.

Finally, you set the color and alpha operators of texture stage one to disabled. This tells Direct3D that you're using only texture stage zero. (Actually, you only set the color operator to disabled. Direct3D doesn't allow you to disable just one operator; it's all or nothing. When you set the color operator to disabled, the alpha is also disabled.)

> **CAUTION**
>
> **Direct3D freaks out if you set just the alpha operator to disabled. The SDK says that setting only the alpha operator to disabled results in undefined behavior.**

Figure 9.4 illustrates what sort of beast you've assembled.

Of course, for an even more interesting effect, you could change the constant alpha value over time by slightly incrementing or decrementing it each frame. This would give you walls that pulse red. Cool, isn't it?

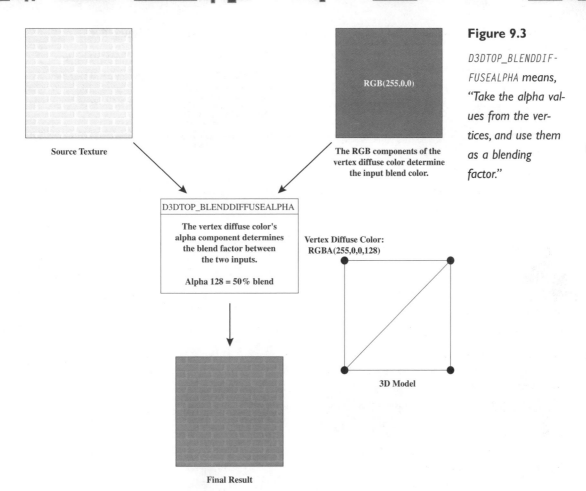

Figure 9.3

D3DTOP_BLENDDIF-FUSEALPHA means, "Take the alpha values from the vertices, and use them as a blending factor."

Source Texture

RGB(255,0,0)

The RGB components of the vertex diffuse color determine the input blend color.

D3DTOP_BLENDDIFFUSEALPHA

The vertex diffuse color's alpha component determines the blend factor between the two inputs.

Alpha 128 = 50% blend

Vertex Diffuse Color: RGBA(255,0,0,128)

3D Model

Final Result

A More Complex Example

You can achieve even more complex effects by chaining the texture stages together. To build on the example, say that your wall is glowing red, and now you want to apply some scorch marks to it. You have a separate scorch mark texture that you want to blend in with your glowing wall texture.

To do this in a single rendering pass, you need three texture stages and must re-arrange the processing order.

Look at Figure 9.5. Here you're using the first texture stage to get your first wall texture into the system. The second stage blends the wall and scorch marks, and the third stage tints everything red.

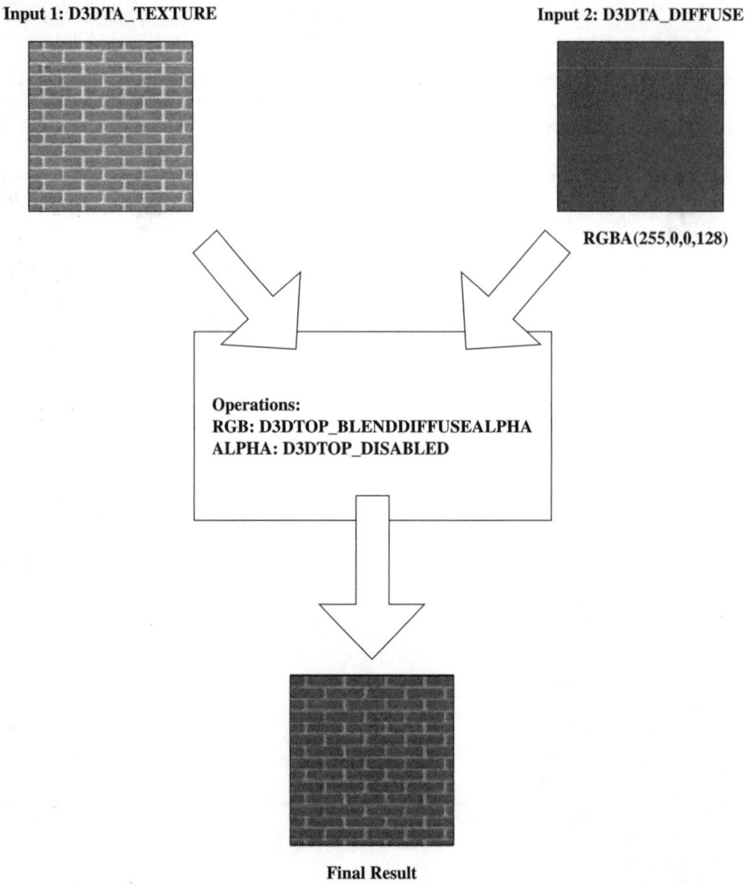

Input 1: D3DTA_TEXTURE

Input 2: D3DTA_DIFFUSE

Figure 9.4

The final set of texture stage states for your glowing red wall.

RGBA(255,0,0,128)

Operations:
RGB: D3DTOP_BLENDDIFFUSEALPHA
ALPHA: D3DTOP_DISABLED

Final Result

TIP

Note that when you're using more than one texture stage, all the stages except the first one have only one input because you pass the results of the preceding stage into the current stage through the other input.

Also note that even though each texture stage has two inputs, only one of those inputs can be a texture. You can't set up one stage that blends two textures because SetTexture allows you to specify only one texture per stage. To blend two textures, you need two stages. The first stage uses a select operation on the first input (the texture), and the second stage does the actual work by blending the output of the first stage (which is just the first texture) with the second texture (refer to Figure 9.5).

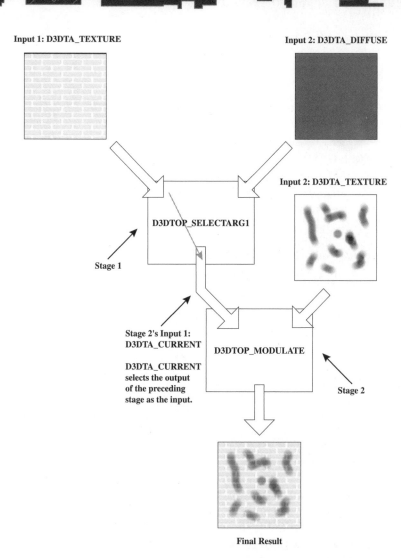

Input 1: D3DTA_TEXTURE

Input 2: D3DTA_DIFFUSE

Input 2: D3DTA_TEXTURE

D3DTOP_SELECTARG1

Stage 1

Stage 2's Input 1:
D3DTA_CURRENT

D3DTA_CURRENT
selects the output
of the preceding
stage as the input.

D3DTOP_MODULATE

Stage 2

Final Result

Figure 9.5

A set of texture stage states for blending a glowing red wall with a scorch mark texture.

Programming Texture Stages

Now that you know exactly how texture stages work, you can learn how to write code to get them to do your bidding.

Believe it or not, for all their complexity, you set up everything about texture stages using only one method: SetTextureStageState of IDirect3DDevice8. It takes three parameters (see Table 9.2):

```
HRESULT SetTextureStageState(
  DWORD Stage,
```

```
D3DTEXTURESTAGESTATETYPE Type,
DWORD Value
);
```

The following are states you can specify for the `Type` parameter:

- **D3DTSS_COLOROP.** Sets the color operation of this texture stage.
- **D3DTSS_ALPHAOP.** Sets the alpha operation of this texture stage.
- **D3DTSS_COLORARG1.** Sets the first color input of this texture stage.
- **D3DTSS_COLORARG2.** Sets the second color input of this texture stage.
- **D3DTSS_ALPHAARG1.** Sets the first alpha input of this texture stage.
- **D3DTSS_ALPHAARG2.** Sets the second alpha input of this texture stage.

You can pass other things in here as well, to set other parameters of the texture stage. See the preceding chapter and the SDK help for the full details.

If you put `D3DTSS_COLOROP` or `D3DTSS_ALPHAOP` in the `Type` parameter, the `Value` parameter tells Direct3D the operation you'd like the stage to perform. You have many choices for operations. The SDK contains the full list, but some of the more common ones include

- **D3DTOP_DISABLE.** Disables this operation. This tells Direct3D that it should use the output of the last stage as the final color.
- **D3DTOP_SELECTARG1.** Tells Direct3D to use this stage's first input as the output, unchanged.

Table 9.2 The SetTextureStageState Parameters

Parameter	Description
Stage	This specifies the texture stage you're modifying. Because Direct3D supports eight texture stages and they're zero-based, the valid values here are 0–7.
Type	This specifies the attribute (state) of the texture stage you want to modify. Each stage has several states, but you're concerned with only a few of them (see the preceding list).
Value	This specifies what you're setting the state of the texture stage to. What you can put here depends on what you've put in the `Type` parameter.

- **D3DTOP_SELECTARG2.** Tells Direct3D to use this stage's second input as the output, unchanged.
- **D3DTOP_MODULATE.** Modulates (multiplies) the two input colors together.
- **D3DTOP_ADD.** Adds the two input colors together.
- **D3DTOP_SUBTRACT.** Subtracts the second input from the first.
- **D3DTOP_BLENDDIFFUSEALPHA.** Blends the two inputs using the interpolated alpha value of the diffuse color of the vertices. For example, if you make a quad in which the left vertices have a 0.0 alpha value and the right vertices have 1.0, this blends the two inputs so that at the left side of the quad, the second input is at full intensity and the first input is transparent, and at the right side, the first input is at full intensity and the second input is transparent.
- **D3DTOP_BLENDTEXTUREALPHA.** Blends the two inputs using the alpha value of the appropriate texel of the texture of this stage.
- **D3DTOP_BLENDFACTORALPHA.** Blends the two inputs using a constant alpha. You set the alpha by setting the D3DRS_TEXTUREFACTOR render state, using a call to SetRenderState:
  ```
  // constant alpha value of 0.5 (128 is about 50% of 255)
  pDevice->SetRenderState(D3DRS_TEXTUREFACTOR, D3DCOLOR_RGBA(0,0,0,128)
  ```
- **D3DTOP_BLENDCURRENTALPHA.** Blends the two inputs using the alpha value outputted by the preceding stage.

If you put any of the color or alpha argument states into Type, you're using the Input parameter to tell Direct3D where to get the color information for that input. Your choices include

- **D3DTA_DIFFUSE.** Direct3D uses the diffuse color (interpolated from vertex to vertex if you're using Gouraud shading) as the input. If your flexible vertex format doesn't include vertex colors, Direct3D uses RGB(255,255,255) as the diffuse color.
- **D3DTA_SPECULAR.** Direct3D uses the specular color as the input. If your vertices don't have specular colors, Direct3D uses RGB(255,255,255).
- **D3DTA_TEXTURE.** Direct3D uses the texture as the input. That is, Direct3D uses the color of the appropriate texel of the texture you specify (by calling SetTexture) as the input.
- **D3DTA_CURRENT.** Tells Direct3D to use the output of the preceding texture stage as the input. If you specify this for stage zero, Direct3D uses the diffuse color, as if you had specified D3DTA_DIFFUSE instead. Note that if you're doing bump mapping, the texture stage you use for bump mapping is skipped. If you set an input for stage three to D3DTA_CURRENT, and stage two is a bump map, Direct3D uses the output of stage one for the input of stage three.
- **D3DTA_TEMP.** Certain graphics cards have a temporary holding place for color data, which you can read from and write to at will. This tells Direct3D to use that temporary place as the input color. Note that you should check the D3DPMISCCAPS_TSSARGTEMP capability to make sure that the device has a temp slot before you use it!

You can also combine (logically OR) these D3DTA_ flags with either of these two modifiers:

- **D3DTA_ALPHAREPLICATE.** Tells Direct3D to replicate the alpha information to all color channels, giving you an input color that's a shade of gray.
- **D3DTA_COMPLEMENT.** Tells Direct3D to invert the arguments (that is, the original argument value *x* becomes 1.0-*x*).

That, gentle reader, is how you multi-texture!

> **Sample Program Reference**
>
> Microsoft supplies a sample program named MFCTex as part of the DirectX SDK. MFCTex is a great tool that allows you to string together texture stages with various inputs and operations and see the results applied in real time. It's great for cooking up combinations of texture stages. Be sure to check it out.

LIGHT MAPPING

Light mapping is one of the most common real-life uses of multitexturing. 3D programmers use light mapping to create the illusion of light shining on a surface (or texture).

What Is Light Mapping, and Why Should I Care?

To see why light mapping is important, imagine for a moment that you need to generate an arena for your shooter game. Say that your arena has only three wall textures—a brick wall, a shiny plastic wall, and a granite wall.

You want your game to have very beautiful lighting. For example, if your level designers create a pillar and put a light in front of it, you want the wall behind the pillar to show the pillar's shadow.

Humanity has figured out the math that will give you correct light calculations for each of the pixels on your back wall to make the pillar's shadow appear. I'm not going to go into those equations here.

Assume that you do the math and end up with a new wall texture that includes the pillar's shadow. That's not what you want, though. If you did that for every shadow in your game, you'd end up with many more than three wall textures. You'd have a texture for each part of the wall that is illuminated differently. You'd have the texture of the wall with the pillar's shadow and myriad other textures with different shadows on them. You'd quickly use up your available graphics memory.

Another approach is to keep the same wall texture and blend it with what's known as a *light map*. A light map is usually a gray-scale texture; the near-white texels in the light map represent areas that have the most light, and the near-black texels represent areas with no light. The light map of your pillar's shadow would resemble Figure 9.6.

Figure 9.6

The light map of a pillar's shadow.

Of course, you still haven't gained anything because now you have your three original wall textures and all your light maps. What saves you is that your eyes can't tell the difference between really high-resolution light maps and really low-resolution ones. The resolutions of your light maps don't have to be nearly as big as the wall texture resolutions. Even if your wall texture is, say, 256×256 pixels, a light map of 16×16 pixels—making each texel of your light map represent a 16×16 area of light intensity on your wall—produces good-looking results. Also, light maps don't need the color depths that regular textures often do. You don't need 16 or 32 bits for each color; 8 bits gives you all the precision you need. In fact, if you're not using colored lights, you can use monochrome light maps, which save a huge amount of space!

All these optimizations bring the light maps' sizes down to a level where it *is* practical to store one base texture and dozens of light maps for the various shadows that appear on that texture. You *can* fit all these small light maps into graphics memory and can therefore give your scene realistic lighting.

Of course, all this depends on your being able to combine the original wall texture with the shadow texture, and that's where you use multitexturing.

You use multitexturing to blend the light map with the original texture, which creates the appropriate shadows and highlights.

Programming Light Mapping

To blend the texture with the light map—or as it's sometimes called, the *dark map*, because it darkens the texture, not lightens it—you set up your texture stages as shown in Figure 9.7.

The first stage outputs the original wall texture; the second stage blends the wall texture with the light map, using the D3DTOP_MODULATE operation, which darkens and lightens the correct areas. Here's how that looks in code:

```
m_pd3dDevice->SetTextureStageState(0, D3DTSS_COLORARG1, D3DTA_TEXTURE);
m_pd3dDevice->SetTextureStageState(0, D3DTSS_COLOROP, D3DTOP_SELECTARG1);
m_pd3dDevice->SetTextureStageState(0, D3DTSS_ALPHAARG1, D3DTA_TEXTURE);
m_pd3dDevice->SetTextureStageState(0, D3DTSS_ALPHAOP, D3DTOP_SELECTARG1);
```

```
m_pd3dDevice->SetTextureStageState(1, D3DTSS_COLORARG1, D3DTA_CURRENT);
m_pd3dDevice->SetTextureStageState(1, D3DTSS_COLORARG2, D3DTA_TEXTURE);
m_pd3dDevice->SetTextureStageState(1, D3DTSS_COLOROP, D3DTOP_MODULATE);
m_pd3dDevice->SetTextureStageState(1, D3DTSS_ALPHAARG1, D3DTA_CURRENT);
m_pd3dDevice->SetTextureStageState(1, D3DTSS_ALPHAARG2, D3DTA_TEXTURE);
m_pd3dDevice->SetTextureStageState(1, D3DTSS_ALPHAOP, D3DTOP_MODULATE);

m_pd3dDevice->SetTextureStageState(2, D3DTSS_COLOROP, D3DTOP_DISABLE);
m_pd3dDevice->SetTextureStageState(2, D3DTSS_ALPHAOP, D3DTOP_DISABLE);
```

Figure 9.7

A typical texture stage setup for light mapping.

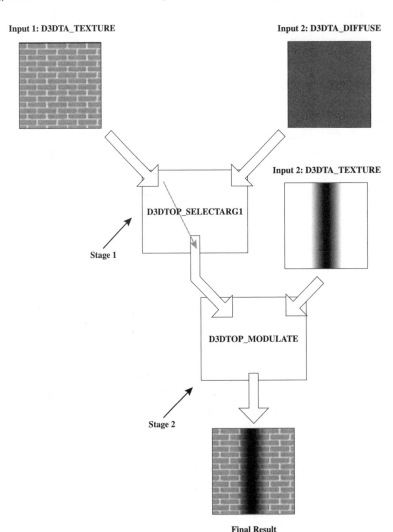

ENVIRONMENT MAPPING

Environment mapping could very well be the most beautiful 3D programming technique you learn. When I first learned how environment mapping worked, I was overwhelmed by the sheer realism of it, and I spent 18 straight hours learning about it and playing with its code.

Take the phone off the hook, and if you listen to music while coding, make sure that you have many songs in your play list because you, too, are about to be overwhelmed by environment mapping!

What Is Environment Mapping, and Why Should I Care?

Environment mapping allows you to render *stunningly* realistic metal or chrome objects by using a simple technique and some creativity in your texture coordinates.

The concept of environment mapping is devilishly simple. Say that you have a metal teapot floating in space. (What sort of game would call for such a scene is beyond me, but let's just suppose.)

The teapot is chrome, so you want it to look chrome. Chrome isn't a color, though. Chrome looks the way it does because it reflects the environment around it, like a mirror. In fact, chrome *is* a mirror, except that it's not flat like most mirrors. Chrome is a mirror bent in the shape of an object.

But wait! Textures are just rectangles, also! If you render a scene and then use that rendering *as a texture*, you can create realistic chrome!

That's what environment mapping is all about. In essence, you render the scene (or environment) as viewed from the position of the metal object. You then map this rendering onto an object. Instant chrome! Also, by using multitexturing to blend the rendered texture with a solid color, you can create painted metal. This is how all the cars in racing games look as though they've just been waxed.

3D programmers use two forms of environment mapping. If they need the other animated objects in the scene reflected off the metal object, they use cubic environment mapping because it's the fastest. That's important when you have to re-render the environment map texture every frame.

If the scene their objects reflect is static, 3D programmers most often use spherical environment mapping because it requires no additional calculations per frame (cubic environment mapping requires some extra calculations on each vertex in the metal object).

Here are both types, explained in more detail.

Spherical Environment Mapping

The technique of spherical environment mapping requires only one texture. This texture is a 360-degree, fish-eye rendering of the scene, shown in Figure 9.8.

Figure 9.8

Spherical environment mapping uses a texture of a 360-degree, fish-eye view of the environment.

Most of the time, 3D programmers render their fish-eye textures using a ray tracer or commercial 3D package. Because the scene is static, they don't have to render it once each frame. They can take their time rendering it during development and just have their application load it and use it as if it were any other texture.

That's exactly how the technique works. You derive the (u,v) coordinates from the vertex coordinates using the two formulas shown in Figure 9.9.

$$U = \frac{N_x}{2} + 0.5$$

$$V = \frac{N_y}{2} + 0.5$$

Figure 9.9

The formula for determining (u,v) coordinates, given a vertex's (x,y) coordinate components.

Many a math professor could tell you why and how these equations relate to the vertices when using a spherical environment map, but you don't have to know the math behind them just yet. Put your faith in geometry, and realistic metal, by way of spherical environment mapping, will surely come your way.

Sample Program Reference

The DirectX sample program SphereMap demonstrates spherical environment mapping in action.

Cubic Environment Mapping

Spherical environment mapping can't be used when your metal object has to reflect the other objects moving around in your scene. It takes too long to generate the 360-degree, fish-eye texture each frame. Instead, for dynamic reflections, you use cubic environment mapping.

> **Sample Program Reference**
>
> The DirectX sample program CubeMap demonstrates cubic environment mapping in action.

Cubic environment mapping uses a cube of six textures (left, right, top, bottom, front, and back) instead of just one fish-eyed texture. Each face of this texture cube has a rendering of the environment as seen from that position, looking in a certain direction (see Figure 9.10).

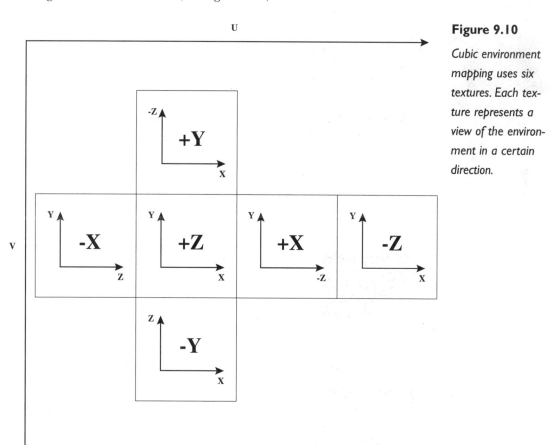

Figure 9.10

Cubic environment mapping uses six textures. Each texture represents a view of the environment in a certain direction.

OTHER USES FOR MULTITEXTURING

Multitexturing makes several other nifty, yet not as widely used, techniques possible. This section mentions other uses for multitexturing.

Glow Mapping

In essence, glow mapping is the same as light mapping, only instead of making things darker, you're applying a glow to certain objects. The technique itself is exactly the same. You still have your base texture, as well as a glow map texture. The only difference lies in the operation the second texture stage uses to combine the two textures. Use D3DTOP_ADD for the texture operation, instead of D3DTOP_MODULATE.

Detail Mapping

You can also use multitexturing to add an extra level of detail to surfaces that are close to the viewer. For example, you have a brick wall, and you'd like the brick wall to appear rough when viewed up close. For now, never mind that you could use bump mapping to achieve the same effect. Detail mapping and bump mapping have very similar purposes.

To achieve your bumpy brick wall, you simply take the brick texture and blend it with the bumpy texture, using a D3DTOP_BLENDDIFFUSEALPHA operation. Direct3D blends these two textures to create the appearance of a bumpy brick texture.

> **TIP**
>
> Note that you can use the same bumpy texture to make anything bumpy. If you had a stone wall that you wanted to appear bumpy, you could blend the stone wall texture with the same bumpy texture and achieve good-looking results.
>
> Note also that frequently you can algorithmically generate the bumpy textures you use for detail mapping, which means that you might not even have to store the bumpy textures on disk. Just have the program generate them when it loads, and you will be good to go. In Part 3, "3D Effects," I discuss algorithmically generating textures.

Color Saturation (a.k.a. Really Bright Objects)

In real life, when a strong beam of light (such as light from the sun) shines directly onto an object, that object appears saturated with white. There are no dark spots on the faces of an object that are exposed directly to sunlight.

You can emulate this effect in your games by combining the object's texture with a white diffuse color. In essence, the white diffuse color ups the brightness on the texture, creating the illusion of strong light hitting its surface.

USING EFFECTS

DirectX 8 includes a new feature—effects—that is nifty enough to warrant its own section in this chapter.

What Are Effect Scripts, and Why Should I Care?

It's no secret that 3D graphics card development moves at a blinding pace. It seems that, no matter what, the top of the line in January is considered primitive by March.

This would be great, except that, if you shell out $300 for a graphics card in January, you might not have another $300 for an upgrade in March. In fact, the majority of computer users *never* upgrade their graphics card (gasp!)—they're perfectly content with what's in the box to begin with. This means that a wide mix of new and old graphics cards is on the market at any given time.

As a game developer, you have three goals:

1. To make your game run on as many systems as possible.
2. To take advantage of the advanced features (such as single-pass multitexturing) on the newest graphics cards to create eye-popping 3D scenes.
3. To keep your sanity.

In the past, you had the freedom to choose any two of these goals (and many game developers chose options 1 and 2 because sanity is highly overrated anyway). Using effect scripts, however, it's easy to nail all three.

An *effect script* is a set of instructions that tells Direct3D how to perform several techniques it can use to render an effect. Some of these techniques look great but work only on high-end cards capable of single-pass multitexturing, advanced blending modes, and so on, and other techniques use fewer features, which enables them to run on older cards at the cost of speed or quality.

Say that you wanted to render water. If you were running on a high-end 3D card, it would make sense to use multitexturing and maybe even a little environment mapping to create a killer water effect. Conversely, on an older card, you would have to use multipass rendering, and for ancient cards, you would have to settle for using a single water texture (yuck!).

In the old days, to support as many graphics cards as possible, you'd hard-code all these techniques into your game, along with the code that looks at the graphics card capabilities and decides which technique to use. After you released your game, if you wanted to remake an effect to take advantage of the latest features on the newest batch of cards, your only option was to add the code, recompile, and redistribute the binary as a patch.

DirectX 8 allows you to store techniques as a set of texture stage states inside human-readable (text) effect files. You tell DirectX to load these effect files, and you can easily ask it whether a certain technique will work on a certain video card. Based on its answer, you decide which technique to use and tell DirectX. It uses the contents of the effect file to set up the correct texture stages, blending modes, and so on, for your chosen technique.

When a new graphics card comes out—and with it, new features—you can easily update your effect file and add techniques that use the new features. You don't have to change any code. You just update and distribute the new text file and let Direct3D take care of the rest.

The Process for Using Effects

Follow this basic process to use an effect:

1. Create your effect file. When you're done with this step, you will have created a text file that contains techniques. Each technique contains one or more *passes* (rendering loops). Each pass contains one or more state assignment commands (for example, setting the alpha blend state or color operation for a certain texture stage). I cover the process of creating an effect file in much more detail in the next section.
2. To begin using your effect file in your code, call the D3DXCompileEffectFromFile function to load your effect file and compile it into an ID3DXBuffer interface. As with texture creation, D3DX includes variants of D3DXCompileEffectFromFile that allow you to specify a chunk of memory instead of a filename, so you can store the effects however you like.
3. When you have an ID3DXBuffer interface, you call the D3DXCreateEffect function. D3DXCreateEffect takes your ID3DXBuffer interface, along with the IDirect3DDevice8 interface of the device on which you're rendering, and returns a new ID3DXEffect interface. The effect interface contains all your techniques.
4. Now that you have the effect interface, you probably want to find out which of its techniques will work with your device. To do this, you call the GetTechnique method of ID3DXEffect, which gives you a technique interface (ID3DXTechnique). Then you call the Validate method of that technique interface, which returns S_OK if the technique can run on the device. (Remember, you don't have to specify the device here because you already gave it to D3DX when you created the effect in step 3.)
5. To use the technique, call the Begin method of ID3DXTechnique after you call BeginScene. Begin returns to you the number of passes your code must execute for the technique to work. The next step, then, is to loop for the number of passes it tells you to, calling the Pass method of the ID3DXTechnique interface before you begin pumping the vertices for that pass.

Step 5 deserves sample code. Here you have a simple code segment that illustrates how to use techniques. Assume that pTechnique points to an ID3DXTechnique interface and pDevice points to an IDirect3DDevice8 interface.

```
UINT uPasses = 0;
pTechnique->Begin(&uPasses); // uPasses now contains # of passes
pDevice->BeginScene(); // begin the scene
// loop for the required number of passes...
for(UINT uPass = 0; uPass < uPasses; uPass++) {
  // call Pass method of technique so that it can set up the
  // render states.
  pTechnique->Pass(uPass);
  // pump the vertices into Direct3D.
  pDevice->SetStreamSource(0, pvbVertices, sizeof(WATER_VERTEX));
  pDevice->SetIndices(pIB, 0);
  pDevice->DrawIndexedPrimitive(D3DPT_TRIANGLESTRIP, 0,
                                uVertices, 0, uIndices -2 );
} // go to the next pass!
// scene done!
pDevice->EndScene();
```

The two most important things to remember are to call the Begin method of ID3DXTechnique and to call Pass each time you enter a new rendering pass.

That constitutes the basic process. Now you will learn how to create effect files.

Creating Effect Files

Effect files have simple syntax, as shown here:

```
{type} {id};
{type} {id} = {const};
// comments start with two forward slashes
TECHNIQUE {id}
{
    PASS {id}
    {
        {state}      = {const};
        {state}[{n}] = {const};
        {state}      = <{id}>;
        {state}[{n}] = <{id}>;
    }
}
```

In essence, an effect file can be divided into two main sections: a variable declaration section and a series of technique/pass blocks that describe how to render the various effect techniques. You assign values to different texture stages using equals statements, one per line.

Note that each technique and pass block has an ID, and you can get to these IDs in your code.

Variable Declarations

At the top of the file, you have your variable declarations. You have two choices here. Either you declare a variable equal to a constant, or you simply declare a variable.

Table 9.3 shows the available variable types.

TIP

Variable names must be valid four-character codes (FOURCCs). They cannot be longer than four characters.

HELP REFERENCE

For more information on legal variable types and how to assign constants to them, consult the DirectX SDK under DirectX 8\DirectX Graphics\Effect File Format\Constant Value Syntax.

Table 9.3 The Available Effect Variable Types

Type	Description
DWORD	A 32-bit integer value.
FLOAT	A floating-point value.
VECTOR	A vector of one, two, three, or four elements.
MATRIX	A 4×4 matrix of floats.
TEXTURE	A texture. You tie the texture to an IDirect3DTexture8 interface inside your code.
VERTEXSHADER	A vertex shader or customized vertex format, and/or vertex shader assembly code. See Chapter 24, "Vertex and Pixel Shader Effects," for more information.
PIXELSHADER	Shader assembly code describing a pixel shader. See Chapter 24 for more information.

Technique and Pass Blocks

After the variable declarations, you declare a technique by using the TECHNIQUE keyword, an ID for the technique, and a few braces. Within that technique declaration, you can define one or more PASS blocks. Each PASS block contains state assignments that set up the appropriate texture stages, blending modes, and so on, for that pass. In other words, this is where you tell D3DX what to do when you call the Pass method of ID3DXTechnique inside your rendering pass loop.

What sort of state commands can you put inside a pass block? Virtually anything you want—materials, lighting, and all the various states for each texture stage, as well as blending modes, and the like.

> **HELP REFERENCE**
>
> I could kill a bunch of trees here by listing the entire set of available state commands, but that doesn't make sense, considering that the SDK help already lists them all. Check out DirectX 8.0\DirectX Graphics\Effect File Format\List of Valid States.

Effects Wrap-Up

Effects are a deep little rabbit hole, much deeper than I have time to describe here, and they're worthy of detailed study. Effects combined with custom vertex and pixel shaders make a powerful duo, so be sure to check out Chapter 24.

> **HELP REFERENCE**
>
> For more information about how to create and use effects, look to the SDK help at DirectX 8.0\DirectX Graphics\Advanced Topics In DirectX Graphics\Effects and Techniques. For a reference guide to the effect file format, look at DirectX 8.0\DirectX Graphics\Effect File Format.
>
> The help also contains an example of an effect file at DirectX 8.0\DirectX Graphics\Advanced Topics in DirectX Graphics\Effects and Techniques\Using Effects and Techniques\Sample Effect File.
>
> Finally, the DirectX SDK includes a sample program, Water, demonstrating effects.

CHAPTER WRAP-UP

Congratulations, you're a texturing monster.

From here, you move to shaders, which give you ultimate power over your 3D card by allowing you to program it directly.

> **NOTE**
>
> The DirectX SDK has several sample programs that demonstrate the concepts in this section. Check out the following:
>
> - `CubeMap`. Demonstrates how to use cubic environment mapping.
> - `SphereMap`. Demonstrates spherical environment mapping.
> - `Fisheye`. Illustrates how to use cube mapping to achieve a fish-eye effect.
> - `Water`. Illustrates how to use effects by showing water rendered using several techniques.

ABOUT THE SAMPLE PROGRAMS

No enhancements to the coding style this chapter. Here are the programs:

- `Ch9p1_GlowingWall`. A simple demonstration of multitexturing techniques in action.
- `Ch9p2_AnimGlowingWall`. Builds on the first sample program, showing you how to animate your glowing wall.

EXERCISES

1. Take the `Ch9p1_MultiTexture` program and change the texture stage states around. Change the various input arguments and operators so that you figure out what each does.
2. Come up with a set of texture stage states that renders glass objects.
3. Take the `Ch9p1_MultiTexture` program and make it use effects. Write an effect file containing two techniques to achieve multitexturing. One technique should use multiple passes; the other technique should use single-pass multitexturing.

CHAPTER 10

VERTEX AND
PIXEL SHADERS

*"To know a thing well, know its limits. Only when pushed
beyond its tolerances will true nature be seen."*
——*Paul Mu'adib, from the movie* Dune

In this chapter, you are going to learn how to program *shaders*—specifically, vertex and pixel shaders. In essence, Direct3D allows you to code little functions that operate on each vertex of your world or finished pixel of your scene, using a special Direct3D minilanguage that looks a lot like assembly language. This enables you to create spectacular effects and still be sure that your code will run as fast as possible on all graphics cards. Behind the scenes, your vertex and pixel shader code can run on different hardware, depending on the graphics card used. For advanced cards, your code can run *on the card itself* if the card has a little CPU just for running shader code. On less advanced cards, Direct3D can push the shader code through your main CPU or do a combination, pushing some code through the CPU and the rest through the graphics card.

You don't have to worry about where your code actually runs. All you need to know is that on a given system configuration, Direct3D can set up things so that the vertex and pixel shader code runs as fast as possible. This means that any effects you create using the shaders will run as fast as possible(!).

Prepare yourself—shaders are weird little creatures. You might not immediately see the benefits to using a pixel or vertex shader, but stick with them. You will soon appreciate the power they possess.

WHY SHADERS?

In the beginning of 3D graphics programming, the graphics cards were simple, which meant that the API controlling them could also be simple. For example, if the state of the art in graphics cards does one texture stage and maybe a handful of blending operations, it makes sense to control that card by using a set of modes. You make API calls to set the texture mode and the blend mode, and you're done. Your API is simple, and it can do everything your card does.

Now let's crank up the complexity of the card. All of a sudden, you need more and more mode API calls to deal with the card's various features. You have multiple texture stages, different color- and alpha-blending operations for each stage, and more addressing modes, bump mapping, and so on. As you can see by the size of the Direct3D API, you need a huge number of API functions to deal with all those modes.

Because graphics cards continue to become more complex, Microsoft implemented a far better approach. Rather than use API calls to set modes on the card, you just write code for a virtual machine in an assembly-like programming language. With a code paradigm in place, you no longer have to worry about carefully setting each of the card's dozens of available modes to achieve the effect you're going for. Instead, you learn the architecture of the virtual machine and write code for that architecture to accomplish your task.

Vertex and pixel shaders make it much easier for you to create unique special effects for your applications. They're a much cleaner, more elegant solution than the texture stage states and rendering states, and they also enable you to do much more interesting things.

Now you will see how they work, starting with vertex shaders.

VERTEX SHADERS

First, I will nail down what exactly a vertex shader is.

Vertex shaders replace the transformation and lighting pipeline you learned about in Chapter 5, "3D Concepts" (see Figure 10.1).

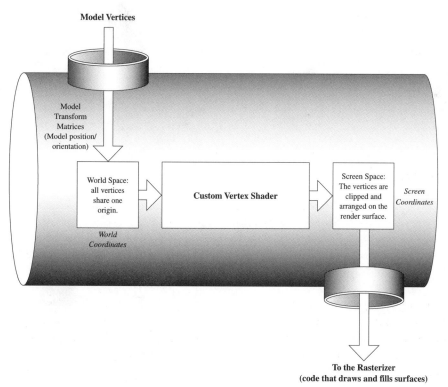

Figure 10.1

Vertex shaders replace most of the transformation and lighting pipeline.

A *vertex shader* takes a vertex as input and outputs a transformed, lit vertex. Now, depending on how you define your vertex format, a vertex can consist of many things: diffuse color, texture coordinates, a normal, you name it. This means that your vertex shader can have several inputs and outputs. In essence, though, a vertex shader is nothing more than a function (see Figure 10.2). It has a specific set of inputs, it runs some code against those inputs, and it outputs a specific set of things.

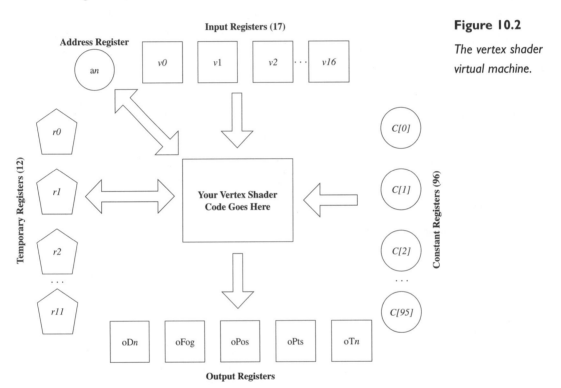

Figure 10.2

The vertex shader virtual machine.

To use a vertex shader, you first write the code for it and store the code in a text file, usually with the extension .s. After that's done, inside your main program, you use D3DX functions to load that file and compile it. When the D3DX functions succeed, they give you back a handle to your vertex shader. You then give this handle to the SetVertexShader method of IDirect3DDevice8, and that sets your vertex shader active.

Wait a minute, though—you have seen SetVertexShader before, in the first 3D sample program. You might not realize it, but you have been using a vertex shader ever since you rendered your first 3D scene. Direct3D comes with a default vertex shader. To use that default vertex shader, you call SetVertexShader, but rather than give it a vertex shader handle, you give it a combination of flexible vertex flags—which is exactly what you have been doing.

The default shader is special because various Direct3D interfaces can control its calculations. For example, you influenced the calculations of the default vertex shader when you set up different light types using IDirect3DDevice8 methods such as SetLight or LightEnable, in Chapter 7 "Lighting".

You can't control your custom vertex shaders the same way, but that's okay—you're not losing any functionality. Your custom vertex shaders can still do everything the default shader does, only now, rather than call methods, you get your vertex shader to do your bidding by manipulating its inputs directly. In addition to the required vertex inputs, vertex shaders also take constants as inputs. These constant values can be set inside your main program, before you start pumping vertices. This means that you can communicate with your shader code by passing values from your main program into its constants.

Effects You Can Make Using Vertex Shaders

The ability to write your own vertex-processing code blows the doors open for many interesting effects. Here are just a couple examples, taken from the DirectX SDK help file:

- **Waves**. As your vertex shader processes each vertex of your landscape, it can manipulate the vertex's z value to create a wave or ripple effect. This is a killer technique for generating realistic water. You use the constants to pass in the parameters of the wave you want the shader to create.
- **Muscles**. As your vertex shader processes each vertex of your model, it can distort some of the vertex's coordinates, based on the shape and position of a sphere. You can use this to simulate some guy's ripped bicep moving as he lifts something. You can also use this technique to achieve the "There's something crawling under my skin!" effect, such as when Neo dives into the agent at the end of *The Matrix*. You can pass the coordinates and shape of the perturbing sphere into your shader through the constant registers, so by specifying different spheres, you can use the same shader for several effects.
- **Bones**. Your shader can move the vertices of your model, based on the position and weight of your model's "bones," enabling you to create a skeletal animation system for the characters in your game.

That should be enough to sell you on the power and flexibility of vertex shaders. Now you will get technical and start learning how they work.

Determining Whether a Device Supports Vertex Shaders

First things first—all this discussion is no good if the device you're on doesn't support vertex shaders. Use the members of the D3DCAPS8 structure to answer your questions (see Table 10.1).

Table 10.1 D3DCAP8 Shader Members

Member	Description
MaxPrimitiveCount	The maximum number of primitives you can specify in each call to DrawPrimitive.
MaxVertexIndex	The maximum size of the vertex indices you can use for hardware vertex processing.
MaxStreams	The maximum number of concurrent data streams you can have.
MaxStreamStride	The maximum data stream for one data stream stride.
MaxVertexShaderConst	The maximum number of vertex shader constants you can use.
VertexShaderVersion	The level of support for vertex shaders.

VertexShaderVersion indicates the following levels of support:

- **0: DirectX 7.0.** This device does not support vertex shaders.
- **1.0: DirectX 8.0.** You can use vertex shaders, but you do not have the address register A0.
- **1.1: DirectX 8.0.** You can use vertex shaders, and you have the A0 address register. 1.1 is what you're hoping for, but the only difference between 1.0 and 1.1 is the missing address register A0.

Most of the cards out there now support vertex shaders, but it never hurts to check.

Specifying the Inputs to a Vertex Shader

After you verify that your card supports vertex shaders, the next order of business is to define exactly the inputs your vertex shader function will take.

You specify the inputs as an array of DWORDs. Direct3D deduces your vertex shader's inputs from an array of DWORDs, filled with certain flags and numbers. You don't usually specify these flags and numbers directly. Instead, you use the D3DVSD_ macros, which save you the headache of making sure that you flip the right bits in the array.

Here is an example, which I will decipher. Say that your vertex structure looks something like this:

```
struct Vertex
{
    D3DXVECTOR3 Position;
    D3DXVECTOR3 Normal;
    D3DCOLOR    Diffuse;
    D3DXVECTOR2 TexCoord0;
};
```

As you can see, you have a position (specified by a three-element vector), a normal, a diffuse color, and one set of (u,v) texture coordinates (specified by a two-element vector). That's typical, so, given what you learned in Chapter 6, "An Introduction to DirectGraphics," your flexible vertex flags would look like this:

```
DWORD dwFvf = D3DFVF_POSITION | D3DFVF_NORMAL | D3DFVF_DIFFUSE |
              D3DFVF_TEX0 | D3DFVF_TEXCOORDSIZE2(0);
```

Now you will learn how to tell Direct3D that your vertex shader takes these parameters as inputs. It all begins, of course, with an array of DWORDs. You don't know (or care) how long this array will be, so you define it like this:

```
DWORD dwVertexInputDecl[] =
{
};
```

To specify your inputs, you rely on the macros shown in Table 10.2.

For the first parameter of the D3DVSD_REG macro, you use any of the following values:

- D3DVSDE_POSITION
- D3DVSDE_BLENDWEIGHT
- D3DVSDE_NORMAL
- D3DVSDE_PSIZE
- D3DVSDE_DIFFUSE
- D3DVSDE_SPECULAR
- D3DVSDE_TEXCOORD0
- D3DVSDE_TEXCOORD1
- D3DVSDE_TEXCOORD2
- D3DVSDE_TEXCOORD3
- D3DVSDE_TEXCOORD4

Table 10.2 D3DVSD Macros

Macro	Example	Description
D3DVSD_STREAM	D3DVSD_STREAM(0)	Tells Direct3D from which stream to get the vertex data. This is usually the first macro you use.
D3DVSD_END	D3DVSD_END()	Tells Direct3D that this is the end of the DWORD array.
D3DVSD_REG	D3DVSD_REG(D3DVSDE_POSITION, D3DVSDT_FLOAT3) D3DVSD_REG(D3DVSDE_DIFFUSE, D3DVSD_REG(D3DVSDE_POSITION, D3DVSDT_FLOAT3) D3DVSD_REG(D3DVSDE_DIFFUSE, D3DVSDT_D3DCOLOR)	Specifies a data element of your vertex structure, along with that element's data type. You will use this macro the most often. The first parameter is the ID of the vertex component (color, position, and the like). All these IDs are #defines that start with D3DVSDE_ (for *Direct3D Vertex Shader Data Element*). The second parameter is the type of the data element. All these IDs start with D3DVSDT_ (for *Direct3D Vertex Shader Data Type*). Remember, the order in which you specify data elements must be the same as the order of the data members in your vertex structure so that things line up inside the vertex buffer.
D3DVSD_CONST	D3DVSD_CONST(8, 1), *(DWORD*)&diffuse[0], *(DWORD*)&diffuse[1], *(DWORD*)&diffuse[2], *(DWORD*)&diffuse[3], ...	Specifies a constant value. The first parameter tells Direct3D which constant register to begin filling with data, the second parameter tells Direct3D the number of constant *vectors* (not bytes—vectors are four DWORDs each!) to load.

Table 10.2 Continued

Macro	Example	Description
D3DVSD_NOP	D3DVSD_NOP()	Generates a NOP (*no operation*) token.
D3DVSD_SKIP	D3DVSD_SKIP(2)	Tells Direct3D to skip the specified number of DWORDs in the vertex. This can be useful if you have additional information in your vertex structure that you don't want to send to your shader.
D3DVSD_STREAM_TESS	D3DVSD_STREAM_TESS()	Sets the tesselator stream (for advanced vertex shader operations).
D3DVSD_TESSNORMAL	D3DVSD_TESSNORMAL(0,1)	Specifies that you want to enable tesselator-generated normals. The first parameter specifies the input stream; the second parameter specifies the stream where the normals will be written to. This command is used for advanced shader techniques.
D3DVSD_TESSUV	D3DVSD_TESSUV(5)	Specifies that you want to enable tesselator-generated surface parameters. The parameter specifies the output stream where you'd like the parameters to go.

- D3DVSDE_TEXCOORD5
- D3DVSDE_TEXCOORD6
- D3DVSDE_TEXCOORD7

For the second parameter of the D3DVSD_REG macro, you use any of the following values:

- **D3DVSDT_D3DCOLOR.** A D3DCOLOR
- **D3DVSDT_FLOAT1.** One float
- **D3DVSDT_FLOAT2.** Two floats
- **D3DVSDT_FLOAT3.** Three floats
- **D3DVSDT_FLOAT4.** Four floats
- **D3DVSDT_UBYTE4.** 4 bytes

As you can see, you probably won't use some of the D3DVSD_ macros. The most important ones are D3DVSD_REG, which registers an element of your structure, D3DVSD_STREAM, which tells Direct3D which vertex stream you want to use, and D3DVSD_END, which ends the array.

Given this simple vertex structure, you can now define the shader inputs:

```
struct Vertex
{
    D3DXVECTOR3 Position;
    D3DXVECTOR3 Normal;
    D3DCOLOR    Diffuse;
    D3DXVECTOR2 TexCoord0;
};
DWORD dwDecl[] =
{
    D3DVSD_STREAM( 0 ),
    D3DVSD_REG( D3DVSDE_POSITION,  D3DVSDT_FLOAT3 ),
    D3DVSD_REG( D3DVSDE_NORMAL,    D3DVSDT_FLOAT3 ),
    D3DVSD_REG( D3DVSDE_DIFFUSE,   D3DVSDT_D3DCOLOR
),
    D3DVSD_REG( D3DVSDE_TEXCOORD0, D3DVSDT_FLOAT2 ),
    D3DVSD_END()
};
```

See how your vertex structure and input declaration fit together? For each element in the vertex structure, you put a corresponding D3DVSD_REG command inside the input declaration.

> **CAUTION**
>
> You must specify the inputs to your shader in the exact order you declare them in the structure. Otherwise, your vertex data will not line up correctly in memory. If you have a member of your vertex structure that you don't want to input to your shader function, use the D3DVSD_SKIP macro to skip over it.

Vertex Shader Assembly Language

After you specify your inputs, you can write the code for your vertex shader. You do this using a language that resembles assembly language. To learn this language, you have to know the registers (variables) with which you can work and the operations you can perform on those variables.

You will start with the registers.

Vertex Shader Registers

Table 10.3 summarizes the registers available for vertex shader programming. Keep in mind that when you see an *n* in the register name, it stands for an integer—for example, vn stands for v0, v1, v2, and so on.

Table 10.3 Vertex Shader Registers

Register	Description
an	Address registers.
	Currently, there is only one address register, a0, that only has one element, x (so a0.x). You can use the address register as a relative address into the array of constants, as in c[a0.x + n]. In this line, you're using the a0.x address register as in index into the array of constants. You can also do the following: c[a0.x + 5]. That is, you can add a number onto the address register and use that sum as an index into the array of constants.
c[n]	Constant registers.
	The vertex shader language supports at least 96 constant registers— the D3DCAPS8 structure gives the exact number of constants supported.
	If you try to read a constant whose index is out of range, you get back (0.0, 0.0, 0.0, 0.0).
	Your program can put values into the constant registers using the SetVertexShaderConstant method of IDirect3DDevice8.

Table 10.3 Continued

Register	Description
rn	Temporary registers you can use for calculation.
	The vertex shader language supplies 12 temporary registers—each register is four floating-point values. You can use up to three temporary registers per operation.
	Note that Direct3D destroys the contents of the temporary registers each time your shader finishes executing. This means that your vertex shader code must write to a temporary register before it reads from it—failure to do so results in a compile error.
vn	The input registers. The vertex shader language supplies 17 input registers.
oDn	Output data registers used to output vertex color data. These data registers are interpolated by the system and then sent into a pixel shader. You use them most often for color information.
oFog	The output fog factor. Direct3D uses only the x component of this 4D float.
oPos	The output position. Arguably the most important thing you calculate, this register contains the final position in homogenous clipping space.
oPts	The output point-size registers. Direct3D uses only the x component of this 4D float.
oTn	The output texture coordinate registers. Direct3D uses these values to determine which texels correspond to this vertex.

The vertex shader language provides several different inputs, detailed here:

- **v0.** Position
- **v1.** Blend Weight
- **v2.** Blend Indices
- **v3.** Normal
- **v4.** Point Size

- **v5.** Diffuse Color
- **v6.** Specular Color
- **v7.** Texture Coordinates 0
- **v8.** Texture Coordinates 1
- **v9.** Texture Coordinates 2
- **v10.** Texture Coordinates 3
- **v11.** Texture Coordinates 4
- **v12.** Texture Coordinates 5
- **v13.** Texture Coordinates 6
- **v13.** Texture Coordinates 7
- **v13.** Position 2
- **v13.** Normal 2

To recap in more detail, the purpose of a vertex shader is to take the inputted vn registers, perform calculations on them (using the cn constant registers, the an address register, and the rn temporary registers if needed), and finally output the o registers your program uses: oDn, oFog, oPos, oPts, and oTn—the color, fog factor, position, point size, and texture coordinates of the inputted vertex.

> **HELP REFERENCE**
>
> The DirectX SDK help file has more detailed descriptions of each register. See DirectX 8.0\DirectX Graphics\Direct3DX Shader Assemblers Reference\Vertex Shader Assembler Reference\Registers.

Now you will look at the operations you can perform on these registers.

Vertex Shader Instructions

Table 10.4 summarizes the instructions available in the vertex shader language.

Note that the lit instruction assumes that the source vector vSrc0 contains the following information:

- vSrc0.x = N*L (the dot product between the vertex's normal and its direction to the light)
- vSrc0.y = N*H (the dot product between the vertex's normal and its half vector)
- vSrc0.z = ignored
- vSrc0.w = The power, in the range of –128 to +128

The Direct3DX team has also included the macro instructions shown in Table 10.5. These macros wrap up several instructions into one macro instruction, making for more readable and less error-prone coding.

Table 10.4 Vertex Shader Instructions

Instruction	Syntax	Description
add	add vDest, vSrc0, vSrc1	Adds vSrc0 and vSrc1 together and puts the result in vDest.
dp3	dp3 vDest, vSrc0, vSrc1	Calculates the three-component dot product of vSrc0 and vSrc1 and puts the result in vDest.
dp4	dp4 vDest, vSrc0, vSrc1	Calculates the four-component dot product of vSrc0 and vSrc1 and puts the result in vDest.
dst	dst vDest, vSrc0, vSrc1	Calculates the distance vector and puts the result in vDest.
		This instruction assumes that vSrc0's components are (*ignored*, d*d, d*d, *ignored*), and vSrc1's components are (*ignored*, 1/d, *ignored*, 1/d). When the instruction is finished, vDest will contain (1, d, d*d, 1/d).
expp	expp vDest, vSrc0	The expp instruction allows you to calculate "2 to the power of vSrc0," with partial precision. This instruction stores the answer in vDest.z.
		Note that this operation is undefined if you pass in a negative number.
lit	lit vDest, vSrc0	The lit instruction allows you to calculate lighting coefficients from two dot products and a power.
log	log vDest, vSrc0	Provides $\log_2(x)$ calculations with partial precision. This instruction stores the answer in vDest.z.
mad	mad vDest, vSrc0, vSrc1, vSrc2	Multiplies vSrc0 and vSrc1, adds vSrc2 onto the product, and puts the results in vDest.
max	max vDest, vSrc0, vSrc1	Fills vDest with the largest components of vSrc0 and vSrc1. For example, if vSrc0.x = 0.5 and vSrc1.x = 0.75, then vDest.x = 0.75.

Table 10.4 Continued

Instruction	Syntax	Description
min	max vDest, vSrc0, vSrc1	Same as max but uses the smallest components. Fills vDest with the smallest components of vSrc0 and vSrc1. For example, if vSrc0.x = 0.5 and vSrc1.x = 0.75, then vDest.x = 0.5.
mov	mov vDest, vSrc0	This instruction simply moves the contents of vSrc0 into vDest.
mul	mul vDest, vSrc0, vSrc1	Multiplies vSrc0 and vSrc1 and puts the result in vDest.
rcp	rcp vDest, vSrc0	Computes the reciprocal (1/x) of the source scalar and puts it in vDest.
rsq	rsq vDest, vSrc0	Computes the reciprocal square root of the source scalar and puts it in vDest.
sge	sge vDest, vSrc0, vSrc1	If vSrc0 >= vSrc1, then vDest = 1.0. Otherwise, vDest = 0.0. Even though the vertex shader programming language doesn't support conditional statements per se, you can use this function to achieve some primitive if statement functionality.
slt	slt vDest, vSrc0, vSrc1	Just like Store Greater Than/Equal (sge), only it's Store Less Than (slt). If vSrc0 < vSrc1, then vDest = 1.0. Otherwise, vDest = 0.0. Even though the vertex shader programming language doesn't support conditional statements per se, you can use this function to achieve some primitive if statement functionality.
sub	sub tDest, tSrc0, tSrc1	Subtracts two sources. When this instruction finishes, tDest = tSrc0 − tSrc1.

Table 10.4 Continued

Instruction	Syntax	Description
def	def vDest, fVal0, fVal1, fVal2, fVal3	Allows you to define a constant register by putting four floating-point values into it. You can accomplish the same thing by calling SetVertexShaderConstant; this is just another means to the same end.
vs	vs.MainVer.SubVer	Allows you to specify a version number for this shader. Version numbers can consist of a main version, followed by a sub version, that is, 1.0. Note that Direct3D requires this instruction to be at the beginning of all vertex shaders.

Table 10.5 Vertex Shader Macro Instructions

Instruction	Syntax	Description
exp	exp vDest, vSrc0	Provides "two to the power of vSrc0" with full precision. This takes 12 instructions to do, but hey, when you need the precision, those 12 instructions are a small price to pay. This operation takes its input from the w channel of vSrc0 (vSrc0.w).
frc	frc vDest, vSrc0	Puts the fractional component of vSrc0 into vDest. Each component of vDest will be in the range of 0.0–1.0. This takes three instructions to do, and it only writes the x and y components.

Table 10.5 Continued

Instruction	Syntax	Description
log	log vDest, vSrc0	Provides $\log_2(x)$ calculations, with full precision. This macro also expands into 12 instructions.
m3x2	m3x2 rDest, vSrc0, mSrc1	Computes the product of vSrc0 and the 3×2 matrix mSrc1. This macro expands into two instructions.
m3x3	m3x3 rDest, vSrc0, mSrc1	Computes the product of vSrc0 and the 3×3 matrix mSrc1. This macro expands into three instructions.
m3x4	m3x4 rDest, vSrc0, mSrc1	Computes the product of vSrc0 and the 3×4 matrix mSrc1. This macro expands into four instructions.
m4x3	m4x3 rDest, vSrc0, mSrc1	Computes the product of vSrc0 and the 4×3 matrix mSrc1. This macro expands into three instructions.
m4x4	m4x4 rDest, vSrc0, mSrc1	Computes the product of vSrc0 and the 4×4 matrix mSrc1. This macro expands into four instructions.

As you can see, the language supports essentially all the math tasks you will likely need to do while calculating vertices.

HELP REFERENCE

You can learn more about the instructions supported by the vertex shader language by looking in the DirectX documentation at DirectX 8.0\DirectX Graphics\Direct3DX Shader Assemblers Reference\Vertex Shader Assembler Reference\Instructions.

Vertex Shader Instruction Modifiers

The vertex shader language supports the component modifiers listed in Table 10.6. You can apply these modifiers to any of the an, c[n], rn, or vn registers or any of the output registers.

Table 10.6 Vertex Shader Instruction Modifiers

Modifier	Description
r.{x}{y}{z}{w}	Destination mask. This allows you to mask off all but one of a vector's four components.
r.[xyzw][xyzw][xyzw][xyzw]	Source swizzle.
-r	Source negation.

Creating a Vertex Shader in Your Program

You can write all the vertex shader assembly code you want, but it won't do you a lick of good unless you can load and use the functions you've written inside your 3D application. Luckily, the process of loading and using a vertex shader is simple:

1. Write your vertex shader code, and store it in a text file, typically with the extension VSH (for *Vertex SHader*). This is the hard part.
2. Inside your application, call the D3DXAssembleShaderFromFile function, which loads and assembles your shader file. D3DXAssembleShaderFromFile gives you back an ID3DXBuffer interface containing the token stream of your assembled shader function.
3. Create the actual vertex shader by calling the CreateVertexShader method of IDirect3DDevice8, giving it the contents of the buffer you got in step 2. CreateVertexShader gives you back a DWORD handle to your shader.
4. Release the ID3DXBuffer interface you got in step 2.

In code, this process looks like the following:

```
LPD3DXBUFFER pCode;
DWORD dwShader;
DWORD dwDecl[] = { // the declaration for your shader
  D3DVSD_STREAM(0),
```

```
    D3DVSD_REG(D3DVSDE_POSITION,  D3DVSDT_FLOAT2),
    D3DVSD_END()
};
// Assemble the vertex shader from the file
if (FAILED(D3DXAssembleShaderFromFile( "MyCoolShader.vsh", 0,
    NULL, &pCode, NULL))) { /* handle errors! */ }
// Create the vertex shader
if (FAILED(m_pd3dDevice->CreateVertexShader( dwDecl,
    (DWORD*)pCode->GetBufferPointer(), &dwShader, 0 )) {
        /* handle errors! */
}
// Release the token buffer
pCode->Release();
```

CAUTION

When you're done with the vertex shader, remember to call DeleteVertexShader, giving it the DWORD of the vertex shader you want to delete.

Rendering, Using the Shader

The logical next step after loading a vertex shader is to tell DirectGraphics that you'd like to use this shader when you render. This is surprisingly easy. When you have your vertex shader's DWORD, you can pass that DWORD to the SetVertexShader method of IDirect3DDevice8, which activates your vertex shader. Here's a code snippet showing how that might look:

```
// Begin the scene
g_pd3dDevice->BeginScene();

// Make our quad the source for the vertex data
g_pd3dDevice->SetStreamSource( 0, g_pVB, sizeof(CUSTOMVERTEX) );

// set our vertex shader active
g_pd3dDevice->SetVertexShader( g_dwShader );

// draw some triangles
g_pd3dDevice->DrawPrimitive( D3DPT_TRIANGLELIST, 0, 2 );

// End the scene
g_pd3dDevice->EndScene();
```

It really is that easy. Simply set your shader active, and then draw your triangles.

Passing Data to Your Shader, Using Constant Registers

You must do one last thing before your vertex shader will work correctly. Even the simplest vertex shader needs data above and beyond what it's getting from the geometry. For example, to transform, clip, and project your geometry properly, your shader has to know what the world, view, and projection matrices are. As you've seen, the vertex shader gets its data from the constant registers, but you haven't yet looked at how the constant registers are filled up in the first place.

The way you do this is by calling the SetVertexShaderConstant method of IDirect3DDevice8, explained in Table 10.7:

```
HRESULT SetVertexShaderConstant(
  DWORD Register,
  CONST void* pConstantData,
  DWORD  ConstantCount
);
```

For example, say that your vertex shader is going to color all your vertices. It expects you to put the color you'd like it to use into constant register four (c4). Therefore, you use SetVertexShaderConstant to load up four floating-point values (corresponding to red, green, blue, and alpha) into c5. This translates into code that looks like the following:

Table 10.7 SetVertexShaderConstant Parameters

Parameter	Description
Register	The number of the constant register you want to load up, or, if you're loading many constant registers at once, the number of the constant register at which you want to start.
pConstantData	The data you want to plug in to the constant register(s). Make sure that the size of this data is four floats for every constant register you're setting. For example, if you're setting three registers, you must make sure that the data size is 12*sizeof(float).
ConstantCount	The number of registers you're setting.

```
// plug the diffuse color into constant register 5
float color[4] = { 1.0f, 1.0f, 0.0f, 1.0f };
g_pd3dDevice->SetVertexShaderConstant(5, color, 1);
```

In this code, you are setting the color to RGBA(1,1,0,1)—opaque yellow—and calling `SetVertexShaderConstant` to push those four floats into constant register four.

CAUTION

A common mistake involves incorrectly setting the constant count (the last parameter to `SetVertexShaderConstant`). Remember, each constant register is four floats, so if you're pushing four floats into one register, make sure that this is one, not four. Incorrectly specifying the number of values (instead of the number of registers) can trash your constants behind your back and lead to really hard-to-find bugs.

NOTE

You can also use the `def` command to set constant registers in a vertex shader. If the constants you're using aren't changing frame by frame, it might be better to set them inside the shader code itself, using `def`, rather than bother with setting them inside your actual C code.

A Simple Vertex Shader Example

You now have a complete understanding of how to use vertex shaders in your programs, but I'll bet that you're still a little confused about how to write the shader code itself. Let me walk you through a series of progressively more complex shaders and show you how these work.

Here is a very simple vertex shader. Fire up the `Ch10p1_SimpleVertexShader` program. Run it, and you will see nothing terribly interesting, just a yellow rotating square on a blue background (see Figure 10.3). However, plenty of new techniques are going on under the surface. Rather than use the fixed function pipeline to generate this image, you are using your own vertex shader.

Because we don't care about texturing or anything fancy, the shader behind this image is very small. Ready? Here it is:

```
vs.1.0
m4x4 oPos , v0, c0
mov  oD0, c4
```

That's it! Three lines, and they're not even long lines. The first line is the mandatory vs command, which DirectX requires at the beginning of all shaders. It simply tells the system that you will be using vertex shader 1.0 commands.

Figure 10.3

A simple vertex shader in action.

The next line is a matrix multiply. This line takes the incoming vertex position data (v0) and multiplies it by the matrix you've put in constant register zero. It stores the result of this multiplication in oPos, which is the position output register—what DirectGraphics looks at after the shader is done to determine the final position of the vertex.

"Wait a minute," you're probably saying, "What happened to the world, view, and projection matrices?" In the fixed function pipeline, the vertex position was first multiplied with the world matrix to get its position in world space. Then, the result of that was multiplied by the view matrix to get its position, as seen from a certain point in 3D space (the camera). Finally, that result was multiplied again, this time by the projection matrix to determine its position within the defined viewport.

As you know, you can combine several matrix multiplications into a single matrix. Multiply a matrix that scales something with a matrix that rotates something, and you end up with a matrix that does both the scale and the rotation at once. That's what's going on here. This code has multiplied the world, view, and projection matrices together and stuffed the combined world/view/projection matrix into c0. Here's the code that does this:

```
D3DXMATRIX mat;
D3DXMatrixMultiply( &mat, &g_matWorld, &g_matView );
D3DXMatrixMultiply( &mat, &mat, &g_matProj );
D3DXMatrixTranspose( &mat, &mat );
g_pd3dDevice->SetVertexShaderConstant(0, &mat,  4);
```

Ah-ha! Here you can see the multiplication fusing the three matrices together, followed by the call to SetVertexShaderConstant that places the fused matrix into constant register zero (c0).

You should now see how that second line of this little shader works. The m4x4 macro multiplies the vector position and the fused world/view/projection matrix and puts the result in oPos. The result of all this is a vertex position equivalent to what you would end up with using the fixed function pipeline. The differences lie in how you get there and in the amount of freedom you have along the way. You could choose to leave the three matrices separate and let the shader combine them. You could use a different matrix for different vertices (for example, you could store the number of the matrix you would like to use for each vertex inside that vertex's data structure). Also, you could get fancy and use dozens of matrices, along with some vertex weight values, to calculate the final vertex position (as programmers do for bone calculations). The key idea here is that the shaders give you the freedom to do whatever you need to do.

That takes care of the vertex position. Now there's the third and final line, which sets the vertex color. It does this by copying constant register four (c4) into output data register zero (oD0).

As you might have guessed, you use SetVertexShaderConstant to stuff the vertex color you want (opaque yellow) into constant register four. The shader simply grabs that constant and uses it as the final color. Again, it doesn't have to be this way. If you want to do something bizarre, see what happens when you change c4 to c0, causing the vertex shader to make the vertex's diffuse color dependent on the matrix you pass it.

Here's another simple shader:

```
vs.1.0
m4x4 oPos , v0, c0
mov  oD0, v5
```

In this code, you replace c4 with v5. This subtle change makes the vertex shader obtain the color information from the diffuse color stored within the vertex structure. You can see this shader in action by making the Ch10p1_SimpleVertexShader program load SimpleShader2.vsh instead of SimpleShader1.vsh.

> **NOTE**
>
> It might seem strange to you that oD0 isn't named oColor or something similar. Instead, it's named *output data register zero*, a much less precise name. This is because oD0 doesn't necessarily have to be the color. The default DirectGraphics pixel shader uses oD0 as the diffuse color, but if you write your own pixel shaders, you can use oD0 for whatever you want—usually the color but occasionally not.

A Complex Vertex Shader Example

Are you starting to see how all this works together? Now take a look at a more complex vertex shader—one that does texturing and lighting, in addition to position and diffuse color. Here it is:

```
vs.1.0
m4x4 oPos, v0, c0

// lighting calculations
dp3 r0, v3, c4
mul oD0, r0.x, v5

// texture pass-through
mov oT0.xy, v7
```

> **Sample Program Reference**
>
> To see this shader in action, run the Ch10p2_TexturingVertexShader sample program.

The only thing terribly interesting in this new shader is the lighting calculation. A quick and easy way to calculate the amount of light falling on a vertex is to take that vertex's normal and dot it with the light vector (the vector specifying the direction in which the light is shining). Then, multiply that value by the vertex diffuse color to arrive at the final, lit color.

That's essentially what the shader does, in the two instructions under the light heading. The c4 register contains the light vector, which you set up using the following code:

```
// set up the light
D3DXMatrixInverse(&matinv, NULL, &g_matWorld);
D3DXVECTOR3 vLight(0.0f, 0.0f, 1.0f);
D3DXVec3TransformNormal(&vLight, &vLight, &matinv);
D3DXVec3Normalize((D3DXVECTOR3*)&vLight, (D3DXVECTOR3*)&vLight);
vLight = -vLight;
g_pd3dDevice->SetVertexShaderConstant(4, &vLight, 1);
```

The light vector starts out as (0,0,1), which makes the light point directly into the scene. You then have to transform the light vector's normal by the inverse of the world matrix and normalize that result (remember, *normalization* means making the length of the vector equal to 1).

Don't worry about the math here. The important thing is that, in the last line of code, you plug a correct light vector in to register c4.

Now, back to the first lighting line in your shader. You are taking the dot product of v3 and c4 and putting the result in r0. You know where c4 comes from, so look at where you get v3.

In the fixed function pipeline, v3 is the normal, just as v0 is the position and v5 is the diffuse color. However, to use the normal in the first place, you must first add it to your vertex data structure:

```
struct CUSTOMVERTEX
{
  D3DXVECTOR3 position; // The position
  D3DXVECTOR3 norm;     // normal
  D3DCOLOR    color;    // The color
  FLOAT       tu, tv;   // The texture coordinates
};
```

Here you can see the new element, norm, sandwiched right in between position and color.

While you're at it, you should also change the custom FVF specification to match your structure. This is always a good habit to get into.

```
#define D3DFVF_CUSTOMVERTEX
  (D3DFVF_XYZ|D3DFVF_NORMAL|D3DFVF_DIFFUSE|D3DFVF_TEX1)
```

Here you can see the added `D3DFVF_NORMAL` tag.

Next, you tell DirectGraphics where inside your vertex structure it can find the normal. You do this by adding a line to your vertex shader declaration:

```
DWORD dwDecl[] = {
  D3DVSD_STREAM(0),
  D3DVSD_REG(D3DVSDE_POSITION,  D3DVSDT_FLOAT3),
  D3DVSD_REG(D3DVSDE_NORMAL,    D3DVSDT_FLOAT3),
  D3DVSD_REG(D3DVSDE_DIFFUSE,   D3DVSDT_D3DCOLOR),
  D3DVSD_REG(D3DVSDE_TEXCOORD0, D3DVSDT_FLOAT2),
  D3DVSD_END()
};
```

In this code, notice that you add an additional binding for `D3DVSDE_NORMAL`. You tell DirectGraphics that the normal comes immediately after the position in your structure and that you consider a normal to be three floating-point values (the x, y, and z components of your vector).

The only order of business left is to set the normals for each vertex. You do this at the same time you set the rest of the vertex data:

> **CAUTION**
>
> I'll say it again here. It's very important to keep your declaration and your actual vertex structure in sync. If they're out of sync, your shader won't run, or it will run against incorrect vn input registers.

```
pVertices[0].position = D3DXVECTOR3(-2.0f, -2.0f, 0.0f);
pVertices[0].norm     = D3DXVECTOR3(0.0f, 0.0f, 1.0f);
pVertices[0].color    = D3DCOLOR_ARGB(255, 255, 0, 0);
pVertices[0].tu       = 0.0f;
pVertices[0].tv       = 0.0f;
```

The next line of the vertex shader lighting calculations multiplies the result of the dot product with your diffuse color and puts the result of that multiplication in the oD0 output register. Now you have a vertex shader that calculates light.

The last line of the shader passes your texture coordinates unchanged from the input register (v7) to the output register (oT0). Note that you use the `.xy` modifier on oT0 so that you store only the x and y components of the texture (because that's all you need—you're not using 3D textures).

That's it for the more complex shader.

Vertex Shader Wrap-Up

This section should give you at least a rudimentary understanding of how to write your own vertex shader. I hope that you will take what you learned and try to write more complex shaders. Vertex shaders enable you to create amazing effects (some of which are discussed in the 3D effects section of this book), so you should spend time learning and playing with them.

HELP REFERENCE

For more information on vertex shaders, go to DirectX 8.0\DirectX Graphics\Advanced Topics in DirectX Graphics\Vertex Shaders. Also, be sure to check out the .vsh files in the Samples\MultiMedia\Media directory of your SDK installation. Those are sample vertex shader files that show you how to implement many effects.

PIXEL SHADERS

Pixel shaders are similar to vertex shaders in that they are little snippets of code resembling assembly language. However, vertex shaders deal with vertex information—pixel shaders allow you to specify how different pixels and texels are blended together to create a final color value.

Effects You Can Make Using Pixel Shaders

Pixel shaders allow you to create and augment, using the pixel shader assembly language, all the texture stage setups discussed in Chapter 9, "Advanced Texturing." This includes the texture stage setups for light mapping, glow mapping, detail mapping, and multiple-texture blending. Additionally, pixel shaders allow you to do all sorts of neat things with light, including dot product lighting. What I'd like for you to do is to forget all that Chapter 8 and 9 stuff about texture stages and such because you're going to replace it with something even more powerful.

Pixel Shader Assembly Language

The pixel shader assembly language is very similar to the vertex shader assembly language, only it has different registers and instructions (see Figure 10.4 and Table 10.7).

Pixel Shader Registers

Table 10.8 summarizes the registers available in a pixel shader.

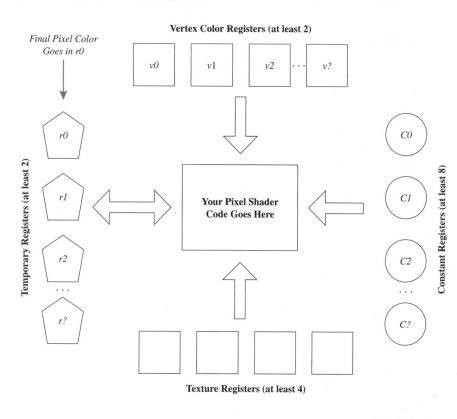

Figure 10.4

The pixel shader virtual machine.

In essence, all the color values come in through the tn and vn registers, and the job of the pixel shader is to calculate the final color value and put it in r0.

HELP REFERENCE
The DirectX SDK help file has more detailed descriptions of each register. See DirectX 8.0\DirectX Graphics\Direct3DX Shader Assemblers Reference\Pixel Shader Assembler Reference\Registers.

Generic Pixel Shader Instructions

To accomplish your goal, you can use any of the generic instructions listed in Table 10.9.

Table 10.8 Pixel Shader Registers

Register	Description
cn	Constant registers, which you set by calling the `SetPixelShaderConstant` method of `IDirect3DDevice8`.
	Constant registers are read-only. Direct3D supports at least eight constants, but you may only use up to two in each instruction.
rn	Temporary registers, which you can use to store intermediate results of a calculation.
	Temporary registers are read/write, and you can use up to two of them in a single instruction. Just like vertex shader temporary registers, however, these lose their values when the pixel shader completes, and it's illegal for you to read one without first writing something into it.
	Note that Direct3D takes r0 as the final output value of the pixel shader. That's the color Direct3D eventually puts on the screen.
tn	Texture registers. You will have the same number of texture registers as maximum simultaneous supported textures. For each pixel, Direct3D initializes the texture registers so that they contain the texture colors of the appropriate texels from the various textures you've specified using the `SetTexture` command.
vn	Vertex color registers. Direct3D guarantees that you will have at least two input color registers, maybe more, depending on your 3D card.
	Direct3D initializes these registers with the color values obtained by iterating the color values output by the vertex shader (in other words, the vertex colors).

Table 10.9 Generic Pixel Shader Instructions

Instruction	Syntax	Description
add	add tDest, tSrc0, tSrc1	Puts the sum of tSrc0 and tSrc1 into tDest.
cnd	cnd tDest, r0.a, tSrc0, tSrc1	Compares the alpha value in r0.a to see whether it's greater than 0.5. If so, it puts tSrc0 into tDest; otherwise, it puts tSrc1 into tDest.
dp3	dp3 tDest, tSrc0, tSrc1	Puts the three component vector dot product of tSrc0 and tSrc1 into tDest.
lrp	lrp tDest, tSrc0, tSrc1, tSrc2	Linearly interpolates between tSrc1 and tSrc2 by the amount specified in tSrc0. Puts the result in tDest.
mad	mad tDest, tSrc0, tSrc1, tSrc2	Multiplies tSrc1 by tSrc2, then adds tSrc0, and puts the result in tDest.
mov	mov tDest, tSrc0	A simple move operation. Puts tSrc0 into tDest.
mul	mul tDest, tSrc0, tSrc1	Multiplies tSrc0 and tSrc1 and puts the result in tDest.
sub	sub tDest, tSrc0, tSrc1	Subtracts tSrc1 from tSrc0 and puts the result in tDest.
def	def vDest, fVal0, fVal1, fVal2, fVal3	Defines a constant, vDest, using four floating-point values.
ps	ps.MainVer.SubVer	Allows you to specify a version number for this shader. Version numbers can consist of a main version, followed by a subversion (that is, 1.0). Note that Direct3D requires this instruction to be at the beginning of all pixel shaders.

Texture-Addressing Instructions

Additionally, you can use the texture-addressing instructions and macros shown in Table 10.10.

Table 10.10 Texture-Addressing Instructions

Instruction	Syntax	Description
tex	tex tDest	Takes the current texel from the texture set at texture stage zero and puts it in tDest.
texbem	texbem tDest, tSrc0	Takes tSrc0 as DuDv perturbation data and calculates the result in tDest. Typically used for bump mapping. Going into more detail on this would be beyond the scope of the book; however, I encourage you to crack open the online help and the DX SDK sample programs to see how this instruction works. This is a macro that expands into two instructions.
texbem1	texbem1 tDest, tSrc0	Takes tSrc0 as DuDv perturbation data with luminance information and calculates the result in tDest. Typically used for bump mapping. This is a macro that expands into two instructions.
texcoord	texcoord tDest	Puts the iterated texture coordinates for this stage into tDest as a color. You use this when declaring the texture registers you're using. For example, the line texcoord t0 declares register t0 as a color derived from its texture coordinates.
texkill	texkill tDest	Masks out the pixel if any texture coordinates are less than 0.
texm3x2pad	texm3x2pad tDest, tSrc0	Partially performs a 2×3 matrix multiply.

Table 10.10 Continued

Instruction	Syntax	Description
texm3x2tex	texm3x2tex tDest, tSrc0	Performs a 3×2 matrix multiply on the tSrc0 color vector.
texm3x3pad	texm3x3pad tDest, tSrc0	Partially performs a 3×3 matrix multiply.
texm3x3spec	texm3x3spec tDest, tSrc0, tSrc1	Performs specular reflection and environment mapping using a 3×3 matrix.
texm3x3tex	texm3x3tex tDest, tSrc0	Performs a 3×3 matrix multiply on the tSrc0 color vector.
texm3x3vspec	texm3x3vspec tDest, tSrc0	Performs specular reflection and environment mapping where the eye vector is not constant, using a 3×3 matrix.
texreg2ar	texreg2ar tDest, tSrc0	Samples this stage's texture at the 2D coordinates specified by the alpha and red components of tSrc0. In other words, it uses tSrc0.a as the u coordinate and tSrc0.r as the v coordinate and returns the color there.
texreg2gb	texreg2gb tDest, tSrc0	Samples this stage's texture at the 2D coordinates specified by the green and blue components of tSrc0. In other words, it uses tSrc0.g as the u coordinate and tSrc0.b as the v coordinate and returns the color there.

Pixel Shader Modifiers

The pixel shader language supports several modifiers:

- **Alpha-replicate**. You can replicate the alpha channel of a certain register across all channels before performing an instruction, by putting a .a after the register name. For example, the command mul r0, r0, r1.a replicates the alpha channel of r1 into all four color channels, then multiplies using those channels, effectively modulating with the alpha value.

- **Invert**. You can invert the color components in a certain register by putting 1- in front of that register. For example, the command `mul r0, r0, 1-r1` multiplies r0 by the inverse of the color in r1.
- **Negate**. You can negate the color components in a register by putting a minus sign (–) in front of that register. For example, the command `mul r0, r0, -v1` multiplies r0 by the negation of the color in v1.
- **Bias**. You can shift each channel in a register down by 0.5 by putting _bias after the register name. For example, the command `add r0, r0, t0_bias` shifts t0 down 0.5 before adding it to r0.
- **Signed Scaling**. You can subtract 0.5 from each channel in a register and then scale the result by 2, by putting _bx2 after the register name. For example, the command `dp3_sat r0, t1_bx2, v0_bx2` shifts the t1 and v0 registers down by 0.5 and then scales them by 2.

Creating and Using Pixel Shaders in Your Program

The process of setting up and using a pixel shader is, in my opinion, easier than what you must do for vertex shaders, so I'm not going to go through every step in mind-numbing detail.

> **Sample Program Reference**
>
> The `Ch10p3_PixelShader` sample program illustrates the process of loading and using a simple pixel shader.

You create a pixel shader the same way you create a vertex shader. First, you assemble the shader, via a call to `D3DXAssembleShaderFromFile` (or something). Then, you create the pixel shader by calling the `CreatePixelShader` of `IDirect3DDevice8`. You don't have to worry about passing `CreatePixelShader` a declaration, as you do for a vertex shader. Just pass it your buffer pointer and the address of the integer where you'd like it to put the pixel shader handle. You delete a pixel shader by calling the `DeletePixelShader` method of `IDirect3DDevice8`.

After you have a pixel shader loaded, you set it active by calling the `SetPixelShader` method of `IDirect3DDevice8`. Again, this is exactly how you use vertex shaders (only you call `SetVertexShader` instead). Keep in mind that you must still set your textures to point to the correct texture interfaces. If you need to set up any constant registers, call the `SetPixelShaderConstant` method of `IDirect3DDevice8`. Otherwise, just draw your primitives, end your scene, and DirectGraphics will execute your pixel shader code when the time comes.

A Simple Pixel Shader Example

Here's a really easy example, just to give you an idea of how to write a pixel shader. Later in this book you will be writing more advanced shaders.

The little pixel shader contained in the `Ch10p3_PixelShader` sample program contains three action-packed lines:

```
ps.1.0
tex t0
mov r0, t0
```

The first line is the obligatory header line, telling DirectGraphics that what follows is a pixel shader based on version 1.0 of the pixel shader language.

The next line declares a texture. This is something unique to pixel shaders. Essentially, declaring a texture gives you an opportunity to change the addressing mode for that texture. The texture declaration is the only place where you can manipulate the addressing for the texture (as opposed to the texel colors themselves). For example, it's in the texture declaration that you tell DirectGraphics that a certain texture is a bump map and should therefore be used to influence the colors of a different texture.

Yes, I'm being intentionally vague here because it's difficult to illustrate without going into a lot of graphics theory. The bottom line is, there are several texture-addressing instructions, but you use one more than all the others. The `tex` instruction tells DirectGraphics that what you're working with is a plain old texture. In other words, when you say `tex t0`, you're really saying, "DirectGraphics, I want you to figure out which texel we're on, given the (u,v) coordinates and the pixel we're currently processing. Then I want you to copy the color of that texel into t0."

After you have the appropriate color in t0, the next line copies it into r0. Recall that r0 is the special register that DirectGraphics takes as the final pixel color. When you combine this line with the lines above it, all you are doing is taking the color of the texel to which this pixel corresponds, putting that color in t0, and copying t0 into r0. This means that the output color (r0) is nothing more than the color of the texel this pixel corresponds to (t0).

This is texturing at its simplest. If you were writing a more complex pixel shader, you could play with t0—perhaps multiply it or add it to another texture color before you finally place it into r0. Additionally, you could choose to use a different texture-addressing instruction and change the way you calculate the appropriate texel or what you do with the texel color after you have found it. The sky is the limit. It just takes time and experimentation to understand all the instructions.

Sample Program Reference

As part of the DirectX SDK, Microsoft includes a great tool for writing pixel shaders and seeing the results of your shader code in real time. The program is named `MFCPixelShader` and can be found inside your DirectX SDK samples directory (<SDK Root>\Samples\Multimedia\Direct3D\ MFCPixelShader).

Pixel Shader Wrap-Up

Using pixel shaders can greatly enhance the quality of your scenes, so take time to become familiar with their operations. The time you spend learning them will pay off big-time in the long run.

The PixelShader sample program on your CD (Ch10p3_PixelShader) illustrates how to set up and use a pixel shader. The program uses a pixel shader to texture a quad, instead of using the traditional fixed-function pipeline.

HELP REFERENCE

For more information on Pixel Shaders, go to DirectX 8.0\DirectX Graphics\Advanced Topics in DirectX Graphics\Pixel Shaders.

CHAPTER WRAP-UP

Wow! Talk about an amazing journey. Just a few hundred pages ago, you were learning how to write a Win32 program. Now you're programming graphics hardware on an assembly language level and have covered everything in between.

At this point, you should feel that you have all the programming and 3D knowledge necessary to make a 3D game. Of course, this doesn't mean that you *do* feel as though you know enough to write the next killer 3D game, but you certainly know much more about the internals of 3D programming (and Windows and DirectX programming in general) than when you began reading this book.

From here on, I'm going to talk about the special effects most games use, dissecting each one so that you can learn how to code it. I wouldn't suggest that you dive right into the effects just yet—you have come a long way, so take a breather and spend some time experimenting.

NOTE

The nVidia Web site contains many additional resources designed to help you understand and implement vertex and pixel shaders. On the Web site at http://developer.nvidia.com you'll find a virtual cornucopia of shader knowledge, in the form of white papers, sample programs, and tutorials.

ABOUT THE SAMPLE PROGRAMS

No enhancements to the coding style this chapter. Here are the programs:

- **Ch10p1_SimpleVertexShader.** Demonstrates a simple vertex shader in action. You walked through segments of this sample program in the section on vertex shaders.

- **Ch10p2_TexturingVertexShader.** Demonstrates a slightly more complex vertex shader—one that calculates texture coordinates for the vertices it processes. Most of this program is exactly the same as Ch10p1_SimpleVertexShader. The only difference is that the program loads a different vertex shader file (VSH) and manages a texture handle.
- **Ch10p3_PixelShader.** Demonstrates a simple pixel shader in action. You walked briefly through segments of this sample program in the section on pixel shaders.

EXERCISES

These are tough exercises, but you can tackle them.

Write vertex and pixel shaders that demonstrate some of the sample effects listed at the beginning of the chapter (waves, muscles, and bones). For vertex shaders, this means that you

1. Write a vertex shader that perturbs an incoming vertex stream into waves (for water).
2. Write a vertex shader that distorts an incoming vertex based on a sphere (for muscles).

For pixel shaders, this means that you

1. Write a pixel shader that performs a texture-blending operation of your choice.

Also, find something you can accomplish with a pixel shader that you can't do using texture stages.

Part 2

2D Effects

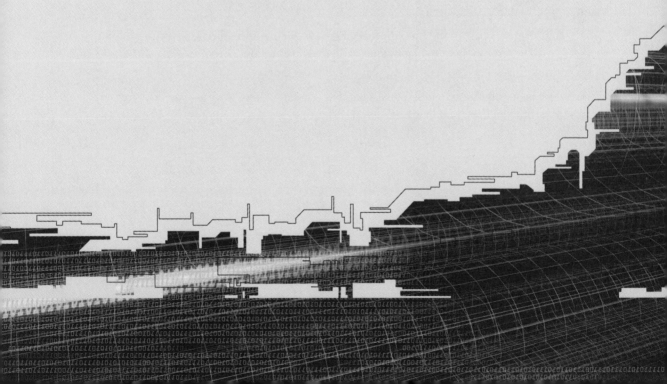

One part down, two to go! Now it's time to sink your teeth into some actual special effects code.

Part 2 is all about 2D effects. Now, you may be thinking, "Hey, what gives? I'll never use 2D effects in a 3D game!" However, you'll find that even 3D games benefit from 2D effects. At the very least, these are good to know so that you can add some eye candy to your title screen and game-over screens. Also, 2D effects often form the foundation of 3D effects, as you'll see in Part 3.

You'll start this second part with a brief tour of fire and water effects. The fire effect and the water effect are two well-known special effects, and programmers have used them in both games and demos for several years.

Next, you'll look at some image manipulation tricks. In Chapter 13, you'll learn the fine art of image feedback, and in Chapter 14 you'll learn how to do real-time image warping using the 3D hardware.

After that, you'll check out some code that renders clouds, using Perlin noise. In Chapter 16, you'll learn how to do some basic 2D image-manipulation: we'll cover algorithms for blurring, sharpening, and edge detection.

You'll complete this part of the book by learning how to code several different types of scene transitions. The simple "fade to black" and "fade to white" will be covered, along with more complex transitions, such as the static dissolve and the cross fade.

Now might be a good time to grab some snacks and create a new playlist—you're about to do some heavy-duty coding (and learning!).

CHAPTER 11

FIRE

"They say time is the fire in which we burn."
——*Soran, from* Star Trek: Generations

epending on how you look at things, all science and technology started with the discovery of fire. I'm no anthropology expert, but I believe that on the list of human achievements, the discovery of fire ranks right up there with the wheel, the printing press, and the invention of nacho cheese Doritos. It's somehow fitting that your first special effect pay homage to the first dramatic discovery we humans made—fire.

Of course, you're not going to be modeling real fire in this chapter. To model the flames of a real fire accurately would require much more CPU power than you have. Like so many other things in game programming, you're going to look at a technique that mimics real fire at a fraction of the processing cost.

This technique has raised its head in virtually every demo scene production since the early '90s because it is easy to learn and looks great when running. If you haven't done so already, you should pause now and run the fire sample programs on your CD. You will see for yourself how convincing a simple algorithm can look. To see the fire in action, look at Figure 11.1.

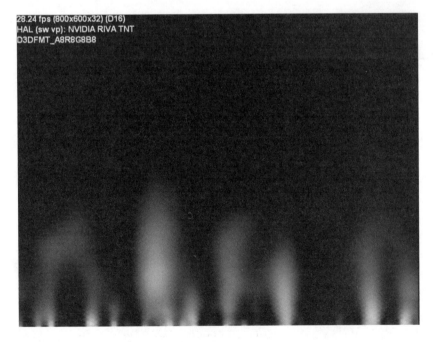

Figure 11.1

Ch11p1_SimpleFire in action.

How Does It Work?

In essence, your fire algorithm is nothing more than a blend function combined with careful use of color and clever dampening functions. You're about to be amazed at how simple this is.

Take a look at Figure 11.2.

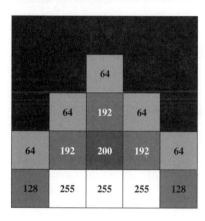

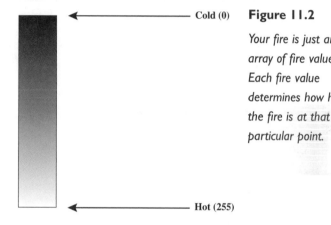

Cold (0)

Hot (255)

Figure 11.2

Your fire is just an array of fire values. Each fire value determines how hot the fire is at that particular point.

Each pixel of the fire is 1 byte; 0 means cold, and 255 means as hot as possible. These fire values are mapped to an appropriate color by using a 255-color palette. For example, you'd probably choose to map fire value 255 to RGB(255,255,255) and fire value 0 to (0,0,0), with red, yellow, and blue colors for the fire values in between. You use these fire values to put texels on a fire texture. You then use the fire texture to texture the objects on which you want the flames to appear.

You start with an array of bytes, equal in dimension to your fire texture size and all 0 except for the bottom row, which you set to random values between 0 and 255. This is the "fuel" for the fire.

Every frame, you process the entire fire array. For each fire value in the array, you do the following (see Figure 11.3):

1. Get the fire values immediately above and below and to the left and right of the fire value you're processing. For fire values on the edge of the fire array, you can wrap around, or you can say that their neighbors are 0.
2. Add all four of these values, and then divide that sum by 4.
3. Subtract an amount, usually a small amount, from the calculation. This emulates your fire flames cooling.
4. You now have your new fire value.

That blends the pixels together, but one piece is still missing—you need to get your flames burning upwards. To do this, you take all your new fire values and move them up by 1 so that a calculation for the fire value at (x,y) is stored at (x,y–1) in the fire array.

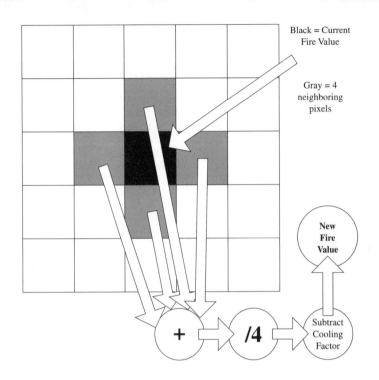

Figure 11.3

The algorithm for calculating the fire.

Black = Current Fire Value

Gray = 4 neighboring pixels

New Fire Value

+   /4   Subtract Cooling Factor

Note that because you have to move the new fire values, you can't use just one fire array. To process a frame of fire, you need two arrays: one array describing the fire array currently and a blank "scratchpad" array into which you can put your calculations.

When you're done with all the calculations, you use your filled-up scratchpad array to color the texels of your fire texture. You determine the color of each texel by looking at the corresponding fire value and using that as an index into your fire color palette (see Figure 11.4).

Finally, after you're done with one frame, you swap buffers so that your new calculations become current and the old array becomes a scratchpad for the next frame (see Figure 11.5).

You also need to fuel the fire by adding random amounts to each fire on the bottom row.

That is how you create a great-looking fire effect. Now that you know the algorithm, look at how to implement it in Direct3D.

WRITING THE CODE

The process of implementing your fire algorithm on Direct3D is tricky but nothing serious. Most of the pain stems from your taking an effect that was originally made for a 320×200, 8-bit paletted surface (the VGA Mode 13h screen) and modernizing it to use 3D hardware.

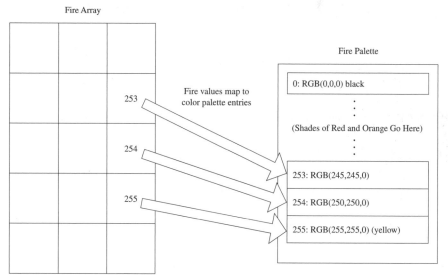

Fire Array

Fire values map to
color palette entries

Fire Palette

0: RGB(0,0,0) black

(Shades of Red and Orange Go Here)

253: RGB(245,245,0)

254: RGB(250,250,0)

255: RGB(255,255,0) (yellow)

Figure 11.4

You use the fire values as indices into your fire palette.

Creating the Fire Texture

The first order of business is to create the texture to which you're going to render the fire. To do this, you have to decide on your texture's dimensions, its surface format, in which memory pool it will reside, and whether you will be using mipmapping. Table 11.1 summarizes all these decisions.

Of course, you must experiment to figure out the best set of texture characteristics for your needs, but that's the fun part.

When you've decided on all of this, creating the texture is as simple as calling
D3DXCreateTexture.

CAUTION

Be sure to check the surface format of the texture after you create it using D3DXCreateTexture. If your device does not support the texture format you requested, D3DXCreateTexture picks a new format that it does support. It's possible that your texture's surface format will be different from what you said you wanted.

Creating the Fire Color Palette

Before you can render your fire, you must have a color palette that tells you how the fire values are mapped to RGBA colors. In essence, what you need are 1,024 bytes (1 byte for each red, green, blue, and alpha component of your 256 colors).

Figure 11.5

When you're done calculating, you swap the arrays.

Frame X

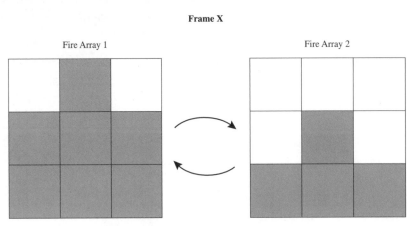

When we're done processing all the fire values for a frame,
we flip the arrays so that the previously active array becomes a scratchpad
for the next frame.

Frame X+1

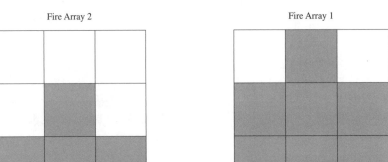

For simplicity's sake, the `Ch11p1_SimpleFire` program has its palette directly embedded into the code, but usually, your best bet is to populate your color palette from a file on disk (or in a resource). That way, you can change the palette of the fire without having to recompile the code.

Now the question becomes, What sort of file format do I use for my palettes?

Palette Files

Your first option is to use a palette file. This is a 1,024-byte file that contains the red, green, blue, and alpha components for each of the 256 colors, and nothing more. The advantage to using

Table 11.1 Texture Creation Decisions

Texture Characteristic	Sensible Decision
Texture dimensions	Usually some power of 2 between 32×32 and 256×256. Any higher, and you start using a lot of CPU time to process the fire. Also, some cards do not support texture sizes above 256×256. Any lower, and you tend to lose so much quality that you can't tell that the fire is fire.
Surface format	Ideally, a paletted-texture surface format, D3DFMT_P8 (see the section "Optimizing the Fire Effect" for more information about this). However, not all cards support this paletted format, so you can use a D3DFMT_A8R8G8B8 format instead, or some 16-bit RGBA or RGB surface, depending on the kind of color quality you need and texture memory you have to spend.
Memory pool	It depends. You have three choices: managed, default, or system. The default pool is out immediately because Direct3D won't let you lock textures that are in the default pool. That leaves managed and system.
	Neither pool is optimal. If you put it in the managed pool, Direct3D does a lot of work each time you lock and change the texture. If you put it in system memory, Direct3D wastes a lot of time moving the texture from system memory over the bus and to the card.
	Ultimately, you have to experiment and figure out which pool is faster for your target system.
Mipmapping	Mipmapping isn't really applicable. However, if your card can generate mipmaps in hardware, and you will be using the additional layers (that is, your fire isn't always up close and personal, so Direct3D would use only the most detailed mipmap level), turn it on. Otherwise, leave it off.

these is that they are incredibly easy to load and save. In fact, if you're using an array of structures to represent your palette, your load code can be only one line:

```
read(hFile, &m_Palette[0], 256*4);
```

Your save code can be

```
write(hFile, &m_Palette[0], 256*4);
```

It doesn't get much easier than that, folks. Of course, because you control the file format, you can add some more features—a header block, for example.

The disadvantage to using palette files is that somehow you have to create one. This means that you need an editor or, at least, a tool that can rip a palette from somewhere else and write it as a 1,024-byte palette file.

Grabbing a Palette out of an Image File

If palette files aren't your cup of tea, you can load a palette that's attached to an 8-bit image file. In many scenarios, this is a very good solution because the functions to load a palette out of an image file already exist (in D3DX!), and you can also use the actual image data for something else (say, a heating or cooling map, discussed later). Of course, it's perfectly okay if you decide to create a dummy 1×1 or 2×2 image and put your fire palette inside the dummy image. Then, in code, you just call D3DXCreateTextureFromFileEx, which gives you your palette. If you're not using the image data for anything, you release the texture right after you load it, saving only the palette information, which you can then store in your own color array for use later.

The following code shows how to grab a palette out of an image file:

```
LPDIRECT3DTEXTURE8 pTexture;
if (FAILED(D3DXCreateTextureFromFileExA(m_pd3dDevice,
    strBMPfile, 0, 0, 1, 0, D3DFMT_UNKNOWN, D3DPOOL_MANAGED,
    0, 0, 0, NULL, m_Palette, &pTexture))) { return(false); }
SAFE_RELEASE(pTexture);
```

You let D3DX do most of the real work. You call the D3DXCreateTextureFromFileExA function to load the image. This function does many things, but what you care most about is that it puts the palette the image uses into m_Palette. After the function completes, you have the palette of the image. Because you don't care about anything else, you immediately turn around and release the texture you just created.

The advantage to this method is that you can use virtually any paint program out there to create your palette. As long as you can get the palette into an image file format (such as BMP), you're set. Even if you create a 1×1 image, the file will be bigger on disk than a plain palette would be, but in this age of 80GB drives, the difference isn't enough to worry about.

Processing the Fire

Now that you have created your texture and color palette, you can enter your frame loop and start rendering frames of the fire. To do this, you follow the algorithm you learned about at the start of the chapter. To illustrate, here's a section of code (refer to Figure 11.3, earlier in this chapter):

```
// loop through all the fire values...
for (int y=0; y < m_iTextureSize; y++) {
  for (int x=0; x < m_iTextureSize; x++) {
    // these will store the fire values immediately to the
    // left, right, top, and bottom of this fire value.
    unsigned char firevalue_left, firevalue_right,
      firevalue_bottom, firevalue_top;
    int finalfirevalue;
    // we must account for wrapping
    // around the horizontal edge (not vertical, however),
    // so we calculate x/y +- 1 and store them temporarily.
    int xplus1, xminus1, yplus1, yminus1;
    xplus1 =x+1; if (xplus1 >= m_iTextureSize) xplus1=0;
    xminus1=x-1; if (xminus1 < 0) xminus1 = m_iTextureSize-1;
    yplus1 =y+1; if (yplus1 >= m_iTextureSize) yplus1=m_iTextureSize-1;
    yminus1=y-1; if (yminus1 < 0) yminus1 = 0;

    // now we can get the fire values of the neighboring pixels
    firevalue_right = m_pActiveBuffer[(y*m_iTextureSize)+xplus1];
    firevalue_left  = m_pActiveBuffer[(y*m_iTextureSize)+xminus1];
    firevalue_bottom= m_pActiveBuffer[((yplus1)*m_iTextureSize)+x];
    firevalue_top   = m_pActiveBuffer[((yminus1)*m_iTextureSize)+x];
    // now, the most important part-  calculate the new fire value.
    finalfirevalue =
     (firevalue_left+firevalue_right+firevalue_top+firevalue_bottom)/4;
    // subtract a certain amount to simulate the fire "cooling."
    // this is where you'd apply your cooling map.
    finalfirevalue -= m_iCoolAmount;
    // make sure that the subtraction of the cool amount didn't take us
    // below zero.
    if (finalfirevalue < 0) finalfirevalue = 0;
    // store the fire value on the scratch array, up one line from
    // where it originally was.  This simulates the flames rising.
    m_pScratchBuffer[((yminus1)*m_iTextureSize)+x] = finalfirevalue;
  }
}
```

In essence, this code does exactly what I described at the start of the chapter. To calculate each fire value, it takes the four neighboring fire values, adds them up, divides by 4, and applies a cooling factor (in this case, m_iCoolAmount) to arrive at the new fire value. It stores all these new fire values into a separate scratchpad array. Sure, some red tape is associated with making certain that you wrap around the edges of your array, but that's about it.

When it's done, it adds a bit to the bottom of the scratchpad array, which gives some numeric fuel to the fire to keep it burning. Here's that section of code:

```
// we work in blocks of 2x1...
for (int x=0; x < m_iTextureSize; x+=2) {
  // we add fuel only to the last row.
  int y=m_iTextureSize-1;

  // determine whether this particular spot gets fuel added or taken
  // away from it, by adding a number between (-31 and 31)
  int fuel = m_pActiveBuffer[(y*m_iTextureSize)+x]+(rand() % 64) - 32;
  // we must be between 0 and 255.
  if (fuel > 255) fuel = 255;
  if (fuel < 0) fuel = 0;
  // apply the new fuel value to two adjacent pixels.
  // This helps reduce the "dithering" effect that the fire
  // is prone to.
  m_pScratchBuffer[(y*m_iTextureSize)+x] = (unsigned char)fuel;
  m_pScratchBuffer[(y*m_iTextureSize)+x+1] = (unsigned char)fuel;
}
```

Again, having to account for the wrapping and minimum/maximum values obscures the true task this code is performing, but I hope that you still see it. You basically add (or subtract) a random amount from the bottom row of the fire. You operate in blocks of two fire values. Doing so creates my favorite form of the fire effect—the illusion that there are little jets of flame at the bottom of the fire, like a natural gas fireplace or stove.

Putting the Fire on the Texture

Now comes the final hurdle—putting your calculated fire values onto the texture as texels.

In Direct3D, to access the texels of a texture directly, you lock it, which tells the system that you're currently changing the bytes of the texture and that it shouldn't do anything. When you finish manipulating the texture's texels, you unlock the texture, which tells the system that you're done and that it can now do whatever it needs to with the texture.

The process for writing directly to a texture is

1. Call the `LockRect` method of `IDirect3DTexture8`, which locks down the texture and returns two crucial bits of information: a void pointer to the texture's texels and an integer named `Pitch`, which tells you the number of bytes between two rows of data (more about this later).
2. Play with the texels by using the pointer you got from `LockRect`.
3. When you're done, call the `UnlockRect` method of `IDirect3DTexture8` to unlock the texture.

Now you will look at each of those steps in more detail.

Locking the Texture

The method you use to lock the texture, `LockRect`, looks like this:

```
HRESULT LockRect(
  UINT Level,
  D3DLOCKED_RECT* pLockedRect,
  CONST RECT* pRect,
  DWORD Flags
);
```

Table 11.2 explains the parameters to `LockRect`.

That `D3DLOCKED_RECT` structure is worth its weight in gold, as you will see in a moment.

Filling the Texture

Now you fill up the chunk of memory given to you in the `pBits` member of the `D3DLOCKED_RECT` structure, but what's the `Pitch` member for?

In Direct3D, there is a definite distinction between the width of a texture and the amount of memory one row of the texture takes up. The amount of memory one row of the texture takes up is called the *pitch* of the texture. It's the number of bytes between any two points that have the same x-value and y-value within +/– 1 of each other—for example, (5,88) and (5,89) or (73,87) and (73,88).

Your pitch will never be less than your texture's width, but it's very common for pitch to be greater than width. This is because Direct3D and/or your video card might need pixels aligned on a certain boundary, or they might use memory after the texel data as a cache for some of their internal calculations (see Figure 11.6).

You can't assume that all graphics drivers use some bit of extra memory after every line of texel data. It's *very* foolish to assume that pitch = width. In fact, it's so foolish, I'd better make a warning box.

Table 11.2 The LockRect Parameters

Parameter	Description
Level	Specifies the mipmap level that you want to lock. For your purposes, you put a 0 here, which tells Direct3D that you're interested in the most detailed mipmap level (the only one you have!).
pLockedRect	This is a pointer to a D3DLOCKED_RECT structure, which contains two members: pBits, the pointer to the texture's surface, and Pitch, which specifies how wide, in bytes, a row is.
	You create a D3DLOCKED_RECT structure, empty it, and then pass its address here. Direct3D fills it in for you, so when the call completes, you have the two pieces of information you need for navigating the texture surface.
pRect	A pointer to a rectangle that specifies which area of the texture you want to lock. If you want to lock the whole thing (as you do here), put in a NULL.
Flags	Allows you to specify flags that control how Direct3D locks the surface. For example, you put D3DLOCK_READONLY here to tell Direct3D that you're going to be reading from, not writing to, the surface.
	In this case, you don't need any flags, so leave this as 0.

CAUTION

When calculating the memory position of a certain texel, always use the texture's pitch, not its width. This is important to do, yet it's also easy to forget, especially if you've programmed Mode 13h DOS graphics or something where you can just assume that a pixel at (x,y) can be accessed in memory as memory[(y*width)+x]. Wrong!

In DirectX, that calculation should *always* be memory[(y*Pitch)+x]. If you're getting strange images or access violations on the textures you lock, check your code to make sure that you're using Pitch, not width.

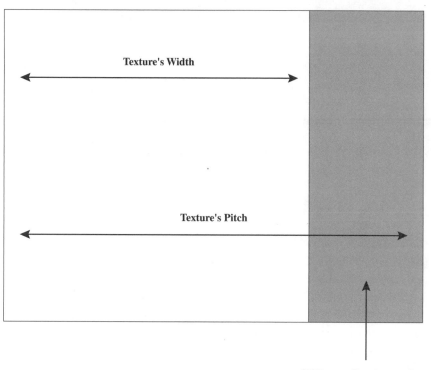

Figure 11.6

A texture's pitch is usually greater than its width.

Texture's Width

Texture's Pitch

D3D may allocate extra bytes
at the end of each row

With that that warning out of the way, you can turn your attention to filling up your texture. Here's the code that does the deed:

```
// lock texture
D3DLOCKED_RECT lockedrect;
::ZeroMemory(&lockedrect, sizeof(lockedrect));

if (FAILED(hr = m_pTexture->LockRect(0, &lockedrect, NULL, 0)))
  return(false);

// our texture surface is now locked, and we can use the pitch to
// traverse it.
unsigned char *pSurfBits =
  static_cast<unsigned char *>(lockedrect.pBits);
int index=0;

for (int y=0; y < m_iTextureSize; y++) {
  for (int x=0; x < m_iTextureSize; x++) {
```

```
        // the fire value at this pos determines the color of this texel
        pSurfBits[index++] =
          m_Palette[m_pActiveBuffer[(y*m_iTextureSize)+x]].peBlue;
        pSurfBits[index++] =
          m_Palette[m_pActiveBuffer[(y*m_iTextureSize)+x]].peGreen;
        pSurfBits[index++] =
          m_Palette[m_pActiveBuffer[(y*m_iTextureSize)+x]].peRed;
        pSurfBits[index++] =
          m_Palette[m_pActiveBuffer[(y*m_iTextureSize)+x]].peFlags;
      }
    // next line
    index += lockedrect.Pitch - (m_iTextureSize*4);
}
// unlock texture surface
if (FAILED(hr = m_pTexture->UnlockRect(0))) return(false);
```

As you see, you're in two for loops, one each for the y and x coordinates. For each pixel, you're taking the fire value, using it as an index into your color palette, and then writing out the color's red, green, blue, and alpha components to your texture's memory.

Unlocking the Texture

This is easy. Just call the UnlockRect method, which takes a single parameter—the mipmap level you want to unlock (in your case, 0).

A Warning about Locking Textures

Now that you know how to lock a texture, I want you to promptly forget that you can do it.

CAUTION

Remember, you *must* call UnlockRect to unlock your surface after you're done. Not doing so causes your application, and potentially your entire system, to crash. No fun!

Many beginning graphics programmers crave the ability to manipulate a texture's texels directly, and after they learn how, they lock textures for *everything*. This in itself isn't a bad thing, but you must remember that when you lock a texture, you relegate your CPU to spending a lot of time dealing with pixels, a job that your graphics card is much better suited to doing.

Think carefully about the decision to lock and modify a texture directly. Locking should be used only as a last resort, when there's no other good way to accomplish what you're doing. For example, don't lock a texture and manually move the rows and columns of textures so that you can "scroll" the texture in a certain direction. Instead, change the (u,v) texture coordinates of your vertices to emulate scrolling. Don't lock a texture so that you can stretch or scale it. Instead, create a quad, put the texture on it, and then change the size of the quad (perhaps rendering the quad to another texture, if you're trying to scale one texture onto another).

To ensure that your game runs as fast as possible, think carefully about when you lock textures.

Making the Fire Texture Fill the Viewport

One final thing is left to do before your effect is done. You must set up things so that the quad using your fire texture takes up the entire viewport. Now, technically, this isn't part of the fire effect—the fire effect's job is to put a flaming image onto a texture. However, you can make your effect demonstration program look good by making it display the entire fire-textured quad. This is more complex than it seems.

Why Perspective Projections Are Sometimes a Pain

Imagine that I told you right now to stop reading and to write a piece of code that displays any bitmap in a window. This program should load an image of any size and display the entire image (and nothing but the image) inside its window. Simple, right? Now imagine that I said not to use the Win32 API and to use only Direct3D. All of a sudden, what was once easy becomes not so easy.

To get the bitmap file displayed on the screen, you'd first use D3DX to load the image into a texture. Then you'd create a quad and render the quad using the image texture. By this point in the book, you should consider writing the code to do all that a trivial task.

The hard part is making the textured quad exactly fill the view. Assume that you set up a situation shown in Figure 11.7. You have a quad that's exactly perpendicular to the z-axis, and you're pointing your camera directly at that quad.

The perspective projection you're using makes things close to the viewer appear bigger than things far away. To get your quad to fill the screen, you must fiddle with the z distance between the quad and the camera until your camera and quad are exactly far enough away from each other that you see the whole quad and nothing but the quad.

This is the 3D programming equivalent of trying to set up a slide projector, finding the magic distance between the projector and the screen so that the slides are as big as possible but not cropped.

In principle, you could conceivably find the right distance between quad and camera, but doing things this way is what I call an RNH (*Really Nasty Hack*). You don't have enough precision in your floating-point numbers to ensure that you will always see the whole quad and nothing but the quad in all screen resolutions. You can spend hours carefully fiddling with the z distance, only to increase your resolution and find that you have a narrow sliver of "not-quad" showing.

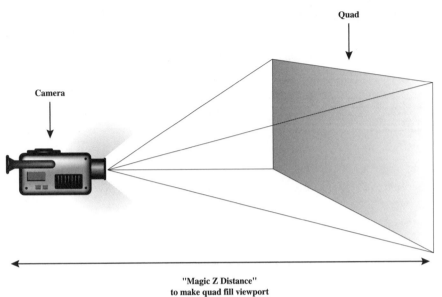

Figure 11.7

An initial attempt at making a quad fill the screen.

Of course, there's also a mathematical way to figure out the exact magic z distance, but let's not go there. Ever since you set up your scene, you've been walking down a progressively darker path, as though you're pushing against Direct3D rather than working with it.

You don't need a magic z distance. You need a way to tell Direct3D, "Hey, I want this rectangle of world space to fill the viewport completely."

You need an orthogonal projection.

Using Orthogonal Projections to Make a Quad Fill the Screen

Think (or flip) back to Chapter 5, "3D Concepts," where I talk about projections. I only briefly mention the orthogonal projection and concentrate on the perspective projection instead. Now it's time to learn orthogonal projections.

In essence, orthogonal projections don't adjust the size of an object based on its distance, the way perspective projections do. In a perspective projection, a 5×5×5 cube can take up the entire screen or be just a blip, depending on how close or far away from it you are. This is great in that it simulates reality, but it's a pain when you're just trying to copy a texture.

In an orthogonal projection, that 5×5×5 cube always takes up the same amount of screen space, regardless of how far away from you it is. This is due to the shape of the viewing volume. Perspective projections use view frustums, but orthogonal projections use view boxes (see Figure 11.8).

Perspective Projection

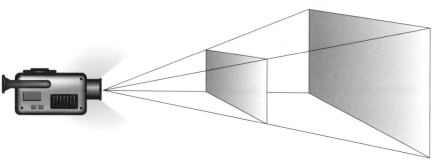

Orthogonal Projection

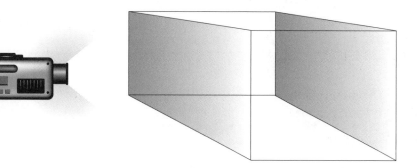

You set up an orthogonal projection the same way you've always done: You call SetTransform, specifying D3DTS_PROJECTION, along with your orthogonal projection matrix.

How do you get the orthogonal projection matrix? Use a D3DXMatrixOrtho function! D3DX includes several D3DXMatrixOrtho functions. The one you use is D3DXMatrixOrthoLH, which looks like this:

```
D3DXMATRIX* D3DXMatrixOrthoLH(
  D3DXMATRIX* pOut,
  FLOAT w,
  FLOAT h,
  FLOAT zn,
  FLOAT zf
);
```

Table 11.3 shows the parameters of D3DXMatrixOrthoLH.

To render-copy a texture, you usually create a projection that's exactly the same dimensions as your target rendering texture. If you wanted to render something onto a 256×256 texture, you'd tell D3DX that you want the width and height of your view volume to be 256. This creates a situation in which one camera-space unit corresponds exactly to 1 pixel.

When you have your 1:1 projection, the rest of the tasks become easy. You set the width and height of your quad equal to the width and height of your projection (and your destination texture). You then set the (u,v) coordinates, clockwise from the top-left, as (0,0), (1,0), (1,1), (0,1), as in Figure 11.9, and you render your scene.

TIP

It's up to you how you get the quad's dimensions equal to those of the projection. You can choose to make a quad with 1×1 dimensions and rely on the world transformation matrix to scale it up, or you can choose to make your quad's vertices match your texture dimensions and set your world transformation to the identity.

I prefer to use a standard 1×1 quad and rely on the world transformation matrix to scale it up. This is mainly so that I can reuse the same quad vertices for several texture sizes.

Table 11.3 The D3DXMatrixOrthoLH Parameters

Parameter	Description
pOut	D3DX stores the calculated orthogonal projection matrix here. (It also returns the same matrix, so you can use this function inside another function call.)
w	The width of the view volume, in camera space.
h	The height of the view volume, in camera space.
zn	The minimum z-value of the view volume, in camera space.
zf	The maximum z-value of the view volume, in camera space.

(0.0,0.0)　　　　　　　　　　　　　(1.0,0.0)

(0.0,1.0)　　　　　　　　　　　　　(1.0,1.0)

Figure 11.9

Setting the (u,v) coordinates for your quad.

Texel/Pixel Alignment in Direct3D

A question I am asked most often from beginning 3D graphics programmers is, "How do I blit using 3D hardware?" They want to know how to set up their textures and polygons so that no stretching, rotating, or other funny business is done to the texture—so that Direct3D copies the texels directly onto the back buffer.

To answer this question, you must dive into the internal workings of Direct3D's texture processing.

As you know, you reference texels on a texture by using texture coordinates—(u,v) values in your vertex data. These coordinates are usually between 0.0 and 1.0; 1.0 always represents the texels at the right (or for v coordinates, the bottom) of the texture, and 0.0 represents the leftmost (or topmost) texels. Therefore, (0.0,0.0) is the texel in the top-left corner, and (1.0,1.0) is the texel in the lower-right corner, regardless of how big your texture is.

The problem is that these (u,v) values are floating-point numbers. Eventually, Direct3D must convert these floating-point numbers into integers because the 3D hardware needs integer coordinates for texel addresses. After all, at some level, your texture is just a 2D array of color values, and Direct3D can't use a floating-point number as an array index. It needs an integer.

It must convert your floating-point numbers into integers. It does this by using the following formulas:

$$T_x = (u \times M_x) - 0.5$$

$$T_y = (u \times M_y) - 0.5$$

Tx and Ty represent the integer values (array indices) Direct3D will use. Mx and My are the width and height of your texture surface, and, of course, u and v are the texture coordinates you gave Direct3D, along with your vertex data.

To view this formula in action, take a peek at Figure 11.10.

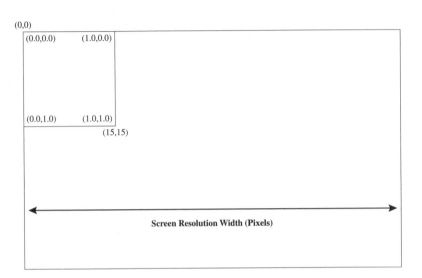

Figure 11.10

The setup for the numeric example of converting floating-point texture coordinates to integers.

Say that you have a 16×16 texture and a 16×16 quad on which you'd like the texture to appear. By using an orthogonal projection equal in size to your screen dimensions, you've set things up so that this 16×16 quad has screen coordinates of (0,0), (15,0), (15,15), (0,15). You've set up the (u,v) values as usual: (0.0,0.0) for the top-left corner of the quad and (1.0,1.0) for the bottom-right.

Now see what happens behind the scenes. To determine the texel color that belongs at screen position (0,0), Direct3D employs the preceding formula. Uh oh, it's come up with (–0.5,–0.5) for the texel's address—no good. If you want the pixels to correspond directly to the texels, you need Direct3D to come up with (0.0,0.0) for the screen position (0,0).

What you do is move your geometry. You subtract 0.5 from the x and y screen space coordinates of your quad so that its top-left corner is at (–0.5,–0.5), and its bottom-right corner is at (14.5,14.5). This seems weird, so work through the numbers again to see why it works.

Again look at the screen point (0,0). Check out Figure 11.11.

Moving your quad introduces one big difference. Your (u,v) values for screen point (0,0) are no longer (0.0,0.0). Because you pinned (u,v) coordinates (0.0,0.0) to screen space position (–0.5,–0.5), the screen space position (0.0,0.0) no longer corresponds to (u,v) coordinates (0.0,0.0). Your (u,v) coordinates are going to be slightly greater than 0.0 because you're 0.5 units

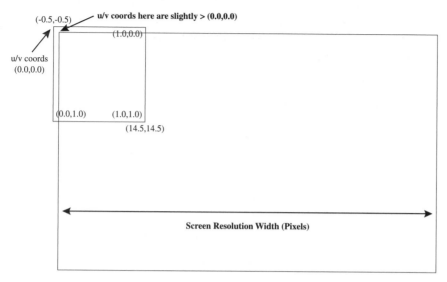

Figure 11.11

Moving the quad so that the texels line up with the screen pixels.

away from the point you've designated as (u,v) (0.0,0.0). Now, if you work through the numbers, you will see that they work out to exactly 0.0.

TIP

If that doesn't make sense to you, maybe you will have better luck visualizing it like this. Imagine that you're making a 2D side-scroller. When your character walks far enough to the right of the screen, you want to scroll the background. When you scroll the background, you move all the background pixels left so that your character appears to move to the right. That's exactly what you did with the quad. By subtracting 0.5 from its (x,y) screen position, you scrolled it left, giving the illusion that the screen moved to the right.

Subtracting 0.5 from the screen position of your quad lines up the center of the texels with the center of the pixels on the screen.

CAUTION

The bottom line here is that to align pixels and texels properly in Direct3D, you must subtract 0.5 from their screen coordinates. Otherwise, things don't line up, and your textures can blur or exhibit ugly stretching artifacts.

Code Wrap-Up

That's all there is to it! By using an orthogonal projection and remembering to shift your geometry 0.5 units up and left, you can easily tell Direct3D that you want a certain quad to fill up the entire viewport. You can use this in your fire demo to ensure that your viewport is filled completely with your beautiful fire-textured quad.

Sample Program Reference

The Ch11p1_SimpleFire program demonstrates everything you've learned so far. Check it out to see the effect in action!

MODIFYING THE FIRE EFFECT

By changing the variables that the fire algorithm uses, you can create a wide variety of fire effects. You will examine each of the variables you can change and the effect those changes have on your flames.

Cooling Arrays

By changing the amount that you subtract from each fire value every time you process it, you change how tall the flames of the fire are. Try setting this to 1 for tall flames and to 5 or 10 for shorter flames (see Figure 11.12).

You can also make each pixel cool at a different rate, creating flames that lick and move. In fact, rather than subtract a constant or random value, you can use a third array, a *cooling array*. The cooling array has the same dimensions as your fire array, and you use the number at a specific (x,y) position in the cooling array to determine how much to cool the corresponding (x,y) position in your fire array.

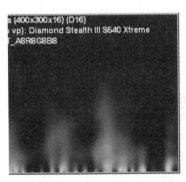

Cooling Value = 1

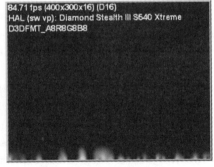

Cooling Value = 10

Figure 11.12

Lower cooling values create tall frames; higher cooling values make short flames.

Now the question becomes, "How do you generate a cooling array?" You make a cooling array two ways: by hand or not by hand. Before you accuse me of being flippant, let me explain. You can create the cooling array by hand, that is, by whipping out your favorite paint program and using the airbrush tool to draw splotches of dark gray on a black background. You then import this into your program and use the red, green, or blue component of each pixel as the amount to subtract from the fire array.

The alternative is to create a cooling array automatically. Chapter 15, "Clouds," explains how to use Perlin noise generation to create unique cloud patterns. You retrofit that cloud code to generate your cooling array automatically, when your program starts.

Regardless of how you generate the array, after you have it, it's very easy to apply it to the fire algorithm to create flames that lick or twist their way up.

You can also choose to animate the cooling array, which, in turn, animates your fire, causing it to appear much more realistic. After all, real fire does not move and swirl in patterns; it's completely erratic. By animating your cooling array, you achieve that sort of behavior.

Fuel

You can also change how much you "heat" the bottom row of the fire each frame. Adding a lot to the last row of the fire puts those fire values closer to 255, creating a hotter fire with taller flames. Adding small (or no!) amounts to the bottom row creates less heat and a more subdued fire.

You're not limited to fueling the fire at the bottom row. You can fuel the bottom two rows for a strong fire. You can also do something drastically different, such as adding heat at random locations in the bottom 50 percent of the fire.

Of course, just as you use a cooling array, you can employ a heat array. If you will forgive the expression, heat arrays are cool. They allow you to make words and images appear inside the flames. For example, you can make a simple text bitmap inside your favorite paint program, and if you use that bitmap as your heat array, you can generate flames in the shape of your text.

Color

The third big variable you can play with is the color of the flames. Changing the fire's color palette gives you the freedom to make tiny adjustments to how the flames look or to change the appearance of the fire so that it doesn't even look like fire any more. For example, rather than use a red/yellow color palette and grow from the top up, you can use a blue/white color palette and grow your flames from the top downwards, creating a convincing waterfall effect.

Also, by playing around with the alpha parameter of your color palette, you can create spooky effects. For example, you can create a hovering, ghost-like shape by using a palette with alpha values and mirroring the texture horizontally or vertically. It's so simple and looks so sweet on-screen.

You can also make the fire appear to fade in and fade out by increasing or decreasing the alpha values of all the colors over time. This isn't terribly realistic (when was the last time you saw a fire fade in?), but it's useful for, say, fading the fire in underneath letters that are already on the screen. If you're interested in fading the entire screen, however, a better option is to use the gamma controls, as described in Chapter 6, "An Introduction to DirectGraphics."

Additionally, you can animate the color palette. When I was a kid, my parents had a wood-burning fireplace. One day my parents bought me a can full of powder (basically, ground up copper). When I threw this powder into the fire, the flames turned blue and green, to my complete and utter amazement. You can create a similar effect by animating your color palette; your fire can start out red/yellow and slowly or quickly shift to a blue/green appearance. You can also create magical fire (whatever *that* is) by changing the colors of the flames as they flicker.

USES FOR THE FIRE EFFECT

One of the great things about putting fire on a texture is that you can then use the texture for just about anything. Put the texture on a cube, sphere, or teapot, and you have firecubes, fire-spheres, or fireteapots. The excitement!

You can also move beyond that simple, gleeful state and use the fire code in conjunction with other techniques to create even more mouth-watering goodness.

Fire Environment Mapping

As you know, *environment mapping* is a technique for drawing metal or shiny surfaces by using a texture to represent the environment around an object. Imagine the fun if you made your fire texture the environment map—your metal objects would appear to be surrounded in animating flame!

The fire technique is best suited to cubic environment mapping. If you use fire environment mapping, you must decide whether to use the same fire pattern on all six faces of the cube or to generate a separate fire sequence. Generally, you can get away with using the same flames on all six faces, but if you want a more realistic effect and can afford the CPU use associated with maintaining six fires, go for it.

Also, you can usually get away with using a smaller fire size (say, 64x64 or even 32x32) when you're doing fire environment mapping. This helps because you have to deal with six faces instead of just one.

Fire Multitexturing

Another way to make the fire effect look better is to use multitexturing. You can use the same fire texture but with different (u,v) texture coordinates to simulate a big, multilevel fire. For example, your second texture stage can combine the source fire texture with, say, the bottom one-third or one-half of the same fire texture, creating the appearance of multiple levels of flame.

OPTIMIZING THE FIRE EFFECT

I believe that the fire effect is best suited to areas of your program where you can waste a lot of CPU time on special effects. You're probably better off putting this effect on a title or end game screen than inside the actual game because most games don't have enough CPU cycles to do a fire effect and still have time set aside for, say, physics, AI, and the like.

Of course, you can also perform a lot of optimizations on the fire effect, and if you're really diligent, you might be able to get a small in-game fire going.

Here are a few optimizations you can try.

Use the Smallest Possible Texture Dimensions

This one's obvious. The larger your fire array, the more CPU cycles you will spend calculating it. Note also that your CPU cycles grow exponentially as your textures increase in size by powers of 2.

It's also possible to write some code that uses different fire array dimensions depending on how close or far away the viewer is from the fire. For example, if the fire is far away from the user, your code can choose to calculate only a 16×16 array, and if the fire is close, it can use a 128×128 array. It's easy to write code that takes a fire array of one size and converts it to an array of another size. Remember the bitmap stretching code you wrote as an exercise for Chapter 7, "Lighting"? It's the same principle: Skip over or duplicate fire array values to arrive at the correct size for the new array.

> **TIP**
>
> In essence, what you're doing here is simulating mipmapping, only you're doing it for different reasons. 3D cards generate mipmaps to localize access to memory. You're doing it because each texel is painfully expensive to calculate.

Use Paletted Textures

If the device on which you're rendering supports paletted texture formats (that is, D3DFMT_P8), use them! By using a paletted texture, you offload all the work of converting the fire values to a color to the graphics card. You simply set up a palette for your fire colors by calling the SetPaletteEntries method of IDirect3DDevice8. Then you make that palette active for your fire texture by calling the SetCurrentTexturePalette method. The graphics card automatically uses the palette to convert your fire values (which are now just indices into the color palette) into colors!

In fact, if you use paletted textures, you can do your fire calculations right there on the texture surface, instead of needing an in-memory array of bytes. Create two paletted textures, and use them as the two fire arrays you need for your processing. Flip back and forth between the two textures when you render your fire so that you're always rendering using the texture with the most current calculations.

Using this method, you speed up the fire effect tremendously.

CHAPTER WRAP-UP

The fire effect is one of the easiest effects you can produce, yet it looks unbelievably nice. It does require significant CPU power, so, again, it might not be appropriate for areas where the CPU needs to concentrate on many things at once. For title screens or end game screens, though, it's a very nice fit indeed.

Indirectly, this chapter also teaches you a few new 3D programming techniques. First, it teaches you how to lock textures to get at their texels directly. You will be locking textures throughout the next several chapters because most 2D effects need direct surface access to work correctly.

Next, you learned about orthogonal projections and how they can be used to generate a 1:1 mapping between world coordinates and screen pixels. Make sure that you understand exactly how this works before you move on. You will be using it in the next few chapters, and I'll assume that if you're reading those chapters, you are an orthogonal projection expert.

Finally, you learned that to align texels and pixels properly, you shift your geometry up and left 0.5 screen space units. This is very important to remember, especially if you're writing a 2D game or planning on integrating 2D and 3D graphics.

You learned a few new concepts. None of them are particularly painful, but they form a strong foundation on which you can learn how to generate more advanced effects.

ABOUT THE SAMPLE PROGRAMS

From here on, the sample programs for each chapter follow a pattern so that it's as easy as possible for you to call up the code and follow along with me. The first program of a chapter is very simple, usually existing in just one source file. In this first program, I sacrifice extendibility and robustness for the benefit of having code that's very straightforward and easy to follow. The first program can crash if things aren't set up just right, but it also presents the algorithms described in the chapter in the most understandable way possible. These programs are named *Simple* programs, like this chapter's `Ch11p1_SimpleFire`.

The remaining programs either build on the simple program or take detours into areas mentioned in the text. I strongly suggest that you read and understand the simple program before diving into these because these programs assume that you know the basics. It's hard enough to learn a new algorithm for an effect. Don't make it more difficult on yourself by skipping the first program and diving into the one that looks the most interesting.

Here are the sample programs:

- **`Ch11p1_SimpleFire`.** This demonstrates the fire effect, without any bells and whistles to distract you. `Ch11p1_SimpleFire` displays a single quad, rendered using the fire texture. Each frame, the fire texture is processed and updated, creating the illusion of fire.
- **`Ch11p2_FireClass`.** This encapsulates the fire effect into a C++ class ready for you to pick up and drop into your own code. It's functionally the same as `Ch11p1_SimpleFire`, but it uses different fire palettes to generate different-colored flames.
- **`Ch11p3_OrthoProj`.** This demonstrates the principles of orthogonal projections. This is the program I challenged you to write. It loads an image and uses orthogonal projections to render the whole image and nothing but the image.

EXERCISES

1. Create a palette maker program that enables your game artists to create palettes for the fires in your game. The palette maker should allow them to choose a start and end color index and a start and end color, and it should interpolate between the start and end colors over the number of colors specified. (Hint: Use floats to represent your colors internally.)
2. Try different blending operations in the core of your fire-processing routine. For example, what happens if you use the neighboring eight fire values (north, east, west, south, northeast, northwest, southeast, and southwest) and divide by 8 instead of 4 to produce the final fire value?
3. Experiment with the various D3DX functions for generating orthogonal projection matrices. All of them are useful in certain situations; see whether you can find a reason for using each of them.

CHAPTER 12

2D WATER

King Arthur: "The swallow may fly south with the sun,
or the house martin or the plover seek warmer climes
in winter, yet these are not strangers to our land."
Soldier: "Are you suggesting coconuts migrate?"
—from Monty Python's Quest for the Holy Grail

Generating realistic water in 3D graphics programming is tantamount to searching for the Holy Grail. From the beginning, game programmers have struggled with creating realistic water. Water appears in most of the games created to date. The side-scrolling action games of yesteryear used three shades of blue, along with some color cycling, to generate ocean waves and waterfalls. Today's games use alpha blending, light mapping, and environment mapping to generate water, but the outcome still isn't quite right. The quest continues and will continue until we have enough processing power to simulate fluid dynamics and generate 3D ray-traced water in real time.

Game programmers have devised many ways to render water for different situations. This chapter looks at a simple yet good-looking technique for rendering water as seen from above. It's a completely 2D effect, so don't use it when your player can walk around and view water from arbitrary angles—the water will appear 100-percent flat, so it won't look right. In the 3D effects section of this book, I cover some alternative techniques you can use in this situation, in Chapter 23, "3D Water."

If you're looking for an astounding 2D, ray-traced water effect and don't mind paying for it in CPU cycles, this is it.

You can see a screenshot of this 2D water effect in action in Figure 12.1. It doesn't look like much. The secret to good water is realistic animation, but we humans haven't yet figured out a way to print an animation onto a page. Run the sample program!

Did you run it? Do you like it? Here's how it works.

How Does It Work?

If you read and understood Chapter 11, "Fire," you already know nearly half of what there is to learn about the water effect. You must do two distinct things to generate this water effect:

- You must use two arrays (which behave very similarly to the fire arrays) to track the height of the water.
- You must use the values of these arrays to perform ray tracing to create your final frame of animation.

You will start with the water arrays.

12.24 fps (800x600x32) (D16)
HAL (sw vp): NVIDIA RIVA TNT
D3DFMT_X8R8G8B8

Figure 12.1

A screenshot of our `Ch12p1_SimpleWater` *sample program.*

The Water Arrays

The water effect uses two independent arrays, just like the fire effect you have come to know and love. Unlike the fire effect, however, these two water arrays are of signed integers. Each array element represents the height of the water at that particular point. Figure 12.2 shows a one-dimensional representation of this. The values can be positive and negative, so they can represent high and low points in the water waves.

One array represents the water height at time t; the other represents the height at time t–1. In other words, you have a new water array and an old water array. Every frame, you take the values

Water array values . . .

0	2	4	2	0	-2	-4	-2	0

Figure 12.2

We store the water height in the water height arrays.

Represent the height of the water wave at various locations

from the *old* water array (which was rendered to the screen in the preceding frame) and use them to calculate new values, which you put onto the *new* water array (the array you will use when rendering this frame).

To make the water move, you blend the values of neighboring array elements. Specifically, you take the water array from the preceding frame, smooth it, apply a dampening factor, and put your calculated values onto the new array for displaying (see Figure 12.3). The arrays then flip-flop so that in the next frame, the second water buffer becomes the source buffer. Sounds awfully similar to fire, doesn't it?

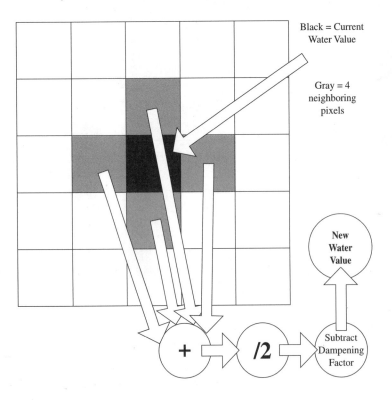

Black = Current
Water Value

Gray = 4
neighboring
pixels

Figure 12.3

Illustrates the algorithm for calculating the new water value.

The primary difference between the two effects is how you use the arrays. In the fire effect, you take the values in the fire array and map them to colors. For the water effect, you take the values in the water array and use them in your ray-tracing calculations. Your ray-tracing calculations tell you which pixel of your source image should appear at each point of your destination image. You will learn about that in more detail in the next section.

That's the overview. Now you will look specifically at the algorithm for processing the water arrays. You start with the two water arrays; these are signed integer arrays and should be initially set to 0. Then, with every frame, you do the following to each water value in the array:

1. For each water value in the array, you need four other water values—the water values immediately above, below, and to the sides of the water value you're processing. For water values on the edge of the water array, you can wrap around, or you can say that their values are 0. If you wrap, your waves will wrap as well. If you call all out-of-range values 0, the waves will stop at the edges.
2. Add all four of these values, and divide that sum by 2. Then subtract the current value in your new water array from the value you calculated (more about this in a moment).
3. Divide by an amount slightly greater than 1 so that any ripples on the water will eventually fade out, leaving a calm surface. This simulates the waves losing energy as they move up and down.
4. You have your new water value. Store it in the new water array.

You now have an updated snapshot of the height of the water at each point in your array. You use this height array, along with some ray-tracing calculations, to copy a source image texture onto your destination texture.

One last thing—you might be wondering about step 2. Why do you divide by 2 and then subtract the current value?

If you were interested in the exact mathematical average of the four pixels, you would divide by 4. To get the average value, because you're adding four things, you should be dividing by 4. I prefer to divide by 2, which makes the waves a little thicker (it takes them longer to die down).

Also potentially puzzling in step 2 is that you subtract the current value from the value you just calculated. In other words, you use the value in the *new* array, not the value in the last frame— that's in the old array. The value in the new array is the value you are about to replace. What's up with using it inside the calculation?

Subtracting the current value is what gives the wave its flowing motion because the subtraction forces the wave to hone in on its average level. We will call the value you calculate by adding and dividing the neighboring values the *new value*. We will call the value currently in your array, about to be clobbered, the *old value*. If the old value is lower than the new value, the wave is going to rise toward average. Conversely, if the old value is greater than the new value, the wave is going to lower toward average.

I realize that it's difficult to see why all the steps in the algorithm are necessary. The quickest way to learn their importance is to load the `Ch12p1_SimpleWater` demo program, take out a certain step, and watch the results. Who knows, maybe you will stumble on an entirely different effect!

Now you will learn how to use ray tracing to convert your water heights into a finished image.

Realistic Water, Using Ray Tracing

Yes, that title doesn't lie—what you're going to do here is ray tracing.

To render your water effect, you must take the water array you calculated and use it to distort your source image so that it looks like it's under water. To do this, you have to take a brief detour into physics.

Water Bending Light

In the real world, a ray of light that hits the surface of a liquid is *refracted*, that is, bent slightly because of the density of the medium through which it's passing (see Figure 12.4). Every substance has a different refraction index that dictates how much the light is bent when it travels into that material.

Common sense dictates that the sooner the light is bent, the farther away it ends up from where it was originally going. Light that hits the

TIP

It's easier to visualize the refraction if you subtract one dimension. Don't worry, the behavior will be exactly the same—you just do the same thing twice. You do all the refraction calculations for x and then turn around and perform those same calculations for y.

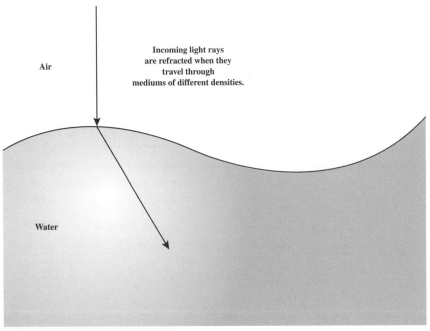

Incoming light rays
are refracted when they
travel through
mediums of different densities.

Air

Water

Figure 12.4

Light rays bend as they pass through materials with different densities.

top of a water wave is bent earlier than light that hits the bottom of a wave (see Figure 12.5). In other words, the high values inside your water array make the light wave refract sooner than the low values. A light wave that hits a high water value ends up very far away from where it was originally headed, but a light wave that hits a low value ends up only slightly off course. That's what makes the water effect work. The ripples you see in the sample program come from the variations caused by the various heights of the waves. Your brain is used to seeing this happen in real life, so it assumes that you're looking at real water.

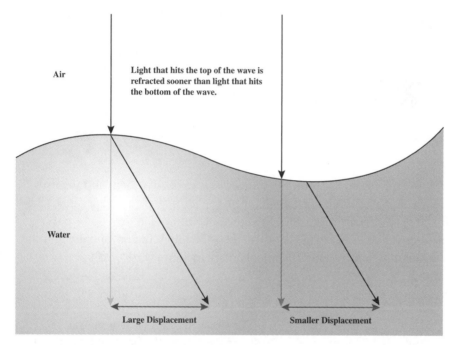

Figure 12.5

The height of the water determines the displacement amount.

Air

Light that hits the top of the wave is refracted sooner than light that hits the bottom of the wave.

Water

Large Displacement

Smaller Displacement

Your program constructs the illusion of water by looking at the height values and determining how soon the light is bent. This determines which texel in the source image you put onto the destination image. In other words, for every texel in your destination surface, you trace one light ray through a certain amount of water. The water bends the light ray. You do some number crunching to determine the new path of the bent light ray and, thus, which source texel you should draw. This is the basic concept of ray tracing.

To copy a texture unchanged onto another texture, you say that the texel at (x,y) on the destination image is the same color as the texel at (x,y) on the destination image. To get an image to appear underwater, however, you use the water heights to skew where the source texels end up on the destination.

If the water height at a particular location, say (x,y), is very high, your light ray is bent early, so it might land three texels away from where it started. In that scenario, you take the source texel at (x–3,y) and put it on your destination at (x,y). Alternatively, if the water height at (x,y) is lower (closer to 0), your light ray is bent later and can end up only one texel away or even on the same texel. This means that you can put source texel (x–1,y) or even (x,y) at destination position (x,y).

That's the idea. Now all you need are a few formulas to nail down everything into numbers.

The Physics Formulas for Bending Light

Believe it or not, this entire effect relies on only two laws of physics.

In 1621, a really smart guy with a really funny name (Willebrord Snell) figured out, through careful experimentation, that the angles between the surface normal and the original and bent light rays are related mathematically. The following equation, now known as *Snell's Law*, expresses the relationship:

$$n_1 \sin(\theta_1) = n_2 \sin(\theta_2)$$

The players in this equation are the two ns, which represent indices of refraction, and the two thetas, which represent the initial and refracted angles from the normal. Figure 12.6 shows all the variables graphically. The shaded surface represents the material into which the light is passing, in this case, water. The dotted line is the surface normal, the solid line is the ray of light, and the thetas are the angles between the normal and the initial and bent light ray.

Snell's Law tells you that the two thetas are related. If you multiply each theta by its corresponding index of refraction, you get the same number.

The refraction index of water is 1.333, and the refraction index of a vacuum is 1.000. (There's probably an interesting story about how we humans figured that out, but it's not of concern right now.) You can find other refraction indices for other liquids

> **TIP**
>
> **An interesting Java applet at http://www.physics.nwu.edu/ugrad/ vpl/optics/snell.html demonstrates Snell's Law graphically.**

in nearly any high-school physics textbook. I've duplicated a few of them in Table 12.1, in case your game design calls for, say, an accurately rendered pool of carbon disulfide.

Returning to the problem at hand, you have a ray of light coming straight down onto your water. That ray bends when it hits the water. You need to know how much it bends and, when you know that, which texel it finally hits. (If the water doesn't bend the light ray, you already know which texel the light ray hits—the texel right underneath it. That is, the light ray corresponding to destination texel (x,y) hits source texel (x,y)). Because the water does bend the light ray, you must do some math to figure out where it ends up.

Figure 12.6

Snell's Law.

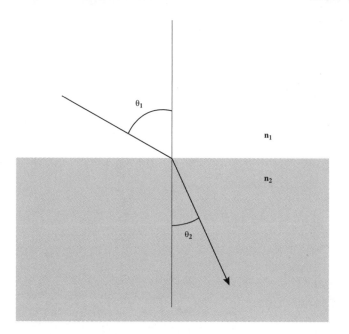

Table 12.1 Refraction Indices of Various Liquids

Material	Refraction Index
Vacuum	1.000
Alcohol (methyl)	1.329
Alcohol (ethyl)	1.361
Water	1.333
Glycerin	1.473
Sugar solution, 25%	1.372
Sugar solution, 50%	1.420
Sugar solution, 75%	1.477
Benzene	1.501
Mineral oil	1.514
Carbon disulfide	1.628

The first order of business is to use algebraic manipulation to coax Snell's Law into telling you how to bend a normal angle into a refracted angle, using a refraction index. Let's shuffle things around:

$$n_1 \sin(\theta_1) = n_2 \sin(\theta_2)$$

$$\frac{n_1 \sin(\theta_1)}{n_2} = \sin(\theta_2)$$

$$\arcsin\left(\frac{n_1 \sin(\theta_1)}{n_2}\right) = \theta_2$$

That equation is much more useful to you. If you give it an original angle and a couple refraction indices, it tells you the refracted angle. This formula is your basic tool for calculating your light rays' paths.

Now it's just a matter of feeding the formula what it needs—the refraction indices you already know: n_1 is the refraction index of the original material the light is passing through. For the sake of simplicity, say that your light is initially inside a vacuum, so you set n_1 = 1. You set n_2 to the refraction index of water, glycerin, or whatever you want your liquid to be.

TIP

Realize that if your indices of refraction are the same, the equation accomplishes nothing—the indices drop out, and you end up taking the sine of an angle and then doubling back and taking its arcsine, which gives you back the angle you started with in the first place.

This is what you would expect—a light ray that travels through water into more water shouldn't bend. The bending occurs only when the light moves from one substance to another.

Calculating the Angle between Surface Normal and a Light Ray

You have two of the three variables you need, but plugging the original angle into the formula is tougher. You have to calculate it. For each (x,y) point, you must know how to figure out the angle between the light coming in and the surface normal.

This takes a little trigonometry. To figure out the angle between the light and the surface normal, you must first know the surface normal. To find the surface normal, you need a flat surface, and you need to know the slope of that surface. Your water wave is nothing more than straight lines between all your water array elements. Because the water array elements contain water heights, it makes sense to approximate the water surface as a straight line between the two array elements.

If this is confusing to you, consider this. Your water waves aren't smooth waves. They're the best approximations of smooth waves you can make, given that you have only so many elements in your water array. Take a peek at Figure 12.7, which shows how you approximate a simple water wave by using five data points. As you can see, you approximate the surface of the water at any point by drawing a straight line between any two data points. For all intents and purposes, the straight line you draw between the two points is the surface of your water. It's not 100-percent accurate, but it gets the job done.

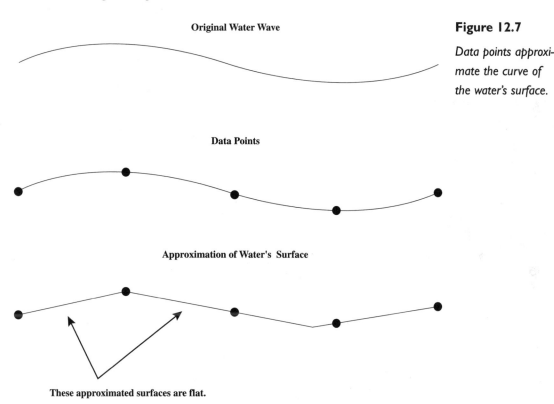

Original Water Wave

Figure 12.7

Data points approximate the curve of the water's surface.

Data Points

Approximation of Water's Surface

These approximated surfaces are flat.

Now you know your surface. It's time for another illustration—check out Figure 12.8. Here you see a zoomed-in view of the water wave, or should I say the approximation of the water wave. You also see a gray line, which is the surface normal. Also, for no apparent reason, I drew a triangle right next to the water surface. I labeled the triangle's dimensions and noted that one of its angles is called *theta*.

Again, your goal here is to find the angle between the incoming light ray and the surface normal. Check out what happens when you rotate that triangle counterclockwise 90 degrees (see Figure 12.9).

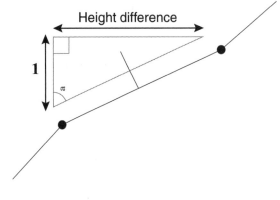

Figure 12.8

You can form a tri-angle using the sur-face normal and the distance.

Height difference

1

a

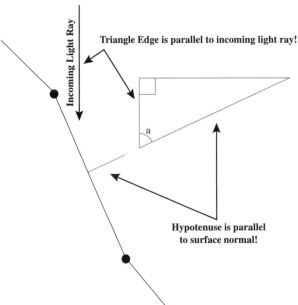

Figure 12.9

Determining the angle between the normal and the incoming light ray.

Incoming Light Ray

Triangle Edge is parallel to incoming light ray!

a

Hypotenuse is parallel to surface normal!

So, theta is the angle between the normal and the incoming light ray!

Sweet! There it is. The hypotenuse of your triangle is now parallel to the surface normal of your water, and theta is now measuring the angle between a line coming straight down and the surface normal. In other words, theta now measures the angle between the incoming light ray and the surface normal.

Now all you do is use some trigonometry to figure out theta. *Tangent* is defined as *opposite over adjacent*. That is, the tangent of an angle is the value you get when you divide the length of the side opposite that angle by the length of the side adjacent to that angle. In this case, the tangent of theta is height difference over 1, or simply height difference. Therefore, if tan(theta) is height difference, theta is arctan(height difference). It's that easy.

Here it is in mathematical terms:

$$\tan(\theta) = \frac{opposite}{adjacent}$$

$$\tan(\theta) = \frac{height\ difference}{1}$$

$$\tan(\theta) = height\ difference$$

$$\theta = \arctan(height\ difference)$$

You now have all the bits necessary to plug in to Snell's Law.

Determining Where the Light Ray Hits

You know how to use Snell's Law, and for each water value in your array, you can figure out the refracted angle. Now you use the refracted angle to determine which exact texel the light ray hits. Specifically, you're interested in calculating a *relative displacement* value, that is, a number that tells you the number of texels the bent ray will move. As you've probably guessed, this takes more trigonometry.

I'll give it away up front and say that you can calculate the displacement by multiplying the height difference by the tangent of the refracted angle:

$$displacement = \tan(refracted\ angle) * height\ difference$$

You're sort of cheating by using the height difference instead of the actual water value. Technically, the displacement is equal to the tangent of the refracted angle, multiplied by the height of the water. However, as you will see when you begin coding the water effect, you can't easily use the actual height because doing so prevents you from using a lookup table to speed up the effect. The effect isn't an exact simulation of reality, but it's close enough to look good.

Ray Tracing Wrap-Up

Yes, there's a little math behind this effect, but I'm sure that you have a good handle on it. I will be honest and say that you probably don't need to understand every equation perfectly, but it will help if you want to tweak the water effect later.

> **TIP**
>
> Demo scene programmers, back in the day, came up with many variations on the water effect algorithm, mostly having to do with the math on which the algorithm relies. Like the one I just walked you through, not all of them are based totally on reality. For example, a common variation is to use the height difference as the displacement, without even bothering to calculate the refracted angle. This saves much work but, in my opinion, isn't as interesting.
>
> The bottom line is, experiment—it's completely up to you to decide whether you want to skip some of these steps (or do additional ones). The important thing isn't the math. It's that the effect look good, run fast, and do everything you want.

Generating Waves

One last key piece to the puzzle involves how data gets into the arrays in the first place. You have all this code set up to generate realistic water ripples, but nothing's going to happen by default. The water arrays will stay at 0, and you will end up with a very expensive way to copy a source texture onto a destination texture.

In the fire effect, with every frame, you add a certain amount to the bottom of the fire array to "fuel" your fire. In the water effect, you don't do this. The water effect simulates the waves and ripples of water as seen from above. Therefore, to get the effect moving, you have to select a point and start a ripple there, as if you had dropped a stone into the water.

When you drop a stone into water, some water is pushed upwards. This initial push upwards is what starts the wave; it's what makes the ripples.

To generate a ripple, all you have to do is push the water up at a certain point. Because your arrays contain the height of your water, raising a point of water is as easy as bumping up the value of a certain array element. To make a wave, you pick a spot where you want the wave to start, give it a high value, and let the effect algorithm do the rest. With every frame, the high number propagates outward, and you see your wave travel along the surface of your water. The wave naturally diminishes over time, thanks to your array processing, and as it travels, you see it refract light realistically, thanks to your ray-tracing efforts.

Obviously, the more you add to a certain point, the stronger the wave moving out from that point will be. Adding 50 to a certain array element generates a stronger wave than adding 25 or 10.

Making Bigger Waves

What if you want to create a really big splash? There's a practical limit to how much you can increase the array element. If you add too much, you wrap around the range of your signed integer and end up with a negative number.

The solution is to add to more than one point. You can decide to add to four adjacent points or to even more points.

You can also add the same value to a circular set of points to create even stronger ripples. This is easy to do. Say that you want to start a circular wave of radius 5 at position (x,y), as in Figure 12.10. The smallest square enclosing that circle goes from (x–5,y–5) to (x+5,y+5). For each point in that square, you can use the distance formula to determine how far away from (x,y) it is and, therefore, how much to add to it. If it's less than or equal to 5, you know that it's within your circle, so you add to it.

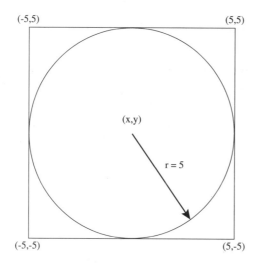

Figure 12.10

A circle with radius five.

Water Effect Wrap-Up

The water effect's bark is worse than its bite. That is, understanding why and how the effect works is much more complicated than coding it. Everything I've talked about so far can be condensed into a few lines of code.

The important things to remember are that you use an array to represent the water height and then use ray tracing, along with the water height array, to map source texels onto a destination surface.

WRITING THE CODE

Why stop now? Take a look at how to program the water effect.

Speeding It Up—Making a Displacement Lookup Table

If you performed the ray-tracing calculations for each texel of each frame of your water animation, you would never achieve a decent frame rate. There is too much math for each texel. Therefore, your first task is to speed up that process. You do this by using a common optimization technique: a lookup table. You will create an array, called the *displacement lookup* table.

Take a peek back at the ray-tracing calculations. Notice that the final displacement value you calculate depends on only one thing: the height difference of the water. (Okay, yes, as I said before, a proper ray-tracing calculation would also take the absolute height of the water into account, but you can get by with substituting actual height for height difference. Remember, it doesn't always have to be realistic to look good).

Because the calculations depend on only one input variable, you will make an array. Each element in the array will contain the results of the ray-tracing calculation for a particular height difference. You know that your height differences aren't going to vary tremendously; even if the valid range is from –500 to 500, that's only 1,000 array elements. If you used integers, they would be 4 bytes each, so your array would be about 4K—a drop in the bucket of today's hardware.

Now, rather than perform the slow ray-tracing calculations for every texel, all you do is look up a value in the array. This is much faster and is the key to generating ray-traced water in real time.

For example, say that you decide to make a 1,024-byte displacement lookup table. Because the height differences can be positive or negative, you dedicate the first half of this array (512 bytes) to the negative values and the other half of the array to the positive values (putting 0 right in the middle at position 512). Then, if a certain texel you're processing has a height difference of –10, you look at position 502 in your array to determine the displacement amount.

> **TIP**
>
> The array doesn't even have to be an array of integers. Each light ray isn't going to be deflected by more than a few texels, so it's perfectly okay to use a signed char (–128 to 128) for the displacement values.

That's how you use the lookup table. You will see that code in a moment, but first, you must make the array. The following code segment shows how it's done:

```
void MakeDisplacementLookupTable(char *pDisplacement, int iArraySize,
                                 float fRefractionIndex,
                                 float fDepth)
{
  for (int i=-iArraySize/2; i < (iArraySize/2)-1; i++) {
    float heightdiff = i*fDepth;

    // the angle is the arctan of the height difference
    float angle = (float)atan(heightdiff);
    // now, calculate the angle of the refracted beam.
    float beamangle = (float)asin(sin(angle) / fRefractionIndex);
    // finally, calculate the displacement, based on the refracted beam
    // and the height difference.
    pDisplacement[i+(iArraySize/2)] = (int)(tan(beamangle) * heightdiff);
  }
}
```

This function fills up the char array you give it, using the refraction index and water depth you provide. It's a relatively clear-cut chunk of code; it just loops through all the height differences and performs the calculations you learned earlier for each height difference. It multiplies each height difference by the given depth, takes the arc tangent of that calculation, and plugs that in to the modified version of Snell's Law you calculated. That gives it the refracted beam angle. The final step is to multiply the tangent of that beam angle by the height difference to determine how many pixels the light ray is skewed.

Creating the Image and Water Textures

You need two textures for your water effect. The first texture holds your *source* image—the image you want to put underneath the water. The second texture holds the completed frame of water animation, ready to be put on the surface of your choice.

TIP

You have to experiment to determine into which memory pool to put the textures. Depending on your system, it can be faster to have the textures reside in system memory instead of video memory. Do some performance tests on your target hardware to determine this.

Processing the Water Arrays

The water array–processing code (the code that loops through each water array element and calculates its new value) looks very similar to the fire-processing code you learned about in Chapter 11. Here's how it works:

```
// loop through all the water values...
for (int y=0; y < iWaterHeight; y++) {
  for (int x=0; x < iWaterWidth; x++) {
    // add up the values of all the neighboring water values...
    int value;
    int xminus1 = x-1; if (xminus1 < 0) xminus1 = 0;
    int xminus2 = x-2; if (xminus2 < 0) xminus2 = 0;
    int yminus1 = y-1; if (yminus1 < 0) yminus1 = 0;
    int yminus2 = y-2; if (yminus2 < 0) yminus2 = 0;
    int xplus1 = x+1; if (xplus1 >= iWaterWidth) xplus1=iWaterWidth-1;
    int xplus2 = x+2; if (xplus2 >= iWaterWidth) xplus2=iWaterWidth-1;
    int yplus1 = y+1; if (yplus1 >= iWaterHeight)yplus1=iWaterHeight-1;
    int yplus2 = y+2; if (yplus2 >= iWaterHeight)yplus2=iWaterHeight-1;
    value  = oldwater[((y)      *iWaterWidth)+xminus1];
    value += oldwater[((y)      *iWaterWidth)+xplus1];
    value += oldwater[((yminus1)*iWaterWidth)+x];
    value += oldwater[((yplus1) *iWaterWidth)+x];

    // average them (/4) and then multiply by two
    // so that they don't die off as quickly.
    value /= 2;

    // subtract the previous water value
    value -= newwater[(y*iWaterWidth)+x];
    // dampen it!
    value = (int)((float)value / 1.05f);
    // store it in array
    newwater[(y*iWaterWidth)+x] = value;
  }
}
```

There's nothing out of the ordinary going on here. You do a double for loop so that you can calculate each element of the water array. For each element, you first figure out whether the neighboring values wrap around. When you know that, you add all the values and divide by 2. Next comes the all-important step of subtracting the preceding water value—the technique that gives the wave its motion. Finally, you apply a slight dampening factor and then store the new value.

Except for a few minor differences, it's identical to fire processing.

Animating the Water

How do you make the water move? As discussed earlier, all you have to do to get a wave going is to add a certain amount at the place from which you want the wave to radiate. If you want bigger waves, you add the same amount to a circular section of water values.

The following code creates a water droplet:

```
void CreateWaterDroplet(int iX, int iY, int iSize, int iSplashStrength,
                        int *waterbuf, int iWaterWidth,
                        int iWaterHeight)
{
  for (int x=iX-iSize; x <= iX+iSize; x++) {
    for (int y=iY-iSize; y <= iY+iSize; y++) {
      // make sure we're in bounds
      if (x < 0 || x >= iWaterWidth || y < 0 || y >= iWaterHeight)
        continue;

      // see if the point at (x,y) is within the circle of radius size
      int square_x    = (x-iX)*(x-iX);
      int square_y    = (y-iY)*(y-iY);
      int square_size = iSize*iSize;
      if (square_x+square_y <= square_size) {
        // it's within the size circle!  apply it to the water buffer.
        waterbuf[(y*iWaterWidth)+x] +=
          (int)((float)iSplashStrength*sqrt(square_x+square_y));
      }
    }
  }
}
```

The point is going to be centered at (iX, iY) and have a radius of iSize. Therefore, you know that the maximum area of water values influenced will be a square, with corners at (iX-iSize,iY-iSize) and (iX+iSize,iY+iSize). Refer again to Figure 12.10 if you're unclear about this.

You must check every value inside this square. You use a weird version of the distance formula to determine whether you need to add to a particular point and, if so, how much. Here's the original distance formula, in case you forgot:

$$d = \sqrt{x^2 + y^2}$$

Remember, you're in 2D, so you don't have to worry about z.

Calculating a square root takes time, so to speed things up, you change the formula around by squaring both sides of it:

$$d^2 = x^2 + y^2$$

Now you can tell whether your point is inside the circle by comparing the squared values. If the sum of x and y squared is less than or equal to the square of iSize, you're in the circle. There are no slow square root operations to bog you down.

Now that you've worked through that, most of the preceding code should make sense. The one remaining puzzle is why you multiply the splash strength by the square root of x and y squared.

Well, it turns out that simply adding the same value to all points within the circle doesn't make for a very interesting wave (try it out—comment out the line of code, and replace it with water-buf[(y*iWaterWidth)+x] += iSplashStrength). To make a better-looking ripple, you have to add different amounts to different places. Specifically, you must add a lot to the edges of your circle and slowly reduce the amount as you move in toward the circle. This gets a nice crisp ripple moving across the water.

The water droplet code multiplies the splash strength by the distance of the particular point from the center of the splash. This elevates the water points on the edge of the circle much more than the ones closer to the middle.

Essentially, that's how you create the illusion of a droplet hitting the water's surface.

Rendering the Source Texture onto the Destination

Okay, you've learned how to make waves and how to process your water array. Now you need to know how to use the values in the array to put the source image onto the destination. Using your displacement lookup table, this process is quick and easy and bears a striking resemblance to the code that renders a fire array onto a texture.

I'm going to walk you through a lengthy section of code from Ch12p1_SimpleWater. You can find this code inside the PutWaterOntoTexture function.

You start by locking the source and destination textures:

```
// lock texture
D3DLOCKED_RECT rect_src, rect_dest;
::ZeroMemory(&rect_src, sizeof(rect_src));
::ZeroMemory(&rect_dest, sizeof(rect_dest));

if (FAILED(hr=pSrcTex->LockRect(0, &rect_src, NULL, 0)))   return(hr);
if (FAILED(hr=pDestTex->LockRect(0, &rect_dest, NULL, 0))) return(hr);
```

Next, you grab the pointers Direct3D has returned to you, and you figure out the source pitch in integers by dividing the number Direct3D gave you by 4:

```
// our texture surface is now locked, and we can use the pitch to traverse it.
DWORD *pSrc = (DWORD *)(rect_src.pBits);
DWORD *pDest= (DWORD *)(rect_dest.pBits);

int dest_index=0;
int src_pitch = rect_src.Pitch/4; // in DWORDS
```

Now you enter the two for loops, which traverses you through the entire water array:

```
for (int y=0; y < iWaterHeight; y++) {
  for (int x=0; x < iWaterWidth; x++) {
```

Inside the for loops, the first order of business is to calculate the height differences in the x and y directions (remember, you're following the same process you learned about earlier, but now you're doing it for two dimensions instead of one):

```
int xdiff = (x == iWaterWidth-1)  ? 0 : waterbuf[(y*iWaterWidth)+x+1]   -
waterbuf[(y*iWaterWidth)+x];
int ydiff = (y == iWaterHeight-1) ? 0 : waterbuf[((y+1)*iWaterWidth)+x] -
waterbuf[(y*iWaterWidth)+x];
```

Now for the slick part. You look up the correct displacement value for your given x and y height differences. These two lines do all the math associated with the ray tracing:

```
int xdisp = lutDisplacement[(xdiff+256) % 512];
int ydisp = lutDisplacement[(ydiff+256) % 512];
```

Now that you know the displacement, it's time to figure out which texel color should be put at this position. Because of the way the trigonometry works, you know how many texels the light ray is skewed, but you don't know which way the light ray goes. Fortunately, figuring this out is easy, based on whether the height difference is positive or negative.

Also, you must keep careful watch on your displacements to make sure that you don't end up referencing a texel that's outside your destination image. For example, if you're calculating the position (0,0) and your math tells you that the displacement is (–5,–5), you can't just plug (–5,–5) into the locked texture memory. There is no texel at (–5,–5). You must be clever enough to intercept the cases in which the light ray falls off the texture. Then you simply default to the color that's at index 0 of your source texture (in other words, the color of the texel at (0,0)). As you read this code, keep in mind that TEXSZ represents the maximum size of your texture:

```
if (xdiff < 0) {
  if (ydiff < 0) {
    if (y-ydisp < 0 || y-ydisp >= TEXSZ || x-xdisp < 0 || x-xdisp >= TEXSZ)
      pDest[dest_index++] = pSrc[0];
    else
      pDest[dest_index++] = pSrc[((y-ydisp)*src_pitch)+x-xdisp];
  }
  else {
    if (y+ydisp < 0 || y+ydisp >= TEXSZ || x-xdisp < 0 || x-xdisp >= TEXSZ)
      pDest[dest_index++] = pSrc[0];
    else
      pDest[dest_index++] = pSrc[((y+ydisp)*src_pitch)+x-xdisp];
  }
}
else {
  if (ydiff < 0) {
    if (y-ydisp < 0 || y-ydisp >= TEXSZ || x+xdisp < 0 || x+xdisp >= TEXSZ)
      pDest[dest_index++] = pSrc[0];
    else
      pDest[dest_index++] = pSrc[((y-ydisp)*src_pitch)+x+xdisp];
  }
  else {
    if (y+ydisp < 0 || y+ydisp >= TEXSZ || x+xdisp < 0 || x+xdisp >= TEXSZ)
      pDest[dest_index++] = pSrc[0];
    else
      pDest[dest_index++] = pSrc[((y+ydisp)*src_pitch)+x+xdisp];
  }
}
}
```

That's it! You loop in this manner through the entire row of texels. When you hit the end, you have to move your dest_index ahead slightly—remember, you use the pitch value here because Direct3D might have extra bytes hanging off the end of each row. You've been adding on to dest_index every time you calculate a new texel, so to move your index down a row properly, you first subtract the number of bytes across the surface you've come so far—this puts you back at x position 0. Then you add the pitch value, which jumps you down a line:

```
// next line
dest_index += (rect_dest.Pitch - (TEXSZ*4))/4;
}
```

Then you start on the next row, and so on, until you have put a color inside every texel of your destination image. Finally, when all the work is done, you clean up your mess by unlocking the textures you locked at the start of this procedure:

```
// unlock texture surface
if (FAILED(hr = pSrcTex->UnlockRect(0))) return(hr);
if (FAILED(hr = pDestTex->UnlockRect(0))) return(hr);
```

It's a lengthy section of code, I know, but after you cut through all the hassle of indexing the texels, it's a simple matter of looking up the displacement for a height value and using that displacement to figure out a source texel to use.

Code Wrap-Up

After you use the water array to copy the texels from the source texture onto the destination, you can do whatever you want with your destination texture. The simple demo program attaches it to a quad and displays it, using an orthographic projection so that it fills the viewport.

MODIFYING THE WATER EFFECT

The water effect has a whole slew of virtual knobs you can turn to adjust its behavior. Take a quick peek at some of the things you can change.

Wave Speed

Using this algorithm, the only way you can change the speed of the wave is by adjusting how frequently the algorithm calculates the new water values. Ordinarily, you would calculate new values every frame, but if you want slower-moving waves, you can decide to calculate the new values every other frame, every third frame, and so on.

Of course, at some point, you can skip too many frames and change your water effect from an animation into a sequence of still images. In other words, there's only so long you can leave any given frame up on the screen and still trick a human brain into thinking that your image is moving.

Unfortunately, this length of time is very small. I'd say that at about 10–15 frames per second, your brain begins to say to itself, "Hey, this isn't moving. It's just a bunch of pictures." This means that if your system is running at 70 frames per second (which is normal for a video game), you're pushing your luck if you try to process the water less than every four frames (70 divided by 4 is 17.5).

As a result, you have only a handful of speed settings for your waves.

You can compensate for the lack of speed settings by using another technique. You can increase the size of the water arrays and then scale these large arrays down before you render the water. This creates the appearance of waves moving slower, but it comes at a high price—the larger your water arrays, the more CPU time you spend calculating the water. As with the fire effect, if you use any water array larger than 512×512, you're likely to run into a performance problem. Even small arrays, of 128×128, put a heavy load on the CPU.

Maybe this is okay. After all, on title screens and other out-of-game screens, frame rates as low as 20 FPS are acceptable. Believe it or not, a GUI running at 20 FPS still feels responsive to the average computer user, and you might get away with even lower frame rates, provided that you keep the mouse cursor motion fluid (either by using a separate thread or by letting Windows handle the cursor).

In general, however, there is a very practical limit to the size of your water arrays. This limit varies, depending on the type of hardware to which you're targeting your game. This means that you have to investigate your own unique situation to come up with other ways to vary the wave speed.

Wave Lifetime

Fortunately, wave lifetime is very easy to manipulate. Two things control wave lifetime: the dampening factor and the strength of the wave.

The Dampening Factor

This is my name for the number you divide by inside your array-processing loop. The *dampening factor* is a positive real number (float) that determines how quickly water values that aren't 0 return to being 0. The dampening factor must be greater than 1. If it's equal to 1, your waves will never die out. If it's between 0 and 1, your waves will become bigger each frame, and your system will eventually balloon out of control.

I like a dampening value of 1.05. It creates what I think of as a deep, calm pond effect—the waves linger around a while. I consider 1.01 and 2.00 the practical limits for the dampening value. It's very hard for me to see the difference between dampening values that are larger. Some people prefer to use high dampening values—2, 3, or 4—to generate very short-lived waves. This doesn't look as realistic to me as the 1.05 value, but you should experiment with various numbers until you arrive at one you like.

The Strength of the Wave

The strength of the wave is determined by the value you add to the water array element to start the wave. Waves with higher power last longer, but even the highest-powered wave is no match for a high dampening value. In other words, the dampening factor has much more influence over how long waves last than the wave's power does.

When you press a key, the Ch12p1_SimpleWater program creates waves ranging in strength from 10 to 25. Here, too, you should experiment to find values that work for you.

Water Currents

You can use some quick-and-dirty techniques to make the water flow over the surface of your image. The easiest trick is to shift both the water arrays up, down, left, or right by 1 with every frame (it doesn't look right if you do it to only one array).

This isn't the only way to generate water currents, but I like this one because it's easy to understand and relatively flexible. You can choose to move different parts of the array by different amounts for more complex, flowing effects, or you can choose to change the flow direction in response to a user action or game event.

> **TIP**
>
> The Ch12p1_SimpleWater demo has a section of code inside the water-processing function that's remarked out. Remove the remarks to see a demo of a water current effect.
>
> The code in the demo is a brute-force way to move the arrays. It's easy to understand but very slow and not optimized. If you choose to employ water currents like this in your programs, you will probably want to optimize the array movement into the array calculations somehow or, at least, move whole rows of the array at once, rather than do a double for loop. Many assembly language resources in print and on the Internet can tell you how to optimize this breed of bulk data movement.

The Depth of the Water

You can use different depth values as you calculate your displacement lookup table. This enables you to create the illusion of the water being very deep or very shallow. All you have to do is change the number by which you multiply your height difference.

The `Ch12p1_SimpleWater` demo uses a depth value of 0.5. Decreasing this makes the ripples on the water less prominent; increasing the depth value makes them easier to see. I'd say that the practical range here is somewhere between 0.02 and 2.0, but that's based on my sense of aesthetics. Your range might vary.

> ## CAUTION
>
> Beware of values that are too deep. The deeper the water, the more the light rays divert from their original path, so more light rays end up outside the boundaries of your texture. This might be acceptable to you if you decide to wrap the displacements (thereby tiling your source image underneath the water), but as always, you should experiment with different depth values to determine whether they're suited for you.

A Better Blending Function

Until now, you have looked at using only one formula to average your water values. In your water array–processing routine, you have always taken the top, left, right, and bottom values, added them, and then divided by 2.

That's not the only way to blend values. A slightly slower but, in my opinion, better-looking way is to add 12 (count them, 12!) points and then divide by 6. It's virtually the same idea, but you're using more data samples, which produces a more accurate average.

Figure 12.11 shows the 12 values you use. They form a diamond shape around your current value.

> ## TIP
>
> Inside the water array–processing function of the `Ch12p1_SimpleWater` program sits a section of commented-out code that implements this blending algorithm. I encourage you to remove the comments, compile the demo, and see whether you can notice a difference in how the ripples look.

> ## TIP
>
> Graphics programmers have devised even better-looking ways to blend. You will learn a couple additional tricks in Chapter 16, "Blurs and Other Forms of Image Manipulation," when we start learning about blurring. Unfortunately, most of these higher-quality blends are too slow—they drop the frame rate of your water so much that they ruin the effect.

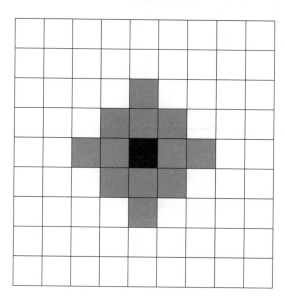

Black square = (x,y) point.
The gray squares are the 12 neighbors
you use in the calculation.

Figure 12.11

A better blending function.

You should use this super-blending technique only if you have loads of CPU time to spare. I don't expect everyone to use this. I mention it here in case you want very good-looking ripples and are willing to take the speed hit that comes with them.

Different Ways to Render the Water

The ray tracing you learned about earlier in this chapter is only one of several ways you can use the values in the water array. Here are a few ways to render the water after you have the water array calculated:

- **Lighten and darken colors**. Here, you always copy the texel at (x,y) on the source surface to (x,y) on the destination—you don't calculate the refraction of the light rays. However, you do play with the source texel's color. If a particular water array element is below 0, you darken the color; if it's above 0, you lighten the color. This creates the illusion of highlights and shadows on the waves of the moving water.
- **Use a bump map**. You can create a bump map using the water arrays and let the hardware take care of shading your texture for you. On newer cards that support hardware bump mapping, this method is much faster than manually lightening or darkening the colors.

Uses for the Water Effect

I hate to say it, but this water effect is useful in only a handful of situations because of its drain on the CPU. Maybe, through careful optimization, you can get it running fast enough to be used in-game, but most of the time it is useful only on title screens, end game screens, and other places where there's less need to keep a high frame rate.

Having said that, here are a few ways to use the water effect.

Rain

Creating a realistic overhead view of raindrops falling is painfully easy, using this effect. All you do is add random values to random water array elements. You change the number of additions you perform every frame to simulate everything from a light sprinkle to a torrential downpour.

> **TIP**
>
> If you hold down a key while running the `Ch12p1_SimpleWater` demo, you can see a good approximation of a rain effect.

Drippy Mouse Cursors

The other popular use for the water effect is to make it appear as though your mouse cursor is dripping water. To simulate a drippy cursor, figure out over which water array element the mouse cursor is currently poised, and add to that array element.

You can use DirectInput to determine the current mouse position, or you can call on the power of the Win32 API function `GetCursorPos`. Either way, you have to do math to convert the cursor position into an (x,y) index into your water array, but it's nothing complex. Assuming that you're using an orthogonal projection so that your water texture fills up the whole screen, all you do is divide the width of your window by the width of your water array. This gives you the pixel width of each water array element. You then take the current mouse cursor x position and divide it by the width of a single water array element, giving you the x index you need.

Repeat the same steps for the y coordinate, using heights instead of widths. I'm leaving out sample code here on purpose—I want you to write this one because you need to understand innately these sorts of pixel-to-array element conversions. If you're in bad need of a hint, read Chapter 14, "Image Warping," and pay careful attention to the section on creating the vertex grid.

Parallel Waves

When you add values to individual points, you get ripples, but when you add the same value to several points in a line, you generate a parallel wave (see Figure 12.12). If you periodically add

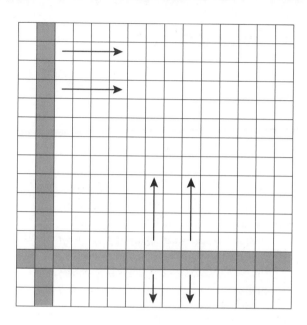

Add the same value to a row
or column of the water array
to generate parallel waves.

Figure 12.12

*How to generate
parallel waves.*

values to the same line, you generate the illusion of a sea or another large body of water, where
the waves are parallel to each other.

Boat Wakes

Everyone probably remembers the code that makes a ball bounce around the screen. You give
the ball an initial x and y velocity and multiply the velocities by –1 when the ball hits a horizontal
or vertical wall.

Rather than draw the ball, add a bit on to the water array element corresponding to the ball's
current position. As it bounces around, the ball will generate a wake.

You can also give wakes to the objects in your game, using this method. If you're making a top-
down boat game, add a value to the water array corresponding to each moving boat's current
position.

OPTIMIZING THE WATER EFFECT

Talk about a resource hog! This water effect demands a lot of attention from the CPU. Here are a
couple things you can do to ease the pain.

Don't Calculate What You Don't Show

If you need a clear, unobstructed pool of water, this optimization technique probably isn't for you. However, very few programs need such a pool. Most of the time, parts of your water effect are covered by title-screen text, rocks, status areas, and other obstructions.

There is no reason to spend time calculating the array values and copying the texels for portions of the water that won't show up on the screen. By spending time maintaining the water you can see, you increase your game's frame rate.

A good way to keep track of what you can and cannot see is to divide the water pool into tiles of a certain size (say, 32×32). If anything fully obstructs a tile, you know from the get-go that you don't have to calculate that 32×32 section of water. You can skip it and go straight to a section that is visible.

> **CAUTION**
>
> Be careful with this tiling method. It doesn't work if something is temporarily obscuring a section of water. You can't start and stop water calculations as the water animation is going—you experience some strange effects if you do. For title screens or other places, though, where you know a certain portion of the water will never be seen, this tiling method works well.

Reduce the Size of Your Water Array

If you're in a pinch, you can cut your water array dimensions in half and make each element in the array represent a 2×2 block of texels. This cuts down on your processing time but also lowers the quality of your image—your water effect will appear slightly blockier than normal.

Of course, you can cut it further than just 2×2. You can cut your array in half again, making each array element represent a 4×4 block of texels. You don't get as much of a speed increase as you did originally, but it should run slightly faster and appear even chunkier on-screen.

> **TIP**
>
> Note that if you cut your water array dimensions in half, you also double the speed at which your waves move.

I wouldn't advocate going down beyond 8×8—that is, reducing your water array dimensions to any more than one-eighth of your texture dimensions. At that point, the waves start to move too fast, and the effect looks too blocky.

Multithread!

If all else fails, the least you can do is move the water processing out into another, lower-priority thread. This enables you to maintain a smooth mouse cursor, which can buy you enough of a speed illusion to render acceptable results.

As with the fire algorithm, you run into some issues when you decide to multithread this code. The biggest problem involves making sure that the textures aren't locked when you need them. There are also many different synchronization issues involved with rendering.

CHAPTER WRAP-UP

Isn't it weird how two vastly different effects can have virtually the same code underneath them? If someone had shown me the fire effect and the water effect before I knew the underlying algorithms, I would have never guessed that the two are so similar. They look so different!

This proves how easy it is to generate entirely new effects by slightly changing an existing effect algorithm. Demo scene programmers have been doing this for years—creatively changing a few lines of code here and there to build an even more interesting effect atop an already existing one. Here, you built a water effect by adding basic ray tracing to what is essentially your fire algorithm.

I encourage you, gentle reader, to do some experimenting on your own. Take the water effect and play with it until you break it—and then continue playing with it. You will learn very quickly how many nifty things you can make by using two arrays along with some math.

However, know that the water effect, like the fire effect, comes with severe speed problems. Whenever you have the CPU doing processing for an individual pixel or texel, you take a significant speed hit. The fire and water effects are great starter effects because they teach the basics of effect programming without relying on your having a vast knowledge of 3D hardware. That's why I put them at the beginning. As you will see in the next chapters, though, a good effect shouldn't rely on a multitude of CPU calculations. Instead, a good effect should offload the work to the graphics card—after all, graphics cards pump pixels much better (and faster) than CPUs.

After you get the graphics card to do the work for you, you open many doors. All of a sudden, it's possible to use advanced effects in-game and still maintain a decent frame rate. The two title-screen tricks you've learned so far are interesting, but I'm sure that by this point you're dying for something you can use inside your game.

For that, all you have to do is keep reading.

ABOUT THE SAMPLE PROGRAMS

Nothing new to report as far as coding style or organization goes. Here is the program:

- Ch12p1_SimpleWater. This sample program demonstrates the 2D water effect without any bells and whistles to distract you.

EXERCISES

Forgive the bad joke: now that you've gotten your feet wet, here are some additional exercises for the water effect:

1. Write a drippy mouse cursor program based on the Ch12p1_SimpleWater sample program.
2. What happens when you use chars instead of integers for your water array elements? Are there enough unique values in a char array to simulate the water accurately? Try it and find out!
3. Experiment with the water arrays. What happens when you add random values to an entire row or column of array elements? What happens when you lock an array element at a certain value (that is, every frame, you set it equal to the same value)? As you've seen, you can create nifty ripple effects by adding values to single array elements, but you can create numerous other effects by playing with multiple array elements simultaneously.
4. From Chapter 11, you know how to use a palette and how to map array values to palette colors. Try this with the water effect. Rather than do all the ray-tracing business to put a source image underwater, use the water values as indices into a color palette. You will create a trippy effect that's begging for image feedback (which you will get to in the next chapter).

CHAPTER 13

1MAGE FEEDBACK

"Every time I learn something new, it pushes some old stuff out of my brain. Remember when I took that home winemaking course, and I forgot how to drive?"

——Homer Simpson

Image feedback is one of the most popular effects in use today. For some reason, MP3 players and jukebox programs love feedback effects. Windows Media Player 7, along with virtually every other MP3 player out there, has a visualization capability that treats you to a shifting, colorful display of oscilloscopes, spectrum analysis, and the like. Most of the time, these effects use image feedback to enhance their appearance. Older versions of WinAMP also use the image feedback effect in their credits dialogs. Figure 13.1 treats you to an example of image feedback.

Just in case you've never played with an MP3 player that uses image feedback and you have no idea what I'm talking about, let me explain the effect in the real world. Hook up a video camera to a TV so that whatever the camera sees is displayed on the TV. Now point the camera at the TV, and put an object in between the two (see Figure 13.2).

When you turn on everything, you end up with a space-warpy, tunneling effect, like the one shown in Figure 13.1. This effect is caused by the camera feeding the TV's image back onto itself, creating an image feedback loop.

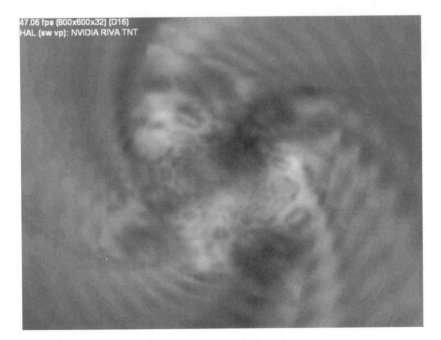

47.06 fps (600x600x32) (D16)
HAL (sw vp): NVIDIA RIVA TNT

Figure 13.1

A screenshot of the `Ch13p1_SimpleFeed` `back` *program in action.*

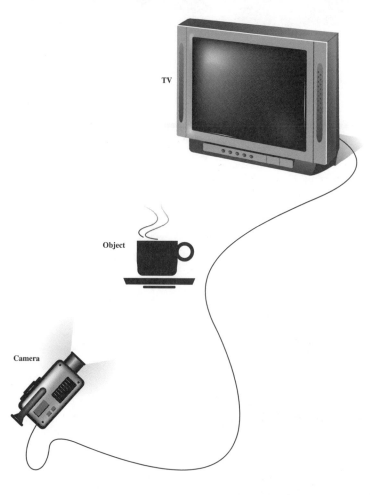

Figure 13.2

Creating image feedback in real life, using a TV and a camera.

TV

Object

Camera

You can also see this effect in action by using two mirrors. Put one mirror in front of your face and the other mirror behind you. When you look into the front mirror, you see several instances of your own head, stretching off in a slightly curved line toward infinity. That's another form of the feedback effect—light repeatedly bounces back and forth between the two mirrors, creating a tunnel of images.

How Does It Work?

This might sound silly, but in essence, the code for the image feedback effect works just like the TV and camera setup, only without the TV and camera. Instead, you use two textures. You take the image on one texture, transform it somehow (usually you rotate and/or shrink it), and then blend the transformed image back in with the original image (see Figure 13.3).

Start with the original image ...

Do something to it
(in this case, rotate and scale it) ...

Figure 13.3

*The algorithm for
image feedback.*

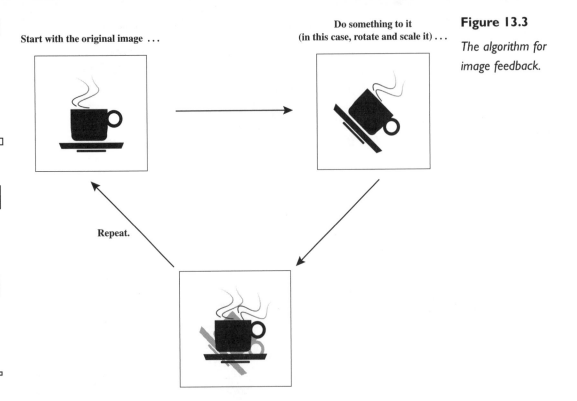

Repeat.

You need two textures because one texture holds the original and final images and the other texture acts as a place for you to store the transformed image temporarily before you blend it back in with the original.

In essence, the first texture (which I call the *primary texture*) holds the start and end images, and the second texture (which I call the *scratch texture*) holds the transformed image you eventually blend back onto the primary texture to complete the effect. Figure 13.4 shows how iterating through this effect a couple times produces the feedback trails.

To make things absolutely clear, here's the process you go through, every frame, to achieve an image feedback effect:

1. You start with the image currently on the primary texture.
2. You take the primary texture and render a transformed version of it onto the scratch texture.
3. You blend the scratch texture back onto the primary texture.

That's how image feedback works, but to use it, you need one more thing. Somehow, you have to get a fresh image into the feedback loop; that is, you need to have some color feed back onto itself in the first place. Otherwise, you end up feeding a completely black image onto itself over and over—all the excitement of watching paint dry, without the hassle of actual paint!

Figure 13.4

Several iterations go by, and feedback trails form.

It's not enough to put just the transformed image onto the scratch texture. Each frame, you also put a fresh image onto the scratch texture before you blend it back onto the primary texture. Rendering something onto the scratch texture before you blend it with the primary texture is the 3D programming equivalent of putting something between the TV and the camera pointing at the TV (refer to Figure 13.2).

TIP

Even if you start with an image on the primary texture, it takes only a few frames before the image stops animating, because each iteration reduces the image size a little. You can shrink an image only so far before it disappears.

CAUTION

It's very important that you not clear the primary texture when you render onto it. You should never clear the primary texture. Doing so wipes out the feedback effect. You should, however, clear the scratch surface each time because you are generating fresh images for the feedback loop on it every frame.

WRITING THE CODE

That's probably hard to follow, so have a look at some sample pseudocode. Say that you have a program that bounces a spinning 3D cube around the screen. Ordinarily, the code to render this animation would go something like this:

1. Set the back buffer as the active rendering surface (usually, you don't do this explicitly, but it's still a step).
2. Clear the rendering surface.
3. Render the cube.
4. Present the back buffer.
5. Move and rotate the cube a little for the next frame.

To put the cube between the TV and the camera—in other words, to use the image feedback effect to give your spinning cube little trails—you do the following:

1. Set the scratch texture as the active rendering surface.
2. Clear the active rendering surface (the scratch texture).
3. Take the image on the primary texture, and transform it onto the scratch texture.
4. Render your cube onto the scratch texture.
5. Set the primary texture as the active rendering surface.
6. Blend the scratch texture onto the primary texture.
7. Set the back buffer as the active rendering surface.
8. Bind the primary texture to the vertices you want so that the image feedback is displayed on whatever surface you prefer.
9. Render your scene, and present the back buffer.
10. Move and rotate the cube a little for the next frame.

Each of these steps is explained in detail in the subsequent sections. However, before even beginning to explore what's going on inside the frame loop, you must first look at how to create the two image feedback textures (the primary texture and the scratch texture).

> **TIP**
>
> Usually, in step 8, you use an orthogonal projection to arrange a quad so that it completely fills the viewport. Then you put the primary texture onto that quad so that, in essence, your primary texture is copied unchanged to the back buffer. However, you're not limited to doing just that. As with the fire effect, after you have your final effect image rendered to a texture, you can use that texture on anything. You can put it on a surface of a 3D model TV so that in your finished scene, the TV appears to be displaying the feedback image. You can also use it as a texture for environment mapping. The power is yours.

Creating the Textures

There's only one trick to creating the image feedback textures: creating them as render targets. Direct3D states that if you want to render a scene onto a texture, you must specify that texture as a render target when you create it.

This means that you have to use the D3DUSAGE_RENDERTARGET flag. That, in turn, means that you can't use the D3DXCreateTextureFromFile function because it doesn't give you any place to put flags. Instead, you must use the superpowerful D3DXCreateTextureFromFileEx function.

The other parameters you pass into D3DCreateTextureFromFileEx are nothing new. Table 13.1 summarizes some good texture decisions.

Table 13.1 Texture Decisions

Texture Characteristic	Sensible Decision
Texture dimensions	Ideally, you should be able to fill up the entire screen with your feedback effect. Unfortunately, because textures must be powers of 2, to use a single texture, you need one with dimensions of 1024×1024 or 2048×2048.
	That usually isn't plausible; a better solution is to use multiple 256×256 textures tiled together so that they cover the entire screen. I will leave implementing that as an exercise for you, gentle reader. For the purpose of simplicity, you set your texture sizes to 256×256.
Surface format	It doesn't matter, as long as your primary texture's format is the same as your scratch texture's format. You can't go wrong if you set both texture formats to the same format used by your back buffer.
Memory pool	Textures that are render targets must reside in D3DPOOL_DEFAULT.
Mipmapping	Because most cards have hardware-mipmapping capabilities, this usually doesn't matter. The sample programs turn it off. If it were on, they would use only the most detailed mipmap level because they render all their textures so close to the viewer.

Here's the code that creates a typical render target texture for the image feedback effect:

```
// create scratch texture that's the same size as the image texture.
// this must be created as a render target.
if (FAILED(hr = D3DXCreateTexture(
    m_pd3dDevice, m_iTextureWidth, m_iTextureHeight, 1,
    D3DUSAGE_RENDERTARGET,
    D3DFMT_A8R8G8B8, D3DPOOL_DEFAULT, &m_pOrigTexture))) {
  return(hr);
}
```

As you can see, the only thing unusual in the call to D3DXCreateTexture is the D3DUSAGE_RENDERTARGET flag. Also, you're storing the texture in D3DPOOL_DEFAULT instead of D3DPOOL_MANAGED.

> **CAUTION**
>
> Render targets must be in the default memory pool. Make sure that you set your memory pool to D3DPOOL_DEFAULT for render target textures. Otherwise, your texture creation calls will fail.

Rendering to a Texture

Now that you have created your textures, the next thing you need to figure out is how to render to them. In other words, you must tell Direct3D, "Hey, rather than render this scene on the back buffer, put it on this texture."

Not all graphics cards support rendering to textures. Most modern cards allow you to set the render target to any texture, but some older cards won't let you change the render target at all. Some insist on having textures in certain memory pools. (As always, just when you think something's going to be easy, along comes the army of old video cards!)

You can, of course, check the capabilities of your particular card to see whether it allows you to set a certain texture as the render target. To do this, use the CheckDeviceFormat method of IDirect3D8. If you find that for some reason you can't set your texture as a render target, you have the following options:

1. Find a texture the card can use as a render target, and use that instead. On some cards, render targets must have a certain color format or be in a certain memory pool, so you can try different color formats and memory pools and hope that a certain combination works. If need be, you can copy the rendered pixels off this texture and into the texture you originally wanted to use.
2. Render to the back buffer, and then copy the rendered pixels directly onto a texture. This isn't recommended, because you usually take a severe speed hit, but it can be done.

3. Give up and don't use this effect. If this effect is just eye candy in your game, it is perfectly acceptable to substitute a different effect (or no effect at all) for these older cards.

I am not going to explore any of these alternatives in detail because on the majority of cards out there, you don't run into any problems. You should know what your options are, though.

Getting back to the task at hand. If your card supports it, you set the render target by calling the `SetRenderTarget` method of `IDirect3DDevice8`. This tells Direct3D that you want the rendering to be put on a texture rather than on the back buffer.

```
HRESULT SetRenderTarget(
  IDirect3DSurface8* pRenderTarget,
  IDirect3DSurface8* pNewZStencil
);
```

Table 13.2 shows the parameters for `SetRenderTarget`.

As you can see, the `SetRenderTarget` command does double duty—it also allows you to change the depth-stencil buffer.

Also, note that `SetRenderTarget` wants surface interfaces, not texture interfaces. You can't pass `SetRenderTarget` a texture because it won't know which mipmap level of the texture to render to. You have to get surface interfaces from your textures by calling the `GetSurfaceLevel` method of `IDirect3DTexture8`:

```
HRESULT GetSurfaceLevel(
  UINT Level,
  IDirect3DSurface8** ppSurfaceLevel
);
```

Table 13.3 shows the parameters for `GetSurfaceLevel`.

Table 13.2 The SetRenderTarget Parameters

Parameter	Description
pRenderTarget	The interface of the surface to which you would like Direct3D to render. If this is NULL, Direct3D doesn't change the render target.
pNewZStencil	The interface of the surface Direct3D should use as a depth-stencil buffer. This also can be NULL, in which case Direct3D doesn't change the current depth-stencil buffer.

Table 13.3 The GetSurfaceLevel Parameters

Parameter	Description
Level	The mipmap level of the surface you want. For top-level (the most detailed) mipmaps or textures without mipmaps, put in a 0 here.
ppSurfaceLevel	The address of a pointer into which Direct3D should put the surface interface.

CAUTION

When you call GetSurfaceLevel, Direct3D increases the internal reference count on the particular surface you request. This means that you must eventually call Release on the surface to decrement the reference count and ensure that you don't end up with any leaks.

SetRenderTarget also has a companion, GetRenderTarget, which you will use occasionally:

```
HRESULT GetRenderTarget(
  IDirect3DSurface8** ppRenderTarget
);
```

No need for a table on this guy—all GetRenderTarget wants is the address of a surface pointer. It fills this address so that it points to the current render target.

Now that you have been properly introduced to the three functions you will be using, here's a snippet of code from

CAUTION

Just like GetSurfaceLevel, GetRenderTarget also increments the reference count on the surface it returns, so you must remember to call Release here as well.

Ch13p1_SimpleFeedback that illustrates the process of setting a render target (in this snippet, assume that m_pScratchTexture is a texture interface you want to set as the render target):

```
// get the current rendering target (we'll set it back later)
LPDIRECT3DSURFACE8 pOldRenderTarget;
m_pd3dDevice->GetRenderTarget(&pOldRenderTarget);
```

```
// get surface interfaces for our textures, so we can set them as rendering
// surfaces later.
LPDIRECT3DSURFACE8 pScratchSurf, pOrigSurf;
m_pScratchTexture->GetSurfaceLevel(0, &pScratchSurf);
m_pOrigTexture->GetSurfaceLevel(0, &pOrigSurf);

// set scratch surface active and clear it.
// SetRenderTarget will also set our viewport so that it completely fills
// pScratchSurf.
m_pd3dDevice->SetRenderTarget(pScratchSurf, NULL);
/////////////////////////////////////////////////////
// clear, BeginScene, DrawPrimitive, EndScene go here
/////////////////////////////////////////////////////
// release the surface of the scratch texture.
pOrigSurf->Release();
pScratchSurf->Release();

// set the rendering target back to the old target.
m_pd3dDevice->SetRenderTarget(pOldRenderTarget, pDepthSurf);
m_pd3dDevice->SetRenderState(D3DRS_ZENABLE, D3DZB_TRUE);
pOldRenderTarget->Release();

// release the depth surface interface.
pDepthSurf->Release();
```

In essence, you begin by squirreling away the current render target. You then call GetSurfaceLevel to get the surface interface. Next, you call SetRenderTarget and go about the business of rendering your scene. Finally, to clean up, you release the surface interface and render target interface you previously had, and you set the render target back to whatever it was before you changed it.

As you have no doubt already construed from the preceding

TIP

If possible, try to avoid calling GetRenderTarget as shown in the preceding code. If you know for sure which render target was active before your change, it's better to set that render target back explicitly. For example, most of the time you can assume that the back buffer was the previous render target, so you don't have to bother with calling GetRenderTarget—you just set the render target to the back buffer when you're done.

I chose to use GetRenderTarget in this example because I wanted to show you how to use it. It makes the code easier to understand and also slightly more robust for those of you who want to cut and paste the effect into your own engines.

code, the process you go through to set a render target is virtually identical to what you do when switching a GDI resource. You make a note of which "thing" you're currently using, you set the new "thing" active, do whatever you need, and then put the old "thing" back when you're done.

Transforming the Primary Texture onto the Scratch Texture

Now that you know how to create (and render to) your image feedback textures, you can code the first step of the effect: the code that takes the contents of the primary texture and transforms it onto the scratch texture.

Before you learn how to transform one texture onto another, you must first learn how to copy one texture onto another. Direct3D provides a CopyRects function that copies texels directly from one texture to another. You will ignore that for now because it won't help you when it comes to transforming the texture.

Instead, you will learn how to copy a texture by setting the destination texture as the render target, setting up a quad, tying the source texture to that quad, and then rendering it, so that Direct3D indirectly copies the source texture to the destination as it draws the quad. When you know how to copy a texture in that way, you can apply whatever transformations you want by fiddling with the quad's vertices and/or texture coordinates. For example, you can rotate the quad 180 degrees and end up with an upside-down copy of your texture.

It's time to learn how to do what I call *render-copying*.

Render-Copying for Beginners

The basic idea behind render-copying is to use an orthogonal projection and a textured quad to move texels from one texture onto another. In essence, you set up an orthogonal projection equal in size to your source texture. You set the render target to your destination texture, begin the scene, draw the quad, end the scene, and you're done.

Here is render-copying code from the D3DHelperFuncs.cpp source file, inside your Common Code directory:

```
HRESULT RenderCopy(LPDIRECT3DTEXTURE8 ptexSource,
  LPDIRECT3DTEXTURE8 ptexDest, int iDestWidth, int iDestHeight,
  LPDIRECT3DDEVICE8 pDev, LPDIRECT3DVERTEXBUFFER8 pvbQuad)
{
  HRESULT hr;
  // get the current depth buffer (we have to pass this
  // into SetRenderTarget so that we don't inadvertently drop our
  // depth buffer.)
  LPDIRECT3DSURFACE8 pDepthSurf;
```

```
pDev->GetDepthStencilSurface(&pDepthSurf);
// get the current rendering target (we'll set it back later)
LPDIRECT3DSURFACE8 pOldRenderTarget;
pDev->GetRenderTarget(&pOldRenderTarget);
// get surface interfaces
LPDIRECT3DSURFACE8 psurfDest;
ptexDest->GetSurfaceLevel(0, &psurfDest);
// set new rendering target & clear
pDev->SetRenderTarget(psurfDest, NULL);
pDev->Clear( 0L, NULL, D3DCLEAR_TARGET, 0x000000, 1.0f, 0L );

// turn off z buffering
pDev->SetRenderState(D3DRS_ZENABLE, D3DZB_FALSE);

// set up texture stages for simple texture stage copy
pDev->SetTextureStageState(0, D3DTSS_COLOROP,   D3DTOP_SELECTARG1);
pDev->SetTextureStageState(0, D3DTSS_COLORARG1, D3DTA_TEXTURE);
pDev->SetTextureStageState(0, D3DTSS_COLORARG2, D3DTA_DIFFUSE);
pDev->SetTextureStageState(1, D3DTSS_COLOROP,   D3DTOP_DISABLE);
pDev->SetTextureStageState(0, D3DTSS_ALPHAOP,   D3DTOP_SELECTARG1);
SetupOrthoProjForRenderCopy(pDev, iDestWidth, iDestHeight);
// set the source texture active
pDev->SetTexture(0, ptexSource);
// begin rendering the scene
if (FAILED(hr = pDev->BeginScene())) return hr;
pDev->SetStreamSource( 0, pvbQuad, sizeof(VERTEX_XYZ_DIFFUSE_TEX1));
pDev->SetVertexShader( D3DFVF_XYZ_DIFFUSE_TEX1 );
// this "blits" the texture
pDev->DrawPrimitive( D3DPT_TRIANGLELIST, 0, 2 );
// end scene
pDev->EndScene();

// release the dest surface
psurfDest->Release();
// set the rendering target back to the old target.
pDev->SetRenderTarget(pOldRenderTarget, pDepthSurf);
pDev->SetRenderState(D3DRS_ZENABLE, D3DZB_TRUE);
pOldRenderTarget->Release();
// release the depth surface interface.
pDepthSurf->Release();
return S_OK;
}
```

There's a lot of red tape there, but I hope that you get the idea. In essence, you squirrel away your current render target and depth buffer. Then you grab a surface interface and set that as your render target. You disable your z-buffer, clear the render target (destination texture), and set up your texture stage states for a simple copy. You set up your orthogonal projection so that one texel on your destination image is equal to one world unit. Then you activate your source texture, begin the scene, pump in the vertices for your quad, and end the scene. Finally, you clean up your mess by releasing the texture and depth-buffer surface interfaces and setting the render target and depth buffer back to how they were before you changed them.

Transforming as You Render-Copy

Let's take it one step further. It's a trivial task to write code that transforms the image as it copies it. In essence, all you do is manipulate the world transformation matrix so that your quad is scaled or rotated.

Here's some code from the Ch13p1_SimpleFeedback program, showing how to set up the world matrix to perform a typical transformation:

```
// set up world matrix so that it rotates the quad slightly.
D3DXMATRIX scalemat,destmat,rotmat;
D3DXMatrixIdentity( &mat );
D3DXMatrixRotationZ(&mat, D3DXToRadian(m_fFeedbackRotation));

// scaling: dividing by 2 will make the texture completely fill the
// rendering surface (because our ortho projection made one texel=
// one pixel, and the quad's local origin is in its exact center.)
// So, dividing by 1.8 will enlarge the image slightly, creating
// the "tunneling" effect of this feedback system.
D3DXMatrixMultiply(&destmat, &mat,
D3DXMatrixScaling(&scalemat, (float)m_iTextureWidth1.8,
  (float)m_iTextureHeight1.8, 1.0));
m_pd3dDevice->SetTransform( D3DTS_WORLD, &destmat );
```

This code starts by putting a rotation matrix into mat. You tell D3DX to give you a matrix that rotates a certain number of radians around the z-axis. The m_fFeedbackRotation is a variable that changes as the program runs. If a constant value were used instead of m_fFeedbackRotation, you would have a feedback system that spins at a constant speed. Using m_fFeedbackRotation, you can change the rotation amount so that the feedback system spins at different speeds (and, when it goes negative, in the opposite direction) as the program runs.

Next, you create a scaling matrix and store it in scalemat. Recall that you're using an orthogonal projection and that your quad is 2×2 units—remember, its corners are at (–1,–1) and (1,1), and its center is at (0,0). Therefore, if you wanted the texture to fill your rendering surface complete-ly, you would scale the quad by half your texture dimensions. This causes –1 to scale into `-m_iTextureWidth/2` and 1 to scale to `m_iTextureWidth/2`.

However, you're not scaling by the texture dimensions divided by 2. You're dividing by 1.8 instead. What this means is that your quad will end up slightly bigger than the screen. This is what gives the feedback effect its tunneling, zooming appearance. You're constantly stretching the quad as you rotate it, so eventually the pixels in the center are stretched out to the edges (see Figure 13.5).

Figure 13.5

Stretching the quad as you rotate it eventually moves the pixels in the center out to the edges.

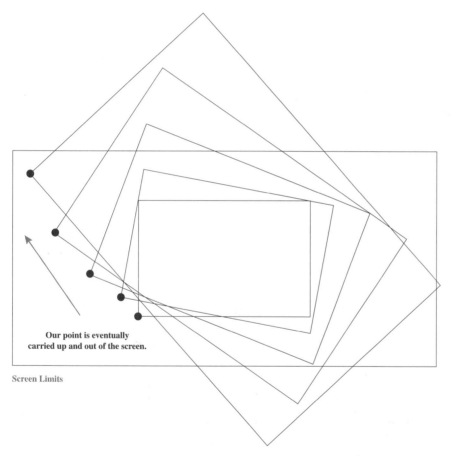

Our point is eventually carried up and out of the screen.

Screen Limits

Finally, you multiply the scaling and rotation matrices by calling `D3DXMatrixMultiply`, storing the result in `destmat`. You then tell Direct3D that `destmat` is the new world matrix with a call to `SetTransform`.

This is, of course, only a rudimentary example of the fun you can have with the feedback effect. I encourage you to spend a lot of time experimenting with other transformation matrices to see what other trippy effects you can produce.

Rendering New Image Data onto the Scratch Texture

In this step of the process, you render any objects you want "in between the TV and the camera" onto the scratch texture.

What you specifically render here is entirely up to you. It can be as simple as a quad zooming in and out (for basic feedback effects) or can be an entire, complex scene. If you're writing an MP3 player, this is where you put the code that draws the wave onto the scratch texture.

Blending the Scratch Texture Back onto the Primary Texture

Because you learned how to render-copy in the previous sections, this section should be a no-brainer. Your goal here is to blend the scratch texture back onto the primary texture, completing the feedback effect.

To blend the textures, you use alpha blending. You enable alpha blending and set up your source and destination blend modes. To achieve a normal alpha blend, you set the source blend mode to source alpha (D3DBLEND_SRCALPHA) and the destination blend to inverse source alpha (D3DBLEND_INVSRCALPHA). All of this is done through a handful of SetRenderState calls, as shown in the following code:

```
m_pd3dDevice->SetRenderState(D3DRS_ALPHABLENDENABLE, TRUE);
m_pd3dDevice->SetRenderState(D3DRS_SRCBLEND, D3DBLEND_SRCALPHA);
m_pd3dDevice->SetRenderState(D3DRS_DESTBLEND, D3DBLEND_INVSRCALPHA);
```

So far so good, but now you must also set up your first texture stage state so that it outputs the correct alpha value. You can do this many ways. I prefer to store alpha values in the quad's vertices, so I set up my texture stage so that the alpha operation selects the diffuse color, as in the following code:

```
m_pd3dDevice->SetTextureStageState(0, D3DTSS_ALPHAARG1, D3DTA_DIFFUSE);
```

After you enable alpha blending and have your texture stage states outputting the correct values, you're all set. Direct3D uses the alpha values stored in the quad's vertices to blend the two images. All you do is render-copy the scratch texture back onto the primary texture.

MODIFYING THE IMAGE FEEDBACK EFFECT

The image feedback effect has several parameters you can use to change its behavior. This section describes a few key variables you can play with. These are by no means the only things you can change, but they give you a jumping-off place.

Feedback Transformation

You can change the type of transformation you apply to the primary texture when you render it onto the scratch texture.

For this effect, the two most common transformations are *scaling* and *z-axis rotation*. Scaling the primary texture as you copy it creates a tunneling effect, and rotating it around the z-axis adds a spin to this tunneling effect, resulting in a feedback loop that seems to spiral out to infinity.

Keep in mind that you're not bound to using a constant rotation or scale amount. You can vary these amounts per frame. For example, every frame, you can apply a rotational acceleration or a scale acceleration so that the feedback system appears to rotate or tunnel faster or slower as time goes on. You can add or subtract constants from these acceleration variables to achieve smooth movement of your feedback system. The possibilities are endless.

Transparency of the Scratch Texture

You can adjust how transparent the scratch texture is when you blend it with the primary texture. By changing the alpha values, you can create slightly different effects.

You can also change the alpha blend modes themselves. For example, you can try additive alpha blending instead of normal alpha blending. This results in a feedback system that eventually fades to white.

USES FOR IMAGE FEEDBACK

As mentioned at the start of this chapter, virtually every MP3 player I've seen uses the image feedback effect. Usually, the MP3 players insert a squiggly line representing the waveform of the sound into the feedback loop. As the song plays and the feedback effect runs, the users are treated to a hypnotizing display of their song's sound wave.

Also, you can combine image feedback with other nifty effects to create, well, even niftier effects. For example, you could put a feedback loop on your fire texture to create flames of fire that have feedback trails!

CHAPTER WRAP-UP

I believe that the most difficult part of learning how to code the image feedback effect is figuring out the orthogonal projections. When you know the basics of how to copy one texture onto another, the entire effect becomes very easy to write.

The good news is that you use the render-copy method in a few other effects, besides image copying. You're going to look at image warping in the next chapter, which is incredibly similar to image feedback. Knowing how to render-copy a texture using an orthogonal projection will be a great help to you in the next chapter.

ABOUT THE SAMPLE PROGRAMS

There are no new enhancements to the coding style or organization this chapter. Here is the program:

- **Ch13p1_SimpleFeedback.** This sample program demonstrates the image feedback effect, without any bells and whistles to distract you.

EXERCISES

Here are a few exercises designed to lock in your understanding of the image feedback concepts we've discussed in this chapter:

1. Write a program that can render-copy a texture of arbitrary size. Yes, you can piece together one from the examples in the book, but render-copying is an important skill, so take the time to learn it correctly by writing your own code.
2. Experiment with various transformation matrices inside the feedback effect–processing function of Ch13p1_SimpleFeedback. In particular, see what effects you get when you rotate about other axes or shrink rather than enlarge the texture.
3. Play with different alpha-blending modes in your feedback-processing loop.

CHAPTER 14

IMAGE WARPING

"Nothing is more terrible than activity without insight."
——*Thomas Carlyle*

Before we start this chapter, I have a confession to make: I'm a sucker for science-themed, kids' TV shows. Back in the day, when I was a wee lad, I used to watch *Mr. Wizard* and *3-2-1 Contact* incessantly—nowadays, I'll still stop channel surfing to watch *Bill Nye, The Science Guy*.

I don't remember what TV show it was, but one of the coolest demonstrations I saw was about fluid dynamics—the whole demo revolved around a rectangular, Plexiglas container full of water. By putting drops of food coloring into the water and gently stirring, the host of the show taught us the basics of fluid dynamics—how the little red swirl mixed with the blue swirl to create little purple swirls that eventually just turned the water into a flat shade of purple. Of course, there were no messy fluid dynamics equations—it was just water, food coloring, and a heavy dose of "hey, neat."

The best part about this chapter's Image Warping effect is that it, too, doesn't involve any real math—it's just a clever trick that produces spectacular results (as you can see in Figure 14.1).

Figure 14.1

Four successive screen-shots showing how Ch14p1_SimpleWarp *warps an image.*

In fact, I'm sure that if someone were to make a kids' show about DirectX special effects, they could cover this one in half an hour and still have time for a little cartoon. That's because this technique is nothing more than a little clever texture coordinate manipulation. By cleverly rendering using different texture coordinate settings, we can "stir up" an image, just as if it were made out of thousands of little drops of food coloring in a Plexiglas container.

HOW DOES IT WORK?

Let's talk about the concept first. To warp an image, you lay a grid of squares on top of it (see Figure 14.2).

Then, you perturb each square a little, so that your grid looks a little messed up, like in Figure 14.3.

Note that at this point you haven't done anything to the image itself—you've just put a messed up grid on top of it.

Next, you pin the grid down onto the image, and you straighten out all the grid squares, which pulls and stretches the image, as if you had just pinned your messed up grid onto a piece of cloth and then straightened the grid, stretching the cloth. What you end up with is, of course, a distorted image.

This by itself isn't terribly nifty, but things get really interesting when you do this repeatedly, creating an animation. I can't think of a word that precisely describes how the image animates—verbs like "melt," "stir," or "swirl" come to mind, but the effect really defies description. Suffice it to say that it's just cool.

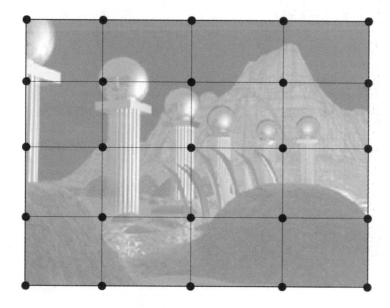

Figure 14.2

Putting a grid of squares down on top of an image, in preparation to warp it.

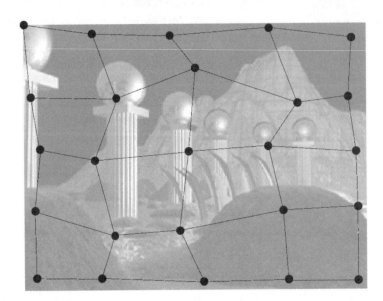

Figure 14.3

Jiggle each grid square a bit, but leave the image underneath unchanged.

Writing the Code

Creating this algorithm in the wonderful world of Direct3D is painfully easy—all we really need is a grid of vertices, each with a (u,v) texture coordinate. Recall from Part 1 that the (u,v) texture coordinate tells Direct3D which vertices are pinned to which texels. The basic idea is to distort the (u,v) texture coordinates for each vertex, then render the mesh (thereby distorting the image) onto another texture of the same dimensions. For the next frame, we flip textures so that our newly messed up image becomes the source image for the next frame, causing it to become further and further distorted with each frame.

It's important to realize that the vertices themselves never actually move. We'll use an orthogonal projection so that there's a 1:1 correspondence between texels and world coordinates. If we were rendering to a 256×256 destination surface, we'd want the four corners of our distortion grid to be at world space coordinates (-128,128), (128,128), (128,-128), and (-128,-128), as shown in Figure 14.4).

Assuming our source image is 256×256, and we want to use a 16×16 distortion grid, we'd set up our grid so that we'd have one vertex every 16 pixels.

These vertex coordinates form little tiled quads, which represent the destination points of our final rendering. Note that these quads will never change position.

Now, we could also set up our texture coordinates so that they corresponded exactly to the position of each vertex. For example, the vertex at (0,0) would have texture coordinates (0.0,0.0)—

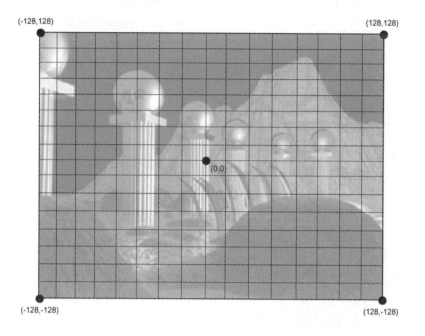

(-128,128) (128,128)

(0,0)

(-128,-128) (128,-128)

Figure 14.4

Coordinates for the four corners of our distortion grid.

the vertex at (256,256) would have texture coordinates (1.0,1.0), and every vertex in between would have texture coordinates calculated by dividing that vertex's row or column by the total number of rows or columns in our grid. That is, a vertex at (32,48) is actually at row 2, column 3 in our 16×16 distortion grid, so its texture coordinates would be (2/16, 3/16), or roughly (0.125, 0.1875) (see Figure 14.5).

If we did this, when we rendered our image, we'd end up with nothing more than our original texture applied to a big quad.

That isn't interesting—what we want is to perturb the (u,v) texture coordinates for each vertex so that when we render, our source texture is "wobbled" across the surface of our grid. That effectively warps the image, and by feeding this warped image back into the system as the texture for the next grid we render, we can create the swimming animation.

That's really all there is to it. Now let's look at each of the steps in more detail.

One Effect, Two Textures

The entire effect starts and ends with textures. So, we'll need two textures—one texture holds the image we want to warp, the second texture will contain the warped image. For the next frame of animation, we'll swap the two textures so that the warped image from the first frame becomes the source image for the second frame (overwriting the original picture—see Figure 14.6).

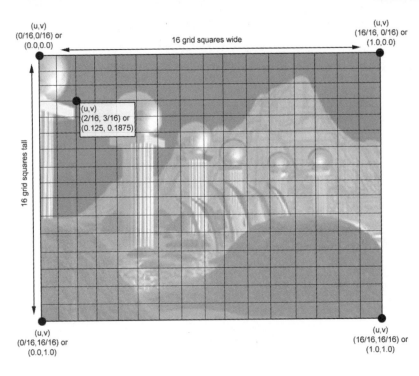

(u,v)
(0/16,0/16) or
(0.0,0.0)

16 grid squares wide

(u,v)
(16/16, 0/16) or
(1.0,0.0)

(u,v)
(2/16, 3/16) or
(0.125, 0.1875)

16 grid squares tall

(u,v)
(0/16,16/16) or
(0.0,1.0)

(u,v)
(16/16,16/16) or
(1.0,1.0)

Figure 14.5

Calculating the texture coordinates for a particular grid point.

Frame X

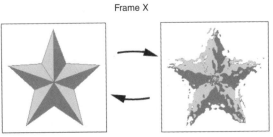

Figure 14.6

Swapping textures to feed the warped image back onto itself.

The warped texture of this frame becomes the
source image for the next frame's warp, thereby
warping the image more and more as time goes on.

Frame X+1

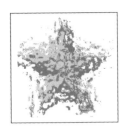

Source Image

Destination Image

If you plan on animating this effect (warping more than once), you'll want your two textures to be the same width and height. Ideally, they will also have the same pixel format.

Here's the code that sets up the two textures:

```
// create the two texture buffers that we'll use for the effect
// these must be created as render targets.
if (FAILED(hr = D3DXCreateTexture(m_pd3dDevice,
  GetLowestPowerOf2(m_iImageWidth),
  GetLowestPowerOf2(m_iImageHeight), 1, D3DUSAGE_RENDERTARGET,
  D3DFMT_A8R8G8B8, D3DPOOL_DEFAULT, &m_pTex1))) { return(hr); }

if (FAILED(hr = D3DXCreateTexture(m_pd3dDevice,
  GetLowestPowerOf2(m_iImageWidth),
  GetLowestPowerOf2(m_iImageHeight), 1, D3DUSAGE_RENDERTARGET,
  D3DFMT_A8R8G8B8, D3DPOOL_DEFAULT, &m_pTex2))) { return(hr); }
```

TIP

Note that we need to create both textures using the D3DUSAGE_RENDERTARGET flag. This is because we'll eventually be rendering scenes directly onto both textures.

Setting Up the Vertex Grid

The next step is to set up our vertex grid. This means that we'll have to look at the texture's texel dimensions, and generate a vertex grid that fits exactly on top of those dimensions. Our vertex grid will ultimately be put into a vertex buffer. The question is, should we also use an index buffer?

It doesn't take much investigation to see that each triangle of our finished grid is going to be sharing a bunch of vertices. In fact, our triangles use each vertex of the grid at least twice (for the corners), with the majority of vertices each contributing to six different triangles (see Figure 14.7).

This means that an index buffer will save us a good chunk of memory.

The next question concerns which primitive type to use. As you recall from Chapter 5 "3D Concepts," we have three different types to choose from: triangle lists, triangle strips, or triangle fans. For the sake of simplicity, I've used triangle lists in all the examples. That isn't to say that triangle lists are the fastest or best approach—for me, the clarity of code that using triangle lists provides is worth the small price of one or two extra bytes per triangle. However, if you're into

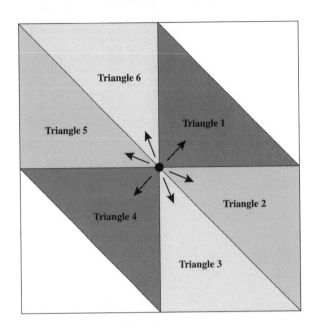

Figure 14.7

The reason we should use an index buffer: most vertices in our grid contribute to the shape of six different triangles.

optimization, you're more than welcome to investigate and figure out how to save a few bytes by using a different primitive type.

So, we've decided to use triangle lists, in conjunction with an index buffer. The next order of business is to write the code that fills up the buffers.

Filling the Vertex Buffer

This is nothing terribly complex. To create the vertices for our grid, we set up a double `for` loop—one loop for x, one loop for y. Our x `for` loop goes from 0 to the number of grid spaces we want horizontally; our y loop goes from 0 to the number of spaces vertically.

Inside the double `for` loop, we need to assign each vertex a position, and a pair of (u,v) texture coordinates.

To figure out each vertex's position, we use the x and y `for` loop indices, along with some basic math. We know that our finished grid must span from (-1.0,-1.0) to (1.0,1.0), with its exact center at (0,0). This means that the grid itself is 2×2 units (see Figure 14.8).

> **TIP**
>
> It doesn't really matter whether you loop first on x and then on y, or if you choose to loop on y first and then on x (in other words, whether you choose to fill up the grid row by row or column by column). However, you need to remember which way you choose, because you'll need to know in what order you created the vertices when it comes time to fill up the index buffer.

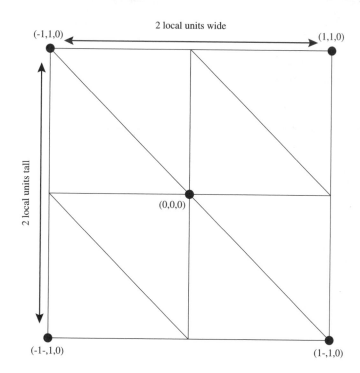

Figure 14.8

Our grid mesh will have dimensions of 2×2 local units, with its local origin in the center.

So, if we're trying to fit, say, 50 grid points inside that grid, we need one grid point every (2/50), or 1/25, or 0.04 units. This means that as we loop, we calculate each individual vertex position by taking the current x and y for loop index, dividing that index by the total number of grid rows or columns, multiplying by 2, and then subtracting 1.0 from that (because our origin is in the center, not at the top/left).

Here's the function, straight from Ch14p1_SimpleWarp, that will loop and create our vertex positions:

```
void SetupVertexGrid(LPDIRECT3DVERTEXBUFFER8 pVBGrid, int iGridWidth,
  int iGridHeight)
{
  HRESULT hr;
  CUSTOMVERTEX* pVertices;

  if(FAILED(hr = pVBGrid->Lock(0,
    iGridWidth*iGridHeight*sizeof(CUSTOMVERTEX),
    (BYTE**)&pVertices, 0))) return;
  for (int x=0; x < iGridWidth; x++) {
    for (int y=0; y < iGridHeight; y++) {
```

```
pVertices[(y*iGridWidth)+x].position =
  D3DXVECTOR3(
    (((float)x/(float)(iGridWidth-1))*2.0f)-1.0f,
    ((((float)(iGridHeight-1-y)/(iGridHeight-1))*2)-1.0f,
    0.0f);
pVertices[(y*iGridWidth)+x].color = D3DCOLOR_ARGB(255,0,0,0);
pVertices[(y*iGridWidth)+x].tu = (float)x/(float)(iGridWidth-1);
pVertices[(y*iGridWidth)+x].tv = (float)y/(float)(iGridHeight-1);
// the four lines above will create a grid that doesn't warp
// the image at all.  But now, we jiggle the texture coordinates
// slightly to achieve the image warp.

// get 2 random numbers - the range of possible values is
// slightly lopsided, because the effect has a tendency to
// move to the lower-right.
float fRandAmtX = RandomNumber(-75,100)/50.0f;
float fRandAmtY = RandomNumber(-75,100)/50.0f;
// use the random numbers to calculate the final amount to move.
pVertices[(y*iGridWidth)+x].tu += fRandAmtX/iGridWidth*2.0f;
pVertices[(y*iGridWidth)+x].tv += fRandAmtY/iGridHeight*2.0f;
    }
  }
  if(FAILED(hr = pVBGrid->Unlock())) return;
}
```

As you can see, the calculations to determine the positions and (u,v) coordinates are very similar. The only major difference is that when calculating the (u,v) coordinates, our target dimensions are 1×1 instead of 2×2, so we don't have to bother with multiplying—we just calculate each individual texture coordinate by taking the appropriate for loop index (x or y) and then dividing by the number of rows or columns in our grid.

Since we don't want an exact texture copy, we need to randomly add or subtract a certain amount from each (u,v) coordinate so that the image warps itself.

TIP

It's worth mentioning here that there are alternative ways to make a grid of points. You could have calculated the width and height of a single grid space, and then "stepped" that amount every time you completed an iteration of your for loop. If you don't need to worry about speed of execution, each approach is perfectly okay—whatever you want to use. I usually think of things in formulas rather than steps, so I tend to code things as shown, but that's just my own style.

Filling the Index Buffer

Now let's look at the second part to making this whole thing work. In the preceding section, we created the vertices that form our vertex grid. But vertices are no good without triangles—we need an index buffer to tell Direct3D how to clump the vertices we've created into triangles.

This process isn't terribly difficult to follow. Our primary mission is to divide each grid space into two triangles.

We know from the get-go that our code will have a double `for` loop so that it can visit each cell in the grid. For each cell in the grid, we need to add six indices to our index buffer. These six indices tell Direct3D how to draw the two triangles for that particular grid space.

Now the only question is, what indices do we store? To form our two triangles, we need four vertices, arranged in a square. We know the order all of our vertices were stored in our vertex buffer, because we just wrote the code that filled the vertex buffer. Because when I filled the vertex buffer I looped first on x, and then on y (that is, filling my vertex buffer up column by column), I know that to get the index of any vertex of my grid, I multiply the vertex's x coordinate by the number of rows in the grid, and add to that product my vertex's y coordinate. In other words, the vertex's index can be calculated as `(x*grid_height)+y`, where x and y are the grid coordinates of the vertex, and `grid_height` is the height of the grid.

> **TIP**
>
> Keep in mind that all of these measurements are in grid spaces—we're not talking about the vertex's local coordinate triplet—we're talking about its position on the vertex grid. The grid position and local coordinate position are two very different things.

Let's take an example. Imagine we have a vertex grid that's 20×20 vertices. We can calculate the index of the vertex at (5,7) in that grid by multiplying 5 times 20, then adding 7: our final answer is 107. This makes sense—our x loop was outside our y loop, which means before we moved from column 1 to column 2, we filled our vertex buffer with 20 vertices. That's where the multiplication comes from.

However, if you programmed your vertex fill code differently, you'll have a different formula for determining a vertex's index. For example, if you swapped your x and y loops so that you looped first on y, and then, inside your y loop, you looped on x, your formula would be `(y*grid_width)+x`.

The point here is that regardless of what the formula is, we know it, because we created our vertex fill code. So filling up the index buffer becomes a simple task of using the formula to arrive at the indices of the vertices we need.

Now let's look at a code snippet—this chunk of code will fill up our index buffer:

```
WORD *pIndices;
if(FAILED(hr = m_pIBGrid->Lock(0,
  VERTEX_GRID_DENSITY*VERTEX_GRID_DENSITY*2*3*2,
  (unsigned char **)&pIndices, 0))) return hr;

WORD *pIndex = pIndices;
for (int x=0; x < VERTEX_GRID_DENSITY-1; x++) {
  for (int y=0; y < VERTEX_GRID_DENSITY-1; y++) {
    // first triangle
    *(pIndex++) = ((y)*VERTEX_GRID_DENSITY)+x;
    *(pIndex++) = ((y)*VERTEX_GRID_DENSITY)+x+1;
    *(pIndex++) = ((y+1)*VERTEX_GRID_DENSITY)+x+1;
    // second triangle
    *(pIndex++) = ((y)*VERTEX_GRID_DENSITY)+x;
    *(pIndex++) = ((y+1)*VERTEX_GRID_DENSITY)+x+1;
    *(pIndex++) = ((y+1)*VERTEX_GRID_DENSITY)+x;
  }
}
if(FAILED(hr = m_pIBGrid->Unlock())) return hr;
```

Pretty amazing, isn't it? All of that talk above boiled down to just a few lines of code! In essence, for each cell of our grid, the code above drops six indices into the index buffer—the first three indices form one triangle of our grid space, and the second three form the other triangle.

CAUTION

If you're using backface culling, beware of the order in which you specify indices. You must specify the indices in a clockwise order for each triangle; otherwise, Direct3D will interpret your triangle as facing away from you instead of toward you, and it will cull (clip) it out of existence!

MODIFYING IMAGE WARPING

Image warping has several key variables; changing these will allow you to modify the image warping effect.

Grid Density

The density of your vertex grid (in other words, the number of squares in the grid) plays a big part in determining how the Image Warping effect looks. In general, smaller squares will give you finer control over the warping process, creating a more turbulent and detailed animation. A courser grid will give you fewer points to perturb the texture, resulting in a simpler, more "linear" animation.

CAUTION

You need to make sure you keep your grid density small. As you increase your grid density, the size of your index buffer increases exponentially. Too many grid vertices, and your index buffer will become larger than 64K. Dealing with index buffers larger than 64K is a big pain, and it may not even be possible, depending on your version of Direct3D and your graphics card. It's better to always keep your vertex grids under 100×100 so that you're guaranteed to have enough room for all your indices.

Perturbation Amount

The other obvious variable is how far you randomly perturb each (u,v) coordinate of your vertices. A smaller random amount creates a slower-moving, more flowing image; a higher amount creates a much more quick and volatile stirring up of the image.

Cumulative Versus Non-Cumulative Warps

I tried and tried to think of a better title for this modification, but the word "cumulative" really says it best. Up to this point, we've been talking only about cumulative warps—warps where you take the warped image of one frame and use it as the source image for the next frame so that the image gets more and more jumbled over time.

It's also possible to do a non-cumulative warp—in other words, to not feed the image back onto itself each frame. You can set up a vertex grid, tie that grid to a texture, and then jiggle the vertex grid's (u,v) coordinates each frame. This creates a really cheap and good-looking water effect—your image will appear to be underneath clear, turbulent water.

Alpha Blending

In the previous chapter, you learned about using alpha blending to generate an image feedback effect. So, take a page from that chapter and apply it here! Use alpha blending when you render your vertex grid. You can choose to make each vertex of the grid have the same alpha value, or you can jumble things up a bit and assign a random alpha to each vertex of the grid—your choice.

The end result looks pretty psychedelic—it looks a lot like the original warp effect, only with "trails" (if you can imagine that).

USES FOR IMAGE WARPING

If you studied the sample programs, you probably realized right off the bat that there's an astounding number of 2D effects you can create, just by keeping the vertex positions constant, and varying their (u,v) coordinates.

It's my opinion that the best places to use an Image Warp effect are when your player's character dies or steps into a transporter. Both effects work really well in those situations.

Image Warping also makes a great transition effect; we'll talk more about that in a couple of chapters.

OPTIMIZING IMAGE WARPING

The nifty thing about the Image Warping effect is that the graphics card is doing all the actual work. Before 3D acceleration, we would have needed to manually calculate the warped image based on pixel positions, which would have burned a ton of CPU time—but now, we just make the image into a texture, and the 3D card crunches all the numbers. So the effect is pretty fast right out of the gate.

Unfortunately, however, to properly use the image warping effect in your scene, you'll need to use two BeginScene/EndScene blocks. You'll need one block to render and warp the old texture into the new texture, and then you'll need a second block to actually render your scene using that warped texture. This is disappointing, but it's a necessary evil.

Also, you have a trade-off to make between the level of detail you want in your image warps, and the number of triangles that must be rendered. You have to choose how fine your grid is; that is, how close each vertex is to the next (and therefore the total number of vertices used for your grid). If you use more vertices to create a grid with smaller squares, you gain more control over the image warp, but you burn through a lot of triangles; conversely, larger grid squares save triangles but sacrifice control. Normally, however, this isn't an issue, because it's doubtful that the number of triangles forming your grid will come anywhere near your 3D card's maximum.

CHAPTER WRAP-UP

Image Warping is fun stuff. It's easy to program, versatile, and fast. If you can stand the hit of having to call `BeginScene`/`EndScene` twice, you can use Image Warping to achieve some really interesting effects.

ABOUT THE SAMPLE PROGRAMS

Nothing new to report for this chapter, as far as the coding style and organization is concerned, anyway. Here is the program:

- **Ch14p1_SimpleWarp**. This sample program demonstrates Image Warping, without any bells and whistles to distract you.

EXERCISES

1. Modify the `Ch14p1_SimpleWarp` program so that it uses alpha blending in conjunction with the Image Warp effect.
2. Modify `Ch14p1_SimpleWarp` so that it uses non-cumulative warping.
3. Vary the perturbation amount inside `Ch14p1_SimpleWarp`, and notice the effect that has on the warping.

CHAPTER 15

CLOUDS

"Revelations are found in clouds."
——*Serge Kahili King*

reating fun video games often involves making those games mimic reality. This 2D effects section started out with a very realistic fire effect, but since then, we've taken a slight detour from reality. All fine and dandy, but now it's time to come back.

This chapter, like the fire chapter, is concerned with mimicking reality—in particular, finding an algorithm that allows us to generate realistic, beautiful clouds and still maintain a decent frame rate (see Figure 15.1).

That sounds like a pretty tall order, but I think you'll be pleasantly surprised at the simple elegance of the concepts.

HOW DOES IT WORK?

Like so many other 2D effects in this section, this technique's output is a texture—a cloud texture. In the next section on 3D effects, we'll learn how to apply the cloud texture to a skybox or skysphere to create a world with an atmosphere; for now, however, let's just concentrate on how to make the texture itself.

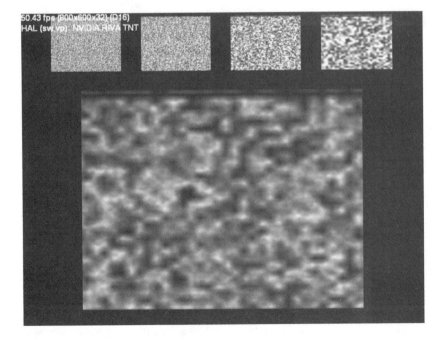

Figure 15.1

Making beautiful clouds that don't drag.

Clouds, like so many other things in nature, are fractals. This means that the overall pattern of a cloud is similar whether you're viewing it up close or far away. In other words, just as the sky as a whole has patches of cloud separated by clear air, each cloud also has patches of subclouds separated by clear air. The subclouds have subclouds, and so on.

Perlin Noise

To create our clouds, we'll be using a technique called Perlin noise, named after Ken Perlin, the guy who created it. You'll see why we call it noise in the next section.

What Is Perlin Noise?

Perlin noise is an amazingly simple tool that can create textures resembling all sorts of natural phenomena—clouds, marble, rock, wood, and everything in between. Because these textures don't use images, but are instead generated through one or more procedures, the industry refers to them as "procedural textures." Perlin noise is one way to generate procedural textures.

Perlin noise is so simple that it's difficult to explain. Consider for a moment a rectangular patch of *regular noise* (see Figure 15.2).

> **TIP**
>
> You could write a whole book on how to code procedural textures. In fact, Ken Perlin teamed up with other industry pioneers of procedural texturing and did just that. The book is called *Texturing and Modeling: A Procedural Approach* (ISBN: 0122287304), and if you find yourself dying to explore procedural texturing in depth, it's the book to buy.

Figure 15.2

A patch of regular noise.

You could generate a noise patch like this by simply assigning each pixel a random gray value. This regular noise is useful for simulating TV static and such, but it's a horrible attempt at making realistic clouds.

Now take a peek at the Perlin noise in Figure 15.3.

Figure 15.3

Perlin noise is smoother than regular noise.

As you can see, it's a smoother, gentler noise (if there can be such a thing)—it's a noise that more closely mimics what you'd see in nature. It's not hard to imagine that figure as the surface of an island-filled planet, the bumps on the bark of a tree, a gas nebula, or thousands of other natural phenomena. Because the variations throughout the noise are gradual, it's great for mimicking nature.

Using the 3D Card to Generate Perlin Noise

Caution: what you're about to learn is a trick. The real algorithm for generating Perlin noise doesn't fit our needs—it relies on a lot of math, and as we all know, math kills frame rates. So, we're going to learn how to generate Perlin noise quickly, by using the features of your 3D card as a substitute for mathematical equations.

What makes Perlin noise so cool is that there's no sharp contrasts, no areas where a black pixel is directly next to a white pixel. Instead, it looks almost as if the whole image has been smoothed out. In fact, if you've ever played a first person shooter, you could say that the Perlin noise looks like what happens to a wall when you get to close to it, and bilinear filtering kicks in—the wall becomes fuzzy and indistinct. (See where I'm going with this?)

We can generate quick approximations of Perlin noise by generating regular noise and then upsampling it (increasing its dimensions), and having the 3D card perform bilinear filtering to smooth it out. In other words, we could generate a 16×16 patch of regular noise (random black and white values), turn bilinear filtering on, and then tell our 3D card to render-copy that 16×16 texture onto a 256×256 destination texture (see Figure 15.4).

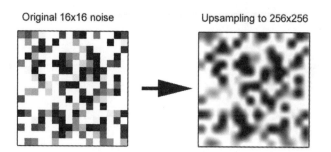

Original 16x16 noise   Upsampling to 256x256

Figure 15.4

A 16×16 texture smoothed into a 256×256 one.

The card's bilinear filtering process will smooth out our noise, and we'll end up with a 256×256 texture that looks really close to something Ken Perlin's algorithm would generate. The texture isn't quite as good as something generated using the Perlin algorithms, but the 3D card can make it very quickly. Once again, we sacrifice a bit of quality for a tremendous speed boost.

Okay, so now you're probably thinking, "Cool, but what does this have to do with clouds?" Read on!

> **TIP**
>
> **Think about how slick this is for a minute. By using bilinear interpolation, we're effectively letting the graphics card interpolate between two data points (colors). The whole interpolation process can be done *on the graphics card itself*, which is a tremendous speed gain. Aren't 3D cards wonderful?**

Layering Perlin Noise to Create Clouds

A block of Perlin noise, by itself, looks very similar to a cloud, but it's not quite believable. Real clouds, being fractal in nature, have many distinct levels of detail—they have an overall shape or form, but they also have very fine variations in color that form highlights and subclouds within that form.

So, we can generate a pretty convincing cloud texture by combining several different layers of Perlin noise. That's how this cloud effect works. In essence, you combine multiple layers of Perlin noise onto a single surface to arrive at your final cloud texture (see Figure 15.5).

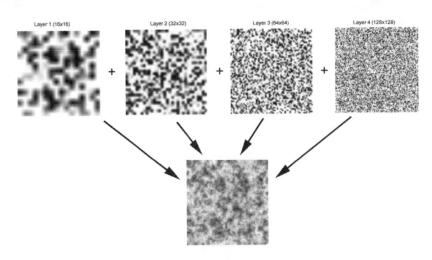

Layer 1 (16x16)   +   Layer 2 (32x32)   +   Layer 3 (64x64)   +   Layer 4 (128x128)

Figure 15.5

Combine multiple layers of Perlin noise onto one surface and voilà! A cloud texture!

Each layer is randomly generated according to two key parameters—amplification and frequency.

- **Amplification** is the range of colors that are allowed for that layer. High amplification means we'll be using black, white, and all grays in between for our clouds, whereas low amplification means we'll only be using colors that are very close to what I call "center gray," RGB(128,128,128)—an exact 50% gray color.
- **Frequency** determines how blurry the layer is. Lower frequencies create very gradual changes in color (see Figure 15.6), whereas higher frequencies create more and more turbulent variations in color.

Figure 15.6

Frequency determines blurriness; use lower frequencies for gradual changes.

Essentially, the dimensions of the source regular noise texture determine the frequency of the finished Perlin noise texture. Think about that for a minute. If we start with a 4×4 block of regular noise (that is, 16 texels of random color), and blow that up to 256×256, we create a very low frequency Perlin noise texture. Our 3D card's bilinear interpolation does a lot of smoothing. Conversely, if we start with a 128×128 block of regular noise, and blow that up to 256×256, there's very little room for the bilinear filtering to smooth things out, and we end up with a much higher frequency Perlin noise texture.

To generate cool-looking clouds, we'll start with a low frequency Perlin noise texture, blend a higher frequency texture onto that one, blend another, even higher frequency texture onto that, and so on, until we arrive at a cloud texture that has rolling, low frequency variations, combined with higher frequency details and highlights (see Figure 15.7).

Figure 15.7

Creating cool-looking clouds through a combination of high and low frequencies.

When I first learned about this technique from an article by Kim Pallister, I didn't believe that something so simple could create such amazing results, but it does.

Usually, I've found that using four octaves (layers) results in a pretty good-looking cloud, so we'll be using four textures. We want octaves; that is, we want the frequency ratios of the layers to be 2:1. That, in turn, means that each texture must be exactly twice the size as the texture before it, sort of like reverse mipmaps. To generate a 256×256 cloud texture, our first (lowest) octave needs to be 32×32; to maintain the 2:1 frequency, we must make our second octave 64×64, our third 128×128, and our fourth and finest octave 256×256.

> **TIP**
>
> Programmers call the individual layers of Perlin noise *octaves*, because usually their frequency is double or half that of the next or previous layer; that is, the frequency ratio is 2:1. In music, if you take a note and double or halve its frequency, you end up with a note that's one octave higher or lower than your original.

So that takes care of the frequency of each octave. To further enhance our cloud image, we can put the amplitude of each layer into a 2:1 ratio. That's easy enough to do, because amplitude is really just a color range. We simply limit the range of gray we can randomly choose from for each layer. For example, we might say that octave one could use any gray value between 0 and 255, whereas octave two could only use half of that—a 64–192 range. We might say that octave three could only use colors 96–160, and octave four could only use 112–144, so that each octave is grayer and less contrasted than the previous one.

Once we have all of these layers generated, we just combine them using alpha blending, and almost magically, a really neat texture comes out. At this point, we're really close to our final cloud texture, but there's still a couple of things we can tweak to make it look better.

Making the Cloud Texture Look Better

You may be perfectly happy with the texture you get by combining octaves of Perlin noise, or if you're using this effect in-game, you might say to yourself, "well, it doesn't look perfect, but it's good enough, and I don't want to waste any more resources on it," which, believe me, is a per-fectly okay thing to say. In fact, if saying such a thing saves you from blowing past your ship date, by all means, say it!

However, if you have some extra time to code, and your target system has a bit of extra time and memo-ry, here are a couple of things you can do to make your cloud texture look better.

TIP

The Ch15p1_SimpleClouds sample program uses all of these tech-niques so that you can see the cloud texture in all its glory.

Square the Combined Texture's Colors

One thing you can do to make your clouds look a little better is to square the colors of your com-posite texture (the texture that contains the combined noise layers). This will increase the con-trast of the texture, which, in turn, creates a more convincing cloud.

To square the colors of a texture, you simply modulate (multiply) that texture by itself. We'll see the code for this a little later on, in the programming section.

Filter the Noise Layers Before You Combine Them

Another trick to generate cool-looking clouds: use bilinear filtering on each noise layer before you combine the noise layers together.

True Perlin noise is "smoother" than just assigning random values to random pixels. A block of true Perlin noise will gently fade from color to color. The exact calculations to do this take too much time for us to use them in this cloud effect; however, we can approximate what those calcu-lations do by simply filtering the texture onto a texture of the same size. Again, we'll look at the code for this a little later.

Subtract the Texture

There's still one last thing we can do to improve the quality of our cloud texture: we can subtract it from a flat color.

Doing this enables us to vary the amount of "cloud" on the texture. By subtracting our cloud tex-ture from a flat color, we effectively *clip* certain values out of existence. This clipping removes some of the cloud pattern from the texture, leaving us with a *partly cloudy* texture (that is, some areas of the texture are cloud, while other areas are completely clear—see Figure 15.8).

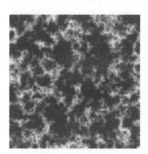

Figure 15.8

Creating a partly cloudy skyscape.

Animating the Cloud Texture

Of course, anyone who's spent a lazy summer afternoon cloud gazing knows that clouds don't just stay in one shape. They animate; they change shape. So, in order for our clouds to be realistic, we must make our clouds change shape as well.

We do this by regenerating the noise layers, then slowly interpolating the "old noise" with the "new noise." This gives us an individual noise texture that constantly fades between random layouts of noise. The process for doing this is very similar to how you'd perform a very slow cross fade (more details on that in a few chapters), but essentially all it takes is some clever texture stage setups. We'll see precisely how this works in the code section.

WRITING THE CODE

The code to create the cloud texture isn't terribly complex, but it does force you to keep track of quite a few textures, and employ quite a few blending modes. However, you'll be happy to hear that there's no math involved; no pesky equations to fiddle with.

Okay, let's get started.

Creating the Textures

The cloud effect begins and ends with textures, so the first step to coding it is to create all of the various textures we'll be using. Here's the list:

- **Noise textures.** These are the individual layers of noise.
- **Smoothed noise textures.** Recall that one of the things we do to make our cloud texture look better is to smooth out the noise textures before we combine them. So, we'll need textures in which we can store this smoothed image.

- **Composite texture.** This is the texture that all the other textures get combined into.
- **Square texture.** This texture holds the results of modulating the composite texture with itself (in other words, squaring the colors of the composite texture).
- **Final texture.** Finally, we need a texture to hold the result of subtracting the square texture from a flat color (to reduce the amount of clouds in the texture). This texture holds that result; it's also the texture where our final cloud image will end up once everything's been done.

It All Starts with a Random Number Generator

Looking at it from a certain angle, one could say that the entire cloud effect depends on a good random number generator. In particular, we need a random number generator that's seeded; that is, if we plug in the same values we'll always get the same results. At first this may seem counterintuitive. I mean, what good is a random number generator if it doesn't give you random values?

As you'll see, a seeded random number (or should I say pseudo-random number generator?) is a must-have for doing cloud animation.

Here's a good example of a pseudo-random number generator:

```
inline float Noise2D(int x, int y)
{
  int n = x + y * 57;
  n = (n<<13) ^ n;
  return ( 1.0f - ( (n * (n * n * 15731 + 789221) + 1376312589) &
  0x7fffffff) / 1073741824.0f);
}
```

As you can see, all this function does is run some bizarre math on the x and y seeds. I could write an entire book on how the math works, but the details of it aren't important right now.

> **TIP**
>
> I got the above pseudo-random number generator from Hugo Elias's Web site—http://freespace.virgin.net/hugo.elias/. Hugo's site describes not only the cloud effect but also various other effects. It's definitely a site worth spending some time at.

Here's another example, but this one uses three seeds instead of two. I got this one from Kim Pallister's cloud generation code:

```
inline float Noise3D(int x, int y, int z)
{
  int n = x + y * 57 + z * 131;
  n = (n<<13) ^ n;
  return ( 1.0f - ( (n * (n * n * 15731 + 789221) + 1376312589) &
  0x7fffffff)
    * 0.000000000931322574615478515625f);
}
```

It's essentially the same as Noise2D, only it calculates n using three seeds instead of two.

Making Some Noise

Now that we've got our pseudo-random number generator, we can use it to create the beginnings of our cloud. The first step is to use the pseudo-random number generator to fill up a texture with random grayscale values.

Once again, I'll spoil the surprise and give you the code up-front:

```
// lock the textures
D3DLOCKED_RECT lockedrect;
::ZeroMemory(&lockedrect, sizeof(lockedrect));

if (FAILED(hr = m_ptexOctave->LockRect(0, &lockedrect, NULL, 0)))
  return(hr);

// our texture surface is now locked, and we can use
// the pitch to traverse it.
unsigned char *pSurfBits =
  static_cast<unsigned char *>(lockedrect.pBits);

int index=0;
for (int y=0; y < m_iOctaveSize; y++) {
  for (int x=0; x < m_iOctaveSize; x++) {
    char cIntensity = (char)((1.0f+Noise2D(x,y)) * 128);
    // the intensity determines the color of this texel
    pSurfBits[index++] = cIntensity; // blue
    pSurfBits[index++] = cIntensity; // green
    pSurfBits[index++] = cIntensity; // red
    pSurfBits[index++] = 0xff;       // alpha
  }
```

```
    // next line
    index += lockedrect.Pitch - (m_iOctaveSize*4);
}
// unlock texture surface
if (FAILED(hr = m_ptexOctave->UnlockRect(0))) return(hr);
```

No surprises here! Most of this code, by now, is fairly commonplace—we've been locking textures for several chapters now, so you should be able to recognize the basic pattern of locking the texture, using the double for loop (x and y) to touch each texel, using the pitch to move through the chunk of locked memory, unlocking the texture when you're done, and so on.

What's of interest to us is the stuff inside the double for loop. As you can see, we start by having our pseudo-random number generator give us the number that corresponds to the position at (x,y). We then do a little math on that value to arrive at a value called cIntensity, between 0 and 255. Then, we simply assign the same cIntensity value to the red, blue, and green components of our current texel, which will give us a texel with a random grayscale value. Nothing to it—an instant noisy texture!

Smoothing the Noise Layers

At this point, we have a texture resembling the one shown in Figure 15.9.

Now, it's time for an optional step—smoothing the noise layer. You don't necessarily have to do this, but if you can spare the processing time and graphics memory, it helps to render-copy your

Figure 15.9

Another cool cloud texture.

noise texture onto another texture (of the same dimensions), with bilinear filtering turned on. You do this so that the graphics card will smooth out your noise, reducing the sharp areas of contrast.

Thankfully, for once, the code is as simple as it sounds. Take a peek:

```
// no alpha blending or lighting
pDev->SetRenderState(D3DRS_ALPHABLENDENABLE, FALSE);
pDev->SetRenderState(D3DRS_LIGHTING, FALSE);
// turn on bilinear filtering (this is what "smooths the noise")
pDev->SetTextureStageState( 0, D3DTSS_MAGFILTER, D3DTEXF_LINEAR);
pDev->SetTextureStageState( 0, D3DTSS_MINFILTER, D3DTEXF_LINEAR);
pDev->SetTextureStageState( 0, D3DTSS_MIPFILTER, D3DTEXF_LINEAR);


// render-copy the texture
return(RenderCopy(ptexSource, ptexDest, iDestWidth,
                  iDestHeight, pDev, pvbQuad));
```

Cake! All the code does is fiddle with the rendering and texture stage states—specifically, we turn off alpha blending (no need for it yet), and lighting (so that we're sure our texels don't end up black because of lack of light). Then, we turn on bilinear filtering by setting the D3DTSS_MAGFILTER, D3DTSS_MINFILTER, and D3DTSS_MIPFILTER to D3DTEXF_LINEAR. Then we just render-copy the noise texture; since bilinear filtering is turned on, the graphics card will smooth our texture for us.

Combining the Noise Layers

Running each noise layer through both snippets of code, we end up with several smoothed noise textures of various sizes. Now we need to combine those layers onto a single destination texture. We do this by using a single quad comprised of four vertices. Each vertex has a diffuse color alpha value of 128—in other words, the quad is exactly halfway transparent. Then, we simply assign each texture to the quad, render it, and move on to the next texture.

The code to do this goes something like this:

```
// set new rendering target & clear
m_pd3dDevice->SetRenderTarget(psurfComposite, NULL);
m_pd3dDevice->Clear( OL, NULL, D3DCLEAR_TARGET, 0x000000, 1.0f, OL );

// set up orthogonal projection matrix
SetupOrthoProjForRenderCopy(m_pd3dDevice, m_iTextureSize,
  m_iTextureSize);
```

```
// begin rendering the scene
if (FAILED(m_pd3dDevice->BeginScene())) return;
m_pd3dDevice->SetStreamSource(0, m_pvbAlphaBlendingQuad,
  sizeof(VERTEX_XYZ_DIFFUSE_TEX1));
m_pd3dDevice->SetVertexShader(D3DFVF_XYZ_DIFFUSE_TEX1);
// set up texture stages for simple texture stage copy
m_pd3dDevice->SetTextureStageState(0, D3DTSS_COLOROP, D3DTOP_MODULATE);
m_pd3dDevice->SetTextureStageState(0, D3DTSS_COLORARG1, D3DTA_TEXTURE);
m_pd3dDevice->SetTextureStageState(0, D3DTSS_COLORARG2, D3DTA_DIFFUSE);
m_pd3dDevice->SetTextureStageState(1, D3DTSS_COLOROP, D3DTOP_DISABLE);
m_pd3dDevice->SetRenderState(D3DRS_ALPHABLENDENABLE, TRUE);
m_pd3dDevice->SetRenderState(D3DRS_ALPHATESTENABLE, FALSE);
m_pd3dDevice->SetRenderState(D3DRS_ZENABLE, D3DZB_FALSE);
m_pd3dDevice->SetRenderState(D3DRS_SRCBLEND, D3DBLEND_ONE);
m_pd3dDevice->SetRenderState(D3DRS_DESTBLEND,D3DBLEND_SRCCOLOR);

// render each layer
for (CloudOctaveVector::iterator i = m_vOctaves.begin();
  i != m_vOctaves.end(); ++i) {

  CCloudOctave *octave = (*i);

  // set the source texture active
  m_pd3dDevice->SetTexture(0, octave->m_ptexSmoothOctave);
  // this "blits" the texture
  m_pd3dDevice->DrawPrimitive( D3DPT_TRIANGLELIST, 0, 2 );
}
// end scene
m_pd3dDevice->EndScene();
```

Again, the first few lines of this code should look familiar—we're just setting our rendering surface to our composite texture. Next, we clear our canvas, and set up our world, projection, and view matrices so that one world unit equals one texel on our destination (yeah, I made a helper function to do this, called SetupOrthoProjForRenderCopy, in D3DHelperFuncs.cpp).

After we've taken care of that, we begin the scene, and prepare to render our special, halfway transparent quad. Then, we set up our texture stage and rendering states. We tell texture stage zero that it should combine our source texel colors with the diffuse color of the quad's vertices. This effectively merges the two colors so that we end up with a halfway transparent version of our source image texels (which is what we want). The render states also are nothing out of the ordinary—we need to turn on alpha blending, but we don't need any alpha testing or depth buffers.

The D3DRS_SRCBLEND and D3DRS_DESTBLEND states are important. We set the source blend factor to one, and the destination blend factor to the color (alpha component) of our texels. In effect, this creates what 3D programmers refer to as an *additive blend*; this means that as layers are applied to the destination texture, they will only lighten it, and never darken it. This is important, because without it, our cloud texture would come out looking incorrect (well, at least incorrect for what I think a cloud should look like—your opinions may differ).

After we have our stages set up, we enter a for loop. If you've never seen the STL in action before, the for loop might look a little funny to you. If it does, go read the appendixes, or take my word for it that the for loop iterates through all of the layers, and that each time, the layer corresponding to the current iteration is put in i. In other words, if it's the second time around, i will correspond to m_vOctaves[1].

We don't really do much with each cloud layer; we simply put it into our first texture slot, and then we draw our semitransparent quad using that first texture. This effectively blends that layer onto the destination texture. Rinse, lather, and repeat for all cloud layers, and you end up with a nicely combined cloud texture.

Squaring the Cloud

We're almost there, but we're not quite done yet. At this point we need to square our cloud layer, which enhances the contrast of the texture and makes for a better-looking cloud. To do this, we just blend the cloud texture onto itself.

Subtracting

This step, like the last one, is optional. If you want to be able to vary the amount of cloud cover during your game, you can subtract the squared cloud texture from a flat gray quad. Depending on how gray the quad is, you'll either end up with more or fewer clouds on your texture. If the quad is close to black, you'll end up with a cloud texture that's basically unchanged from the previous step (it has a lot of clouds). If the quad is closer to white, you'll end up with a mostly clear-sky texture with just a patch of cloud here and there.

MODIFYING THE CLOUD EFFECT

This effect has a lot of tweaking potential, mainly because it takes several steps to create, and each step has its own set of things with which you can play. Here are some of the more common things to try.

Blending Factors

You can change the shape of your clouds drastically by messing with the blend factors when you combine all of the individual cloud layers onto a single texture. By default, we've used alpha values of 128 (halfway transparent), but you should try different factors for different layers and see what happens. You could even adjust the blend factors over time and create some interesting animation effects.

Color Clouds

This whole time, we've been working with grayscale textures. Grayscale suits our needs just fine for creating real-life, mostly white clouds, but if we move beyond black and white we can create some really weird (yet cool) looking patterns, which I call *color clouds*.

To generate color clouds, keep everything the way it is, only change your pseudo-random number generator so that it takes three seeds instead of just two (or, if you're doing animation, you'll already have three seeds, so you'll have to add a fourth). The new seed you add will allow you to generate random numbers for each of the red, green, blue (and if you want to, alpha) components of your texture. This new seed should take a number between 0 and 2 (0 is red, 1 is green, 2 is blue), and should use that to influence the number it gives back.

TIP

To further enhance this effect, you could severely granulize the color values available. For example, instead of saying, "Okay random number generator, give me a red value between 0 and 255," you could say, "Random number generator, give me a red value between 0 and 4 (inclusive)," and then you could multiply the value it gives you by 64. This will give you one of five possible red values—0, 64, 128, 192, or 256 (remember to cap at 255 so that 256 really just means 255).

Do the same thing for green and blue, and you effectively limit the palette of colors that your program can randomly choose from. The end result is a brighter, less "muddy" color cloud, because there's a higher chance that you'll get very high or very low RGB values.

Alternatively, as a different means to the same end, you could just set up a color palette of 16 or 32 colors, and let the random number generator create a random index into that color palette.

Any way you cut it, if you reverse the bell curve, so that the majority of random RGB values fall at either end of the range (very close to 0 or 255), instead of in the middle, you'll end up with a brighter color cloud.

However you do it, you'll eventually end up with individual noise textures that have random color variations, instead of just grayscale values. Blend and animate these together, and you'll have a very colorful, cloud-like pattern, ideal for all sorts of special effects (spells in RPGs, especially).

> **TIP**
>
> **Alternatively, you could make different random number generators for each channel of color—a red generator, a green generator, and a blue generator.**

Uses for the Cloud Effect

You can only use the cloud effect to generate clouds.

Just kidding. I feel like every chapter, I start this section with a sentence like "there are many things you can do with this effect." So, I'm instead going to say the same thing a little differently: You can use cloud effect for myriad different things in your game. Let's take a look.

Slime, Lava, and Plasma

In the early 1990s, there were several demos that used Perlin noise, along with some color cycling, to generate *plasma* displays—screens full of hypnotic patterns that slowly changed color. You can accomplish something similar using this technique, along with some alpha blending or diffuse coloring.

By varying the colors of the noise textures, you can create many different effects. Turn the noise layers green and yellow, and you've got a pretty convincing slime texture. Turn it red and orange, add a bit of animation, and you've got some great lava. In a pinch you could probably create a fairly good simulation of water by using shades of blue and white, along with some alpha channel variations.

One of the reasons Ken Perlin is so famous is because his techniques can be used for so many different things. We've just learned about one form of Perlin noise; you can use many other forms to generate marble, wood, fabric, and other materials. Unfortunately, most of the other forms of noise are difficult to do in 3D hardware, but there are plenty of things you can emulate just with this one noise effect.

Dynamically Generated Landscapes

One of the techniques 3D programmers use to generate landscapes is called "height mapping," wherein a texture is used to represent the altitudes of a landscape. Black values represent low altitudes, and white values represent higher elevations.

Our cloud texture can be used, without any modifications, as a height map for generating landscapes on-the-fly. In fact, you could take a screenshot of Ch15p1_SimpleClouds, use a paint program to grab the cloud texture out of that screenshot, and drop that cloud texture into Bryce 4 to generate a landscape.

If you're planning on distributing your game on CD or DVD, this probably isn't much of a benefit to you, but if you're relying on an Internet distribution, it behooves you to make your game have as small a footprint as possible. One way to reduce your footprint is to generate your game data at runtime (or maybe install-time), and anything that can replace megabytes of randomly generated landscape vertex data with a handful of bytes of executable code is a Good Thing.

Optimizing the Cloud Effect

Luckily, you can do several things to make the cloud effect work faster or on systems without as much graphical power as others. Here are the big things you can change.

Use Fewer Octaves

The higher frequency octaves take up the most graphics memory and processing time, yet they contribute the least to the overall cloud texture. So, they're one of the first things you can kick to the curb when dealing with older systems. In fact, on really old systems, you can ditch all octaves but the first one, and still come out with an effect that resembles reality (your clouds will be a little square, if you can imagine that, but if you're just putting them on a skybox or leaving them in the background, the user will probably be too involved in the rest of your game to notice the clouds' squareness).

Use Smaller Textures

Going hand in hand with the idea of using fewer octaves is using smaller textures. The cloud texture tiles very well, so you can usually get away with some very low resolution textures, especially if you're animating. In fact, 256×256 is probably overkill for most applications—128×128 would be more realistic, and 64×64 might serve you in a pinch.

Don't Lock the Textures Very Often (or At All)

There's a high cost associated with locking down those noise layers and regenerating the noise on them during animation, so doing it only occasionally will save you some speed. And, as always, you can spawn a separate, low priority thread to handle the re-creation of the noise textures.

Alternatively, you can do away with in-game noise texture updates altogether, and still have some nicely animating clouds. The trick is to generate, during load or init time (when the user has to wait anyway), several different noise patterns for each layer of noise. Store them in system memory (which is cheap), and then, inside the game, instead of actually locking the noise texture and using the random number generator to make a new pattern, just swap out the old pattern from graphics memory and swap in a new pattern.

Caveat emptor: doing this will make your cloud animations somewhat predictable. How predictable depends primarily on the number of different noise patterns you generate for each texture, and how you choose a new pattern when it's time (hint: don't just go in a loop—select one at random). Of course, as mentioned previously, that might not matter—if your player is tearing down a raceway at 240MPH she probably won't have time to notice that the clouds in the sky are repeating.

Minimize the Number of BeginScene/EndScene Calls

There's a rule in 3D programming that says, "don't use any more BeginScene/EndScene pairs than you have to." Unfortunately, the cloud effect requires a handful of scenes, because it has to switch the rendering target several times. However, it doesn't have to be that way. There's no rule that says you have to use different textures for each noise layer—you could make a big texture and then tile the different noise layers on that. Just remember to carefully manipulate the (u,v) texture coordinates of your quads as you're making your clouds.

You're not going to be able to completely fit the cloud generation into one or two scene blocks, but you can easily beat what the sample programs are doing (remember, I write the sample programs for clarity, not speed).

CHAPTER WRAP-UP

The cloud effect requires a lot of little steps, which makes it seem tougher than it really is. In reality, you'll find that the code for the cloud effect is long, but not really complex.

The type of Perlin noise we explored here is not the only type Ken Perlin created. Several different variations of Perlin noise exist, and you can use them to generate different effects. Unfortunately, you'll have a hard time implementing most of these noise variations on 3D hardware; you'll have to do complex calculations and you won't be able to trick your graphics card into doing them for you (by using bilinear interpolation or whatnot). However, they're still interesting, and I encourage you to check them out.

ABOUT THE SAMPLE PROGRAMS

The time has come. Our simple sample programs are becoming complicated. I believe that C++, when used properly, is a great tool that can significantly reduce the complexity of a program. So, this chapter's examples use more C++ than the previous sample programs.

Also, this chapter's sample programs use the STL (Standard Template Library), which is essentially a big toolbox. The STL provides us with a toolbox full of "standard" computer science constructs, like stacks, deques, vectors (no, not the 3D kind—an STL vector is a resizable array), sorting algorithms, and so on. If you're not familiar with the STL, I've included an appendix that will give you a crash course.

And now, the program:

- `Ch15p1_SimpleClouds`. This sample program demonstrates the cloud effect, without any bells and whistles to distract you.

EXERCISES

1. Experiment with the blending weights in the `Ch15p1_SimpleClouds` sample program. How does the image differ if you use a 75% or 25% alpha value?
2. Write a derivative program based on `Ch15p1_SimpleClouds` that uses 16 octaves, or maybe just two. See the speed difference?

CHAPTER 16

BLURS AND OTHER FORMS OF IMAGE MANIPULATION

Ray: *"Egon, this reminds me of that time
you tried to drill a hole in your head."*
Egon: *"That would have worked if you hadn't stopped me."*
——From the movie Ghostbusters

O kay, yes, I'll admit it—image manipulation probably isn't the first thing that people think of as a "special effect." However, games today are beginning to use image manipulation techniques for a wide variety of purposes: reducing their footprints by generating graphics at install-time or runtime, or creating special focus transition effects using blurred and sharpened textures, just to name a few. So, even though CPUs won't be fast enough to perform image manipulation in real time for a few years, these basic techniques are still great tools to have in your big intra-ear toolbox.

This chapter will examine the basics of image manipulation, including blurring, sharpening, and edge detection. Your first thought might be that these manipulations are very different from each other, but as we'll see they're all very closely related—just variations on a central theme.

How Does It Work?

Just to make sure we're all starting from the same spot, let's state the obvious—image manipulation is all about touching each pixel of an image (or, in our case, texel of a texture), and performing some operation on it—for example, to create a "negative" of an image, all we'd have to do is visit each pixel of that image, and invert the red, green, and blue values (subtract them from 255 so that values that were previously 255 become 0, and vice versa).

So, regardless of what kind of image manipulation we're doing, we're going to be using a double for loop to visit each texel of our image. The question now becomes, "what do we do inside the for loop?"

Hold that thought for a moment, as we define some new terminology.

Talk the Talk

Image manipulation, like 3D programming, is an old and relatively large area of study, so it has its own set of new vocabulary words. You don't necessarily have to know the terminology to understand what's going on, but it definitely helps when speaking to a fellow programmer, so let's spend a bit of time up-front learning the terminology.

What we're officially doing is called "image convolution using kernels." The word *convolution* in this sense just means "messing with." We're using kernels to mess with the color values of an image.

So what's a kernel?

What's a Kernel?

To answer that question, we first need to know how image manipulation works.

As explained before, we visit each pixel using a double `for` loop. We perform a calculation on the red, green, and blue components for each pixel we visit, in order to arrive at a new color value for that pixel. A kernel defines what that calculation is.

All of these image-processing effects use weighted averages for their calculations. That is, to arrive at a certain color component value for a certain pixel, you average the values neighboring that pixel. This is similar to what you did with the fire effect.

For example, let's say we have a setup shown in Figure 16.1.

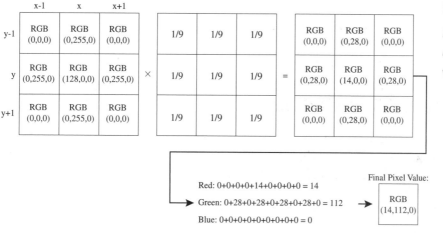

Figure 16.1

Blurring an image using an array of weight values.

To calculate the new RGB value for the pixel at (x,y), we'd add up the RGB values for all nine pixels. We'd then divide by nine, effectively averaging the values. This doesn't seem like it should blur the image, but in reality it does.

Let's look at it another way. In the preceding example, you could say that since we're dealing with nine pixels, each pixel contributes 1/9th to the final value. So, this means that instead of adding all the pixels together and then dividing by nine, we can divide each pixel's value by nine, then add all those divided values together. The math is the same, we're just doing things in a different order—in this case, we're multiplying each value by 1/9th, or about 0.11, then adding up the results of the multiplications to arrive at our final value.

We don't have to multiply each value by the same amount, however. We could choose to multiply different pixels by different amounts—in other words, we could choose to take a weighted average of the pixel values.

All image processing follows this basic pattern. The only difference lies in what pixels you choose to use, and the weights you give each one. This is where the kernel comes into play.

A kernel, simply put, is a 2D array of weights. The array element at the center of the array represents the pixel you're currently processing. The other elements represent the factors by which you should multiply the other pixels' values. For example, Figure 16.2 shows a kernel describing the situation we just talked about (averaging the nine pixels around a point).

1/9	1/9	1/9
1/9	1/9	1/9
1/9	1/9	1/9

Figure 16.2

A blurring kernel.

As you can see, we have simply assigned 1/9th to all the elements of our kernel, plus our center pixel (kernel arrays have an odd number of rows and columns so that there is always a definite center pixel).

Now, to process our image, we overlay the kernel onto the image we're currently processing. In other words, we set things up so that the pixel we're processing corresponds to the element at the center of our array (row or column size divided by two, rounded down). Then, we do a double for loop through our kernel array, multiplying each underlying pixel value by the corresponding kernel array "weight." We add all of these up, and we have our new (x,y) value.

Some Kernels to Use

I'm not a gambling man, but if I were, I'd put money on the fact that since you now know how kernels work, you're dying to see some kernels for various effects. Wait no more!

Blurring

Figure 16.2 shows a blurring kernel. In essence, the blur kernel makes the image-processing code take an exact average of the pixels within one pixel of the pixel in question. This results in a nicely blurred image.

Stronger Blurring

You can achieve better blurring by including more pixels in your kernel. The wider and taller your kernel, the more blurry your image gets. For example, a kernel like that shown in Figure 16.3 creates a significantly more blurry image than the kernel shown in Figure 16.2.

CAUTION

Unfortunately, the bigger your kernel, the longer it takes to calculate the color values for each pixel. Strong blurring filters can take a significant amount of time to calculate, so beware.

Sharpening

Figure 16.4 shows a sharpening kernel.

1/25	1/25	1/25	1/25	1/25
1/25	1/25	1/25	1/25	1/25
1/25	1/25	1/25	1/25	1/25
1/25	1/25	1/25	1/25	1/25
1/25	1/25	1/25	1/25	1/25

Figure 16.3

A stronger blurring kernel.

Figure 16.4

A sharpening kernel.

This is a weird kernel, because it has negative ones in it. The negative ones actually invert the colors of the neighboring pixels, and the positive nine amplifies greatly the original pixel value. This combination of inverting and brightening creates the illusion of a much sharper image.

Edge Detection

To detect the edges of an image, use a kernel like that shown in Figure 16.5.

The kernel operates very similarly to the sharpening filter; the key difference is that only the values immediately above, below, and to the sides of the pixel are negated.

WRITING THE CODE

You're probably thinking there won't be much to this section. After all, the image manipulation algorithms are pretty easy. Right now, without learning anything you haven't studied so far, you should be able to sit down and write a program that blurs, sharpens, or performs edge-detection on a texture. You know everything you need—how to create a texture, how to lock it, and how to traverse the texels using the texture's pitch (not width!). You know how to manipulate the color components of each texel independently, and you can probably figure out how to write a function that implements a certain kernel. All you do for each texel is pass the color components into your kernel function, and it hands you back the new color components. Easy!

0	-1	0
-1	9	-1
0	-1	0

Figure 16.5

An edge-detection kernel.

So, let's crank it up a notch. We're going to write a set of C++ classes that enable us to apply any kernel. Through the magic of polymorphism (virtual functions), we're going to write a framework for image manipulation. This framework will allow us to drop in kernels of arbitrary sizes and functions; the framework will take care of iterating through every texel of our image and applying our kernel.

> **TIP**
>
> If you've done any Java programming, the system we're going to create will look suspiciously similar to the image processing functions of the Java AWT library.

Class Layout

One of the first steps to designing a C++ program is to determine what classes you want and how those classes will interact. In this case, we can see already the immediate need for two classes: CImageManipulator and CImageManipulatorKernel.

- **CImageManipulator.** This is the class that will encapsulate our image manipulation code. The idea here is that when we want to manipulate an image, we'll instantiate this class and point it at our source texture, and the destination texture. We'll also provide it with basic information about our texture—its width, height, and color format.
- **CImageManipulatorKernel.** This class encapsulates an image manipulation kernel. In essence, it's nothing more than a glorified two-dimensional array that contains the weight values that make up a certain kernel.

Now that you know the two main players, let's look at each in detail.

CImageManipulator

This is the "mother class." CImageManipulator does the work of traversing the image and calling CImageManipulatorKernel to do the work on each pixel.

Because the class is so small, I'm just going to give you the whole thing up-front:

```
class CImageManipulator
{
public:
  CImageManipulator() { }
  virtual ~CImageManipulator() { }

  bool ProcessImage(LPDIRECT3DTEXTURE8 pSrcTexture,
    LPDIRECT3DTEXTURE8 pDestTexture,
    int iWidth, int iHeight, CImageManipulatorKernel &kernel,
    bool bRedEnable = true, bool bGreenEnable = true,
    bool bBlueEnable = true, bool bAlphaEnable = false);

  D3DXCOLOR ReadPixelRel(int iRelPosX, int iRelPosY);

private:
  void WritePixelRel(D3DXCOLOR color,
    bool bRedEnable, bool bGreenEnable,
    bool bBlueEnable, bool bAlphaEnable);

  LPDIRECT3DTEXTURE8 m_pSrcTexture;
  LPDIRECT3DTEXTURE8 m_pDestTexture;
  int m_iWidth;
  int m_iHeight;
  int m_iPitch;
  int m_iCurPosX;
  int m_iCurPosY;
  unsigned int m_iSrcIndex;
  unsigned int m_iDestIndex;
  unsigned char *m_pSrcBits;
  unsigned char *m_pDestBits;
};
```

As you can see, there isn't much to this class. We have a whole bunch of private members that store the properties of the image we're dealing with—texture handles, as well as width, height, and pitch.

We also have a couple of methods. First, we have ReadPixelRel and WritePixelRel. These two enable us to read the color value of pixels, and write new color values to pixels in our source and destination images, respectively. The Rel stands for Relative, because the functions don't take an absolute (x,y) pixel coordinate. Instead, they take a coordinate that's relative to the current position stored in m_iCurPosX and m_iCurPosY. For example, suppose

> **TIP**
>
> Remember, *pitch* is how many bytes separate two vertical pixels. It must be at least as large as the width of the image, but is often larger, to accommodate extra bytes that Direct3D puts at the end of each row in memory.

m_iCurPosX equals 10, and m_iCurPosY is 20. If I pass in –3 for x and 9 for y to ReadPixelRel, I'll end up reading the value at x=7 (10–3), y=29 (20+9). This is useful because the kernels want to read values relative to the current pixel they're processing.

Finally, we have a beast of a member function, ProcessImage. That's the money function—it's what you call to manipulate an image. As you can see, ProcessImage take a boatload of parameters—it wants texture handles for the source and destination textures, the width and height of the image, a kernel to use, and a whole bunch of Booleans that specify which color channels you'd like the kernel to change. I put that in because often you only want to play with the RGB channels of an image, leaving the alpha value unchanged. It also opens up some pretty cool features—blur just the red and blue channels of an image and you wind up with a pretty nifty looking picture.

Now, let's take a closer look at that ProcessImage method. Like I said, ProcessImage is *El Jefe*. Here's an abridged version:

```
bool CImageManipulator::ProcessImage(
  LPDIRECT3DTEXTURE8 pSrcTexture,
  LPDIRECT3DTEXTURE8 pDestTexture, int iWidth, int iHeight,
  CImageManipulatorKernel &kernel,
  bool bRedEnable, bool bGreenEnable, bool bBlueEnable,
  bool bAlphaEnable)
{
  HRESULT hr;
  try {
    m_pSrcTexture = pSrcTexture;  m_pDestTexture = pDestTexture;
    m_iWidth = iWidth; m_iHeight = iHeight;

    int index=0;  m_iSrcIndex = 0; m_iDestIndex = 0;

    // lock source and destination textures, set m_iPitch to the pitch
    // of the locked rectangle, and set m_pSrcBits and m_pDestBits to
    // the locked memory.
```

```
     for (m_iCurPosY = 0; m_iCurPosY < iHeight; m_iCurPosY++) {
       for (m_iCurPosX = 0; m_iCurPosX < iWidth; m_iCurPosX++) {
         D3DXCOLOR finalcolor;
         kernel.ProcessPixel(finalcolor, this);
         WritePixelRel(finalcolor, bRedEnable,
           bGreenEnable, bBlueEnable, bAlphaEnable);
       }
       m_iDestIndex += DestLockedRect.Pitch - (iWidth*4);
     }
     // unlock textures [snip]
   }
   catch(...) {
     // unlock textures [snip]
     return(false);
   }
   return(true);
 }
```

A lot of things are going on in that section of code. We begin by squirreling away some of the parameters into member variables. Then, we lock the surfaces.

After we do that, we enter a double for loop, using m_iCurPosY and m_iCurPosX. This means that those two variables will always contain the (x,y) coordinates of the pixel we're currently processing.

For each pixel, we call the ProcessPixel method of the kernel object our caller supplied. We give ProcessPixel ourselves, because we're the only class that knows how to read pixels from the source image. Internally, each kernel's ProcessPixel method will call our ReadPixelRel class (see how this all fits together?).

The kernel's ProcessPixel method eventually gives us back the final color value for the pixel. We then write that color value to the destination image, and move on to the next pixel.

As you can see, I designed this so that the kernel class would take care of performing all of the calculations for a given image convolution kernel.

So, let's have a gander at CImageManipulatorKernel.

CImageManipulatorKernel

This class is responsible for doing the actual kernel calculations. All of the various image convolution kernels derive from a common base class called CImageManipulatorKernel. That way, we can pass any kernel we like to the ProcessImage method of CImageManipulator. This is a good example of the power of polymorphism—CImageManipulator doesn't know (or care) what kind of kernel it's applying to the image, or what sorts of calculations that kernel is performing. It only cares about making sure each pixel of the image gets calculated, and about handling the source and destination textures.

A Word about Speed and Program Design

Every programming language comes with its own set of features. As you're programming in any language, you need to pay careful attention to what features of that language you're using, and what impact using those features has on your program's performance.

For example: C++ has a "virtual functions" feature. The benefit of using virtual functions is that they can make several classes look the same—that is, they can expose a common interface, a powerful tool in certain situations (like this one!) where we may have several classes that should all behave a certain way.

But, virtual functions also have a drawback. In C++, the cost of using a virtual function is that you perform some pointer dereferencing, because behind the scenes the C++ compiler keeps an array of function pointers (known as the vtbl, or "v-table"), which it uses to figure out where your virtual function calls actually go.

Ordinarily this wouldn't be anything to worry about, but in our situation, we're calling a virtual function inside a double for loop, which means that we're dereferencing pointers a lot—thousands of times, if not hundreds of thousands. This can slow things down noticeably.

Many people tend to jump on C++ as being a "slow language," and it's often situations like these that they cite to prove their point. "In C," they'll say, "there's no need for that pointer dereferencing, so C is a faster language!"

The logic error these folks are making is that they're not comparing apples to apples. By removing the pointer dereferencing associated with the virtual function call inside the double for loop, of course they've made the program faster, but they've also made the program less flexible, because they've scrapped the ability to plug in different kernels easily. They've changed the design! Of course the C program will run faster—if we scrapped the ability to plug in different kernels, our C++ program could run just as fast.

The point I'm making here is that language flame wars are the trademark of novice programmers. An experienced programmer knows that it's usually not the language that matters; it's the program's underlying design. Saying C++ is unequivocally faster than Visual Basic is a fallacy—a well-designed VB program can run circles around a poorly designed C++ program. Conversely, if both C++ and VB programs are designed well—that is, each is using only the features of the language they need to get the job done—their performance will be comparable. (Unless, of course, the VB program is being interpreted at runtime, and not compiled, in which case, again, we're not comparing apples to apples.)

Programmers who do not understand the features of the language in which they're coding typically use that language's features incorrectly, and end up creating bad program designs (and therefore, slow programs, which lead to comments like "This language is slower than that one!"). If you indiscriminately use the features of C++ without realizing how they work (and therefore, what performance costs are associated with them), your C++ programs will be fat and slow. On the other hand, if you use the right tool for the job, and think carefully about the underlying design, you can create programs that run as fast as possible in *any* language.

So, now that you know the architecture of this system, let's take a look at the base class, CImageManipulatorKernel:

```
class CImageManipulatorKernel
{
public:
  CImageManipulatorKernel() { }
  virtual ~CImageManipulatorKernel() { }

  virtual void ProcessPixel(D3DXCOLOR &finalcolor, CImageManipulator
  *manip) = 0;

protected:
  D3DXCOLOR ApplyKernelToPoint(D3DXCOLOR &finalcolor, int iKernelWidth,
  int iKernelHeight,
    CImageManipulator *manip);

  std::vector<float> m_KernelValues;
  int m_iWidth;
  int m_iHeight;
};
```

`CImageManipulatorKernel` isn't a very big class, because most of the real work is done in the individual derived kernel classes. Notice that `ProcessPixel` is a pure virtual function, which means you can't ever instantiate a generic `CImageManipulatorKernel` class. You must instantiate a specific derived class (that is, `CBlurKernel`), instead. The pure virtual function also means that all derived classes must implement the `ProcessPixel` function. So, you could say that `CImageManipulator` doesn't actually do anything; it just sets up the ground rules for what the derived classes must do. In other words, it's an interface, because the pure virtual function describes the interface between the kernels and the class that uses them—`CImageManipulator`.

`CImageManipulatorKernel` does provide some help, however. The individual derived kernel classes can use the `ApplyKernelToPoint` method. We'll look at that method a little later.

Note also that our beloved kernel base class contains only a few member variables. We have a vector of kernel values, and a width and height (here, the width and height specify the dimensions of the kernel, not of the image).

So, since there's nothing interesting to see here, let's look now at a derived kernel class, `CBlurKernel`:

```
class CBlurKernel : public CImageManipulatorKernel
{
public:
  CBlurKernel();
  virtual ~CBlurKernel() { }

  void ProcessPixel(D3DXCOLOR &finalcolor, CImageManipulator *manip);

private:
};
```

Not much to see in the class declaration. In fact, the only thing `CBlurKernel` does is implement a constructor, and the `ProcessPixel` function.

The constructor is fairly simple as well—it just creates a blur kernel using the vector `CBlurKernel` has inherited from the base class:

```
for (int y=0; y < 3; y++) {
    for (int x=0; x < 3; x++) {
      m_KernelValues.push_back(1.0f/9.0f);
    }
  }
```

All we're doing in that section of code is putting nine values into the kernel vector. All values are 1/9, or about 0.11. Refer again to Figure 16.2: these nine values correspond to the nine weights that we need for our blur kernel.

Now, let's look at the body of the `ProcessPixel` function:

```
void CBlurKernel::ProcessPixel(D3DXCOLOR &finalcolor, CImageManipulator
*manip)
{
  finalcolor = ApplyKernelToPoint(finalcolor, 3, 3, manip);
}
```

Hey, what's up with that? We were expecting some huge calculations to take place, but there's nothing here but a call to a method of the base class!

That's because the calculations all the kernels do are very similar. Essentially, all a kernel does is look at each color underneath the kernel, multiply it by the corresponding kernel weight, and add it to a running total. After it does this for all the kernel elements, it divides the running total by the number of kernel elements to arrive at the final color value.

As you've probably guessed by now, that's exactly what the `ApplyKernelToPoint` method of `CImageManipulatorKernel` does:

```
D3DXCOLOR CImageManipulatorKernel::ApplyKernelToPoint(
  D3DXCOLOR &finalcolor, int iKernelWidth, int iKernelHeight,
  CImageManipulator *manip)
{
  D3DXCOLOR runningtotal; runningtotal *= 0.0f; // clear it!
  std::vector<float>::iterator i = m_KernelValues.begin();

  for (int y=0; y < iKernelWidth; y++) {
    for (int x=0; x < iKernelHeight; x++) {
      D3DXCOLOR pixcolor = manip->ReadPixelRel(
        ((int)(-iKernelWidth/2))+x,((int)(-iKernelHeight/2))+y);
      pixcolor *= (float)(*i);
      runningtotal += pixcolor;
      i++;
    }
  }
  return(runningtotal);
}
```

Ah-ha—there's where the calculation is occurring. Since we have this `ApplyKernelToPoint` function, all we need to do to create any type of kernel is supply the appropriate kernel dimensions and kernel weights, just like we did in the `CBlurKernel` constructor. `ApplyKernelToPoint` takes care of performing the calculations. This is much better than copying and pasting this code into the `ProcessPixel` method of each kernel class. Imagine if we found a bug in the logic—we'd have to change the `ProcessPixel` methods of every kernel we'd written!

> **TIP**
>
> Just because `ApplyKernelToPoint` is there doesn't mean we must use it for all kernels. If, in the future, we dreamed up a kernel that operated differently from what we'd coded in `ApplyKernelToPoint`, we could very easily just write that unique code into the `ProcessPixel` method of that particular kernel.

That's essentially all there is to the code for this chapter. Like I said, I wanted to achieve two simultaneous goals here: first, to show you how image manipulation works, and second, to show you an example of how good object-oriented programming can create a flexible system.

Uses for Image Manipulation

The most common use for image manipulation is to generate textures as your program loads. If your game calls for a blurry version of a scene or a texture, you don't have to waste disk space (and more importantly, ZIP file space if you're doing an Internet distribution) storing a blurred version of a texture. Instead, you can create that blurred texture at install-time, or when a level is loading.

A good example of this might involve creating window shadows for your game's user interface. Let's say that you're using a dialog-based system that enables your users to set up the game options before they start playing. Let's say you get fancy, and decide that it'd be cool if your dialogs cast a shadow. Let's further say that your dialog windows are individually hand-crafted by your artists—they're not just rectangles, they have protrusions of images and odd shapes that add a little flair to your GUI.

In this scenario, if you didn't know how to blur an image, you'd be forced to create your dialogs' shadows in Photoshop or Paint Shop Pro, and store those blurred images on disk. A better solution would be to use an image manipulation kernel that blurs the image and removes its color information (creating a grayscale image). You could run each dialog image through this *shadowing* kernel when your program loads instead of loading them from disk, thereby significantly reducing your program's footprint.

OPTIMIZING IMAGE MANIPULATION

Image manipulation is a slow process, because each pixel of an image must be individually touched. Also, if your kernel is large, there can be several dozen (if not hundreds) of multiply instructions for each pixel. Following are just a few ways to speed up the image manipulation effect.

Use Pixel Shaders

You can use a pixel shader to perform simple image manipulation operations on the GPU, giving you tremendous speed improvements. Additionally, you don't need to bother with traversing the texture surface directly; the pixel shader handles all that.

We'll look at how to implement basic image manipulation using pixel shaders in Chapter 24, "Vertex and Pixel Shader Effects."

Use Lookup Tables

If you know you're going to be performing a lengthy calculation for each color component of each pixel, it may make sense to create a lookup table. After all, each color component can only range from 0 to 255, which means you'll only need a 256-byte array. It's much faster to look something up in a table of precalculated values than it is to recalculate the same thing for every single pixel.

CHAPTER WRAP-UP

Image manipulation is fun stuff—fun stuff made easy by careful use of the power of C++. You learned two things in this section. First, you learned how most image manipulations are performed. You learned how to set up some common kernels, and how to traverse each texel in a texture to apply those kernels.

You also received a good lesson in C++ design—how to use the features of the language to create clean, well-designed classes that operate through strict and well-defined interfaces. You also learned about the hidden costs associated with some of C++'s language features.

I believe the second lesson is more important than the first. What we walked through was, on a very small scale, the process you'd also go through when designing a 3D engine and an entire game. Proper design of your C++ classes up-front will save you hours of frustration down the road, so I can't stress enough how important it is to spend time on design.

ABOUT THE SAMPLE PROGRAMS

No enhancements to the coding style this chapter. Here is the program:

- **Ch16p1_SimpleBlur**: This sample program demonstrates the blur effect, without any bells and whistles to distract you. It also contains code for sharpening, "Xtreme Blurring," and edge detection, not to mention a spiffy island image I generated one lazy Saturday several months ago.

EXERCISES

1. Spend some time creating random filters, or making intelligent guesses to create new filters. For example, what happens to your image if you process it using a kernel filter that randomly changes for each pixel? What happens if you exceed the maximum allowed value for a kernel?
2. Do some speed comparisons to determine how fast one kernel is relative to another. How much does the speed decrease when you add a few rows and columns to a kernel?
3. As it's currently written, the sample code for this chapter works only on 32-bit RGBA surfaces. Enhance the ReadPixelRel and WritePixelRel functions so that they work on several of the most common texture formats, or, even better, write one read function and one write function that work on all texture formats (yes, it can be done).

CHAPTER 17

FADES, WIPES, AND OTHER TRANSITIONS

"Details matter."
—*Neal Stephenson,* Snow Crash

Transitions are one of the details that separate a well-made game from an average one. They're one of those little "detail points" that can help make your game more fun. After all, which would you rather have: a game that locks up for 15 seconds when you click start, only to instantly pop you into the action, or a game that slowly fades out and then fades back in?

Of course, transitions are a low priority. You probably shouldn't spend time perfecting that dissolve effect when your main graphics engine is still halfway done. But, if you've got a solid title and a bit of time to spare, consider adding a little extra oomph to your games with some cool transition effects.

This chapter is broken down differently than the chapters you've read so far. It consists of two sections. The first section is devoted to explaining some simple transitions, which don't require a lot of coding, or a lot of 3D card features. The second section builds on this by showing you some more advanced things you can do.

TIP

What follows is by no means an exhaustive list of every effect possible. I've tried to cover most of the more common effects so that you have a good foundation from which to jump and create your own, nifty transitions. Today, the things you can do on 3D hardware to transition from one scene to another are truly limitless. Experiment!

Also, this chapter is a little light on sample code and sample code walk-throughs. That's because I wanted to give you a wide variety of effects, instead of just focusing on one or two. By this point, you should be familiar enough with everything to decipher the algorithms directly from the sample programs I've provided. Of course, I'll walk you through the harder stuff.

SIMPLE TRANSITIONS

Let's start with some simple fading and wiping techniques. The fade is by far the most widely used transition out there. Smooth fading has been around ever since we've had palette registers, and even before that, a few games used non-smooth fades, which were basically a succession of gradually darker images to simulate a smooth fade. A lot of old-school, 8-bit Nintendo games did this, and even though the effect wasn't perfect, it got the idea across quite well.

Fading to Colors Using Alpha Blending

In Chapter 6, "An Introduction to DirectGraphics," we discussed a way to fade the screen to an arbitrary color by messing with the gamma controls of D3D. If you're interested in doing simple, full screen fades to various colors, the gamma controls are the way to go. However, there is a different technique that you can use to fade, and it's useful enough to learn even if you already know how to do gamma fades.

You can use alpha blending to generate great-looking fades. In essence, all you have to do is create a quad of a solid color (to fade to black, you'd make all vertices of the quad RGB(0,0,0)). Then, you draw the quad on top of your scene using progressively more opaque alpha values. At first, because the alpha is near zero, the scene will be darkened only a little; as the alpha value increases, the solid-colored quad will become more and more opaque, and your scene will fade to the color of your quad.

This method is typically used much more than the gamma controls, because it has a couple of key advantages:

- Not everything on the screen has to fade. For example, if you have a play area and some status indicators (health icons, ammo counts, etc.) also on the screen, you can fade the play area to a certain color and keep the other stuff as-is. All you need to do is remember to turn off your depth buffer, and then render your status indicators after you render the "fading quad" (the quad you're using to fade your scene). Your play area will appear to fade out, but your status indicators will remain normal.
- You can fade in a window. Gamma controls only work if your game has exclusive access to the display—that is, if you're running in full screen mode. So, if you're using gammas for your fading, you'll have to use a backup method if you want your users to see your fades when they run your game in a window. Frequently it's easier to use alpha blending fades than to write two different chunks of fading code.
- You can fade different parts of the screen. By using various quads of different alpha values (or by using different alpha components on the vertices of one quad), you can fade parts of the screen independently. With gamma controls, you either fade the whole screen, or none of it.

An alpha blend fade requires us to add a little bit to our rendering function, to render the second quad. Here's what that code looks like:

Sample Program Reference

The `Ch17p1_AlphaBlendFade` sample program demonstrates how to fade by putting partially transparent quads in front of your scene.

When to Fade

Don't overuse the fade effect. For that matter, don't overuse any of the transitions I'm about to teach you. I guarantee you, no matter how cool you think an effect is, your players will hate you if you make them sit through 10-15 seconds of transition every time they encounter a monster or enter a room.

This isn't a game design book, but here's a tip: There's a difference between scene changes inside a game and mode changes *of* a game. Knowing the difference between these two should help you decide when to fade.

A scene change inside a game is similar to a scene change in a movie—for example, your player walks into a cave or enters a room. The player is still playing, and nothing's really changed except the scenery. In these types of situations, you typically would not want a transition effect—and if you absolutely wanted to use one, it should be a really quick transition (two seconds tops). This is because players may be changing scenes hundreds of times as they play your game. Most games require players to constantly move to various locations, so the transitions can get really old.

On the other hand, a mode change is almost always a great place for a longer, more interesting transition. A mode change occurs when the user switches in and out of the game, or switches between screens that set up the game. For example, when users select "Single Player" from the title screen and hit go, they're performing a "mode change"—they're leaving "title screen mode" and entering "game mode." At this point your game will typically have to swap a lot of data—it'll have to get rid of all the graphics, sounds, and other resources it had been using for the title screen, and it will need to load up all of the resources it needs for the first level of the game. Sadly, this is typically a lengthy process, so the least you can do is treat your users to a couple of cool transitions to let them know that your game is working and no longer listening to them (transition out), or that your game has finished setting everything up and is ready for them to start playing (transition in).

So, take a suggestion—save your cool transitions for the mode changes, and use simple transitions (or even none at all, aka "cuts," just like in a movie) for your in-game scene changes.

Of course, it's only a suggestion, and there are rarely any hard and fast rules in game design. For example, if you're making an RPG or adventure game, your players may switch in and out of combat mode frequently as they play the game and encounter monsters. It might be perfectly fine to use a transition to tell the players, "You are moving into combat mode now—get ready!" On the other hand, it may just irritate them after a while. Listen to your play testers.

```
// [snip] calculate projections, clear, etc.
// draw scene (for this sample program, the scene is simply 1 quad)
m_pd3dDevice->DrawPrimitive( D3DPT_TRIANGLELIST, 0, 2 );

// if we're fading, we need to also draw a 2nd quad on top.
if (m_fFadeTime > 0.0f) {
  // set up texture stage states for this quad
  m_pd3dDevice->SetTextureStageState(0, D3DTSS_COLORARG1,
    D3DTA_DIFFUSE );
  m_pd3dDevice->SetTextureStageState(0, D3DTSS_ALPHAARG1,
    D3DTA_DIFFUSE );

  // put the correct colors into the quad's verts
  FadeQuadVerts(m_FadeToColor, m_fFadeTime, 5.0f, m_pVB);

  m_pd3dDevice->SetRenderState(D3DRS_ALPHABLENDENABLE, TRUE);
  m_pd3dDevice->SetRenderState(D3DRS_SRCBLEND, D3DBLEND_SRCALPHA);
  m_pd3dDevice->SetRenderState(D3DRS_DESTBLEND, D3DBLEND_INVSRCALPHA);

  // draw 2nd quad
  m_pd3dDevice->DrawPrimitive( D3DPT_TRIANGLELIST, 0, 2 );
  // turn off alpha blending
  m_pd3dDevice->SetRenderState( D3DRS_ALPHABLENDENABLE, FALSE );
}
```

The biggest change here is that immediately after we draw our scene, we check to see if we're currently fading. If so, we set up our texture stages so that both color and alpha information comes from the diffuse color of the vertices. This means that if the alpha component of our vertices is close to zero, the quad will be very transparent (at the beginning of our fade); if it's closer to one, it will be more opaque (like what we want at the end of our fade).

We then call the FadeQuadVerts function to calculate the colors of the quad's vertices, based on the color we're fading to (m_FadeToColor), how much time has gone by since we started fading (m_fFadeTime), and how long we want the fade to last (5 seconds).

Once FadeQuadVerts has calculated the correct diffuse colors, we set up the rendering states to enable alpha blending, and then we draw our quad. Nothing to it!

Here's the FadeQuadVerts function:

```
void FadeQuadVerts(D3DXCOLOR FadeToColor, float fFadeTime,
                float fEffectTime, LPDIRECT3DVERTEXBUFFER8 pVB)
{
```

```
HRESULT hr; CUSTOMVERTEX* pVertices;

// calculate the new color value
FadeToColor.a = FadeToColor.a * (fFadeTime / fEffectTime);
if (FadeToColor.a > 1.0f) FadeToColor.a = 1.0f;

if(FAILED(hr = pVB->Lock(0, 6*sizeof(CUSTOMVERTEX),
  (BYTE**)&pVertices, 0))) return;

pVertices[0].color = (DWORD)FadeToColor;
pVertices[1].color = (DWORD)FadeToColor;
pVertices[2].color = (DWORD)FadeToColor;
pVertices[3].color = (DWORD)FadeToColor;
pVertices[4].color = (DWORD)FadeToColor;
pVertices[5].color = (DWORD)FadeToColor;

if( FAILED( hr = pVB->Unlock() ) ) return;
}
```

There's nothing complex going on here. We calculate the diffuse color by taking the color our caller wants to end up with (FadeToColor) and adjusting its alpha based on the fade time and total effect time. At fade time zero, we calculate the alpha channel as zero, which means the "fading" quad isn't visible at all. However, as fade time approaches total effect time, we get nearer and nearer to multiplying the alpha channel by one, which makes our quad more solid and our fade color stronger.

After we've calculated the correct diffuse color, all we need to do is lock the vertex buffer, plug in the color for each vertex, unlock, and we're done!

Dissolves (Cross Fades)

A close cousin to color fading, in the dissolve effect (or as it's sometimes known, the cross-fade), you fade one image out while fading another in on top of it. If you've ever seen a high-dollar slide show display—like the ones they used to make everyone in my high school sit through that used like 18 slide projectors simultaneously!—you've probably seen your share of dissolves.

Cross fading on the PC used to be a tricky thing to do, but now it's as easy as putting two quads on top of each other and messing with the alpha component of their vertices' diffuse colors. Put the image you're cross fading out of on top, and the image you're cross fading into on the bottom (see Figure 17.1).

Figure 17.1

A few frames of a dissolve transition.

Then, slowly decrement the alpha values to fade out your top image and reveal the image underneath (or, if you prefer, put your original image on the bottom, and slowly increment the top image's alphas). Here's the code that does that:

```
void CDissolveTransition::FadeQuadVerts()
{
  HRESULT hr;
  VERTEX_XYZ_DIFFUSE_TEX1* pVertices;
  D3DXCOLOR FadeToColor(0.0f, 0.0f, 0.0f, 1.0f);

  // calculate the new color value
  FadeToColor.a = FadeToColor.a * (m_fFadeTime / m_fDuration);
  if (FadeToColor.a > 1.0f) FadeToColor.a = 1.0f;

  if( FAILED( hr = m_pVB->Lock(
    0, 6*sizeof(VERTEX_XYZ_DIFFUSE_TEX1), (BYTE**)&pVertices, 0 ) ) )
    return;

  pVertices[0].color    = (DWORD)FadeToColor;
  pVertices[1].color    = (DWORD)FadeToColor;
  pVertices[2].color    = (DWORD)FadeToColor;

  pVertices[3].color    = (DWORD)FadeToColor;
  pVertices[4].color    = (DWORD)FadeToColor;
  pVertices[5].color    = (DWORD)FadeToColor;

  if( FAILED( hr = m_pVB->Unlock() ) ) return;
}
```

> **TIP**
>
> If you wanted to simultaneously tint the image to a certain color and dissolve it, you could play with the other color components at the same time you're doing this alpha calculation.

In the preceding code, we first start by making color that's black, but with an alpha value dependent on the time the effect has been running divided by the total duration of the effect. We then lock the vertex buffer, and apply that calculated color to each vertex. In this way, we fade the image over time.

I'm sure you can devise many different types of dissolves in addition to the one I've coded for you.

Sample Program Reference

The `Ch17p2_TransitionPageant` sample program contains a class called `CDissolveTransition` that contains the code for this effect.

Wipes

George Lucas made wiping transitions famous in *Star Wars*. In a wipe transition, the new scene wipes itself over the old scene, usually from left to right or right to left. It's not just a simple pan; it's more like laying down wallpaper (see Figure 17.2).

Figure 17.2

The wipe effect in action.

Directional Wipes

The most basic wipe is a directional wipe. You have eight directions from which to choose; your directional wipes may start at any edge or corner and progress to the opposite edge or corner. (Of course, you also can choose to write code that wipes at an arbitrary angle, but that's a little more complex and in my opinion isn't really worth the effort.)

I prefer to do directional wipes by stretching a single quad over the image, adjusting the texture coordinates as I go. The only slightly difficult part of coding this is getting the texture coordinates of the quad to correlate with where that quad is on-screen. Remember, you're not actually messing with either of the images, you're just showing a progressively larger section of the new image in every frame. So, the (u,v) coordinates of your quad must always match up with where that quad is on-screen, or you'll end up inadvertently distorting your new image.

Here's some code:

```
void CWipeTransition::CalcQuadVerts()
{
  HRESULT hr;
  VERTEX_XYZ_DIFFUSE_TEX1* pVertices;

  float fRatio = m_fFadeTime / m_fDuration;
```

```
float fNewVertX1, fNewVertY1, fNewVertX2, fNewVertY2;
float fNewU1, fNewV1, fNewU2, fNewV2;

switch(m_Direction) {
  case Up:
    fNewVertX1 = -1.0f; fNewVertX2 = 1.0f; fNewVertY2 = -1.0f;
    fNewVertY1 = -1.0f + (2.0f * fRatio);
    fNewU1 = 0.0f; fNewU2 = 1.0f;
    fNewV1 = 1.0f - (1.0f * fRatio); fNewV2 = 1.0f;
    break;
  case Down:
    fNewVertX1 = -1.0f; fNewVertX2 = 1.0f; fNewVertY1 = 1.0f;
    fNewVertY2 = 1.0f - (2.0f * fRatio);
    fNewU1 = 0.0f; fNewU2 = 1.0f;
    fNewV1 = 0.0f; fNewV2 = 1.0f * fRatio;
    break;
  case Left:
    fNewVertY1 = 1.0f; fNewVertY2 = -1.0f; fNewVertX1 = -1.0f;
    fNewVertX2 = -1.0f + (2.0f * fRatio);
    fNewV1 = 0.0f; fNewV2 = 1.0f;
    fNewU1 = 0.0f; fNewU2 = 1.0f * fRatio;
    break;
  case Right:
    fNewVertY1 = 1.0f; fNewVertY2 = -1.0f; fNewVertX2 = 1.0f;
    fNewVertX1 = 1.0f - (2.0f * fRatio);
    fNewV1 = 0.0f; fNewV2 = 1.0f;
    fNewU1 = 1.0f - (1.0f * fRatio); fNewU2 = 1.0f;
    break;
};
```

There's a bit of math at play here. First, we switch based on the direction we're wiping. As you can see, all four cases follow the same pattern, it's just a matter of whether the calculations use negative or positive values.

The key to the entire wipe animation is the fRatio variable. This variable is simply the time we've been doing the transition (m_fFadeTime) divided by the total time the transition is supposed to take (m_fDuration). At the beginning of the transition, m_fFadeTime will be close to zero, making fRatio also close to zero. Conversely, when the transition is almost over, fRatio will be close to one (and for one frame at the very end, it will equal one).

TIP

For a smoother wipe, set the alpha components on your strips. One side of the strip (the side that is adjacent to the edge of the screen, or to other strips) should be opaque, and the other side should be transparent (see Figure 17.3).

Sample Program Reference

The `Ch17p2_TransitionPageant` sample program contains a class called `CWipeTransition` that contains the code for this effect.

So, given that, let's take a look at the `Up` case. Three of the four (x,y) coordinates of our quad have been hard-coded. The last, `fNewVertY1`, we calculate using `fRatio`. If you don't see immediately how the equation works, plug in the boundary cases: when `fRatio` is close to zero, we'll end up adding very little to –1.0, which means the top of our quad will be very near to the bottom (–1.0). However, when `fRatio` is close to one, we'll end up adding close to 2.0 onto –1.0, which gives us 1.0, effectively placing the top of our quad at the top of the screen. That's how we use `fRatio` to stretch a quad slowly up the screen.

The logic is similar for the texture coordinates and for the other three cases. If it's not clicking for you yet, try running it in the debugger, where you can see the numbers move.

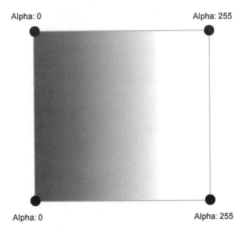

Figure 17.3

Cleverly assigned alpha values make for a smooth wipe.

Split Wipes

A split wipe comes in from two opposite directions simultaneously, like a pair of doors closing. You can create a split wipe very easily—just use two quads, start them at opposite sides, and slowly pull their edges together.

Window Blinds

To create a horizontal or vertical window blinds effect (see Figures 17.4 and 17.5), you use many quads instead of just one or two.

Figure 17.4

The horizontal window blinds effect.

Figure 17.5

The vertical window blinds effect.

You can choose to have each quad expand at the same rate, or you can randomly adjust the rate, so that certain quads "fill up" before others.

ADVANCED TRANSITIONS

So, those are the simple transitions. Now the gloves come off—here's some harder hitting, more advanced transitions you can do.

Melts

Set the way-back machine; remember DOOM? Remember how the screens melted away?

You too can make your images appear to melt and slip down the screen by using a variant of the Image Warping technique we learned about a few chapters ago.

To make the image melt, instead of using a grid of vertices, use skinny columns of vertices (see Figure 17.6). Of course, if we wanted our screen to melt to the left or right instead of the bottom, we'd use skinny rows, but let's concentrate on the classic top-to-bottom melt for now.

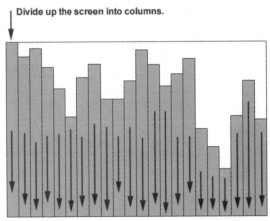

Divide up the screen into columns.

Each column moves downward at its own pace.

Figure 17.6

The basic concept of a melt transition.

After you have your strips in place, you simply start them all at the top of the screen, and then randomly move each strip down a bit every frame. Here's how that looks in code:

```
void CMeltTransition::DoTransition(float fTransTime)
{
  m_fFadeTime += fTransTime;

  HRESULT hr;
  VERTEX_XYZ_DIFFUSE_TEX1* pVertices;

  if( FAILED( hr = m_pVBMelt->Lock( 0, m_iNumVertsX*m_iNumVertsY*sizeof
(VERTEX_XYZ_DIFFUSE_TEX1),
      (BYTE**)&pVertices, 0 ) ) )
    return;

  for (int x=0; x < m_iNumVertsX; x++) {
    for (int y=0; y < m_iNumVertsY; y++) {
      pVertices[(y*m_iNumVertsX)+x].position.y -=
      m_FallSpeed.GetRandomNumInRange()*fTransTime;
    }
  }
  if(FAILED(hr = m_pVBMelt->Unlock())) return;
}
```

In this code, we lock the buffer, and then enter a double for loop. Inside the loop, we subtract a random amount from each vertex's y value, which slowly pulls it down the screen. Note that because I've decided the speeds are in seconds, we need to multiply them by fTransTime, which is number of seconds that have passed since the last frame.

That effect looks good, but because we're using random numbers, statistics dictate that over time all of our vertices will move downward at roughly the same rate. To achieve a different (and, in my opinion, better) melt effect, we should assign a different speed to each vertex, and use that speed every frame, instead of randomly selecting a speed for each frame. Here's that code:

```
void CConstSpeedMeltTransition::DoTransition(float fTransTime)
{
  m_fFadeTime += fTransTime;

  HRESULT hr;
  VERTEX_XYZ_DIFFUSE_TEX1* pVertices;

  if( FAILED( hr = m_pVBMelt->Lock( 0, m_iNumVertsX*m_iNumVertsY*sizeof
(VERTEX_XYZ_DIFFUSE_TEX1),
      (BYTE**)&pVertices, 0 ) ) )
    return;

  for (int x=0; x < m_iNumVertsX; x++) {
    for (int y=0; y < m_iNumVertsY; y++) {
      pVertices[(y*m_iNumVertsX)+x].position.y -= m_ColumnDropSpeed[x]
      * fTransTime;
    }
  }
  if(FAILED(hr = m_pVBMelt->Unlock())) return;
}
```

I call this "constant speed melting." In this code, there's a new variable, m_ColumnDropSpeed, which is an STL vector containing the speeds for each column. Instead of subtracting a random value, we now subtract the same value each frame, which causes certain columns over time to move significantly faster than others. This creates, in my opinion, a cooler melting effect.

Sample Program Reference

The Ch17p2_TransitionPageant sample program contains classes called CMeltTransition and CConstSpeedMeltTransition that demonstrate random speed and constant speed melting.

Fades to Static

This isn't anything you don't know how to do already, but I wanted to mention it here just because I like it and I wanted to make sure you didn't forget about it when choosing transitions.

In Chapter 15, "Clouds," we learned how to fill a texture with random grayscale noise. That noise makes a very good static texture, especially if we ditch the smooth animation we learned about back then and instead just replace completely the entire noise pattern every frame. Here's the code for the job:

```
void CStaticDissolveTransition::DoTransition(float fTransTime)
{
  m_fFadeTime += fTransTime;

  // lock texture
  D3DLOCKED_RECT lockedrect;
  ::ZeroMemory(&lockedrect, sizeof(lockedrect));

  if (FAILED(m_texStatic->LockRect(0, &lockedrect, NULL, 0))) return;

  // our texture surface is now locked, and we can use the
  // pitch to traverse it.
  unsigned char *pSurfBits = static_cast<unsigned char
  *>(lockedrect.pBits);

  for (int y=0; y < m_iStaticSize; y++) {
    for (int x=0; x < m_iStaticSize; x++) {
      // the fire value at this position determines the
      // color of this texel
      unsigned char s = RandomNumber(0,255);
      *(pSurfBits++) = s; // blue
      *(pSurfBits++) = s; // green
      *(pSurfBits++) = s; // red
      *(pSurfBits++) = 255; // alpha
    }
    // next line
    pSurfBits += lockedrect.Pitch - (m_iStaticSize*4);
  }

  // unlock texture surface
  if (FAILED(m_texStatic->UnlockRect(0))) return;
}
```

Essentially, all we're doing is locking a texture and randomly assigning grayscale values to each texel inside it. We select a random value between 0 and 255, then drop that value into the red, green, blue channels. That's all we need for some good looking static.

Once we've got that realistic static, we can cross fade from our existing scene into the static texture to create a nice-looking "communications are breaking up!" effect. Combine this effect with some static sound (also easy to create, just put random values into a sound buffer), and you've got the beginnings of a great sci-fi plotline.

> **TIP**
>
> You can create a better looking "communications break-up" effect by using a vertex grid, instead of just one quad, when you cross fade. Assign each vertex of this grid a random alpha value, so that different areas of the source image appear to be fading out more quickly than others. Best of all, if there's nothing else important going on during your transition, you can make a fairly dense vertex grid.

> **Sample Program Reference**
>
> The `Ch17p2_TransitionPageant` sample program contains a class called `CStaticDissolveTransition` that shows you how to write static dissolves.

Crunches

I'm not quite sure what to call this effect, so I figured "crunch" was as good a name for it as any other. In essence, the effect involves crunching the old scene down into the center of the screen, revealing the new scene as the old scene crunches (see Figure 17.7).

You set this up the way you would a cross fade, only instead of using a quad for your top image, you use a rectangular layout similar to a vertex grid, but with all the internal vertices removed (see Figure 17.8).

You have vertices only on the periphery of the object. Set the (u,v) coordinates of each vertex so that initially, D3D places your texture unchanged onto your mesh (just like if you were doing a render copy).

 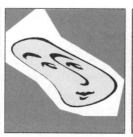 

Figure 17.7

Crunch time! A shot of the crunch transition.

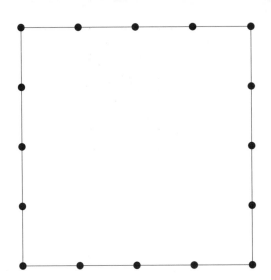

Figure 17.8

A vertex grid, minus the internal vertices, stands at the core of the crunch fade.

Then, each frame, you take each vertex of this mesh and move it a little closer to the center of the screen. You do this by calculating the slope of the line that runs between the vertex's current position and the center point. (Be sure to make a special case for those points directly above or below the center point, otherwise your program will crash with a divide by zero error.) Leave the (u,v) coordinates unchanged throughout this process, and your graphics card will distort the image to fit this bizarre shape.

If you vary the distance each vertex moves each frame, you can create the illusion of a vacuum cleaner or something sucking the image into the center of the screen. For added emphasis, you could play a slurping, sucking sound as the effect runs!

> ## Sample Program Reference
>
> I didn't include any crunch code here, but the `Ch17p2_TransitionPageant` sample program contains a couple crunch effect classes: `CCrunchTransition` and `CConstSpeedCrunchTransition` that show you how to do constant speed and random speed crunches.

Warp-Dissolves

Another variation on the dissolve theme, warp-fading is a combination of image warping and dissolving (see Figure 17.9).

You can create the flashback transition used in the movie *Wayne's World*, where the old image first begins to swim and then slowly dissolves into the new image, by using this technique. All that's required is a few slight modifications to the image warping code. First off, we'll be using a non-cumulative warp, so don't worry about having to feed the warped image back into itself each

Figure 17.9

The warp-fade combines warping and dissolving.

frame. Instead, just create your vertex grid, and jiggle each vertex (or each texture coordinate) as you slowly increase its alpha value—the image will swim as it fades out.

That gets us a watery effect, but not the transition used in one of The Funniest Movies Out There. To get the *Wayne's World* effect, we first ditch the vertex grid, and replace it with strips that run horizontally (not vertically!). Then, we move each strip according to a sine (or cosine) wave.

For each vertex of each strip, we use the sine (or cosine) of that vertex's y value, plus a global y value you increment each frame (to get the wave moving), to determine the vertex's x position. You can adjust how far left and right the vertices undulate by multiplying them by an arbitrary constant (two, four, whatever).

> **Sample Program Reference**
>
> The Ch17p2_TransitionPageant sample program contains a warp-dissolve class called CWarpDissolveTransition. It does a random image warp as it dissolves instead of a sine wave warp.

To generate a truly realistic *Wayne's World* warp-dissolve, you increment the constant you're multiplying the sine values by each frame, so that at first the source image ripples just a little, but as time goes on the image starts to ripple violently. Doodly-doo! Doodly-doo! Doodly-doo!

Tile Transitions

Before 3D programming came along, game programmers were obsessed with tiles. Back in the day, 8- and 16-bit consoles used tiling extensively for everything from backgrounds and characters to text and status bars. So, it's no surprise then that programmers eventually created several nifty transitions based on tiles. I really like all the tile transitions, because they remind me of retro gaming. This section will take a peek at some of the more popular ones.

The Secret to It All: Don't Use an Index Buffer

To create a tile transition, you first divide the old image into tiles. The key to implementing tile transitions is *not* to use an index buffer for your vertex grid. The index buffer doesn't suit us here, because eventually all of the tiles will be separate from one another, and so we'll end up not sharing any vertices. Instead, just make a mesh full of tiles, and duplicate vertices.

The only other thing you need to consider when creating your tile mesh is the dimensions of your tiles—how many texels wide and tall you'd like them to be. This, of course, depends on your screen resolution, but in general if you divide your screen up into 30 tiles, the effects look great. 30×30 triangles equates to 900 tiles, and at two triangles per tile, that's 1800 triangles your 3D card has to handle—a drop in the bucket for contemporary 3D cards.

Things You Can Do with Tiles

I considered saving myself some time and replacing this section with a section called "Things You Can't Do with Tiles," and then just writing "nothing." But, I figured that probably wouldn't be very useful to you.

Once you've got your "tile mesh," you can do all sorts of things to each individual tile within the mesh. Here are just a few ideas:

- **Shrinking.** In this effect, the tiles slowly shrink to reveal the new image behind them. It's similar to how a fly would probably see the crunching effect. In each frame, shrink each tile a bit—keep the (u,v) coordinates the same, but move each tile's four vertices closer to that tile's center. You can also choose to decrease the vertices' alpha components, so that the tiles fade out as they're shrinking.

- **Spinning.** Spin each tile as you slowly shrink it, for an even more interesting effect. You can, of course, spin on any axis, or you can spin each tile randomly on several axes. My personal favorite is to spin the tiles on the z axis.

- **Smashing.** This one takes a bit of physics math to do, but essentially, you explode tiles, as if a bomb had just exploded in the center of the screen right behind the tiles. We'll look at the equations to do this later, when we get to the chapter on 3D explosions, but essentially it just involves applying a force in a particular direction to each tile. You can choose to have the tiles eventually fragment and vanish, or you can choose to fade the whole effect out as the tiles are flying—both approaches look cool.

- **Tile MetaEffects.** Imagine that each tile is itself a separate screen, capable of displaying a separate transition. You could apply any of the transitions we've talked about so far on a per-tile basis; for example, you could create a "tile-dissolve" effect by performing a separate dissolve effect for each tile using random speeds. Some tiles would dissolve faster than others, which would look pretty cool. You could also create "tile-crunches" or "tile wipes." You truly could go out of control and create "tile-tile" effects, where each tile is divided into subtiles, and each subtile is given a different effect. Recurse down as far as you want.

Delay Patterns for Tile Transitions

For even more creativity, consider the fact that all of the tiles don't have to start and stop moving at the same time. If you're spinning or shrinking your tiles, you can add a little spice to your effects by starting the animation at different times for different tiles.

Now the question becomes when should each tile start and a whole new set of "meta-transitions" appear? Here are just a few of the patterns you could apply to the tile start times:

■ **Spirals.** Start with the center tile (or the group of 2×2 center tiles)—these tiles start animating immediately. Then, you just spiral around the center, starting each tile as you visit it, so that the tiles at the edges of the screen are the last to start moving (see Figure 17.10).

7	6	6	6	9
7	2	2	5	9
7	3	1	5	9
7	3	4	4	9
8	8	8	8	9

Figure 17.10

The spiral delay pattern.

Low-numbered tiles start their effects first.

■ **Concentric Rectangles.** Again, start with the center tile, but this time move outward in concentric rectangles. After a brief pause, start all of the tiles adjacent to your center tiles, then after another brief pause, start all the tiles adjacent to those, and so on, until finally the tiles at the edge of the screen all start simultaneously (see Figure 17.11).

3	3	3	3	3
3	2	2	2	3
3	2	1	2	3
3	2	2	2	3
3	3	3	3	3

Figure 17.11

The concentric rectangle delay pattern.

Low-numbered tiles start their effects first.

■ **Wipes.** Start at one edge of the screen (or at a corner, if you're doing a diagonal wipe), and slowly move across, starting each tile as you go (see Figure 17.12).

1	2	3	4	5
1	2	3	4	5
1	2	3	4	5
1	2	3	4	5
1	2	3	4	5

Figure 17.12

The wipe delay pattern.

Low-numbered tiles start their effects first.

Of course, countless other variations exist—you could also choose to start random tiles at random times, or you could use the position of the player or a recently defeated boss or something to determine which section of the screen fades out first (or last).

Templates to the Rescue

One of the things I noticed when I was designing my tile transition class was that all of the tile transitions used essentially the same rendering and updating code. So, I created a template-based system that allows you to plug in different tile behaviors to the same CTileTransition class. CTileTransition takes one template argument, which needs to be a class derived from CTileBehavior.

CTileBehavior is an abstract base class with a couple of virtual functions—Render and Setup, and one pure virtual function, Update. Classes derived from CTileBehavior implement these functions to create their own unique tile transition effect. Meanwhile, the base class takes care of storing all of the tile objects (CTileTransition creates one CTileBehavior-derived class for each tile in the transition).

Sample Program Reference

The Ch17p2_TransitionPageant sample program contains a few classes for tile transitions. Check out the template class CTileTransition—it contains the essential code for tile transitions. You can plug in any number of CTileBehavior classes into CTileTransition—check out the two CTileBehavior derived classes, CTileTransitionBehavior_Shrink and CTileTransitionBehavior_TwirlAndShrink, to see how to implement some basic tile effects.

Also, if you want to see how to implement a tile effect using just one call to DrawPrimitive, check out the Ch17p2_TileTransition_OneVB.cpp and Ch17p2_TileTransition_OneVB.h source files.

Tile Transition Wrap-Up

Be warned: playing with the tile effects can be addictive. My recommendation is to have plenty of caffeine and nothing else to do before you sit down to write your tile transitions, because once you're in the code, you're going to want to spend all night playing with these silly tiles.

A CLASS HIERARCHY FOR TRANSITIONS

You now know how some of the most common effects work, and you've seen snippets of the code for each of those transitions. One thing may have struck you as you were reading this chapter: all of the transition effects are similar to each other. They all transition from an old image to a new image, which means all transitions share a set of variables—if nothing else, the texture handles for the old and new images.

So, let's build a class hierarchy (see Figure 17.13). To do this, we need to think about what sorts of things each transition does, and what sorts of things all transitions do. All transitions move from an old image to a new image within a certain amount of time; true, they differ on how they accomplish that movement, but in a way they're all doing the same thing.

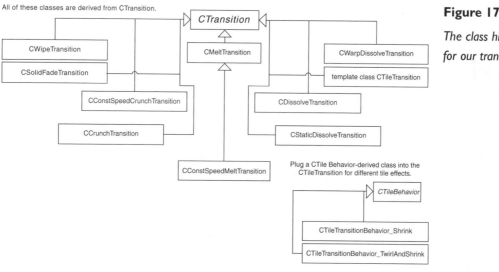

Figure 17.13

The class hierarchy for our transitions.

TIP

Whenever you have a situation like that—where "what to do" remains constant, but "how to do it" can vary—you should consider implementing a class hierarchy. Essentially, put the "what" inside the base class, and the "how" inside the derived class(es).

For us, this means our base class, CTransition, should keep the handles to the old and new textures, as well as the duration of the transition effect. Additionally, we know that each transition will need to calculate some animation each frame, and obviously each transition will need to render itself. So, we can create two pure virtual functions, DoTransition and DoRender, to handle animation calculation and rendering, respectively.

The beauty of doing things like this is that the code that's using the transitions doesn't need to know about what specific transition it's performing. All it needs to do is say, "Transition, please calculate your animation," or "Transition, render thyself!" We can swap transition effects all we want, and C++ will automatically take care of calling the appropriate calculation or render function based on the type of the transition object we're using.

Also, a possibility exists where some transitions may derive from others. For example, a constant-speed melt transition is a melt transition with some changes involving what's subtracted from each vertex's y value. The rendering and setup of the two melt transitions is exactly the same; only the update function is different. This kind of situation just begs for a class derivation.

I haven't taken this class hierarchy as far as I probably should have. More classes create more flexibility, which is good, but also less readability, which isn't so good (especially when you're writing a book trying to teach this stuff). For this reason, I only went about halfway as far as I could have gone with the transition class hierarchy—you are invited to take the classes I have so far and break them apart even further to create as flexible a system as you need.

CHAPTER WRAP-UP

We covered a lot of techniques in this chapter, and didn't go into much detail on most of them. Thankfully, most of the effects are nothing complex—they're just clever manipulations of quads and alpha components.

The main thing you should take away from this chapter is that there are really an endless variety of effects you can create, and if you have the time to code them, they can really add a lot of polish to your game.

ABOUT THE SAMPLE PROGRAMS

I haven't added anything to the coding style or organization this chapter, so let's dive straight into the program list:

- **Ch17p1_AlphaBlendFade.** This sample program demonstrates how to fade using alpha blending (that is, a partially transparent quad layered on top of your scene).

■ **Ch17p2_TransitionPageant.** It's a pageant! Specifically, it's a pageant of transitions. This sample program demonstrates all of the different transitions effects we've covered. It's also a good example of how you can use templates for extendible class hierarchies.

EXERCISES

1. Throw all the stuff from this chapter into a blender! Make your own effects by combining the techniques I've outlined for you here.
2. Write a "transition editor" that will allow your artists to interactively select a fade and set up parameters for it. The program should save the information to disk, so that your games can load it.
3. Write a program that compares gamma ramp fades and alpha-blended quad fades side-by-side. Does either look significantly different than the other?
4. Add tile delays to the tile transition class. Make a second template argument for a new CTileDelay base class that allows your users to specify which type of delay pattern they'd like to apply to the tile transition.

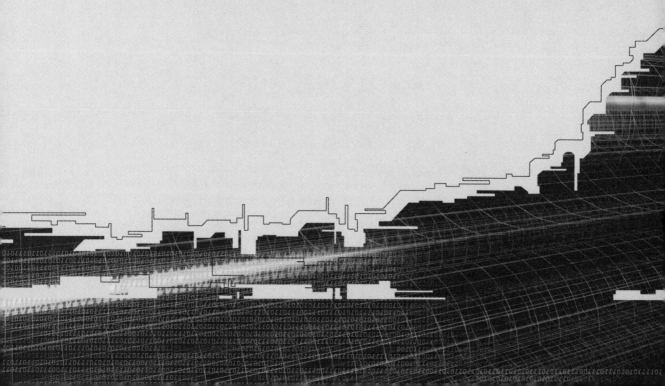

Part 3

3D Effects

You've already learned much about Direct3D programming in general, and about several different forms of 2D special effects. Now it's time to complete the trinity, and learn the final piece of the puzzle. Now it's time for the 3D effects.

Part III starts with two chapters designed to teach you about particle systems, one of the most widely used techniques for implementing special effects of every kind. In Chapter 18, you'll learn about the basics of particle systems. Chapter 19 will build on that knowledge, and show you how to create an advanced particle system engine.

Next, you'll look at some effects that rely, in part, on particle systems. Chapter 20 is all about making things blow up, and Chapter 21 explains weaponry and projectiles.

After that, you'll look at some general 3D effects. Chapter 22 teaches you how to create a lens flare, in some respects the king of all special effects. Chapter 23 shows you one way to create ultra-realistic looking 3D water in your games.

The final chapter is all about shader effects. You'll learn a variety of techniques for creating special effects using vertex and pixel shaders.

Without further ado, let's get started.

CHAPTER 18

Rain, Smoke, Magic, and More! The Joy of Particle Systems

"The beginning of knowledge is the discovery
of something we do not understand."
—*Frank Herbert*

W e will start this section on 3D effects by looking at what many programmers consider the most useful special effect technique of them all—learning how to make a particle system.

Programmers use particle systems for a wide variety of effects. Particle systems can create convincing weather effects, like rain or snow, as well as magic effects, smoke, fire, debris, jet streams, and more. In fact, you could say that particle systems form the basis of virtually all 3D effects. That's why we're learning about them right now, as we kick off this 3D section.

One of the coolest things about using particle systems is that you can create all sorts of different effects simply by adjusting variables inside the system. This means that the same code that implements your rain and snow effect may also drive your magical spell or smoke effects. You could even re-use the same particle system code across games with little or no modification, and you could even expose the particle system variables to your artists (through a WYSIWYG particle system "editor"), so that they could quickly and easily generate killer effects without you ever having to write one line of code!

Those are just a few of the reasons why particle systems rock. I could list more, but you've probably already played games that show firsthand the magic of particle systems, and you even may have read chapters of other books that touch on how to create particle systems.

I'm going to spend the next two chapters on particle systems. In this chapter, we're going to cover the basics of particle systems—what they are and how to write their code. Next, we'll spend some time learning how to make a particle system editor. If you already know what a particle system is, and have written an editor for one, you may want to skip to the next chapter to learn how to go beyond the simplistic, and make a truly advanced, flexible particle system, using a simple scripting language.

This is going to be a very long roller coaster ride, so strap yourself in. Right now your car has just moved away from the loading area. You feel the chain latch on underneath, and start carrying you up the hill…

WHAT IS A PARTICLE SYSTEM?

In real life, a "particle" is a really small piece of something. For example, when you smash a brick with a hammer, you get little brick particles (bricklets?) that go everywhere. A raindrop, a snowflake, a drop of blood, or flaming piece of debris from a dying starship could also all be considered particles. Check out Figure 18.1 for a screenshot of a particle system in action.

In video game programming, a particle is a texture attached to a two-dimensional quad just like the textured quads we've dealt with in the previous part of this book (see Figure 18.2).

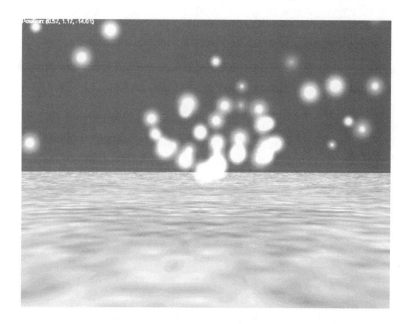

Figure 18.1

A screenshot of a particle system in action.

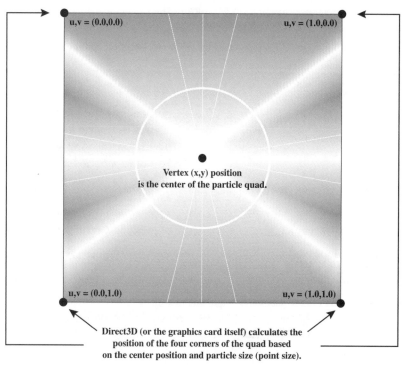

Figure 18.2

A particle is really just a textured quad.

u,v = (0.0,0.0)   u,v = (1.0,0.0)

Vertex (x,y) position
is the center of the particle quad.

u,v = (0.0,1.0)   u,v = (1.0,1.0)

Direct3D (or the graphics card itself) calculates the
position of the four corners of the quad based
on the center position and particle size (point size).

These quads are typically small, and programmers usually render them using alpha blending, so that they're partially transparent. Some programmers (along with the DirectX docs) also refer to these as *point sprites* because they're essentially a 2D sprite (image) centered on a particular point.

By modeling the physics of each particle, you can create dozens of complex special effects. For example, you could create a snowstorm by keeping an array of hundreds of particles. Every frame, you would loop through this array, adjust each particle's y position (moving it down a little, to simulate gravity), and possibly adjusting its x position as well (snowflakes wiggle as they fall). In this way, you create a very convincing snowstorm effect, because you're essentially modeling what happens in nature. You have a big set of particles, and you simulate the natural forces at play on each of those particles. Render each particle as a quad with a snowflake texture on it, and you've got a very convincing snowstorm.

All particle systems have three things at their core:

- **An array of particles.** All particle systems have an array of particles. In C++, these are usually particle objects (CParticle is a very common name). Raindrops and snowflakes are obvious examples of particles. A less obvious particle example: simulating a waterfall or water fountain using water droplets, or simulating a pillar of smoke using "smokelet" objects, or even simulating the energy released during a magic spell by throwing brightly colored "spell particles" around.
- **An update function.** The particle system's update function loops through all the particles in the array, and performs processing on each one. Typically, the update function moves the position of the particle based on some physics calculations. It uses physical variables in these calculations, like gravity, wind direction, weight of the particle, etc. The update function also may mess with other particle properties (for example, its color or opacity—as smoke rises, it becomes more transparent).
- **A render function.** This function takes care of setting up the rendering state (that is, turning alpha blending on), and putting the particle system on the screen. It loops through all particles in the system, and issues the appropriate graphics calls (SetTexture and DrawPrimitive) needed to get those particles on the screen at the correct position.

> **TIP**
>
> Notice how the pattern here is the same as the overall pattern for a game. You have a core set of objects (in this case, the array). Several times per second, you update those objects, and render them.

That's really all it takes to make a particle system.

Typically, in a C++ particle system, you'll have a CParticleSystem class that takes care of managing all the CParticles. The update and render functions are typically public methods of CParticleSystem, and the CParticle array is usually a private or protected member (so that nothing except the CParticleSystem class can modify it). The following code summarizes what we've learned so far:

```
class CParticle
{
public:
  D3DXVECTOR3 m_vPosition; // position of particle in world space
  // additional particle properties...
};
class CParticleSystem
{
  public:
    void Update(void);
    void Render(void);
  protected:
    CParticle m_aParticles[2000]; // big array of particles
};
```

If the particle system technique were a cupcake, that code would be the creamy filling—it's the stuff that makes everything else worthwhile. The particle array, and the update and render functions are the three essential things that make a particle system.

Now, of course, I glossed over the hard part—the implementation of Update and Render. That's where we'll be spending the rest of this chapter.

HOW COMPLEX SHOULD YOU MAKE YOUR PARTICLE SYSTEM?

The first question you should ask yourself when designing a particle system is: How flexible do I want it? Recall that the core goal of a particle system is to move all the particles somehow, and then render those particles. Usually, the update code relies on physics calculations to move the particles. These physics calculations can be really simple, or really complex.

The advantage to creating a simple particle system is that the code is easy to understand, and your update method is usually pretty fast. At the same time, the disadvantage is that simple particle systems may not do everything you want, or be flexible enough for your game.

For example, let's say that you implement a very simple particle system designed for snow. Your update function does a great job of looping through each particle (snowflake), applying gravity to it, and making it wiggle a bit as it falls. No problems—simple to understand, but not very flexible.

Say you want to add a water fountain to the same game that uses your snow particle system. Now you're faced with a choice: either implement a whole new particle system—that means redoing all of the array management code (yuck!)—or, somehow extending the update function in your snow particle system so that it can handle water fountains. This might mean removing the hard-coded gravity value, and replacing it with a variable that you can set to be "down" for snow and "up" for the water fountain.

As you can see, the more things you want a particle system to handle, the more complex it's going to be. I'm going to start out very simple, but by the time you've reached the end of this chapter, you will have walked through the implementation of a very complex particle system—a system that can handle the bulk of effects out there.

CAUTION

Notice I didn't say that my particle system could handle every effect. This is because no particle system can handle every effect out there. Don't try to create a particle system that will do everything under the sun—you'll spend way too much time designing it, and it'll be slow and bulky (if it works at all). A much better approach is to try to capture most of the common things, and put in some flexibility (through carefully placed virtual functions) so that you can code a specialization of your system to handle the really weird or complex stuff.

In general, my answer to the question "how complex should my particle system be?" is "not very." Do what you need to do in order to ensure you can use your particle system for the effects you see yourself making. Do nothing more.

The rest of this chapter outlines the features I decided to implement in my system, so that it could handle the bulk of the effects I consider common or useful. We're going to start this chapter by building a simple, yet still surprisingly flexible, particle system. We're going to spend the next chapter piling features onto this simple system, so that in two chapters, we'll have a complex system that can handle a ton of very different effects.

Now let's take it to the mat, by looking at the details of particles and particle systems. There's not a lot of code yet, as we're still just grasping the concepts.

TIP

Keep in mind that everything in this chapter is really my own personal solution. It fits my needs, and I believe it will fit most of the requirements of most games. But, like everything else, you'd need to put my implementation up against your requirements, and see if it's worth using. It could be that for what you're doing in your game, you won't need much of what I illustrate in the coming sections. It could be that your game calls for a vastly different particle system with a vastly different update function, or that my system is overkill for what you're doing. You just never know.

CORE PARTICLE PROPERTIES

It all starts with our friend, Mr. Particle. The core idea is that particles are "born" at a certain position in 3D (world) space. As the system's update function moves them around, they live their short, happy lives. Eventually, for some reason, they die. So right away we have our first particle property: lifetime.

Most particle systems implement a particle lifetime that dictates how long (usually in seconds) the particle lives. The update function keeps track of how long the particle has been living—if it exceeds the lifetime, the particle dies. Alternatively, some particles may also die if they hit a wall or another game object (for example, snowflakes and raindrops usually disappear as soon as they hit something).

So, we'll need a particle lifetime, and of course we'll need a 3D vector to hold this particle's position in world space, but what else will we need? Here's a full list of the particle properties I consider essential. We will add to this list as we move from simple particle systems to more advanced ones:

- **Position.** A no-brainer. We'll use a 3D vector to represent the particle's (x,y,z) position in world space. We don't care about local space for particles.
- **Lifetime.** We just talked about this.
- **Velocity.** This determines where the particle is moving. This is typically expressed in world units per second. Every frame, we'll add this velocity to the particle's position to move it.
- **Color.** Not all particles need to be the same color. We can set the vertex colors of our particle quads to whatever we want, which will in turn "tint" the texture toward that color. This is useful—for example, if we were creating an explosion effect, we'd want particles to be different shades of red, orange, yellow, and white—not just a single color. So, we need to keep track of the color of each particle.
- **Size.** Same idea—in an explosion, we might want some big bits and some little bits. Keeping track of each particle's size will give us this flexibility.

Those properties form the nucleus of our particle class.

CORE PARTICLE SYSTEM PROPERTIES

Now that we know specifically what a particle is, the next key step is to figure out what sort of variables we want in the system itself.

- **Gravity.** We need a vector that describes the direction and strength of gravity (measured in world units/sec). Since earth's gravity pulls everything straight down at 9.8 meters per second squared, a good choice for a gravity vector might be (0,–9.8,0). Choosing that also gives us some idea of the scale of our world: one world space unit is equal to one meter.

- **Texture.** This controls the appearance of each particle. For example, for snowflakes, we might use a snowflake image, for our particle texture.
- **Emission Rate.** The emission rate (or emit rate, to its friends) controls how quickly the particle system creates new particles. The particle system will use this number in its update method to determine how many new particles to make. Game programmers typically measure emission rates in particles per second, so 1.0 means "make one new particle every second" (a relatively slow emission rate).

TIP

As you can see, there's a pattern at play here: essentially, any variable that can't change from particle to particle is a system property. Any variable that *can* change on a particle-by-particle basis must of course be a particle property.

This leads you to a lot of choices—for example, you may decide that you want to give each particle a random texture from a pool. In that case, you'd move your texture variable from the system level down to the individual particle level, so that each particle could have a different texture. See the flexibility? Of course, the drawback to that is that each particle would have to keep track of its own texture interface, and the system would have to ensure that there's enough memory for everything.

But wait! Those aren't all the properties for our system. Remember, our update function must create new particles. When the update function creates a new particle, it must assign values to each of the properties of that particle (color, lifetime, etc.). So, our system needs variables that will tell the update function how to choose those values.

One way to go is to make the update function pick a random value within a certain range. If we gave the update function minimum and maximum values for the new particle's properties, it could pick a value at random. This means we'll also need the following properties:

- **Minimum, Maximum Lifetime.** The update function will pick a number in between these two floats to determine the lifetime of the specific particle it's creating.
- **Minimum, Maximum Velocity.** A set of two vectors; the update function will create a specific particle velocity by choosing random x, y, and z values that fall in between the x, y, and z values of the minimum velocity, and the x, y, and z values of the maximum velocity. For example, if our minimum velocity were (0.0, –1.0, –2.0), and our maximum velocity were (5.0, 10.0, 15.0), the update function would pick a number between 0.0 and 5.0 for x, between –1.0 and 10.0 for y, and between –2.0 and 15.0 for z. It would then take these random x, y, and z values and put them into the particle's velocity vector.
- **Minimum, Maximum Color.** This is the same idea as the min/max velocity, only instead of vectors we're using RGBA color values. The update function will pick a

number between minimum color and maximum color, and assign that as the particle's color.

■ **Minimum, Maximum Size.** Again, same idea—the update function picks an initial size for the particle between minimum size and maximum size.

Now we have the properties we need for our particle system. I'm sure by this point you've probably thought of several additional properties you could add to the system to make it cooler. Be patient—we'll add more properties as we move through the chapter.

WRITING THE CODE FOR A BASIC PARTICLE SYSTEM

We've got enough concepts to start implementing. At this point, you should load up the Ch18p1_SimpleParticles sample program, and follow along using that code.

CParticle

Let's begin the process of coding a basic particle system by defining our CParticle class. We'll use CParticle to represent one particle in our particle system.

```
class CParticle
{
public:
  CParticle() {
        m_fSize = 1.0f; m_fLifetime = 1.0f; m_fAge = 0.0f;
  }
  virtual ~CParticle() { }
    float m_fSize;
  float m_fLifetime;
  float m_fAge;

  D3DXCOLOR m_Color;
  D3DXCOLOR m_ColorStep;

  D3DXVECTOR3 m_vPos; // current position of particle
  D3DXVECTOR3 m_vDir;
  inline bool Update(float fTimeDelta)
  {
    /* don't worry about this just yet! */
  }
};
```

TIP

D3DXCOLOR and D3DXVEC-TOR3 are helper classes provided by D3DX, which encapsulate a color and a vector. They're cool because they redefine operators, so that, for example, you can add vectors by using the + operator.

TIP

A good rule of OOD says that you really shouldn't expose members as public—you should make accessor functions instead. For example, instead of making m_fSize a public member, I should have made m_fSize protected, and make GetSize and SetSize functions to allow users of the class to change the particle size.

For the sake of readability, I chose not to implement accessor functions. In a real particle system, you probably should.

As you can see, CParticle is nothing complex. There's a whole bunch of public variables—the properties of the particle system—plus a constructor that sets some default values, and an inline function called Update.

Don't worry about the Update function—you'll see how it works in a few pages.

So that's CParticle. Now let's take a look at CParticle's mom: CParticleEmitter.

CParticleEmitter

This class contains our particle array, along with the properties for the system as a whole (gravity, texture, etc.).

```
class CParticleEmitter
{
public:
  CParticleEmitter();
  virtual ~CParticleEmitter();
  virtual void Update(float fElapsedTime, float fTimeDelta);
  virtual HRESULT Render();
  virtual HRESULT RestoreDeviceObjects(LPDIRECT3DDEVICE8 pDev,
    const char *strTextureFilename);
  virtual void InvalidateDeviceObjects();
  //////////
  // accessor functions deleted to save space
  //////////
```

```
private:
  // particle system attributes
  D3DXVECTOR3 m_vGravity;
  D3DXVECTOR3 m_vPos; // position of emitter
  float m_fMinEmitRate; // in particles/sec
  float m_fMaxEmitRate; // in particles/sec
  // these vars determine starting values for each particle

  D3DXCOLOR m_Color1;
  D3DXCOLOR m_Color2;

  float m_fMinSize;
  float m_fMaxSize;
  D3DXVECTOR3 m_vSpawnDir1;
  D3DXVECTOR3 m_vSpawnDir2;
  // other stuff
  int m_iVBSize; // size of the vertex buffer ( < NUMPARTICLES)
  LPDIRECT3DDEVICE8 m_pd3dDevice;
  LPDIRECT3DVERTEXBUFFER8 m_vbParticles;
  LPDIRECT3DTEXTURE8 m_texParticle;
  CRecyclingArray<CParticle, NUMPARTICLES> m_Particles;
};
```

The most important methods of CParticleEmitter are Update and Render. RestoreDeviceObjects and InvalidateDeviceObjects are really init and uninit routines, with names that match the DirectX sample program framework. I've taken the liberty of declaring everything virtual just in case someone wants to derive from CParticleEmitter.

Note also that CParticleEmitter has a few member variables that aren't system properties.

TIP

I deleted the accessor (Get/Set) functions from this code listing to save space. I didn't use accessors back in CParticle, but I decided to use them here. I was thinking about how often client code would be messing with the variables of CParticle and CParticleEmitter. It's probably a rare occurrence when client code will want to change the properties of a CParticle directly; most of the time, the only class touching CParticle will be CParticleEmitter. However, client code will touch CParticleEmitter's properties very often, if not always. This means that without accessor functions, there's a significantly higher chance that if I change the type of a CParticleEmitter property, I'd have to modify additional code files (not a good thing). So, I bit the bullet and spent the little bit of extra time required to make accessor functions.

CParticleEmitter squirrels away the Direct3D device inside m_pd3dDevice, and uses m_vbParticles and m_texParticle to keep track of the vertex buffer used for rendering the particles (we'll see that in a second), and the texture used by the particles.

I've saved the most confusing line for last. Time to answer that little demonic question that's been hiding just below the surface of your mind as you've been reading this: What on earth is m_Particles? As seen in the preceding code, m_Particles is a CRecyclingArray. CRecyclingArray is a new class, so let's talk about it a bit.

CRecyclingArray

Stop! Before reading any further, if you don't know what a C++ template is, go and read the appendix and then come back.

Now that you've wrapped your brain around templates, let's figure out what exactly a CRecyclingArray is.

What Is CRecyclingArray?

CRecyclingArray works like std::vector, with one key difference: it doesn't use dynamic memory allocation. Instead, you give it a maximum number of objects as a template parameter. To client code, CRecyclingArray looks and acts like a vector—you can add objects to it, and delete them from it. Behind the scenes, however, CRecyclingArray isn't allocating memory—it's just using some Boolean flags to tell it which members of the static array are allocated, and which are available. When you "new" something using CRecyclingArray, the array picks the next available free object and gives it to you. When you "delete" something, CRecyclingArray marks the object you delete as free. There's no actual memory allocation or deallocation going on; instead, CRecyclingArray "recycles" the memory as you create and destroy things. Hence the name CRecyclingArray.

Now you're asking: What's wrong with using new and delete? Two things:

- **Memory allocation is slow.** Over the course of a typical particle system's lifetime, thousands of particles will be created and destroyed. We'd lose a lot of time if every particle creation and destruction triggered a memory allocation or de-allocation. Don't take my word for it though—try it out yourself and see the speed hit!

- **Allocating several small chunks of memory fragments the heap.** If the speed hit wasn't enough to scare you away from new and delete (for this purpose), here's another reason—allocating tons of little objects is a great way to fragment your heap. Imagine the heap is a slab of cookie dough. If you poke 50 little holes in the dough in random locations, you'll be lucky if you can find a big enough hole-free area for one cookie (see Figure 18.3).

Figure 18.3

Too many holes; no cookie.

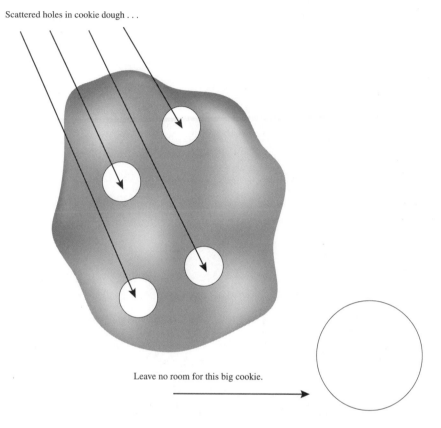

Scattered holes in cookie dough . . .

Leave no room for this big cookie.

But, poke the same 50 little holes right next to each other, and you'll still have enough space for several cookies (see Figure 18.4), even though you took the same amount of dough out each time.

That's essentially what heap fragmentation is—poking several little holes in random locations. Heap fragmentation can lead to slow performance (the system has to shuffle things behind your back), or worse, "out of memory" errors. No fun!

So, that's the impetus for using CRecyclingArray. It gives us the best of both worlds—the ability to allocate and free objects as we need them (like a standard dynamic array), without the speed or heap fragmentation worries typically associated with allocating/de-allocating small objects. Whoo-hoo!

Using a Recycling Array

Now that you know why I created CRecyclingArray, I'd like to show you how to use it. After you know how to use it, I'll show you how it works internally.

Cluster all the holes together, however . . .

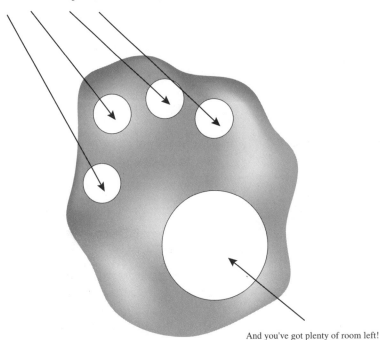

Figure 18.4

Holes clumped together—cookie!

And you've got plenty of room left!

First lesson: how to create a recycling array. CRecyclingArray takes two template arguments: the type of object in the array, and the maximum array size (that is, the maximum number of objects the array will ever hold). For example, the following code will create a recycling array containing up to 50 CMyClass objects:

```
CRecyclingArray<CMyClass, 50> m_MyArray;
```

So far, so good. Next lesson: how to create and destroy objects. To create an object, call the New method. (I dislike overloading the new operator, so I chose this way instead, for clarity.) You'll get back a pointer to your new object, like in the following code:

```
CMyClass *newclass = m_MyArray.New();
```

To delete an object, call Delete—there's a Delete method that takes an index into the particle array, and a version that takes the actual pointer:

> **CAUTION**
>
> **Be careful with that maximum value. If you've got 50 objects allocated and you try to allocate one more, CRecyclingArray will throw an out_of_range error. (I like C++ structured exception handling for cases like that.)**

> **CAUTION**
>
> **CRecyclingArray doesn't call the constructor of the object you new. Instead, it just sets the new object equal to a blank object, so be sure you have a working operator= overload for any objects you use with CRecyclingArray.**

```
m_MyArray.Delete(5); // delete object at position 5
m_MyArray.Delete(newclass); // delete newclass
```

Keep in mind that the Delete function doesn't NULL the pointer you pass to it.

Table 18.1 shows other useful, but self-explanatory, methods of CRecyclingArray.

Table 18.1 Methods of CRecyclingArray

Method	Description
GetNumFreeElements()	Returns the number of free elements currently available (dead).
GetNumUsedElements()	Returns the number of elements currently in use (alive).
GetTotalElements()	Returns the total number of elements (that is, the maximum number of elements you can have alive simultaneously—yes, the same thing you specified as a template argument).
GetAt(index)	Returns the object at the array index given. Ambitious readers could also make an overloaded [] operator.
IsAlive(index)	Returns true if the object at the given index is in use; false otherwise.
DeleteAll()	Kills all elements in the array.

How the CRecyclingArray Works

Now that I've given you the tour, let's take a peek inside the guts of CRecyclingArray.

It's actually a very simple system. Internally, CRecyclingArray has an array of Booleans equal in size to the maximum number of objects. True means the object is in use (allocated), and false means it's free.

Let's look at the New method, which is the most complex thing in the array:

```
TArrayElement *New()
{
  // assert that we have space for this one
  if (GetNumFreeElements() < 1)
```

```
    throw(std::out_of_range(
        "CRecyclingArray::New: too many objects!"));
// find first element not in use.  as an optimization, we start at
// the position that was allocated last, in the hopes that the next
// position will be free.
int i = m_iLastNew;
for (int q=0; q < iNumElements; q++) {
  if (!m_bAlive[i]) {
    // we've found our free spot!  use it!
    break;
  }
  else {
    i++; if (i >= iNumElements) i = 0;
  }
}
// clear it
m_aElements[i] = m_NewTemplate;
// increment used count
m_iUsedElements++;
m_bAlive[i] = true;
m_iLastNew = i;

// return it
return(&m_aElements[i]);
}
```

The New method starts at the object after the one it allocated last time, and looks for a false flag. As soon as it finds the false flag, it sets the flag true, increments the used object count, and sets the object equal to a new blank object (see Figure 18.5).

No constructor is called; instead, New relies on the equals statement to "clean" the object.

The other methods are simple, so I'm not going to cover them here. The only other tricky one is the Delete overload that takes a pointer to the object instead of an index—there's some pointer arithmetic going on there to determine the index of the object. I tried to make this pointer math as obvious as possible, by doing some ugly things—casting pointers to ints, etc. If you don't get it by just looking at the code, I encourage you to fire up a debugger and step through it—all things should become clear.

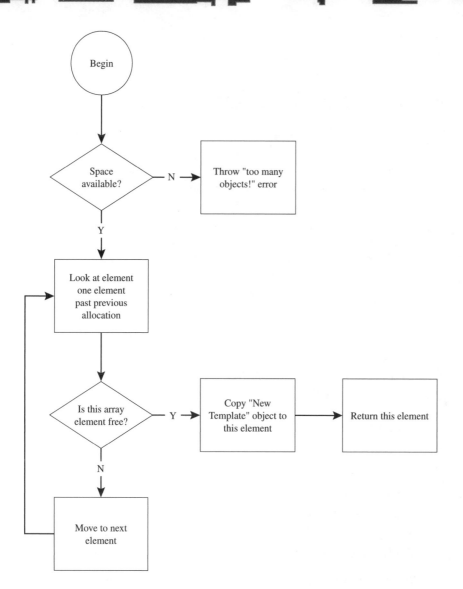

Figure 18.5

Logic for the New method.

CRecyclingArray **Wrap-Up**

CRecyclingArray won't wash your dog or make your teeth whiter, but it will make managing objects of your video game much easier—you'll no longer have to worry about speed hits associated with badly timed memory allocations and de-allocations. You'll also never have to worry about running out of memory at some random point in your game—because all the memory is allocated up front, if you need to support a maximum of 5,000 bullets but the system you're running on can't give you that much memory, you'll know about it when you create your array, not at some random point inside your game. I use CRecyclingArray in several places in my games—I hope you'll find it as useful as I do.

Setting Up a Particle System

Enough with this CRecyclingArray stuff, let's get back to the task at hand—building a simple particle system.

The first step toward coding a working particle system is to set up the Direct3D resources the particle system needs. In our case, that means putting some code in the particle system's initialization routine (RestoreDeviceObjects) that creates a texture and vertex buffer for our particles.

Neither task is anything worth losing sleep over. Let's look the init function in all its glory:

```
HRESULT CParticleEmitter::RestoreDeviceObjects(LPDIRECT3DDEVICE8 pDev,
  const char *strTextureFilename)
{
  HRESULT hr;
  m_pd3dDevice = pDev;
  m_Particles.DeleteAll();
  // load up the particle system texture
  if (FAILED(hr = D3DXCreateTextureFromFile(m_pd3dDevice,
    strTextureFilename, &m_texParticle))) {
    return(hr);
  }

  // create vertex buffer
  if(FAILED(hr = m_pd3dDevice->CreateVertexBuffer(
    m_iVBSize * sizeof(VERTEX_PARTICLE),
    D3DUSAGE_DYNAMIC | D3DUSAGE_WRITEONLY | D3DUSAGE_POINTS,
    D3DFVF_PARTICLE, D3DPOOL_DEFAULT, &m_vbParticles))) return(hr);
  // all is well!  return OK.
  return S_OK;
}
```

The first thing we do is squirrel away a pointer to the Direct3D device we'll be using. Next, we clear the particle array, just for the sake of being clean. A simple call to D3DXCreateTextureFromFile will give us our texture interface (the users of CParticleSystem will pass a texture filename into RestoreDeviceObjects), and a call to CreateVertexBuffer takes care of creating our vertex buffer.

Several things are different about creating the vertex buffer, however. For starters, there are the D3DUSAGE_DYNAMIC and D3DUSAGE_POINTS flags. These flags tell Direct3D specific things about how we're planning on using the vertex buffer. The D3DUSAGE_DYNAMIC flag tells Direct3D that the data in the vertex buffer will be dynamic (constantly changing). The D3DUSAGE_POINTS flag tells it that the data elements in the buffer represent particles (or "point sprites" as Direct3D calls them).

> **TIP**
>
> Yes, it may come as a shock to you, but there's actually significant support for particle systems embedded in DirectX. Particle systems really are that common.

Point Sprites and a New Vertex Format

The other thing that's different about the creation of our vertex buffer is the vertex format we're using. In the past, we had always used a vertex structure I call VERTEX_XYZ_DIFFUSE_TEX1 that contains the position, color, and texture coordinates of our vertex:

```
typedef struct
{
  D3DXVECTOR3 position; // The position
  D3DCOLOR    color;    // The color
  FLOAT       tu, tv;   // The texture coordinates
} VERTEX_XYZ_DIFFUSE_TEX1;
```

That vertex structure works for many things, but for particle systems we need a new structure, containing some different information:

```
typedef struct
{
    D3DXVECTOR3 position;
    float       pointsize;
    D3DCOLOR    color;
} VERTEX_PARTICLE;
```

As you can see, this new vertex structure, VERTEX_PARTICLE, is very similar to VERTEX_XYZ_DIFFUSE_TEX1, with two main differences: we've ditched the texture coordinates and added a pointsize member.

The reason we removed the texture coordinates is simple. There is a rendering state called D3DRS_POINTSPRITEENABLE. When this rendering state is set to true, Direct3D automatically maps the entire texture onto each point. In other words, with D3DRS_POINTSPRITEENABLE set to true, the vertex position of our vertex structure no longer represents just one point of a triangle—it represents the center of a particle. How Direct3D accomplishes this isn't our concern—it may "expand" out these particle positions into a two-triangle quad, putting texture coordinates of (0.0, 0.0), (1.0,0.0), (1.0,1.0), and (0.0, 1.0) onto the four vertices of that quad. Or, if the 3D card supports point sprites in hardware (some do), Direct3D may just pass along the information it gets, along with a note that says, "Hey Mr. Graphics Card, these are particle center points, please draw them using this entire texture, as if they were quads."

So, because of that, we no longer have to keep texture coordinates in our vertex structure. We can rest assured that Direct3D knows enough to map our entire texture onto the particle, and to put the center point of that particle at the position we specify. Wonderful, isn't it?

Okay, so what's up with pointsize, then? Essentially, pointsize tells Direct3D the "point size" of our point sprite; in other words, how big the particle should be, in camera-space units. A particle with a point size of 2.0 is twice as big as one with a size of 1.0. It isn't a requirement that you have a point size member in your vertex structure; however, putting one in there gives you the freedom to make your particles different sizes.

> **CAUTION**
>
> If you do include a point size in your vertex format, however, Direct3D does require that it come before the color member in memory (which is why we list it before color in our VERTEX_PARTICLE structure).
>
> Direct3D has very specific rules regarding the order of vertex members, and it shows no mercy to programmers who disobey these rules. Consult Chapter 6, "An Introduction to DirectGraphics," for more information.

That's our new vertex structure. Remember, you can switch vertex structures at any time—usually, in our case, we'll be using this structure to render our particles, but will switch back to using VERTEX_XYZ_DIFFUSE_TEX1 (our "normal" structure) to render other geometry.

That solves the last remaining mystery regarding setting up a particle system, and creating a vertex buffer. Now that we know how to initialize a system, let's look at how to render one.

Rendering the Particles

If you didn't know any better, you'd probably write your system one of two ways:

1. **One DrawPrimitive Call for Each Particle.** In this approach, you'd make a for loop going from zero to the number of particles. For each particle, you'd lock the vertex buffer, put in its coordinates, unlock the buffer, and call DrawPrimitive to render that particle. You'd use a very small vertex buffer—in fact, since you're calling DrawPrimitive for every particle, you'd only need a 1-element vertex buffer!

2. **One DrawPrimitive Call for All the Particles.** In this approach, you'd lock the vertex buffer, then loop and put every alive particle into the buffer. You'd unlock, and then just call DrawPrimitive once to render the entire particle system. For this situation, you need a huge vertex buffer—one that's big enough to hold the maximum number of alive particles in your system.

As it turns out, neither one of these approaches is optimal. This situation is what I call a "Goldilocks Situation"—you've got one bowl of porridge that's way too hot, and one that's way too cold. What you need is a bowl that's "just right."

Option 1 isn't great, because you waste a lot of time calling DrawPrimitive—you could potentially be calling it thousands of times *each frame*. Not good. Option 2 is also less than ideal, because your graphics card is sitting idle while your CPU is working hard assembling the vertex buffer. This situation would be akin to hiring an artist to work on your game, and then telling him he couldn't start on the artwork until the code was 100% complete.

The "just right" situation is to hand small chunks of particles to the graphics card. This way, nothing sits idle—the graphics card begins processing the first chunk of particles while the CPU moves on and starts preparing the vertex buffer for the next chunk.

The next question involves how big the chunks should be. There is probably an exact optimal value somewhere—I leave finding this number as an exercise for you. I use 10% in the particle system code, and I've found that gives me decent frame rates. Figure out if that's optimal or not.

So, to get the best possible performance, our rendering code must be a glorious ballet of setting render states, locking the vertex buffer, pumping in a bunch of particle system coordinates, unlocking the buffer, calling DrawPrimitive, and then repeating the process on the next bunch of particles.

Setting Render States

Now we're ready to tackle the entire render function. I'm going to walk you through the Render method of CParticleEmitter implemented in Ch18p1_SimpleParticles.cpp. Instead of giving the Render code here in one big chunk, I've broken it down into several segments, so that it's easier to follow.

Here's the first segment of code:

```
HRESULT CParticleEmitter::Render()
{
  HRESULT hr;
  // Set the render states for using point sprites
  m_pd3dDevice->SetRenderState(D3DRS_POINTSPRITEENABLE, TRUE );
  m_pd3dDevice->SetRenderState(D3DRS_POINTSCALEENABLE,  TRUE );
  m_pd3dDevice->SetRenderState(D3DRS_POINTSIZE_MIN, FtoDW(0.00f) );
  m_pd3dDevice->SetRenderState(D3DRS_POINTSCALE_A,  FtoDW(0.00f) );
  m_pd3dDevice->SetRenderState(D3DRS_POINTSCALE_B,  FtoDW(0.00f) );
  m_pd3dDevice->SetRenderState(D3DRS_POINTSCALE_C,  FtoDW(1.00f) );
```

Yep, the only exciting thing going on here is that we're setting some render states. Don't worry about the FtoDW function—all it does is take a float and convert it to a DWORD (which is what SetRenderState wants as a second parameter). For the morbidly curious, here's what FtoDW looks like:

```
// Helper function to stuff a FLOAT into a DWORD argument
inline DWORD FtoDW( FLOAT f ) { return *((DWORD*)&f); }
```

That's it—nothing more than a way to wrap an ugly cast into an innocent-looking function.

And now, Table 18.2 explains all of those SetRenderState flags.

Table 18.2 SetRenderState Flags

Flag	What It Does
D3DRS_POINTSPRITEENABLE	Setting this flag to true tells Direct3D that when you send points into the system, Direct3D should automatically assign texture coordinates so that the entire texture is applied to each point. In other words, you're saying "Hey Direct3D, the vertices I'm sending you are actually the center points of quads, and I want the texture coordinates of the four corners of the quad to be (0.0,0.0), (1.0,0.0), (1.0,1.0), and (0.0,1.0)."
D3DRS_POINTSCALEENABLE	This flag controls two subtly interwoven things. First, setting this flag to true tells Direct3D that it should scale the size of the particles based on their distance from the camera. (If we turned this off, all particles would be the same size, regardless of how far away they were—sort of like if we were using an orthographic projection.) This flag also controls whether the point size member of our particle vertex format is in camera-space units or screen-space units (pixels). With this set to true, it's in camera-space units (and the particle gets smaller as you move the camera away from it). With this flag false, Direct3D interprets the point size as screen-space units (pixels), and the particle stays that same size regardless of how far away it is.

Table 18.2 Continued

Flag	What It Does
D3DRS_POINTSIZE_MIN, D3DRS_POINTSIZE_MAX	These two render states accept floating-point values (courtesy of the FtoDW function) that specify the smallest and largest possible size of a point sprite. Sizes less than D3DRS_POINTSIZE_MIN are enlarged to that minimum, and sizes greater than D3DRS_POINTSIZE_MAX are shrunk to that maximum.
D3DRS_POINTSCALE_A, D3DRS_POINTSCALE_B, D3DRS_POINTSCALE_C	These three values together determine how the particle's size is calculated given its distance from the camera. Think back to Chapter 7, "Lighting," these states work somewhat similarly to how the Attenuation0, Attenuation1, and Attenuation2 variables work.
	If that doesn't ring a bell: Essentially, A, B, and C are coefficients in the equation shown in Figure 18.6. As you can see, by setting A, B, and C to either 1.0 or 0.0, we can change how Direct3D calculates the particle's size.
	It's okay if you don't completely understand that—most of the time you'll want to just use the square of the distance, so set A and B to 0.0 and C to 1.0. Experiment around with the other combinations to see how they influence Direct3D's behavior.

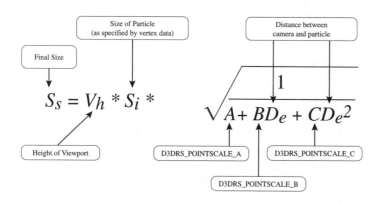

Figure 18.6

The point scale equation.

Set Texture and Vertex Buffer Active

After we set the render states, we set a few other states that should look more familiar:

```
// Set up the vertex buffer to be rendered
m_pd3dDevice->SetStreamSource(0, m_vbParticles,
  sizeof(VERTEX_PARTICLE));
m_pd3dDevice->SetVertexShader(D3DFVF_PARTICLE);
m_pd3dDevice->SetTexture(0, m_texParticle);
```

These three function calls set our vertex buffer and texture active. Note also that in our call to SetVertexShader we specify D3DFVF_PARTICLE:

```
#define D3DFVF_PARTICLE (D3DFVF_XYZ|D3DFVF_DIFFUSE|D3DFVF_PSIZE)
```

We need to set this vertex format so that Direct3D knows we're playing with a different kind of vertex structure (one that has a position, a diffuse color, and a point size—hence the flags D3DFVF_XYZ, D3DFVF_DIFFUSE, and D3DFVF_PSIZE). See Chapter 6 if this is unclear to you.

Lock the Vertex Buffer

Now we're getting down to the task at hand. The following code locks our vertex buffer:

```
VERTEX_PARTICLE *pVertices;
DWORD dwNumParticlesToRender = 0;
if(FAILED(hr = m_vbParticles->Lock(
  0,
  m_iVBSize * sizeof(VERTEX_PARTICLE),
  (BYTE **) &pVertices,
  D3DLOCK_DISCARD)))

  return hr;
```

Here we have a member variable m_iVBSize that dictates how many particle vertices we'll be working with at one time. Again, as I said before, I typically set this variable to 10% of my total particles, so that in a system with, say, a maximum of 2,000 particles, the system processes the first 200, hands those off to the graphics card, and then starts on the next 200.

Pump the Particles Into the Vertex Buffer

Now it gets interesting. After we've locked the vertex buffer, we need to start filling it up. To do that, we need to enter a for loop:

```
// Render each particle
for (int q=0; q < NUMPARTICLES; q++) {
  if (m_Particles.IsAlive(q)) {
    CParticle &part = m_Particles.GetAt(q);

    pVertices->position = part.m_vPos;
    pVertices->pointsize = 1.0f;
    pVertices->color = (DWORD)part.m_Color;
    pVertices++;
```

We loop through each particle, and determine whether that particle is alive. If it is, that means we need to render it, so we add its position, color, and size information into our vertex buffer (pVertices). We then increment the pVertices pointer, so that we move to the next structure inside the vertex buffer.

Keep in mind we haven't closed the for loop just yet.

Push the Vertex Buffer Out to the Graphics Card

Now it's time for the next chunk of code:

```
if(++dwNumParticlesToRender == m_iVBSize) {
  // Done filling this chunk of the vertex buffer - unlock & draw!
  m_vbParticles->Unlock();
  if(FAILED(hr = m_pd3dDevice->DrawPrimitive(
    D3DPT_POINTLIST, 0, dwNumParticlesToRender)))
    return hr;
  // Lock the next chunk of the vertex buffer.
  if(FAILED(hr = m_vbParticles->Lock(
    0, m_iVBSize * sizeof(VERTEX_PARTICLE),
    (BYTE **) &pVertices, D3DLOCK_DISCARD)))
    return hr;
  dwNumParticlesToRender = 0;
}
```

After we increment the pointer, we need to make sure there's still room in the vertex buffer (for the next particle). If there is room, no problem—we just move on to the next particle. However, if there isn't room, we need to do a little work.

Take a look at the first line in the preceding section of code. Here, we're incrementing a dwNumParticlesToRender count, and then comparing it to the size of the vertex buffer. If the count is equal to the size, that means we've filled up the buffer, and that it's now time to push that chunk of vertex data out to the 3D card via a call to DrawPrimitive.

As you can see from the code inside the `if` block, once we've determined the vertex buffer is full, we unlock it, and draw it (using the `D3DPT_POINTLIST` flag, which tells Direct3D that we're pushing point data, as opposed to triangle lists or strips). After we're done drawing, we lock the buffer again, specifying the `D3DLOCK_DISCARD` flag (now that we've sent that chunk of vertex data to the card, we have no real need for it anymore, so we can discard it).

Cleanup: Push Out the Stragglers

One last little thing before we're done:

```
// Unlock the vertex buffer
m_vbParticles->Unlock();
// Render any remaining particles
if(dwNumParticlesToRender)
{
  if(FAILED(hr = m_pd3dDevice->DrawPrimitive(
    D3DPT_POINTLIST, 0, dwNumParticlesToRender )))
    return hr;
}
// Reset render states
m_pd3dDevice->SetRenderState(D3DRS_POINTSPRITEENABLE, FALSE);
m_pd3dDevice->SetRenderState(D3DRS_POINTSCALEENABLE,  FALSE);
```

Essentially, all we're doing here is making sure that even if the vertex buffer size doesn't divide evenly into the number of particles, we still render all the particles. For example, if the maximum number of particles is 10, and your vertex buffer size is seven, it's possible that you'd come out of the `for` loop with three particles in the vertex buffer, but not rendered yet (no call to `DrawPrimitive`). So, we put in one last call to `DrawPrimitive`, to make sure everything in the vertex buffer gets drawn.

We finish the rendering function by turning off point sprite mode (by setting the `D3DRS_POINTSPRITEENABLE` render state to `false`).

Rendering Wrap-Up

And that, gentle reader, is one way to render a particle system.

> **TIP**
>
> There are other ways—for example, the Microsoft point sprite sample program renders using slightly different logic. It essentially tacks vertex data onto the end of the vertex buffer as the buffer is being rendered (yes, you can do such a thing, by specifying the `D3DLOCK_NOOVERWRITE` flag). This is a great optimization, but it's more than a little confusing, and as such isn't the best way to teach someone the basics.

Updating the Particles

Now that you've seen how to render the particle system, it's time to fill in the other half of the puzzle: the Update function. You'll be happy to hear that I consider rendering to be a lot more difficult than updating.

The update function does two main things:

- **Move and Animate the Particles.** The function needs to move each particle according to its velocity. It also needs to do whatever's required for animation—changing the particle's size, changing its color, whatever. As part of this process, the function also needs to make sure that particles die when they're supposed to.
- **Create New Particles.** The update function also needs to create new particles, to replace the particles that have died.

Let's look at both of those responsibilities in more detail, starting with the animation.

Moving and Animating Particles

In essence, all we need to do for our Update function is touch each of the particles that are alive, move them, and make sure they're still alive. We do this using the following code:

```
void CParticleEmitter::Update(float fElapsedTime, float fTimeDelta)
{
  // update existing particles
  {
    for (int q=0; q < m_Particles.GetTotalElements(); q++) {
      if (m_Particles.IsAlive(q)) {
        CParticle &part = m_Particles.GetAt(q);
        if (!part.Update(fTimeDelta)) {
          m_Particles.Delete(&part);
        }
      } // is alive
    } // next particle
  } // update block
}
```

That code is really just a loop framework—most of the heavy lifting actually occurs in part.Update(). Notice that we check the return value of part.Update(); if it returns false, we delete the particle (effectively marking it as free in our recycling array).

> **TIP**
>
> Designing things so that most of the work was accomplished inside a particle Update function seemed more object-oriented than just having the code right in this function—after all, the particle system shouldn't care about how the particle is actually updated; it seemed to me like the particle should take care of updating itself.

So, let's look at the Update code:

```
class CParticle
{
  . . . // see the first section for this stuff
  inline bool Update(float fTimeDelta)
  {
    // age the particle
    m_fAge += fTimeDelta;
    // if this particle's age is greater than it's lifetime, it dies.
    if (m_fAge >= m_fLifetime) return(false); // dead!
    // move particle
    m_vPos += m_vDir * fTimeDelta;
    return(true); // particle stays alive
  }
}
```

Notice that we're given fTimeDelta, a variable containing the amount of time in seconds that has passed since the last frame—and presumably since the last call to Update. The first thing we do is add this value onto the particle's lifetime. If the particle was only supposed to live for three seconds, and adding that put m_fLifeTime over that amount, then we return false, which tolls a bell for the particle, causing a little "Particle Grim Reaper" to come along and take that particle to a better place.

Assuming the particle is still alive, the next task is to move it. To do this, we take the particle's velocity (a vector described in world units per second), and multiply it by the elapsed time since the last frame. For example, if half a second has gone by, fTimeDelta would equal 0.5, and we'd end up cutting the velocity in half (which makes sense, because m_vDir contains the number of world space units the particle should move in a full second).

That's all we need to do for this simple example. In more complex examples, however, we'll see a whole

TIP

I made Update inline because it satisfies the two criteria for inline functions: it is a highly critical section of code, running at least once per particle per frame, potentially hundreds of thousands of times per second. Also, Update doesn't really do a lot, which means that if it weren't inline a fair amount of its time would be spent dealing with the overhead of actually calling the function.

As they say, premature optimization is the root of all evil, so don't optimize until your code is close to finished, but do keep these things in mind—sometimes you can get a fairly good speed boost out of inlining a heavily used function.

bunch of things going on—the particle Update function may change the particle's size and color, its direction, and so on.

Creating New Particles

The final ingredient needed to make this whole concoction work is the code that creates new particles.

Let's look at what's going on there. Here's the second segment of code from the Update function:

```
{
  // determine the number of particles we need to create
  float fEmitRateThisFrame =
    RandomNumber(m_fMinEmitRate, m_fMaxEmitRate);
  int iNumNewParts = fEmitRateThisFrame * fTimeDelta;
  m_fNumNewPartsExcess += (float)(fEmitRateThisFrame * fTimeDelta) -
    iNumNewParts;

  if (m_fNumNewPartsExcess > 1.0f) {
    iNumNewParts += (int)m_fNumNewPartsExcess;
    m_fNumNewPartsExcess -= (int)m_fNumNewPartsExcess;
  }

  for (int q=0; q < iNumNewParts; q++) {
    try {
      CParticle *part = m_Particles.New();

      // determine a random vector between dir1 and dir2
      float fRandX = RandomNumber(m_vSpawnDir1.x, m_vSpawnDir2.x);
      float fRandY = RandomNumber(m_vSpawnDir1.y, m_vSpawnDir2.y);
      float fRandZ = RandomNumber(m_vSpawnDir1.z, m_vSpawnDir2.z);
      part->m_vDir = D3DXVECTOR3(fRandX, fRandY, fRandZ);
      part->m_vPos = m_vPos;
      float fRandR = RandomNumber(m_Color1.r, m_Color2.r);
      float fRandG = RandomNumber(m_Color1.g, m_Color2.g);
      float fRandB = RandomNumber(m_Color1.b, m_Color2.b);
      float fRandA = RandomNumber(m_Color1.a, m_Color2.a);
      part->m_Color = D3DXCOLOR(fRandR, fRandG, fRandB, fRandA);

    } catch(...) { q = iNumNewParts; }
  }
}
```

The first order of business is to determine how many new particles we need to make. We do this by multiplying the emission rate (in particles per second) by the elapsed time (in seconds). For example, if half a second went by, we'd multiply the emission rate by 0.5.

It seems like it should be as easy as that, but in reality we need to account for something else: we can't create "half" of a particle. For example, let's say that our emit rate is 1 particle per second, and that we're running at 70 frames per second. That means, every frame, fEmitRateThisFrame comes out to be 1.0/70.0, or roughly 0.014 particles. This means that to create one particle every second, we need to generate 0.014 particles every frame. Huh? We can't do that!

To account for this, we use a new variable, m_fNumNewPartsExcess. Every frame, we split fEmitRateThisFrame into two parts: a whole number of particles to create and a floating-point excess value which we add to m_fNumNewPartsExcess. For example, if fEmitRateThisFrame is 1.6, we'd create one particle, and add 0.6 to m_fNumNewPartsExcess. Every frame we check to see whether m_fNumNewPartsExcess is greater than one, and if it is, we take the whole number portion and move it from m_fNumNewPartsExcess into fEmitRateThisFrame. This creates a holding area that can slowly build up as frames are processed.

Once we know how many particles to make, we go into a for loop and start making them. We ask the recycling array for a new particle object; we then pump in some randomly selected values for the properties of that new particle.

I've written a couple overloads of RandomNumber that use floats and integers. Feel free to continue this tradition and write overloads that take colors and vectors—I chose not to here, for readability's sake.

> **TIP**
>
> Remember that CRecyclingArray will throw if there's not enough space to create a new object. That's why the whole thing is surrounded in a try/catch block—if anything goes wrong, we'll end up inside the catch handler, where we simply set our loop index equal to the number of new particles we need to create, effectively saying "I give up!" We'll drop immediately out of the for loop, and we won't try to create any more new particles (for that frame).

Basic Particle System Code Wrap-Up

We've explored the three key pieces to the particle system puzzle—how to render a particle system, how to update a particle system, and how to create the individual particles that comprise that particle system.

I hope you feel comfortable with the basic structure of how a particle system works, because now it's time to take off the training wheels. The next step is to build an editor for our particle system, and throw in some additional properties as we go. After we have a basic system and editor in place, we can take it to the next level, by looking at how events can give us a truly versatile particle system.

MAKING A PARTICLE SYSTEM EDITOR

Even the coolest particle system won't do you a lick of good (whatever that is) if you can't configure it. So, the next order of business is to create a particle system editor.

Chindogu and the Question "Why Make an Editor?"

Chindogu is a Japanese art form invented by Kenji Kawakami, a noted Japanese designer (and anarchist). I don't do it justice here in just a few sentences, but essentially, Chindogu is the fine art of creating elaborate and ingenious inventions that are completely useless. Examples of Chindogu include feather dusters you strap on your cat's feet ("let your cat dust your house as it walks!") and the infamous Butter Stick (like lipstick, only with butter). No, I'm not making this up, and a quick Web search for "Chindogu" will prove it.

Far too often, I see developers practice the fine art of Chindogu, by successfully producing an ingeniously designed, but completely useless, chunk of software. So it's always a good idea to ask yourself "Why am I coding this? Is there a need? Will this be used?"

So, why make an editor? The particle system editor, and specifically, the save and load functions we're going to write for our particle system class, allow us to separate "particle system changes" from "code changes." Without these functions, you would need to hard code the particle system properties you wanted directly into your game. This means that every time you want to change the properties, you must recompile. If you're working with game artists who are picky about the appearance of the particle systems in the game, you may find yourself spending most of your time changing the hard-coded properties, recompiling, and redistributing the new compile. Not fun.

Pushing these properties out to a text file (that the game reads in and acts on) solves this problem. Now your artists can change the particle system without a recompile. Unfortunately, it still isn't very optimal, because they have to launch the game to see their changes in action. The optimal solution would be to create a WYSIWYG particle system editor. That way, your artists could change the particle system's properties and see their changes take effect instantly. This eventually leads to happier artists, which in turn leads to better game art.

> **TIP**
>
> Of course, if you're a lone wolf developer, you may not need an editor. You may be perfectly content with having to recompile each time you want to change a particle system property.

Form Follows Function

Now that you've decided to make an editor, the next step is to decide how much time you want to spend on it. You can really go hog wild here, but I'd suggest keeping it simple—run in a window, use the Win32 API for your GUI, and only implement the most basic functionality. Keep the focus on making a tool, not on making something "cool." Sure, it can be slick, and it may need to be if you're distributing it to your end users (players)—but in general it doesn't have to be completely polished; it's being used primarily in-house.

You should also talk to the people who will be using your editor (lone wolfs can talk to themselves). Ask them about what features they'd like to see, and keep them in the loop as you add features. What I'm really talking about here is the software development process, and since many people have written many great books on this topic, I'll just leave it at that—keep your users in the loop, and they'll tell you what you need to develop.

Saving and Loading Particle System Properties

Enough of this design talk—let's write some code. Go ahead and open the `Ch18p2_ParticleProps` sample program to get started.

The heart and soul of the particle system editor is the code that saves and loads particle system properties. Fortunately, this is fairly simple stuff. Just write each property out in a format you'd like. My only suggestion is to make it human-readable, so that even if they don't have your particle system editor, your team can go in and edit a particle system using Notepad. I prefer a

human-readable text file that looks a lot like an INI file, but other choices (such as XML) are also cool. As always, in the end it comes down to what your requirements are, what you've worked with before, and just in general, what you like.

I'm not going to talk much about the `Save` function, because you should be able to follow it on your own. Essentially, it just calls `fprintf` to write out the property file in a format resembling an INI file.

> **TIP**
>
> I wrote these save and load routines to be as easily understandable as possible. So, I opted to use the C-style `FILE*` routines (`fprintf`, etc.). This is not the most "C++" way to do it—a better alternative would be to use the stream operators (`<<` and `>>`). You guessed it—this is left as an exercise for the reader.

The load method is much more interesting. This method has to correctly read and parse the properties file, and to do that requires a bit of text manipulation. Essentially, there are two steps: first, we read the entire file into an STL map. This gives us a set of property names (to the left of the equal sign) and their associated values (to the right of the equal sign). Once we have the map, we look for specific property names in it. We use the values we find to set the properties of our system.

Let's examine both of those steps in more detail.

Creating the Map

Here's a snippet of code taken from the Load method of CParticleEmitter, taken from the Ch18p2_ParticleEmitter.cpp.

```
// read the entire contents of file into a map.
int count=0;
while (!feof(file) && count < 1000) {
  // read a line
  fgets(buf, sizeof(buf), file);

  if (strlen(buf) >= 2) { // if there's something on that line,
    // separate that line into left and right side of = sign
    memset(leftside, 0, sizeof(leftside));
    memset(rightside, 0, sizeof(rightside));
    PluckFirstField(buf, leftside, sizeof(leftside), "=");
    PluckFirstField(buf, rightside, sizeof(rightside), "\n");

    if (valuemap.find(leftside) != valuemap.end()) {
      throw("Duplicate value encountered.");
    }
    // insert left and right sides into map.
    valuemap.insert(
      std::make_pair(std::string(leftside), std::string(rightside)));
  }
  // increment safety count
  count++;
}
if (count == 1000) {
  throw("File too big (most likely not a particle system file)");
}
```

The basic flow of this code goes something like: read a line into buf (blank lines are discarded). Presumably buf has an equal sign in it; using the PluckFirstField function, separate buf into the stuff to the left of the equal sign, and the stuff to the right. Put these in leftside and rightside.

The details of `PluckFirstField` aren't important; you give it a field delimiter (in this case, =), and it puts that field into the destination you specify (in this case, `leftside` or `rightside`). `PluckFirstField` also removes that field from `buf`, so that if before `buf` were `ThisProp=ThisValue`, after the first call (using = as a delimiter), `buf` would be `ThisValue`, and `ThisProp` would be in `leftside`. It plucks the field off the source string and puts it into the destination string.

> ### TIP
>
> **This code has virtually no error checking, and is generally fragile. For example, there's nothing that removes extra white space from the property names before checking for duplicates in the map.**
>
> **This code isn't written to be robust; it's written to teach a concept, and error checking would have obfuscated the main logic. I encourage you to add some error checking.**

After we have the left and right values, we check to see if a property by that name already exists in the map. If it does, we throw an error (because this is a syntax error—the user specified two different values for the same property). If we don't find any duplicates, we insert the pair into the map, and we move to the next line.

One last thing: we keep a count of the number of lines we've processed. This count is stored in the very aptly named variable, `count`. There's no way a real property file would come close to 1,000 lines in length, so if our count ever exceeds 1,000, we assume we're not reading a property file and we bail out. This prevents the system from locking and running out of memory if you accidentally throw it a wrong file.

Searching the Map and Setting Properties

After we've created our map, it's a simple thing to look through it for the specific properties we want. After creating the map, the `Load` method calls numerous `ReadProperty` overloads, which scan the map for the requested property (to the left side of the equal sign), extract the corresponding right-side text, and then put that extracted property into the appropriate variable.

I'm not going to go over this entirely, but I do want to step through the function named `GetRightSideFromValueMap`, which does most of the heavy lifting for all the `ReadProperty` functions. `GetRightSideFromValueMap` looks like this:

```
void CParticleEmitter::GetRightSideFromValueMap(
  std::map<std::string, std::string> &valuemap,
  const char *strName, char *dest, int destsize)
{
  std::string str;
  if (valuemap.find(strName) == valuemap.end()) {
    std::string errorstr;
```

```
    errorstr = std::string("Missing property \"") +
       std::string(strName) + std::string("\"!");
    throw(errorstr);
  }
  strncpy(dest, valuemap[strName].c_str(), destsize);
}
```

We hand GetRightSideFromValueMap several things—we give it a map of values to search through (valuemap), the name of the property we want (strName), and the destination buffer (dest) and its size (destsize). GetRightSideFromValueMap searches valuemap for strName; if it finds it, it puts the corresponding right-side text into dest. If it doesn't find it, it throws an error, which is caught by the top-level Load method.

Loading Code Wrap-Up

That's the tricky area in loading a particle system property file. Loading isn't anything terribly unwieldy, but it does have its rough points.

TIP

Yes, I know there are functions in Windows (GetPrivateProfileInt, etc.) that read and write INI files. I didn't use these because I wanted to show you the internal workings of parsing a text file, which you'll need when we get to the section on compiling a particle script. Besides, using these functions (already declared obsolete by Microsoft) to read files that don't have anything to do with program settings is bending the rules a bit, and creates apprehension in me.

However, they're worth checking out—you may decide that it's okay to use them in your game.

Presenting a GUI

The other important feature we need for our editor is a GUI. Essentially, we need a front-end so that we can easily edit our particle system properties, and see our results in real time.

I implemented my GUI as a big tool window, pictured in Figure 18.7.

This probably isn't the most efficient or sweet-looking GUI on the planet, but it gets the job done, and serves as a simple example.

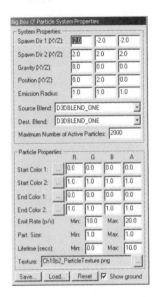

Figure 18.7

The GUI for my parti-cle editor is a simple tool window.

Creating a Tool Window (Really Just a Modeless Dialog)

The title says it all, really. If you know how to create a modeless dialog, then you know how to create a tool window. A careful combination of checks in the resource editor will turn a normal dialog box into a tool window—check out Figure 18.8.

I'm not going to talk about the rest of the work you need to do in the resource editor—you can layout your edit boxes and such however you'd like, and name them whatever makes sense to you.

Making a modeless dialog is surprisingly easy—all we need to do is create a dialog box (using the Win32 API function CreateDialog) inside our RestoreDeviceObjects method, and destroy that window (using DestroyWindow) when we do the rest of our clean up.

Here's the creation code:

```
// initialize the dialog
{
  g_theSystem = &m_PartSys; // so dialog box can get at it.
  m_hWndPropDlg = CreateDialog(NULL,
    MAKEINTRESOURCE(IDD_PARTICLEPROPS), m_hWnd,
    (DLGPROC) PropDlgProc);
  ShowWindow(m_hWndPropDlg, SW_SHOW);
}
```

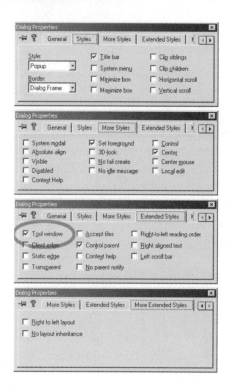

Figure 18.8

The set of checks that turn a normal dialog box into a tool window.

CreateDialog and ShowWindow are the dynamic duo of dialog creation. To create the dialog, we call CreateDialog, and pass it the resource ID of our dialog template (IDD_PARTICLEPROPS), the window handle of the parent of the dialog (m_hWnd), and the message processing procedure (PropDlgProc). The MAKEINTRESOURCE macro simply casts our integer resource ID into a LPTSTR, because that's what the API function is expecting. Remember, the Win32 API is C, and there's no notion of function overloading in C. If the Win32 API were C++, there would be two CreateDialog overloads— one that took an integer (which we would use), and another one that took a string (which most Windows programmers don't use).

One last thing I want to point out—the g_theSystem variable. PropDlgProc, our message-handling procedure, is a global function. We're going to be messing with the properties of our particle system from within this global function. We can't just access our particle system properties directly within our global

TIP

If you check the visible checkbox in the resource editor's dialog properties tab, you don't need the call to ShowWindow. However, since I always seem forget to do this and then end up spending time trying to debug why the dialog doesn't appear, I've gotten in the habit of always putting a ShowWindow call after my CreateDialog call.

function, because it doesn't belong to `CParticleEmitter`, and even if it did, it would have to be static method (aka, no `this` pointer). So, we setup a global pointer, `g_theSystem`, to point to the particle system we're editing, so that inside `PropDlgProc` we can get it by saying something like `g_theSystem->SetPos()`.

Message Processing Madness

A dialog box is just a window, and like all windows, it has a message processing function. It's inside this message processing function that we tie GUI actions to changes in our particle system. For example, our dialog's message processing procedure will receive an event whenever the contents of an edit box changes. When an edit box changes, we will need to read its new value, and plug that new value into the particle system (by calling the appropriate method of `CParticleEmitter`). For example, if we get an event saying that the edit box corresponding to the emission rate has changed, we will use a Win32 API call to get the contents of the edit box (as a string). Then, we will convert that string into a float, and we will use that float in our call to `g_theSystem->SetEmitRate()`.

That's essentially the pattern. Now, inside the actual code, I use a lot of little helper functions to avoid doing massive amounts of cut and paste. I have several helper functions that stuff primitive data types (floats, but also colors and vectors) into edit boxes. For example, there's a `Stuff3EditsIntoVector` function that reads the values of three different edit boxes and puts them into a 3D vector. There's also a `Stuff4EditsIntoColor` function that reads from four edit boxes— red, green, blue, and alpha, and creates a color from those values.

TIP

Little helper functions like these really make working with GUIs easier. If you do a lot of bare-bones Win32 GUI programming, you probably already have a set of very small (but very valuable) functions that automate the most routine aspects of working with the Windows GUI.

There are entire frameworks (such as the Microsoft Foundation Classes) that are designed to make GUI programming easier. People have mixed feelings about MFC— some swear by it, others consider it a bloated and over-designed waste of time.

I chose not to include it in this book because it isn't really a prerequisite for learning DirectX or special effects. However, if you're doing serious GUI development strictly in Windows, it's worth checking out. MFC has many features designed to present a more object-oriented view of the Windows GUI world.

Pushing Initial Values Into the GUI

There's one more thing you have to do before you have a basic GUI interface to your particle system. You know how to convert GUI edit boxes into particle system properties, but you also need to go the other way—you need to know how to convert particle system properties into GUI edit boxes. When your particle editor starts, the first thing it has to do is pump the default particle system properties into the modeless tool window. It also must pump new properties into the tool window whenever your user decides to load a particle system from disk.

Pushing values into the GUI is relatively easy—in the end, we're just using edit boxes, so it all comes down to pushing strings into those edit boxes using the Win32 API function SetWindowText.

CAUTION

Many Windows GUI programmers tend to write GUI code that follows a "read, validate, update" pattern. When an edit box changes, Windows generates a message. In response to that message, the GUI code first reads the new data out of the edit box. Then, it validates that data—for example, if someone has typed "asdf" into an edit box that is supposed to be a number, the validation code needs to do something about that—either ignore the change or perhaps treat "asdf" as "0". Finally, because the data may have changed when it was validated, the program also needs to update the GUI with the new (correct) data (in this case, pushing "0" into the edit box that previously contained "asdf").

This "read, validate, update" pattern is a fine paradigm, but you can get burned by stack overflow errors if you're not careful. The read and validate code are fine, but when the update code puts the new value back into the edit box, that triggers a Windows message, which, if you're not careful, will trigger the read code, inadvertently closing the circle and creating an infinite loop—not a good thing.

So, if you choose to employ the "read, validate, update" pattern of GUI coding, you need to put in some sort of mechanism that will break the circle. For example, the Ch18p2_ParticleProps program uses a Boolean flag that tells the system whether it should respond when Windows says "hey, your edit box changed." Before the update code starts pushing new values into the GUI, it sets this flag, effectively telling itself, "ignore these update messages, because they're coming from me." When it's finished updating, it flips the flag back so that it handles any future (actual) changes to the edit boxes' contents.

Such a method is only one way to do it. Just make sure you have something so that you don't enter an infinite loop.

Adding Flair—Putting Common Dialog Boxes to Use

We've got the basics down, and we've covered a lot of ground, but we don't really have a lot to show for it. At this point we have what's essentially a functional, but really irritating, GUI. By spending more time and harnessing the power of Windows Common dialog boxes, we could create a much more friendly GUI.

For example—we currently have four edit boxes that in tandem specify a color. That's a brutal interface, because our Particle Systems Artist (or Particle Systems Engineer, if you prefer) must know the red, green, and blue values

> **TIP**
>
> I gave a quick overview of Windows Common dialog boxes in Chapter 2, "Advanced Win32 API Programming." If you're not sure what a Common dialog is, flip back to that chapter and read through that section.

of the color they want. A much better interface would allow them to select a color on-screen, instead of worrying about RGB values. This is a great time to whip out the Windows Common Color dialog (see Figure 18.9).

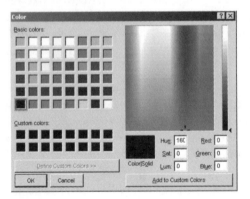

Figure 18.9

The Windows Common Color dialog.

Using the Common Color dialog is easier than you might think. Here's the code for a function that uses it:

```
void BrowseForColor(HWND hWnd, UINT idR, UINT idG, UINT idB, UINT idA)
{
  static COLORREF custcolors[16];
  CHOOSECOLOR cc;
  memset(&cc, 0, sizeof(cc));
  cc.lStructSize = sizeof(cc);
  cc.hwndOwner = hWnd;
```

```
cc.Flags = CC_RGBINIT | CC_FULLOPEN;
cc.lpCustColors = custcolors;
// get current values, convert to 0-255 range
D3DXCOLOR color = Stuff4EditsIntoColor(hWnd, idR, idG, idB, idA);
cc.rgbResult = D3DXColorTo255RGB(color);
if (ChooseColor(&cc)) {
  color.r = (float)GetRValue(cc.rgbResult) / 255.0f;
  color.g = (float)GetGValue(cc.rgbResult) / 255.0f;
  color.b = (float)GetBValue(cc.rgbResult) / 255.0f;
  StuffColorInto4Edits(color, hWnd, idR, idG, idB, idA);
}
}
```

This function presents a Common Color dialog box to the user, allows him to choose a color from it, and then puts the RGB value of that color into the three edit boxes with IDs idR, idG, idB, and idA. We don't really do anything with idA, the alpha component, because the Common dialog has no notion of an alpha value for colors.

The ChooseColor function does the heavy lifting—that's the Win32 API call that shows the Common Color dialog box. The code before the ChooseColor call sets up various elements of the CHOOSECOLOR structure that the ChooseColor function uses. We put our window handle into the structure. We call the Stuff4EditsIntoColor function to grab the color that's currently in the four edit boxes. Next, we use the D3DXColorTo255RGB function (my own creation) convert the D3DXColor (with floating-point RGB values in the range of 0.0 to 1.0) to a Win32 color (with integer RGB values in the range of 0 to 255). We put this value in the rgbResult structure member, so that ChooseColor selects it as the initial color (that's what the CC_RGBINIT flag is for).

Finally, we can call ChooseColor. If ChooseColor returns true, that means the user has selected a color and clicked OK, which in turn means that we need to grab the color they've selected (which ChooseColor puts in the rgbResult member of the structure), convert it back into a 0.0–1.0 range D3DXColor, and finally stuff that D3DXColor back into the four edit boxes.

One last thing to explain—the custcolors array, declared at the top of the function. ChooseColor needs an array of 16 COLORREF values, which act as storage spots for any custom colors the user sets up when inside the Common Color dialog box. We don't need to do anything other than provide space for these custom colors—ChooseColor does the rest. I've made the array static so that the user's custom colors are preserved for the life of the application.

Now we're on a roll. We've implemented one common dialog that will save our users all sorts of irritations as they're designing particle systems. Why stop now? Let's implement another one, a common file dialog, so that our user can easily browse for a texture filename (see Figure 18.10).

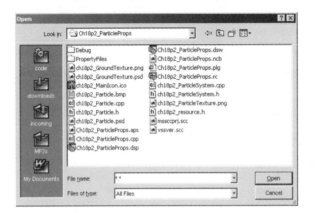

Figure 18.10

Browsing for a file-name—the common file dialog in action.

Here's the code for that:

```
OPENFILENAME ofn;        // common dialog box structure
char szFile[260];        // buffer for filename

// Initialize OPENFILENAME
ZeroMemory(&ofn, sizeof(OPENFILENAME));
ofn.lStructSize = sizeof(OPENFILENAME);
ofn.hwndOwner = hWnd;
strncpy(szFile, g_theSystem->GetTextureFilename().c_str(),
  sizeof(szFile));
ofn.lpstrFile = szFile;
ofn.nMaxFile = sizeof(szFile);
ofn.lpstrFilter = "PNG Files (*.png)\0*.png\0Bitmap Files
(*.bmp)\0*.bmp\0All Files (*.*)\0*.*\0\0";
ofn.lpstrFileTitle = "Choose Texture File";
ofn.Flags = OFN_PATHMUSTEXIST | OFN_FILEMUSTEXIST;
// Display the Open dialog box.
if (GetOpenFileName(&ofn)==TRUE) {
  g_theSystem->SetTexture(ofn.lpstrFile);
  SetWindowText(GetDlgItem(hWnd, IDC_TEXTURE),
    g_theSystem->GetTextureFilename().c_str());
}
```

Most of the work we need to do to use common file dialogs involves plugging the right things into the huge OPENFILENAME structure that GetOpenFileName, the Win32 API call that shows the dialog box, uses. We start by putting in the simple stuff—the size of the structure, and our window handle. Next, as a courtesy, we put our current texture filename into the lpstrFile structure member, which the Win32 API uses as the initial filename that's displayed in the dialog.

Next comes the filter string. This looks weird, but it follows a pattern. We're setting the values in the drop-down list at the bottom of the dialog (see Figure 18.11).

Each entry in the drop-down box has two strings associated with it—a description (for example, "All Files") and a mask (for example, "*.*"), as illustrated in Figure 18.12.

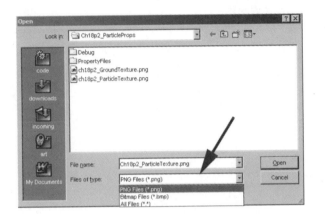

Figure 18.11

We're setting the values in this drop-down list.

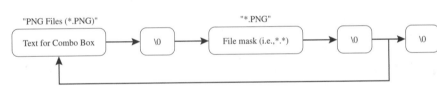

Figure 18.12

Layout of the string that specifies the drop-down list values.

We specify these two strings one right after the other, with a NULL character (\0) separating them. Two NULLs in a row tell Windows it's reached the end of the list. So, in the preceding code, I'm putting three entries into the combo box. The description of the first is "PNG Files (*.PNG)." Its mask is "*.PNG". The next description is "Bitmap Files (*.bmp)", with a mask of "*.bmp". Finally, I put in the obligatory "All Files (*.*)", with a mask of (surprise!) "*.*".

The rest of the structure filling code is easy. The lpstrFileTitle member holds the title of the dialog box, and the flags specify that the user must select a path and filename that actually exist.

If GetOpenFileName returns true, it means that the user has selected a file and clicked OK. Windows puts the file they selected in the lpstrFile member of the OPENFILENAME structure. It's as easy as that!

GUI Wrap-Up

Now that you've got the basic idea of how to write an editor, I encourage you to go wild and write something with a much cooler GUI on it. Here are a few ideas to get you warmed up:

- Replace the edit boxes with something niftier. For example, if you know that a certain property won't exceed a maximum value or fall below a minimum value, you could put a horizontal slider control in place of an edit box (see Figure 18.13).

Figure 18.13

A horizontal slider control.

- The tool window right now is pretty massive. You could make it smaller by organizing the controls into two sections—system properties and particle properties—and then creating a tab control with tabs that show the properties for each of those sections (see Figure 18.14).

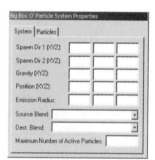

Figure 18.14

A hypothetical tab control for the particle system editor.

- You could put spin controls on your edit boxes (see Figure 18.15). Personally I think spin controls are something straight out of the Ninth Level of Hell, so I choose not to use them. But if you disagree, feel free to implement them.

Figure 18.15

Spin controls on the edit boxes!

Editor Wrap-Up

In this section we took a look at the basics of building a particle system editor, then went a bit further and used some nifty Win32 API features to make our GUI a little better. The code for all of this excitement, and more, can be found in the `Ch18p2_ParticleProps` sample program. I encourage you to check it out and become familiar with it now, before you dive into the advanced section.

CHAPTER WRAP-UP

As the saying goes, "we must be butter, because we're on a roll!" (Boo, hiss!)

You've got the basics of how a particle system works, and you have a good start on creating a GUI-driven particle system editor. At this point, you have several choices:

- If you're new to Win32 GUI programming and want to learn more, you may want to spend some time fiddling with the editor we've created here. It's the perfect environment to play with GUI programming.
- If you've never seen particle system code before, you need to make sure you fully understand what I've presented here before going on to the next chapter.
- You may want to spend some time and add additional properties and features to the particle system code I've given you. In the next chapter, I'm going to present some ideas on additional properties, but you probably already have a couple in mind right now.

Here are some additional resources for particle systems:

- www.particlesystems.com has a ton of information, mostly for non-real-time particle systems (used in 3D renderers like 3D Studio MAX). However, just because it's not written specifically for real-time stuff (games) doesn't mean you can't adapt the concepts.
- Richard Benson gave a great talk on particle systems for the 1999 XGDC (eXtreme Game Developer's Conference). He has posted the slides to his talk at http://home.earthlink.net/~rbenson/ParticleHTML/Particles_files/frame.htm.
- Jeff Lander wrote an excellent article on particle systems, called "The Ocean Spray in Your Face," for the July 1998 issue of *Game Developer Magazine*. It's considered by many to be the place to start reading to learn about particle systems.
- John Van der Burg wrote an article titled "Building an Advanced Particle System," accessible at http://www.gamasutra.com/features/20000623/vanderburg_01.htm. In it he discusses several advanced topics, including how to link a particle system into a 3D engine, and how to link multiple particle systems together underneath a particle manager.

ABOUT THE SAMPLE PROGRAMS

After all these chapters of me saying, "Nope, nothing new to report about the coding style," I bet you thought this chapter would say the same thing. Gotcha!

These aren't really coding style changes, but this chapter is the first in the section on 3D effects, so it makes sense to spend some time now enhancing our demo programs to accommodate the third dimension. There are several new things that we'll be using throughout this section, and I need to spend a quick few pages explaining them so that you're not confused and distracted by them as you learn the new particle system stuff.

Let's first look at the programs on tap for this chapter, and then we'll talk about the specific enhancements.

The Programs

This chapter comes with two fairly complex programs, one for each major section:

- **Ch18p1_SimpleParticles.** This sample program demonstrates particle systems, without any bells and whistles to distract you. You should be working through this while reading the section on particle system basics.
- **Ch18p2_ParticleProps.** Shows some additional particle system properties. This program also shows you one way to create a basic particle system editor—it shows how to create a modeless "particle properties" tool window that allows the user to edit the properties of the particle system and see the results of their editing in real time. Work with this as you read the section on creating a particle system editor.

Now let's take a look at the generic enhancements to support 3D.

A Camera Class

The most obvious new thing about this chapter's demos is that you can move around in them. The new camera code makes it easy for you to use the keyboard and mouse to move around the scene and take a peek at the action from any angle.

Camera Basics

All of the camera code ultimately is concerned with one thing—creating a view matrix. The camera code is responsible for taking the camera's position in 3D space, along with its current yaw, pitch, and roll settings, and creating from that a view matrix that we can plug into Direct3D to have it accurately render our scene.

It does this using a few simple quaternion calls:

```
// Set the view matrix
D3DXQUATERNION qR;
D3DXQuaternionRotationYawPitchRoll(&qR, m_fYaw, m_fPitch, m_fRoll);
D3DXMatrixAffineTransformation(&m_matOrientation, 1.25f,
  NULL, &qR, &m_vPosition );
D3DXMatrixInverse( &m_matView, NULL, &m_matOrientation );
```

These function calls shield you from a lot of math going on behind the scenes. Without derailing into how quaternions work, here's what we do: we create a quaternion and populate it using the camera's current yaw, pitch, and roll (the m_fYaw, m_fPitch, and m_fRoll). We then transform that quaternion into an orientation matrix by supplying the camera's position in 3D space. Finally, we invert that orientation matrix to get our view matrix. Again, we don't need to go into the mathy details of how this all works right now (although it certainly is fascinating).

This new camera functionality is encapsulated entirely by a C++ class called CUserControlledCamera.. CUserControlledCamera's job is to keep track of the camera's position and orientation, and spit out a view matrix when asked.

Inside CUserControlledCamera, to keep track of the camera's position, we use a vector called m_vPosition. We also have three additional floating-point numbers, m_fYaw, m_fPitch, and m_fRoll, which keep track of the orientation of the camera.

Mouselook

Now that we have a camera class that can convert its position, along with its yaw, pitch, and roll, into a view matrix, it becomes really easy to create a mouselook system. Movement along the mouse's x-axis corresponds to changes in the camera's yaw; y-axis mouse movement means changes to the camera's pitch.

The camera's roll isn't controlled with the mouse (at least in this "Quake-esque" style of mouselook—I've seen other styles of mouselook that mess with the roll).

So, implementing mouselook in code is as easy as taking the mouse's relative x- and y-axis movements, and converting those into camera yaw/pitch changes, like so:

```
// mouse look
DIMOUSESTATE2 dims2;
m_InputManager.ReadMouse(dims2);
m_Camera.AddToYawPitchRoll(
  (float)dims2.lX/0.8f,
  (float)dims2.lY/0.8f,
  0.0f);
```

This section of code, from CMyD3DApplication::ProcessInput(), begins by reading the mouse, as described in Chapter 3, "DirectX." After the call to ReadMouse, the mouse's relative x and y movement is stored in dims2.lX and dims2.lY. The code simply tells the camera class to add the movement to the camera's yaw and pitch. And you thought mouselook was difficult!

The Ground Plane

One last thing—I put a ground plane in most of the 3D sample programs as a point of reference. Seeing ground allows you to orient yourself in 3D space much easier than if you're just floating in space. So, I made a `CGroundPlane` class, responsible for creating and keeping track of the ground's texture handle, vertex buffer, and so on. Most of the 3D sample programs use this `CGroundPlane` class to draw the ground.

I draw the ground as a vertex grid, complete with an index buffer—very similar to what we learned how to do for image warping back in Chapter 14, "Image Warping." I've played with the texture coordinates a little, so that the ground texture is tiled across the vertex grid, instead of stretched.

Other than that, the code and concepts are the same. A quick glance at the source and header files should be all you need to attain complete understanding.

EXERCISES

1. Modify a sample program so that it uses dynamically allocated particles. In other words, instead of using a fixed-size array, make the program `new` particles when it needs them and `delete` them when it's done (or, if you're more into strict C programming, use `malloc` and `free`). See for yourself why dynamic memory isn't a good choice here.
2. Change the save and load code for the particle system, to make it use the stream C++ operators, << and >>, instead of the old C stuff.
3. When rendering the particles in a particle system, what "chunk size" creates the highest frame rate? 10%? 20%? 70%? Find the optimal number, and figure out how big of an additional speed gain that optimal number creates.
4. Experiment around with the three rendering states that control how Direct3D calculates the size of a point sprite (`D3DRS_POINTSCALE_A`, `D3DRS_POINTSCALE_B`, and `D3DRS_POINTSCALE_C`). Do you see a need to make your particle system flexible enough to handle these different size calculation factors? I didn't; you might.

CHAPTER 19

Advanced Particle Systems

"Powers of observation lie with the mind,
Luke, not with the eyes."
—*Obi Wan Kenobi*

e ended the last chapter after learning how to create a nice, user-friendly editor for our particle system. Have you got a good handle on all that GUI code we talked about? Good—now throw it all out the window! (Now is the time to throw your head back and gasp dramatically, so that everyone around you thinks you're reading something containing plot twists and drama.)

We're going to spend this chapter talking about Ch19p1_AdvancedPartSys, the advanced demo contained on your CD, so go ahead and fire up that sample program. The first thing you'll notice is that the GUI we spent so much time developing in the previous chapter isn't around any longer. Instead, we just have a big edit box alongside our 3D view (see Figure 19.1).

The big edit box is where we can input a particle system script. Stop reading for a bit and play around with the new script-based editor—you can load up some sample scripts from the Scripts directory to test drive it.

Figure 19.1

Hey, where did the GUI go?

MAKING AN ADVANCED PARTICLE SYSTEM

This chapter's main focus is on creating what I call scriptable particle systems. We're going to take the existing particle system code from the last chapter and do two things. First, we're going to enhance it by giving our particles and particle systems a few extra properties. Second, we're going to look at a different and, in my opinion, more flexible paradigm for particle systems—the script.

Adding Flexibility to the Current System

We want the most bang for our buck. Translated into this context, that means we want as flexible a particle system as we can get, but still keeping the code lean and mean. By moving to a script-based paradigm, we have freed ourselves from having to maintain a complex GUI—a GUI that fronts the same amount of flexibility of our scripts would require several complex dialogs.

The reason for this complexity has to do with arrays. Take, for example, the particle color property. In the last chapter we could specify a start color and an end color. Not bad, but not flexible either—what if we were creating a fire ember that we wanted to start white, fade to yellow, then orange, then red, then black? Similarly, what if we wanted the size or velocity of the particle to change?

Now, we could tackle these enhancements on a case-by-case basis. Changing the color member from a single variable into an STL vector of colors would take some code, but it's nothing that would take days of effort. It is the same thing with the particle size and the velocity.

So now, instead of just a simple particle with a core set of properties, we now have a more intelligent particle that can change over time. For example, we might go from this code:

```
class CParticle {
  /* snip */
protected:
  D3DXCOLOR m_StartColor;
  D3DXCOLOR m_EndColor;
};
```

Into this code:

```
class CColorChange {
public:
  float m_fTime;
  D3DXCOLOR m_NewColor;
};
```

```
class CParticle {
  /* snip */
protected:
  std::vector<CColorChange> m_ColorChanges;
};
```

In other words, we've gone from a simple start color and end color (m_StartColor and m_EndColor) into an arbitrary number of color changes, each associated with a particular time. That's a more flexible method.

Now, imagine also if we did something similar with all of the other particle properties. At first it might seem that we would have a pretty good solution, but on closer examination we would realize we messed up because all of the code that kept these vectors arranged neatly and in order would be duplicated for each property. We would have to loop through the color vector of every frame, and see if there were any changes to process. Then, we would have to do the same thing with the vector of sizes and the vector of velocities. Not good—we would have code duplicated all over the place.

Events

There's a better way to achieve that same sort of flexibility, but it requires a different mode of thinking. Instead of having a vector for each individual property, just have the particle contain one big vector that contained all of the changes—color changes, size changes, whatever.

Polymorphism comes to our rescue here. Imagine an abstract base class, CEvent, which defined a pure virtual function that "applied" the event to a particle:

```
class CEvent {
public:
  virtual void DoItToIt(CParticle &part) = 0;
protected:
  float m_fTime; // time the event occurs
};
```

Each CEvent derivative would implement DoItToIt differently—the DoItToIt method of a CColorChangeEvent would apply a new color to the given particle, while other event derivatives might mess with the particle's size or color. Since all events need to be associated with a certain time in the particle's life, we would add a time member to the CEvent base class.

With this design in place, things become a lot easier to manage. The particle just keeps a vector of CEvent derivatives.

Event Sequences

Or does it? It's easy to see how this change gives our particle system a lot more flexibility, but we don't have to stop there. Imagine that we wanted to extend our fire particle system so that it generated not only embers, but smoke as well. The embers would have one event sequence—their colors would change from white, to yellow, orange, and red. But the smoke particles would have a very different sequence of events: they might start out opaque gray, but slowly turn black and become transparent.

To handle this level of flexibility, we would need our particle system as a whole to keep track of several different vectors of events. Whenever a new particle was born, the system would decide which event sequence it would use. We could set up some additional properties governing how the system decided on the event sequence—we could assign a probability to each event sequence in our system. For example, we could say that a particle has a 25% chance of becoming an ember and a 75% chance of becoming smoke.

As you can see from the architecture overview shown in Figure 19.2, we're about to do some drastic things to our particle system.

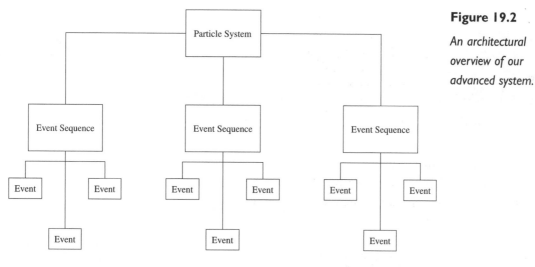

Figure 19.2

An architectural overview of our advanced system.

We are going to add the concept of events. Each event is essentially a particle property change bound to a time. Next, we're going to add the notion of event sequences, which are vectors of events that tell the particle how to behave over the course of its life. Finally, we're going to create a vector of event sequences, and write code to make the particle system randomly assign each created particle to a particular event sequence. Implementing these enhancements will create a particle system capable of handling many very different types of effects.

Goodbye, GUI

Now that we've decided on a more flexible design, we need to think about what this means for our user interface. I spent a lot of time kicking around ideas, but finally came to the conclusion that the best thing to do was eliminate the GUI entirely. If we kept the GUI, we would need to make separate dialogs to configure each event, plus more dialogs to handle adding, editing, and deleting event sequences. Additionally, we would need to add dialogs each time we wanted to add a new event or particle property.

That's a lot of GUI work, and while it's certainly doable, I didn't want to spend a lot of time in this book working through it. Instead, I opted to do away with the GUI entirely and rely on a very simple, text-based scripting "language" instead. I put the word language in quotes because what we'll be creating isn't really a language—it has no concept of variables, loops, conditionals, etc. In fact, at the end of this chapter we'll end up with something more like a really complex property file (like the .X file format) than a true scripting language. However, the foundation will be in place. If you decide to take what's presented here and enhance it, adding support for language features, you could very well end up with a "real" language.

Also, there are a couple of fringe benefits to doing things this way. By writing code to read in and parse a complex properties file, you should learn several things about how DirectX reads X files, and a little about how it handles shader compiling. You also will end up with a good library of routines should you ever need to create other complex, text-based property file formats.

The Birth of a Simple Scripting Language

I started designing the property file format by launching Notepad and just typing things. Right away, I realized that the first order of business was to create a hierarchy of events and event sequences. I decided that the top level of this hierarchy should be the particle system itself; contained within the particle system would be the event sequences, and contained within the sequences would be the events. So, let's do that.

A good way to separate these sections is to use curly braces—{ and }. After all, in C++, curly braces were used to contain code chunks inside parent code. This leads us to a very rough skeleton that looks something like this:

```
ParticleSystem {
  EventSequence 1 {
    Event 1 {
      /* event properties */
    }
```

```
      Event 2 {
        /* event properties */
      }
    }
    EventSequence 2 {
      Event 1 {
        /* event properties */
      }
      Event 2 {
        /* event properties */
      }
    }
  }
}
```

This is good, but that's a lot of braces. Let's forego using braces for the events, and use equal signs instead:

```
ParticleSystem {
  EventSequence 1 {
    Event 1 = /* event properties */
    Event 2 = /* event properties */
    }
  }
  EventSequence 2 {
    Event 1 = /* event properties */
    Event 2 = /* event properties */
    }
  }
}
```

We should also define some completely arbitrary ground rules for the script:

- White space doesn't matter. Just like in C/C++, things may be separated by any number of newline characters, tabs, and spaces.
- Two forward slashes in a row denote a line comment, just as they do in C++.
- Our properties file is case insensitive; however, it should preserve the case of any string literals (such as names of things) it comes across.

That gives us a fairly good skeleton on which to hang everything, but before we can start draping properties onto these bones, we need to clean house a bit.

The Property Shuffle

We ended the last chapter with a particle system containing several different properties. Now that we have this new notion of events and event sequences, we need to take another peek at all of those properties and determine where they fit. Are they an event? Are they a property of a given event sequence? Or, are they a property of all event sequences, that is, of the particle system itself?

The flexibility of our system depends directly on which of these three levels get which properties. For example, take gravity, currently a property of the particle system. We could choose to put gravity on one of three levels:

- **Event Level.** On this level, each particle keeps track of its own gravity value. Gravity is a property of the particle itself.
- **Sequence Level.** On this level, gravity is a property of an event sequence. This means that all particles belonging to the same event sequence share the same gravity.
- **System Level.** On this level, gravity is a property of the particle system as a whole. All particles share one gravity value, regardless of which event sequence they belong to.

So, which one do we want? In this case, my choice was to have gravity on the event sequence level. In other words, I decided to make gravity be a property of an event sequence. I chose this because, to me, it seemed like having a per-particle gravity setting was overkill. On the other hand, I could see situations where I'd want one set of particles to fall, and another set of particles to rise (for example, in a fire particle system, the embers would fall but the smoke would rise). This told me it was wrong to make gravity a property of the particle system as a whole.

Essentially, we have to make that decision for each particle property and each particle system property from the last chapter. As always, we'll need to strike a balance between flexibility and code complexity. Making all of these properties events creates a very flexible system, but also one that is needlessly complex. Conversely, putting all of these properties at the particle system level creates a very simple system, but one that can't do much.

Table 19.1 shows how I've chosen to organize the properties.

In my mind, this strikes the best balance between flexibility and complexity. You may have a different idea—the important thing is that you go through the process of design up front, so that you end up implementing something that's going to serve you well.

The Element of Randomness

Sheesh! More design! Be patient, we're almost there!

Now that we have the properties grouped, we need to think about one last thing—randomness. Inside our property file, it's not acceptable to just say that each particle has a size; we need to say "all particles have a size between this and that," and let the particle engine decide on a random

Table 19.1 Property Shuffle

Property	Level
Particle System Position	Particle System
Emit Rate	Event Sequence
Source Blending Mode	Event Sequence
Destination Blending Mode	Event Sequence
Lifetime	Event Sequence
Texture	Event Sequence
Emission Radius	Event Sequence
Gravity	Event Sequence
Spawn Direction	Event Sequence
Color	Event
EventTimer	Event
Size	Event
Velocity	Event
Position	Event

value within that range when the time comes. To accommodate randomness, then, all we need to do from a property file standpoint is make sure that we store ranges for properties, instead of just numbers. For example, instead of just saying that the property "size" is an int, we say it's two ints—a minimum size and a maximum size. The particle system code takes care of picking a value in this range when it needs to.

We can also extend this to colors and vectors, since colors are ultimately just four numbers lumped together (RGBA) and vectors are three numbers lumped together (x,y,z).

Planning It Out: BNF Grammar

Now we have everything we need to start mapping out all of these properties into a set of rules that define our properties file. To do this, we're going to borrow a technique from compiler design, called BNF Grammar. BNF stands for Backus Naur Form. A BNF grammar, commonly used to create compilers, is a way of writing down rules specifying what's legal syntax and what isn't. I've found that it's really easy to write complex property file parsing code if you have a grammar in front of you (and conversely, it's really hard without one), so we're going to invest time up front for design (always a good idea), and write a grammar.

> **TIP**
>
> I've taken liberties on the BNF Grammar notation standards a little, so don't get freaked out if you happen to be a BNF expert and see weird things in my grammar.

A grammar, written out, is simply a series of equality statements, combined with some logic operators. At its simplest, it allows us to say stuff like "this thing is either this, or this, but nothing else."

I've found that the easiest way to construct a grammar is to start with the simple things and then build your way up. Another equally valid approach is to start at the top and build down—whichever is easiest for you. Going from the bottom up is easier for me, so that's what I'm going to walk you through in the next few pages.

We can start defining our grammar by defining what a Number is, so that later we can define the other data types in terms of Numbers—in other words, we can say things like "a Vector is three Numbers" or "a Color is four Numbers." Once we have all the data types defined, we'll zoom out a little more, and start defining properties in terms of the data types—"ParticleColor is a Color" or "Velocity is a Vector." We'll continue doing this until we finally have the entire format of the property file specified.

Then, once we have all of the definitions, we can start with the code. For example, we could write a function called ReadNumber that reads in a Number from our properties file. Then, we could implement the function that reads a Vector (with three calls to ReadNumber), followed by the function to read a Velocity, and so on.

Starting Simple—What's a Number?

So, let's start simple. Here's a line from our grammar, specifying what a RealNumber is, and what a Number is:

```
RealNumber ::= --< float datatype >--
Number ::=  <RealNumber> | Random(<RealNumber>,<RealNumber>)
```

The first line simply says "a RealNumber is a float." I've used a special syntax (not standard BNF Grammar) to denote C++ primitive types. I could have written out the actual definitions for floats and other primitive types, but there's no value in doing that—once we know something's a float, we know enough to parse and load that item effectively. For example, there's no reason for me to specify that a float is one or more numbers, optionally followed by a decimal point, then more numbers, when realistically the C API function atof is going to handle all those details for me anyway.

So, the first line just aliases RealNumber to float. It says, "A RealNumber is a float." The next line is a little more complex. In this BNF Grammar, the pipe symbol, |, means "or," and anything in < > angle brackets denotes another BNF definition. Anything without angle brackets is literal—we're expecting that string or character at that exact point.

So, we're defining Number as either a RealNumber, or the string "Random," followed by an opening parenthesis, followed by a RealNumber, a comma, another RealNumber, and a closing parenthesis. This means, for example, that a number is either "0.5", or "Random(1.0,2.0)".

Vectors Are Just Numbers

Can you see what I'm doing here? I'm essentially designing in the ability for the user to write "Random(min,max)" anywhere I'm expecting a number in my properties file. To more clearly illustrate this, let's look at the definition for a vector:

```
Vector ::= XYZ(<Number>,<Number>,<Number>)
```

Here, you can see that a vector is made up of the string "XYZ," followed by an open parenthesis, but then it gets interesting. We specify that next come three Numbers, separated by commas. Here's the neat part: because we've already defined a Number as either a RealNumber (float), or as this Random thing, we have given the property file writer the ability to specify random ranges wherever they would like. This means that all of the following are valid vector specifications:

```
XYZ(0, 1, 0) // straight up
XYZ(0, Random(-1,1), 0) // either straight up or down
XYZ(Random(-1,1), 1, 0) // up and to the left or right
XYZ(Random(-1,1), Random(-1,1), Random(-1,1)) // any direction!
```

This is one of the reasons I chose to make a property file interface for this advanced particle system, instead of a GUI. A GUI that captured this flexibility would have been somewhat complex, whereas this property file solution (to me, at least) seems like a much more intuitive way to specify things. In fact, you could almost call it programming!

Also, keep in mind that we can easily specify the places we need a concrete number, and not a random number range, by putting RealNumber instead of Number into our grammar file. For example, if for some bizarre reason we didn't want to allow a random number range on the X component of our vector, we could write the following:

```
Vector ::= XYZ(<RealNumber>,<Number>,<Number>)
```

See how the first thing after the opening parenthesis is a RealNumber instead of a Number? That means we are expecting only a number—no randoms allowed.

The Other Primitive Data Types

Moving right along, here's some more grammar that defines the rest of the data types we will be using in our properties file:

```
Name ::= "{--< char >--}"
AlphaBlendMode ::= D3DBLEND_ZERO |
                   D3DBLEND_ONE |
                   D3DBLEND_SRCCOLOR |
                   D3DBLEND_INVSRCCOLOR |
                   D3DBLEND_SRCALPHA |
                   D3DBLEND_INVSRCALPHA |
                   D3DBLEND_DESTALPHA |
                   D3DBLEND_INVDESTALPHA |
                   D3DBLEND_DESTCOLOR |
                   D3DBLEND_INVDESTCOLOR |
                   D3DBLEND_SRCALPHASAT
Color ::= RGBA(<Number>,<Number>,<Number>,<Number>)
VersionNumber ::= <RealNumber>
```

Let's walk through that quickly. That top line is probably the most confusing, so let's take it apart piece by piece. We are defining a Name, and the first thing we are expecting is a quote. After that though we have this funny {A-Z,a-z,0-9}* business. The curly braces mean "zero or more things from this set." Inside the set we have a C++ char data type, so, from the beginning, the line reads, "A Name is a quote, followed by zero or more chars, followed by a quote."

Of course! What we are effectively doing is saying that a Name is a string of letters and numbers, enclosed in quotes. Simply put, Name is our property file's string data type!

The next definition is easier. We are just saying that AlphaBlendMode is one of several different literals. This is basically an enumeration—we are saying "these are the only things that are legal anywhere we are expecting an AlphaBlendMode."

Next, we define a Color, as simply RGBA(followed by four Numbers separated by commas, ending with a close parenthesis. Again, remember that a Number is either a simple "0.5" affair, or it's something like "Random(0,1)," so we're allowing our property file writer to specify random ranges here.

Finally we have VersionNumber. This chunk of grammar started hard, but ends easy—VersionNumber is just another name for a RealNumber.

The View from the Top of the Grammar, Down

So, those are our primitive data types. We've specified the little things, and in so doing we've created a set of building blocks we can use to create the more complex statements. Now, let's shift perspective a little and look at the very top of the grammar tree.

The whole point of the properties file is to specify a particle system. So, this definition sits at the very top of the tree:

```
ParticleSystem ::= ParticleSystem <VersionNumber> <Name>
  "{" {<SysProperty>} {<EventSequence>} "}"
```

This definition says that a `ParticleSystem` starts with the string "`ParticleSystem`," followed by a version number, a name, and an open brace, {. (Notice that the open brace is in quotes to distinguish it from the BNF open brace meaning "repeat.") Next come one or more `SysProperties` and one or more `EventSequences` (remember, these braces, without quotes, mean "repeat"). Finally, the particle system is closed by a closing brace, }.

So, according to that grammar, the simplest particle system we can create is something like this:

```
ParticleSystem 1.00 "SimpleParticleSystem" { }
```

That won't do anything—a particle system will be created with the default values for every property.

So, that's the top level grammatical entry. Now let's look at the definitions for `SysProperty` and `EventSequence`:

```
SysProperty ::= <VectorProperty> = <Vector>
EventSequence ::= EventSequence <Name> "{" {<SeqProperty>} {<Event>}
"}"
```

`SysProperty` is fairly easy—it's just something called a `VectorProperty`, followed by an equal sign, and then a `Vector`. `EventSequence` is more complex—it's the string "`EventSequence`," followed by a `Name`, an {, any number of `SeqProperties`, and any number of `Events`, ending with a }.

Now that I've set you in motion, I'll sit back and let you deduce the rest of the file structure. Follow each new definition you come across and you will eventually end up down at a primitive data type. See how the grammar has enabled us to dice up a very complex property file format into little manageable chunks?

Notice also that essentially, the flow of the grammar follows the flow of code. Immediately after the code opened the text file, it would try to match against a `ParticleSystem` definition—it would expect the string "`ParticleSystem`," followed by a version number, and so on as specified in our

ParticleSystemDefinition. When it got to the {EventSequence} spot, it would enter a while loop that repeatedly called a function named, say, ProcessEventSequenceBlock.

Now we would be at the EventSequence line in our grammar. ProcessEventSequenceBlock would eventually call a function to process an Event, and we would enter a new subroutine (and move down to a new definition in the grammar). Writing each individual processing function is easy, because we have a grammar that tells us exactly what to look for, and when to look for it.

Events

Tying an event to a particular time in a particle's life is the core task around which all of this other stuff is built, so it's important that we make sure we handle this in the most flexible way possible. In particular, we need a syntax that makes it easy to see when each event occurs. Here's a brief description of how I designed my grammar to solve this problem.

I decided that the easiest way to implement the events was to use an at keyword, so that the events would appear to be sentences. For example, if we wanted to change the particle's color to red after one second of its life, I decided a line like the following was fairly intuitive:

```
at 1.0 color = RGBA(1,0,0,1)
```

Here, the at keyword designates an event. The number immediately after the at is the number of seconds into the particle's life when the event occurs (in this case, one second). Anything after that number is the event itself. I decided to let the exact syntax from that point on vary depending on the event. All of the events we are actually going to code take the form of a simple assignment—a particle property, followed by an equal sign, followed by the new value for that particle, that is, "color = RGBA(1,0,0,1), but it doesn't have to be that way. For example, if we had an event that changed two particle properties simultaneously, we might want to use something other than the equal sign construct. I decided that as long as the events fit on one line, they should be able to take whatever format is most intuitive.

I also wanted an intuitive way to set the starting and ending values for the particle properties. When you think about it, you can set all of your starting properties by creating events that fire zero seconds into the particle's life. However, writing something like the following seemed non-intuitive:

```
at 0.0 color = RGBA(1,0,0,1)
```

Sure, this sets the particle's color to red as soon as it's created, but I decided to improve the readability of the scripts slightly, by creating an initial keyword that stood for at 0.0, so that the property file could contain lines like this:

```
initial color = RGBA(1,0,0,1)
```

This seemed much more intuitive to me.

Dealing with Fades

Just setting properties is fun, but it's not very useful. The particle system of yester-chapter gave us the ability to fade between a starting an ending color. I wanted to expand on that for this chapter, and give this chapter's particle system the ability to fade between any two properties through any specified time.

Essentially, what I wanted was a way to say "this event doesn't happen instantly, instead, it fades in over time." This led me to create a fade so key-phrase for my grammar. Here's an example of how fade so works:

```
initial color = RGBA(1,0,0,1)
fade so at 2.0 color = RGBA(0,0,1,1)
```

The two preceding lines should create a particle that starts out red and slowly fades to blue, so that by the time it's two seconds old, it's completely blue.

Also, I wanted the capability to do more complex fades, such as the following:

```
initial color = RGBA(1,0,0,1)
fade so at 2.0 color = RGBA(0,0,1,1)
fade so at 3.0 color = RGBA(0,1,0,0)
fade so at 4.5 color = RGBA(0,0,0,0)
```

In those four lines, you can see that the particle is supposed to start out red, fade to blue, then green, and finally black/transparent, so that when it's 4.5 seconds old it's pure RGBA(0,0,0,0).

The Final Keyword

With the ability to fade came the issue of how to specify an ending property. Notice that our grammar gives the property file creator flexibility when setting particle lifetimes. Thanks to our Number definition, the author can say LifeTime = 5, or they can say LifeTime = Random(5,10).

This makes it impossible to use the at keyword to create an event that happens exactly at the end of the particle's lifetime. Say we wanted to make the particle fade to black as it died. Since we can't know for sure how long the particle is going to live, we can't simply write a fade so at line, because we're lacking something to put in the time field.

This stumped me for a while, until I realized that the way around it was to simply create a new keyword, final, that stood for the end of the particle's life. This allowed me to write a line like the following:

```
fade so final color = RGBA(0,0,0,0)
```

That gave me an easy and intuitive way to fade a certain particle property to a final value. The particle processing code would be responsible for substituting final with the lifetime of the specific particle being processed.

Note that we could have just as easily faded the particle size, causing it to shrink into oblivion:

```
fade so final size = 0
```

Nothing to it!

Rudimentary Loops: The `EventTimer` Property

The ability to create random particle lifetimes also threw a monkey wrench into another feature. Based on what we have now, we can create particles that change color in a timed pattern—for example, starting out red, then turning green after one second, blue after two, and so on.

However, what we can't really do is loop the color pattern, because again we don't know specifically how long the particle will live. Say, for example, that we wanted a particle to blink between red and blue every second, so that at zero seconds it would be red, and one second blue, two seconds red, three seconds blue, and so on. Now granted, if we knew that our particle lifetime was Random(2,3) we could just expand the loop out for three seconds, guaranteeing that even the oldest possible particles would follow the pattern until they died:

```
initial color = RGBA(1,0,0,1)
at 1.0 color = RGBA(0,0,1,1)
at 2.0 color = RGBA(1,0,0,1)
at 3.0 color = RGBA(0,0,1,1)
```

That works for a particle with a maximum three-second lifespan, but what if the particle could live for 10 or 20 seconds? It's wasteful to have to write out 20 lines of the same two events, alternating.

It became clear to me that what would be really cool is if you could play with the ages of each particle. This led me to create a new particle property called EventTimer. When the particles are born, both their EventTimer and their lifetime are set to zero. EventTimer increments in the exact same way that the particle's lifetime does. The difference is that you can create an event that "resets" the EventTimer back to a certain value. Also, every time specified in every at event line is no longer compared against the particle's lifetime, but is instead compared against the EventTimer. This gives you some very primitive looping capabilities:

```
initial color = RGBA(1,0,0,1)
at 1.0 color = RGBA(0,0,1,1)
at 2.0 color = RGBA(1,0,0,1)
at 3.0 EventTimer = 1
```

Follow the flow of this: at `EventTimer` = 0 seconds (the `initial` keyword), the particle is red. At `EventTimer` = one second, it turns blue. At `EventTimer` = two seconds, it turns red again. At `EventTimer` = three, `EventTimer` is reset to one, which causes the blue event at one to fire, changing the particle back to blue. One second later, `EventTimer` is back to two, and the particle changes to red. See how resetting the event timer has looped the pattern?

> **TIP**
>
> Keep in mind that throughout all of this, the particle's lifetime is forever stepping forward, and can't be set backwards. So at the end of the preceding walk-through, the `EventTimer` is set to two, but the particle's lifetime is four, because the lifetime wasn't ever reset to zero. This allows us to maintain accurate aging and destruction of particles, regardless of what pattern their `EventTimer`s are forcing them to follow.

The First Steps to Writing the Property File Loader

So, we're feeling pretty smug. We're armed with a complete grammar for our properties file, and we've addressed how we're going to maintain all of the functionality from last chapter's simple particle system. We've also added a couple of additional events and grammatical constructs that make our system much more flexible than what we had last chapter.

Now, our mission is clear: write code that reads in the entire properties file and translates it into a particle system object (that contains any number of event sequence objects, that each contain any number of events). Oh, and parse specific event level, event sequence level, and particle system level properties, too. After that, we'll change the `Update` function so that it uses and acts on the appropriate vector of events—but that's a topic that can wait for a few pages.

For now, let's just concentrate on getting the property file loaded. That alone sounds like a tall order, but it's doable and actually quite easy, provided we know how to do a couple of things up front.

Dealing with White Space and Comments

The first issue we need to deal with is white space. Somehow we need to disregard all the white space and just pick out the things we're looking for—text strings, opening and closing braces/parentheses, and so on. It's not enough to just blindly remove any whitespace characters, because we need to keep the white space potentially embedded in strings (that is, if someone names a particle system "My Cool System," we don't want to change it to "MyCoolSystem" inadvertently).

At the same time, we need to somehow deal with the comments. It would be nice to simply remove them before we get started with the code that actually used the grammar to walk through the file and convert text lines into objects or properties of objects.

It turns out we can kill both these birds with one stone: a chunk of code called a tokenizer, or, if we were writing a real compiler, a preprocessor. I'm going to go with the term tokenizer because tokens remind me of Chuck E. Cheese's, one of my favorite hangouts as a kid.

Essentially, a tokenizer takes as input a big text string (say, the contents of a properties file), and creates as output a vector of "tokens." A token is like an atom; it's the smallest "thing" defined by our grammar. Tokens may be numbers, like "10.05," strings, like "This is a string" (notice the white space in there), or they may be single characters, like {, }, = , (,), etc.

Here's a class definition for a token:

```
class CParticleEmitterToken {
public:
  std::string m_strValue;
  enum TokenType m_Type;
 /* member functions snipped */
};
```

Each token has a type, which we use when we actually process the grammar file. For example, a token may be a Name and contain the string MyParticleSystemName, or it may be a RealNumber and contain the string 10.05. Here are all of the token types we'll be using:

```
enum TokenType {
  // the basics
  RealNumber = 1,
  Equals, Comma, OpenParen, CloseParen, OpenBrace, CloseBrace,
  Quote,
  // keywords
  KeywordParticleSystem, KeywordEventSequence, KeywordRandom,
  KeywordXYZ, KeywordColor, KeywordTexture, AlphaBlendMode,
  // system property tokens
  SysVectorProp, SeqAlphaBlendModeProp,

  // event time tokens
  KeywordFade, KeywordSo, KeywordAt, KeywordInitial, KeywordFinal,

  // particle properties (event types)
  ParticleNumericProp, ParticleVectorProp, ParticleColorProp,
```

```
   // event sequence props
   SeqNumericProp, SeqVectorProp,
   Unknown
};
```

We'll use the type to validate that the property file is syntactically correct—for example, if we're processing a RealNumber, and we're at a token with type Keyword and contents Random, we expect that the next token will be of type OpenParen, and the one after that will of type RealNumber. If not, we've got a syntax error.

Let's create a class, CParticleEmitterTokenizer, whose sole responsibility is to convert a text stream into a vector of tokens. Follow along in the source code if you like, by opening Ch19p1_ParticleEmitterTokenizer in your IDE.

Creating the Tokenizer

The process of taking a text string and converting it into a vector of tokens is actually pretty simple, because we can use a very simple state machine to do the work. For those of you unfamiliar with a state machine, think of a traffic light. It can only be in one of three states—red, yellow, or green. It also has rules that define its behavior—for example, there's a rule that says it can't go from red to yellow, or from yellow to green—it must progress from red to green, green to yellow, yellow to red, then back to red to green (see Figure 19.3).

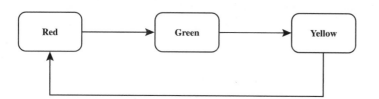

Figure 19.3

A traffic light is a simple state machine.

Our tokenizer code is a state machine summarized in the flowchart (see Figure 19.4).

Since this is a fairly complex chart, let's spend some time going through each process and decision.

The basic flow involves iterating through the entire string we've been given, and letting the tokenizer process each character in that string. One of two things will happen to each character—either the tokenizer will discard it (as white space, or inside a comment), or it will be added to a token. The tokenizer's main function is called Tokenize.

Inside Tokenize, the tokenizer can be in one of four states: InWhiteSpace, InText, InComment, or InQuote. What state the tokenizer is in determines how it acts when it's processing each character.

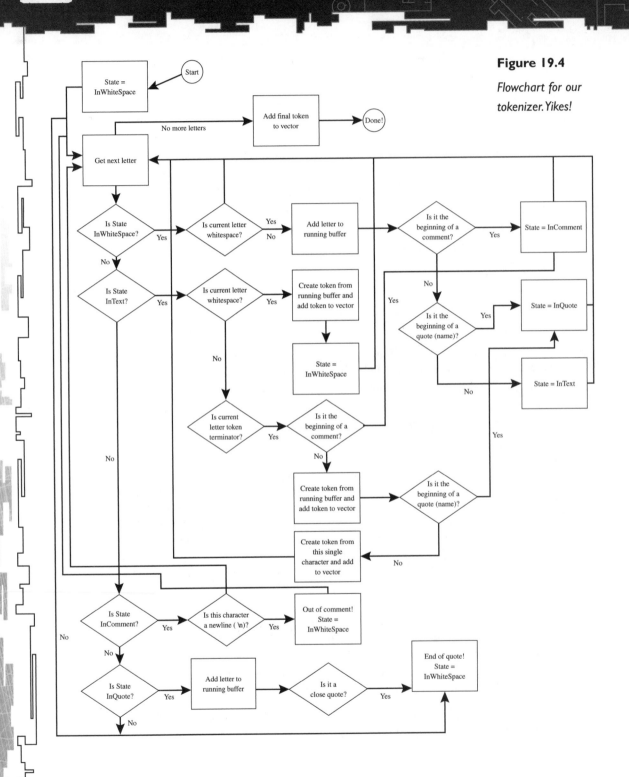

Figure 19.4

Flowchart for our tokenizer. Yikes!

For example, the tokenizer starts off in the InWhiteSpace state, which means that it's simply look-ing for the next non-whitespace chunk to start processing. All whitespace characters are discard-ed. If the first two non-whitespace characters the tokenizer comes across are two forward slashes, it enters into the InComment state. Once it's InComment, the tokenizer discards all characters until it sees a newline (\n), when it transitions back to the InWhiteSpace state. In this way, all characters from the start of a comment to the end of the line are discarded.

The InText state is a bit more complex. When the tokenizer's InText, it appends each character onto a buffer that will eventually become the token. It keeps appending characters until it hits white space, or a special token separator character (parentheses, brackets, commas). At that point, it stops appending characters to the buffer, turns the buffer into a token, determines what type of token it is, and adds it to the token vector (the AddToken method accomplishes all this work).

I needed to make a special exception for quoted strings, because they can contain white space. The InQuote state operates by unconditionally adding the character it's processing to the token array. This includes white space characters. When the InQuote state sees a closing quote, it con-verts the running buffer into a token, and transitions back to the InWhiteSpace case.

The best way for you to see all of this logic in action is to simply fire up the Ch19p2_TokenizerTester program and step through it in the debugger.

Determining the Token Type

When the tokenizer finally amasses a string of characters that constitute a token, it needs to figure out what kind of token it has found. It does this by calling DetermineTokenType, a func-tion that performs a simple series of string searches on the token to determine its type. For example, it first tries to deter-mine if the token starts with a number, or with the negative sign. If it does, the tokenizer knows it's got a RealNumber. Similarly, if the token contains "Random" or "XYZ" the tokenizer knows it's got a Random token or a KeywordVector token.

> **TIP**
>
> The DetermineTokenType function converts the token string to all uppercase (if it's not a Name). This effectively makes the properties file case insensitive.

The Beginning of the Actual Loading Code

Now that we've written a parser to convert our text stream into a vector of tokens, we can begin writing the actual loading code. Take a look at the Ch19p1_AdvancedPartSys program—specifically, the Compile method of CParticleEmitter, contained in Ch19p1_ParticleSystem.cpp This is the main method, responsible for converting a text string into a set of event sequences, events, and properties.

Handling Errors

Before we start writing the actual compiling code, we need to determine how we're going to handle errors. What happens if we're expecting a parenthesis but see a string instead? What happens if we see a number where a keyword is supposed to be?

Obviously, we need some sort of robust error-handling mechanism. This is where C++ exceptions can really save us (if you're not familiar with exceptions, I give a brief overview of them in the appendix). By wrapping a try/catch construct around our compiling code, we give ourselves the ability to throw an error from anywhere within the compiling code—we might be deep within our grammatical structure, and see something go wrong, and we can easily just throw and have the error caught back up in the Compile method.

For now, we can just throw strings that say roughly what the error is. We don't want to spend a lot of time on really robust error handling, because it's not like we're doing a very complicated compilation that takes minutes to run. Even a large property file will compile in the blink of an eye, so we don't need to waste time attempting to go on after we've found one error. We can just throw.

> **TIP**
>
> Also, we don't really need to throw more than a string—for now, anyway. I purposely left out the ability to associate a file/line with an error message, because I wanted you to implement this yourself—it's fairly easy and it's a great way to get familiar with the compiling code.

The Beginning

The compile function starts innocently enough. We clean the particle system by calling InvalidateDeviceObjects, then calling Init. After that we tokenize our text string by instantiating a CParticleEmitterTokenizer object and calling its Tokenize method. Whoosh! Our tokenizer follows the flowchart explained earlier many times to parse our input file; the Tokenize function gives us back our token stream, and we're ready to begin interpreting it in accordance with our grammar.

The beginning is easy—our grammar mandates that our properties file start with the keyword ParticleSystem, followed by a version number and an opening brace. So, these first several lines ensure that happens:

```
std::vector<CParticleEmitterToken>::iterator TokenIter =
  tokenizer.m_TokenVector.begin();
std::vector<CParticleEmitterToken>::iterator EndIter =
  tokenizer.m_TokenVector.end();
if (tokenizer.m_TokenVector.size() < 2)
  throw("This script is too small to be valid.");
// make sure the first four tokens are ParticleSystem, Quote,
// VersionNumber, and OpenBrace
```

```
if (TokenIter->m_Type != KeywordParticleSystem)
  throw("First word must be ParticleSystem"); }
CParticleEmitterTokenizer::NextToken(TokenIter, EndIter);
if (TokenIter->m_Type != Quote) throw("Must name particle system");
m_strName = RemoveQuotes(TokenIter->m_strValue);
CParticleEmitterTokenizer::NextToken(TokenIter, EndIter);
if (TokenIter->m_Type != RealNumber)
  throw("Must have version number"); }
CParticleEmitterTokenizer::NextToken(TokenIter, EndIter);
if (TokenIter->m_Type != OpenBrace)
  throw("Missing opening brace for ParticleSystem block");
```

This code starts by creating a token iterator, TokenIter, and pointing it to the beginning of the token stream. It also stashes the end of the stream into another iterator, EndIter.

There are no guarantees regarding how many tokens we have. Any token we process could actually be the last token in the vector. This means that we need to be careful when incrementing to the next token. Specifically, we need to make sure that we don't increment our way straight off the edge of the vector and out into open memory.

To ensure we handle this correctly, we have a static method of CParticleEmitterTokenizer called NextToken. NextToken is simple:

```
static void NextToken(
  std::vector<CParticleEmitterToken>::iterator &TokenIter,
  std::vector<CParticleEmitterToken>::iterator &EndIter)
{
  if (TokenIter == EndIter) throw("Unexpected end-of-file.");
  TokenIter++;
}
```

Yep, it's just a safeguard. NextToken simply increments our token iterator (TokenIter) and then makes sure that we're not at the end of the token vector. If we are, it throws an "unexpected end-of-file" error, because if we had expected the end of file we wouldn't have called NextToken in the first place. In this way, we're guaranteed to recover gracefully from an abrupt end to our properties file.

Now let's get back to the grammar. Now that you know what NextToken is all about, the code I gave you to begin with should be fairly easy to follow. All we're doing is checking that we do in fact have the correct tokens in the correct order. Notice also that when we get to where the particle system name is supposed to be, and we ensure that we've got a Name token, we strip the quotes off the value of that token and set that equal to our particle system name. Bing! We've just interpreted our very first property—at this point our code knows how to extract the name of our particle system from the properties file!

If we had more than one version of our property file grammar floating around, we would probably want to analyze the version number that the user supplied. However, since this is version 1.0, there are no previous versions to worry about, so there's no need to spend time messing with the version number. If you change the grammar, I encourage you to rev it to version 1.1 or something, and add code that looks at the version number supplied and either accommodates that version (by using a different, older grammar) or issues an error ("hey, you must write a properties file as defined by the version 1.1 grammar, not the 1.0 one!").

Processing the Particle System Block

After it has ensured the first few tokens are okay, the `Compile` method calls a subroutine named `ProcessParticleSystemBlock`. Not surprisingly, this method is responsible for interpreting a particle system block, starting with the opening brace (notice that we didn't increment the token iterator before calling it) and ending with the closing brace of the particle system block.

The Beginning

Our grammar defines a particle system block as any number of system properties, followed by any number of event sequences, followed by a closing curly brace. If you look at the structure of the `ProcessParticleSystemBlock` method, you'll see that it mirrors exactly our defined grammar:

```
bool CParticleEmitter::ProcessParticleSystemBlock(
  std::vector<CParticleEmitterToken>::iterator &TokenIter,
  std::vector<CParticleEmitterToken>::iterator &EndIter)
{
  bool StartedProcessingSequences = false;

  // move past the opening brace...
  CParticleEmitterTokenizer::NextToken(TokenIter, EndIter);
  while (TokenIter->m_Type != CloseBrace) {
    CParticleEmitterToken savedtoken;
    savedtoken = *TokenIter;
```

```
    switch (TokenIter->m_Type) {
      case SysVectorProp:
      {
        /* details of this to be discussed later! */
      }
      break;
      case KeywordEventSequence:
      {
        /* details of this to be discussed later! */
      }
      break;
      default:
      {
        char buf[256];
      _snprintf(buf, sizeof(buf),
          "Unexpected \"%s\" in Particle System Block!",
          TokenIter->m_strValue.c_str());
        throw(&buf[0]);
      }
      break;
    }
  }
  CParticleEmitterTokenizer::NextToken(TokenIter, EndIter);
  return(true);
}
```

The method starts by incrementing the token iterator, moving past the opening brace and onto a new token. It then essentially just keeps looking for SysVectorProp or KeywordEventSequence tokens until it hits a CloseBrace token. When that occurs, it jumps over the close brace and returns.

Processing the Particle System's Vector Properties

Now that we've got the structure, let's look at what happens inside the SysVectorProp case:

```
case SysVectorProp:
{
  if (StartedProcessingSequences)
    throw("Cannot specify any particle system properties after"
        " specifying sequences.");
```

```
CMinMax<D3DXVECTOR3> v;
CParticleEmitterTokenizer::NextToken(TokenIter, EndIter);
if (TokenIter->m_Type != Equals) throw("Expected equals sign!");
CParticleEmitterTokenizer::NextToken(TokenIter, EndIter);
CParticleEmitterTokenizer::ProcessVector(v, TokenIter, EndIter);
if (savedtoken.IsPosition()) {
  m_vPosRange = v;
}
else {
  throw("Unknown particle system property!");
}
}
break;
```

The first thing we do is check to make sure that we haven't started processing event sequences. Remember, our grammar says that we can't start doing sequences until we're done with system properties—we enforce this by using a simple static `bool` that starts out `false` but gets set to `true` when we enter the `case KeywordEventSequence` block. If it's `true` now, that means we've had at least one event sequence already, so we throw an error.

Assuming everything so far is cool, we increment the token iterator, moving off the name of the particular vector property we're setting, and (hopefully) onto an equal sign. If not, we throw an error. Note that before we moved off the vector property token, we saved it in a variable called `savedtoken`—this occurred above the `switch` statement.

Since we're in a `SysVectorProp`, we know that the property we're actually setting is a vector of some sort. So, we call the `ProcessVector` method of `CParticleEmitterTokenizer` to take care of the details of converting the next several tokens into a `CMinMax<D3DXVECTOR>`. (If you're unfamiliar with my `CMinMax` creation, I explain it in the templates section of the appendix.)

`ProcessVector` looks like this:

```
bool CParticleEmitterTokenizer::ProcessVector(CMinMax<D3DXVECTOR3> &v,
                                    std::vector<CParticleEmitterToken>::iterator
&TokenIter,
                                    std::vector<CParticleEmitterToken>::iterator
&EndIter)
{
  // this token needs to be a XYZ keyword.
  if (TokenIter->m_Type != KeywordXYZ) throw("Expecting XYZ(...)!");
  NextToken(TokenIter, EndIter);
```

```
  if (TokenIter->m_Type != OpenParen) throw("Expecting ( after XYZ!");

  CMinMax<float> x;
  CMinMax<float> y;
  CMinMax<float> z;
  NextToken(TokenIter, EndIter); ProcessNumber(x, TokenIter, EndIter);
  if (TokenIter->m_Type != Comma) throw("Vector components must be
separated by a comma.");
  NextToken(TokenIter, EndIter); ProcessNumber(y, TokenIter, EndIter);
  if (TokenIter->m_Type != Comma) throw("Vector components must be
separated by a comma.");
  NextToken(TokenIter, EndIter); ProcessNumber(z, TokenIter, EndIter);
  if (TokenIter->m_Type != CloseParen) throw("Expecting ) to close vector.");
  NextToken(TokenIter, EndIter);

  v.m_Min = D3DXVECTOR3(x.m_Min, y.m_Min, z.m_Min);
  v.m_Max = D3DXVECTOR3(x.m_Max, y.m_Max, z.m_Max);
  return(true);
}
```

Here you can see the code starting to fall into the same groove as the grammar. The code validates that the tokens are syncing up with the grammar, and calls the ProcessNumber function three times, exactly when it's expecting a Number token. ProcessNumber takes care of interpreting the grammar stream and returning a min/max value. Just for the sake of completeness, here's ProcessNumber:

```
bool CParticleEmitterTokenizer::ProcessNumber(CMinMax<float> &number,
  std::vector<CParticleEmitterToken>::iterator &TokenIter,
  std::vector<CParticleEmitterToken>::iterator &EndIter)
{
  // the first token is either random keyword, or an actual number.
  switch(TokenIter->m_Type) {
    case KeywordRandom:
    {
      // parse random number into minmax
      NextToken(TokenIter, EndIter);
      if (TokenIter->m_Type != OpenParen)
        throw("Expecting opening paren after Random keyword.");
      NextToken(TokenIter, EndIter);
      if (TokenIter->m_Type != RealNumber)
        throw("Expecting first number within Random(...).");
```

```
          number.m_Min = atof(TokenIter->m_strValue.c_str());
          NextToken(TokenIter, EndIter);

          if (TokenIter->m_Type != Comma)
            throw("Expecting comma within Random(...).");
          NextToken(TokenIter, EndIter);

          if (TokenIter->m_Type != RealNumber)
            throw("Expecting second number within Random(...).");
          number.m_Max = atof(TokenIter->m_strValue.c_str());
          NextToken(TokenIter, EndIter);
          if (TokenIter->m_Type != CloseParen)
            throw("Missing close paren on Random(...).");
          NextToken(TokenIter, EndIter);
        }
        break;
      case RealNumber:
        // min and max both equal realnumber
        if (TokenIter->m_Type != RealNumber) throw("Expecting number.");
        number.m_Max = number.m_Min =
          atof(TokenIter->m_strValue.c_str());
        NextToken(TokenIter, EndIter);
        break;
      default: throw("Expecting either Random(...) or a number value.");
    }
  return(true);
}
```

Again, this code follows a pattern. It was really easy to write these functions, because I essentially just translated my grammar rules into switch statements and if statements—nothing to it! The ProcessNumber method either fills in the min/max class with two different values (if the user has said something like "Random(5,10)"), or it sets min and max to the same value (if the user has just specified a plain old float, like "5.0").

We started at ProcessParticleSystemBlock and have drilled our way down, all the way to the bottom—the ProcessNumber method. Again, if you're having trouble keeping a picture of the call stack in your head, I encourage you to fire up a debugger and step through all this code—it's really very easy to follow once you understand how the grammar correlates to the shape of the methods.

Processing the Particle System's Event Sequences

Now, let's return back to the top. We've looked at the `SysVectorProp` case, and have drilled down through `ProcessVector` and `ProcessNumber`. Now let's look at the other case inside `ProcessParticleSystemBlock`: the `KeywordEventSequence` case. Here's that code:

```
case KeywordEventSequence:
{
  StartedProcessingSequences = true;
  CParticleEventSequence *newseq = new CParticleEventSequence;
  m_Sequences.push_back(newseq);
  CParticleEventSequence *seq = *(m_Sequences.end()-1);
  seq->Reset();
  if (!ProcessEventSequenceBlock(*seq, TokenIter, EndIter)) {
    delete seq;
    m_Sequences.pop_back();
  }
}
break;
```

The first thing we do is set the Boolean `StatedProcessingSequences` to `true` (so that if there's a `SysVectorProp` later we can throw an error). Next, we instantiate a new `CParticleEventSequence` object and add it to our particle system's vector of event sequences. This code is optimistic—it assumes there won't be any problems interpreting the event sequence block. If there are problems, `ProcessEventSequenceBlock` returns `false`, and we remove the bad event sequence from our vector.

Dive! Dive! Let's see what's inside the `ProcessEventSequenceBlock` function:

```
bool CParticleEmitter::ProcessEventSequenceBlock(
  CParticleEventSequence &seq,
  std::vector<CParticleEmitterToken>::iterator &TokenIter,
  std::vector<CParticleEmitterToken>::iterator &EndIter)
{
  bool StartedProcessingEvents = false;
  // move past the event sequence keyword...
  CParticleEmitterTokenizer::NextToken(TokenIter, EndIter);
  // next token should be the name of the sequence...
  if (TokenIter->m_Type != Quote)
    throw("Must name particle sequence block!");
  seq.SetName(TokenIter->m_strValue);
  CParticleEmitterTokenizer::NextToken(TokenIter, EndIter);
```

```
// next token should be opening brace...
if (TokenIter->m_Type != OpenBrace)
  throw("Expected opening brace for particle sequence block!");
CParticleEmitterTokenizer::NextToken(TokenIter, EndIter);
while (TokenIter->m_Type != CloseBrace) {
  CParticleEmitterToken savedtoken;
  savedtoken = *TokenIter;
  switch (TokenIter->m_Type) {
    case SeqNumericProp: { /* snip! */ } break;
    case SeqVectorProp: { /* snip! */ } break;
    case SeqAlphaBlendModeProp: { /* snip! */ } break;
    case KeywordTexture: { /* snip! */ } break;
    case KeywordFade: case KeywordAt: { /* snip! */ } break;
    case KeywordInitial: case KeywordFinal: { /* snip! */ } break;
    default: { /* snip! */ } break;
  }
}
seq.NailDownRandomTimes();
seq.SortEvents();
seq.CreateFadeLists();
CParticleEmitterTokenizer::NextToken(TokenIter, EndIter);
return(true);
}
```

I snipped most of the details out of the preceding code so you could more easily see its overall structure. Notice the similarity to ProcessParticleSystem—we start by verifying that the first few tokens conform to our grammar. Then, we enter a while loop, processing the sequences numeric, vector, and alpha blend mode properties (the SeqNumericProp, SeqVectorProp, and SeqAlphaBlendModeProp cases), the texture for this event sequence (KeywordTexture), and the event lines themselves (KeywordFade, KeywordAt, KeywordInitial, and KeywordFinal)—our events can start with either fade, at, initial, or final.

I'm not going to bore you with the details of the sequence property interpreters. Those case statements operate virtually identically to the SysVectorProp case of the ProcessParticleSystemBlock method. The only somewhat interesting one is the SeqAlphaBlendModeProp, which interprets the D3DBLEND_ enumerations. Step through the code to see how that works.

Processing the Events of an Event Sequence

I would like to draw your attention to the event processing keywords (KeywordFade, KeywordAt, KeywordInitial, and KeywordFinal). Let's take a look at that piece of code:

```
case KeywordFade: case KeywordAt: case KeywordInitial:
case KeywordFinal:
{
  StartedProcessingEvents = true;
  bool IsFade = false;
  CMinMax<float> TimeRange;
  // parse the time range section of the event line
  CParticleEmitterTokenizer::ProcessTime(
    TimeRange, IsFade, 0, seq.GetLifetime().m_Max, TokenIter, EndIter);
  if (TokenIter->m_Type != ParticleNumericProp &&
      TokenIter->m_Type != ParticleVectorProp &&
      TokenIter->m_Type != ParticleColorProp)
    throw("Expecting particle property after time specifier!");
  CParticleEvent * NewEvent = NULL;
  try {
    // create the appropriate event
    NewEvent = EventFactory(TokenIter->m_strValue, TokenIter, EndIter);
    if (!NewEvent)
      throw("Unknown event type or error creating event!");
    // let the event parse the rest of its properties from
    // the token stream.
    if (IsFade && !NewEvent->FadeAllowed())
      throw("Fading is not supported on this event.");
    NewEvent->ProcessTokenStream(TokenIter, EndIter);
    NewEvent->SetTimeRange(TimeRange);
    NewEvent->SetFade(IsFade);
    seq.m_Events.push_back(NewEvent);
  }
  catch(char *e) { SAFE_DELETE(NewEvent); throw(e); }
  catch(...) { SAFE_DELETE(NewEvent);
    throw("Unhandled exception creating event!");
  }
}
```

This code breaks down the task of interpreting an event line into three distinct pieces. First, it parses the time element of the event, by calling the static method ProcessTime of CParticleEmitterTokenizer. After that, it calls EventFactory to create an event. Finally, it tells the event to interpret the rest of its parameters by calling ProcessTokenStream, and adds the event to the sequence's vector of events.

Parsing the Time Element of an Event

That's the overview, now let's look at each of those three tasks in more detail, starting with the parameters of ProcessTime. The first two are references—ProcessTime hands back a TimeRange (remember, they could have written something like "at random(2,4) color = ...", so we need a CMinMax to store our time). ProcessTime also gives us a bool, IsFade, which is true if they've specified a fade so event. On the other hand, for ProcessTime to function correctly, we must give it the minimum and maximum particle lifetimes (the zero is the minimum lifetime), plus the token iterators. ProcessTime uses the minimum and maximum particle lifetime values we've given it to correctly interpret the initial and final keywords.

Using a Factory to Create an Event

In case you've never heard of it, a factory is a design pattern that programmers use to simplify code. Essentially a factory just creates an object of a specific type, given a set of input values. The benefit to using a factory is that it keeps all of this logic in one place.

Here's the code for our EventFactory method:

```
CParticleEvent *CParticleEmitter::EventFactory(
  std::string EventName,
  std::vector<CParticleEmitterToken>::iterator &TokenIter,
  std::vector<CParticleEmitterToken>::iterator &EndIter)
{
  CParticleEvent *event = NULL;
  if (EventName.find("SIZE") != std::string::npos)
    event = new CParticleEvent_Size();
  else if (EventName.find("EVENTTIMER") != std::string::npos)
    event = new CParticleEvent_EventTimer();
  else if (EventName.find("REDCOLOR") != std::string::npos)
    event = new CParticleEvent_RedColor();
  else if (EventName.find("GREENCOLOR") != std::string::npos)
    event = new CParticleEvent_GreenColor();
  else if (EventName.find("BLUECOLOR") != std::string::npos)
    event = new CParticleEvent_BlueColor();
  else if (EventName.find("ALPHA") != std::string::npos)
    event = new CParticleEvent_Alpha();
  else if (EventName.find("COLOR") != std::string::npos)
    event = new CParticleEvent_Color();
  else if (EventName.find("VELOCITYX") != std::string::npos)
    event = new CParticleEvent_VelocityX();
```

```
else if (EventName.find("VELOCITYY") != std::string::npos)
  event = new CParticleEvent_VelocityY();
else if (EventName.find("VELOCITYZ") != std::string::npos)
  event = new CParticleEvent_VelocityZ();
else if (EventName.find("VELOCITY") != std::string::npos)
  event = new CParticleEvent_Velocity();
return(event);
}
```

Nothing terribly complex going on here—essentially, EventFactory just looks at the EventName we give it and instantiates the corresponding CParitcleEvent derivative class. Remember, we get the event name from the value of the token.

Processing the Event Properties and Storing the Event

Finally, our code must give the event derivative class the chance to parse the rest of the tokens. Keep in mind that the event interpretation code doesn't care how many tokens are after the event name, or what they are. All we care about is the name of the event—our factory uses that to create the appropriate CParticleEvent derivative. After that token, we don't care—we simply call the ProcessTokenStream virtual function, and the specific event takes care of loading and interpreting the rest of its properties.

All of the events currently in our code have very simple ProcessTokenStream implementations, because like I said before, all of our events are essentially just "event name, equal sign, value." In fact, all of the ProcessTokenStream methods of the various events really just turn around and call a ProcessPropEqualsValue method, implemented in the CParticleEvent base class. This method has several overloads, but they all do the same thing: they read the next token, make sure it is an equal sign, and then call ProcessVector or ProcessNumber or whatever to read the actual property and return it.

Writing these methods saved me from doing a lot of copy-and-paste work in the event derivatives' ProcessTokenStream implementations.

> **TIP**
> It's always a good idea to avoid copying code—in fact, it's such a good idea that if they would let me, I'd carve "Don't Cut And Paste" on the back of that "Release What You Create" plaque.

After the event derivative completes its interpretation of the tokens, the ProcessTokenStream method returns. We finish by setting a few properties for the event (its TimeRange and whether or not it's a fading event), and adding it to our event sequence's vector of events.

Loading Code Wrap-Up

At this point we've looked at all of the big pieces of how to load a properties file. We've seen how event sequences are added to a particle system, and how events are added to an event sequence. We've looked at the code that interprets particle system properties and event sequence properties.

At this point, I now hope you have a good understanding of how our Compile function converts a property file into a particle system.

Using What We Have Loaded

There's still one huge piece missing, however. Now that we've got a particle system, containing event sequences, and event sequences containing events, how do we update and render all that? In other words, we've got this particle system loaded—now what?

That's what this next section is all about. Let's start with the update function.

Our New Event-Based Update Function

Scrap all that code you learned last chapter—here's our new update function:

```
void CParticleEmitter::Update(float fElapsedTime, float fTimeDelta)
{
  for (std::vector<CParticleEventSequence *>::iterator i =
      m_Sequences.begin(); i != m_Sequences.end(); i++)
  {
    (*i)->Update(fElapsedTime, fTimeDelta, m_vPos);
  }
}
```

As you can see, most of the real work isn't done here. Since a particle system is now just a collection of event sequences, all we have to do to render the system is render all the event sequences. Here's that code, taken from the Ch19p1_ParticleEventSequence source file:

```
void CParticleEventSequence::Update(float fElapsedTime,
  float fTimeDelta, D3DXVECTOR3 m_vPartSysPos)
{
  if (!m_Particles) return;
  // update existing particles
```

```
{
  for (int q=0; q < m_Particles->GetTotalElements(); q++) {
    if (m_Particles->IsAlive(q)) {
      CParticle &part = m_Particles->GetAt(q);
      if (!part.Update(fTimeDelta)) {
        m_Particles->Delete(&part);
      }
      else {
        // apply gravity to this particle.
        part.m_vDir += fTimeDelta * m_vGravity.GetRandomNumInRange();
        // run all the particle's events
        RunEvents(part);
      }
    } // is alive
  } // next particle
  float fEmitRateThisFrame = m_EmitRate.GetRandomNumInRange();
  int iNumNewParts = fEmitRateThisFrame * fTimeDelta;
  m_fNumNewPartsExcess +=
    (float)(fEmitRateThisFrame * fTimeDelta)-iNumNewParts;

  if (m_fNumNewPartsExcess > 1.0f) {
    iNumNewParts += (int)m_fNumNewPartsExcess;
    m_fNumNewPartsExcess -= (int)m_fNumNewPartsExcess;
  }
  for (int q=0; q < iNumNewParts && m_Particles->GetNumFreeElements();
       q++) {
    try {
      CreateNewParticle(m_vPartSysPos);
    } catch(...) { q = iNumNewParts; }
  }
}
```

You can sort of see parts of the update code from the last chapter peeking out through this code. Our framework is still the same: we still update before we create new particles, and within the update section, we still call the particle's Update function, and we still check to see if the particle's alive. However, after that we've got some new code.

Most interesting is the call to RunEvents. RunEvents looks like this:

```
void CParticleEventSequence::RunEvents(CParticle &part)
{
  // apply any other events to this particle
  for (std::vector<CParticleEvent *>::iterator i = part.m_CurEvent;
       i != m_Events.end() &&
       (*i)->GetActualTime() <= part.m_fEventTimer; i++) {
    float oldeventtimer = part.m_fEventTimer;
    (*i)->DoItToIt(part);
    if (part.m_fEventTimer != oldeventtimer) {
      // event timer has changed, we need to recalc m_CurEvent.
      for (std::vector<CParticleEvent *>::iterator RecalcIter =
           m_Events.begin(); RecalcIter != m_Events.end() &&
           (*RecalcIter)->GetActualTime() < part.m_fEventTimer;
           RecalcIter++); // do nothing, just loop!
      // set our main iterator to the recalculated iterator
      // the -1 just compensates for the i++ in the main for loop
      i = RecalcIter-1;
    }
  }
  part.m_CurEvent = i;
}
```

This method is responsible for figuring out which events happened in between the last frame and this frame, and for running all of those events. Inside the CParticle class is a new member, called m_CurEvent, which is an event iterator. When the code first creates the particle, m_CurEvent is set to the beginning of the event vector. Each time an event occurs, m_CurEvent gets incremented, so that it always points to the last event that fired.

We begin this code by looping from m_CurEvent to the end of the event vector, or to the first event that has a firing time greater than our particle's current event timer (part.m_fEventTimer)— remember, we discussed before that the event timer is exactly like the particle's lifetime, only it can be reset through an event. So, the for loop essentially says "loop through every event that was supposed to occur between the last frame and this frame."

The DoItToIt call actually runs the event on the particle. DoItToIt is a pure virtual function that's implemented by every CParticleEvent derivative class. It's inside this function that the event applies itself to the particle—for example, a color event's DoItToIt function would set the particle's color; a size event's DoItToIt would set a particle's size. Effectively, this is where the event "strikes" the particle—whammo!

Notice that before the call to DoItToIt we squirrel the particle's current event timer away, into a variable called oldeventtimer. After the DoItToIt call, we compare the particle's event timer to the one we stashed away; if they're different, that means that the event changed the particle's event timer, and we need to recalculate our event iterator.

The for loop inside the if statement does just that. It looks at the particle's new event timer and recalculates the iterator so that it points to the next event that's supposed to fire. It does this by starting at the beginning of the event array, and incrementing the iterator until it comes either to the end of the array, or to an event with a time that's greater than the event timer.

After we recalculate the array, we set our main iterator, i, to the recalculated value. Notice that this has the potential to "rewind" our main iterator and cause us to loop, which is As It Should Be.

This is a bit complex, so let's walk through an example together. Let's say we're processing a set of events that look like this:

```
at 0.001 color = rgba(1,0,1,1) // event 0
at 0.5 color = rgba(0,1,0,1) // event 1
at 1 eventtimer = 0.001 // event 2
```

Nothing too complex—we want the particle to start off purple, fade to green in half a second, fade back to purple in another half second, and loop. I've taken the liberty of labeling each of the events here from zero to two so that they're easier to refer to.

Let's start from the beginning—our particle event timer is zero, and our particle's m_CurEvent member is pointing to the beginning of the event array. Some frames go by, and our particle event timer and m_CurEvent member increment, until eventually the particle event timer is 0.99 and m_CurEvent is pointing to event 2. Our frame delta is 0.02 seconds. The particle's Update function adds 0.02 onto the event timer, making it 1.01, and then the code calls RunEvents.

The RunEvents main iterator, i, starts at event 2, and loops until the end of the event vector, effectively saying that we just need to process event 2. So far, so good. We call event 2's DoItToIt, and notice that the method changed the event timer—it overwrote the existing value of 1.01 with the new value of 0.001.

At this point we know we have to recalculate the event iterator, because at this point the event iterator and m_CurEvent are both out of sync with the event timer. So, the code says, "forget it! Let's just start from the beginning and keep incrementing until we find an event with a time greater than or equal to our new event timer value, 0.001." We do this, and immediately realize that event 0 is equal to 0.001, so set our master iterator, i, to point to event 0. Next, we decrement the iterator by one, but as we come to the end of the for loop and loop around we increment it, so the next effect is that i points to event 0. Event 0 fires, as it should, and since event 1 doesn't occur until time 0.5, our for loop's conditional statement fails, and we break out of the for loop. Finally, we set m_CurEvent to i, essentially reminding ourselves that the next event in line is event 1.

That's how the logic works, but again, if you still can't wrap your brain around it, fire up the debugger and step through it until you can. You can find this exact sequence of events inside the BlinkingGreenAndPurpleLights.txt file inside your particle scripts directory.

Our New Event-Based Render Function

We're halfway there—now let's learn about the new Render mechanism. Starting from the top, CParticleSystem's Render method looks like this:

```
HRESULT CParticleEmitter::Render()
{
  for (std::vector<CParticleEventSequence *>::iterator i =
m_Sequences.begin(); i != m_Sequences.end(); i++) {
    (*i)->Render(m_vbParticles, m_iVBSize);
  }
  return S_OK;
}
```

Again, just like with the Update method, all this Render method does is loop through the event sequences, calling their Render methods.

CParticleEventSequence's Render method is exactly the same as the previous chapter's Render function. It sets up the render states, texture, and texture states, then repeatedly locks the vertex buffer, fills it, unlocks it, and calls DrawPrimitive to Render a batch of particles.

So when you get right down to it, the only difference between last chapter's Render function and this one is that this one has to loop through each event sequence. It's cool how sometimes, in the midst of the entire world getting torn down and rebuilt, some methods manage to escape the carnage completely unchanged.

Scriptable Particle Systems Wrap-Up

Wow! Not that I've ever done it, but right now I feel a bit like I imagine I would after I had hiked through the Amazon rainforests and emerged into an open field. We've walked through the jungle, seen many interesting things, and have arrived out the other side, back into the light of day.

I wrote this section to give you just one example of how you can take a basic particle system and enhance it to suit the needs of your game. Maybe this event-based approach will work for you, or maybe it won't—either way, you've learned that even though all particle systems share a common core, the advanced features of each one may vary from game to game.

USES FOR SCRIPTABLE PARTICLE SYSTEMS

It's now time for us to enjoy what we've just worked so hard to create. This section gives you a few ideas on how you can use this scriptable particle system to create several different types of effects. (Because really, that's what it's all about—if you can't make something cool looking with what you code, why code it?)

Snow

The secret to good snow is in your snowflake texture (see Figure 19.5).

Figure 19.5

The snowflake texture for our snow particle system.

There isn't much to the actual snowflake script:

```
particlesystem "snow" 1.00 {
  position = XYZ(0,18,30)
  eventsequence "snow" {
    sourceblendmode = D3DBLEND_SRCALPHA
    destblendmode = D3DBLEND_DESTALPHA
    numparticles = 100
    gravity = XYZ(0,-1,0)
    emitrate = 10
    emitradius = XYZ(random(-20,20),0,0)
```

```
    lifetime = 10
    texture = "Snowflake1.png"
    initial color = rgba(1,1,1,1)
    initial size = random(0,2)
    initial velocity = XYZ(random(-1,1),0,0)
    at 0.5 velocityX = random(-1,1)
    at 1 eventtimer = 0.01
  }
}
```

Note the last two lines of that script—they cause each snowflake to randomly change its x velocity every half second. This creates the illusion that the snowflakes are drifting back and forth in the wind. Pretty cool, isn't it?

Also note that the emit radius is huge (in the x direction)—this allows the snowflakes' starting positions to be randomly dispersed over a 40 unit area.

Figure 19.6 shows this script in action.

TIP

Some people prefer to create another particle property that stores the weight of the particle. The code then uses the weight value to calculate the gravitational pull on each particle. We could have done something like this—we could have made each snowflake have a different weight value, causing them to drift downwards at different rates. Again, if you find yourself needing this flexibility, I encourage you to add the notion of weights to your particle system.

Figure 19.6

It's snowing!

Magic Spells

You can create dozens of good magic spell scripts. Here's one I like:

```
particlesystem "magic" 1.00 {
  position = XYZ(0,2,0)
  eventsequence "swirl1" {
    sourceblendmode = D3DBLEND_ONE destblendmode = D3DBLEND_ONE
    numparticles = 100 gravity = XYZ(0,0,0)
    emitrate = 3 lifetime = 4.5
    texture = "Ch18p3_ParticleTexture.png"
    initial color = RGBA(random(0,1),random(0,1),random(0,1),1)
    initial velocity = XYZ(random(-0.5,0.5),random(-0.5,0.5),0)
    fade so at 1 velocity = XYZ(-1,-1,0)
    fade so at 2 velocity = XYZ(-1,1,0)
    fade so at 3 velocity = XYZ(1,1,0)
    fade so at 4 velocity = XYZ(1,-1,0)
    at 4 eventtimer = 0.001
  }
  eventsequence "swirl2" {
    sourceblendmode = D3DBLEND_ONE destblendmode = D3DBLEND_ONE
    numparticles = 100 gravity = XYZ(0,0,0)
    emitrate = 3 lifetime = 4.5
    texture = "Ch18p3_ParticleTexture.png"
    initial color = RGBA(random(0,1),random(0,1),random(0,1),1)
    initial velocity = XYZ(random(-0.5,0.5),random(-0.5,0.5),0)
    fade so at 1 velocity = XYZ(1,-1,0)
    fade so at 2 velocity = XYZ(1,1,0)
    fade so at 3 velocity = XYZ(-1,1,0)
    fade so at 4 velocity = XYZ(-1,-1,0)
    at 4 eventtimer = 0.001
  }
  eventsequence "swirl3" {
    sourceblendmode = D3DBLEND_ONE destblendmode = D3DBLEND_ONE
    numparticles = 100 gravity = XYZ(0,0,0)
    emitrate = 3 lifetime = 4.5
    texture = "Ch18p3_ParticleTexture.png"
    initial color = RGBA(random(0,1),random(0,1),random(0,1),1)
    initial velocity = XYZ(random(-0.5,0.5),random(-0.5,0.5),0)
    fade so at 1 velocity = XYZ(1,1,0)
    fade so at 2 velocity = XYZ(-1,1,0)
```

```
      fade so at 3 velocity = XYZ(-1,-1,0)
      fade so at 4 velocity = XYZ(1,-1,0)
      at 4 eventtimer = 0.001
    }
  eventsequence "swirl4" {
    sourceblendmode = D3DBLEND_ONE destblendmode = D3DBLEND_ONE
    numparticles = 100 gravity = XYZ(0,0,0)
    emitrate = 3 lifetime = 4.5
    texture = "Ch18p3_ParticleTexture.png"
    initial color = RGBA(random(0,1),random(0,1),random(0,1),1)
    initial velocity = XYZ(random(-0.5,0.5),random(-0.5,0.5),0)
    fade so at 1 velocity = XYZ(1,-1,0)
    fade so at 2 velocity = XYZ(-1,-1,0)
    fade so at 3 velocity = XYZ(-1,1,0)
    fade so at 4 velocity = XYZ(1,1,0)
    at 4 eventtimer = 0.001
    }
  }
```

That script will create a cloverleaf pattern around the center of the particle system, sort of like a swirling field of magical energy (see Figure 19.7).

Add a spice of random color and sizes to it, if you like.

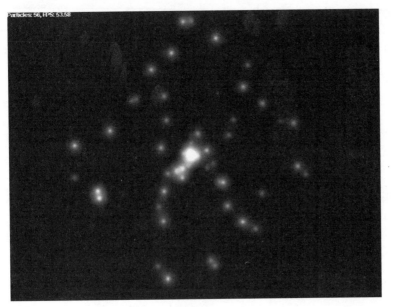

Particles: 56, FPS: 53.58

Figure 19.7

A particle system for magic spells.

The script works by adjusting the particle velocities at key times. Each event sequence causes the particles of that event sequence to drift in a circle. The script includes four circles—northeast, northwest, southeast, and southwest.

Jetstreams and Rockets

Here's an example of a fire jet I created:

```
particlesystem "FireJet" 1.00 {
  position = XYZ(0,1,3)
  eventsequence "FireJet" {
    sourceblendmode = D3DBLEND_SRCALPHA
    destblendmode = D3DBLEND_DESTALPHA
    numparticles = 50
    gravity = XYZ(0,-1,0)
    emitrate = 200
    lifetime = Random(0.01,1)
    texture = "JetExhaust.png"
    initial color = rgba(1,1,1,1)
    initial size = 0.15
    at random(0.1,0.3) redcolor = 1
    at random(0.1,0.3) greencolor = 1
    at random(0.1,0.3) bluecolor = 0
    fade so at 0.5 color = rgba(1,0,0,random(0,1))
    fade so at 0.7 color = rgba(1,0,0,1)
    fade so final color = rgba(1,0,0,0)
    initial velocity = XYZ(random(-0.25,0.25),random(1,5),0)
  }
}
```

Notice the color fade sequence in this script—we go from pure white, to yellow, to red, and finally to transparent black. This is similar to the fire palette we used for 2D fire back in Chapter 11, "Fire."

Of course, if you're making a sci-fi game and are using a particle system for your spaceship engines, you might want them a different color. Play around with greens and blues instead of reds and yellows to create some cool engine effects.

Faeries

If one of your game scenes is inside a magical forest, try this script for some cool-looking faeries (see Figure 19.8):

Figure 19.8

Faeries!

```
particlesystem "faeries" 1.00 {
  position = XYZ(0,2,0)
  eventsequence "faeries" {
    sourceblendmode = D3DBLEND_SRCALPHA
    destblendmode = D3DBLEND_DESTALPHA
    numparticles = 500
    gravity = XYZ(0,0,0)
    emitrate = 10
    emitradius = xyz(1,1,1)
    lifetime = 6
    texture = "Ch18p3_FaerieTexture.png"
    initial color = rgba(random(0,1),random(0,1),
      random(0,1),random(0,1))
    initial velocity =
      XYZ(random(-0.5,0.5),random(-0.5,0.5),random(-0.5,0.5))
    at 1 velocity =
      XYZ(random(-0.5,0.5),random(-0.5,0.5),random(-0.5,0.5))
    at 2 velocity =
      XYZ(random(-0.5,0.5),random(-0.5,0.5),random(-0.5,0.5))
    at 3 velocity =
      XYZ(random(-0.5,0.5),random(-0.5,0.5),random(-0.5,0.5))
    at 4 velocity =
      XYZ(random(-0.5,0.5),random(-0.5,0.5),random(-0.5,0.5))
```

```
    at 5 velocity =
      XYZ(random(-0.5,0.5),random(-0.5,0.5),random(-0.5,0.5))
    fade so final color = rgba(0,0,0,0)
    fade so final size = 0.01
  }
}
```

The velocity changes make the faeries seem to drift aimlessly before fading out.

If you wanted to enhance this, you could animate the particle texture so that the faeries' wings flapped gently as they flew.

Lightning Bugs

You can also use the same basic faerie code to create cool-looking lightning bugs. I won't write out the entire script here, for that reason, and because the script is rather long, but I encourage you to take a look at it on your CD.

Noteworthy things about this script: I decided that there could be two kinds of bugs—yellow ones and white ones. So, I created two different event sequences—yellowbugs and whitebugs. I decided that the white bugs should appear less often than the yellow bugs, so I decreased the white bugs' emit rate slightly.

Other Scripts

I found particle scripts fun to create, so I made a bunch of extra ones that I didn't discuss here. Cruise the scripts directory on your CD to see these other particle systems.

OPTIMIZING SCRIPTABLE PARTICLE SYSTEMS

By far, the biggest factor in determining how fast your particle system will run is how complex it is. By that, I mean its functionality, and also the number of events and event sequences you have. The moral to this is that you should strive to make your property files as simple as they can be, and also to make your particle system only support features that you actually use.

That being said, there's one obvious thing you can do to optimize this system. The number of particles you need to create a realistic looking effect varies depending on how far the camera is from the particle system itself. If the camera is close, you may need a lot of particles; if it's far away, you may be able to get by with only a dozen or so. Therefore, many game programmers write code that scales back the number of particles used in a particle system if that system is far away.

OTHER POTENTIALLY NIFTY ENHANCEMENTS

I hope that our adventure through this jungle of code has inspired you to take the current source and augment it with your own features. To further inspire you, here are a few things I think would be cool to add to our scriptable particle system:

- **Black Holes.** Right now our particle system has the notion of gravity, but it's only a vector. It might be useful to enhance it so that you can input a point at a given position (relative to the particle system's origin) and designate it as a "black hole," so that the particles that got close to that point would get diverted or even sucked into the hole. You could write code that killed the particles that got sucked into the hole.
- **Reverse Black Holes (White Holes?).** The same idea as with black holes, only instead of making the particles get sucked in, make them get pushed away from these points. I'm sure that by creating a few random black and (what I call) white holes, you could create some truly nifty particle systems.
- **Random Flicker Values.** You could create four new numeric particle properties that controlled how much the red, green, and blue values of a particle's color "flicker" each frame. Inside the Render function, the code could pick four random values within these ranges, and add those random values onto the particle's color before drawing it. In this way you could create particles that flickered randomly.
- **Wiggle Values.** Same idea as above, only instead of adding random values onto the RGBA components of a particle's color, you add random XYZ values onto the particle's position. This would allow you to create particles that wiggle as they move.
- **Trails.** You can easily add code that remembers the last few positions of each particle, and uses those positions to draw particle trails, just like mouse cursor trails. This is useful for creating effects, but it can also bog down your graphics card easily. If each particle has 5 phantoms of itself forming a trail, then with 100 particles you're pushing 1,000 triangles to the card. The numbers add up quickly.
- **Multiple Textures.** This is a big one. Currently our particle system only allows one texture per event sequence. It would be great to enhance this so that it supported multiple textures. Also, you could add events that changed the particle's texture—great for animating the particle sprites as they're being drawn.

Again, you should make the decision regarding which of these features to implement based on the particle system needs of your game. Don't implement things you'll never use, because at best, that will just waste your time, and at worst, those "improvements" could cause a performance hit in your particle system.

CHAPTER WRAP-UP

In the last two chapters, we've gone from learning what a particle system is, to implementing an editor, to implementing an advanced, scriptable particle system. We've covered a huge amount of ground. What you need to do now is just spend some time and let all of these concepts sink in. Play around with a particle system editor, and then with the scripted systems, until you've got a pretty good handle on what all the code is doing. I consider particle systems to be one of the most important techniques for generating any type of 3D effect, so having a rock-solid understanding of particle systems now can only help you as we move to the other chapters, and as you make your own killer game.

ABOUT THE SAMPLE PROGRAMS

No code style changes, and just two sample programs this chapter, but they're both somewhat complex. Here they are:

- **Ch19p1_AdvancedPartSys.** This program is the essence of the entire chapter—it implements an advanced, and what I call "scriptable," particle system. Note that I had to disable the space and enter hotkeys (stop/go and single step) because we need to be able to enter spaces and line feeds in our script edit window.
- **Ch19p2_TokenizerTester.** A testing program for you to use to see how the tokenizer works. This program takes as input a filename and writes as output the list of all the tokens (and their types).

EXERCISES

You can do all sorts of stuff to the particle systems—I've outlined some of those enhancements in a previous section. However, if you're still thirsty for more, here are some additional things to try:

1. Create a pluggable factory system for your events. Currently, if you add a new event, you have to go and add a few lines to the EventFactory function so that it properly creates the event. A pluggable factory system here will allow you to add events to the system without changing the EventFactory code. If you're unfamiliar with pluggable factories, check out the article I wrote on them—"Why Pluggable Factories Rock My Multiplayer World"—included on your CD.
2. Enhance the compiler so that it gives line numbers along with the error messages. This is as easy as adding an m_iLineNum member to CParticleEmitterToken. As you tokenize, keep track of what line you're on, and stuff that line number into the tokens you create. Then, when you throw an error, throw the token along with it (make an error class), so that you can display not only the error message, but the line number and actual token that generated the

error. If you wanted to get really slick, you could keep track of the column number as well, so that you could spit out the exact line number and column that generated the error.

3. You might want to consider changing things so that your property file supports what I call "event blocks." By event block, I mean the ability to specify that two or more events all occur at the same time. For example, notice the braces in the line `fade so at Random(3,5) { redcolor = 0.5 bluecolor = 1.0 }`. You can't currently do something like this, because if you write two lines that both occur at a random time, there's no guarantee that those two lines will take effect at the *same* random time.

CHAPTER 20

EXPLOSIONS

"Where's the explosion?"
"They never show the good stuff."
——*Beavis & Butt-head*

1’m an explosion aficionado. I study video game explosions the way some people study Picasso or fine wine. From the simple “dot” explosions of the old-school vector-based games, through the 8-bit era of what I call “glorified asterisk” explosions, all the way to today’s lush effects and 3D fire, explosions have played an integral part in many video games.

In this chapter, we’re going to show the good stuff. We’ll take a look at how to code explosions, starting simple, but adding features as we go.

STARTING SIMPLE: EXPLOSION SPRITES

Let’s start with the smallest and easiest explosion technique—explosion sprites. This involves nothing more than replacing the object that’s getting blown up with an animation, created by drawing quads with different alpha-blended explosion textures. For a view of this in action, see Figure 20.1.

> **TIP**
>
> Follow along with this section by loading the `Ch20p1_SimpleExplosion` program into your IDE.

Figure 20.1

A screenshot of our `Ch20p1_SimpleExplosion` *sample program.*

Creating the Explosion Textures

A good place to start is with the explosion images themselves. You have several options when it comes to the images—you can choose to make them, or pull an existing graphic or animation from somewhere else. Here are a few ideas:

- **Render them in 3D Studio MAX.** 3D Studio has some great tools for creating explosions, and when 3D Studio is placed in the hands of an experienced 3D artist, the results can be breathtaking. Unfortunately, this option really isn't suited for those of us strapped for cash—the cost of the software, combined with the time and talent needed to use it, prohibits the smaller development shops from using this.

- **Use something from the Pyromania CD.** A company by the name of VCE sells several "Pyromania" CD-ROMs full of video snippets of real-life explosions and other cool fire effects. It's relatively easy to convert these images into a sequence of textures for use in your own game. The Pyromania CD-ROMs are cheap—about $100–$200 depending on how many CDs you want, and that's for royalty-free usage. However, beware: the Pyromania images are very popular, so most experienced game developers and visual effects people can instantly recognize any clip from Pyromania. The average game player probably won't notice, but you might need to do something else if you don't want your game explosions looking like everyone else's.

> **TIP**
>
> **You can read more about the Pyromania CDs at http://www.vce.com.**

- **Draw them yourself!** Explosions are easier to draw than you might think. The trick is to create a whole bunch of red and yellow splatters of color, and then to simply blur them together several times. There are several good tutorials on the Net, as well.

After we know how to get or make the images, the next question is, "How many frames of animation should my explosion sprite contain?" More frames create higher explosion quality, but use more texture memory. I've found that this sprite-based explosion technique is best suited to small explosions—rockets hitting walls, oil cans exploding, that sort of thing. So, we shouldn't go wild when it comes to our animation. I've found that using seven 64×64 textures is usually adequate. Assuming you want 32-bit color textures, that's 16,384 bytes per explosion frame, or about 114K for the whole animation.

> **TIP**
>
> **You don't need 32-bit color. It's not like your player is going to be staring at these explosions for minutes on end. They're going to see a flash of animation, and that's it—they'll have hardly any time to notice if your images look slightly pixelated. 32-bit color may be overkill; you may decide to spend your precious graphics card memory elsewhere.**

Creating the explosion textures is a two-step process. First, we need to create our actual explosion artwork. However, since the explosion images aren't perfectly square, our second task is to combine our artwork with an alpha channel so that the correct parts of the texture are marked as transparent. Check out Figure 20.2—it shows each frame of our explosion animation.

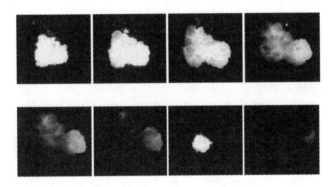

Figure 20.2

Frames of our explosion animation.

Conveniently enough, Microsoft provides, as part of the DirectX SDK, a program called the DirectX Texture Tool. This program allows you to combine images with alpha channels to create partially transparent textures.

Here are the specific steps involved in creating a texture using this tool:

1. Select New Texture from the File menu, then specify the texture settings you want your new texture to have.
2. Once your new texture is created, select Open Onto This Surface from the File menu, and open your image file.
3. Now that you have your image on the texture, you need to load your alpha channel. Select Open Onto Alpha Channel of This Surface from the File menu, and open your alpha channel.
4. You should see your alpha channel merge onto your image. If you like, you can change the background color to a different color by using the Change Background Color command from the View menu. You'll be able to see, through the transparent areas of your texture, your chosen background color.
5. When everything's just right, choose Save As from the File menu to save your texture as a DDS file.

Do this for each frame of your explosion, and you'll end up with a set of DDS files, which you can load using the D3DXCreateTextureFromFile command.

> **TIP**
>
> This isn't the only way to create textures with alpha channels. If you have another method that you prefer, go for it!

Creating Sprite and Animation Classes

We've got our images; now let's write some code to load them and store them in an organized way.

This means that we need to create a set of C++ classes that handle animations. This is one of those "classic" moments in game programming. The male children of ancient tribes had to go out and kill large, toothy animals to prove themselves as warriors. Novice game programmers write sprite and animation classes. If you've never written a sprite or animation class before, don't worry; this won't be the last time you write one.

Over the course of writing many different sprite classes, I've come to realize two important things about creating a solid design:

- Create a frame class that holds the image for one frame of animation, and then create an animation class that contains one or more frame classes.
- Keep your animation timing and positioning information separate from your animation image collection.

Let's look at those two things in more detail.

Frame Classes and Animation Classes

The first thing I've learned is that it's best to have a separate class that takes care of each individual frame of an animation, and then to have another class that keeps track of a group of animation frames. Let's start with the frame class:

```
class CAnimFrame
{
public:
  CAnimFrame() { m_pTexture = NULL; }
  virtual ~CAnimFrame() { SAFE_RELEASE(m_pTexture); }
  LPDIRECT3DTEXTURE8 m_pTexture;
  float m_fTime;
};
```

Yep—essentially, it's just a texture handle and a time value. The time value dictates how long this particular frame of animation will stay visible. I've found that having per-frame times is useful in a number of situations where your

TIP

One other thing to mention: over the years I've found that hiding data members of the frame class is more trouble than what it's worth. I've never run into a situation where I've needed to change the data type of the timing or image storage variable. However, if you're bent on following the rules of C++ design, don't let me stop you—go ahead and create accessor functions.

animation needs to "delay" on a certain frame for a certain amount of time. We won't be facing these situations with our explosions, but since we're creating a generic animation class I thought I'd mention it.

Now let's have a gander at the animation class:

```
class CAnimSequence {
public:
  CAnimSequence(LPDIRECT3DDEVICE8 pDev);
  virtual ~CAnimSequence() {
    ClearAllFrames(); SAFE_RELEASE(m_pVBQuad);
  }

  bool AddFrame(const char *strFilename, float fTime);
  void DeleteFrame(int index);
  void ClearAllFrames();
  int GetCurFrame(CTimer &timer);
  LPDIRECT3DTEXTURE8 GetCurFrameTexture(CTimer &timer) {
    try {
      int iCurFrame = GetCurFrame(timer);
      return(m_vFrames[iCurFrame]->m_pTexture);
    } catch(...) { }
    return(NULL);
  }
  void Render(CTimer &timer, D3DXMATRIX mat);
protected:
  LPDIRECT3DVERTEXBUFFER8 m_pVBQuad;
  LPDIRECT3DDEVICE8 m_pd3dDevice;
  std::vector<CAnimFrame *> m_vFrames;
};
```

At the heart of the CAnimSequence class is m_vFrames, the vector of animation frames. The other key data member is m_pVBQuad—the vertex buffer of the quad that we use to render the animation.

Using this class is fairly simple—we create an instance, and add the appropriate frames and times via multiple calls to the AddFrame method:

```
// create explosion animation
m_pExploAnim = new CAnimSequence(m_pd3dDevice);
m_pExploAnim->AddFrame("Ch20p3_Explosion_Frame01.dds", 0.03f);
m_pExploAnim->AddFrame("Ch20p3_Explosion_Frame02.dds", 0.03f);
m_pExploAnim->AddFrame("Ch20p3_Explosion_Frame03.dds", 0.03f);
m_pExploAnim->AddFrame("Ch20p3_Explosion_Frame04.dds", 0.03f);
```

```
m_pExploAnim->AddFrame("Ch20p3_Explosion_Frame05.dds", 0.03f);
m_pExploAnim->AddFrame("Ch20p3_Explosion_Frame06.dds", 0.03f);
m_pExploAnim->AddFrame("Ch20p3_Explosion_Frame07.dds", 0.03f);
m_pExploAnim->AddFrame("Ch20p3_Explosion_Frame08.dds", 0.03f);
```

Here you can see us pumping in the individual frames of animation, and telling the sequence how long each frame should be displayed. Drilling down, the AddFrame method loads up the file, creates a new sequence, and adds it to the vector:

```
bool CAnimSequence::AddFrame(const char *strFilename, float fTime)
{
  if (!m_pd3dDevice) return(false);
  if (fTime <= 0) return(false);
  CAnimFrame *newframe = new CAnimFrame();

  // create a texture for this frame
  if (FAILED(D3DXCreateTextureFromFile(m_pd3dDevice,
               strFilename, &newframe->m_pTexture))) {
    delete newframe;
    return(false);
  }

  // add to vector
  newframe->m_fTime = fTime;
  m_vFrames.push_back(newframe);
  return(true);
}
```

> **TIP**
>
> You could add a load function so that instead of assembling the animation inside your source, you could simply tell the animation object to load a properties file that, in turn, told it the images it should load. But, for the purposes of this chapter, this will work just fine.

Creating a Timer Class

We now have a set of animation frames, but before we continue we need to speak briefly about time. Time is an integral part of animation. We need to keep track of the number of seconds since we've told the animation to start. Let's use a simple timer class to do this:

```
class CTimer
{
public:
  CTimer() { /* snip! */ }
  virtual ~CTimer() { /* snip! */ }
```

```
    void Start() { m_bIsRunning = true;  }
    void Pause() { m_bIsRunning = false; }
    void Stop()  { Pause(); m_fTime = 0; }
    void Begin() { Stop(); Start(); }
    void BeginWithDelay(float fDelay) { m_fTime = -fDelay; Start(); }

    void SetTime(float t) { m_fTime = t; }
    float GetTime() { return(m_fTime); }
    bool IsRunning() { return(m_bIsRunning); }

    void Update(float fElapsedTime) {
      if (m_bIsRunning) {
        m_fTime += fElapsedTime;
      }
    }
    // these are here so you can call 1 function to update all timers
    static std::vector<CTimer *> m_Timers;
    static void UpdateAll(float fElapsedTime) { /* snip! */ }
protected:
  bool m_bIsRunning;
  float m_fTime;
};
```

This is the C++ equivalent of a simple stopwatch. We can start, stop, and pause our timer, and we can reset it to zero. Or, if we'd like the timer to start in, say, two seconds, we can call the BeginWithDelay function. We also have a function called Update that's used to increment the timer value. Our main code calls Update every frame, providing the number of seconds that have passed since the last frame. If it's running, the timer simply adds this value onto its internal counter.

> **TIP**
>
> We'll add some stuff to the timer class later in this chapter, but this is a good start for now.

Keeping Timing and Position Information Separate from the Animation

Okay, returning to the main topic after that brief diversion: We've covered the first of two nuggets for architecting animation/sprite functions—first create a frame class, then create an animation class that contains multiple frame classes.

The second good design philosophy I've discovered is to keep your animation timing and positioning information separate from your animation images. The main reason for this is that you can have the same animation playing at different times and different places in your game.

For example, let's say you're making an *Asteroids* clone. You've skimped on the graphics, so you have only one asteroid animation. However, you have several different asteroids on the screen—each is using the same set of animation images, but each asteroid is at a different place, and they were all created at different times. It's silly to load a separate set of animation images for each asteroid—that would waste graphics memory like crazy! Instead, a better approach is to have all the asteroids share the same animation class (and animation images), but to keep their own position and timing information.

That's why it's better to keep the animation images separate from the animation timings and position information, even though your gut instinct may tell you to lump all this stuff together in one sprite class. Another way to look at it: the timing and position is unique to each "instance" of the animation, but all instances share the same set of animation images.

What we've stumbled on here is the difference between a *sprite* and an *animation*. I call an animation instance a sprite. A sprite contains a reference to a particular animation sequence, plus a position and a timer (for determining which frame of the animation to display). In the above example, I'd consider each individual asteroid a sprite.

Here's what a sprite class looks like:

```
class CSprite
{
public:
  CSprite();
  CSprite(CAnimSequence *anim);
  virtual ~CSprite();
  CTimer &Timer() { return(m_Timer); }
  void SetAnim(CAnimSequence *anim) { m_pAnim = anim; }
  CAnimSequence *GetAnim() { return(m_pAnim); }
  D3DXVECTOR3 &Pos() { return(m_vPos); }
  void Render(D3DXMATRIX view);
  // SNIP! accessor functions SetSize/GetSize,
  // SetRotationYaw/GetRotationYaw,
  // SetRotationPitch/GetRotationPitch, and
  // SetRotationRoll/GetRotationRoll removed!
private:
  float m_fSize;
  D3DXVECTOR3 m_vPos;
```

```
    float m_fRotationYaw, m_fRotationPitch, m_fRotationRoll;
    CTimer m_Timer;
    CAnimSequence *m_pAnim;
};
```

CSprite contains three important data members: the m_Timer, m_vPos, and m_pAnim elements. The m_Timer element keeps track of how many seconds have passed since we've told the sprite to begin playing its animation. Notice that other code has direct access to m_Timer, through the Timer method.

The m_vPos member keeps track of the sprite's position in 3D world space. The other critical member, m_pAnim, tells the sprite which animation sequence it should use.

This sprite class also has a rotation feature. By specifying different values for m_fRotationYaw, m_fRotationPitch, and m_fRotationRoll, we can rotate our sprite arbitrarily.

TIP

I know what you're thinking, and you're right—I probably could have made m_pAnim a reference instead of a pointer. I chose not to, because after much deliberating and internal strife, I decided that a sprite doesn't necessarily *need* to have an animation sequence associated with it. Sometimes, you may want a sprite to be a timer floating out in 3D space somewhere, or you may decide to *display* something other than a sprite at that location. For example, you may want an *audio* sprite—a particular sound effect, wired to a timer, and tied to a position. You could use this audio sprite to simulate flies or mosquitoes, or anything else your players can hear moving around but not see.

However, there are myriad other valid ways to design things. My hope is not that you use my designs outright; rather, that you take my architecture as advice when building your own system.

Deciding which Frame to Display

The core function of our animation class works like this: we give it the number of seconds into the animation we're at, and it gives us back the correct frame to display for that time. Let's look at that code:

```
// determine the correct frame to be on given this new time
int iCurFrame = 0; float fTimeCount = 0.0f;
for (std::vector<CAnimFrame *>::iterator i = m_vFrames.begin();
     i != m_vFrames.end(); ++i) {
```

```
  fTimeCount += (*i)->m_fTime;
  if (timer.GetTime() <= fTimeCount) break;
  iCurFrame++;
}

if (iCurFrame >= m_vFrames.size()) return;
```

This is a brute force algorithm, but it gets the job done. We start with the first frame of animation, and with a time count (fTimeCount) of zero. We add the frame's delay time onto the time count, and compare that value against the timer's current time. If the timer's time is greater than the time count, we know that the frame of animation we're currently touching has already been displayed (or should have

> **TIP**
>
> Note that this isn't the fastest code on the planet. A better approach might be to cache the last frame of animation displayed, and then just start the search from that point. These changes improve speed but also make the code more complex, so I chose not to implement them here.

been displayed). If, on the other hand, the timer's time is less than the time count, we stop, because we've found the animation frame we're supposed to display.

The Problem with CTimer

I promised you we'd return to CTimer—here we are. There's a subtle problem with our timer design—if you forget to call Update, the timer never steps forward. I first noticed this when I was trying to figure out why an animation I had linked to a timer wasn't playing, even though I had wired the animation and the timer together, and I had called the Begin method of the timer. After debugging several other, more complex functions, I realized the reason things weren't animating was because I wasn't calling the Update method of CTimer. D'oh!

The first time I ran into this bug, I called myself stupid, added the Update call, and went on with my life. The *second* time I ran into this bug, I called myself *really* stupid for designing such a high-maintenance class. Every time I made a new timer, I had to make sure I was calling its update function! What a chore! It was at that point I decided to revise the design of CTimer so that I'd never again fall into the same pit.

My solution was to make all of the timers put a pointer to themselves in a static vector when they were created, and to remove that pointer from the vector when they were deleted. You can see this occurring in the constructor and destructor of CTimer:

```
class CTimer
{
public:
```

```
CTimer() {
  // register timer by adding it to static vector
  m_Timers.push_back(this);
  Stop();
  char buf[256];
  _snprintf(buf, sizeof(buf),
    "Timer created! Total Timers: %d\n", m_Timers.size());
  OutputDebugString(buf);
}
virtual ~CTimer() {
  // delete timer from vector
  for (std::vector<CTimer *>::iterator i = m_Timers.begin();
       i != m_Timers.end(); i++) {
    if ((*i) == this) {
      m_Timers.erase(i);
      char buf[256];
      _snprintf(buf, sizeof(buf),
        "Timer deleted! Total Timers: %d\n", m_Timers.size());
      OutputDebugString(buf);
      break;
    }
  }
}
static std::vector<CTimer *> m_Timers;
/* etc... */
};
```

Now I had a list of every timer in existence. Notice also that I put in some debugging lines (via the API function OutputDebugString), so that when I was in DevStudio I could see the timer counts rising and falling as my code created and destroyed timers.

> **TIP**
>
> **In case you've never heard of it before: a static member variable is a member variable that all instances of a particular class share. In this example, all of the CTimer instances share the same pointer list.**

Next, I created a new method, UpdateAll, which called Update for each timer in that list:

```
static void UpdateAll(float fElapsedTime) {
  for (std::vector<CTimer *>::iterator i = m_Timers.begin();
       i != m_Timers.end(); i++) {
    (*i)->Update(fElapsedTime);
  }
}
```

Now, all I had to do was make one call to `UpdateAll` and I was set! That's much better than having to remember to call each individual timer's `Update` method!

Billboarding

Returning to the topic of animation—I purposely didn't talk about how to draw a frame of animation when I was discussing the sprite and animation classes, because drawing a frame in a 3D world brings up another pesky issue.

Our sprites are 2D images. We put these 2D images onto quads as textures. In order to create the illusion that these 2D images are actually 3D explosions, we need to ensure that our quads always face the camera. If we slip, and somehow let the camera see the quad from an angle, we'll have shattered our illusion.

This technique is called *billboarding*, and it's an important tool in rendering high-quality 3D scenes at high frame rates. Billboarding gets its name from the fact that what we're essentially doing here is creating a billboard with a picture on it. This billboard always faces the camera.

You can use billboarding in many different situations—for example, you could create pictures of a tree and substitute a billboarded tree image (a 2-triangle quad) for a 2,000-triangle tree model. Of course, if the user gets close enough to the tree billboard he'll be able to tell it's not a model. However, if the user will never get close, you can get away with it, and save yourself the effort of drawing those extra 1,998 triangles.

> **TIP**
>
> **Billboarding works really well for simple explosions because the explosions don't exist long enough for your player to notice the fact that they're just images. Why waste a bunch of graphics-processing power on something that's not going to be noticed?**

Implementing Billboarding

As it turns out, the code to implement billboarding is really simple. All we need to do is rotate our quad so that it faces the camera. The following code chunk accomplishes this:

```
void CSprite::Render(D3DXMATRIX view)
{
  if (!m_pAnim) return;
  // Set up a rotation matrix to orient the explo sprite
  // towards the camera.
  D3DXMATRIX matScale, matTranslate, matTranspose,
    matBillboardRot, matWorld;
```

```
D3DXMATRIX matRot; // user-specified rotation
D3DXMatrixTranspose(&matTranspose, &view);
D3DXMatrixIdentity(&matBillboardRot);

matBillboardRot._11 = matTranspose._11;
matBillboardRot._12 = matTranspose._12;
matBillboardRot._13 = matTranspose._13;
matBillboardRot._21 = matTranspose._21;
matBillboardRot._22 = matTranspose._22;
matBillboardRot._23 = matTranspose._23;
matBillboardRot._31 = matTranspose._31;
matBillboardRot._32 = matTranspose._32;
matBillboardRot._33 = matTranspose._33;

D3DXMatrixTranslation(&matWorld, m_vPos.x, m_vPos.y, m_vPos.z);
D3DXMatrixRotationYawPitchRoll(&matRot, m_fRotationYaw,
   m_fRotationPitch, m_fRotationRoll);
D3DXMatrixScaling(&matScale, m_fSize, m_fSize, 1);
m_pAnim->Render(m_Timer,
   matScale * matRot * matBillboardRot * matWorld);
}
```

There's some clever math at play here. We start by taking the view matrix (the position and orientation of the camera) and transposing it. We then take the upper-left 3×3 block of numbers from our transposed matrix and use that as our rotation matrix. I encourage you to play with the numbers on your own to see exactly why we do this and how it works. We then combine this rotation matrix with the position, rotation, and scaling matrices we've created from the m_vPos, m_fRotationYaw, m_fRotationPitch, m_fRotationRoll, and m_fSize members. With this, we have achieved billboarding—no matter where our camera is, if we use the combined scale, rotation, and world matrices, our quads will always be drawn facing the camera.

Rendering the Explosion

Billboarding was the last of a set of obstacles on the road to rendering an explosion. Now that we've gone through all of those, it's time to finally look at how to render these sprites.

I prefer to use additive alpha blending for my explosions. Additive blending means that instead of averaging the texel color and the existing pixel color together, you add them, to arrive at the final color (see Figure 20.3). This creates bright-looking explosions that look cooler to me.

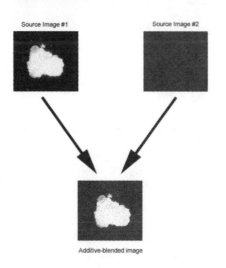

Figure 20.3

A graphical example of additive blending.

To do this requires some render state changes:

```
m_pd3dDevice->SetRenderState(D3DRS_ALPHABLENDENABLE, TRUE);
m_pd3dDevice->SetRenderState(D3DRS_SRCBLEND, D3DBLEND_SRCALPHA);
m_pd3dDevice->SetRenderState(D3DRS_DESTBLEND, D3DBLEND_DESTALPHA);
```

Also, we'll need to turn off z-buffering. We can see through our explosion sprite, so we don't want it to occlude anything behind it.

```
m_pd3dDevice->SetRenderState(D3DRS_ZENABLE, FALSE);
```

TIP

Be careful when you turn depth-buffering off. When you do this, Direct3D no longer sorts and draws triangles correctly; that is, if you have one triangle completely covering up another, Direct3D will still draw both triangles. This completely ruins any illusion of realistic 3D images. The rule of thumb is to draw all of your opaque triangles first, then turn off depth-buffering and draw all your partially transparent objects. Even then, however, you still have to worry about drawing two partially transparent objects on top of each other. Code carefully.

Now we're ready to draw the explosion. We call `m_sprExplo.Render`, and our sprite class takes care of the details of setting up the world matrix. It then calls the `Render` method of `CAnimSequence`, which determines the correct texture (animation frame) to display, and calls `DrawPrimitive` to render the quad.

EXPLOSION CLUSTERS

If you want something a little more dramatic than just one puny explosion sprite, you can code a sequence of explosion sprites at random locations around a center point. I call this an "explosion cluster." Figure 20.4 shows one in action.

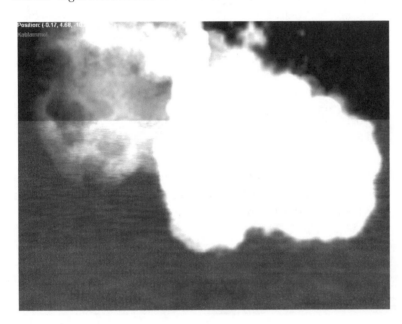

Figure 20.4

A screenshot from our second sample program, Ch20p2_ExplosionCluster.

Explosion clusters are really easy to create—instead of using just one explosion sprite, use several, and create all of them at different positions, at different times, and with different sizes. We accomplish this by using an array of explosion sprites, instead of just one:

```
const int NUMSPRITES = 5;
CSprite m_sprExplo[NUMSPRITES];
```

Now that we've got our array, when an explosion needs to happen, we can just assign each sprite a random position and size:

```
if (uMsg == WM_KEYUP && (wParam == 'b' || wParam == 'B') &&
    !m_timObjectRebirth.IsRunning()) {
  // they've pressed b! time to blow up the object!
  // create one big explosion in the middle
  CreateExplosion(m_sprExplo[0],
    0.0f, 4.0f, 0.0f, // position
    0.0f, 0.0f, 0.0f, // radius
```

```
    15.0f, 5.0f,       // size
    0.0f, 0.0f);       // time
  // create several smaller explosions around it
  for (int q=1; q < NUMSPRITES; q++) {
    CreateExplosion(m_sprExplo[q],
      0.0f, 4.0f, 0.0f, // position
      1.0f, 1.0f, 1.0f, // radius
      10.0f, 5.0f,       // size
      0.0f, 0.25f);      // time
  }
  m_timObjectRebirth.Begin();
}
```

The preceding code comes from the message-processing function of our sample application. The first line checks to see whether the user has clicked the B key, and whether there's an object ready to be blown up. If so, we create one big explosion by calling `CreateExplosion` (which we'll discuss in a moment). We then create several smaller explosions. Notice that the `for` loop starts at one, not zero—we've already used the zero index for the big explosion.

Now I'll show you `CreateExplosion`:

```
void CMyD3DApplication::CreateExplosion(
  CSprite &spr,
  float PosX, float PosY, float PosZ,
  float RadiusX, float RadiusY, float RadiusZ,
  float Size, float SizeDelta,
  float Time, float TimeDelta)
{

  spr.Pos() = D3DXVECTOR3(PosX, PosY, PosZ) +
    RandomNumber(
      D3DXVECTOR3(-RadiusX, -RadiusY, -RadiusZ),
      D3DXVECTOR3(RadiusX, RadiusY, RadiusZ));
  spr.SetSize(Size + RandomNumber(-SizeDelta, SizeDelta));
  spr.Timer().BeginWithDelay(Time+RandomNumber(-TimeDelta, TimeDelta));
}
```

`CreateExplosion` takes a bunch of parameters, but isn't really that complex. The first parameter is the most important—it's a reference to the sprite we're going to be manipulating. All this function really does is play with that sprite. It starts by setting the sprite's position by taking the center point (`PosX`, `PosY`, and `PosZ`) and adding a random vector based on the `RadiusX`, `RadiusY`, and

RadiusZ parameters. This is, in essence, saying "give me a position at PosX plus or minus RadiusX, PosY plus or minus RadiusY, and PosZ plus or minus RadiusZ."

Next we select a random size of our sprite, which can be anywhere between Size+SizeDelta and Size-SizeDelta. This enables us to give an "average" size and a variance.

Finally, we start the explosion sprite's timer. This causes the explosion to animate as it's drawn—remember, thanks to our static UpdateAll method of CTimer, this sprite's timer is going to tick every frame, and every frame this CSprite class will give its associated CAnimSequence the value of this timer, which the CAnimSequence class uses to determine which frame to display.

The only step left is to change our Render function so that it draws all the sprites in the array instead of just one:

```
if (m_timObjectRebirth.IsRunning()) {
  for (int q=0; q < NUMSPRITES; q++) {
    m_sprExplo[q].Render(m_Camera.GetViewMatrix());
  }
}
```

Nothing to it! We just use a for loop and call Render for each sprite in our array.

DROPPING IN THE PARTICLE SYSTEM CODE

Now this explosion is starting to look interesting. The explosion clusters look cool; however, we're still missing something. When things blow up, little pieces of debris fly everywhere. We can leverage our particle system code to provide this "debris" effect.

We've already developed a set of particle system classes for situations just like this. Thanks to the beauty of object-oriented design, we can drop those classes directly into this explosion program without any hassle. However, when we do that we'll discover that the particle system code isn't quite ready for prime time.

So, let's back up a bit and complete it. What do we need to add? Two things:

- **A loop command**. All of the particle scripts last chapter played continuously—particles were constantly created to keep the system running inside the editor. This is good inside an editor, but to put the particle system to actual use, we need to be able to control whether the particle system should run continuously, or if it should simply create its particles once, and stop running when those particles die. As you'll soon learn, this translates into a loop command in our particle system script.

■ **Start and Stop methods**. In the Chapter 19 editor, we wanted the particle system to start as soon as the script was parsed, and to never stop. Again, however, in real life we need the ability to start and stop the particle system—in this specific case, we need to be able to start the system when we create the explosion, and we need to stop the system when the explosion has died out.

The next two sections will examine each of these new things in more detail.

Adding a Loop Command to Our Particle Sequence

As explained previously, we need to add a loop command to the lexicon of our particle system scripts. The loop command should be a property of a particle sequence, which would give us the freedom to make certain sequences "one time" and others infinite. For example, in the particle system script for our explosion, we might want a one-time sequence of fire (red and orange particles), and an infinite sequence of smoke (black particles).

So, this new loop command will be a property of a sequence. What values will it contain? For starters, I didn't see any reason to allow random cycles of looping, so I just made it a RealNumber (as opposed to a Number, which if you'll recall from the previous chapter, can either be an explicit floating-point value or a random keyword, specifying a range of values from which to randomly pick).

Now the property is starting to take shape. We know it's a numeric property of a sequence. We can squeeze in the notion of an "infinite" loop by making a special rule—if the loop property is −1, then that particular sequence should loop infinitely. This is better than forcing the scriptwriter to enter 9999 or some other obscenely high value.

That finalizes our design for this loop property. The next step is to look at how we're going to add the necessary mechanics to the particle system to support this property. There are two main steps to doing this:

1. Add the code to the particle system compiler so that it will interpret the loops keyword in the script correctly and will store the loops setting we've specified into the CParticleEventSequence class.
2. Enhance the event sequence class so that it looks at its loops property to determine whether more particles can be created.

Let's start with the first step.

Interpreting the Loop Keyword Inside the Particle Script

We're enhancing our particle system scripting files slightly so that we can add things like this:

```
particlesystem "Explosion" 1.00 {
  eventsequence "Flaming Debris" {
    loops = 1 // this sequence should loop once
    // debris properties
  }
  eventsequence "Smoke" {
    loops = -1 // this sequence should loop infinitely
    // smoke properties
  }
}
```

This means we need to add code to correctly interpret that `loops` keyword; we need to take the loop value we've specified in the script and put it inside the particle sequence class. For starters, we need someplace to put the loop value. This is easy:

```
class CParticleEventSequence
{
public:
  /* blah */
  int GetLoops(void) { return(m_Loops); }
  void SetLoops(const int data) { m_Loops = data; }
private:
  int m_Loops; // number of loops to run
  /* blah */
};
```

In the preceding code, you can see that we've added an `m_Loops` member that will contain the number of loops this particle sequence should do. We don't want to support the notion of looping 3.457 times, so an integer is appropriate.

Next, we need to add the code that can recognize this new item, parse it, and interpret it successfully so that we end up with a meaningful value inside `m_Loops`. Since this is a new property of the particle event sequence, the logical place to start is by adding the appropriate parsing code to the `ProcessEventSequenceBlock` method of `CParticleEmitter`:

```
bool CParticleEmitter::ProcessEventSequenceBlock(
  CParticleEventSequence &seq,
  std::vector<CParticleEmitterToken>::iterator &TokenIter,
```

```
      std::vector<CParticleEmitterToken>::iterator &EndIter)
{
  // move past the event sequence keyword... (clipped)
  // next token should be the name of the sequence... (clipped)
  // next token should be opening brace... (clipped)
  while (TokenIter->m_Type != CloseBrace) {
    CParticleEmitterToken savedtoken;
    savedtoken = *TokenIter;
    // the first token here can be a SysNumberProperty,
    // SysAlphaBlendModeProperty, SysVectorProperty,
    // or an EventSequence.

    switch (TokenIter->m_Type) {
      case SeqNumericProp:
      {
        /* snip */
        // the next 2 tokens should be an equals, and a number.
        CParticleEmitterTokenizer::NextToken(TokenIter, EndIter);
        if (TokenIter->m_Type != Equals)
          throw("Expected equals sign!");
        CParticleEmitterTokenizer::NextToken(TokenIter, EndIter);
        CParticleEmitterTokenizer::ProcessNumber(number, TokenIter,
          EndIter);
        if (savedtoken.IsEmitRate()) {
          seq.SetEmitRate(number);
        }
        else if (savedtoken.IsLifeTime()) {
          seq.SetLifetime(number);
        }
        else if (savedtoken.IsNumParticles()) {
          seq.SetNumParticles(number.m_Max);
        }
        else if (savedtoken.IsLoops()) { // this one is new!
          seq.SetLoops(number.m_Max);
        }
        else {
          throw("Unknown sequence numeric property!");
        }
      }
      break;
      /* code from this point forward clipped out */
```

I didn't recopy the whole function here. Instead, I just gave you enough surrounding code so you could see how the new lines fit in. The section of code inside the `SeqNumericProp` case is responsible for determining the type of numeric property we have, and setting the appropriate value. Here you can see the lines added to check and see whether the token type is a loop (via the call to the `IsLoops` method of `CParticleSystemToken`), and to set the sequence's loop value if so. Note that because the loop value can't be a random number, we just use the max value of the random range.

The next logical thing to code is the `CParticleEmitterToken` member `IsLoops`. This is easy:

```
class CParticleEmitterToken {
public:
  std::string m_strValue;
  enum TokenType m_Type;
  /* other similar functions snipped! */
  bool IsLoops(void) {
    return(m_strValue.find("LOOPS") != std::string::npos);
  }
};
```

`IsLoops`, like the other members of its ilk, just does a string compare to determine whether this token is in fact a loop token.

Now we need to add the code that identifies the loop token as a particle sequence property. We do this inside the `DetermineTokenType` method of `CParticleEmitterTokenizer`:

```
void CParticleEmitterTokenizer::DetermineTokenType(
  CParticleEmitterToken &token)
{
  /* snip */
  if (token.m_strValue.find("LIFETIME") != std::string::npos ||
      token.m_strValue.find("EMITRATE") != std::string::npos ||
      token.m_strValue.find("NUMPARTICLES") != std::string::npos ||
      token.m_strValue.find("LOOPS") != std::string::npos) { // here!
    token.m_Type = SeqNumericProp; return;
  }
  /* snip */
}
```

Here, I've added another condition for the if statement. If the token's value is `LOOPS` this code will set its type to `SeqNumericProp`, so that the rest of the code can identify and interpret it correctly.

TIP

We don't have to worry about case when comparing the token values. Remember, the parser converts everything to uppercase as it parses.

> **TIP**
>
> This process is somewhat painful. As you use your particle system scripts more, you're going to slowly be adding features and new script keywords. I encourage you to take what I've done and enhance its design so that additions to the lexicon are simple—ideally, you should only need to touch one place in the script interpretation code to add a new property.

With these modifications in place, our script interpretation code now properly recognizes the loops property and puts the appropriate value into m_Loops.

Implementing the Loop Keyword

We now have a valid m_Loops value; the next question is, "How do we act on that?"

This is surprisingly simple. First, we need to add a new member to CParticleEventSequence. This new member will keep track of the total number of particle lifetimes that have passed. We'll call this m_iTotalParticleLives:

```
class CParticleEventSequence
{
public:
  /* snip! */
private:
  /* snip! */
  long int m_iTotalParticleLives;
};
```

Now, all we need to do is add a couple of lines to the Update method of CParticleEventSequence:

```
void CParticleEventSequence::Update(
  float fElapsedTime, float fTimeDelta, D3DXVECTOR3 m_vPartSysPos)
{
  if (!m_Particles) return;
  // update existing particles
  { /* snip! */ }
  float fEmitRateThisFrame = m_EmitRate.GetRandomNumInRange();
  int iNumNewParts = fEmitRateThisFrame * fTimeDelta;
  m_fNumNewPartsExcess +=
    (float)(fEmitRateThisFrame * fTimeDelta)-iNumNewParts;
```

```
    if (m_fNumNewPartsExcess > 1.0f) {
      iNumNewParts += (int)m_fNumNewPartsExcess;
      m_fNumNewPartsExcess -= (int)m_fNumNewPartsExcess;
    }
    /* this part is new! */
    if (m_Loops > 0 &&
        m_iTotalParticleLives+iNumNewParts > m_Loops * m_iNumParticles) {
      iNumNewParts = (m_Loops*m_iNumParticles)-m_iTotalParticleLives;
      if (iNumNewParts <= 0) { iNumNewParts = 0; }
    }
    for (int q=0; q < iNumNewParts && m_Particles->GetNumFreeElements();
         q++) {
      try {
        CreateNewParticle(m_vPartSysPos);
      } catch(...) { q = iNumNewParts; }
    }
}
```

As you can see, the loop mechanism works based strictly on mathematics. We don't really care about how many times each individual particle has been created. Instead, we just track how many lifetimes altogether have occurred since the beginning of the particle system. The total number of lifetimes should always be less than the maximum number of particles multiplied by the number of loops. For example, if we had a particle system with a maximum of 500 particles, and a loops value of two, then the total lifetimes should not exceed 1000 (500 * 2).

The lines of code above enforce that rule. If the number of new particles this frame (iNumNewParts) would exceed the maximum allowed lifetimes, we subtract from it. This gives us the ability to "kill" certain sequences after a certain number of loops—exactly what we need.

Integrating the Particle System

Now that we have everything else squared away, we can turn our attention to the particle script itself. Here's the script I used in the Ch20p3_ComplexExplosion sample program:

```
particlesystem "Explosion" 1.00 {
  position = XYZ(0,0,0)
  eventsequence "Flaming Debris" {
    sourceblendmode = D3DBLEND_ONE
    destblendmode = D3DBLEND_ONE
    loops = 1
    numparticles = 50
```

```
        gravity = XYZ(0,0,0)
        emitrate = 1000
        emitradius = XYZ(random(-1,1),random(-1,1),random(-1,1))
        lifetime = random(1,4)
        texture = "Ch20p3_FlamingDebris.png"
        initial size = random(0.1,1)
        initial color = rgba(1,1,1,1)
        fade so at 0.5 color = rgba(1,1,0,1)
        fade so at 1 color = rgba(1,0,0,1)
        fade so final color = rgba(0,0,0,1)
        initial velocity = XYZ(random(-10,10), random(-10,10),
           random(-10,10))
    }
    eventsequence "Spaceship Debris" {
        sourceblendmode = D3DBLEND_SRCALPHA
        destblendmode = D3DBLEND_DESTALPHA
        loops = 1
        numparticles = 20
        gravity = XYZ(0,0,0)
        emitrate = 1000
        emitradius = XYZ(random(-1,1),random(-1,1),random(-1,1))
        lifetime = 1
        texture = "Ch20p3_FlamingDebris.png"
        initial size = random(0.1,2)
        initial color = rgba(0,1,0,1)
        fade so final color = rgba(0,0,0,1)
        initial velocity = XYZ(random(-24,24), random(-24,24),
           random(-24,24))
    }
}
```

I've created two event sequences for this particle system: the "flaming debris" and the "spaceship debris." They're similar to each other—they both use the same texture, emit rate, and emit radius. However, notice that the spaceship debris is a little bigger, has a little faster velocity. This creates a "double-explosion" effect, where the spaceship debris comes flying out first, followed by the bits of flaming debris. Of course, this is all just my personal artistic tastes—the fun part here is creating your own sequences for your own explosion effects.

There's a little bit of code inside the RestoreDeviceObjects method that's responsible for loading this particle script and compiling it:

```
// initialize particle system
std::string strScript;
LoadFileIntoString("Ch20p3_ParticleScript.txt", strScript);
m_ParticleEmitter.RestoreDeviceObjects(m_pd3dDevice);
m_ParticleEmitter.Compile(strScript.c_str());
```

Here you can see us loading the particle script into an STL string via the `LoadFileIntoString` function. After we've got the STL string containing our script, we tell our particle system to `RestoreDeviceObjects`, and then we tell it to compile the script we've loaded.

That's in essence all there is to it. The only thing left is to add a couple of lines to our `FrameMove` and `Render` methods. In `FrameMove`, we call `m_ParticleEmitter.Update`, and in `Render` we call `m_ParticleEmitter.Render`. Our particle system is wired up and ready to go!

ADDING A SHOCKWAVE

Sometimes, explosion sprites and particles just won't cut it. When your players blow up that giant mechanized camel at the end of level 15, they expect to see something more—something *big*.

Give it to them! Let's add a shockwave to our explosions. As you can see in Figure 20.5, often a shockwave makes an explosion look significantly more dramatic.

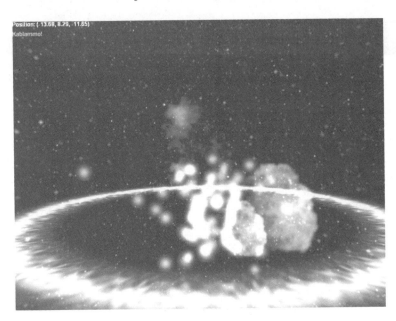

Figure 20.5

A screenshot from our third sample program, `Ch20p3_ComplexExplosion`.

Creating the Shockwave Texture

Let's start developing our shockwave effect by creating the texture we'll use for the wave itself.

We don't need a very large image—a 32×32 texture works just fine. Check out Figure 20.6—we start by creating a simple gradient.

Figure 20.6

The shockwave texture we'll use.

I chose to make my shockwave fade from blue on the edges to white in the middle. Then, I applied a distortion to the gradient to make it appear less even. Next, I faded the top and bottom edges of the texture to black.

At this point I had a good-looking shockwave texture, but it didn't tile. I needed to cut this image in half and mirror it against itself so that there was no seam when I tiled the image horizontally. I did that, and arrived at the final shockwave texture.

> **TIP**
>
> Several good paint programs facilitate this kind of image manipulation. Adobe Photoshop is expensive, but it's the industry standard (in the immortal words of Ferris Bueller, "if you have the means, I highly recommend picking one up"). JASC's Paint Shop Pro is also a good alternative.

Setting Up the Vertices and Texture Coordinates

Now that we've got a texture, the next step is to create the shockwave mesh, which requires a bit of trigonometry. Our goal is to end up with a set of triangles that accurately depict a ring. We can then scale this ring progressively bigger to create our shockwave.

Figure 20.7 shows the layout of our ring model.

At first glance, that may seem complex, but when you think about it all we really need to create that model are the coordinates of several points along the inside of the ring, and several points along the outside of the ring (see Figure 20.8).

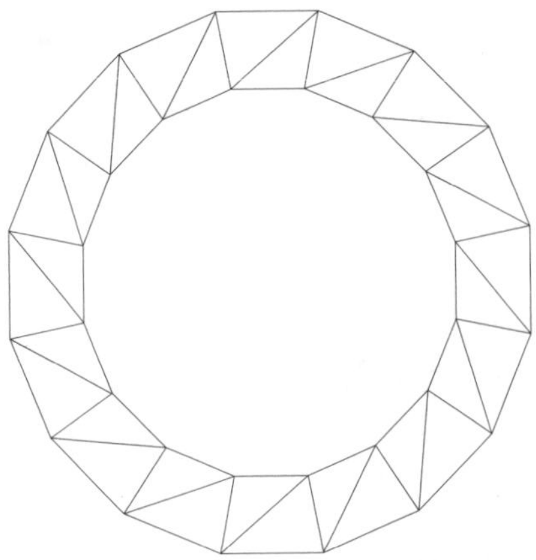

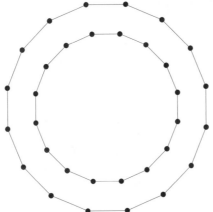

Figure 20.7

The layout of our ring model.

Figure 20.8

The coordinates we need to create our ring.

Note that since the ring is lying flat, like an Aerobie on a table, the y coordinates for each vertex in the ring are going to be the same. What we care about are the x coordinates and the z coordinates—varying the x and z values enables us to create a ring that has width and depth but no height.

Trig to the rescue! The trigonometric sine and cosine functions allow us to plug in an angle and a distance, and get back a coordinate pair. We can use the following formula to figure out an x and z coordinate given a distance d and an angle theta:

$$x = d(\sin(\theta))$$

$$z = d(\cos(\theta))$$

As the formula says, to get the x coordinate, we multiply the distance by the cosine of the angle; to get the z coordinate, we multiply the distance by the sine of the angle. Armed with this tool, we can easily determine the coordinates of all the vertices of our shockwave (see Figure 20.9).

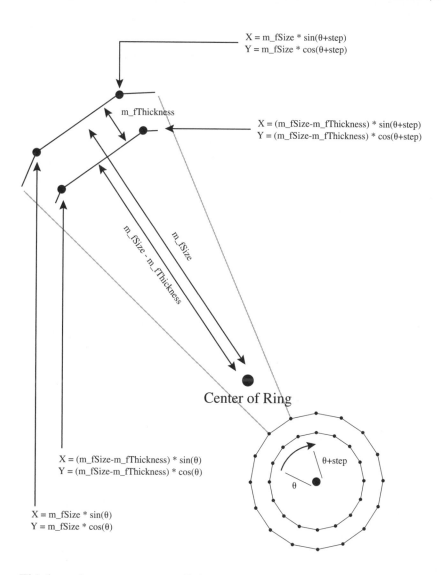

$X = m\_fSize * \sin(\theta+step)$
$Y = m\_fSize * \cos(\theta+step)$

m_fThickness

$X = (m\_fSize-m\_fThickness) * \sin(\theta+step)$
$Y = (m\_fSize-m\_fThickness) * \cos(\theta+step)$

m_fSize - m_fThickness

m_fSize

Center of Ring

$X = (m\_fSize-m\_fThickness) * \sin(\theta)$
$Y = (m\_fSize-m\_fThickness) * \cos(\theta)$

$X = m\_fSize * \sin(\theta)$
$Y = m\_fSize * \cos(\theta)$

$\theta+step$

θ

Figure 20.9

Figuring out the coordinates of the shockwave.

This has a bonus—we can easily increase or reduce the number of triangles in our ring by varying the number of angles for which we calculate points. To create a highly detailed ring, we'd create a point for every angle from 0 to 360 degrees. To create a less detailed ring, we'd step by 10 degrees, 20 degrees, or even 50 degrees (see Figure 20.10).

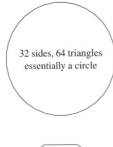

Figure 20.10

Bigger angle steps reduce the number of triangles, but make the ring less round.

This concept plays out in code as follows:

```
// create shockwave
{
  m_iNumVerts = iNumDivisions * 6;
  // Create vertex buffer for shockwave
  hr = m_pd3dDevice->CreateVertexBuffer(
    m_iNumVerts*sizeof(VERTEX_XYZ_DIFFUSE_TEX1),
    D3DUSAGE_WRITEONLY, D3DFVF_XYZ_DIFFUSE_TEX1,
    D3DPOOL_MANAGED, &m_pVB);
  if(FAILED(hr)) return(hr);
  // Fill vertex buffer
  VERTEX_XYZ_DIFFUSE_TEX1* pVertices;
  if(FAILED(m_pVB->Lock(0, 0, (BYTE**)&pVertices, NULL))) return hr;
  // calculate number of vertices
  float fStep = 360.0f / iNumDivisions;

  for (float q=0.0f; q < 360.0f; q+= fStep) {
    // calculate x1, z1, x2, z2, x3,z3 and x4,z4 points
    float x1 = m_fSize * sin(TORADIANS(q));
    float z1 = m_fSize * cos(TORADIANS(q));
    float x2 = (m_fSize-m_fThickness) * sin(TORADIANS(q));
    float z2 = (m_fSize-m_fThickness) * cos(TORADIANS(q));
    float x3 = m_fSize * sin(TORADIANS(q+fStep));
    float z3 = m_fSize * cos(TORADIANS(q+fStep));
```

```
    float x4 = (m_fSize-m_fThickness) * sin(TORADIANS(q+fStep));
    float z4 = (m_fSize-m_fThickness) * cos(TORADIANS(q+fStep));
    /* assign these coordinates to 2 triangles... */
  }
  m_pVB->Unlock();
}
```

As you can see, we start by figuring out the number of vertices we're going to need. This is always going to be the number of divisions we have in our ring multiplied by six (two triangles at three vertices each for each division in our ring). Next, we create and lock a vertex buffer of the correct size.

After that, we calculate our "step" value (fStep). Then, we enter a for loop, going from 0 to 360 degrees, stepping by the step value we calculated. Inside the for loop we calculate the x and z coordinates of the four vertices: the inner and outer coordinates of the ring at our current degree (q), plus the inner and outer coordinates of the ring at the next step (q+fStep). Refer again to Figure 20.9 for a graphical depiction of this. We get the outer coordinate by multiplying by m_fSize, the desired size of the ring. We get the inner coordinate by multiplying by m_fSize-m_fThickness.

When we have the x and z coordinates of all four vertices, we can create the two triangles that form this segment of the ring. I left that code out of the listing above, because it's really easy and somewhat lengthy. Essentially, the code makes two triangles—one from vertices two, one, and four, and the other from vertices one, three, and four. After we create the triangles, we loop, and do the same thing for the next segment.

> **TIP**
>
> You may want to consider reimplementing this using an index buffer. Because each segment of the ring shares its vertices with the segment before it and the segment after it, in the current code there's a fair amount of duplication of vertex data that should be eliminated. I wanted to give you the most straightforward code, so I opted not to include this feature in the demos and leave it to you as an exercise, instead.

Rendering the Shockwave

Time once again to fiddle with the render states. Like my explosions, I prefer my shockwaves additive-blended, so I use the same render states as defined in the previous section.

There's one additional requirement: we need to turn off culling. Normally, we tell Direct3D to cull the triangles that are not facing us so that we don't waste time rendering them. This works well for solid objects, but it breaks for this shockwave effect.

That's because the shockwave really only has one side to it. If we left culling on, our shockwave would become invisible when we viewed it from the bottom (looking up at it). That's because Direct3D would have culled all of the shockwave's triangles, because the normals of all of the triangles are pointing away from the camera. So, in order to keep our triangle viewable from all directions, we need to turn off culling when we draw it.

This is accomplished through a SetRenderState call:

```
m_pd3dDevice->SetRenderState(D3DRS_CULLMODE, D3DCULL_NONE);
```

After we've turned off culling and set up our alpha blending states, we can call the Render method of CShockwave to create the appropriate transformation matrix and actually pump the triangles into Direct3D. CShockwave's Render method looks like this:

```
void CShockwave::Render()
{
  D3DXMATRIX matWorld, matScale, mat;
  D3DXMatrixIdentity( &matWorld );
  D3DXMatrixIdentity( &matScale );
  D3DXMatrixTranslation(&matWorld, m_vPos.x, m_vPos.y, m_vPos.z);
  D3DXMatrixScaling(&matScale, m_fScale, 1.0f, m_fScale);
  mat = matScale * matWorld;

  m_pd3dDevice->SetTransform( D3DTS_WORLD, &mat);
  m_pd3dDevice->SetTexture(0, m_pTexture);
  m_pd3dDevice->SetVertexShader(D3DFVF_XYZ_DIFFUSE_TEX1);
  m_pd3dDevice->SetStreamSource(0, m_pVB,
    sizeof(VERTEX_XYZ_DIFFUSE_TEX1));
  m_pd3dDevice->DrawPrimitive(D3DPT_TRIANGLELIST, 0, m_iNumVerts/3);
}
```

That's nothing we haven't seen before. We start by setting up the world transformation matrix, which is really just a combination of a translation matrix (to move the shockwave model to the right position in our 3D world) and a scale matrix (which allows us to animate the shockwave's movement out from the explosion, by increasing the x and z scale factor).

It's all downhill from there. We set the texture, wire up our vertex shader, and call DrawPrimitive to render the shockwave.

Making the Shockwave Fade Out

There's one last thing we need to add to our shockwave before it's perfect. The shockwave needs to fade out as it expands.

To accomplish this, all we need to do is change the alpha values of the shockwave's vertices every frame. Granted, this isn't the only way to do it, but I like doing it in this manner because it gives us the freedom to get fancy later—for example, we could choose to fade individual vertices of the shockwave faster or slower, or we could choose to fade the inner ring out before or after the outer ring.

For now, though, let's just start simple. Here's a quick function that sets the alpha values of all the vertices in our shockwave:

```
void CShockwave::SetAlpha(int i255Alpha)
{
  VERTEX_XYZ_DIFFUSE_TEX1* pVertices;
  if(FAILED(m_pVB->Lock(0, 0, (BYTE**)&pVertices, NULL))) return;
  for (int q=0; q < m_iNumVerts; q++) {
    pVertices->color = D3DCOLOR_ARGB(i255Alpha,255,255,255);
    pVertices++;
  }
  m_pVB->Unlock();
}
```

As you can see, this method takes one parameter—an integer alpha value. I named it i255Alpha to note explicitly that it doesn't want a floating-point value between zero and one; instead, it wants an integer value between 0 and 255.

We start by locking the vertex buffer. Then, we tromp through each of the vertices in our vertex buffer, and assign them their new alpha value. When we're through, we unlock the buffer. It doesn't get much easier than that.

And with that, we come to the end of our journey. We've now developed a rather dramatic explosion that uses multiple explosion sprites, a particle system, and a shockwave.

CHAPTER WRAP-UP

In this chapter, we learned how to blow up things. We learned how to create pyrotechnics—small sprite-based explosions, as well as catastrophic events, complete with debris and shockwaves. We also looked briefly at skyboxes—a way to create static background images in 3D scenes.

Explosions are one of those things that you'll need to spend some time on for your game. I've provided you with a core, and have illustrated one way to create an explosion. Now you get to do the fun part: you get to take this code and twist it into making explosions that are unique for your game.

ABOUT THE SAMPLE PROGRAMS

This chapter's sample programs walk you through the process of creating a cool explosion effect. There are three programs:

- Ch20p1_SimpleExplosion. This program illustrates how to create the simplest form of an explosion effect—the explosion sprite. It also illustrates how to use a skybox to create a deep space background.
- Ch20p2_ExplosionCluster. Building on the first program, this program shows how to enhance the code to draw several explosions around a central point, instead of just one.
- Ch20p3_ComplexExplosion. This program takes the code from the second program and adds to it a particle system (from the last chapter) and a shockwave.

SKYBOXES

There's one more topic we need to discuss before bringing this chapter to a close. The sample programs of the previous chapter used a ground plane and a completely black sky, which got the job done but was a bit lackluster, graphically. This chapter, I decided to fix that, by replacing the ground plane with a skybox.

What is a skybox? Simply put, it's a way to create background images for 3D programs. We do this by making a huge cube, and putting the camera directly in the middle of it (see Figure 20.11).

This cube is called a *skybox*. On the inside of the cube we paint the far background as seen from different directions, sort of like the sequences of six images we'd use for environment mapping (more on that in a few chapters). For example, if we wanted to create a landscape background, on the top of the cube we'd paint sky, on the bottom we'd paint dirt, and on the four remaining walls we'd paint a horizon scene.

The trick is to make this cube move with the camera, so that the six "walls" are always the same distance away from the camera. That way, regardless of where the camera moves, the background always stays the same. As the camera pans and rotates, the background moves as it should; however, it never gets any closer or farther away.

There are two steps to using skyboxes. First, we must create the six images for the skybox. Second, we must write the code to render the skybox.

> **TIP**
>
> You don't necessarily need to use a cube. You can also use sky-spheres, which cut down on distortion somewhat but use more triangles.

Figure 20.11

Our camera is in the middle of a huge cube!

Camera is in
exact center

Creating the Skybox Images

There are several ways to create good skybox images:

- **Draw them "by hand."** If your environment's suited for it, the easiest way to draw skyboxes is to just make six different images. For example, I used a program called "Universe," by Diard Software (www.diardsoftware.com), to create six different starfield images. I randomly assigned these images (one of which is shown in Figure 20.12) to walls of the box, and my starfield background was good to go.

> **TIP**
>
> There's a great article by Gavin Bell entitled "Creating Backgrounds for 3D Games" that talks a lot about skyboxes and how to generate them. Check it out on Gamasutra: http://www.gamasutra.com/features/visual_arts/19981023/skybox_01.htm.

- **Use a 3D renderer.** If you need to maintain cohesion between the six images—for example, you need mountain ranges to wrap around the sides of your box, a sky above it, and some dirt below, the creation of a skybox becomes a bit more complex. In this situation,

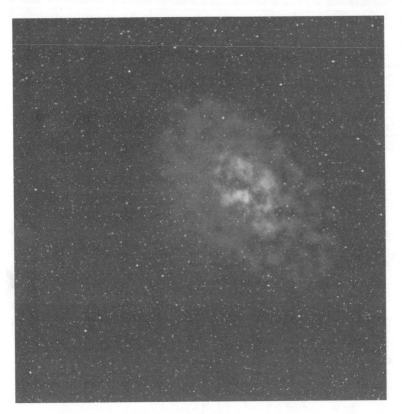

Figure 20.12

One of the images for my deep space skybox.

you could create a 3D scene of your world, and then render it as seen from the six different directions. For example, you could create a Bryce scene, position your camera in the middle of it, and then render six different views with different camera rotations for your six skybox images.

■ **Use a program specifically designed to draw skyboxes.** Another alternative is to use a skybox paint program, which allows you to paint on a skybox as if it were a single image. You draw the picture you want to see, and this program takes care of converting what you've drawn into the six images for the six skybox walls.

The Skybox Code

However you do it, eventually you wind up with your six images. The next step is to write the code to manage and render the skybox.

I created a class, CSkyBox, which does this. The Skybox.h and Skybox.cpp source files contain this class. Here's the definition of it:

```
class CSkyBox
{
public:
  static const int NUMFACES;
  CSkyBox();
  ~CSkyBox();
  HRESULT RestoreDeviceObjects(
    LPDIRECT3DDEVICE8 pDev,
    const char *strTopTextureFilename,
    const char *strBottomTextureFilename,
    const char *strFrontTextureFilename,
    const char *strBackTextureFilename,
    const char *strLeftTextureFilename,
    const char *strRightTextureFilename);
  void InvalidateDeviceObjects();
  void DeleteDeviceObjects();
  enum BoxFace { Top = 0, Bottom, Left, Right, Front, Back };
  LPDIRECT3DTEXTURE8 GetTexture(BoxFace face) {
    return(m_Texture[face]);
  }

  void Render(CCamera &camera);
  float GetSize(void) const { return(m_fSize); }
  void SetSize(const float data) { m_fSize = data; }

private:
  float m_fSize;
  LPDIRECT3DDEVICE8 m_pd3dDevice;
  LPDIRECT3DTEXTURE8 m_Texture[6];
};
```

This skybox class boils down to a size and six textures. We don't really even need a vertex buffer—since there are relatively few vertices for a skybox we can get by with just storing the vertex data on the stack, in system memory, which saves us a little bit of hassle because we don't have to worry about creating, locking, unlocking, and releasing a vertex buffer. You'll see how this plays out in a bit.

TIP

3D programmers have different preferences when it comes to naming the sides of the skybox. I prefer the up, down, right, left, front, back notation, but others like naming them based on their axis and position (+y, -y, +x, -x, +z, -z). Use what you'd like, just be consistent.

In an effort to write more readable code, I created an enumeration that mapped an array index to one of the six sides of the skybox. So instead of wondering which face was stored in m_Texture[3], you could write m_Texture[Right] and know automatically.

Loading the textures is a straightforward matter, but rendering a skybox is more interesting, so let's look at that:

```
void CSkyBox::Render(D3DXMATRIX &matView)
{
  float f;
  VERTEX_XYZ_DIFFUSE_TEX1 vert[4];
  D3DXMATRIX mat = matView;
  mat._41 = mat._42 = mat._43 = 0.0f;
  m_pd3dDevice->SetTransform(D3DTS_VIEW, &mat);
  D3DSURFACE_DESC desc;
  m_Texture[Front]->GetLevelDesc(0, &desc);
  f = 0.5f / (float)(desc.Width);
  vert[0].tu = 0.0f + f; vert[0].tv = 0.0f + f;
  vert[1].tu = 0.0f + f; vert[1].tv = 1.0f - f;
  vert[2].tu = 1.0f - f; vert[2].tv = 0.0f + f;
  vert[3].tu = 1.0f - f; vert[3].tv = 1.0f - f;
  m_pd3dDevice->SetVertexShader(D3DFVF_XYZ_DIFFUSE_TEX1);
  f = m_fSize * 0.5f;
  // left (negative x)
  vert[0].position = D3DXVECTOR3(-f,  f,  f);
  vert[1].position = D3DXVECTOR3(-f, -f,  f);
  vert[2].position = D3DXVECTOR3(-f,  f, -f);
  vert[3].position = D3DXVECTOR3(-f, -f, -f);
  m_pd3dDevice->SetTexture(0, m_Texture[Left]);
  m_pd3dDevice->DrawPrimitiveUP(D3DPT_TRIANGLESTRIP,
    2, (LPVOID) vert, sizeof(VERTEX_XYZ_DIFFUSE_TEX1));
  // SNIP! Same idea for the other sides.
}
```

There are lots of subtle (yet interesting) things going on here. First, look at what we do to the view matrix, in the first chunk of code. We zero out the bottom row, which in effect removes any translation and scaling. This is what keeps the skybox at the same distance regardless of where the camera moves. If we also wanted to lock the skybox's rotation, we'd zero out some other elements, leaving us with an identity matrix.

Next we set up our texture coordinates. Now, you'd expect that we'd just set these to the standard 0.0 and 1.0 so that our full texture is displayed, but as you can see we've got some funny f variable in there. The f variable contains the amount we should offset our texture coordinates by if we want to skim a pixel. Without the f amount, the seams of our skybox would be visible. However, with the f in there, we can adjust our textures ever so slightly to remove the cracks.

> ## CAUTION
> It's very important that we use `DrawPrimitiveUP` any time our vertices aren't stored in a vertex buffer. Attempting to use `DrawPrimitive`, and then trying to force your memory pointer into `SetStreamSource`, doesn't work. Sure, you can get it to compile using a `reinterpret_cast` (just as you can get an elephant into a Volvo by squeezing the elephant hard enough), but Direct3D won't actually display your vertices. Always use `DrawPrimitiveUP` if you're not using a vertex buffer.

Next come the vertices. Setting their coordinates is fairly simple. We change the f value so that it's now equal to half the specified size of our skybox (`m_fSize`). We then set up the vertices as appropriate for this particular side of the skybox. Finally, we set our texture and render. Notice that we're using `DrawPrimitiveUP` instead of the normal `DrawPrimitive`. The `DrawPrimitiveUP` method is specially designed to take a user memory pointer instead of a vertex stream.

I clipped out the code that renders the other sides of the skybox, because the process is exactly the same. That's all there is to it!

EXERCISES

1. See if you can prove, mathematically, why the billboarding code works.
2. Change the code that determines what frame to display given a timer value. Enhance this code so that it operates as fast as possible under "normal" conditions (that is, the timer hasn't been reset or moved backward).
3. Enhance the animation class so that it allows you to create animations that loop, run backward, or ping-pong (go forward to the last frame then backward to the first frame). This will require some significant changes to the code that determines what frame to display given a particular time. You may want to segment the `CAnimation` class into several subclasses—`CReverseAnimation`, `CForwardAnimation`, and `CPingPongAnimation`, for example.
4. Enhance the `CAnimSequence` class so that it can load animations from a file and save them back to a file. The animation file should contain a list of images to load, plus information on how long to display each one. I've learned from experience that, in general, it is better to store information in text files rather than binary files so that anyone with a text editor can

edit them. If you use binary files you lock yourself in to having to create some sort of "editor" or front-end program that takes the user's input and converts it into a file. Hint: use the parser code we made in the preceding chapter as a starting point.

5. Enhance the shockwave class so that it uses an index buffer for the shockwave model.

CHAPTER 21

GUNS AND PROJECTILES

Tank: "So, what do you need, besides a miracle?"
Neo: "Guns. Lots of guns."
——*from* The Matrix

In the old days, every gun in every video game shot little white dots. Today, however, 3D hardware has provided us with a veritable garden full of projectile fruits. In this chapter, we'll pick a few of those tastier fruits to analyze.

This chapter is going to teach you some techniques you can use to make your in-game weaponry look better. We're going to look at three different types of weaponry—a machine gun, which shoots invisible bullets, a plasma cannon that shoots bullets you can see, and a bolt weapon that shoots laser-like beams of energy.

However, before we go there, we need to establish a framework. If you like, follow along by firing up the Ch21p1_FiringRange sample program.

THE FIRING RANGE FRAMEWORK

This chapter's sample program drops you in the middle of a desert and allows you to test-fire all of the weapons. There are no enemies or targets to hit. That's because collision detection is outside the scope of this chapter (and really, this book).

> **TIP**
>
> However, I don't want to leave you completely out in the cold on this subject. There are many excellent techniques that you can use to determine if a bullet hits a target. If the bullet is invisible, use a ray cast/intersection technique similar to the one we will cover in the next chapter. If the bullet is visible, you can use bounding boxes and bounding spheres to determine whether two objects overlap.

The Gun Base Class

I designed the framework of the example program to leverage polymorphism, because to me polymorphism seemed like an intuitive solution. You have many different types of guns, so it makes sense that you'd have a base class (CGun) with several derivations (CLaserGun, CMachineGun, and CPlasmaGun). CGun contains several methods common to all types of guns, as you can see here:

```
class CGun
{
public:
```

```
CGun();
virtual ~CGun();
virtual HRESULT RestoreDeviceObjects(LPDIRECT3DDEVICE8 pDev,
  const char *strMeshFilename);
virtual void InvalidateDeviceObjects();
virtual void Render(CCamera &camera) = 0;
virtual void Update(float fElapsedTime) = 0;
virtual bool CanFire() = 0;
virtual void Fire(CCamera &camera) = 0;
CD3DMesh *GetMesh() { return(m_pMesh); }
CTimer &Timer() { return(m_Timer); }
D3DXVECTOR3 &Pos() { return(m_vPos); }

protected:
  void AssembleWorldMatrix(CCamera &camera, D3DXMATRIX &matWorld,
    D3DXVECTOR3 vTranslation = D3DXVECTOR3(0,0,0));
  CD3DMesh* m_pMesh;
  CTimer m_Timer;
  D3DXVECTOR3 m_vPos;
  LPDIRECT3DDEVICE8 m_pd3dDevice;
};
```

CGun is an abstract base class, thanks to the pure virtual definitions of Render, Update, CanFire, and Fire. These four methods form the core of our common interface—all the different types of guns must implement these methods to be used in our framework.

CGun also contains a lot of data elements common to all guns. We store the model, timer, position, and device pointer here, because all guns need these. There's also a protected method, AssembleWorldMatrix, which we'll look at a bit later.

Switching Weapons

It's time to put this polymorphism to use. Switching weapons is pretty easy now that we know all of our guns are going to conform to the same interface. However, before we can switch weapons we need to load them:

```
m_PlasmaGun.RestoreDeviceObjects(m_pd3dDevice, "Ch21p1_Gun.x");
/* SNIP: init bullet array (we'll discuss this later)
m_LaserGun.RestoreDeviceObjects(m_pd3dDevice, "Ch21p1_Gun.x");
m_MachineGun.RestoreDeviceObjects(m_pd3dDevice, "Ch21p1_Gun.x");
m_PlasmaGun.Pos() = D3DXVECTOR3(0.5f, -0.6f, 1.0f);
```

```
m_LaserGun.Pos() = D3DXVECTOR3(0.5f, -0.6f, 1.0f);
m_MachineGun.Pos() = D3DXVECTOR3(0.5f, -0.6f, 1.0f);
m_pCurGun = &m_MachineGun;
```

In this code, which was taken from the RestoreDeviceObjects method of CMyD3DApplication, you can see that I'm a programmer, not an artist. I've done the unthinkable: I'm using the same model, Ch21p1_Gun.x, for all three guns! If you're into 3D modeling, I encourage you to create different gun models and replace them. As it is now, however, we'll be using the same model, but using different light colors to tint the various guns, so that the machine gun is white, the plasma cannon is green, and the bolt weapon is red.

After I get all the guns loaded, I set their positions. You'll see how these positions come into play a bit later. Finally, I set m_pCurGun to the address of the machine gun (&m_MachineGun). We use the m_pCurGun member to keep track of the current gun. It's nothing more than a pointer to our abstract base class:

```
class CMyD3DApplication
{
  // snip!
  CGun *m_pCurGun;
};
```

To switch weapons, we first need to monitor the appropriate input events. Because I'm an avid FPS fan, I chose to use the one, two, and three number keys to switch weapons. I decided machine gun was one, plasma cannon was two, and the bolt weapon was three.

When a key is pressed, we need to follow this rough sequence of events:

1. Figure out, based on what key was hit, which gun they're switching to. Also figure out if the gun switch is legal (that is, they own the gun they want, they're not currently switching weapons, etc.)
2. Start moving the old gun down, out of the scene.
3. Once the gun is out of the picture, switch to the new gun—stop rendering the old gun and start rendering the new one.
4. Bring the new gun back up into the scene.

There are two main pieces of code that make these events happen. First, we need to check for the keypress. We do this inside the ProcessInput method:

```
void CMyD3DApplication::ProcessInput()
{
  const float fSpeed = 0.5f;
  unsigned char m_bKey[256];
```

```
    ZeroMemory( m_bKey, 256 );
    GetKeyboardState(m_bKey);
    // Process keyboard input
    // SNIP! I removed the standard keyboard control checks
    // because they're not new.
    if(m_bKey['1'] & 128) BeginGunTransition(&m_MachineGun);
    if(m_bKey['2'] & 128) BeginGunTransition(&m_PlasmaGun);
    if(m_bKey['3'] & 128) BeginGunTransition(&m_LaserGun);
    // SNIP! I removed mouselook because again, it's nothing new.
}
```

Here you can see the beginnings of the logic. If the one, two, or three keys are down, we call BeginGunTransition with a single parameter: the new weapon we want to use. Here's what BeginGunTransition looks like:

```
void CMyD3DApplication::BeginGunTransition(CGun *pNextGun)
{
    if (typeid(*pNextGun) == typeid(*m_pCurGun)) return;
    if (m_TransitionTimer.IsRunning()) return;
    m_pNextGun = pNextGun;
    m_TransitionTimer.Begin();
}
```

In this function, we do two things. The top two lines concern themselves with making sure that the gun switch is legal. Notice the typeid at play here. We use typeid (part of C++'s RTTI capabilities) to derive the class that the pNextGun and m_pCurGun pointers are pointing to. If the type of *m_pCurGun is equal to the type of *pNextGun, then our user is being dumb. They're trying to switch to the weapon type they're currently using, and we disregard their request.

The second if line checks to see if the transition timer is running. If it is, that means we're already in the middle of switching from one weapon to another, so we ignore the user's request.

The next two lines concern themselves with actually setting up the transition. First, we

> **CAUTION**
>
> Notice that we're dereferencing the pointers before we compare them. That's because typeid(pNextGun) is always going to be CGun *. However, typeid(*pNextGun) (notice the star in there) will vary depending on what pNextGun is actually pointing to. This is one of the most common mistakes I see programmers make when they're first learning RTTI. If you're trying to compare types of objects through a pointer, make sure you dereference it.

store the gun we're switching to inside the m_pNextGun member. Second, we start our transition timer.

From here, the FrameMove method implements the rest of the logic:

```
HRESULT CMyD3DApplication::FrameMove()
{
  // irrelevant code snipped out here
  if (m_pCurGun) m_pCurGun->Update(m_fElapsedTime);
  if (m_TransitionTimer.IsRunning()) {
    if (m_pCurGun) {
      if (m_TransitionTimer.GetTime() < 0.25f) {
        m_pCurGun->Pos() = D3DXVECTOR3(
          0.5f, -0.6f-(m_TransitionTimer.GetTime()*4), 1.0f);
      }
      else {
        m_pCurGun = m_pNextGun;
        m_pCurGun->Pos() = D3DXVECTOR3(
          0.5f, -1.6f+(m_TransitionTimer.GetTime()*4)-1.0f, 1.0f);
      }
      if (m_TransitionTimer.GetTime() > 0.5f) {
        m_TransitionTimer.Stop();
        m_pNextGun = NULL;
      }
    }
  }
  return S_OK;
}
```

After updating the current gun, we check to see whether the transition timer is running. A running transition timer means that we're transitioning weaponry, and we enter into the main section of logic.

The total transition time is half a second. That half second is further divided into two sections. During the first 0.25 seconds, we are moving the current gun down off the screen. From 0.25 to 0.5 seconds, we're moving the new gun up into the scene. During each chunk of movement, we use the timer's actual value to set the gun's position.

When we hit (or exceed) half a second, we stop our timer and set m_pNextGun to NULL, reminding ourselves that we're done with this transition. That's it! Weaponry switched!

Positioning and Rendering the Gun Model

During our discussion of switching weaponry, I sort of sidestepped a very important issue, which is, how do we render the gun in the first place?

The secret to rendering weaponry first-person-shooter style is to invert the view matrix, as this listing of CMachineGun::Render illustrates:

```
void CMachineGun::Render(CCamera &camera)
{
  if (!m_pd3dDevice) return;
  // create a light - SNIPPED!
  // if firing, render machinegun flare - also snipped.
  // We'll discuss this in the next section.
  // render gun model
  {
    D3DXMATRIX matWorld;
    // snip! Some logic right here will be discussed later!
    AssembleWorldMatrix(camera, matWorld,
      D3DXVECTOR3(0.0f, 0.0f, 0.0f));
    m_pd3dDevice->SetTransform( D3DTS_WORLD, &matWorld );
    m_pd3dDevice->SetRenderState( D3DRS_ALPHABLENDENABLE, FALSE);
    m_pd3dDevice->SetRenderState(D3DRS_ZENABLE, TRUE);
    m_pd3dDevice->SetRenderState( D3DRS_CULLMODE,  D3DCULL_CCW );
    m_pd3dDevice->SetRenderState( D3DRS_LIGHTING, TRUE);
    m_pMesh->Render(m_pd3dDevice);
  }
}
```

Here you can see the overarching structure of the Render method. I've cut out the first two sections of code, which create a white light and render the flare of the machine gun. We'll discuss them in a moment. For now, though, focus your attention on the block of code that renders the weapon.

Most of the good stuff is hidden inside AssembleWorldMatrix. That method (which belongs to CGun) sucks in the camera, along with an offset value, and spits out the world matrix needed to render the gun appropriately. The second parameter to AssembleWorldMatrix is actually a reference, and that's where AssembleWorldMatrix stores the correct matrix. Here you can see this code turn around and set the matrix calculated by AssembleWorldMatrix as the world matrix for the scene. It then sets up some render states, and calls the Render method of m_pMesh to pump out the triangles.

So, now that you've got the zoomed-out view, let's look at `AssembleWorldMatrix`:

```
void CGun::AssembleWorldMatrix(CCamera &camera,
  D3DXMATRIX &matWorld, D3DXVECTOR3 vTranslation)
{
  D3DXMATRIX matTrans, matScale, matRot;
  D3DXMATRIX matView = camera.GetViewMatrix();
  D3DXMATRIX matViewInverse;
  float fDet;
  D3DXMatrixInverse(&matViewInverse, &fDet, &matView);
  D3DXMatrixTranslation(&matTrans,
    m_vPos.x+vTranslation.x,
    m_vPos.y+vTranslation.y,
    m_vPos.z+vTranslation.z);
  D3DXMatrixScaling(&matScale, 0.15f, 0.15f, 0.15f);
  D3DXMatrixRotationYawPitchRoll(&matRot,
    (float)PI-((float)PI/15.0f),
    (float)PI/16.0f, 0.0f);

  matWorld = matRot * matScale * matTrans * matViewInverse;
}
```

There is lots of math at play here. We start by grabbing the view matrix from the camera, and inverting it. Here's a kernel of truth: if you set your world matrix to be the inverse of your view matrix, a point at local coordinates (0,0,0), when run through that world matrix, will move to the exact position of your camera. (I invite you to prove it by working some actual numbers!)

So, inverting the view matrix takes care of moving our gun along with our camera. In the next section of code, we convert the translation vector we are given, along with our gun's position, into a translation matrix. The gun position (`m_vPos`) is a vector that describes the position of the gun relative to the camera. It's understood that if you set `m_vPos` to (0,0,1), you're saying, "hey, I want this gun to be one unit in front of the camera, regardless of where the camera is or which direction it's actually facing." Imagine that we've mounted the gun on the camera.

Recall that in our `RestoreDeviceObjects` method of `CMyD3DApplication`, we set the position of all the guns to be (0.5, –0.6, 1.0). This positions the gun a half unit off to the right, 0.6 units down, and one unit in front of the camera. Those numbers seemed to position the gun realistically for a right-handed person. If I had wanted a lefty player instead, I could have used –0.5 instead of 0.5 for the x component.

Now, let's get back to `AssembleWorldMatrix`. After we create our translation matrix, we create two more matrices—`matScale` and `matRot`—which scale down our gun model and rotate it so that the barrel is pointing out away from us. The numbers I've plugged into these matrices have no significance; I simply played around with some numbers until I got the gun size and orientation that I wanted.

The final line of code is where it all comes together. We multiply all of our matrices together. Remember, the order matters when doing matrix multiplication.

We start by rotating the model and scaling it down. At this point, we have a world matrix that positions the gun correctly, but leaves it at world position (0,0,0). The next step is to translate the gun based on the gun position relative to the camera. Finally, we multiply all that by the inverse of the view matrix, which moves the gun to the camera's position and orientation.

TIP

If you're having trouble following the math, one of the best ways to learn how it all works is by taking certain matrices out of the big multiplication chain and seeing how the program changes. That, combined with tracing through the code, should allow you to visualize what's going on.

Firing the Gun

We now know how to render a gun, and how to switch weapons. But we are still missing the most important piece: getting the gun to fire.

Firing of the gun starts when `ProcessInput` detects that the mouse button is down:

```
DIMOUSESTATE2 dims2;
m_InputManager.ReadMouse(dims2);
// mouselook snipped!
if (dims2.rgbButtons[0] && m_pCurGun && m_pCurGun->CanFire())
  m_pCurGun->Fire(m_Camera);
```

Here you can see `ProcessInput` reading the mouse, and checking to see if the left button (`rgbButtons[0]`) is pressed. If it is pressed, we call the `CanFire` method of the current gun to determine whether we can fire. If `CanFire` returns true, we call the `Fire` method of the current gun.

It's the individual gun's responsibility to determine whether or not it can be fired. This allows us to put in recharge or reloading times, and all sorts of other fun stuff. Likewise, it's the gun's responsibility to actually fire when we call its `Fire` method. Different guns will do different things, and we will examine their different behaviors in the next few sections.

THE MACHINE GUN

Now that you know the framework we are running in, we can look closely at each of the three different gun types, starting with the old favorite, the machine gun.

The main special effect for the machine gun is the muzzle flash—you know, that flash of light or fire that comes out the barrel of a gun when it is shot (see Figure 21.1).

Figure 21.1

A screenshot of our machine gun in action.

The machine gun implements this effect using a simple muzzle sprite and some creative scaling and positioning code.

Let's start by looking at the class definition for CMachineGun:

```
class CMachineGun : public CGun
{
public:
  CMachineGun();
  virtual ~CMachineGun();
  virtual HRESULT RestoreDeviceObjects(LPDIRECT3DDEVICE8 pDev,
    const char *strMeshFilename);
  virtual void InvalidateDeviceObjects();
  virtual void Render(CCamera &camera);
```

```
virtual void Update(float fElapsedTime);
virtual bool CanFire();
virtual void Fire(CCamera &camera);

protected:
  CAnimSequence *m_pAnim;
  CSprite m_sprMuzzleFlare;
};
```

Short and sweet—you can see here the derivation from CGun, plus also the animation sequence and sprite members. Now let's look at how to fill up those members.

Loading the Muzzle Flash Sprite

Before we can draw the muzzle flash, we need to load its sprite. Here's the code of CMachineGun::RestoreDeviceObjects:

```
HRESULT CMachineGun::RestoreDeviceObjects(LPDIRECT3DDEVICE8 pDev, const char
*strMeshFilename)
{
  HRESULT hr = S_OK;
  hr = CGun::RestoreDeviceObjects(pDev, strMeshFilename);
  if(FAILED(hr)) return(hr);
  m_pAnim = new CAnimSequence(pDev);
  m_pAnim->AddFrame("Ch21p1_MachineGunFlare.dds", 0.025f);
  m_sprMuzzleFlare.SetAnim(m_pAnim);
  return(S_OK);
}
```

Notice right off the bat that we call the base class implementation of RestoreDeviceObjects. This gives our base class a chance to load up the gun model. After that, we create a new animation sequence, and add a single frame to it, with a delay of 0.025 seconds (really fast). We then attach this animation to our muzzle flare sprite (shown in Figure 21.2).

Firing the Machine Gun

We just finished learning about how the framework calls our Fire method. Now, let's look at firing from the machine gun's perspective. It has just been told to fire; here's what it does:

Figure 21.2

Our muzzle flare image.

```
void CMachineGun::Fire(CCamera &camera)
{
  m_Timer.Start();
  m_sprMuzzleFlare.Timer().Begin();
  m_sprMuzzleFlare.SetSize(RandomNumber(1.0f, 3.0f));
  m_sprMuzzleFlare.SetRotationRoll(RandomNumber(0.0f, 2.0f*(float)PI));
}
```

Here you can see the machine gun start its timer, and start the timer on the muzzle flash sprite. It then assigns a random size and rotation to the sprite, just to give it some variety. If the exact same sprite were used, with the exact same size and rotation, it would look pretty primitive. However, by varying the size and rotation we can create the illusion of several different kinds of muzzle flashes without wasting a lot of graphics memory.

That's cool, but you're probably wondering how we get the machine gun muzzle flash to flicker on and off, simulating the firing of many bullets per second. For the answer to that, we must look at the CanFire and Update methods. Let's start with CanFire:

```
bool CMachineGun::CanFire()
{
  return(!m_Timer.IsRunning());
}
```

Well, that's easy enough. We can fire if the timer is not running. Now let's look at Update:

```
void CMachineGun::Update(float fElapsedTime)
{
  if (m_Timer.GetTime() > 0.05f) {
    m_Timer.Stop();
  }
}
```

Ah-ha! There's the trick! We stop the timer after it has been running for longer than 0.05 seconds. However, recall that our animation sequence only has one frame, and that frame only displays for 0.025 seconds!

That's how the muzzle flashes. Let's assume the player is holding down the left mouse button. On the first frame, the machine gun will think "sure, I can fire," and our framework will call the machine gun's Fire method. At that point, the gun timer and the sprite timer both start. Then 0.025 seconds later, the sprite reaches the end of its animation sequence and stops displaying. However, we've still got another 0.025 seconds to go until our gun timer reaches 0.05 and we can fire again. That's how we get the rapid fire of the machine gun—if we let our sprite display for 0.05 seconds or longer, we would just end up with a constantly drawn muzzle flare, which isn't even close to realistic.

> **TIP**
>
> Remember, because our timers register themselves and our framework is calling CTimer::UpdateAll, the gun and sprite timers will run without us ever having to call their update methods.

Drawing the Muzzle Flash

You've now seen the logic behind firing the machine gun. There is only one thing left, and that's the code that actually renders the muzzle flash on the screen.

Earlier I snipped out an excerpt from CMachineGun::Render. Here's that missing section:

```
// if firing, render machinegun flare
if (m_Timer.IsRunning()) {
  D3DXMATRIX matEmitterWorld, matInvView, matTrans,
    matRot, matGunTrans;
  float fDet;
  D3DXMatrixInverse(&matInvView, &fDet, &camera.GetViewMatrix());
  D3DXMatrixTranslation(&matTrans, 0.0f, 0.0f, 2.8f);
  D3DXMatrixRotationYawPitchRoll(&matRot, (float)PI, 0.0f, 0.0f);
  D3DXMatrixTranslation(&matGunTrans, m_vPos.x, m_vPos.y, m_vPos.z);
```

```
matEmitterWorld = matRot * matGunTrans * matTrans * matInvView;
m_sprMuzzleFlare.Pos() = D3DXVECTOR3(
  matEmitterWorld._41,
  matEmitterWorld._42,
  matEmitterWorld._43);

// snipped - set render states and texture stage states for flare.
m_sprMuzzleFlare.Render(camera.GetViewMatrix());
}
```

Again, the secret to this code is the inverted view matrix. Notice the similarities between this code and AssembleWorldMatrix—in both places, we're combining the inverted view matrix with some other transformations to arrive at a final world matrix. However, here we're not using that world matrix entirely. Once we have it, we just use its bottom row (the translation row) to set our sprite's position. The billboarding code within the sprite itself takes care of rotating the sprite so that it faces the camera.

Also, just like with AssembleWorldMatrix, there are some numbers in this code that are entirely based on my opinion. The (0.0, 0.0, 2.8) translation simply places the muzzle flash on what I perceived to be the end of the machine gun barrel. There's no doubt a more scientific way of doing this—you could probably measure the extent of the vertices in the model or something—but for this simple example program an eyeballed value will work just fine. I leave the more advanced code as an exercise for you.

Recoil

At this point, our machine gun code is almost complete. We've got the flare rendering correctly and the firing timings down. However, there's one piece missing. When a real machine gun fires, it recoils. Let's learn how to simulate that.

The secret to recoil is in the offset parameter that we pass to AssembleWorldMatrix. Here's the chunk of code to look at:

```
// render gun model
{
  D3DXMATRIX matWorld;
  AssembleWorldMatrix(camera, matWorld,
    m_Timer.IsRunning() ?
    D3DXVECTOR3(0.0f, 0.0f, RandomNumber(0.0f, -0.5f)) :
    D3DXVECTOR3(0.0f, 0.0f, 0.0f));
  m_pd3dDevice->SetTransform( D3DTS_WORLD, &matWorld );
  m_pd3dDevice->SetRenderState( D3DRS_ALPHABLENDENABLE, FALSE );
```

```
m_pd3dDevice->SetRenderState(D3DRS_ZENABLE, TRUE);
m_pd3dDevice->SetRenderState( D3DRS_CULLMODE,  D3DCULL_CCW );
m_pd3dDevice->SetRenderState( D3DRS_LIGHTING, TRUE);
m_pMesh->Render(m_pd3dDevice);
}
```

Look at what's happening with the final parameter to `AssembleWorldMatrix`. That mess of conditional expression operators (question marks and colons) is collectively saying, "If the timer is running, give `AssembleWorldMatrix` a vector with x and y components zero, but a z component between 0.0 and 0.5. If the timer isn't running, give `AssembleWorldMatrix` a vector of (0,0,0)."

Let's think about that for a minute. If the timer is running, it means the gun is firing. `AssembleWorldMatrix` will take the translation vector we provide to it and add it to the gun's position when it creates the world matrix. So in essence all this code is doing is randomly subtracting a little bit from the gun's z position, causing it to move back a little bit. Done per frame, this creates the illusion that the machine gun is recoiling like mad. Perfect!

THE PLASMA CANNON

With that, we come to the end of our machine gun discussion. Now let's look at the next weapon in our arsenal, the plasma cannon. To see it in action, check out Figure 21.3.

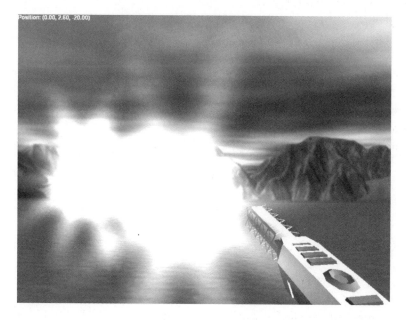

Figure 21.3

A screenshot of our plasma gun in action.

Bullets and Bullet Arrays

The chief difference between the plasma cannon and the machine gun is that you can see the plasma cannon's bullets. This doesn't seem like that big of a difference, but as you'll see, it necessitates a lot of changes under the hood.

For starters, there's the question of who should "own" the bullets. Obviously, we need some sort of array to hold the positions of all the plasma bullets this machination fires. But, should this array be a member of the `CPlasmaGun` class?

I kicked this around a bit and ultimately decided that the bullet arrays should exist independent of the gun classes. The main reason I decided on this was because there may be a situation where we want multiple guns, but, for performance reasons, we also want to set a limit on the total number of bullets that can be fired. With this "bullets separate from gun" paradigm, we can keep one master array of bullets (and have it be a fixed size), and have as many plasma guns as we want use that array when they fire.

This means that our `CPlasmaGun` class requires some additional stuff:

```
class CPlasmaGun : public CGun
{
public:
  CPlasmaGun();
  virtual ~CPlasmaGun();
  virtual HRESULT RestoreDeviceObjects(LPDIRECT3DDEVICE8 pDev,
  const char *strMeshFilename);
  virtual void InvalidateDeviceObjects();
  virtual void Render(CCamera &camera);
  virtual void Update(float fElapsedTime) { }

  virtual bool CanFire();
  virtual void Fire(CCamera &camera);
  void SetBulletArray(CPlasmaBulletArray *array) {
    m_pBulletArray = array;
  }

protected:
  CPlasmaBulletArray *m_pBulletArray;
};
```

Again, just like with `CMachineGun`, you can see the ": public CGun" phrase nailing down `CPlasmaGun` as a class derived from `CGun`. Notice, however, that we've got a new member, `m_pBulletArray`, and a new method, `SetBulletArray`. Together, these link the plasma gun to its bullet array.

Here's what a bullet array looks like:

```
class CPlasmaBulletArray
{
public:
  CPlasmaBulletArray();
  virtual ~CPlasmaBulletArray();
  static const int NUMBULLETS;
  HRESULT RestoreDeviceObjects(LPDIRECT3DDEVICE8 pDev);
  HRESULT InvalidateDeviceObjects();
  void UpdateAll(float fElapsedTime);
  void RenderAll(CCamera &camera);
  void AddBullet(D3DXVECTOR3 vPos, D3DXVECTOR3 vVelocity);
protected:
  LPDIRECT3DDEVICE8 m_pd3dDevice;
  LPDIRECT3DVERTEXBUFFER8 m_pVB;
  CAnimSequence *m_pAnim;
  CRecyclingArrayDyn<CPlasmaBullet> *m_pBullets;
};
```

As the code implies, `CPlasmaBulletArray` is really just a glorified `CRecyclingArrayDyn`. This class wraps access to the recycling array, and enhances it with bullet-specific functionality. The number of bullets is determined by the `NUMBULLETS` constant (remember, you initialize static member variables independent from class definitions). Also in this class are the obligatory `RestoreDeviceObjects` and `InvalidateDeviceObjects`, plus `UpdateAll` and `RenderAll` methods to move and draw all the bullets. The final member, `AddBullet`, allows us to add a bullet to the array by providing its initial position and its velocity.

An individual bullet is nothing spectacular either, as you see here:

```
class CPlasmaBullet : public CBullet
{
public:
  CPlasmaBullet() { }
  virtual ~CPlasmaBullet() { }
  CSprite m_Sprite;
};
```

The only interesting things here are that `CPlasmaBullet` contains a sprite (to draw the actual bullet), and that `CPlasmaBullet` derives from a `CBullet` base class. Here's what `CBullet` looks like:

```
class CBullet
{
public:
  CBullet() {
    m_vPos = D3DXVECTOR3(0,0,0); m_vVelocity = D3DXVECTOR3(0,0,0);
  }
  CBullet(D3DXVECTOR3 vPos, D3DXVECTOR3 vVelocity) {
    m_vPos = vPos; m_vVelocity = vVelocity;
  }
  virtual ~CBullet() { }
  D3DXVECTOR3 &Pos() { return(m_vPos); }
  D3DXVECTOR3 &Velocity() { return(m_vVelocity); }
protected:
  D3DXVECTOR3 m_vPos;
  D3DXVECTOR3 m_vVelocity;
};
```

This base class provides each and every specific bullet type (CBullet derivative) with a position and a velocity, along with some handy constructors and accessor functions.

Updating and Rendering Bullets

Here's an easy topic. Rendering bullets requires nothing more than setting the sprite position equal to the bullet's position. Updating bullets just means adding their velocity to their world position to move them in the direction they're supposed to go. So, the UpdateAll and RenderAll methods of CPlasmaBulletArray are very short, so short in fact that I'm not going to list them here. But, I will show you the texture used for the plasma bullets in Figure 21.4.

TIP

The only other trick is that the bullets have a lifespan. I hard-coded this to five seconds; once a bullet reaches its five-second mark, the bullet array Update method kills it. You may, however, want to change this so that the bullets die when they are a specified distance away from the user or when they hit a wall.

Figure 21.4

The texture used for the plasma bullets.

Firing a Bullet

Now that we know how to draw and move bullets, let's learn how to create one. Here's the code from `CPlasmaGun::Fire`:

```
void CPlasmaGun::Fire(CCamera &camera)
{
  if (m_pBulletArray == NULL) {
    OutputDebugString("\nCPlasmaGun::Fire: error - I can't fire a"
      " bullet because I'm not hooked up to any bullet array.");
    return;
  }
  try {
    D3DXMATRIX matWorld, matInvView;
    D3DXVECTOR3 vPosition = D3DXVECTOR3(0.0f, 0.0f, 0.0f);
    D3DXVECTOR3 vVelocity = D3DXVECTOR3(0.0f, 0.0f, 1.0f);
    D3DXVECTOR3 vPositionOut, vVelocityOut;
    float fDet;
    // invert view and remove translation
    D3DXMatrixInverse(&matInvView, &fDet, &camera.GetViewMatrix());
    matInvView._41 = 0.0f; matInvView._42 = 0.0f;
    matInvView._43 = 0.0f;
    AssembleWorldMatrix(camera, matWorld);
```

```
        D3DXVec3TransformCoord(&vPositionOut,&vPosition, &matWorld);
        D3DXVec3TransformCoord(&vVelocityOut,&vVelocity, &matInvView);
        m_pBulletArray->AddBullet(vPositionOut, vVelocityOut*50.0f);
        m_Timer.Begin();
    }
  catch(...) { return; }
}
```

To correctly fire a bullet, we need to know its position and its velocity. We can get the position by taking a (0,0,0) vector and running it through the world matrix, which translates our (0,0,0) point to the gun's world position.

We can obtain our velocity by starting with a (0,0,1) vector—because the player is firing bullets into the scene—and running it through our inverted view matrix. However, there's a slight catch. When we're calculating the bullet velocity, we don't care about the actual position of the camera, because we've got that covered by the position vector. So, we set the bottom row of the inverted view matrix to zeros, just like we did for the skybox code in the last chapter. This gives us a matrix that can translate our relative direction—(0,0,1), or "straight ahead"—into an absolute direction based on the angle of the camera. So, if our camera is facing backward (that is, looking down the negative z axis), this matrix will transform our (0,0,1) point into (0,0,–1). Nifty!

After we have both the position and velocity vectors, we can call `AddBullet` to create a bullet and add it to the array. Notice that I multiply the velocity by 50 to make the bullet move fast. Note also that I could have just as easily specified a (0,0,50) vector instead of a (0,0,1) vector—same difference, it's just a question of whether you want to do the multiplication first or last.

Plasma Cannon Miscellany and Wrap-Up

The hardest part to rendering the plasma cannon is getting the bullets to behave correctly. We've discussed that, however, so here are a few other details I don't want you to miss:

- `CanFire`. The plasma gun's `CanFire` method forces the user to wait a tenth of a second between firings. It does this by looking at the gun's timer, which is started as part of the `Fire` method.
- `Recoil`. The timer is also used to simulate recoil on the gun. We implemented the machine gun recoil by using a random z modifier; however, for the plasma gun I wanted a slightly different effect. I wanted the gun to jump back quickly when a bullet was fired, and then slowly return to its original position. So, the plasma gun's recoil function calculates the z modifier based on the gun's timer. It starts with –1, then adds five times the timer's value. This, in my opinion, creates a pretty realistic-looking recoil. Play with the numbers if you would like.

And with that, we can end our discussion of plasma guns. Of course, you can make all sorts of different guns based on these same gun, bullet, velocity, and positioning algorithms. For example, replace the velocity with an acceleration, add some smoke particles, and change the bullet sprite, and you've got yourself some pretty sweet rockets.

THE BOLT WEAPON

Time for a discussion of the third and final weapon—the laser gun. This gun is unique from both the plasma and machine guns in that it fires a straight beam of energy. I decided there would be two separate elements to this effect. First and foremost, I had to draw a realistic-looking laser when the gun was fired. Second, I wanted to use a particle system to create some extra energy particles flying out from the gun when it was fired. Yes, I know it is completely un-scientific— whoever heard of a real laser "leaking" energy?—but I thought it would look cool! Check out Figure 21.5 and see if you agree with me.

Figure 21.5

A screenshot showing our bolt weapon (laser gun) in action.

It all starts with a laser texture (see Figure 21.6). I created this by applying a distortion filter to a simple red to white gradient.

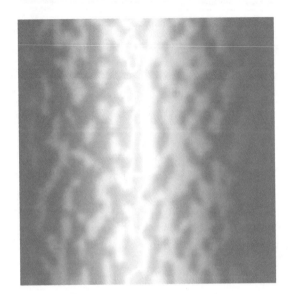

Figure 21.6

Our laser texture.

The CLaserGun Class

After we have the laser's texture, the next logical step is to define our CLaserGun class:

```
class CLaserGun : public CGun
{
public:
  CLaserGun();
  virtual ~CLaserGun();
  virtual HRESULT RestoreDeviceObjects(LPDIRECT3DDEVICE8 pDev,
    const char *strMeshFilename);
  virtual void InvalidateDeviceObjects();
  virtual void Render(CCamera &camera);
  virtual void Update(float fElapsedTime);
  virtual bool CanFire();
  virtual void Fire(CCamera &camera);

protected:
  LPDIRECT3DVERTEXBUFFER8 m_pVBLaser;
  LPDIRECT3DINDEXBUFFER8 m_pIBLaser;
  CAnimSequence *m_pAnim;
  CParticleEmitter m_Emitter;
  D3DXMATRIX m_matWorld;
```

```
  bool m_bIsFiring;
};
```

Right away you can spot some interesting things going on in this class. For example, we're using both a vertex and index buffer. We're also using a particle system, and for some odd reason we're storing a world matrix inside the class. All these mysteries, and more, will soon be solved—just keep reading!

Firing the Laser

What fun is a laser if you can't fire it? Here's the code that gets the job done:

```
void CLaserGun::Fire(CCamera &camera)
{
  m_Timer.Start();
  m_Emitter.Start();
  D3DXMATRIX matEmitterWorld, matInvView, matTrans,
    matRot, matGunTrans;
  float fDet;
  D3DXMatrixInverse(&matInvView, &fDet, &camera.GetViewMatrix());
  D3DXMatrixTranslation(&matTrans, 0.0f, 0.0f, 0.0f);
  D3DXMatrixRotationYawPitchRoll(&matRot, (float)PI, 0.0f, 0.0f);
  D3DXMatrixTranslation(&matGunTrans, m_vPos.x, m_vPos.y, m_vPos.z);
  m_matWorld = matRot * matGunTrans * matTrans * matInvView;
  D3DXMatrixTranslation(&matTrans, 0.0f, 0.0f, 2.8f);
  matEmitterWorld = matRot * matGunTrans * matTrans * matInvView;
  m_Emitter.SetPos(D3DXVECTOR3(
    matEmitterWorld._41,
    matEmitterWorld._42,
    matEmitterWorld._43)
  );
}
```

Most of this code concerns itself with creating the appropriate world matrix, but notice in the first two lines that we set the timer running and we start up the particle system. Notice also that we store the world matrix—we do this because I decided that after a beam fires, it can't move, even if the player that fired it is still on the move. Storing the world matrix inside m_matWorld creates beams that stay in one place as they fade out.

Drawing the Laser

Now that we have our world matrix, drawing the laser becomes pretty easy:

```
// if firing, render laser
if (m_Timer.IsRunning()) {
  WORD* pIndices;
  if( FAILED(m_pIBLaser->Lock( 0, 6*sizeof(WORD),
    (BYTE**)&pIndices, 0 ))) return;
  VERTEX_XYZ_DIFFUSE_TEX1* pVertices;
  if(FAILED(m_pVBLaser->Lock(0, 0, (BYTE**)&pVertices, NULL))) return;
  pIndices[0] = 3; pIndices[1] = 2; pIndices[2] = 1;
  pIndices[3] = 3; pIndices[4] = 1; pIndices[5] = 0;
  float a = 1.0f-(m_Timer.GetTime()*2);
  if (a < 0.0f) a = 0.0f;
  pVertices[0].color = D3DXCOLOR(1.0, 0.0, 0.0, 0.0);
  pVertices[1].color = D3DXCOLOR(1.0, 0.0, 0.0, 0.0);
  pVertices[2].color = D3DXCOLOR(1.0, 0.0, 0.0, a);
  pVertices[3].color = D3DXCOLOR(1.0, 0.0, 0.0, a);
  pVertices[0].tu = 0.0f; pVertices[0].tv = 0.0f;
  pVertices[1].tu = 1.0f; pVertices[1].tv = 0.0f;
  pVertices[2].tu = 1.0f; pVertices[2].tv = 100.0f;
  pVertices[3].tu = 0.0f; pVertices[3].tv = 100.0f;
  pVertices[0].position = D3DXVECTOR3(-0.15f,  -0.05f,  -100.0f);
  pVertices[1].position = D3DXVECTOR3( 0.15f,  -0.05f,  -100.0f);
  pVertices[2].position = D3DXVECTOR3( 0.15f, -0.05f, -2.0f);
  pVertices[3].position = D3DXVECTOR3(-0.15f, -0.05f, -2.0f);

  m_pVBLaser->Unlock();
  m_pIBLaser->Unlock();
  // now render!
  m_pd3dDevice->SetTexture(0, m_pAnim->GetCurFrameTexture(m_Timer));
  m_pd3dDevice->SetTransform( D3DTS_WORLD, &m_matWorld );
  m_pd3dDevice->SetRenderState( D3DRS_CULLMODE,  D3DCULL_NONE );
  m_pd3dDevice->SetRenderState( D3DRS_LIGHTING, FALSE);
  m_pd3dDevice->SetRenderState(D3DRS_ZENABLE, FALSE);
  m_pd3dDevice->SetRenderState( D3DRS_ALPHABLENDENABLE, TRUE);
  // SNIP! Set up texture stages for alpha blending.
  m_pd3dDevice->SetVertexShader(D3DFVF_XYZ_DIFFUSE_TEX1);
  m_pd3dDevice->SetStreamSource( 0, m_pVBLaser,
    sizeof(VERTEX_XYZ_DIFFUSE_TEX1) );
```

```
  m_pd3dDevice->SetIndices( m_pIBLaser, 0L );
  m_pd3dDevice->DrawIndexedPrimitive( D3DPT_TRIANGLELIST,
    0, 4, 0, 2);
  m_pd3dDevice->SetRenderState( D3DRS_ALPHABLENDENABLE, FALSE);
}
```

The trick to drawing the laser is to make a long, skinny quad (see Figure 21.7).

Notice that when we set up the positions of our four vertices, we made the quad have a thickness of 0.30 units, no height, but a length of 98 units! That's huge, and it is that trick that makes the laser appear to be firing off into the distance.

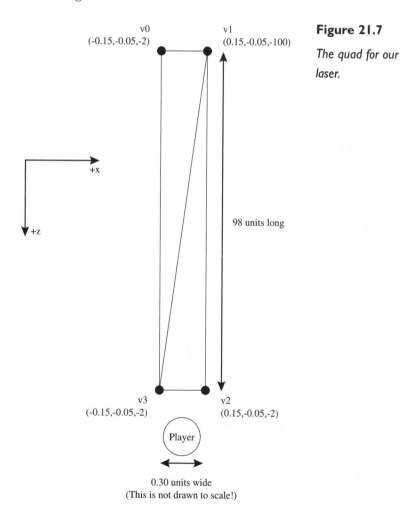

v0
(-0.15,-0.05,-2)

v1
(0.15,-0.05,-100)

+x

+z

98 units long

v3
(-0.15,-0.05,-2)

v2
(0.15,-0.05,-2)

Player

0.30 units wide
(This is not drawn to scale!)

Figure 21.7

*The quad for our
laser.*

Notice also that we mess with the alpha value of the nearest two vertices. By setting the alpha value as one minus twice the timer's value, we create a laser that fades out within half a second.

Integrating the Particle System

The final touch for the laser effect is the particle system. Inside the laser's `Fire` method, we set the position of the particle system to the end of the gun's barrel. We then tell it to execute the script it previously compiled.

The script itself looks like this:

```
particlesystem "Laser Effects" 1.00 {
  position = XYZ(0,0,0)
  eventsequence "ExcessEnergy" {
    sourceblendmode = D3DBLEND_ONE
    destblendmode = D3DBLEND_ONE
    loops = 1
    numparticles = 10
    gravity = XYZ(0,0,0)
    emitrate = 1000
    emitradius = XYZ(
      random(-0.1,0.1), random(-0.1,0.1),random(-0.1,0.1))
    lifetime = 1
    texture = "Ch21p1_LaserParticle.png"
    initial size = random(0.1,0.3)
    initial color = rgba(1,0,0,1)
    fade so final size = 0.0
    initial velocity = XYZ(random(-4,4),random(-4,4),random(-4,4))
  }
}
```

This simple script delivers a few small, bright red particles (see Figure 21.8) that shrink until finally dying. I created this script based on my own ideas of what I wanted; I encourage you to edit it and come up with your own unique effect!

Figure 21.8

Particle texture for our laser's particle system.

CHAPTER WRAP-UP

I hope you enjoyed the fruits from the garden of weaponry!

Obviously, there are a lot more techniques you can use to enhance the quality of your weapon effect. Dynamic lighting plays an important role in most weapons—the rocket that lights the walls as it flies down the hallway. Weapons also typically leave marks when they intersect with walls—craters for rockets, glowing ovals of energy for plasma, and that sort of thing. These additional effects can sometimes mean the difference between an astounding weapon and a ho-hum one, so be sure to fill in the details when you are creating the weapons for your game.

ABOUT THE SAMPLE PROGRAMS

Instead of breaking each gun into its own sample program, I decided to combine all of them into one big example:

- **Ch21p1_FiringRange.** This program illustrates three different types of weaponry—a simple machine gun, a plasma cannon, and a bolt weapon.

EXERCISES

1. Enhance the Ch21p1_FiringRange sample program so that it displays a crosshair in the center of the screen. Probably the easiest way to do this would be to use screen coordinates, rather than trying to fiddle with the z coordinate.

2. Sometimes, hard-coding is a viable solution. However, it can also become a hack. This sample program works great with the existing gun model, but it will go down in flames if you use a different model, because the distances won't be right. To remedy this, see if you can figure out how to remove the hard-coded distances and coordinates from the code, and replace them with values derived from the gun model(s).

3. Here's an easy one: add a check to ProcessInput so that the current gun doesn't fire if we are transitioning between guns.

4. Make a fourth weapon—a rocket launcher—based on the plasma gun. Add Chapter 19's particle system for smoke effects. Hint: The initial rotation of the rocket mesh will be based on the rotation of the camera, so use the inverse view matrix.

CHAPTER 22

LENS FLARES

"Anything can be faked."
—*Philip K. Dick*

The lens flare is a glorious symbol of the 3D gaming era. Pac-Man symbolized the birth of the video game—the time when a completely new form of entertainment burst onto the scene. The lens flare, to me, symbolizes the time when 3D games finally started to have "spare" graphics power. All of a sudden the CPU wasn't 100% busy just with the mechanics of pushing polygons. Thanks to dedicated 3D graphics hardware, we now had some spare time each frame to render effects just for the sake of making the game look good. Depending on who you ask, gaming has been getting better or worse ever since.

In this chapter, we'll dissect the lens flare effect. We'll start by explaining what a lens flare is, followed by a discussion of the concepts of the technique itself. After that we'll dive into the code to render a lens flare in 2D and in 3D, and we'll look at how to figure out programmatically whether a lens flare should be shown. Finally, we'll wrap up by looking at some other effects that go hand-in-hand with lens flares.

WHAT ARE LENS FLARES?

In real life, a lens flare is an artifact of excess light hitting the optics of a camera (see Figure 22.1).

Figure 22.1

A screenshot of the `Ch22p2_InSceneLensFlare` *sample program.*

If you point a camera at a very bright light, some of that light will reflect off the camera's internal lenses and optic mechanisms, creating ghost-like rings, circles, and squares. It's actually somewhat difficult to do with modern cameras, because the normal world sees lens flares as a mistake that should be corrected. As we game programming nerds have been busy creating lens flares, the camera nerds have been busy trying to prevent them. Most cameramen buy expensive solutions designed to eliminate lens flare.

CAUTION

The key to a good lens flare effect is subtlety. As you create your lens flares, try not to go overboard. In the early days of 3D gaming, it was common to see very prominent lens flare effects—some effects were so strong they literally blocked your view of the action! Since then, gamers have gotten over the initial coolness factor of the lens flare and have come to appreciate a more restrained effect. Nowadays, "over-the-top" lens flare effects typically are considered laughable instead of awe-inspiring. Consider yourself warned—just as with pants and restaurant uniforms, too much flare is not a good thing.

The phantom images of the flare depend on the type of glass and optics in the camera, so there's a wide variety of patterns you can generate. Most lens flares have hexagonal spots, because of the way light crystallizes. Other common flare types are rings (sometimes in a rainbow color), dots, and small points of light.

THE CONCEPTS

Lens flares themselves are simple little creatures. You draw a straight line that passes through both the light source and the center of the screen. You then arrange the flare spots along this line (see Figure 22.2).

Give each flare spot a color, an alpha component, a size, and a shape, and you've got the basics.

The Flare Spots

The flare spots can be any shape you think looks good—I like rings and spots, though some other people prefer hexagonal shapes. Figure 22.3 shows my set of flare shapes.

Note that these images are essentially alpha masks—the white pixels denote complete opacity, and the black pixels denote complete transparency. We'll modulate the texture colors with the vertex diffuse colors to colorize these images for the actual flare. We'll then render the flares using additive alpha blending.

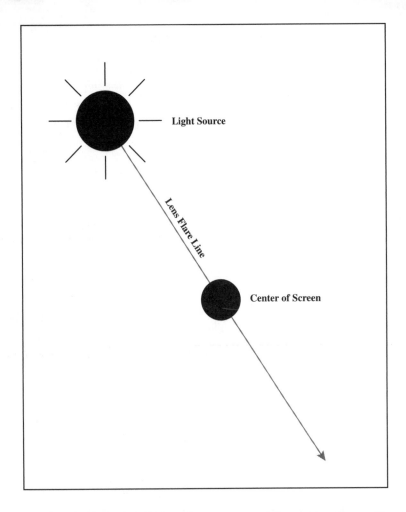

Figure 22.2

Arrange the flare spots on a line between the light source and the center of the screen.

Light Source

Lens Flare Line

Center of Screen

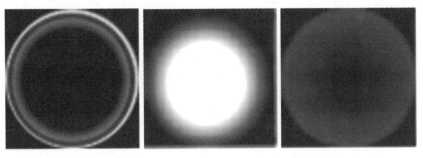

Figure 22.3

My set of lens flare shapes.

Flare without Sun, and Flare Intensities

That's the basic idea—now let's polish it out a bit. Take a camera outside on a sunny day and pan it around the landscape, moving the sun in and out of the picture. As you do, you'll notice two things. First, the lens flare appears even when the sun isn't in the picture. If the sun is just off the edge of view, you'll still get a flare. Second, the flares don't suddenly appear at a certain point— they fade in and fade out.

We'll be implementing both of these behaviors with our software lens flare by coding some additional properties. We'll start by designing a "flare border"—an area that surrounds the outside of the screen. If the sun is outside of this flare border, there's no flare. If the sun is inside this flare border, there's a flare, though this flare may be more or less prominent depending on how close the sun is to actually being in the picture (see Figure 22.4).

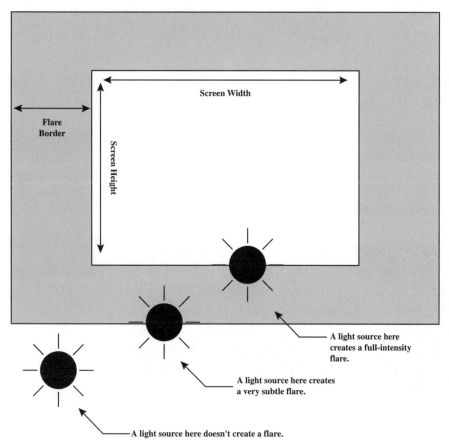

Figure 22.4

The intensity of the flare depends on the distance of the sun from the edge of the screen.

Screen Width

Flare Border

Screen Height

A light source here creates a full-intensity flare.

A light source here creates a very subtle flare.

A light source here doesn't create a flare.

A sun that's just barely off the screen will generate a lens flare at close to full intensity, whereas a sun that's just barely inside the flare border will generate a lens flare at a very low intensity.

Given this, we can determine the intensity (between zero and one, with one being full intensity and zero being no flare) using this logic:

```
if the sun is on the screen
  intensity = 1, and we're done
else
  determine how far away the sun is from the edge of the screen by
  taking the greater of either the horizontal distance or the
  vertical distance.  call this "distance."
  take distance and divide it by the size of the flare border.
  Call this the "inverse intensity."
  if the inverse intensity is greater than one, set it equal to one.
  intensity = 1 - inverse intensity
end if
for each vertex of each lens flare spot
  multiply the alpha component of the vertex's diffuse color
  by the intensity.
  render the flare
next
```

See how that works? Let's look at a couple of examples. Let's say the sun's screen position is (–5,–10), that is, it's just off the upper-left edge of the screen. Our flare border is 50 pixels. The sun is five pixels away from the edge of the screen horizontally and 10 pixels away vertically, so we use 10 as the distance. (We take the absolute value to make it positive, because distances can't be negative.) We then take the distance (10) and divide it by the flare border (50). This gives us 1/5, or 0.2. We then subtract that value from one, giving 0.8. So we draw our flare with an intensity of 80%.

However, if the sun were farther away, our distance would be greater. If the sun were at (–15,–30) we would divide 30 by 50, giving 0.6, and subtract that from one, giving 0.4. This represents a 40% intensity. It works! As the sun moves farther away from the edge of the screen, the intensity decreases.

Notice that we've got a cap on "inverse intensity." By ensuring that inverse intensity never goes above one, we ensure that intensity itself never falls below zero.

This chunk of math solves both problems—the user will still see the flare even if the sun isn't in the picture. However, as the sun moves out of the flare border, the flare will fade out. Conversely, when the sun starts moving into the flare border, toward the screen, the lens flare effect will fade in.

THE LENS FLARE OBJECT

The lens flare code is segmented into two classes—CLensFlare and CLensFlareSpot. CLensFlareSpot represents an individual spot within the flare. It has a color, size, and position, as you can see from the following class declaration:

```
class CLensFlareSpot
{
public:
  CLensFlareSpot();
  CLensFlareSpot(LPDIRECT3DTEXTURE8 pTex, float fSize,
    float fLinePos, D3DXCOLOR Color);

  virtual ~CLensFlareSpot();
  void SetTexture(LPDIRECT3DTEXTURE8 pTexture) {
    m_pTexture = pTexture;
  }
  LPDIRECT3DTEXTURE8 GetTexture(void) { return(m_pTexture); }
  float GetSize(void) const { return(m_fSize); }
  void SetSize(const float data) { m_fSize = data; }
  float GetLinePos(void) const { return(m_fLinePos); }
  void SetLinePos(const float data) { m_fLinePos = data; }
  D3DXCOLOR GetColor(void) const { return(m_Color); }
  void SetColor(const D3DXCOLOR &data) { m_Color = data; }

protected:
  LPDIRECT3DTEXTURE8 m_pTexture;
  float m_fSize;
  float m_fLinePos;
  D3DXCOLOR m_Color;
};
```

Notice that we only use one float (m_fLinePos) to represent position. That's because lens flares are in essence one-dimensional. After you have the line passing through the sun position and the center of the screen, all you need is one number to represent where a flare is on that line. You can call the center of the screen zero, the sun position –1, and the mirrored sun position on the other side of the line 1 (see Figure 22.5).

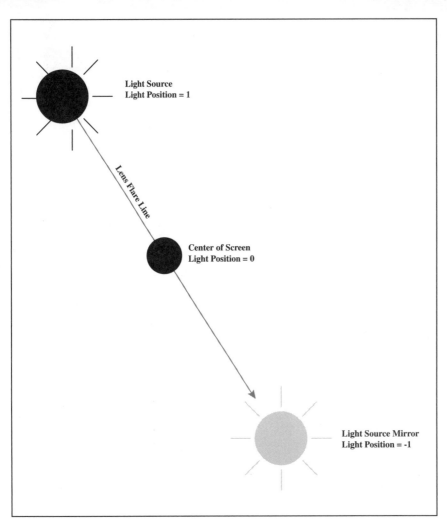

Figure 22.5

The zero, one, and negative points on the 1D lens flare line.

Along with m_fLinePos, we have a size variable, m_fSize. This contains the size of the flare spot, as a percentage of the screen width. A value of 1.0 here creates a gargantuan spot—one that's as wide as the screen. A value of 0.5 creates one that's half the size of the screen, and so on. I did this because I wanted the lens flare effect as a whole to look the same regardless of what screen resolution the player was running.

Now let's look at CLensFlare:

```
class CLensFlare
{
public:
```

```
  CLensFlare();
  virtual ~CLensFlare();
  HRESULT RestoreDeviceObjects(LPDIRECT3DDEVICE8 pDev);
  void InvalidateDeviceObjects();
  void Render(int iLightSourceX, int iLightSourceY, int iScreenWidth,
    int iScreenHeight, bool bFirstOnly = false);
  void Render(CCamera &camera, D3DXMATRIX matProj,
    D3DXVECTOR3 vLightPos, int iScreenWidth, int iScreenHeight,
    bool bFirstOnly = false);
  void CalcLightSourceScreenCoords(CCamera &camera, D3DXMATRIX matProj,
    D3DXVECTOR3 vLightPos, int iScreenWidth, int iScreenHeight,
    int &iCoordX, int &iCoordY, int &iCoordW);
  void DeleteTextures();
  void DeleteSpots();
  LPDIRECT3DTEXTURE8 AddTexture(const char *strFilename);
  void AddSpot(CLensFlareSpot &spot);
  /* SNIP! GetIntensityBorder, SetIntensityBorder, GetIntensity
     accessor functions removed from this listing. */
protected:
  CMinMax<float> m_fIntensity;
  float m_fIntensityBorder;
  HRESULT RecreateVB();
  LPDIRECT3DVERTEXBUFFER8 m_pVBSpots;
  int m_iVBSize;
  LPDIRECT3DDEVICE8 m_pd3dDevice;

  std::vector<LPDIRECT3DTEXTURE8> m_Textures;
  std::vector<CLensFlareSpot> m_Spots;
};
```

CLensFlare, at its most basic, is an object with two vectors. One vector contains all of the lens flare spots (CLensFlareSpot objects). The other vector contains the textures the spots use. We also have a vertex buffer, m_pVBSpots that we use to draw the individual flare spots, and two variables, m_fIntensity and m_fIntensityBorder, which control how bright the lens flare is, and how quickly it fades out as the sun moves off-screen, respectively.

> **TIP**
>
> Notice that it is CLensFlare that keeps track of all the textures, not the individual CLensFlareSpot objects. I did this because I wanted to use the same texture for several different spots.

Notice that m_fIntensity is a CMinMax. This is so the user of the CLensFlare class can control more precisely how the flare fades in and out. The minimum value of this CMinMax represents the intensity of the flare when the sun is very close to being completely outside the border zone. The maximum value represents the intensity of the flare when the sun is on-screen. In this way, the user of CLensFlare has specific control over the intensity of the flare at all times.

To use CLensFlare, you conjure up an instance of it, load it up with textures, and load it up with spots:

```
m_LensFlare.RestoreDeviceObjects(m_pd3dDevice);
LPDIRECT3DTEXTURE8 texHalo =
   m_LensFlare.AddTexture("Ch22p1_LensFlare_Halo.dds");
LPDIRECT3DTEXTURE8 tex1 =
   m_LensFlare.AddTexture("Ch22p1_LensFlare_01.dds");
LPDIRECT3DTEXTURE8 tex2 =
   m_LensFlare.AddTexture("Ch22p1_LensFlare_02.dds");
LPDIRECT3DTEXTURE8 tex3 =
   m_LensFlare.AddTexture("Ch22p1_LensFlare_03.dds");

m_LensFlare.AddSpot(
   CLensFlareSpot(texHalo, 1.20f,  1.0f,
   D3DXCOLOR(1.0f, 1.0f, 1.0f, 1.0f)));

m_LensFlare.AddSpot(
   CLensFlareSpot(tex2, 0.10f, 0.8f,
   D3DXCOLOR(0.7f, 0.5f, 0.0f, 0.2f)));
m_LensFlare.AddSpot(
   CLensFlareSpot(tex2, 0.01f, 0.7f,
   D3DXCOLOR(1.0f, 0.0f, 0.0f, 0.7f)));
/* etc... */
```

As you load textures, CLensFlare returns their handles to you so you can use them as you create the spots.

CLensFlare contains two overloaded Render methods. The first Render method takes in the screen position (in pixels) of the light source that is creating the flare. This method is suitable for 2D games. The second method takes a 3D vector containing the light source's world position, plus a camera object. This is the method of choice for 3D games. We'll cover the inner workings of both methods in the next two sections.

RENDERING LENS FLARES IN 2D

Let's look first at the 2D `Render` method, because it's the simpler of the two.

There are three main steps to get a lens flare displayed on the screen. First, we need to figure out the intensity of the lens flare. Second, we need to figure out the positions of all of the spots that make up the flare. Finally, we need to render each spot.

Let's look at each of those steps in more detail. Follow along inside the `Ch22p1_SimpleLensFlare` sample program if you would like.

Calculating the Intensity

As mentioned previously, to calculate the intensity of the lens flare, we look at the position of the sun (or light source creating the flare). If the sun is on the screen, we should be at max intensity. If the sun is within a border zone, just off the edge of the screen, we should be somewhere between minimum and maximum intensity. If the flare is totally outside the border zone, we should be at minimum intensity.

Notice that I didn't use any actual numbers there. The first time I mentioned this concept, I used 0–1 as an intensity range. Now, however, we're going to crank it up a notch. Instead of hard-coding an intensity range from 0–1, we are going to let the user of `CLensFlare` decide on the range, by setting the `CMinMax` variable `m_fIntensity`. This makes our code a little more flexible—if the user never wants the lens flare to be stronger than half intensity, he can specify a min/max range of 0–0.5. Conversely, if the user never wants the lens flare to fade totally he can bump up the minimum value.

Here's the section of code that implements the calculation we talked about in the previous section:

```
// calculate actual intensity based on the given intensity
// and how far from the edge of the screen the sun is.

float fRealIntensity;
int iAwayX = (iLightSourceX < 0) ? -iLightSourceX :
  (iLightSourceX > iScreenWidth) ?
  iLightSourceX-iScreenWidth : 0;

int iAwayY = (iLightSourceY < 0) ? -iLightSourceY :
  (iLightSourceY > iScreenHeight) ?
  iLightSourceY-iScreenHeight : 0;
```

```
float fAway = (iAwayX > iAwayY) ? iAwayX : iAwayY;
if (fAway > m_fIntensityBorder) fAway = m_fIntensityBorder;

fRealIntensity = 1.0f - (fAway / m_fIntensityBorder);
fRealIntensity = m_fIntensity.m_Min +
  (fRealIntensity*(m_fIntensity.GetRange()));
```

Yep, there's a bit of math here. We start by figuring out how far away the sun is in the X and Y directions (iAwayX and iAwayY). These values can either be zero, which means the sun is on-screen, or they can be greater than zero, if the sun is off the screen.

Once we have iAwayX and iAwayY, we take whichever is bigger and store it in fAway. This is key because fAway now contains the distance from the screen to the sun. Now we can calculate the intensity. We start by calculating an intensity that is between zero and one. We do this by dividing fAway by the size of our intensity border. We then subtract that result from one. For a more detailed explanation of this calculation, refer to the earlier section.

We now have the intensity between zero and one. The final step is to "scale" that intensity into the range the user has supplied. We do this by multiplying fRealIntensity by the range of m_fIntensity, which is really just max-min, then adding the minimum value onto that.

Once we have an intensity within the range the user has specified, we use that to calculate the alpha component of the vertex color. This code is a bit out of order—it doesn't follow immediately after the preceding code. Instead, it's part of a for loop, so it's done for each flare spot in the CLensFlare vector:

```
D3DXCOLOR color = spot.GetColor();
color.a *= fRealIntensity;
if (color.a > 1.0f) color.a = 1.0f;
if (color.a < 0.0f) color.a = 0.0f;
if (bFirstOnly && i != m_Spots.begin()) color.a = 0.0f;
pVertices->color = color;
```

Here you can see us retrieve the spot's current color, multiply the alpha component by fRealIntensity, cap it within the range 0.0–1.0, and finally assign it to the vertex diffuse color.

The if statement regarding the bFirstOnly is a special case—bFirstOnly is a parameter passed to the function. It's true if they only want to draw the first flare object, which is usually the halo or the biggest of them all. The if statement sets the alpha component of the vertex color to zero if bFirstOnly is true, and if the spot we are currently processing isn't at the very beginning of the array.

Calculating Triangle Positions

The next order of business, now that we have the intensity worked out, is to calculate the position of all the flare spots, and fill up the vertex buffer.

Right off the bat, note that we are dealing with a new type of vertex. We are not using our beloved `VERTEX_XYZ_DIFFUSE_TEX1` data type. Instead, we are using a new `VERTEX_LENSFLARE` structure, which contains a position variable that's in 2D screen coordinates, not 3D world space. That's because this `Render` function is strictly 2D. We'll add 3D capabilities in the next section.

This is a fairly large section of code, so we are going to take it bit by bit, starting at the beginning:

```
// calculate spot positions and fill VB
{
  int iCenterOfScreenX = iScreenWidth/2;
  int iCenterOfScreenY = iScreenHeight/2;
  int iDistanceX = iCenterOfScreenX - iLightSourceX;
  int iDistanceY = iCenterOfScreenY - iLightSourceY;
  // lock the vertex buffer
  VERTEX_LENSFLARE *pVertices;

  if(FAILED(m_pVBSpots->Lock( 0,
          m_iVBSize*6*sizeof(VERTEX_LENSFLARE),
          (BYTE**)&pVertices, 0)))
    return;
```

The 2D math at play here is fairly straightforward. We are passed, as parameters, the x and y position of the light source (`iLightSourceX` and `iLightSourceY`). We also are given the screen width and screen height (`iScreenWidth` and `iScreenHeight`). The first thing we do is calculate the (x,y) position of the center of the screen, by dividing the screen's width and height by two. We then compute the distance between the center of the screen and the light source, and store this in `iDistanceX` and `iDistanceY`. This is important—`iDistanceX` and `iDistanceY` contain the numbers around which all of our flare-spot positioning calculations are based.

After we lock the vertex buffer, we enter a `for` loop to set up the vertices for each individual flare spot:

```
// for each spot in this flare...
for (std::vector<CLensFlareSpot>::iterator i = m_Spots.begin();
    i != m_Spots.end(); i++) {
  CLensFlareSpot &spot = (*i);
// calculate this spot's center position
int iSpotCenterPosX = iCenterOfScreenX -
  ((float)iDistanceX * spot.GetLinePos());
```

```
    int iSpotCenterPosY = iCenterOfScreenY -
      ((float)iDistanceY * spot.GetLinePos());
    int iSizeDiv2 = ((float)iScreenWidth * spot.GetSize()/2.0f);
    /* SNIP: mess with vertex's alpha value based on fRealIntensity
       (see code snippets in the previous section for this) */
    // set up the first triangle
    pVertices->position =
      D3DXVECTOR3(iSpotCenterPosX-iSizeDiv2,
                  iSpotCenterPosY-iSizeDiv2, 0);
    pVertices->tu = 0.0f; pVertices->tv = 0.0f;
    pVertices->rhw = 1.0f;
    pVertices++;
    /* SNIP! other vertices are set up the same way, at:
     (iSpotCenterPosX+iSizeDiv2, iSpotCenterPosY-iSizeDiv2, 0)
     (iSpotCenterPosX+iSizeDiv2, iSpotCenterPosY+iSizeDiv2, 0)
     (iSpotCenterPosX-iSizeDiv2, iSpotCenterPosY-iSizeDiv2, 0)
     (iSpotCenterPosX+iSizeDiv2, iSpotCenterPosY+iSizeDiv2, 0)
     (iSpotCenterPosX-iSizeDiv2, iSpotCenterPosY+iSizeDiv2, 0)
    */
} // next spot
m_pVBSpots->Unlock();
```

For each spot in the flare spot vector (m_Spots), we start by calculating that spot's center point on the screen. For the x component, iSpotCenterPosX, we do this by multiplying iDistanceX by the spot's line position, and then subtracting that result from the horizontal center of the screen (iCenterOfScreenX). We then do the same thing with different variables to get the vertical component (iSpotCenterPosY).

Think this through for a minute—if we've got a spot whose position on the line is 1.0, we'll multiply iDistanceX by 1.0, which in turn means we will subtract iDistanceX from iCenterOfScreenX to get iSpotCenterPosX. It works! Conversely, if the spot's line position is –1.0, we will end up flipping the signs and adding iDistanceX onto iCenterOfScreenX, which gives us the same position mirrored from the center of the screen.

Once we've got the spot's center position, everything else is easy. We get the spot's size, multiply it by the width of the screen (remember: the spot size is specified in percentage of screen space to

> **TIP**
>
> **You're right—it's probably better to use an index buffer here, so that we don't duplicate two vertices. I chose not to, because the benefits are trivial and it would increase the complexity of the code I'm trying to teach. However, now that you know how this thing works—go for it!**

maintain resolution independence), and then use that value (`iSizeDiv2`) to calculate the four corners of our quad.

Notice that we set the `rhw` (reciprocal of homogenous w) component of our vertices to 1.0. Behind the scenes, as part of the rasterization process, Direct3D will multiply/divide the x, y, and z components by the w, so we need to make sure it is set to one to prevent any changes in our coordinates.

TIP

You may be wondering why I didn't use point sprites here. It seems like it would be easier to turn point sprites on, and then just deal with the center points of each flare spot, instead of having to manually calculate out the four corner vertices. Indeed, it is; I wish I could have used point sprites, but unfortunately, several graphics cards limit the maximum size of a point sprite. Most cards limit it to 64 or 128 pixels, and that just ain't gonna cut it for a lens flare spot. We usually want the spots to be big— sometimes as big as a quarter or half of the screen—which translates into dimensions much larger than 64 or 128 pixels.

The lesson: even in this age, you can't rely on the hardware to do everything. You need to pay attention to the limitations you face from the card and code around those limitations when appropriate.

Rendering the Triangles

We now have the positions and colors for each flare spot quad calculated—let's draw 'em!

All this requires is some careful setup of our render states and our texture stage states:

```
// render spots
{
  m_pd3dDevice->SetRenderState(D3DRS_LIGHTING,   FALSE );
  m_pd3dDevice->SetRenderState(D3DRS_CULLMODE,   D3DCULL_NONE );

  // turn on additive alpha blending
  m_pd3dDevice->SetRenderState( D3DRS_ALPHABLENDENABLE, TRUE );
  m_pd3dDevice->SetRenderState(D3DRS_SRCBLEND, D3DBLEND_SRCALPHA);
  m_pd3dDevice->SetRenderState(D3DRS_DESTBLEND, D3DBLEND_ONE);
  m_pd3dDevice->SetTextureStageState(0,
    D3DTSS_ALPHAARG1, D3DTA_TEXTURE);
```

```
m_pd3dDevice->SetTextureStageState(0,
  D3DTSS_ALPHAARG2, D3DTA_DIFFUSE);
m_pd3dDevice->SetTextureStageState(0,
  D3DTSS_ALPHAOP, D3DTOP_MODULATE);
m_pd3dDevice->SetTextureStageState(0,
  D3DTSS_COLORARG1, D3DTA_DIFFUSE);
m_pd3dDevice->SetTextureStageState(0,
  D3DTSS_COLORARG2, D3DTA_TEXTURE);
m_pd3dDevice->SetTextureStageState(0,
  D3DTSS_COLOROP, D3DTOP_MODULATE);
// set custom vertex shader
m_pd3dDevice->SetStreamSource(0, m_pVBSpots,
  sizeof(VERTEX_LENSFLARE));
m_pd3dDevice->SetVertexShader(D3DFVF_LENSFLARE);
// this isn't the fastest way to do things, but it's easy
// to understand.  optimization left as an exercise for
// the reader :)
for (int q=0; q < m_Spots.size(); q++) {
  m_pd3dDevice->SetTexture(0, m_Spots[q].GetTexture());
  m_pd3dDevice->DrawPrimitive(D3DPT_TRIANGLELIST, q*6, 2);
  }
}
```

Notice that once we get all the render and texture stage states set up, we enter a for loop. For each spot, we set the texture to the appropriate texture handle for that spot, and then we call DrawPrimitive to draw the two triangles that make up this spot.

CAUTION

This is a terribly inefficient way to do things. There's a lot of overhead associated with a DrawPrimitive call, so you should never call it to draw just one or two triangles. Here, however, I have, and I have a good excuse: the textures. There's no guarantee that all the spots will use the same texture. There's not even any guarantee the spots will share textures. This fact, combined with the fact that we're only drawing a few triangles total for the flare effect, and the fact that optimizing the code would make it significantly harder to understand, makes it okay (but still not good) to do this. However, I encourage you to spend some time and optimize things so that all flares using the same texture are drawn with one call to DrawPrimitive.

RENDERING LENS FLARES IN 3D

We now know how to render a lens flare in 2D, so let's add a dimension. (If you're following along with the code in front of you, now's the time to load up the `Ch22p2_InSceneLensFlare` sample program.)

The `CLensFlare` object comes with two overloaded `Render` methods, shown here:

```
// 2D Render
void Render(int iLightSourceX, int iLightSourceY,
  int iScreenWidth, int iScreenHeight, bool bFirstOnly = false);
// 3D Render
void Render(CCamera &camera, D3DXMATRIX matProj,
  D3DXVECTOR3 vLightPos,
  int iScreenWidth, int iScreenHeight, bool bFirstOnly = false);
```

As you can see, the 3D `Render` method takes slightly different parameters. Instead of just giving `Render` the (x,y) coordinate of the light source, we must now supply a `D3DXVECTOR3` containing the world position of the light. We need to additionally feed it a camera (so it can get the view matrix) and a projection matrix (you'll see why in a second).

Here's what the 3D version of `Render` looks like:

```
void CLensFlare::Render(CCamera &camera, D3DXMATRIX matProj,
  D3DXVECTOR3 vLightPos, int iScreenWidth, int iScreenHeight,
  bool bFirstOnly)
{
  int iScreenX, iScreenY, iScreenW;
  CalcLightSourceScreenCoords(camera, matProj, vLightPos,
    iScreenWidth, iScreenHeight, iScreenX, iScreenY, iScreenW);
  if (iScreenW >= 0.0f) Render(iScreenX, iScreenY, iScreenWidth,
    iScreenHeight, bFirstOnly);
}
```

Here you can see the trickery we're using. All we need to do is calculate the light source's screen coordinates from its world position and the position and orientation of the camera. Once we have the screen coordinates, we can just call the 2D version of render to take care of the specifics of drawing the flare.

So, here's how we calculate the screen coordinates:

```
void CLensFlare::CalcLightSourceScreenCoords(CCamera &camera,
  D3DXMATRIX matProj, D3DXVECTOR3 vLightPos, int iScreenWidth,
  int iScreenHeight, int &iCoordX, int &iCoordY, int &iCoordW)
{
  D3DXMATRIX matWorld, matView, matConcat, matViewportScale;
  D3DXVECTOR4 vResult;

  matViewportScale = D3DXMATRIX(
    iScreenWidth/2, 0, 0, 0,
    0, -iScreenHeight/2, 0, 0,
    0, 0, 1, 0,
    iScreenWidth/2, iScreenHeight/2, 0, 1
  );
  matView = camera.GetViewMatrix();
  D3DXMatrixIdentity(&matWorld); // no need for a world xform
  matConcat = matWorld;
  matConcat *= matView;
  matConcat *= matProj;
  matConcat *= matViewportScale;
  D3DXVec3Transform(&vResult, &vLightPos, &matConcat);
  iCoordX = vResult.x/vResult.w;
  iCoordY = vResult.y/vResult.w;
  iCoordW = vResult.w;
}
```

This method has one clear job: take the 3D world position of our light and convert it to screen coordinates. We give this method the light position (vLightPos), along with the camera (camera), the projection matrix (matProj), and the screen dimensions (iScreenWidth and iScreenHeight), and it in turn gives us back the (x,y) screen coordinates of the light source, plus the w coordinate calculated (the iCoordX, iCoordY, and iCoordW parameters). Notice that these parameters are references, so we can pass values back through them.

This function, in essence, duplicates the process that the 3D card performs in silicon. Recall from the first section of this book that to convert a position in 3D space into 2D screen coordinates requires transforming that point through several matrices. This code performs that transformation.

We first gather up all of the matrices we need. This includes the projection matrix (which we're given as a parameter), the view matrix (which we can get from the camera we're given), the viewport scaling matrix (which we can derive from the width and height of the screen), and the world matrix (which we really don't need, because we already have our light coordinates in world space). We concatenate all these matrices together, and then call a D3DX helper function (D3DXVec3Transform) that transforms our light position vector from world space to screen space.

We haven't really spoken that much about the viewport scaling matrix, matViewportScale. As you can see, I've hard-coded in a viewport scaling matrix (see Figure 22.6).

$$
\begin{bmatrix}
iScreenWidth/2 & 0 & 0 & 0 \\
0 & -iScreenHeight/2 & 0 & 0 \\
0 & 0 & 1 & 0 \\
iScreenWidth/2 & iScreenHeight/2 & 0 & 1
\end{bmatrix}
$$

Figure 22.6

The viewport scaling matrix hard-coded into the program.

Viewport scaling is the last step of the 3D pipeline. In the regular 3D pipeline, after we've multiplied the vertex by the world, view, and projection matrices, we need to do two final things.

■ **First, we need to scale the point into the dimensions of the screen.** At this point our screen spans from −1 to 1 in both the x and y directions, with the (0,0) point in the middle. We need to scale the x component of the vertex so that instead of being within the range −1 to 1, it's within the range −iScreenWidth/2 to iScreenWidth/2. We need to do the same thing with the y coordinate, so that it's between −iScreenHeight/2 and iScreenHeight/2. That's why there's iScreenWidth/2 in the (1,1) position and −iScreenHeight/2 in the (2,2) position (remember, these two positions determine the x and y scaling factor). The (2,2) position is negative because our screen's y coordinates increment as they go down the screen, but 3D coordinates decrement as they go down. Without this step, our scene would render upside-down on the screen. (Hey, that might actually be a cool effect in certain situations!) We flip things over by negating this scaling factor.

■ **Second, we need to translate the vertex's position.** Because the (0,0) point of the screen is at the upper left, but the (0,0) point in 3D graphics is centered on the screen, we need to move the vertex over by half the screen's width and half the screen's height. That's why the bottom elements of the matrix are iScreenWidth/2 and iScreenHeight/2.

> **TIP**
>
> If you're observant, you noticed that back in the 3D overload for Render, we only called the 2D Render if the w coordinate we got back from CalcLightSourceScreenCoords was greater than zero. This check is in place so that the lens flare only appears if the sun is in front of the camera. If the sun is in front of the camera, the w coordinate will be positive, and we'll proceed with drawing the flare. If the sun is behind the camera, we'll end up with a negative w—our cue to skip the flare drawing.

That's how a viewport scaling matrix works. That isn't the only viewport scaling matrix that's valid—you can do all sorts of cool fisheye effects by messing with the scaling matrix—but what I have coded in there is a fairly typical transform. A few matrix multiplies are all it takes to get from 3D world space to 2D screen space. Cool, isn't it?

FIGURING OUT WHETHER YOU SHOULD DRAW A LENS FLARE

There's one critical feature still missing from our lens flare code. The lens flare looks perfect, but we don't yet have any code that can determine whether the light source that's causing the flare is actually visible, or if it's blocked by other objects in the scene. If an object (palm tree, red dragon, mother ship, whatever) moves between the camera and the light source, the flare should disappear. Let's learn how that's done.

CAUTION

Many people erroneously think that the best way to determine whether or not you should draw a lens flare is just to read a particular z-buffer value. You look at the value in the z-buffer for the (x,y) screen coordinate of your sun. If the z-buffer contains the same z-value as your actual sun quad, you know nothing is obscuring the sun, so you draw the lens flare. If the z-buffer contains a different value, it must be because something is in between the sun and the camera, so you don't draw the flare.

This is a good theory, but it falls apart when you actually try to code it. A depth buffer read is a tremendous hack. Most graphics cards won't allow you to do it, and the few graphics cards that will allow you to lock and read the depth buffer have different formats for the data. So, even if you are able to lock the depth buffer you still need to figure out the format of the data. Worst of all, this information is usually proprietary, so you may have to cruise some Web sites, or call every graphics card manufacturer you want to be compatible with and ask them what format you should expect. Ack!

If that weren't enough, it's slow, too. Many other algorithms are often faster than doing a depth buffer read. So, be wary of using this method. We'll look at some better alternatives.

To determine whether we should render a flare, we need to borrow a few chapters from the ray-tracing book. We need to fire an imaginary ray into the scene. We know the (x,y) screen coordinate of our sun. We fire a ray into the 3D scene from this coordinate. If the ray doesn't hit anything (or if it hits the skybox), we know there's no object blocking the sun, so we draw the flare. Conversely, if the ray hits an object, we know that object is blocking the sun, so we shouldn't render the flare.

TIP

From this basic concept you can get pretty fancy. You could fire off several rays from neighboring screen positions to see whether the sun is totally or only partially obscured, and based on that information you could play with the intensity of the lens flare. If a lot of rays made it through, the flare would be pretty intense; or, if only a few rays made it through, the flare would be very subtle. It all comes down to how much CPU time you want to spend firing rays into your scene. (Hint: Make it scale for older hardware. If a user's system doesn't have much processing power, fire one ray. If he is on a beefy box, fire several.)

So, let's learn how to cast a ray into the scene and see if it hits anything. We'll start with the `IsLensFlareObscured` method of `CMyD3Dapplication`:

```
bool CMyD3DApplication::IsLensFlareObscured()
{
  // get screen coordinates of the light source.
  int iLightW;

  m_LensFlare.CalcLightSourceScreenCoords(m_Camera,
    m_matProj, m_vSunPos, m_d3dsdBackBuffer.Width,
    m_d3dsdBackBuffer.Height, m_iSunScreenPosX,
    m_iSunScreenPosY, iLightW);
  m_iNumObjectsAtPoint = NumObjectsAtPoint(m_iSunScreenPosX,
    m_iSunScreenPosY);
  return(m_iNumObjectsAtPoint > 0);
}
```

This method's job is to return `true` if the lens flare is obscured, `false` if it isn't. It accomplishes this by first calculating the screen position of the lens flare (notice this is the same function that the 3D `Render` method calls). Once it has the screen coordinates of the sun, it passes these to the `NumObjectsAtPoint` function, which casts the imaginary ray into the scene and returns the number of objects the ray hits. If the ray hits an object, the flare is obscured, so this function returns `true`; otherwise, it returns `false`.

The NumObjectsAtPoint method has two distinct parts, which we'll cover one by one. First, it calculates the direction and origination of the ray in 3D space based on the screen coordinates. Second, it loops through each triangle in the scene, and determines whether the ray hits that triangle.

> **TIP**
>
> The code I'm presenting in this NumObjectsAtPoint method isn't optimized. Because there's only one object in our scene (the planet), we can afford to use a brute force method like this. In a real game, you'd probably want to wire this function up to your BSP tree or portal paradigm so you could quickly eliminate large numbers of triangles. You'd also probably want to use AABB (axis-aligned bounding boxes) to first check to see if a ray even comes close to a mesh before you bother looking at each individual triangle within that mesh.

Calculating the Ray's Origination and Direction

The first task is to take the screen coordinates given and convert them into two 3D vectors—one vector describing the origin of the ray, and a second vector describing its direction. Here's the code that does the job:

```
// get ray's origin and direction
{
  D3DXVECTOR3 v;
  v.x = ( ( ( 2.0f * iX ) / m_d3dsdBackBuffer.Width  ) - 1 ) /
    m_matProj._11;
  v.y = -( ( ( 2.0f * iY ) / m_d3dsdBackBuffer.Height ) - 1 ) /
    m_matProj._22;
  v.z =  1.0f;
  // Get the inverse view matrix
  D3DXMATRIX matView, m;
  matView = m_Camera.GetViewMatrix();
  D3DXMatrixInverse( &m, NULL, &matView );
  // Transform the screen space pick ray into 3D space
  vRayDir.x  = v.x*m._11 + v.y*m._21 + v.z*m._31;
  vRayDir.y  = v.x*m._12 + v.y*m._22 + v.z*m._32;
  vRayDir.z  = v.x*m._13 + v.y*m._23 + v.z*m._33;
  vRayOrig.x = m._41;
  vRayOrig.y = m._42;
  vRayOrig.z = m._43;
}
```

The code starts by creating a 3D vector (v) from the given screen coordinates (iX and iY). Really, it just reverses the math the viewport scaling and projection matrices did to get the screen coordinates in the first place. We hard-code the z value to 1.0 simply because we don't know the original z value.

After we have that vector, we calculate the inverse of the view matrix. We then perform some math on the vector and the inverted view matrix to arrive at our ray's direction and origin. I'm purposely not going to talk about how this is accomplished because I'd like you to work the numbers and see it for yourself. Pick some matrices that are easy to work with and work the numbers through so you can glean an understanding of how this math works.

Performing Ray/Triangle Intersection Tests

After we have the ray's direction and origin, we can check for intersections between the ray and all the triangles we're concerned about. Here's that section of code:

```
LPDIRECT3DVERTEXBUFFER8 pVB;
LPDIRECT3DINDEXBUFFER8 pIB;
m_pObject->GetLocalMesh()->GetVertexBuffer( &pVB );
m_pObject->GetLocalMesh()->GetIndexBuffer( &pIB );
struct VERTEX { D3DXVECTOR3 p, n; FLOAT tu; FLOAT tv; };
WORD*       pIndices;
VERTEX*     pVertices;
DWORD       dwNumFaces = m_pObject->GetLocalMesh()->GetNumFaces();
pIB->Lock( 0,0,(BYTE**)&pIndices, 0 );
pVB->Lock( 0,0,(BYTE**)&pVertices, 0 );
for( DWORD i=0; i<dwNumFaces; i++ )
{
  D3DXVECTOR3 v0 = pVertices[pIndices[3*i+0]].p;
  D3DXVECTOR3 v1 = pVertices[pIndices[3*i+1]].p;
  D3DXVECTOR3 v2 = pVertices[pIndices[3*i+2]].p;
  float fPickT, fPickU, fPickV;
  // Check if the pick ray passes through this point
  if( DoesRayIntersectTriangle( vRayOrig, vRayDir, v0, v1, v2,
                                &fPickT, &fPickU, &fPickV ) ) {
    iNumObjectsAtPoint++;
  }
}
pVB->Unlock();
pIB->Unlock();
```

```
pVB->Release();
pIB->Release();
return(iNumObjectsAtPoint);
```

Here again you can see we are farming out the dirty work, this time to a function called DoesRayIntersectTriangle. This code concerns itself with locking the vertex and index buffers of the object in question, and looping through each triangle of that object. It calls DoesRayIntersectTriangle for each triangle in the object—if the ray does in fact intersect the triangle, it adds one to its count and goes on its merry way. At the end, it cleans up its mess by unlocking the vertex and index buffers, and releasing the interfaces it acquired from the calls to GetVertexBuffer and GetIndexBuffer.

So, there is only one thing left to look at: DoesRayIntersectTriangle. Here's that code:

```
bool DoesRayIntersectTriangle( const D3DXVECTOR3& orig,
                               const D3DXVECTOR3& dir, D3DXVECTOR3& v0,
                               D3DXVECTOR3& v1, D3DXVECTOR3& v2,
                               FLOAT* t, FLOAT* u, FLOAT* v )
{
  // Find vectors for two edges sharing vert0
  D3DXVECTOR3 edge1 = v1 - v0;
  D3DXVECTOR3 edge2 = v2 - v0;
  // Begin calculating determinant
  D3DXVECTOR3 pvec;
  D3DXVec3Cross( &pvec, &dir, &edge2 );
  // If determinant is near zero, ray lies in plane of triangle
  FLOAT det = D3DXVec3Dot( &edge1, &pvec );
  if( det < 0.0001f )
    return false;
  // Calculate distance from vert0 to ray origin
  D3DXVECTOR3 tvec = orig - v0;
  // Calculate U parameter and test bounds
  *u = D3DXVec3Dot( &tvec, &pvec );
  if( *u < 0.0f || *u > det )
    return false;
  // Prepare to test V parameter
  D3DXVECTOR3 qvec;
  D3DXVec3Cross( &qvec, &tvec, &edge1 );
  // Calculate V parameter and test bounds
  *v = D3DXVec3Dot( &dir, &qvec );
  if( *v < 0.0f || *u + *v > det )
      return false;
```

```
    // Calculate t, scale parameters, ray intersects triangle
    *t = D3DXVec3Dot( &edge2, &qvec );
    FLOAT fInvDet = 1.0f / det;
    *t *= fInvDet;
    *u *= fInvDet;
    *v *= fInvDet;
    return true;
}
```

There is a lot of math at play here. I don't have the space to dive that deep into the geometry that's going on, but I can at least provide you with a summary of what we're doing. First, we calculate the determinant, and see if it's near zero. If so, we know right away that the ray doesn't intersect the triangle (because it is in fact coplanar, that is, it exists on the plane of the triangle).

If we didn't get lucky, we have to keep calculating. We assume that the ray intersects the triangle, and we figure out the (u,v) texture coordinates that it hit. If the ray didn't actually hit our triangle, the (u,v) coordinates will be out of bounds, and we can return false. Otherwise, we know the ray did, in fact, hit the triangle, and we multiply the (u,v) coordinates by the inverse of the determinant to arrive at their final values.

Code Wrap-Up

We've now drilled all the way down to the ray/triangle intersection test. Zooming back out—we test the ray against each triangle in our model, and keep a count of how many triangles intersect. If this count ends up above zero, we know the sun is obscured by this object and we don't draw the flare. Conversely, if it's zero, we know the sun isn't blocked by this object, so we can render the flare.

That's it! Now let's wrap this chapter up by talking about a couple of other cool things you might want to do.

THE EFFECT: MORE THAN JUST THE LENS FLARE

When you point a camera at a light source, a lens flare is just one of many side effects. Consider implementing these other side effects to enhance your eye-candy:

- **Make the whole scene slightly brighter.** You can do this by playing with the gamma ramp as described in the first section of this book, or by drawing a white quad over the entire screen, setting its alpha value to near-transparent.

- **Implement streaking.** If you point most cameras to a bright light source in a dark room for a few seconds and then move the camera away, you usually get a streak corresponding to the path the bright light took on its way out of the frame. It would be cool to see a game implement this same effect. Of course, this only makes sense to do if you're trying to convey to your players that they're watching a camera—glass doesn't do this.
- **Antireflective Coating.** Just a random thought I wanted to pass along: By tinting your lens flares shades of green or purple, you can sometimes create the illusion that your glass has an antireflective coating. I have no idea why, but if you manage to get a lens flare through an antireflective material in real life, the flare is usually tinted green or purple.

CHAPTER WRAP-UP

Again, I can't tell you how important it is that you make your lens flare effects subtle. I'm sure I speak for the vast majority of gamers when I say that lens flares are best when they're only barely noticeable. It's bad enough that you have to fight that huge machine gun–carrying scorpion using only a pistol; it's worse if a programmer decided to go overboard and create a lens flare that obscured your view while you were fighting.

Now that I've said that, there are a couple areas I encourage you to explore on your own. For starters, experiment with generating the lens flare textures themselves, and with randomly assembling flare spots together to form flares. Also, consider implementing lens flares with only a single spot at the light source. Often times these "minor" lens flares are great for torches and other concentrated sources of light. Go wild, but keep it subtle!

ABOUT THE SAMPLE PROGRAMS

Let the eye-candy begin! There are two sample programs for this chapter:

- `Ch22p1_SimpleLensFlare`. This program illustrates a 2D lens flare effect. Use your mouse to move the light source around, and watch as the flare moves with it.
- `Ch22p2_InSceneLensFlare`. This program builds on the previous one. We take our 2D lens flare and go 3D with it, providing a light source position in world space, and the ability to fly anywhere within the scene. This program also demonstrates how to tell whether or not there's something blocking the light source.

EXERCISES

1. Enhance the lens flare class so that it can generate a random flare by randomly choosing the number of spots, size of the spots, colors, and textures.
2. After you have that done, make a WYSIWYG lens flare editor by combining the lens flare object with the GUI code we touched on in Chapters 18 and 19.
3. The preceding chapter's sample program had a skybox of a desert setting, but no lens flare. It needs one badly. Have at it.
4. Enhance the lens flare rendering code so that all the flare spots that use the same texture are drawn with one call to DrawPrimitive.
5. Optimize the NumObjectsAtPoint method so that it uses bounding boxes and/or BSP (binary space partitioning) algorithms instead of the brute force method currently implemented. Yes, this is a tough exercise!
6. Work the math to determine how the ray's origin and direction are computed from the inverted view matrix within NumObjectsAtPoint. Hint: Use a calculator or (better yet) write a program to handle the ugly arithmetic.

CHAPTER 23

3D WATER

"And you may ask yourself: how do I work this?"
——Talking Heads, *"Once in a Lifetime"*

ater is one of the most fascinating special effects. Almost every 3D game uses some form of 3D water—dungeons and battlefields almost invariably have puddles here and there.

This sample program will walk you through the steps needed to create realistic-looking water. The techniques explained in this chapter build on the techniques we learned about in Chapter 12, "2D Water," so if you haven't read Chapter 12 you probably should before you dive into this.

THE CONCEPTS

Creation of 3D water is a difficult task. Good-looking water relies on carefully combining several different techniques. However, as you can see in Figure 23.1, when all of these techniques come together the result can be absolutely stunning.

First and foremost, water needs to move realistically. Fortunately, we covered an algorithm to accomplish this back in the 2D effects section. To get our water to move in 3D, we'll be migrating that algorithm into the third dimension, and tweaking it a little as we go.

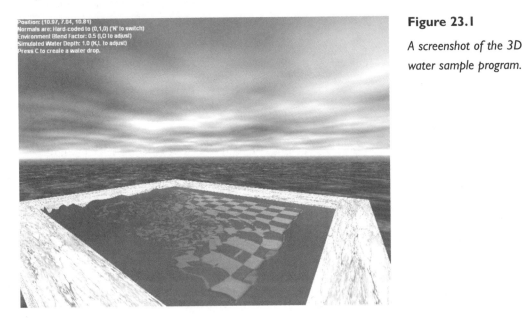

Figure 23.1

A screenshot of the 3D water sample program.

Secondly, water needs to both reflect and refract light. In real life, when a beam of light hits the surface of a liquid, the liquid reflects some of that light, and lets the rest of the light pass through. However, the light that does make it through is refracted (bent) based on the depth of the liquid and its refraction index (sound familiar?).

To create good-looking water, we must simulate both reflection and refraction. Let's start with reflection.

Reflection Using Environment Mapping

If you've ever seen a chrome object in a game or demo, you've witnessed environment mapping. Simply put, *environment mapping* is the art of taking the view from a certain location (the environment), and mapping it onto an object, based on (for example) that object's vertex normals.

We covered this briefly back in the first section of the book, when we learned that there are two main forms of environment mapping: spherical and cubic. *Spherical environment mapping* involves creating a single fisheye texture and using that as your environment map. *Cubic environment mapping*, on the other hand, is similar to a skybox, in that you have six textures. Onto each texture you render a view of a certain direction (positive x, negative x, and so on). After you've rendered the scene six different times, from six different angles, and you have all six textures (called a cube map), you let Direct3D assign texture coordinates based on the normals of your object.

Spherical environment mapping is best suited to static scenes (where nothing is moving). If you have moving objects you'd like to be reflected in your map, cubic environment mapping is the better choice, because the textures are much easier to generate (even if there are six of them).

Even though we don't have any moving objects in our sample program, we'll be using cubic environment mapping. I have only enough space to teach one form of environment mapping, and you'll find that you use cubic far more often than spherical.

Refraction

We implement refraction almost identically to how we did it back in Chapter 12. The major changes for this go-around are that we've ditched the lookup table and are now using floating-point operations to calculate the results. As you'll see, this isn't as terrible of a speed hit as it sounds, because we'll be calculating fewer points than back in Chapter 12.

THE CODE

Let's start learning about 3D water by looking at the Ch23p1_SimpleWater sample program. Load it, and you'll notice that it contains a new class, CWaterPlane, defined in Ch23p1_WaterPlane.h.

```
class CWaterPlane
{
public:
  CWaterPlane();
  virtual ~CWaterPlane();
  virtual HRESULT RestoreDeviceObjects(LPDIRECT3DDEVICE8 pDev,
    int iNumVerts, const char *strInPoolTextureFilename);
  virtual void InvalidateDeviceObjects();
  virtual void Update(float fElapsedTime);
  virtual void Render();
  void CreateWaterDroplet(int iX, int iY, int iSize,
    int iSplashStrength);
  bool GetHardcodeNormals(void) const { return(m_bHardcodeNormals); }
  void SetHardcodeNormals(const bool data = true) {
    m_bHardcodeNormals = data;
  }
  float GetEnvBlendFactor(void) const { return(m_fEnvBlendFactor); }
  void SetEnvBlendFactor(const float data) { m_fEnvBlendFactor = data; }
  float GetDepth(void) const { return(m_fDepth); }
  void SetDepth(const float data) { m_fDepth = data; }
protected:
  void ProcessWater();
  void ApplyHeightArrayToVB();
  float CalcDisplacement(float fHeightdiff);
  HRESULT CreateVertexGrid(LPDIRECT3DVERTEXBUFFER8 *pVB,
    LPDIRECT3DINDEXBUFFER8 *pIB, D3DPOOL pool, float fTotalSize,
    DWORD dwColor, int iNumVerticesX, int iNumVerticesY,
    LPDIRECT3DDEVICE8 pDev);
  LPDIRECT3DVERTEXBUFFER8 m_pVBPool;
  LPDIRECT3DINDEXBUFFER8 m_pIBPool;
  LPDIRECT3DTEXTURE8 m_texInsidePool;
  LPDIRECT3DDEVICE8 m_pd3dDevice;
  int m_iNumVerts;
  float *m_fHeightArray1;
  float *m_fHeightArray2;
  float *m_pActiveHeightArray;
  float *m_pScratchHeightArray;
  float m_fDampValue;
  float m_fRefractionIndex;
  float m_fDepth;
```

```
    float m_fEnvBlendFactor;
    bool m_bHardcodeNormals;
    CTimer m_Timer;
};
```

This class exhibits your typical basic interface. We have our familiar Render and Update methods, as well as the standard RestoreDeviceObjects and InvalidateDeviceObjects. We also have a few accessor methods, plus a method that enables us to create a droplet on the surface of our water.

Under the hood, we have a few protected methods and members. Notice that we have our own version of CreateVertexGrid—you'll see why in a moment. Also notice that CWaterPlane contains a timer, a couple of height arrays, and two pointers (just like in Chapter 12).

Setting Up the Water Plane

Before we can start playing with the water, we need to initialize it. That's where RestoreDeviceObjects comes in:

```
HRESULT CWaterPlane::RestoreDeviceObjects(LPDIRECT3DDEVICE8 pDev,
    int iNumVerts, const char *strInPoolTextureFilename)
{
    m_iNumVerts = iNumVerts;
    m_pd3dDevice = pDev;
    if (FAILED(D3DXCreateTextureFromFile(m_pd3dDevice,
                strInPoolTextureFilename, &m_texInsidePool)))
        return E_FAIL;
    CreateVertexGrid(&m_pVBPool, &m_pIBPool, D3DPOOL_MANAGED, 1.0f,
        D3DXCOLOR(1.0f, 1.0f, 1.0f, 1.0f), iNumVerts,
        iNumVerts, m_pd3dDevice);
    // initialize height arrays
    m_fHeightArray1 = new float[iNumVerts*iNumVerts];
    m_fHeightArray2 = new float[iNumVerts*iNumVerts];
    memset(m_fHeightArray1, 0, sizeof(float)*iNumVerts*iNumVerts);
    memset(m_fHeightArray2, 0, sizeof(float)*iNumVerts*iNumVerts);
    m_pActiveHeightArray = m_fHeightArray1;
    m_pScratchHeightArray = m_fHeightArray2;
    m_Timer.Begin();
    return(S_OK);
}
```

Here you can see the code doing two essential things. First, it creates a vertex grid—the pool of water itself. Second, it allocates and zeros out the two height arrays for the water. Recall from Chapter 12 that the basic algorithm involves swapping these two arrays so that the calculations feed back into themselves every frame.

You may be wondering why `CWaterPlane` defines its own version of `CreateVertexGrid` when there's a perfectly good one inside the common code libraries. The answer is simple: our vertex format has changed. We need a new vertex format because we have to make room in our vertex structure for the vertex normal, as well as an extra pair of texture coordinates:

```
typedef struct
{
  D3DXVECTOR3 position; // The position
  D3DXVECTOR3 normal;   // normal vector
  D3DCOLOR    color;    // The color
  FLOAT       tu1, tv1; // The texture coordinates
  FLOAT       tu2, tv2; // The texture coordinates
} VERTEX_XYZ_NORMAL_DIFFUSE_TEX2;
// Our custom FVF, which describes the
// VERTEX_XYZ_NORMAL_DIFFUSE_TEX2 vertex type
#define D3DFVF_XYZ_NORMAL_DIFFUSE_TEX2
(D3DFVF_XYZ|D3DFVF_NORMAL|D3DFVF_DIFFUSE|D3DFVF_TEX2)
```

Here you can see that we've added a new D3DXVECTOR3, called normal, as well as a new pair of texture coordinates, tu2 and tv2. This new VERTEX_XYZ_NORMAL_DIFFUSE_TEX2 structure is a heavyweight vertex format for a heavyweight effect.

Also, if you look closely, you'll notice that `CreateVertexGrid` isn't exactly the same as the one in the common code base. Check this out:

```
VERTEX_XYZ_NORMAL_DIFFUSE_TEX1 *pVertices;
float fSizeDiv2 = fTotalSize/2;
if( FAILED( hr = (*pVB)->Lock( 0,
    iNumVerticesX*iNumVerticesY*sizeof(VERTEX_XYZ_NORMAL_DIFFUSE_TEX1),
    (BYTE**)&pVertices, 0 ) ) )
  return hr;
for (int x=0; x < iNumVerticesX; x++) {
  for (int y=0; y < iNumVerticesY; y++) {
    pVertices[(y*iNumVerticesX)+x].position = D3DXVECTOR3(
      (iNumVerticesX > 1) ? (((float)x/(float)
      (iNumVerticesX-1))*fTotalSize)-fSizeDiv2 : 0,
       0.0f,
```

```
        (iNumVerticesY > 1) ? (((float)
        (iNumVerticesY-1-y)/(float)(iNumVerticesY-1))*fTotalSize)-
        fSizeDiv2 : 0);
    pVertices[(y*iNumVerticesX)+x].color = dwColor;
    pVertices[(y*iNumVerticesX)+x].tu2 =
        (float)x/(float)(iNumVerticesX-1);
    pVertices[(y*iNumVerticesX)+x].tv2 =
        (float)y/(float)(iNumVerticesY-1);
    }
}
```

A couple of subtle things are at play here. For starters, notice that we're creating the vertex grid on the XZ plane, not the XY plane. Water is flat, so we need to vary the X and Z coordinates, but leave the Y coordinate 0 (for now, anyway).

Notice also that we're setting the second set of texture coordinates, not the first set. The environment map will use the first set of texture coordinates.

Updating the Water

To animate the water realistically, all we need to do is come up with new Y values for each vertex of the vertex grid. You can use a variety of algorithms to do this. Some programmers prefer to use a springs-based physics model. However, rather than learning a whole new algorithm, let's use one that works well, and that we already know. Let's use the water algorithm from Chapter 12.

Recall that in Chapter 12, we were using what's essentially a blend function. We calculated each water height by taking the average height of the water around it. We then took that height value and used a displacement lookup table to determine the exact texel to draw at that point.

The core of that algorithm—the blending—works very well in 3D, we just need to change some of the logic associated with drawing the water. For starters, we won't be operating on a per-texel level. Instead, we'll be operating on a per-vertex level—we'll give each vertex a height value and two sets of texture coordinates, one for reflection and one for refraction. Direct3D will calculate the reflection coordinates based on the vertex's normal. We'll calculate the refraction coordinates based on the height of the vertex, and the displacement formula we learned about in Chapter 12.

Here's CWaterPlane's Update method—the start of our code discussion:

```
void CWaterPlane::Update(float fElapsedTime)
{
    if (m_Timer.GetTime() > 0.04) {
```

```
    ProcessWater();
    ApplyHeightArrayToVB();

    // flip-flop the water buffers.
    float *temp = m_pActiveHeightArray;
    m_pActiveHeightArray = m_pScratchHeightArray;
    m_pScratchHeightArray = temp;
    m_Timer.Begin();
  }
}
```

You should notice two things about that code. First, check out the if block surrounding the processing. We're only going to process the water (animate it) if our timer is greater than 0.04 seconds. I put in this mechanism because the water waves were traveling too fast. Remember, the waves aren't traveling through each texel, they're traveling through vertices. In Chapter 12, to get from one side of the screen to the other, a wave had to move through about 300 texels, and because it could only move one texel per frame, that translated into 300 frames of animation. Now, however, we're using a 32×32 or 64×64 vertex grid, and to get from one side of the screen to the other the wave only has to pass through 32 or 64 points. This takes fewer frames, which creates a much faster wave.

As discussed in Chapter 12, there are only two ways to slow down the water waves generated by this particular algorithm. Either we must add more points to pass through (say, by increasing the density of our vertex grid to 128×128 or 256×256), or we need to do updates less often. Increasing the vertex grid puts a strain on system resources, so the better solution is to put in a small delay (0.04 seconds) between every frame of water animation.

TIP

If you take out the delay, the waves travel fast, and when they travel, to me they create the illusion that our water plane is no longer water, but instead is a piece of cloth pulled very tightly. Conversely, if you increase the delay, your water starts to behave like sludge. I bet if you upped the delay high enough, and replaced the reflection texture map with a molten rock texture, you'd end up with some cool-looking lava! Experiment with delay factors to simulate different things.

Let's get back to the code listing. If 0.04 seconds have passed, we call ProcessWater and ApplyHeightArrayToVB, and then we flip the water buffers (just like in Chapter 12). The ProcessWater method takes care of putting new height values into m_pScratchHeightArray, and the ApplyHeightArrayToVB takes care of putting those height array values into the Y position of each vertex. Let's look at each of those independently.

Calculating the New Height Values

Here's a code snippet showing ProcessWater:

```
void CWaterPlane::ProcessWater()
{
  // loop through all the water values...
  for (int y=0; y < m_iNumVerts; y++) {
    for (int x=0; x < m_iNumVerts; x++) {
      // SNIP! Figure out the exact indices of xminus1, xminus2,
      // yminus1, and yminus2
      float value;
      // Method 1: Slower but yields slightly better looking water
      {
        value  = m_pActiveHeightArray[((y)       *m_iNumVerts)+xminus1];
        value += m_pActiveHeightArray[((y)       *m_iNumVerts)+xminus2];
        value += m_pActiveHeightArray[((y)       *m_iNumVerts)+xplus1];
        value += m_pActiveHeightArray[((y)       *m_iNumVerts)+xplus2];
        value += m_pActiveHeightArray[((yminus1)*m_iNumVerts)+x];
        value += m_pActiveHeightArray[((yminus2)*m_iNumVerts)+x];
        value += m_pActiveHeightArray[((yplus1) *m_iNumVerts)+x];
        value += m_pActiveHeightArray[((yplus2) *m_iNumVerts)+x];
        value += m_pActiveHeightArray[((yminus1)*m_iNumVerts)+xminus1];
        value += m_pActiveHeightArray[((yminus1)*m_iNumVerts)+xplus1];
        value += m_pActiveHeightArray[((yplus1) *m_iNumVerts)+xminus1];
        value += m_pActiveHeightArray[((yplus1) *m_iNumVerts)+xplus1];

        // average them
        value /= 6.0f;
      }
      // subtract the previous water value
      value -= m_pScratchHeightArray[(y*m_iNumVerts)+x];
      // dampen it!
      value /= m_fDampValue;
      if (value > 10.0f) value = 10.0f;
      if (value < -10.0f) value = -10.0f;
      // store it in array
      m_pScratchHeightArray[(y*m_iNumVerts)+x] = value;
    }
  }
}
```

You can see Chapter 12's algorithm in action here. The biggest modifications to it happened because we're using floating-point height arrays rather than integers. The old code that translated the height into an integer has been taken out. Notice that we do cap the range of water values between –10 and 10—this is so that as our water animates, the vertices don't move too far up or down. If they move too far, our player will notice that the water isn't solid, it's just a plane with nothing underneath it.

> **TIP**
>
> You'll need to choose the capping range based on how close your player is able to get to the surface of the water. If the water is unreachable, far away, you can use a higher cap value; if the player will be able to walk right up to the surface of the water and actually touch it, you'll need a much lower cap value.

Applying the Height Values to the Vertex Grid

Now that we have our new height values, we can use them to set the positions and texture coordinates of the vertices in our vertex grid. Here's the code that gets the job done:

```
void CWaterPlane::ApplyHeightArrayToVB()
{
  HRESULT hr;
  VERTEX_XYZ_NORMAL_DIFFUSE_TEX1 *pVertices;
  float fSizeDiv2 = 0.5f;
  if( FAILED( hr = m_pVBPool->Lock( 0,
      m_iNumVerts*m_iNumVerts*sizeof(VERTEX_XYZ_NORMAL_DIFFUSE_TEX2),
      (BYTE**)&pVertices, 0 ) ) )
    return;
  for (int x=0; x < m_iNumVerts; x++) {
    for (int y=0; y < m_iNumVerts; y++) {
      float fValue = m_pActiveHeightArray[(y*m_iNumVerts)+x];
      if (fValue > 2.0f) fValue = 2.0f;


      pVertices[(y*m_iNumVerts)+x].position = D3DXVECTOR3(
        (m_iNumVerts > 1) ?
        (((float)x/(float)(m_iNumVerts-1)))-fSizeDiv2 : 0,
        fValue,
        (m_iNumVerts > 1) ?
        (((float)(m_iNumVerts-1-y)/(float)(m_iNumVerts-1)))-fSizeDiv2
        : 0);
```

```
// calculate texture coordinates
{
  float xdiff = (x == m_iNumVerts-1) ? 0 :
    m_pActiveHeightArray[(y*m_iNumVerts)+x+1] -
    m_pActiveHeightArray[(y*m_iNumVerts)+x];

  float ydiff = (y == m_iNumVerts-1) ? 0 :
    m_pActiveHeightArray[((y+1)*m_iNumVerts)+x] -
    m_pActiveHeightArray[(y*m_iNumVerts)+x];

  float xdisp = CalcDisplacement(xdiff);
  float ydisp = CalcDisplacement(ydiff);
  float tu, tv;
  if (xdiff < 0) {
    if (ydiff < 0) {
      tu = (float)x/(float)(m_iNumVerts-1)-xdisp;
      tv = (float)y/(float)(m_iNumVerts-1)-ydisp;
    }
  // SNIP - same logic, just different pluses and minuses,
  // for the other combinations!
  if (tu < 0.0f) tu = 0.0f; if (tu > 1.0f) tu = 1.0f;
  if (tv < 0.0f) tv = 0.0f; if (tv > 1.0f) tv = 1.0f;
  pVertices[(y*m_iNumVerts)+x].tu2 = tu;
  pVertices[(y*m_iNumVerts)+x].tv2 = tv;
  pVertices[(y*m_iNumVerts)+x].color =
    D3DXCOLOR(1.0f, 1.0f, 1.0f, m_fEnvBlendFactor);
  }
 }
}
```

The bulk of the process happens just past the two for loop lines, where we grab the height value, stick it in fValue, and then use that to set the vertex's Y position. I bounced the value through the fValue variable primarily because it makes the code slightly more readable (all those question marks and colons are bad enough without me doing an array lookup in there as well!). If you wanted to, you could divide fValue by a constant to "dampen" the water as it was pushed out to the vertices. It's not terribly useful, but it may come in handy for certain effects.

The next step is slightly more hairy. We need to calculate the second pair of texture coordinates to create the illusion that our water is refracting light through it. The bulk of this logic is similar to how we did it back in 2D. The primary difference is that instead of using a displacement lookup table, here we're actually calling a function to calculate the floating-point value.

Calculating Displacement

Let's have a peek at that `CalcDisplacement` function:

```
float CWaterPlane::CalcDisplacement(float fHeightdiff)
{
  // the angle is the arctan of the height difference
  float angle = (float)atan(fHeightdiff);
  // now, calculate the angle of the refracted beam.
  float beamangle = (float)asin(sin(angle) / m_fRefractionIndex);
  // finally, calculate the displacement, based on the refracted beam
  // and the height difference.
  return(tan(beamangle) * (fHeightdiff+m_fDepth));
}
```

It's short, but heavy on the math. Again, notice here that we've upgraded everything to use purely floating-point calculations.

This function is slow, and it could be optimized. For starters, notice that we're calculating the `beamangle` from scatch every time this function is called. That's a prime candidate for a lookup table; however, note that in order to do one, we must establish some level of granularity to our angle variable. Lookup tables have finite sizes, but as it stands now our angle could really be any number, at any precision, between 0 and pi times 2. You need to do something—like, say, multiply the float by 100 and then round down to the nearest integer—before you can use a lookup table here.

Calculating Normals

There's one last step we must undertake before we're finished with these water vertices. To properly map the reflection, Direct3D depends on each vertex having an accurate normal. We need to calculate those normals.

Recall from Chapter 4, "3D Math," that we can generate a normal by taking a cross-product of two vectors. So all we really need to do is determine where to get those two vectors. This is fairly easy—we can just use two neighboring vertices, as shown in Figure 23.2.

If we happen to be on the far edge of the vertex grid, we can use the vertices to our left or above us; otherwise, we'll use the vertices to our right, or below us (see Figure 23.3).

Let's look at the code to calculate normals. This code resides inside the `ApplyHeightArrayToVB` method:

```
// since our model has changed, we must now recompute the normals.
for (x=0; x < m_iNumVerts; x++) {
  for (int y=0; y < m_iNumVerts; y++) {
    if (m_bHardcodeNormals) {
      pVertices[(y*m_iNumVerts)+x].normal = D3DXVECTOR3(0,1,0);
    }
```

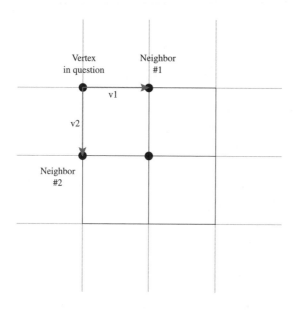

Figure 23.2

Using neighboring vertices as our two vectors.

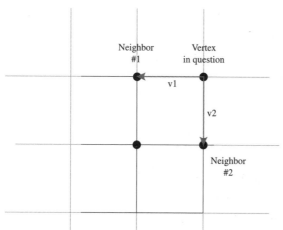

Figure 23.3

If we're on a border, we can use the vertices to our left and above us.

```
      else {
        // calc normal
        int xplus1 = (x == m_iNumVerts-1) ? m_iNumVerts-2 : x+1;
        int yplus1 = (y == m_iNumVerts-1) ? m_iNumVerts-2 : y+1;
        D3DXVECTOR3 v1 = pVertices[(y*m_iNumVerts)+x].position;
        D3DXVECTOR3 v2 = pVertices[(y*m_iNumVerts)+xplus1].position;
        D3DXVECTOR3 v3 = pVertices[(yplus1*m_iNumVerts)+x].position;
        D3DXVECTOR3 vNorm1 = v2 - v1;
        D3DXVECTOR3 vNorm2 = v3 - v1;
        D3DXVECTOR3 vNorm;

        D3DXVec3Normalize(&vNorm1, &vNorm1);
        D3DXVec3Normalize(&vNorm2, &vNorm2);
        D3DXVec3Cross(&vNorm, &vNorm2, &vNorm1);
        D3DXVec3Normalize(&vNorm, &vNorm);
        pVertices[(y*m_iNumVerts)+x].normal = vNorm;
      }
    }
  }
```

As you can see, I couldn't decide whether I wanted to actually calculate the normals, or if I wanted to just hard-code them to point straight up (0,1,0). Both options are valid, and yield equally cool effects. If the normals are pointed straight up, all of the water—even the waves themselves—reflect the sky. If the normals are calculated, you might be able to see some of the horizon or even the ground reflected off the waves. It's a subtle difference, but it's worth leaving the choice up to the user of CWaterPlane.

Anyway, assuming we bother to calculate the normals, there's a sequence of steps we must undertake. First, we grab three vectors—the position of the vertex in question, plus the positions of the vertices immediately to the right of it and below it. We subtract these vectors from each other to get our two coplanar vectors, vNorm1 and vNorm2 (see Figure 23.4 to learn how this works).

We normalize the two coplanar vectors, and then cross them to arrive at vNorm, our normal vector.

One last thing: Direct3D expects the normals to be normalized. This sounds funny, but what it really means is that in order for the environment mapped reflections to display properly, the magnitude of our normal vector must be one. So, we finish with a call to D3DXVec3Normalize, which gives us our final, normalized, normal.

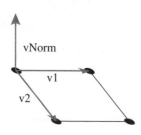

Figure 23.4

This diagram illustrates how to calculate the two coplanar vectors.

TIP

This code could be improved. The chief problem is that because we're using an index buffer, we can't give the same vector two different normals. This means that, for example, on the apogee of a wave, we can't create a sharp transition by using two vectors with different normals (see Figure 23.5).

Fortunately, this small error is very hard to detect visually, since the waves are constantly in motion and the reflections change so quickly. To solve this problem would require us to sacrifice the memory savings we've gained by having an index buffer, and to me, it wasn't worth it. If you'd like to see the difference for yourself I encourage you to change the code appropriately.

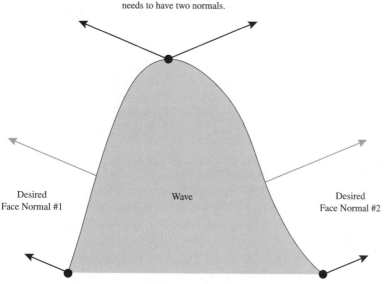

This vertex, at the apogee of the wave, needs to have two normals.

Desired Face Normal #1

Wave

Desired Face Normal #2

Figure 23.5

This figure shows why some vertices need two normals.

Creating the Environment Map

We've calculated the new vertex positions, normals, and texture coordinates. We now need to focus our efforts on the environment map itself. Specifically, we need to create the cube map, and render the scene from six different angles onto the map, so that what's reflected in our water really is what's actually in the scene.

Let's start by looking at how to create an environment map:

```
// Create the cubemap, with a format that matches the backbuffer, since
// we'll be rendering into it
if( FAILED( hr = m_pd3dDevice->CreateCubeTexture(
    CUBEMAP_RESOLUTION, 1, D3DUSAGE_RENDERTARGET,
    m_d3dsdBackBuffer.Format, D3DPOOL_DEFAULT, &m_pCubeMap ) ) )
  return E_FAIL;
if( FAILED( hr = m_pd3dDevice->CreateDepthStencilSurface(
    CUBEMAP_RESOLUTION, CUBEMAP_RESOLUTION,
    D3DFMT_D16, D3DMULTISAMPLE_NONE, &m_pCubeFaceZBuffer) ) )
  return E_FAIL;
```

Here you can see the code performing two tasks. First, it creates the cube texture itself. Direct3D knows what a cube map is, so all we need to do is say, "hey, man, create a cube texture" and behind the scenes it generates six different textures for the six sides of the cube.

However, we also need to generate a depth buffer. We could use the backbuffer's, but remember that the user can change resolutions, so it's possible (albeit unlikely) that he might select a resolution smaller than CUBEMAP_RESOLUTION, which would make our depth buffer smaller than our texture, causing many headaches. So, we play it safe and make our own depth buffer with the same dimensions as the textures of the cube map.

> **TIP**
>
> When we're done, we release the cube map just as we would a normal texture.

Updating the Environment Map

Now it's time to render the six different scenes onto the six different textures of the cube map.

Splitting the Render Function

Rendering environment maps is tricky. For starters, we need to make sure we render the same scene that the camera sees, only from a different perspective. We also need to make sure that as we're rendering the scene onto the cube map textures, we don't draw the object that's actually using the cube map (because if we did, what would we texture it with?). We also need to make sure that we don't render the heads-up display text (the yellow text in the upper-left corner) onto our cube maps; otherwise, we would see the text's reflection inside our water!

These restraints force us to change the architecture of our sample program. Up until now we've always had one single Render method that draws the whole enchilada. We need to break that down slightly. We need a core method that renders the objects in the scene, and then we need two different wrappers around this core. The screen-rendering wrapper needs to call the core rendering function, and then tack on the code that displays the yellow text. The cube map rendering method needs to call the core method six different times using six different view matrices.

Let's look at all three of these methods, starting with the screen rendering method, because it's the most familiar.

The Screen Rendering Method

I want to start by drawing your attention to a single line in our CMyD3DApplication class definition:

```
HRESULT Render() { return(ScreenRender()); }
```

This little line forms a critical link. The sample program framework we're using calls the Render virtual method when appropriate. However, we've renamed the real Render to ScreenRender, which means that without this line our scene would never render. Virtual functions aren't mandatory, and without a Render method our program would use the framework's base-class Render method, which doesn't do anything interesting.

Now that we have that out of the way, let's look at ScreenRender itself:

```
HRESULT CMyD3DApplication::ScreenRender()
{
  if( SUCCEEDED( m_pd3dDevice->BeginScene() ) ) {
    CoreRender(true, m_Camera.GetViewMatrix());
    char buf[256];
    _snprintf(buf, 256, "Position: (%.2f, %.2f, %.2f)",
      (float)m_Camera.GetPosition().x,
      (float)m_Camera.GetPosition().y,
      (float)m_Camera.GetPosition().z);
    m_pFontSmall->DrawText(2,  0, D3DCOLOR_ARGB(255,255,255,0), buf);

    // Other text rendering snipped out!

    // End the scene.
    m_pd3dDevice->EndScene();
  }
  return(S_OK);
}
```

As you can see, we've scooped out most of the tasty rendering goodness and moved it to CoreRender. This render function begins the scene, calls CoreRender to draw most of the objects, draws the text, and then ends the scene.

The Core Rendering Method

I'm not going to copy the entire contents of CoreRender onto these pages, because it's big and there's very little inside it we don't know about (and what little new stuff there is, we'll discuss shortly).

I do, however, want to draw your attention to the method's parameters:

```
HRESULT CMyD3DApplication::CoreRender(bool bRenderWater,
  D3DXMATRIX matView)
```

CoreRender needs two things. First, it needs to know whether to render the water mesh. If we're rendering the cube map textures, we don't want to draw the water, so we set this to false. On the other hand, ScreenRender sets it to true because it wants to draw the whole scene.

The second parameter is even more important. It's the view matrix that we should use when rendering. When ScreenRender calls CoreRender, it passes it the view matrix calculated by the current camera, because it wants to render the scene as seen from the camera. However, the cube maps don't want that—they want to render the scene from a different perspective, which we'll look at shortly. So they pass in a different view matrix.

> ### CAUTION
>
> It's extremely important that you set up this "view matrix parameterization" when rendering using environment maps. One of the common mistakes is to accidentally grab the view matrix of the camera from within your core rendering function. This error means that all six sides of the cube map will be rendered with the same view matrix (namely, the camera's view matrix), which isn't even remotely close to what you probably wanted.
>
> Beware. If you're having environment map headaches, a good place to start your solution is to sweep your code for errant references to the camera's view matrix.

The Cube Map Rendering Method

Now let's look at the third and final method, CubeMapRender. There are several new and interesting things here. Let's take it one step at a time, and look at the code in little chunks.

We'll start with the prep work:

```
HRESULT CMyD3DApplication::CubeMapRender()
{
  // Set the projection matrix for a field of view of 90 degrees
  D3DXMATRIX matProj;
  D3DXMatrixPerspectiveFovLH(&matProj, D3DX_PI/2, 1.0f, 0.5f, 100.0f);
  m_pd3dDevice->SetTransform(D3DTS_PROJECTION, &matProj);
  // Calc reflected view matrix
  D3DXMATRIX matViewDir = m_Camera.GetViewMatrix();
  matViewDir._41 = 0.0f; matViewDir._42 = 0.0f; matViewDir._43 = 0.0f;
  D3DXPLANE plane; plane.a = plane.b = plane.c = plane.d = 0.0f;
  D3DXMATRIX matFlip; D3DXMatrixReflect(&matFlip, &plane);
  D3DXMatrixMultiply(&matViewDir, &matFlip, &matViewDir);
```

In this first section of code you can see us setting up the projection matrix, and doing something funny with the view matrix. Essentially, we're reflecting the view matrix relative to the ground plane. We do this because we need the water to reflect an inverted view of the world. Without this reflection code, our water would resemble a portal. It would always show us the world right-side-up as seen from (0,0,0). We need to see the world from (0,0,0), but we also need it upside-down, so we reflect the view by creating a reflection matrix (matFlip) and concatenating it with our camera's view.

Notice also that before we do that, we lop off the bottom row from our camera's view matrix, effectively repositioning it at the world origin, just like we do when we render a skybox. We don't want the scene to shift in our water just because we move the camera closer or farther away from it (although if we changed the angle of the camera, we'd want the reflection to change appropriately).

Now for the next section of code:

```
  // Store the current backbuffer and zbuffer
  LPDIRECT3DSURFACE8 pBackBuffer, pZBuffer;
  m_pd3dDevice->GetRenderTarget( &pBackBuffer );
  m_pd3dDevice->GetDepthStencilSurface( &pZBuffer );
  // Render to the six faces of the cube map
  for( DWORD i=0; i<6; i++ ) {
    // Set the view transform for this cubemap surface
    D3DXMATRIX matView;
    matView = D3DUtil_GetCubeMapViewMatrix( (D3DCUBEMAP_FACES)i );
    D3DXMatrixMultiply( &matView, &matViewDir, &matView );
    m_pd3dDevice->SetTransform( D3DTS_VIEW, &matView );
```

Now we're getting into the details. Here you can see us squirreling away the current backbuffer and depth buffer—we'll restore those at the end of the function. Next, we enter a `for` loop for each of our six textures. For each texture, we begin by calculating the appropriate view matrix for that particular texture. We use a Direct3D utility function, `D3DUtil_GetCubeMapViewMatrix`, to give us the appropriate view direction for our current texture index. To arrive at the view matrix for this particular face of the cube map, we take the matrix the utility function gave us and multiply it by the inverted view matrix we calculated before we entered the `for` loop.

Marching right along, here's the next section of code:

```
    // Set the rendertarget to the i'th cubemap surface
    LPDIRECT3DSURFACE8 pCubeMapFace;
    m_pCubeMap->GetCubeMapSurface( (D3DCUBEMAP_FACES)i, 0,
      &pCubeMapFace );
    m_pd3dDevice->SetRenderTarget( pCubeMapFace, m_pCubeFaceZBuffer);
    pCubeMapFace->Release();
    m_pd3dDevice->BeginScene();
    m_pd3dDevice->Clear( 0L, NULL, D3DCLEAR_TARGET | D3DCLEAR_ZBUFFER,
      0xffffffff, 1.0f, 0L );
    CoreRender( FALSE, matView );
    m_pd3dDevice->EndScene();
}
```

Here we actually render the scene. We set our rendering target to the appropriate face of the cube map (which we get through a call to the `GetCubeMapSurface` method of the cube map object). After we do that, we begin the scene, clear it, and call `CoreRender` to draw the view. Notice that we specify `false` so as not to draw the water itself, and that we pass in the view matrix we calculated. When `CoreRender` is done, we end the scene and close the `for` loop, moving on to the next cube map texture.

Here's the final section of code:

```
  m_pd3dDevice->SetRenderTarget( pBackBuffer, pZBuffer );
  pBackBuffer->Release();
  pZBuffer->Release();
  return S_OK;
}
```

Here you can see us cleaning up our mess. We set the render target and depth buffers back to their original values, and return "all is well!".

That wasn't so bad! Again, the most important part is setting up the correct view matrix. I encourage you to play around with different view matrices and see what those do to the reflection in the water in the final scene.

Rendering the Water

We've got the positions. We've got the normals. We've got the texture coordinates, and we've got the rendered views on the environment map. Time to pull this all together and push the triangles out to the graphics card. Here's the section of CoreRender that does the deed:

```
if (bRenderWater) {
  D3DXMATRIX matTrans, matScale;
  D3DXMatrixTranslation(&matTrans, 0.0f, 1.1f, 0.0f);
  D3DXMatrixScaling(&matScale, 16.0f, 1.0f, 20.0f);
  matWorld = matScale * matTrans;
  m_pd3dDevice->SetTransform( D3DTS_WORLD, &matWorld );

  m_pd3dDevice->SetRenderState( D3DRS_LIGHTING, FALSE);
  m_pd3dDevice->SetRenderState( D3DRS_ALPHABLENDENABLE, FALSE);

  // Turn on texture-coord generation for cubemapping
  m_pd3dDevice->SetTextureStageState( 0, D3DTSS_TEXCOORDINDEX,
    D3DTSS_TCI_CAMERASPACEREFLECTIONVECTOR );
  m_pd3dDevice->SetTextureStageState( 0, D3DTSS_TEXTURETRANSFORMFLAGS,
    D3DTTFF_COUNT3 );
  m_pd3dDevice->SetTextureStageState( 0, D3DTSS_ADDRESSU,
    D3DTADDRESS_MIRROR );
  m_pd3dDevice->SetTextureStageState( 0, D3DTSS_ADDRESSV,
    D3DTADDRESS_MIRROR );
  m_pd3dDevice->SetTextureStageState( 1, D3DTSS_COLOROP,
    D3DTOP_BLENDDIFFUSEALPHA );
  m_pd3dDevice->SetTextureStageState( 1, D3DTSS_COLORARG1,
    D3DTA_CURRENT );
  m_pd3dDevice->SetTextureStageState( 1, D3DTSS_COLORARG2,
    D3DTA_TEXTURE );
  m_pd3dDevice->SetTextureStageState( 1, D3DTSS_ALPHAOP,
    D3DTOP_SELECTARG1 );
  m_pd3dDevice->SetTextureStageState( 1, D3DTSS_ALPHAARG1,
    D3DTA_TEXTURE );
```

```
m_pd3dDevice->SetTextureStageState( 2, D3DTSS_COLOROP,
    D3DTOP_DISABLE );
m_pd3dDevice->SetTextureStageState( 2, D3DTSS_ALPHAOP,
    D3DTOP_DISABLE );
m_pd3dDevice->SetTexture( 0, m_pCubeMap );
m_Water.Render();
// Restore the render states
m_pd3dDevice->SetTextureStageState( 0, D3DTSS_TEXCOORDINDEX,
    D3DTSS_TCI_PASSTHRU );
m_pd3dDevice->SetTextureStageState( 0, D3DTSS_TEXTURETRANSFORMFLAGS,
    D3DTTFF_DISABLE );
}
```

It's long, but it isn't that complex. We begin by creating a world matrix that will make our water mesh fill the inside of the pool frame (which we've loaded as an X file and rendered separately). I cheated—I knew how big the pool frame was, so I just hard-coded those values into the scaling matrix. A better solution would be to look at the model itself to determine how big to make the water mesh.

Next we set up our texture stage states. The first stage renders the environment map, so we tell Direct3D to automatically generate the texture coordinates based on the reflection vector, which is, in turn, based on the normals we've calculated (or hard-coded!).

So, we have a color from our environment map coming out of the first texture stage. In the second stage, we combine that with the inside of the pool texture (see Figure 23.6). We've set up the texture coordinates so that they refract this texture realistically.

Notice that we blend the two texture colors based on the vertex's diffuse alpha value. We set this up by specifying D3DTOP_BLENDDIFFUSEALPHA for our second stage's color operation. Back when we calculated the vertices, we also set their alpha value to the environment blending factor, which is by default 0.5. We can (and do) change that via a call to SetEnvBlendFactor based on user input (the I and O keys increment and decrement the blending factor).

We complete the chain by disabling the third texture stage, which signals to Direct3D that we'll be using the output from the second stage (the combined environment map color and refracted texture color) as the final color for that particular texel.

TIP

Yes, you could do this with a pixel shader. I leave the task of writing a pixel shader equivalent to these texture stage setups as an exercise for you.

Figure 23.6

The texture for the inside of our pool.

Code Wrap-Up

That completes our tour of realistic water rendering. The only things we didn't touch on were the rendering of the pool frame (it's just a simple X file model), and the management of the water algorithm itself (which we discussed in Chapter 12).

From here, I encourage you to play with the Ch23p1_SimpleWater sample program. Change things and see how the application reacts, for that is one of the best ways to learn all this stuff.

CHAPTER WRAP-UP

The method I've described here is only one of many ways to go about creating water. You may find this approach too complex to use during your actual game, but as faster and faster processors seep their way down into the homes of the game players, this will become less of a worry.

However, I feel I should at least do lip service to a few other methods. Here's a short list of alternatives:

- **Procedural textures.** Many times you can achieve good-looking water using some Perlin noise and some clever alpha blending and diffuse coloring. Tint your water blue, and partially transparent, and continually generate Perlin noise for its texture, and you'll end up with water that looks fairly realistic. The bonus to this method is that all you need to do is change the color palette to create other liquids—green and yellow hues for slime, reds and oranges for lava—you get the idea.
- **Bump mapping.** You can create a good-looking water effect (especially a distant water effect) by combining Chapter 12's algorithm with some bump mapping code. Bump mapping, driven by Chapter 12's algorithm, combined with environment mapping, makes for some really killer-looking "liquid metal" surfaces.
- **Springy water.** One of the best ways to simulate liquids is to model the water as a grid of interlocked springs. Use some physics to calculate the forces each spring exerts on its neighbors when they're stretched, and use this as the basis for your water modeling. The effect created by the springs looks much smoother and less triangular than the method presented in this chapter, but it's also fairly CPU intensive. As a bonus, however, you can use the same "spring mesh" to simulate cloth.

ABOUT THE SAMPLE PROGRAMS

There's just one sample program this chapter:

- `Ch23p1_SimpleWater`. This sample program shows you how to create realistic-looking water, using a combination of environment mapping and refraction techniques.

EXERCISES

1. Rewrite the water calculation using vertex and pixel shaders. On hardware that supports shaders, you'll see a dramatic improvement in the processing time, since you will have off-loaded to the graphics card virtually all of the intense calculation.
2. Rewrite the displacement code so that it uses a lookup table for the beam angle.
3. Change the code so that there's no longer an index buffer, which in turn means that you can generate two normals for the vertices that are at the top of the waves. See if you can notice the (theoretically) improved visual quality.
4. Enhance the water mesh rendering code so that it looks at the X file of the pool frame and determines from that the scaling matrix for the water mesh.

CHAPTER 24

VERTEX AND PIXEL SHADER EFFECTS

"You look at where you're going and where you are and it never makes sense, but then you look back at where you've been and a pattern seems to emerge. And if you project forward from that pattern, then sometimes you can come up with something."

—Robert M. Persig, Zen and the Art of Motorcycle Maintenance

O dds are high that you already knew that vertex and pixel shaders provide you, the graphics programmer, with amazing freedom to create astounding effects. However, up until now you probably haven't had the opportunity to really wrestle in the dirt with any shader code.

In this chapter, we're going to take a look at some of the effects you can create using vertex and pixel shaders. We'll be looking at two forms of cartoon rendering that highlight vertex shaders, plus several pixel shader effects.

I should mention that most of these vertex and pixel shader effects are based (loosely) on code provided by nVidia, as part of their SDK. The entire nVidia SDK is included on your CD.

CARTOON SHADING

One of the best examples of how you can use vertex shaders to create interesting effects is non-photorealistic rendering. All the preceding pages of this book have concerned themselves with the generation of essentially photorealistic scenes. We create some objects, texture them, throw some simulated light on them, hand the whole thing off to the graphics card, and on our screen appears a realistic rendition of our scene. Objects are shaded based on the strength and color of the light sources, just as they are in real life.

Cartoon shading throws that whole thing out the window. This effect allows you to create images that simulate cartoons (see Figure 24.1).

As you can see in that figure, the lighting isn't realistic, and it appears as if the whole scene had been sketched out as a cartoon by a professional animator.

Follow along through the sections below by loading up the `Ch24p1_ToonShader` program in your IDE.

Regular Lighting

Cartoon rendering works its magic by playing with the lighting calculations, so let's first start by looking at how regular lighting calculations work. Once we know that we can learn to "toon render" by moving away from those regular calculations.

Position: (0.01, 2.23, -3.57)
Texture: 3-color (T to change)

Figure 24.1

A screenshot of the Ch24p1_ToonShading *program.*

Light is really all about vertex normals. To calculate the amount of light falling on a vertex, you take the dot product of the vertex normal and the light vector. For example, this is how a normal vertex shader would calculate the diffuse color:

```
dp3 oD0, r0, c4
```

It doesn't get much easier than that! In the preceding code, you can see us storing the dot product of the vertex's normal vector (stored in r0) and the light vector (c4) inside the diffuse color output (oD0).

How Does Cartoon Shading Work?

The lighting calculation inside a cartoon shader operates identically to a regular lighting calculation, with one important difference: instead of storing the dot product as the diffuse color, the cartoon algorithm uses it as an index into a one-dimensional texture.

This is like a graphical equivalent to adding a level of indirection. To achieve regular lighting, you'd use a one-dimensional texture like that shown in Figure 24.2: a smooth gradient from black to white.

Figure 24.2

A cartoon shading texture that creates smooth lighting.

However, to achieve cartoon rendering you use a texture that's a little less smooth (see Figure 24.3).

As you can see, you can segment the light any way you want by using this texture. You're using this texture as a conversion map—in comes the calculated light value, and out comes the appropriate "clamped" value that creates the cartoon rendering look.

Once you have this "clamped" light value, you combine it with the vertex's diffuse color (through texture blending) to arrive at the final color at that point.

Figure 24.3

A cartoon shading texture that creates only a few different light intensities.

Writing the Cartoon Shading Code

Now that we've got a grip on how the effect works, let's look at how to write code to render things as if they were in a cartoon. For starters, you'll use this vertex structure to implement cartoon rendering:

```
typedef struct
{
  D3DXVECTOR3 pos;
  D3DXVECTOR3 normal;
  D3DCOLOR diffuse;
  float uShade;  //texcoord for stage 0
  float uEdge;   //texcoord for stage 1
} VERTEX_XYZ_NORMAL_1DTEX2;
#define D3DFVF_XYZ_NORMAL_1DTEX2 \
  D3DFVF_XYZ | D3DFVF_NORMAL | D3DFVF_DIFFUSE | D3DFVF_TEX2 | \
  D3DFVF_TEXCOORDSIZE1( 0 ) | D3DFVF_TEXCOORDSIZE1( 1 )
```

Here you can see a couple of interesting things. For starters, notice that this vertex format has no diffuse color. We don't need one, at least not yet. Also, notice that we have two separate one-dimensional texture coordinates. We'll use these as lookups into our edge and shade textures, respectively (we'll examine the edge texture coordinate more closely in the next section, on silhouette rendering).

Loading the Vertex Shader

Now let's look at how to load the cartoon vertex shader:

```
// Create vertex shader
{
  LPD3DXBUFFER pCode;
  DWORD dwDecl[] =
  {
    D3DVSD_STREAM(0),
    D3DVSD_REG(0, D3DVSDT_FLOAT3),
    D3DVSD_REG(1, D3DVSDT_FLOAT3),
    D3DVSD_REG(2, D3DVSDT_FLOAT1),
    D3DVSD_REG(3, D3DVSDT_FLOAT1),
    D3DVSD_END()
  };
  // Assemble the vertex shader from the file
  if( FAILED( hr = D3DXAssembleShaderFromFile(
      "Ch24p1_ToonShader.vs", 0, NULL, &pCode, NULL ) ) )
    return hr;
  // Create the vertex shader
  hr = m_pd3dDevice->CreateVertexShader( dwDecl,
    (DWORD*)pCode->GetBufferPointer(), &m_dwShader, 0 );
  pCode->Release();
  if( FAILED(hr) ) return hr;
}
```

Here you can see source code hard at work, defining our vertex shader declaration and assembling the shader from the Ch24p1_ToonShader.vs file.

This process is the same as the one we went through back in Chapter 10, "Vertex and Pixel Shaders," to get our simple vertex shaders to load, so I'm not going to spend a lot of time on it here.

However, I do want to draw your attention to the vertex shader declaration inside the code above. Remember, the job of the declaration is to bind the elements of our vertex structure to inputs for our shader. The code above starts out by saying, "We're now working with vertex stream zero." Since we only use one stream, this makes sense. The next line says "bind the first three floating-point values to input register zero (v0)." In other words, this line is what sets v0 equal to our position vector, inside our vertex shader code. The same story plays out for the next element—the code says, "bind the next three floating-point values to input register one." Since the next three floats are our normal vector, this code binds v1 to the vertex's normal. The next two lines bind v3 and v4 to our shade and edge texture coordinates (remember, our texture is one-dimensional). Finally, the D3DVSD_END line signals to Direct3D that this completes our shader declaration.

Setting the Vertex Shader Constants

Now that we've got the vertex shader loaded and the vertex elements wired up to the v0 and v1 inputs, we're ready to jump into the actual rendering code. Check out this section of the Render method of CMyD3DApplication:

```
// Set up the vertex shader constants
{
  D3DXVECTOR4 vLightDir(0.0f, 0.0f, -1.0f, 0.0f);
  D3DXVec4Normalize(&vLightDir, &vLightDir);

  m_pd3dDevice->SetVertexShaderConstant(4, &vLightDir, 1);

  D3DXMATRIX matWorldViewProj;
  D3DXMATRIX matWorldView, matWorldViewInverse;
  matWorldViewProj = matWorld * m_Camera.GetViewMatrix() * m_matProj;
  matWorldView = matWorld * m_Camera.GetViewMatrix();
  D3DXMatrixInverse(&matWorldViewInverse, NULL, &matWorldView);
  D3DXMatrixTranspose(&matWorldViewProj, &matWorldViewProj);

  m_pd3dDevice->SetVertexShaderConstant(0, &matWorldViewProj, 4);
  m_pd3dDevice->SetVertexShaderConstant(5, &matWorldViewInverse, 4);
}
```

Here you can see the code setting up three different constants for our shader. First, the easy one—we store the light direction in slot four. Notice that I've hard-coded the light value so that it always shines directly into the scene. Also keep in mind that since we'll be transforming this light normal by the view matrix, what this really means is that the light always shines in the direction the camera is facing—as if there were a spotlight mounted to the top of our imaginary camera.

TIP

We could just as easily have stored the separate world, view, and projection matrices in 12 different constant slots. Granted, this would mean that we'd have to use more vertex shader instructions to combine all three matrices, but we could do it.

Think carefully about how you want to use your constant registers. The vast majority of the time it's better to reduce the number of vertex shader instructions, even if it means using more constant registers and more prep work on the C/C++ side of the world.

The interesting code arrives a couple of lines later. We store the combined world, view, and projection matrix as constant zero, and we use slot five to store the inverted world/view matrix. The vertex shader will use constant zero to calculate the final vertex position, and it will use constant five as part of the lighting calculations.

The Cartoon Vertex Shader

Now that we've set up our constants, let's take a look at how the vertex shader uses them. The neat thing about vertex shaders is that they're really short, so you can reprint them in their entirety inside graphics books!

```
vs.1.0
// transform position
m4x4 oPos, v0, c0
// transform normal
m3x3 r0, v1, c5
// normalize normal
dp3 r0.w, r0, r0
rsq r0.w, r0.w
mul r0, r0, r0.w
// l dot n
dp3 oT0.x, r0, c4
// diffuse color pass-thru
mov oD0, v4
```

This is where all the magic happens. Our shader begins by multiplying the vertex position by our combined view, world, and projection matrix. That does it for the vertex position—it's now ready to be clipped and scaled into our viewport.

Next we focus on the normal. We multiply the vertex's normal by the inverse of the world/view matrices, stored in constant registers five, six, and seven. We then normalize the normal, and dot it with our light vector (c4). Ordinarily, this would give us the final diffuse color for this vertex, but since we're cartoon rendering, we store this inside oT0. Since oT0 is a one-dimensional texture, we use the .x modifier so that only the x component is modified.

The shader finishes off by simply moving the diffuse color from the input register v4 into the output register oD0. That's right—we don't do anything with the diffuse color inside the shader. Instead, we rely on texture blending modes to modulate this color with the appropriate brightness value that we get from the texel at the coordinate stored in oT0.

Texture Stage States for Cartoon Rendering

Now it's time for the next piece of the puzzle. Here's the code that sets up the texture stage states:

```
// set up texture blending modes
m_pd3dDevice->SetTexture(0, m_pShadeTexture);

m_pd3dDevice->SetTextureStageState(0, D3DTSS_ADDRESSU,
  D3DTADDRESS_CLAMP);

m_pd3dDevice->SetTextureStageState(0, D3DTSS_COLORARG1,
  D3DTA_TEXTURE);
m_pd3dDevice->SetTextureStageState(0, D3DTSS_COLOROP,
  D3DTOP_SELECTARG1);

m_pd3dDevice->SetTextureStageState(1, D3DTSS_COLORARG1,
  D3DTA_CURRENT);
m_pd3dDevice->SetTextureStageState(1, D3DTSS_COLORARG2,
  D3DTA_DIFFUSE);
m_pd3dDevice->SetTextureStageState(1, D3DTSS_COLOROP,
  D3DTOP_MODULATE);
```

As you can see, we're using two texture stages here. From the first stage, we get a color somewhere in between black and white—our light intensity. We modulate this with the diffuse color to arrive at the final color. Nothing to it!

Notice the very first state setup we do. We set the addressing mode of the u coordinate on texture stage zero to D3DTADDRESS_CLAMP. This clamps the light value, so that even if our shader calculates a light intensity outside of the range 0.0–1.0, we're still okay. As a counterexample, what we certainly don't want here is a wrap addressing mode. That would make a light value slightly higher than 1.0, say, 1.2, wrap around our texture and become equivalent to a light value of 0.2. This creates weirdness, and is best avoided.

Pumping Out the Triangles

The final task is for the code to pump out the triangles to Direct3D. Here's the relevant code snippet:

```
LPDIRECT3DVERTEXBUFFER8 pVB;
m_pTeapot->GetLocalMesh()->GetVertexBuffer(&pVB);
LPDIRECT3DINDEXBUFFER8 pIB;
m_pTeapot->GetLocalMesh()->GetIndexBuffer(&pIB);

SetMeshColor(pVB, m_pTeapot->GetLocalMesh()->GetNumVertices(),
  D3DXCOLOR(1.0, 0.0, 0.0, 1.0));
m_pd3dDevice->SetStreamSource( 0, pVB,
  sizeof(VERTEX_XYZ_NORMAL_1DTEX2));
m_pd3dDevice->SetIndices(pIB, 0);

m_pd3dDevice->DrawIndexedPrimitive(D3DPT_TRIANGLELIST, 0,
  m_pTeapot->GetLocalMesh()->GetNumVertices(), 0,
  m_pTeapot->GetLocalMesh()->GetNumFaces());

pVB->Release();
pIB->Release();
```

Right about now you should be feeling surprised. Ordinarily, the way to render a CD3DMesh object is to simply call its Render method. Unfortunately, that doesn't work when you're using vertex shaders, because the Render method sets the vertex shader back to the legacy one. This is an especially subtle bug, because it appears as though everything is working great when in reality your vertex shader code isn't even being executed!

So Render is not going to cut it here. Instead, we have to manually retrieve the vertex and index buffers of our object, and call DrawIndexedPrimitive directly. Also, after we're done we must remember to release the pointers because the calls to GetVertexBuffer and GetIndexBuffer increment the reference counts on the buffers.

So, you're correct—it's a little more complex than normal, but it's a small price to pay for being able to use both CD3DMesh and custom vertex shaders in the same program.

ADDING PEN STROKES TO CARTOON SHADING

So we've looked at one way to create a cartoon-ish effect. However, there's currently something missing with our cartoon renderer. Real cartoons are more than just color shading—they also have a pen outline where the animator sketched the scene. So, now we're going to look at one way to create a pen-stroke outline for our cartoon renderer.

If you like, follow along inside the Ch24p2_ToonShaderSilo sample program (check out Figure 24.4 for a screenshot).

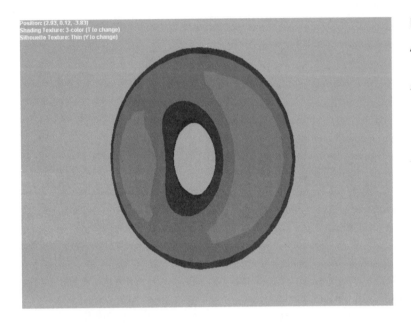

Figure 24.4

A screenshot of the Ch24p2_ToonShaderSilo sample program.

How Does It Work?

To create pen-stroke outlines, we use a second, separate texture—the edge texture. The edge texture, shown in Figure 24.5, uses alpha blending, so that only the very edges of the texture are opaque. The rest of the texture is transparent.

Figure 24.5

The edge texture, used to create pen-style outlines.

By taking the dot product between the vertex's negative normalized position and its normalized normal (say that five times fast), we can determine whether that particular vertex is part of the silhouette of the image—that is, whether or not that vertex is on the edge of the drawing. Lower dot product values indicate that the vertex is part of the silhouette; higher dot product values, not so much. So, adding a pen outline is as easy as using this dot product as an index into the 1D edge texture, just as we did for the shading texture in the previous section.

Adding Edge Support to the Vertex Shader

Now you know why the cartoon rendering vertex structure had two 1D texture coordinates. We use one texture coordinate for the shading texture, and one for this new edge texture.

This means that we need to calculate this second texture coordinate inside our vertex shader. Here's the new vertex shader that adds silhouette support to our program:

```
m4x4    r0,     v0,     c5              ; r0 = View space position
m3x3    r1,     v1,     c0              ; r1 = View space normal
m4x4    oPos,   v0,     c0              ; Spit out projected position
dp3     r2.x,   r0,     r0              ; Normalize r0 (position)
rsq     r2.x,   r2.x
mul     r0,     r0,     r2.x
dp3     r1.w,   r1,     r1              ; Normalize normal
rsq     r1.w,   r1.w
mul     r1,     r1,     r1.w
dp3     oT0.x,  r1,     c4              ; l dot n = shade tex idx
dp3     r3.x,   r0,     -r1             ; Compute dot product
mad     oT1.x,  r3.x,   c9.x, c9.x      ; Scale to [0,1], store as texndx
mov     oD0,    v4                      ; diffuse color = v4 (pass-thru)
```

As you can see, this vertex shader is very similar to the one in the last section. The primary difference is that we compute the dot product of r0 and −r1, and store that in r3.x. We then scale that value to between 0.0 and 1.0, just the range we need for a texture coordinate lookup.

Adding the Edge Texture to the Texture Stage States

The next step is to enhance our texture stage setups so that the edge texture is used.

This is a little more complex. We need to use two rendering passes: one to draw the object with the cartoon shading, and a second pass to draw the edge. Here's how that looks in code:

```
// pass 1
{
  // set up texture blending modes
  m_pd3dDevice->SetTexture(0, m_pShadeTexture);

  m_pd3dDevice->SetTextureStageState(0, D3DTSS_COLORARG1,
    D3DTA_TEXTURE);
```

```
    m_pd3dDevice->SetTextureStageState(0, D3DTSS_COLOROP,
      D3DTOP_SELECTARG1);
    m_pd3dDevice->SetTextureStageState(1, D3DTSS_COLORARG1,
      D3DTA_CURRENT);
    m_pd3dDevice->SetTextureStageState(1, D3DTSS_COLORARG2,
      D3DTA_DIFFUSE);
    m_pd3dDevice->SetTextureStageState(1, D3DTSS_COLOROP,
      D3DTOP_MODULATE);
    m_pd3dDevice->DrawIndexedPrimitive(D3DPT_TRIANGLELIST, 0,
      m_pTeapot->GetLocalMesh()->GetNumVertices(), 0,
      m_pTeapot->GetLocalMesh()->GetNumFaces());
}
// pass 2 - draw silhouette
{
  // set up texture blending modes
  m_pd3dDevice->SetTexture(0, m_pSiloTexture);
  m_pd3dDevice->SetTexture(1, m_pSiloTexture);
  m_pd3dDevice->SetRenderState(D3DRS_ALPHABLENDENABLE, TRUE);
  m_pd3dDevice->SetRenderState(D3DRS_SRCBLEND, D3DBLEND_SRCALPHA);
  m_pd3dDevice->SetRenderState(D3DRS_DESTBLEND, D3DBLEND_INVSRCALPHA);
  m_pd3dDevice->SetTextureStageState(0, D3DTSS_COLORARG1,
    D3DTA_DIFFUSE);
  m_pd3dDevice->SetTextureStageState(0, D3DTSS_COLOROP,
    D3DTOP_SELECTARG1);
  m_pd3dDevice->SetTextureStageState(0, D3DTSS_ALPHAARG1,
    D3DTA_DIFFUSE);
  m_pd3dDevice->SetTextureStageState(0, D3DTSS_ALPHAOP,
    D3DTOP_SELECTARG1);
  m_pd3dDevice->SetTextureStageState(1, D3DTSS_COLORARG1,
    D3DTA_TEXTURE);
  m_pd3dDevice->SetTextureStageState(1, D3DTSS_COLOROP,
    D3DTOP_SELECTARG1);
  m_pd3dDevice->SetTextureStageState(1, D3DTSS_ALPHAARG1,
    D3DTA_TEXTURE);
  m_pd3dDevice->SetTextureStageState(1, D3DTSS_ALPHAOP,
    D3DTOP_SELECTARG1);

  m_pd3dDevice->SetTextureStageState(2, D3DTSS_COLOROP,
    D3DTOP_DISABLE);
  m_pd3dDevice->SetTextureStageState(2, D3DTSS_ALPHAOP,
    D3DTOP_DISABLE);
```

```
m_pd3dDevice->DrawIndexedPrimitive(D3DPT_TRIANGLELIST, 0,
    m_pTeapot->GetLocalMesh()->GetNumVertices(), 0,
    m_pTeapot->GetLocalMesh()->GetNumFaces());
}
```

As you can see, the first pass works the same as it did in the last section. In the second pass, we turn on alpha blending (because we don't want the non-silhouetted areas to overwrite the shading we've already rendered). We set up a two-stage chain. We don't really have to do this; the only reason we do it here is because our vertex shader puts the edge coordinate in oT1, which means we must use texture stage one to access that coordinate.

> **TIP**
>
> Alternatively (and this is probably a better solution), you could use two different shaders—one for each pass—and use only one texture stage on the second pass. I decided not to do this because in my opinion it's harder to read that way. I leave this as an exercise for you.

Cartoon Rendering Wrap-Up

In conjunction, the edge and shade textures go a long way toward creating the illusion of cartoon rendering. Another helpful hint is to put your cartoon-rendered objects on a bright background, either white or bright gray, to enhance the illusion of sketches on paper.

Cartoon rendering is a great example of some of the effects you can create now that 3D graphics hardware has progressed enough to support hardware-based vertex shaders.

Now let's look at the second type of shader—the pixel shader—which gives you even more power!

IMAGE PROCESSING USING PIXEL SHADERS

This section will guide you through creating several different types of effects using simple pixel shaders. We'll be looking at pixel shaders that blur, sharpen, invert, and de-colorize a scene, all in real time.

If you'd like, load up the Ch24p3_ImgManip sample program and follow along in the IDE. You can see a screenshot of this sample program in Figure 24.6.

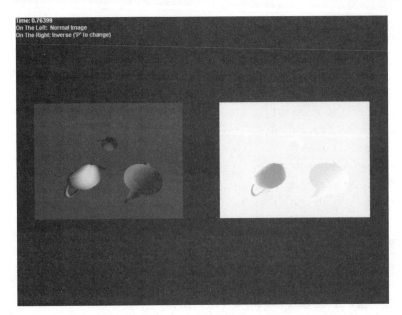

Figure 24.6

A screenshot of the `Ch24p3_ImgManip` *sample program.*

The Framework

Before we start talking about the shaders themselves, we need to create a framework to showcase them. So I've built a sample application that contains two windows. The left window shows a scene rendered without pixel shaders, and the right window shows a scene as seen through a particular pixel shader. The scene images are generated in real time; I render to a separate off-screen texture.

I'm not going to cover the framework that does this in detail right now, because it's very easy to follow, provided you've read the last few chapters (especially Chapter 23, "3D Water," which talks extensively about rendering a scene onto a texture).

There are a few things worth highlighting, however. For starters, I use two separate vertex shaders. One vertex shader renders the teapots inside the scene. This is a simple vertex shader that calculates the position and the diffuse color, given a light direction and a combined world/view/transform matrix. There's nothing particularly noteworthy about this shader.

The second shader is more interesting, and we'll talk about it shortly. Before we talk about it, I need to introduce you to the vertex structure for the quads we'll be pushing through the pixel shaders:

```
typedef struct
{
  D3DXVECTOR3 position; // The position
```

```
D3DCOLOR    color;      // The color
float       tu0, tv0;   // texcoords 0
float       tu1, tv1;   // texcoords 1
float       tu2, tv2;   // texcoords 2
float       tu3, tv3;   // texcoords 3
} VERTEX_IMGMANIP;
#define D3DFVF_IMGMANIP (D3DFVF_XYZ|D3DFVF_DIFFUSE|D3DFVF_TEX4)
```

Several interesting things are in this vertex structure. First, notice that there's no normal information. Since we won't be applying lighting to our quads, there's no need to store the surface normals for them.

Second, notice that there are four—yes, four—pairs of texture coordinates. Amazingly enough, we will be using all four of these texture coordinates for a couple of pixel shaders. We'll see how that works in later sections.

The Framework's Vertex Shader

Now that you've seen the vertex structure, I'd like to acquaint you with the vertex shader we'll be using:

```
vs.1.0
// transform position
m4x4 oPos, v0, c[0]
// transform texture coords
add oT0.xy, v3, c[5]
add oT1.xy, v3, c[6]
add oT2.xy, v3, c[7]
add oT3.xy, v3, c[8]
```

This little guy hides a key concept. We start by transforming the vertex position (v0) by the combined world/view/projection matrix stored in constants zero through three. That's nothing new, however, notice what we're doing after that. We're taking the texture coordinates of the vertex (v3) and adding different constant registers onto them to arrive at the final texture coordinates for each of our four stages.

For this to make complete sense, we need to know what's in constant registers five through eight. Here's the code that sets up those registers:

```
// Set up the vertex shader constants
{
  D3DXMATRIX matWorldViewProj;
```

```
matWorldViewProj = worldmat * projmat;
D3DXMatrixTranspose(&matWorldViewProj, &matWorldViewProj);
float fPerTexelOffset = 0.5 / m_iTextureSize;
D3DXVECTOR4 vConstants0(-fPerTexelOffset, -fPerTexelOffset,
    0.0, 0.0);
D3DXVECTOR4 vConstants1(-fPerTexelOffset,  fPerTexelOffset,
    0.0, 0.0);
D3DXVECTOR4 vConstants2( fPerTexelOffset, -fPerTexelOffset,
    0.0, 0.0);
D3DXVECTOR4 vConstants3( fPerTexelOffset,  fPerTexelOffset,
    0.0, 0.0);

m_pd3dDevice->SetVertexShaderConstant(0, &matWorldViewProj, 4);
m_pd3dDevice->SetVertexShaderConstant(5, &vConstants0, 1);
m_pd3dDevice->SetVertexShaderConstant(6, &vConstants1, 1);
m_pd3dDevice->SetVertexShaderConstant(7, &vConstants2, 1);
m_pd3dDevice->SetVertexShaderConstant(8, &vConstants3, 1);
}
```

This is certainly interesting. We set constant register zero to the combined world/view/projection matrix—this is to be expected. Then, we fill up constant registers five, six, seven, and eight with four constant vectors.

Notice what the vectors contain. We calculate the width of one texel, and store this in fPerTexelOffset. We then set up the constant registers so that they move the texture one texel northwest, southwest, northeast, and southeast.

This means that when we're inside our pixel shader, our four texture stages contain the colors of the texels immediately northwest, southwest, northeast, and southeast of the current texel.

Why We Want This: The Blur and Sharpen Pixel Shaders

We want to know the colors of the neighboring texels so that we can create blur and sharpening pixel shaders. For example, here's what the blur pixel shader looks like:

```
ps.1.1
def c1, 0.25f, 0.25f, 0.25f, 0.25f
tex t0
tex t1
tex t2
tex t3
```

```
mul r0, c1, t0
mad r0, c1, t1, r0
mad r0, c1, t2, r0
mad r0, c1, t3, r0
```

Here you can see that the pixel shader creates the final output color (r0) by adding one-fourth of the t0, t1, t2, and t3 textures. This effectively creates a blur by averaging the northwest, northeast, southwest, and southeast texels. Pretty cool, isn't it? By using several textures, we've "tricked" the pixel shader into letting us read the values of neighboring texels!

Here's another great example of this technique. This is a sharpening pixel filter:

```
ps.1.1
tex t0
tex t1
tex t2
tex t3
// r0 = 4*t0 - t1 - t2 - t3
// rearranged, this is r0 = t0 - t1 + t0 - t2 + t0 - t3 + t0
mov    r0, t0
sub    r0, r0,   t1
add    r0, r0,   t0
sub    r0, r0,   t2
add    r0, r0,   t0
sub    r0, r0,   t3
add    r0, r0,   t0
```

Here you can see the code adding four t0s, a t1, a t2, and a t3 to arrive at the final output color (r0). This corresponds (roughly) to a sharpening kernel.

Other Cool Pixel Shaders

We don't always have to use four texture stages to create cool effects. Here are a few pixel shaders that use only one texture stage to work their magic.

A Simple Black-and-White Shader

Ever wished you could take a color scene and render it in black and white? Imagine how cool it would be if characters might drink a potion that rendered them color-blind for a certain amount of time. Or, imagine looking through the viewfinder of a spy camera. In both of these situations, a pixel shader that took a color image and rendered it in black and white would come in handy.

Here is just such a shader:

```
ps.1.1
def c1, 0.3333f, 0.3333f, 0.3333f, 0.0f
tex t0
tex t1
tex t2
tex t3
dp3 r0, t0, c1
```

Here you can see the code taking the dot product of the first texture stage (t0) and the constant vector c1. Recall the mathematical process you use to take a dot product, and you'll realize that this shader is really multiplying the red, green, and blue components by 0.3333, then adding the results of these multiplications together. This creates a black-and-white image.

A Better Black-and-White Shader

The black-and-white shader in the preceding section works great, but it's a little dark. Here's a better alternative:

```
ps.1.1
def c1, 0.3333f, 0.59f, 0.11f, 0.0f
tex t0
tex t1
tex t2
tex t3
dp3 r0, t0, c1
```

The only thing different between this shader and the last one is the constant vector c1. In this shader, the code uses values for red, green, and blue multiplication that more accurately reflect how sensitive our eyes are to each color. For example, the amount of green in a color (believe it or not) is the biggest factor in determining how bright our eyes perceive that color to be. By modeling our eye's biases through these constant values, we create a shader that renders a more accurate black-and-white scene.

> **TIP**
>
> Note that you could really use any three constants in the shader above. You can tint the image to any color you like simply by messing with the constants.

Inverting an Image

Here's another cool pixel shader. This one simply inverts the colors, like the negatives for color film:

```
ps.1.1
def c1, 0.25f, 0.25f, 0.25f, 0.25f
tex t0
tex t1
tex t2
tex t3
mov r0, 1-t0
```

It doesn't get much easier than that! You can tell the pixel shader to invert something by pre-pending "1–" to the thing that you want to invert. In this example, we're inverting t0, then storing that as our final output color (r0).

Direct3D includes support for several interesting modifiers like this one; check out Chapter 10 for a complete list of them.

CHAPTER WRAP-UP

I feel like I've just played you two notes of a symphony. The range of things you can do with vertex and pixel shaders is truly mind boggling; it blows open the door for tons of interesting effects. I encourage you to experiment on your own!

Sample Program Reference

nVidia provides several really neat examples of vertex and pixel shaders as part of its SDK. Microsoft also provides a couple of examples as part of the DirectX 8.0 (and later) SDK.

ABOUT THE SAMPLE PROGRAMS

These sample programs each highlight a different technique that we've described in this chapter:

- **Ch24p1_ToonShader**. This sample program shows you how to create non-photorealistic rendering using a toon vertex shader.
- **Ch24p2_ToonShaderSilo**. This sample program builds on the preceding one. It shows you how to add simulated pen strokes to your renderings, by using silhouettes.
- **Ch24p3_ImgManip**. This sample program shows you how to create a pixel-shader-based image processor, capable of performing blurs, sharpens, and several other cool effects on your textures.

EXERCISES

1. Go back to Chapter 16 and rewrite the image manipulation code using a pixel shader and multiple texture passes.
2. Make the second pass of the cartoon renderer use only one texture stage, by using two different vertex shaders (one for the edge texture, and one for the shading texture).

CONCLUSION

I was never very good at writing conclusions. My English teachers in high school, and my professors in college, would always criticize my papers for their pathetic closing arguments (they'd also nail me for using triple spacing and 14-point fonts to get around their page requirements, but that's another story).

I suppose I wasn't any good at writing them because I always thought they were pointless. I mean, I've already said everything I wanted. What more is there?

A funny thing happened, however, as I started thinking about what the end of the book would be like. I realized that I needed a conclusion, a final thought that would sum up everything you've learned and give you one last springboard off which to jump. So here it is, that final idea before the cold and lonely tundra of the index.

A good special effects programmer is like a used-car salesperson. Special effects, like selling used cars, is all about tricking the viewer into believing that something exists when it doesn't. It's about using smoke and mirrors to create believable illusions of unbelievable things.

The cool thing about special effects programming is that it doesn't matter how you do it, as long as it looks good. This gives you, the special effects programmer, amazing amounts of freedom to exercise your creativity. Hollywood special effects studios employ everything from puppets to clay to CGI. Good video game special effects programmers also use everything at their disposal—lookup tables, trigonometry, rendering to textures—to create convincing effects.

This book gave you an overview of some of the more common special effects. It also gave you a tour of some basic special effects algorithms. I hope that I've not only answered a lot of your "whoa, how'd they do that?" questions, but also provided you with a grab-bag of techniques that you can employ when creating your own effects.

Also, one last thought: special effects are not a replacement for good gameplay. All of the eye-candy in the world won't save you if your gameplay sucks, but if your gameplay is solid, special effects can turn your game from good into extraordinary. Don't build your games around the effects; build your effects around your game.

That's it; I'm coming off the soapbox. I hope your journey through this book has been enjoyable, as well as informative. If there's anything you want to ask, just e-mail me: mason@spin-studios.com. I'll be happy to answer your questions. Also, one last plug—check out my Web site, www.spin-studios.com, for cool games and useful game development tools.

May your debugging sessions be short and your compile times quick!

Mason McCuskey
Portland, Oregon
November, 2001

APPENDIX A

Advanced C++ and STL

hen I was a kid, I loved flying kites. I grew up in suburban Denver, which was great, but it wasn't exactly the kite-flying utopia that Chicago or someplace windier would be. Frequently, getting a kite off the ground required my brother's help—he'd stand a couple dozen yards away from me, holding the kite. On my signal, he would throw the kite up into the air, and I would run as fast as I could away from him. In this way we could generate just enough wind for the kite to rise up and catch an actual breeze.

That's what this appendix is. To continue this (cheesy?) analogy, the goal of this appendix is to give you just enough knowledge to get you off the ground and flying high enough to catch the actual breeze. This appendix isn't going to cover everything in C++ and STL; it's not even going to really scratch the surface. But if you're not very experienced with these technologies, it's my hope that this appendix will give you what you need to know to understand the rest of the book.

CAUTION

I'm going to move fast, and won't cover each topic in complete detail. If you're completely new to a topic, you should do yourself a favor and devote more time to it than I have. The CD gives you URLs for several great C++ and STL Web sites that you can cruise to and learn some of the finer points. Also, the book *STL Tutorial and Reference Guide: C++ Programming with the Standard Template Library*, by David R. Musser, Gillmer J. Derge, and Atul Saini is a great resource for learning STL.

SELECTED C++ TOPICS

As I wrote the sample code for this book, I used what many programmers refer to as a "sane subset" of C++. C++ is a feature-rich language, and every C++ feature is useful in certain situations. However, the code for the book does not venture into all of those situations. So I've taken a few C++ features and banned their usage, in the hopes that the book would be easier to read and follow. For example, I've tried very hard not to overload operators, even though there are cases where operator overloading would be elegant.

However, some features of C++ are simply too good to pass up. I'm going to devote a little time to each of these features now. I'll progress from what I consider the easier stuff to the more complex features.

Let's start with inline functions.

Inline Functions

Inline functions are especially valuable to game programmers, because oftentimes they can speed up the execution of a program. Careful inlining can give you some good performance gains (at the expense of executable size, which usually isn't an issue).

When you use the C++ keyword `inline` on a certain function, you're telling the compiler that function doesn't necessarily have to be a function. If it saves time, the code can be embedded directly into the "caller," without the need for a function call.

So essentially, an inline function is C++'s answer to C's #define. Inline functions behave exactly like regular functions, with one key difference: When the compiler comes across an inlined function, it doesn't create a machine-language subroutine. Instead, it just places the machine language code for the function directly "inline" with the rest of the code, just as if you had used #define to make a macro.

In this way, you get the best of both worlds—you get the speed of having the function's code directly inline. No time is wasted putting variables onto the call stack before the function is called and popping them off when the function is done.

Also, since you're not just doing string substitutions like with #define, you get the benefit of having the compiler treat your macro as an actual function. To see why this is handy, take a look at the following code (pardon me if you've seen this one):

```
#define BoundsCheck(a) if (a < 5) a = 5; if (a > 10) a = 10;
void Foo(void) {
  int a = 0;
  BoundsCheck(++a);
  printf("%d", a);
}
```

What does that function print? It looks like it should print 1, right? Bzzt, wrong! It prints at least 2, sometimes 3. The reason: the compiler is doing simple string substitution on your #define, so you actually wind up with machine language code that corresponds to this:

```
void Foo(void) {
  int a = 0;
  if (++a < 5) ++a = 5;
  if (++a > 10) ++a = 10;
  printf("%d", a);
}
```

Now it's easy to spot the gotcha—you didn't actually mean for a to be incremented twice—you wanted it to be incremented just once, and then passed to a BoundsCheck "function." Here's equivalent C++ code that works correctly:

```
inline void BoundsCheck(int &a) {
  if (a < 5) a = 5;
  if (a > 10) a = 10;
}
void Foo(void) {
  int a = 0;
  BoundsCheck(++a);
  printf("%d", a);
}
```

That code prints 1, which, if you'll forgive the pun, is more in line with what you'd expect it to do.

Namespaces

One of the problems with traditional C is that of naming. Frequently in C, you'll run into the problem of "name clashing"—essentially, you'll run out of good unique names for global functions. Even worse, let's say you're writing a C API, in other words, you're writing some code and then handing a library (lib file) to another C developer. Let's say that C developer has written a global function called Process, and that you've also embedded a global function called Process into your API library. That's a problem—the name of your API function is clashing with the name of the other developer's function. Unfortunately, the only remedy for this is for one of you to change your function name—no fun.

In C++, however, you can avoid this problem by using namespaces. Essentially, a namespace is a "folder" for your function and variable names. Just as you can group files into hierarchies of folders, in C++ you can group functions and variables into hierarchies of namespaces.

For example, let's say you're writing a 3D game, and you'd like all of the classes for your 3D engine grouped together. You'd use a namespace, and write code something like this:

```
namespace MyCool3DEngine {
  void Initialize();
  void Terminate();
  void Draw();
  // other variables, functions, and classes for 3D engine go here.
};
```

Now, all of the stuff associated with your 3D engine is contained nice and neat in a namespace called MyCool3DEngine.

> **TIP**
>
> You may not realize it, but you've already been dealing with namespaces regularly. Classes, structures, enums, and several other things you're already familiar with exist within namespaces. For example, if you have a static method Foo, of class A, you know you can't access Foo from outside class A without specifying A::Foo.
>
> The keywords class, struct, and enum do things in addition to creating a name-space. The namespace keyword simply creates a namespace, nothing more.

You have two options for accessing the stuff you've put inside a namespace. First, you can use the scope resolution operator, ::, like so:

```
void RunGame(void) {
  // initialize 3D engine
  MyCool3DEngine::Initialize();
  // etc.
}
```

In the example above, we use the scope resolution operator to get to the Initialize function contained in the MyCool3DEngine namespace.

Alternatively, you can specify a "using namespace" line, like so:

```
using namespace MyCool3DEngine;
void RunGame(void) {
  // initialize 3D engine
  Initialize();
  // etc.
}
```

This works similar to how a search path works for files. The "using namespace" line tells the compiler that if it can't find a function, it should look for it within the specified namespace. In the above example, if the compiler doesn't immediately find a function called Initialize, it looks in the name-space MyCool3DEngine.

> **TIP**
>
> The "using namespace" line is only valid within your current scope. For example, if you put using namespace inside a function body, it's only valid when you're inside that function.
>
> Most of the time you'll put using namespace at the top of your C++ file, at global scope.

The "using namespace" feature is handy not only because it saves you some keystrokes but also because if the name of the namespace changes, you only have to adjust the code in one place (that is, you only have to change the "using namespace" line).

You can also "alias" a namespace. Aliasing allows you to change the name of a namespace, which can be handy if you're dealing with code that you can't change (such as code from other developers or companies). For example, if a company's code is irritating you because they've named their namespace something huge like Official3DGraphicsRenderingAPIVersionOne, you can switch that to something easier to type (say, GFXRenderingAPI) by writing code like this:

> **TIP**
>
> In this way, you not only solve the name clashing problem, but you can also do a better job of isolating your code from other people's code. If the company later changes the name of their namespace, all you need to change is this one alias line, and you're good to go.

```
namespace GFXRenderingAPI = Official3DGraphicsRenderingAPIVersionOne;
```

Also—you can nest namespaces. Think of the scope resolution operator, ::, as the equivalent to the backslash in the file system (it's not quite as versatile, but it provides a good analogy for right now). For example, let's say you have namespace A embedded in namespace B, like so:

```
namespace A {
  namespace B {
    void Foo(void);
  }
}
```

> **TIP**
>
> The C++ Standard Template Library is contained entirely within a namespace called std. So frequently, in source files that use STL, you'll see using namespace std lines, or you'll see std:: prefixed to STL functions and data types.

You could get to Foo by writing:

```
A::B::Foo();
```

So, that's a namespace—a simple C++ feature that really adds a lot to the organization of your code. Give it a try sometime—it's handy!

Dynamic Memory Allocation the C++ Way

I'm painting with broad strokes here, but essentially, programmers have two options for memory allocation: dynamic and static. A program can allocate different amounts of dynamic memory each time it runs; however, it always uses the same amount of static memory.

When you declare a variable on the stack, that's a static allocation. Here's an example:

```
char str[256];
```

Every time this piece of code runs, you get 256 chars. There's no way to change how much is allocated, short of cracking open the source code, changing that 256 number to a different value, and then recompiling.

If you don't know for sure how much memory you'll need, static allocation becomes irritating. You have two choices: brace for the worst case and statically allocate the maximum number of objects that you'll support (knowing that you may only use 3 of those 256 chars), or allocate the memory dynamically.

A Quick Recap of How to Dynamically Allocate Memory in C

If you're an experienced C programmer, you're probably good friends with the C standard library functions malloc and free. C programmers use these two functions extensively to perform dynamic memory allocation—that is, to have their programs allocate various amounts of memory as they run. For example, you might write something like this:

```
int iNumberOfCharsNeeded = CalculateNumCharsNeeded();
char *str = (char *)malloc(iNumberOfCharsNeeded);
```

Using malloc, we can allocate just the right amount of memory that we need. That's the C way to do it—malloc and free.

How Not to Dynamically Allocate Memory in C++

However, because you're now a C++ programmer, you need to break the malloc and free habit. Both malloc and free are C library calls, and as such, they have no clue about C++. So, based on that piece of information, see if you can spot the bug in the following code:

```
class MyClass
{
public:
  MyClass() { m_Number = 10; }
private:
  int m_Number;
};
void main(void)
{
  MyClass *newClass = (MyClass *)malloc(sizeof(MyClass));
```

```
    printf("%d", newClass->m_Number);
    free(newClass);
}
```

Looks pretty innocent, right? Careful—contrary to what you'd expect, this program does not print out 10. In fact, there's no telling *what* it will print. The bug is that malloc, being an old-school C function, doesn't know about constructors. Sure, it allocates enough memory to hold a MyClass object, but it doesn't actually call the MyClass constructor. So m_Number never gets initialized to 10.

Proper Dynamic Memory Allocation in C++

So what we need is a way to say, "hey, Mr. Compiler, I'm not just allocating memory here, I'm actually making a new object, so you need to call its constructor." The way we do this is with the new keyword. Here's the same code, only this time the use of new has vanquished the bug:

```
void main(void)
{
    MyClass *newClass = new MyClass;
    printf("%d", newClass->m_Number);
    delete newClass;
}
```

The first thing you should notice is that we've replaced the malloc call with new. That creates the object—notice also there's no longer a need to cast the return value from new. Not only does new properly call the constructor for MyClass, it also hands you back the correct type of pointer, so there's no more messy casting.

So that's half the mystery. But we also need to free the object properly—we must ensure that the destructor (if any) for the object is called. To do this, we use the delete keyword. The delete keyword works just like free, only it also makes sure the object's destructor gets called.

Dynamic Memory Allocation for Arrays in C++

Now that you've got the basics, consider this: let's say we wanted to create five MyClass objects. That situation is a bit trickier, so, if you'll forgive my second bad pun in this appendix, we need to learn some more "new" stuff.

This time I'll give you the code up front:

```
void main(void)
{
    MyClass *newClass = new MyClass[5];
```

```
for (int q=0; q < 5; q++) {
  printf("%d", newClass[q].m_Number);
}
delete[] newClass;
}
```

I've changed a couple of things here. First, notice the [5] at the end of the new line. That tells the C++ compiler that we're creating five objects, and that we'd like the constructors to be called for each of those five objects. Correspondingly, the brackets at the end of the delete keyword tell the compiler that it needs to call the destructors for all the objects

> ## CAUTION
>
> You need to be very careful and ensure that your news and deletes are in sync. That is, make sure you use delete to free single objects and delete[] to delete object arrays. Otherwise, you'll get strange memory errors and probably access violations. Forgetting to put the brackets on the end of delete when killing an array of objects is one of the most common mistakes I've seen beginning C++ programmers make.

in the array (we don't have to specify the size of the array when we call delete[]—the compiler remembers how many we allocated in the first place).

Note also how we get to the individual objects inside that array, just as if newClass were an array of chars or ints. All we have to do is put the index we want (in this example, the variable q) inside brackets.

Pause for a moment here and make sure you understand all of these concepts. Dynamic versus static memory allocation is a vital concept that you need to know inside and out in order to follow the examples in this book.

Polymorphism and Pure Virtual Functions

When most people think of C++, this is the topic in the forefront of their minds. As you know, C++ allows you to create classes, which are like structs but with functions and with the capacity to make things private. This is the first thing most C++ programmers learn.

The second thing is that these classes can be arranged in a hierarchy, and you can leverage this hierarchy inside your programs to address things in a generic manner. For example, say you're writing a game about animals, and you have three classes: cat, dog, and fish. Each animal needs to eat, so you write an eat method for each class. Using a feature of C++ called polymorphism, you can treat the cat, dog, and fish classes as a generic "animal." You can tell that "animal" to eat, and C++ will take care of calling the appropriate function based on the type of object.

This is called *polymorphism,* one of the three key principles of object-oriented programming (the other two key principles are *data abstraction* and *inheritance,* but I'll only deal with the latter here).

Polymorphism is a noun, meaning "the ability to change into different forms." Essentially, that's what C++ classes can do. If you set up the situation correctly, they can change into different things without your ever knowing.

Inheritance versus Aggregation (Is-A versus Has-A)

Every C++ class can be derived from no classes (no inheritance), one class (single inheritance) or from many classes (multiple inheritance). To make one class inherit another, put the inherited class on the declaration line for the new class. For example, to make class Y inherit class X, write the following:

```
class X { /* whatever */ };
class Y : public X { /* whatever */ };
```

That tells the compiler that class Y inherits class X *publicly*, which means that the public methods and members of class X are public in class Y. C++ supports other types of inheritance, but public inheritance is the most common.

In the example above, C++ programmers would say that class Y is "derived from" class X. In other words, class Y derives some of its functionality (methods and members) from class X.

Now, applying that to our cat, dog, and fish example: we know that cats, dogs, and fish are all animals. So, we might want to create a class hierarchy that reflects that:

```
class CAnimal { /* whatever */ };
class CFish : public CAnimal { /* whatever */ };
class CCat : public CAnimal { /* whatever */ };
class CDog : public CAnimal { /* whatever */ };
```

That establishes a class hierarchy. The compiler now knows that fish, dog, and cat classes derive from the animal class (in other words, a fish is an animal, a dog is an animal, and a cat is an animal. For this reason, object-oriented programmers also refer to inheritance as an "is-a relationship"—a fish is-a animal, a dog is-a animal, and a cat is-a animal.

So, that's an "is-a" relationship. There's also a "has-a" relationship. For example, we know that all three types of animals, be they fish, cats, or dogs, have hearts, so we can say that an animal "has-a" heart:

```
class CHeart { /* whatever */ };
class CAnimal {
protected:
  CHeart m_Heart;
};
```

```
class CFish : public CAnimal { /* whatever */ };
class CCat : public CAnimal { /* whatever */ };
class CDog : public CAnimal { /* whatever */ };
```

In this code, we've created a CHeart class and added a member to CAnimal called m_Heart. The cat, fish, and dog classes now automatically get an m_Heart object, because they derive from CAnimal. A derived class inherits the members and methods of its base (or parent) class.

This is called a "has-a" relationship—an animal has-a heart. Some programmers also refer to "has-a" relationships as "aggregation."

> **TIP**
>
> Note also the protected: keyword. That tells the compiler that m_Heart is in protected storage, which means it's only visible to methods of CAnimal and methods of classes derived from CAnimal. Protected storage is somewhere between public (where everything can see the member) and private (where only that class can see the member).

> **TIP**
>
> It can sometimes be tricky to decide between inheritance and aggregation. I've found that using "is-a" and "has-a" in a sentence about the two things in question often helps me decide whether I should make a new base class and derive from it, or if I should just give a variable to an existing class. If the "Is-a" sentence makes sense, that means inheritance is the way to go; if the has-a sentence makes more sense, that means I should use aggregation.
>
> For example, "a fish is-a heart" sounds silly, but "a fish has-a heart" is reasonable, so aggregation wins. As a counterexample, we know the animal/fish relationship is inheritance, because "a fish has-a animal" sounds ridiculous, but "a fish is-a animal" makes perfect sense.
>
> Keep this in mind as you're designing your class hierarchies.

Virtual Functions

Now that we've got hearts for our fish, dog, and cat class, we might decide to give them a little more life. We know that all animals breathe, so we can easily add a Breathe function to our code:

```
class CHeart { /* whatever */ };
class CAnimal {
protected:
```

```
  void Breathe(void);
  CHeart m_Heart;
};
class CFish : public CAnimal { /* whatever */ };
class CCat : public CAnimal { /* whatever */ };
class CDog : public CAnimal { /* whatever */ };
```

This works, but the problem is that our animals breathe in different ways. Fish breathe water; cats and dogs prefer air. Having one `Breathe` function for all three animal types would force us to perform a switch inside the function, and do different things depending on what kind of animal we have:

```
void CAnimal::Breathe(void)
{
  if (ThisAnimalIsADog() || ThisAnimalIsACat()) { BreatheAir(); }
  if (ThisAnimalIsAFish()) { BreatheWater(); }
}
```

There are several painful points in that bit of code. For starters, how do we implement the `ThisAnimalIsADog`, `ThisAnimalIsACat`, and `ThisAnimalIsAFish` functions? Additionally, if we add new animals, we have to go back to this function and add `if` statements. Even worse, if none of the `if` statements is true, the animal doesn't breathe at all!

Polymorphism was designed to solve just this type of problem. C++ contains a feature called "virtual functions." Virtual functions are functions that are defined for both the base and derived classes. When you call a virtual function of a class, the compiler looks at the type of class, and automatically calls the correct function.

Let's see how it looks:

```
class CHeart { /* whatever */ };
class CAnimal {
protected:
  virtual void Breathe(void) { BreatheAir(); }
  CHeart m_Heart;
};
class CFish : public CAnimal
{
protected:
  void Breathe(void) { BreatheWater(); }
};
class CCat : public CAnimal { /* whatever */ };
class CDog : public CAnimal { /* whatever */ };
```

Here we've introduced a couple of things. First, we've put the `virtual` keyword before the `Breathe` prototype in `CAnimal`. This tells the compiler that `Breathe` is a virtual function. Second, we've added a `Breathe` function to `CFish`.

Now let's say we have some code as follows:

```
void Foo(void)
{
  CFish fish;
  CDog dog;

  dog.Breathe(); // calls CAnimal's Breathe
  fish.Breathe(); // calls CFish's Breathe
}
```

That's polymorphism! When we say `dog.Breathe`, the compiler knows that dog is of type `CDog`. Since `CDog` doesn't define a `Breathe` function, we end up inside `CAnimal`'s `Breathe` function. Conversely, when we call `fish.Breathe`, the compiler notices that we've created a `Breathe` function just for `CFish`, and calls that instead of `CAnimal`'s breathe.

Pure Virtuals

At this point our code is starting to become much more object-oriented, but there's still something that should be bothering you—fish aren't the only animals that don't breathe air. For example, if we added a `CEel` class, we'd have to make sure to add a `Breathe` function for it, otherwise, we'd incorrectly be calling `BreatheAir` for eels!

Right now we're saying to the compiler "unless I tell you otherwise, assume that all animals breathe air." It might be better if we could say "don't make any assumptions; I will provide a `Breathe` function for all derived classes." That way, we could be sure that each animal is breathing correctly.

This is where the notion of a *pure virtual function* comes into play. A pure virtual function (or pure virtual, to its friends), is a function that only exists for derived classes. It has no base class implementation.

You declare one by putting `= 0` after the function declaration in your class. Here's how we'd use one in our code:

```
class CHeart { /* whatever */ };
class CAnimal {
protected:
  virtual void Breathe(void) = 0;
  CHeart m_Heart;
};
```

```
class CFish : public CAnimal
{
protected:
  void Breathe(void) { BreatheWater(); }
};
class CCat : public CAnimal
{
protected:
  void Breathe(void) { BreatheAir(); }
};
class CDog : public CAnimal
{
protected:
  void Breathe(void) { BreatheAir(); }
};
```

Essentially, the only thing we've done here is put an = 0 in place of CAnimal::Breathe. That tells the compiler that our Breathe function doesn't exist in our base class, but must exist in every class that derives from our base (we get compile errors if it doesn't).

One important caveat to creating pure virtual functions: Any class with a pure virtual cannot be instantiated. That is, with the pure virtual inside CAnimal, you can't ever create a variable of type CAnimal. This makes sense, because what would the compiler do if you created a variable of type CAnimal, and then called Breathe on it? It would have no idea what kind of animal it would be dealing with, so it wouldn't know what Breathe function to call.

You can still create references and pointers to that base class, however, and in reality, that's where the power of polymorphism really shines, because it allows you to do things like this:

```
CAnimal *CreateRandomAnimal(void)
{
  CAnimal *theAnimal = NULL;
  switch(rand() % 3) {
    case 0: theAnimal = new CCat(); break;
    case 1: theAnimal = new CDog(); break;
    case 2: theAnimal = new CFish(); break;
  }
  return(theAnimal);
}
void Foo(void)
{
  CAnimal *pAnimal = CreateRandomAnimal();
```

```
  pAnimal->Breathe(); // automatically calls the correct function!
  delete pAnimal;
}
```

In the code example above, we've got a function that creates a random type of animal. It returns that random type of animal in a pointer to its base class, CAnimal. (Remember, you can't create CAnimals, but you can create pointers to CAnimals.) When Foo tells the new CAnimal pointer to breathe, the compiler automatically knows which function to call.

Think about how cool that is for a moment. Foo doesn't know or even care what type of animal it's dealing with—it just says Breathe and the compiler does the rest. In fact, we could add 500 different types of animals, and rewrite CreateRandomAnimal so that it randomly picked one of those 500 animals, and so long as all 500 animals derived from CAnimal and all 500 implemented a Breathe function, Foo would work without our changing one line of its code. That's the power of polymorphism!

Virtual Destructors

I want to cover one last, very important topic on polymorphism before moving on. We need to talk about what happens when base and derived classes are destroyed.

Each C++ class has a constructor and destructor, which tells the compiler what to do when that object is created or destroyed. Normally, if the constructor allocates any memory for the class, the destructor frees that memory. For example, let's say we wanted to create a couple of animal parts dynamically:

```
class CHeart { /* whatever */ };
class CGills { /* whatever (for the fish) */ };
class CAnimal {
public:
  CAnimal() { m_pHeart = new CHeart; }
  ~CAnimal() { delete m_pHeart; }
protected:
  virtual void Breathe(void) = 0;
  CHeart *m_pHeart;
};
class CFish : public CAnimal
{
public:
  CFish() { m_pGills = new CGills; }
  ~CFish() { delete m_pGills; }
```

```
protected:
  void Breathe(void) { BreatheWater(); }
  CGills *m_pGills;
};
class CCat : public CAnimal
{
protected:
  void Breathe(void) { BreatheAir(); }
};
class CDog : public CAnimal
{
protected:
  void Breathe(void) { BreatheAir(); }
};
```

Here you can see I've added a couple of things. First, I changed CAnimal so that it dynamically allocates and deletes the heart object.

I've also added a similar mechanism to CFish—the fish object now creates some gills when it's constructed, and destroys those gills when it's destroyed.

Unfortunately, there's a bug in that code, and it's a sneaky one. Let's say I have the same Foo function:

```
void Foo(void)
{
  CAnimal *pAnimal = CreateRandomAnimal();
  pAnimal->Breathe(); // automatically calls the correct function!
  delete pAnimal;
}
```

The problem here is that Foo only knows it's dealing with a CAnimal. So, when it says delete pAnimal, the CAnimal destructor is called, but not the destructor for any derived objects. So if CreateRandomAnimal happens to create a fish, we'll create a heart and some gills, but when we call delete we will end up calling only the CAnimal destructor, and we'll wind up deleting the heart but not the gills. This is bad because we leak memory, to say nothing of the spookiness in having some disembodied gills floating around somewhere.

To fix this problem, we need to make the CAnimal destructor virtual. When we add the virtual keyword to the beginning of the destructor line, we solve our problem.

The virtual keyword has a slightly different meaning when applied to destructors. Ordinarily, virtual means "hey, Mr. Compiler, check the derived classes for this function, and if you find it down there, don't call this one, call the derived one instead." But, when applied to the destructor, the virtual keyword says "hey, Mr. Compiler, you need to call the destructor for the derived classes, *as well as* the destructor for this object." C++ does things this way because if both the base class and the derived class allocate memory, both destructors need to be called.

CAUTION

For the reason you've just seen, you should probably play it safe and make *every* destructor you create virtual. You may be sure you'll never derive another class from a particular class, but if you later change your mind and you don't have a virtual destructor you run the risk of creating really hard-to-spot memory leaks.

Polymorphism Wrap-Up

So those are the details of polymorphism that you need in order to understand the code in this book. What I've just spoken about is by no means a complete rundown on the subject. Many books have been written on how to use polymorphism to create better-designed programs, and you should definitely check them out if you want to become a better C++ programmer.

CAUTION

Yes, you can derive an object from more than one base class. This is called *multiple inheritance*. I'm not going to show you how to do it, though, because most C++ programmers consider MI to be evil. Unless you're doing something very convoluted, you'll never have a good reason to use multiple inheritance. If you find yourself in a situation where MI might make sense, keep thinking about that situation until you come to a better solution. MI causes confusion and is very error-prone. Pretend it doesn't exist and your programs will be much better off.

Exception Handling

The next topic I want to glance at is exception handling, and I'll start by asking a question: How would you characterize the "robustness" of the programs you've written before? In other words, do they handle errors gracefully? Do they recover from abrupt end of files or unexpected data and issue a sensible error message, or do they simply go down in flames?

Writing a robust program has traditionally been a pain, but a C++ feature called exception handling can help make it easy. To learn why, let's first start with an example.

Life Before Exception Handling

Say someone asks you to write a function that reads a file into memory. You gladly oblige them, and hammer out a first version that looks something like this:

```
void ReadFileIntoMem(char *filename, char **pMemory)
{
  int handle = open(filename, O_RDONLY | O_BINARY);
  int len = filelength(handle);
  (*pMemory) = new char[len+1];
  read(handle, *pMemory, len);
  close(handle);
}
```

Pretty easy to write, but not exactly robust. What happens if there's not enough memory, and new returns NULL? Crash! What happens if the filename isn't found? What happens if there's a read error? I could go on, but I hope you see my point. Virtually no error checking is done on this code.

So, let's say you notice that and decide to make a robust ReadFileIntoMem function. You add some code to check for common errors, like so:

```
bool ReadFileIntoMem(char *filename, char **pMemory)
{
  int handle = open(filename, O_RDONLY | O_BINARY);
  if (handle == -1) return(false);
  int len = filelength(handle);
  if (len == -1) close(handle); return(false);
  (*pMemory) = new char[len+1];
  if (*pMemory == NULL) close(handle); return(false);
  if (read(handle, *pMemory, len) != len)
    close(handle); return(false);

  close(handle);
  return(true);
}
```

Now we're a little more robust. The function will detect most errors and gracefully recover by returning false, which lets the calling function know that something went horribly wrong.

The code to do this works great, but it's now a lot harder to follow than our first, non-robust version of the function. The error handling logic is essentially interwoven with the core logic, and it can be difficult to see at a glance what the function is doing. Also, we still haven't caught all the errors. For example, if `filename` is `NULL` coming in, we'll crash.

This painful error-checking problem is a classic irritation of C programming that C++'s exception handling feature was designed to solve.

The Basics of Exception Handling

Exception handling in C++ works by using three main constructs:

- **Try blocks**. These are blocks of code that begin with the statement "`try` {" and end with "`}`". You put code that might bomb inside a try block, effectively saying to the compiler, "try this."
- **Catch blocks**. These are blocks of code that start with "`catch`", followed by a variable declaration, and end with "`}`". These come immediately after each try block, and tell the compiler what to do if something goes wrong.
- **Throw statements**. When something goes wrong, you "throw" the error by using the `throw` keyword. Program flow jumps immediately to the appropriate catch block. You can throw anything you want—strings, ints, even C++ objects.

Here's a simple example that illustrates all three constructs:

```
try {
  // do something risky
  throw("An error has occurred!");
}
catch(const char *e) {
  printf("%s", e);
}
```

First, notice the try block. We've wrapped the risky code inside a try block, and we've immediately followed that try block with a catch block (catch blocks must always come right after try blocks). Inside the try block, we're throwing a string, which is really a `const char` pointer.

That `catch` line may look sort of strange. We're actually declaring a variable e of type `const char`. You can think of e as similar to a parameter of a function. It exists only within the catch block, and it's passed by value, not by reference. The compiler automatically fills in e with whatever error (of type `const char`) the throw statement threw. So this sample code simply prints out the error string using `printf`.

Here's the cool thing about exception handling—you can throw from within a function and catch outside that function. For example, the following code is completely legit:

```
void Foo(void)
{
   throw("Error in function foo!");
}
void main(void)
{
   try {
     Foo();
   }
   catch(const char *e) {
     printf("%s", e);
   }
}
```

Pretty cool, isn't it? When Foo throws, program execution jumps *up the stack* to the nearest catch statement. That is the core of the power of exceptions. Frequently an error will occur in some low-level function, and you won't have enough knowledge of what's actually going on to correctly handle the error. In C, your only recourse has been to communicate that something happened, usually through a return value, and hope that whatever segment of code called that function is paying attention to what it returns.

Another thing to keep in mind: really low-level stuff will also throw an exception. For example, if you access memory that you shouldn't, an exception will be thrown. You can catch this exception and attempt to pull up from the nosedive your program is in. Most standard C++ APIs, including the STL, will also throw exceptions.

Catching Different Types, and Catching Everything

You're not limited to just catching one type of exception. Here's an example that catches both strings and integers:

```
void Foo(void)
{
   if (rand() % 2) throw("Error in function foo!");
   else throw(5);
}
void main(void)
{
   try {
     Foo();
   }
```

```
catch(const char *strError) {
  printf("Caught string: %s", strError);
}
catch(int iError) {
  printf("Caught integer: %d", iError);
}
}
```

I've modified Foo so that it randomly throws a string or an integer. To accommodate this, I've also added a new catch handler that catches integers instead of strings.

TIP

The type you're catching doesn't need to match the type you're throwing exactly. For example, if you throw an object of class Derived, and class Derived is derived from class Base, a catch(Base &e) handler will catch the Derived class you threw. Once you're inside the catch block, you can choose to use RTTI (explained in a few pages) to determine what kind of thing you've caught and act appropriately.

But the order you specify the catch statements in matters. Say you have a catch block for both Base and Derived objects. Be careful: If the Base catch comes before the Derived catch, any Derived objects you throw will end up in the Base catch, because it came first. Example:

```
class Base { /* yada */ };
class Derived : public Base { /* yada */ };
void main(void)
{
  try {
    throw(Derived());
  }
  catch(Base &e) {
    // Derived is caught here...
  }
  catch(Derived &e) {
    // even though you probably want it caught here.
  }
}
```

For this reason, it's always a good idea to make your first catch blocks very specific and put broader catch statements (like base classes) later.

You can also add a special catch statement, which many programmers call a *catch-all*, that will catch anything for which you haven't specifically written a catch handler. You create a catch-all by putting an ellipsis (three dots) inside the parentheses of the catch statement, like so:

```
void Foo(void)
{
  switch(rand() % 3) {
    case 0: throw("Error in function foo!");
    case 1: throw(5);
    case 2: throw(5.08f);
  }
}
void main(void)
{
  try {
    Foo();
  }
  catch(const char *e) {
    printf("Caught string: %s", e);
  }
  catch(int e) {
    printf("Caught integer: %d", e);
  }
  catch(...) {
    printf("I caught something, but I have no idea what it is.");
  }
}
```

In this example, Foo now throws strings, ints, or floats. The string and int throws end up in the string and int handler, but since we haven't defined a handler for floats, the float throw ends up in the catch-all handler.

> **TIP**
> You can't declare a variable for your catch-all handler. After all, what type would it be?

Nested Try Blocks, and Re-Throwing Exceptions

Yep, you can nest try blocks just like you can nest any other block of code. Here's an example:

```
void main(void)
{
  try {
    Foo();
    try {
```

```
      throw("Another Error Occurred");
    }
    catch(const char *e) {
      printf("An error occurred after Foo: %s", e);
    }
  }
  catch(const char *e) {
    printf("Caught string: %s", e);
  }
  catch(int e) {
    printf("Caught integer: %d", e);
  }
  catch(...) {
    printf("I caught something, but I have no idea what it is.");
  }
}
```

In this example, the very first catch handler catches the `"Another Error Occurred"` error. You can nest try/catch blocks as deep as you'd like.

You can also re-throw an exception, if you catch something and you have no idea what to do with it. Here's an example of that:

> **TIP**
>
> **The typical rule is to catch an error as close as possible to where it was thrown. You should catch errors as soon as you know enough about what's going on to properly handle them.**

```
void main(void)
{
  try {
    Foo();
    try {
      throw("Another Error Occurred");
    }
    catch(const char *e) {
      // our error is caught once here
      printf("An error occurred, and I have no idea what to do"
        " about it, so I'm re-throwing.");
      throw;
    }
  }
  catch(const char *e) {
```

```
    // our error is caught again here
    printf("Caught string: %s", e);
  }
  catch(int e) {
    printf("Caught integer: %d", e);
  }
  catch(...) {
    printf("I caught something, but I have no idea what it is.");
  }
}
```

In that example, I changed the innermost catch handler, and made it re-throw the error. The error is caught by the innermost handler, which prints a message saying it doesn't know what to do with it, and then re-throws. The next handler up then catches the error. This is extremely nifty, because it allows you to log errors and then hand them off without actually doing anything about them.

> **TIP**
>
> By the way, when an exception is thrown, the C++ compiler takes care of calling the destructors of any objects that need to be destructed because you're moving up in scope. For example, if you have an object inside Foo and you throw, the compiler will call the object's destructor, ensuring that memory is cleaned up properly as you exit the function.

The Do's and Don'ts of Using Exceptions

As you now know, exceptions can be a powerful tool. However, just like any tool, exceptions are not appropriate in all situations. One of the most common errors I see beginning C++ programmers make is to sprinkle exceptions everywhere in their code. They throw at the slightest hint of something gone wrong, and often don't write catch handlers as close to the error as possible. Ironically, this leads to code that's very difficult to follow and debug.

So, here are a few bullet points on the do's and don'ts of using exceptions:

- **Don't use exceptions as a replacement for errors.** An error simply generates an alternate flow of logic; an exception, however, is truly something out of the ordinary, and usually causes chaos. For example, if you prompt a user for a password to begin play at a certain level of your game, and he enters the incorrect password, that's an error. Your program takes an alternate path of execution, probably displaying an error message like "hey, your password's wrong!" and allowing them to enter it again. However, if you run out of memory while trying to validate the password, that's an exception, because it's something you wouldn't normally expect to happen.

- **Do use exceptions to separate error logic from core logic**. Isolate your error-handling code in a catch block (or many catch blocks), so that you end up with the exceptional cases separated from the normal cases.
- **Don't use exceptions where a normal switch statement or other program feature would suffice**. Again, you should use exceptions only to handle truly bizarre events in your code. The normal flow of logic through your program should be exception-free.
- **Don't just drop a library that uses exceptions into a program that doesn't**. If you must, surround the library interface with a set of wrapper classes that catch the exceptions and convert them into whatever non-exception error-handling system you have (return values, global variables, whatever).
- **Don't convert existing, already robust code to use exceptions**. Also, as a corollary to the last item—it's very tedious and time-consuming to take a robust program that doesn't use exceptions and change it so it does. If your program is working correctly and robustly already, don't change it.
- **Do use a class hierarchy for exceptions**. By this I mean create a base class called CException or something, and derive from it different exception classes— COutOfMemoryException, CArrayOutOfBoundsException, and so on. Use RTTI (discussed later) to figure out what you've caught, or create a virtual function that returns the class name of the exception as a string.
- **Don't worry about using exceptions in small programs**. If you're writing a one-page command-line utility program, exceptions are probably more trouble than they're worth. Just because you have a great tool for making code robust doesn't mean that all of your code needs it to be robust—oftentimes it's better to concentrate on the game itself at the expense of the internal tools. Just make sure that what you're releasing to your end users, the players, is robust!

Exception Handling Wrap-Up

Believe it or not, there are many exception-handling topics that I didn't cover here. Before you go charging off and using exceptions in your next 3D engine, you should spend more time learning about the fine points of their usage. For example: What happens if you throw an exception inside a constructor? What happens if you're creating an array of objects, and midway through the construction of the objects, you throw? How many array objects are valid? Can you write a handler for exceptions that no one catches?

Don't start using exceptions heavily without first being able to answer those questions. Exceptions are new, unlike anything we've seen in C, and we need to move carefully to ensure we're using them correctly.

> **TIP**
>
> STL has several built-in exception classes that you may find useful. Check out your STL documentation for details.

C++ Style Casting

You're probably intimately familiar with casting—you know, saying to the compiler, "yes, I know it's an integer, but pretend it's a char, OK?" You've probably seen code like this:

```
int i = 5;
char c = (char)(i);
```

Essentially, what you're doing here is "casting" the value (i) to a char. It's supposed to be an int, but by doing a cast you're saying "stuff this into a char and don't complain!"

Also, you've probably seen pointer casts, like what you have to do when you use malloc:

```
char *str = (char *)malloc(50);
```

You need the (char *) cast in there because malloc returns a void *, and the compiler doesn't want to automatically convert void *'s into char *'s.

So that's how you do it in C, and C++ still allows you to do this form of casting. But you run into several ugly things when you try it:

- **It isn't something for which you can easily search**. Say you've got a chunk of code, and you want to know every place where that code is casting. How do you do that? You can't just search for parentheses, because they're used everywhere. If your search tool doesn't support wildcards in the search statements, you're basically out of luck, and even if it does, it'll erroneously find prototypes of functions that take one argument: A cast like (char *) looks the same as part of a C function prototype, void foo(char *).
- **It doesn't differentiate between dangerous casts and innocent casts**. Say you've got a pointer to class D, which derives from class B. Casting your pointer to (B *) is safe, because we know B is a base class of D. However, casting your (D *) pointer to, say, (char *), isn't nearly as safe—in that situation, you're playing directly with bytes of memory, and that's risky. In C, you accomplish both safe and risky casts the same way.

C++ style casting was designed to solve these two main problems. C++ style casts are obvious, and they differentiate between safe and unsafe casts.

There are four new cast keywords in C++. Table A.1 summarizes them.

To use the casts, you first type the keyword for the cast you want to use. Put the thing you want to cast to inside < and > symbols immediately after the cast keyword. Then, put the stuff you want to cast from inside parentheses immediately after the >. Here's an example:

```
int i = 50;
char *pMemory = reinterpret_cast<char *>(&i);
```

Table A.1 New C++ Casts

Cast Keyword	Description
reinterpret_cast	Use this cast to do anything. You can use it to convert void pointers to floats, convert chars into pointers, and do all sorts of other risky stuff.
static_cast	Use this cast to do "safe" casting, for example, to convert a derived class pointer into a base class pointer (called "upcasting"). You can also use it to perform implicit type conversions (stuff the compiler would have done anyway, like converting an int to a float if you're adding it to another float). You can also use static_cast to convert a void pointer into something more useful.
	The compiler won't let you use a static_cast for anything that's really dangerous. To program the safest possible cast, always use static_cast; don't use reinterpret_cast until the compiler says that you must.
dynamic_cast	Use this to perform dynamic downcasts (converting from a base class pointer into a derived class pointer). In other words, you can use dynamic_cast to ask, "hey Mr. Compiler, does this base pointer really point to a derived object?"
	If it does, the compiler will give you back a pointer to that derived object. If it doesn't, the compiler will give you a NULL pointer back.
	This cast is a part of doing run-time type identification, which we'll talk about a little later.
const_cast	Use this to add or remove "const-ness" from something. For example, if you have a const class and need to convert it to non-const, you can use this. You can also use it to temporarily make something const.
	You can also use const_cast to add or remove volatility from something. If you've got a volatile object, and you need it not to be, use const_cast. Or if you need something volatile, const_cast is the tool for the job.

That code is functionally equivalent to the old-school

```
int i = 50;
char *pMemory = (char *)(&i);
```

As you can see, using C++ casts, it's possible to easily search for all "dangerous" casts. Just search for reinterpret_cast, a C++ keyword.

CAUTION

Be careful using dynamic_casts with references. When you dynamic_cast a pointer, and the compiler can't safely determine that your cast is legal, it returns NULL. But, if you're dynamic_casting a reference, the compiler can't simply return NULL, because references can't ever be NULL.

So it throws! Yep, you read that right—the compiler will actually throw an exception, of type bad_cast. If you don't have a catch-all handler or a handler specifically for bad_casts, you're probably going down in flames. So be careful any time you dynamic_cast a reference and make sure you've got a catch block in case things go wrong.

Here's a short example showing the new C++ casts in the wild:

```
class CMyClass : public CMyBaseClass { /* whatever */ };
void foo(const CMyClass *myClass, CMyBaseClass *myBaseClass)
{
  // use static cast to convert myclass into my base class
  CMyBaseClass *pStaticCastedClass =
    static_cast<CMyBaseClass *>(myClass);

  // use dynamic cast to see if a base class pointer really
  // points to a derived class
  CMyClass *pDynamicCastedClass =
    dynamic_cast<CMyClass *>(myBaseClass);
  if (pDynamicCastedClass) {
    printf("hey, myBaseClass really does point to a CMyClass.");
  }
  else {
    printf("nope, myBaseClass doesn't really point to a CMyClass.");
  }
```

```
  // use const cast to add or remove constness
  CMyClass *pNotConstClass = const_cast<CMyClass *>(myClass);

  // use reinterpret cast to do dangerous stuff
  char *pClassMemory = reinterpret_cast<char *>(myClass);
}
```

RTTI

Now that you've gotten a grip on C++ casting, we can talk about another C++ feature—*run-time type identification,* or RTTI.

As its name implies, RTTI is a C++ feature that allows you to determine what type an object is. We saw a little of this in the preceding section, where we learned that we can use dynamic_cast to effectively ask the compiler if something is of a given type. Technically, dynamic_cast is part of RTTI.

RTTI isn't just about dynamic_cast, however. There's another equally important keyword—typeid. The typeid keyword works very similarly to how sizeof works—it's not really a function, but you use it as if it were. The sizeof "function" returns the size of whatever you gave it, in bytes. The typeid "function" gives you an object called type_info that contains type information about what you gave it.

> **CAUTION**
>
> The compiler throws an exception if you pass NULL into typeid. The exception is of type bad_typeid. So make sure you've got a bad_typeid catch block anywhere you could potentially be passing NULL into typeid.

Specifically, here's what type_info contains:

```
class type_info {
public:
   virtual ~type_info();
   int operator==(const type_info& rhs) const;
   int operator!=(const type_info& rhs) const;
   int before(const type_info& rhs) const;
   const char* name() const;
   const char* raw_name() const;
private:
   /* you can't see this! */
};
```

As you can see, this type_info class consists of three functions and two overloaded operators. Let's look at each in detail.

type_info::before

The before method isn't terribly useful. You use it to determine if one type ID should be sorted before another. For example, if you have classes X and Y, you could use the before function to determine if X should come before Y:

```
if (typeid(X).before(typeid(Y))) { /* X comes before Y! */ }
else { /* Y comes before X! */ }
```

Like I said, not the most useful thing in the world, but it's handy in certain situations.

type_info::name

This method is much more useful. It returns the name of the thing you pass it:

```
class MyClass { /* yada */ };
void main(void)
{
  MyClass x;
  printf("x is a %s.", typeid(x).name());
}
```

That code will print "x is a MyClass." I'm sure you can find myriad uses for this: For example, you can save the name of class that generates your saved game files *inside* the save file itself, so that you'll always know what class to use to load it.

> **TIP**
>
> Don't use the name you get back from this function to control your program logic. That is, don't use it in if statements, like if (strcmp(typeid(MyClass).name(), "MyClass")). A better way to do that is to use the overloaded operators that you'll learn about momentarily.

type_info::raw_name

This method is very similar to the name method, with one key difference—raw_name returns the decorated name, which isn't human readable. The decorated name has at signs—@—and weird letters all over it, because it's the name the compiler uses to refer to the type internally. Nonetheless, this name may be useful in situations where you need to compare things.

Overloaded Operators of type_info

The type_info class contains overloads for the == and != operators. These overloads allow you to compare the types of two objects directly, without having to do string comparisons on their names (or raw names).

For example:

```cpp
class MyClass { /* yada */ };
class MyOtherClass { /* yada */ };
void main(void)
{
  MyClass x;
  MyOtherClass y;

  if (typeid(y) == typeid(MyOtherClass)) {
    printf("So far, so good...");
  }
  if (typeid(x) != typeid(MyClass)) {
    printf("Something has gone horribly, horribly wrong.");
  }
  if (typeid(MyClass) == typeid(MyOtherClass)) {
    printf("Something is still horribly, horribly wrong.");
  }
  printf("x is a %s.", typeid(x).name());
}
```

Here you can see that we're doing some comparisons to see whether certain variables are of certain types.

> **TIP**
>
> Keep in mind that `dynamic_cast` can tell us the same thing. But `dynamic_cast` can be slightly slower than `typeid`, so only use `dynamic_cast` when you want a pointer to the object, and use `typeid` when you want to see if an object is equal to something.

RTTI Wrap-Up

Pretend this sentence contains the standard disclaimer about how you really should wait to use RTTI in your own projects until you know more about it. Here are some other questions you can research on your own:

- What does `typeid` give you if you pass it a template class?
- What does `typeid` give you if you pass it a void * that actually points to a base class?
- Does `typeid(5) == typeid(int)`? Does `typeid(5) == typeid(float)`?

Templates

C++ supports a powerful feature called *templates,* which can really help you out in certain situations. So here's how they work.

Template Functions

Let's say you're a C programmer who's just spent the last two months coming up with the perfect function to swap two integers:

```
void swap(int *a, int *b)
{
  int temp;
  temp = *a;
  *a  = *b;
  *b = temp;
}
```

Now, let's say you've just recently learned about C++ references, so you've rewritten your swap function to be even more glorious:

```
void swap(int &a, int &b)
{
  int temp;
  temp = a;
  a  = b;
  b = temp;
}
```

Pretty nifty. This code is easy to read, and is reasonably optimized. You've got yourself a great tool for swapping integers.

But what about swapping floats? Arrgh! Now you have to create another function to handle floats. You know that C++ will let you overload the function name so long as the parameters are different, so you write an overload for swap that takes floats:

```
void swap(float &a, float &b)
{
  float temp;
  temp = a;
  a  = b;
  b = temp;
}
```

At this point you should be concerned, because you've used copy/paste inside your IDE. Any time you copy and paste code, you should get worried, because you're creating two identical functions. If you find a bug in the int version of swap, you'll have to go and make the exact same patch to the float version, and that wastes time (to say nothing of the headaches that come if you forget to update the other function—if you've done a lot of copy/paste, you can also waste a lot of time chasing your tail, solving the same bug over and over again for different data types).

This is what C++'s template feature was designed to solve. Templates allow you to write code that operates on things of any data type—ints, floats, classes, structs, whatever. You simply tell the compiler what string you'd like to substitute for the variable type, write your algorithm, and the compiler takes care of "putting in" the correct types. In other words, you create the "template" for the code, and the compiler uses this template, along with a certain data type, to create the actual code.

It's easier to see in code than explain in words, so here's a version of swap that will work for *all* objects:

```
template<class T> void swap(T &a, T &b)
{
  T temp;
  temp = a;
  a   = b;
  b = temp;
}
```

We start out with the keyword `template`, which tells the compiler we're about to define a template function. Next, we put `class T` inside a tag, which tells the compiler, "Any time you see a `T`, you should replace it with whatever type is needed." Next, we write our function, using `T` in place of int or float. `T` is effectively a placeholder for a variable type.

Now, when we call this function, the compiler automatically plugs in the correct types. For example, say we call the function like this:

```
int x=5, y=10;
swap(x, y);
```

The compiler will automatically instantiate (make) a version of swap that works for ints. If we say:

```
double x=5.0, y=10.0;
swap(x, y);
```

Then it'll make a version that works for doubles. Pretty cool, isn't it? We can even have it generate a version for a class:

```
CMyClass x, y;
swap(x,y);
```

That will work, provided we've overloaded the = operator for CMyClass.

So, that's what you *can* do. Here's what doesn't work:

```
CMyClass x; int y;
swap(x,y);
```

In this situation, we're trying to use two different data types. As it's written now, the swap template won't accept two different types. However, we could rewrite it so it does:

```
template<class T1, class T2> void swap(T1 &a, T2 &b)
{
  T1 temp;
  temp = a;
  a = b;
  b = temp;
}
```

It gets a little trickier to make that version of swap work—you'd need to have operator = overloads, or you'd have to rely on implicit conversions (that is, the compiler automatically knowing how to set an int equal to a float). I wrote that example

> **TIP**
>
> The compiler only generates the code that you need. It doesn't automatically generate every possible version of swap or other template functions. When you add code that uses a float version of swap, it creates the float version.
>
> Because of this, it's possible that a template function may compile and link without any errors at first, then start giving you errors if you go back and use it for a different type. For example, if we didn't have an operator = overload for a class we were using swap with, we'd get an error *inside* swap complaining about our trying to set one class equal to another.
>
> The Visual C++ compiler (and most other compilers) will also give you the line of code that caused the compiler to generate the erring template function, but it still sometimes takes a bit of thinking to deduce exactly what broke and why.

mainly to show that you could specify as many different template parameters (type substitutions) as you want.

Template Classes

You've now learned how to create template functions. C++ also lets you create template classes. Here's what that looks like:

```
template <class T>
class MyTemplateClass
{
```

```
public:
  /* use T for the types of some variables here */
  T m_MyData;
};
```

You declare a template class basically the same way you declare a template function: you type the keyword `template` followed by the different template arguments. You then declare the template class just as you would any other class.

To instantiate a template class, you must give the compiler all the argument types the template requires. You do this as follows:

```
MyTemplateClass<int> m_IntClass;
m_IntClass.m_MyData = 5; // m_MyData is of type int
MyTemplateClass<float> m_FloatClass;
m_FloatClass.m_MyData = 5.0f; // m_MyData is of type float
```

In that example, we're instantiating a version of `MyTemplateClass` that uses ints. See how the template argument just hangs off the class name?

You might be thinking, "Okay, that's cool, but it seems totally pointless." Here's a practical example of how you can use templates to make your life easier:

```
template <class T> class CMinMax
{
public:
  CMinMax() { m_Min = T(); m_Max = T(); }
  CMinMax(T tMin, T tMax) { m_Min = tMin; m_Max = tMax; }
  ~CMinMax() { }
  T m_Min;
  T m_Max;
  T GetRandomNumInRange(void) {
    // note: RandomNumber overloads must exist for type T!
    return(RandomNumber(m_Min, m_Max));
  }
  T GetRange(void) { return(abs(m_Max-m_Min)); }
};
```

This is a template class used in many of the sample programs of this book. It's handy when you have a parameter that isn't simply one number, but rather can be any number within a certain range (defined by `m_Min` and `m_Max`). This comes in handy in situations where you want to create something, but want to leave certain things to chance—for example, you may want to create an enemy that has between 50 and 100 hit points.

This class is a good example of how templates work. If I wanted to create a pair of floating-point min/max values, I'd declare something like this:

```
CMinMax<float> m_MyRange;
```

I could then automatically get a random number within this range by writing the following:

```
float fRandValue = M_MyRange.GetRandomNumInRange();
```

Provided that I had an overload of the RandomNumber function for floats, everything would work great. The template would enable me to treat my minimum and maximum values as one atomic unit (a *range*), and I could use any data type I wanted to specify the start and end of the range.

If I wanted to get really fancy, I could make a class that represents a set of enemy attributes: hit points, strength, armor, and so on. Let's say I call this class CEnemyAttrib. I could then make an enemy attribute range CMinMax<CEnemyAttrib>, and plug two different sets of enemy attributes into it, representing the strongest and weakest enemies. Then, provided I wrote a RandomNumber overload, I could automatically generate an enemy that falls within that range simply by calling GetRandomNumInRange!

Continuing to learn about the power of templates: If our class template used more than one type of class, we'd need to separate the data types by commas:

```
template <class T1, class T2>
class MyDualTemplateClass
{
public:
  /* use T for the types of some variables here */
  T1 m_MyData;
  T2 m_MyData2;
};
void Foo(void) {
  MyTemplateClass<int, float> m_MyClass;
  m_MyClass.m_MyData1 = 5; // m_MyData1 is of type int
  m_MyClass.m_MyData1 = 5.0f; // m_MyData2 is of type float
}
```

You can also really warp your head, because you can put template classes in other template classes:

```
template <class T>
class MyTemplateClass
{
public:
  /* use T for the types of some variables here */
  T m_MyData;
};
void Foo(void) {
  // create a template class that uses a template class that uses
  // ints
  MyTemplateClass< MyTemplateClass<int> > m_MyClass;
  // m_MyClass.m_MyData is of type MyTemplateClass, so it has another
  // m_MyData of type int.
  m_MyClass.m_MyData.m_MyData = 5;
}
```

You see this more often than you might think. The STL library includes several template classes that use other template classes as template arguments. It can get downright weird trying to think about some of these, so the best advice I can give you is to simply practice!

C++ Wrap-Up

So, there it is—a quick tour through the C++ features that are used in this book.

I hope this section has given you a deeper understanding of what C++ is all about—giving programmers more tools they can use to make their job easier. As I said before, not all of the C++ features are useful in every situation. An experienced C++ programmer knows which tools fit the job, and uses only those tools. That means you shouldn't waste time using a C++ feature just for the sake of using it—use the feature because it reduces complexity and makes your life easier.

Also, resist the temptation to add in everything under the sun. Not every function needs to be virtual, not every program needs to use exceptions, and not everything needs its own namespace. Pick and choose your weapons carefully, and you'll be fine.

> **TIP**
>
> There's an excellent book on C++ programming called *Thinking In C++*, by Bruce Eckel, that's worth a read if you really want to learn C++ inside and out. Best of all, you can get the electronic version of this book for free from http://www.mindview.net.

THE STANDARD TEMPLATE LIBRARY (STL)

Now that I've given you a crash course in the C++ features you need to understand this book, it's time to talk about the other thing you need to know: STL.

What Is the STL, and Why Should I Care?

STL is an acronym for the Standard Template Library. Let's take that apart word by word. First of all, the STL is *standard*. The powers that be incorporated it into the ANSI standard of C++, so any compiler that's ANSI compliant will have an STL library. This is great, because it means that if you ever need to port your program to Linux or something, you won't have to scrap all the code that relies on the STL.

Second, the library uses *templates*. In fact, some of the most heavy-duty take-no-prisoners template code I've seen resides in the STL. The STL programmers used templates to make the library as useful as possible. For example, they didn't just want to make one algorithm or container class work with just ints, or just floats, or just chars, so they template-ized the whole thing so that it could work with any class you can dream up.

Finally, the L in STL means *library*. Real libraries are huge collections of books. The STL is a huge collection of container classes and algorithms. You will probably never use all of the STL in one program, and you may never use all of it anywhere. For that reason, the STL is broken down into several components. You use each component by including a specific header file, just like what you're used to with the C run-time libraries. Usually, you don't even have to worry about linking in the correct STL libraries—the compiler takes care of that for you.

We're going to concentrate on the two types of STL container classes this book uses: vectors and maps. There are many other container classes (stacks, lists, and so on), and I encourage you to learn more about them—they can be useful in many situations.

STL Strings

One of the most useful things the STL provides is a string class. C programmers spend a lot of time wrangling fixed-length character arrays—char buf[256] and such. This can often lead to frustrating buffer overruns—or "I tried to put a six character string into a five element array"—errors.

C++ string classes solve this problem. The STL library provides a rather lightweight string class, called string. To create an STL string, just type something like this:

```
std::string strFilename;
```

You can then assign a value to this string as follows:

```
strFilename = "C:\\test\\myfile.txt";
```

The string class takes care of the details of allocating the right amount of memory to hold the string.

You can figure out how long a string is by using the size method:

```
printf("The length of the string \"blah\" is: %d",
  std::string("blah").size());
```

Notice also in that section of code how I created a temporary string object by passing in a character array to the string constructor.

If you need to convert your string into a character array, use the c_str method:

```
void Foo(char *strFilename)
{
  /* do something with filename */
}
void main(void)
{
  std::string str = "SomeFile.txt";
  Foo(str.c_str());
}
```

CAUTION

Whenever you want to print a string, and you use the %s tag in your printf statement, remember to use the c_str method, otherwise, you'll get weird printf results, and sometimes program crashes!

For example, don't do this:

```
printf("The string is: %s", strSomeSTLString); // kablooey!
```

Instead, do this:

```
printf("The string is: %s", strSomeSTLString.c_str());
```

That's essentially the basics of using STL strings. Consult the STL documentation to learn about the more powerful features of STL strings that this book doesn't use.

STL Vectors

Think of an STL vector as a resizable array. Once you've got an STL vector created, you can add as many items to it as you want (until you run out of memory, of course), and you can delete any item inside the array without affecting the others.

Making an STL Vector

To create a new vector, all you need to do is declare a variable of that type. Remember, vector is a template class, so you need to give it the type of stuff you'll be storing. For example, to create a vector of ints, write something like this:

```
std::vector<int> m_ArrayOfInts;
```

To create a vector of chars, write

```
std::vector<char> m_ArrayOfChars;
```

Or to create a vector of your own classes, write

```
std::vector<CMyClass> m_ArrayOfMyClasses;
```

Adding Items

The vector class allows you to put objects into it in a few different ways. First, there's the most common: just call the push_back method:

```
std::vector<int> m_ArrayOfInts;
m_ArrayOfInts.push_back(5); // add 5 to array (array is now 5)
m_ArrayOfInts.push_back(3); // add 3 to array (array is now 5, 3)
m_ArrayOfInts.push_back(4); // add 4 to array (array is now 5, 3, 4)
```

The push_back method puts the new item at the very end of the array. (In case you're curious, there's also pop_back, which removes the last item from the array.)

When you push an item into an STL vector, you're actually making a copy of that item. This doesn't matter when dealing with ints, but becomes important if you're using a vector to store classes.

If you want to insert stuff in the middle of the array, you can use insert. The insert method takes two arguments. The first one specifies where you'd like the item placed. The insert method will place the

> **CAUTION**
>
> **Your class needs to implement an operator = overload to make this work, and if your class allocates memory or contains pointers to different things, you need to make sure that your overload copies that memory correctly.**

item immediately before the one specified. The second argument is a reference to the item you want to insert.

Here's an example of insert:

```
std::vector<int> m_ArrayOfInts;
m_ArrayOfInts.push_back(5); // add 5 to array (array is now 5)
m_ArrayOfInts.push_back(3); // add 3 to array (array is now 5, 3)
// add 4 to the *beginning* of the array
m_ArrayOfInts.insert(m_ArrayOfInts.begin(), 4);
// array is now 4, 5, 3
// add 7 between 5 and 3 (that is, before element 3)
m_ArrayOfInts.insert(m_ArrayOfInts.begin()+2)
// array is now 4, 5, 7, 3
```

The only thing weird in that code is probably the m_ArrayOfInts.begin()+2 stuff. Essentially, the begin method returns an iterator. An *iterator* is a pointer to whatever type you're storing; in this case, it's an int *. The begin method of vector returns an iterator that points to the first thing in our vector. Since we want the third object down, we simply add two to this iterator and pass that as the location before which we want the new item inserted.

STL vectors allow you to insert things in many more ways than I've just shown. For example, you can insert a whole range of blank objects, using resize or another insert overload. However, most programmers rarely use more than push_back and the simple insert overload.

> **TIP**
>
> **This sounds more complex than it is. Don't worry, you'll become more familiar with iterators after you have a chance to play with them in your own programs.**

Getting and Editing Items

Once you got some stuff in the vector, you probably want to get at it. You can do this in several ways. First and oftentimes easiest: STL vectors overload the brackets operator, [], allowing you to pretend that your vector is really just an array:

```
std::vector<int> m_ArrayOfInts;
m_ArrayOfInts.push_back(5); // add 5 to array (array is now 5)
m_ArrayOfInts.push_back(3); // add 3 to array (array is now 5, 3)
if (m_ArrayOfInts[0] != 5) {
  printf("All is not right in the universe.");
}
```

You can also loop through the entire vector by doing something like this:

```
for (std::vector<int>::iterator i = ArrayOfInts.begin();
     i != ArrayOfInts.end(); ++i) {
  printf("%d ", *i);
}
```

That's a mammoth `for` statement, but it comes apart fairly easily. First, we declare an iterator for a vector of integers, name it `i`, and set it equal to the beginning of the vector. We keep looping so long as `i` does not equal `end`. The end method of `vector` is very similar to `begin`, except it gives you an iterator that's one past the end of the array.

So, essentially, we're looping from the beginning of the vector to the end. Since `i` is an iterator, and an iterator is just a fancy pointer to our object, all we have to do inside the `for` loop is dereference the pointer and use it. If you were using classes, you would probably want to create a reference to that class element, like this:

TIP

Always use ++i instead of i++ when iterating through a vector. It's faster because the compiler does not have to create a temporary object behind the scenes.

```
for (std::vector<CMyClass>::iterator i =
ArrayOfClasses.begin();
     i != ArrayOfClasses.end(); ++i) {
  CMyClass &ThisClass = *i;
  /* do whatever you need to here, using ThisClass */
} // next!
```

That code makes things a little easier to read, because once you get into your `for` loop, you can use a reference to the class instead of constantly having to dereference the iterator.

CAUTION

Be careful if you add new items, shuffle the item order, or delete items while you're using an iterator to move through the `vector`. The insertion and deletion functions may actually invalidate your iterator, which will cause you to go tromping off into memory somewhere and will probably lead to an access violation.

Check the STL docs for more information on how to get around this.

Deleting Items

To delete an item from a vector, use the clear and erase methods. The clear method kills everything in the array:

```
std::vector<int> m_ArrayOfInts;
m_ArrayOfInts.push_back(5); // add 5 to array (array is now 5)
m_ArrayOfInts.push_back(3); // add 3 to array (array is now 5, 3)
m_ArrayOfInts.clear(); // array is now empty
```

The erase method, on the other hand, allows you to delete a specific item or a range of items. STL vectors provide two overloaded erase methods. The first overload takes one iterator and simply deletes that item. The second overload takes two iterators and deletes all items between them—including the first iterator but not the second:

```
std::vector<int> m_ArrayOfInts;
m_ArrayOfInts.push_back(5); // (array is now 5)
m_ArrayOfInts.push_back(3); // (array is now 5, 3)
m_ArrayOfInts.erase(m_ArrayOfInts.begin()); // (array is now 3)
m_ArrayOfInts.push_back(4); // (array is now 3, 4)
m_ArrayOfInts.push_back(6); // (array is now 3, 4, 6)
// kill everything but the first element
m_ArrayOfInts.erase(m_ArrayOfInts.begin()+1, m_ArrayOfInts.end());
// array now contains 3
```

The code above shows how to use both erase overloads. Again, note that the end method does not return an iterator pointing to the last element of the array. It returns an iterator pointing *past* the last element of the array.

A Clever Way to Delete Vectors Full of Derived Objects

Many programmers use STL vectors to store pointers to different classes. For example, say you have three classes, CCircle, CTriangle, and CRectangle, all of which derive from a common base class, CShape. Now, let's say you need to store an arbitrary number of circles, triangles, and rectangles. An elegant way to do this is to create a vector of CShape *'s, dynamically allocate memory for each object, and then add its pointer to the vector, like so:

```
class CShape { /* blah */ };
class CCircle: public CShape { /* blah */ };
class CTriangle: public CShape { /* blah */ };
class CRectangle: public CShape { /* blah */ };
void main(void)
```

```
{
  std::vector<CShape *> shapes;
  shapes.push_back(new CCircle());
  shapes.push_back(new CTriangle());
  shapes.push_back(new CRectangle());
  // now, how do you delete these shapes?
}
```

So, the question is, "How do you delete the shapes you've just created?" This is where the cleverness comes in. For years, I used to write deletion code like this:

```
for (std::vector<CShape *>::iterator I = shapes.begin();
  i != shapes.end(); ++i) {
  delete i;
}
shapes.clear();
```

As it stands, there's nothing wrong with that code. It gets the job done just great—but it's a bit much to write just to nuke a vector.

However, Yordan Gruchev, a fellow game programmer, has come up with a better way. He has used template programming to create an `stlwipe` function that encapsulates all that code. Here's what `stlwipe` looks like:

```
template<class T>
void stlwipe(T &t)
{
  //get the first iterator
  T::iterator i=t.begin();
  //iterate to the end and delete items (should be pointers)
  for(; i!=t.end();++i) delete(*i);
  //clear the collection (now full of dead pointers)
  t.clear();
}
```

See how that works? Now that we have our template function, we can just call `stlwipe(shapes)` to delete everything from our vector. Pretty slick, isn't it?

Other Useful Vector Stuff

Now that you know the basics of adding, editing, and deleting elements from a vector, here are a few other useful things you can do:

- You can find out if a vector is empty by calling the `empty` method. That method returns `true` if the vector is empty, `false` otherwise.
- You can find out how many items are in the vector by calling the `size` method.
- Behind the scenes, the STL vector allocates memory for each item you pass into it. If you know you're going to be pushing a whole bunch of items in, you can tell the vector to make room in advance, so that it does one big memory allocation instead of fragmenting your memory with several smaller allocations. The vector method to call to do this is `reserve`.

STL Vector Wrap-Up

The best way to become familiar with everything an STL vector can do is to simply crack open the `vector` header file and look at the class declaration. You'll see many more methods than I've covered here, and you'll probably want to go through the STL docs (or an STL book) to learn about the stuff not used in this book.

STL Maps

Another critical container class is the STL map. This section explains what a map is, and shows you some basics on how to use a map.

What Is an STL Map?

An STL map lets you find a "thing" given a "key." Maps work in pairs—every item you put into a map is bound to a key. Once you put these key/item pairs into the map, you can quickly retrieve an item if you know its key.

For example, say we're writing a search program for a library. We know that all books have an ISBN number, so we decide that the ISBN number is the key by which we'll retrieve the other book information—author, title, and the rest. We make a structure that contains all the book information, like so:

```
class CBook
{
public:
  CBook() { }
  CBook(string strAuthor, string strTitle, string strISBNNumber) {
    m_strAuthor = strAuthor;
    m_strTitle = strTitle;
    m_strISBNNumber = strISBNNumber;
  }
```

```
    string m_strAuthor;
    string m_strTitle;
    string m_strISBNNumber;
    /* other info - etc */
};
```

Then, for each book, we insert a key/value pair into a map (see Figure A.1).

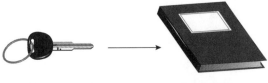

ISBN Number   **Book Object**

Figure A.1

Our map's key is the ISBN number; the map value is the detailed info on the book itself.

Our key is the ISBN number; our value is everything we know about the object that goes with that ISBN number.

After we have all our keys and values inserted into the map, we can retrieve a structure full of information about a book simply by supplying the ISBN number to the map. The map has an internal organization that lets it quickly find the book structure corresponding to the ISBN number we gave it.

Many programmers use maps to accomplish many different kinds of tasks. The example I gave above is only one way to use a map. Another way is to create something resembling a translation table, in which the key and the item the key is attached to are the same data type. For example, let's say we wanted to create an encryption program, which would take a string and jumble the letters (A=G, B=Y, and so on, randomly, for the rest of the alphabet). We could use a map to make the translation easier—our keys could be A-Z, and our values could be the random letter each key corresponds to. That way, when we needed to encrypt the message, we could simply ask the map, "Hey, what letter is attached to key B?" The map would hand us back whatever letter we inserted attached to key B, and to encrypt our string, we'd replace all instances of B in it with that value. When we wanted to decrypt, we could make a reverse-map, where the keys are the jumbled letters and the items are the "real" letters each jumbled letter corresponds to.

In case the lightbulb still hasn't come on, let me try to explain maps in terms of another example, this time with some code to buttress it.

Let's say you're writing a multiplayer game. Each player is playing the game from his own computer, which has its own IP address. Let's say your networking code just received an "I quit this game!" message from a certain IP address, and now it needs to figure out the player name that IP address corresponds to, so that it can display a message saying "<player> left the game" and take the player out of the game.

That's the situation—you've got an IP address, and you need a player name. One way to solve this situation is to create a vector of objects, with each object containing an IP address and a name, like so:

```
class CPlayerInfoObject {
  public:
    CIPAddress m_IP;
    std::string m_strPlayerName;
    /* other player info */
};
std::vector<CPlayerInfoObject> g_vPlayerInfo;
```

You'd fill this vector up with all the players in the game. Then, when you needed a player name for a certain IP address, you'd loop through the elements of this vector until you found the structure you wanted, like so:

```
std::string GetPlayerNameGivenIPAddress(CIPAddress GivenIP)
{
for (std::vector<CPlayerInfoObject>::iterator i =g_vPlayerInfo.begin();
  i != g_vPlayerInfo.end(); i++) {
  if (i->m_IP == GivenIP) {
    // we've found our player! return their name!
    return(i->m_strPlayerName);
}
// we didn't find anything, so return an empty name.
return("");
}
```

This is perfectly acceptable code, but touching every single item isn't exactly the fastest way to search for something.

This kind of situation is what maps were designed to solve. The map container can essentially replace all that slow and error-prone search code:

```
std::map<CIPAddress, CPlayerInfoObject> g_mPlayerInfo;
std::string GetPlayerNameGivenIPAddress(CIPAddress GivenIP)
{
  return(g_mPlayerInfo[GivenIP].m_strPlayerName);
}
```

The bracket operator [] is overloaded for maps, so that you can put in your key and get back the corresponding object (or a "blank" object, made with the default constructor, if the map doesn't find a match).

So, that's essentially what a map is. Now let's look at how to create and use one in code.

Making an STL Map

To use a map, you must first include the <map> STL header:

```
#include <map>
```

Once you include the header file, creating a new map is as simple as the following:

```
std::map<CKey, CValue> myMap;
```

Here we're declaring a new map called myMap. The map template needs two template arguments. The first template argument is the data type you'd like to use as a key—in the example above, the ISBN number was the key. You can use any data type you like here, including the built-in data types.

The second template argument is the "value" data type. This is what you get back when you put in the key. Again, you can put in any type you want.

> **TIP**
>
> You'll probably want to disable warning number 4786 before you include the map header. The STL map makes heavy use of templates, and the template expansions generate gobs of a particular compiler warning—4786. The warning itself isn't terribly important, and it's next to impossible to read the output window with it present. Luckily you can easily disable the warning by typing the following:
>
> ```
> #pragma warning(disable: 4786)
> ```
>
> This will turn off the warning and allow you to make sense of your compiler output once again.

Actually, map has four template arguments, but most of the time you can omit the last two and let the compiler use its default values. In case you're curious, the other two arguments specify how to sort things within a map, and how to allocate memory for the elements in the map.

Adding Items

You might think that the map class would contain two different arrays of objects—one array for the keys, and another array for the values. However, it doesn't work that way. The map stores one array full of std::pair objects.

The std::pair object is a nifty little STL creation; it's a handy tool for "pairing" two objects together into one object. Essentially, pair simply contains two objects (of any type), called first and second. To prove that it's really that simple, here's a typical STL class definition for pair:

```
template<class T, class U>
  struct pair {
    typedef T first_type;
    typedef U second_type
    T first;
    U second;
    pair();
    pair(const T& x, const U& y);
    template<class V, class W>
        pair(const pair<V, W>& pr);
  };
```

See the first and second objects? This pair object just takes two random classes and "binds" them together into one structure.

As you've probably already surmised by now, we need to "bind" our key and our value together using std::pair before we can insert it into our map. And there's an STL function called make_pair that does just that. Here's an example of inserting an object into a map:

```
std::map<std::string, CBook> books;
// declare a new book object
CBook SpecialEffectsBook("Mason McCuskey",
  "Special Effects Game Programming with DirectX", "1-931841-06-3");
// add it to the map
books.insert(std::make_pair(SpecialEffectsBook.m_strISBNNumber,
  SpecialEffectsBook));
```

Notice the call to make_pair in the code above, to bind the ISBN number of the book with the book object itself.

Finding Items

STL maps are no fun unless you can use them to find something. Fortunately, finding something in a map is really easy. The first way to do this is to use the find method of std::map, like so:

```
map<string, CBook>::iterator it;
it = books.find(strISBN);
```

```
if (it == books.end()) { // not found!
  cout << "I don't know about that book.";
}
else {
    CBook &theBook = it->second;
    /* etc. */
}
```

Give the find method a key, and it will return an iterator pointing to the object in the map with that supplied key, or pointing to end() if there's no match. As you can see in the code above, the iterator doesn't point to an object of type CBook, it points to a pair object (remember, when you inserted the object you bound the key and object together in a pair object). The book object you're after is the second member of this pair object.

If you're in a hurry, you can also use the overloaded bracket operators to find something:

```
CBook &theBook = books[strISBN];
```

The only caveat to using this is that if the object doesn't exist in the map, this will actually create a blank

> **TIP**
>
> Keep in mind that a map supports iterators, just as a vector does. So you can make a for loop from map.begin() to map.end() and play with each element individually, just as with a vector.

object and associate it with that key. Note also that the brackets operator gives you back a reference to it->second, so there's no need for you to do anything extra. Just put in a key, get back an object—cool, isn't it?

Deleting Items

You can delete items you've added to a map by calling the erase method. This works the exact same way it does for a vector—simply pass in an iterator and that object is deleted.

You can also clear the entire map in one fell swoop by calling the clear method.

> **CAUTION**
>
> Again, just as with vectors, be careful if you add new items, shuffle the item order, or delete items while you're using an iterator to move through the map.

MultiMaps

Up until now, we've talked only about maps. However, even though we don't use them in this book, I feel compelled to mention the map's sibling. STL provides another class very similar to a map, called a *multimap*.

Essentially, the keys in a multimap can be duplicated, whereas in an ordinary map each key must be unique. For example, the whole ISBN/book database is great for an ordinary map, because we're guaranteed that two books can never have the same ISBN number. However, if you were modeling a school and wanted to key students by their last name, you would probably want to use a multimap because there may be several students with the same last name. (I once knew three Smiths in my elementary school homeroom alone.) Alternatively, you might decide to use another piece of ID, one that more uniquely identifies a student (say, their Social Security number).

> **TIP**
>
> If you're using a multimap, you can use the count function to return the number of items associated with a specific key.

STL Map Wrap-Up

STL maps, like STL vectors, are a very useful tool that can save you a lot of programming time when properly used. By using a map, you're guaranteed to have a fast and very well-tested algorithm for storing and quickly retrieving all sorts of items. Free working code! Now that's something that everyone can enjoy.

STL Wrap-Up

I realize that it's probably painful and discouraging to learn all this new STL stuff. If you're like most programmers, you've probably already got some great tools to do the STL stuff I've covered here. You may be used to a particular C++ string class or exception hierarchy.

I consider the STL valuable because it's cross platform and really is part of the C++ standard. So no matter where you go, as long as you have C++, you have STL. That's something that can't be said for most other array toolboxes.

Also, realize that you can always wrap the STL into a form more suitable for you. For example, if you've been using a string class of your own, there's no reason why you can't reimplement that string class in terms of STL strings (that is, using an STL string behind the scenes). That's a great approach if you've already got a large codebase that's using a proprietary string class, or if you just like keeping the same names.

In general—give the STL a chance. It's a bit ugly at first, but once you spend some time working with it, the larger pattern to it clicks in, and you see the method to its madness. At that point, you start really exploiting the power of the STL—all of a sudden, complex algorithms can be written in one line, using some clever STL types and templates.

ABOUT THE SAMPLE PROGRAMS

The two sample programs for this appendix demonstrate STL vectors and STL maps.

- **ChAp1_STLVectorSample**. This sample program demonstrates STL vectors. I designed it so that you can step through it with the debugger and watch the vectors change as things happen.
- **ChAp1_STLMapSample**. This sample program demonstrates STL maps. Again, step through it with the debugger and watch the maps change as things happen.

EXERCISES

There are no exercises for this appendix. Becoming familiar with C++ and the STL is just something that takes practice with real-life programming.

APPENDIX B

INTRODUCTION TO DEVSTUDIO

"Godzilla. He is a good man… and he is a bad man."
—*Unknown*

This appendix is for all of you who haven't had that much experience using the Microsoft Development Studio (DevStudio, to its friends) to develop applications for Windows. In this appendix, you'll learn the basics of creating a project, adding source code files, setting up library and include paths, and all the other tasks needed to create the sample programs for this book.

DevStudio is like Godzilla. It helps out with a lot of things, but in the blink of an eye can turn evil and cause you a lot of grief. On the good side, DevStudio comes packed with powerful features, all designed to make the life of the programmer easier. On the bad side, it also does a remarkably good job of hiding from you the details of compiling programs. If you've done C/C++ development somewhere else, you're probably familiar with make files. Make files are not at the forefront of DevStudio—make files are present, but they take a back seat to DevStudio's GUI for configuring compiler and linker options. You will more than likely never edit a make file directly. Instead, you'll make changes to the way your source code compiles and links via myriad dialog boxes, property sheets, and drop-down lists. Like I said, it's a double-edged sword.

In this appendix, I'm going to teach you how to take the source code files contained on the CD and create from them an executable. Throughout this appendix we'll be using the `Ch1p2_NormalWindow` sample program as our test subject.

> **TIP**
>
> **All of this information applies to Visual C++ 6.0, but other versions are very similar.**

CREATING A PROJECT AND WORKSPACE

At its core, DevStudio operates on the ideas of projects and workspaces. The hierarchy looks like Figure B.1—a *project* contains a collection of source files and options, and a *workspace* contains one or more projects.

Most of your workspaces will contain only one project. Most programmers only put multiple projects into their workspaces if they're writing a set of DLLs or components that function together, and they need quick access to several different code collections simultaneously.

To write some new code in DevStudio, the first thing you'll want to do is create a workspace and project in which that new code will live. You do this by selecting the New command from the File drop-down menu. This presents you with a dialog. Navigate to the Projects tab of this dialog, and your screen will resemble Figure B.2.

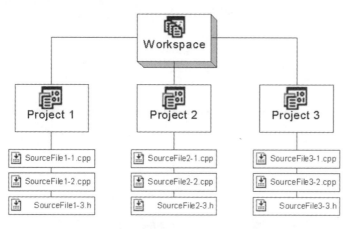

Figure B.1

A workspace is a collection of projects, and a project is a collection of source files.

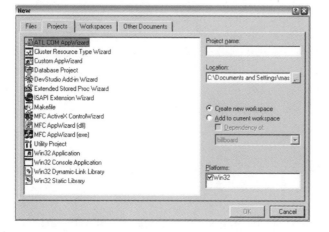

Figure B.2

The New Project dialog.

To create a new project, you must first tell DevStudio what kind of application you want to create. There are many choices here, but you'll more than likely want to use one of the following:

- **Win32 Application**. This is by far the most common selection. This project type is used when you're creating a plain-old Windows application.
- **Win32 Console Application**. This project creates a "console application." Console applications behave very similarly to old DOS programs. They're command-line–based, they have a text window to do their work in, and that's about it. They don't use dialog boxes and they don't have a message pump. If you're creating a simple program that doesn't need a GUI, console applications are the way to go.
- **MFC Appwizard (exe)**. This project is similar to a Win32 Application, but includes support for the Microsoft Foundation Classes (MFC). MFC is a set of classes and a framework designed to make it easy to create applications that conform to most of the user

interface standards for Windows. For example, if you use MFC, you automatically gain the ability to use an MDI (multiple document interface), such as Word, where you can open multiple windows from within one "master" window. We don't use MFC in this book, but since this is a common choice for heavy-duty GUI applications (and even some games), I thought I'd mention it here.

Because Ch1p2_NormalWindow is a windows program that doesn't use MFC, go ahead and select the Win32 Application project from the list. Also, be sure to give your project a name (this is also the name of the EXE) and a location before you click OK.

When you click OK, a new dialog box comes up, asking you if you'd like to create an empty project, a simple Win32 application, or a typical "Hello World" application (see Figure B.3).

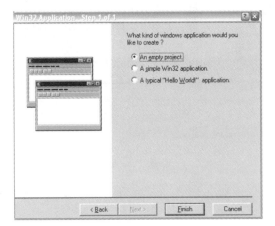

Figure B.3

After inputting a project name and clicking OK, this dialog comes up.

These are shortcuts designed to make your life easier; for example, if you opt to create a simple Win32 application, DevStudio will give you a project and a source code template that's already put together. If you select a "Hello World" application, DevStudio will create a completely functional program. All you need to do is compile it; when you run the EXE you've compiled, a window containing the text "Hello World" will appear on your screen.

That's all fine and dandy, but since we've already got source code and just need a project, go ahead and select "An empty project," and click Finish. Another dialog will come up, summarizing the options you've selected. Click OK at this point and DevStudio will generate your project and workspace!

Notice that out on your hard drive, you now have a DSP file and a DSW file for your project. The DSP file is the project file, and the DSW file is the workspace file. Both are human readable, so you can load them in a text editor, but you shouldn't modify them.

ADDING SOURCE CODE FILES

After you have a project and workspace created, you need to add some source code files to it. If you were creating new code from scratch, you'd again select New from the File drop-down menu, go to the Files tab, and click C++ Source File or C++ Header File to create a blank CPP or H file.

But, if you already have source code files, you can add those directly to your project. Click the FileView tab on your left. You'll see a treeview, with your workspace at the top and your project immediately beneath it. Right-click your project, and you'll be presented with a context menu like the one shown in Figure B.4.

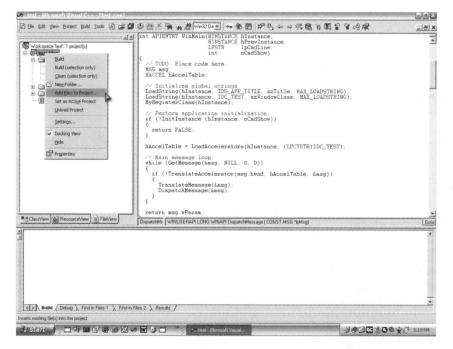

Figure B.4

Right-click on your project, and you'll be presented with this menu.

Click Add Files to Project, and then browse for the source code files you want to add (you can add multiple files at once by holding down Ctrl or Shift as you click their names).

For `Ch1p2_NormalWindow`, navigate to the folder containing the source code and add the source code file `Ch1p2_NormalWindow.cpp` to the project.

Now if you expand the project node in your FileView tree, you'll see three folders underneath it—source code files, header files, and resource files. Under source code files, you should see your `Ch1p2_NormalWindow.cpp` source file (see Figure B.5). Double-click it and you can edit it.

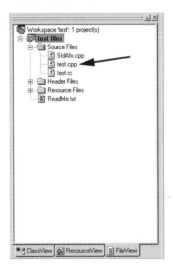

Figure B.5

After you insert a source code file, it should appear in the FileView tree.

SETTING COMPILER OPTIONS

After all of your source code files have been added, you can turn your attention to the task of setting the compiler options for your project.

There's roughly a dozen different ways to get to the Project Settings dialog that contains all of your project options. I prefer to get there by right-clicking on the project in the FileView tree, and selecting Settings from the context menu (see Figure B.6).

Figure B.6

To get to the project settings, right-click on the project in the FileView tree and select Settings.

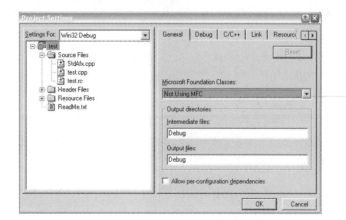

Figure B.7

The Project Settings dialog box.

Figure B.7 shows the Project Settings dialog box.

As you can see, on the left you have the same tree that's in your FileView. On the right are a bunch of controls to set the options. Running along the top are a whole slew of tabs for the various sections of controls.

DevStudio uses two different sets of project settings—one for debug, and one for release. The idea here is that you'll probably want to compile things differently depending on whether it's just a quick build for you to test and debug things, or if it's a finished program that you intend to distribute to your customers (the game players!).

Most of the time you'll be working with debug builds (that is, builds based on the debug set of project settings). Occasionally, as you're writing your program, you should create a release build to guarantee that your project settings are in sync, and that certain compiler settings (optimization, lack of debug information, and so on) don't interfere with the behavior of your program (they shouldn't, but every so often they do).

You can change which set of project settings you build with by selecting Set Active Configuration from the Build drop-down menu. You'll be presented with a dialog box, as shown in Figure B.8—select the settings you'd like to make active, and then click OK. You can also do this from the toolbar.

Figure B.8

The configuration dialog box that appears when you select Set Active Configuration.

I'm not going to cover every single option you can set. For most of the settings, the default values DevStudio provided will work just fine. I will, however, draw your attention to the useful options, or to the options that you'll more than likely need to change.

TIP

You're not limited to just two sets of project settings. You can create additional sets of settings by selecting Configurations from the Build drop-down menu, and then clicking the Add button. You usually won't need to do this, but I wanted to mention it in case you found yourself in a weird situation. For example, sometimes you'll want to build shareware with different options for registered and demo versions—you could set up something like that using four different sets of project settings: demo debug, demo release, registered debug, and registered release.

Setting the Warning Level

Usually the default warning level 3 will work just fine, but occasionally you'll want to increase or (shame on you!) decrease the warning level of the C++ compiler so that you create the illusion that your code isn't broken. To do this, go to the C/C++ tab inside the settings dialog. Select General from the category drop-down, and your dialog will change into something like Figure B.9.

TIP

It's usually a good idea to check the Warnings as Errors checkbox here as well. Bad programmers ignore warnings and face the consequences of badly written code. Good programmers solve the warnings that come up as if they were compiler errors.

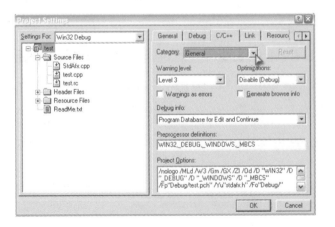

Figure B.9

The Project Settings dialog after selecting General from the Category drop-down.

Immediately below the category drop-down is the drop-down for the warning level. Choose a new value (higher numbers mean the compiler is more strict) to set the warning level you want.

Setting the Optimization Level

Immediately next to the warning level drop-down inside the C/C++ tab of the Project Settings dialog is another drop-down that controls the optimization level of the compiler. Here, you can choose to optimize for size (that is, make the EXE as small as possible, even if it means the code runs slower) or for speed (make things run fast, even if it means a larger EXE). Needless to say, most of the time you'll want to set this for speed.

You can also turn on or off optimizations individually. Select optimizations from the category drop-down, and you'll be able to enable or disable specific optimization techniques. This is extremely useful because very rarely, a certain optimization feature might cause your program to crash or behave in strange ways (Visual C++ isn't perfect when it comes to this sort of thing).

Turning on Run-Time Type Identification (RTTI)

The sample programs need RTTI turned on to operate correctly (if you're not sure what RTTI is, consult Appendix A). To turn on RTTI, navigate to the C/C++ tab inside the settings dialog. Select C++ Language from the category drop-down, and your dialog will change into something like Figure B.10. Make sure the Enable Run-Time Type Identification (RTTI) checkbox is checked.

CAUTION

If you try to use RTTI and the active set of project settings doesn't have RTTI enabled, the compiler will warn you. If you choose to ignore its warning, your program will more than likely crash when it comes to the first chunk of code that uses RTTI.

LIBRARY AND INCLUDE SEARCH PATHS

One of the most vital things to understand in DevStudio is how it handles search paths for source code files, include files, and libraries. For each of the major categories (source code files, include files, library files, and so on), there are actually two completely separate settings. There's a setting that's stored in the specific project you're working on, and a global setting that applies to all projects.

The per-project settings take precedence over the global settings. That is, DevStudio only looks at the global settings if it can't find what it's looking for using the per-project settings.

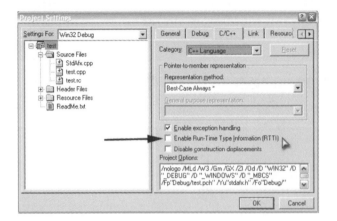

Figure B.10

Enabling RTTI is as easy as checking this checkbox.

Here's an example. Let's say we've added an #include "MyHeaderFile.h" directive to our source code. DevStudio now needs to find this include file. To do this, it first looks in the same directory as the source file it's compiling. If it can't find MyHeaderFile.h there, it looks in the folders you've specified inside the per-project include file search path (in the order you specified them). If it still can't find it, it looks in the global search path for include files (again, in the order you specified). If it can't find it even then, it gives up, and the compiler spits out an error message.

Here's how to set up the two different search paths.

Per-Project Search Paths

Per-project search paths are set up through the Project Settings dialog box. You can set up per-project search paths for include files and for library files.

To set up the include file search path, go to the C/C++ tab, and select Preprocessor from the Category drop-down list (see Figure B.11).

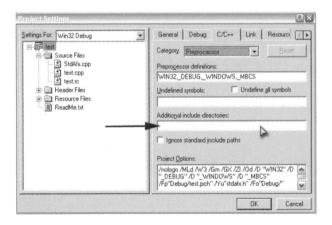

Figure B.11

Setting the per-project search paths.

Near the bottom is an edit box labeled
Additional Include Directories. Insert your
`include` directories here, separated by commas.

To set up the library search path, go to the
Link tab, and select Input from the category
drop-down. At the bottom of the dialog will be
an edit box labeled Additional Library Path.
Enter your search paths here, separated by
commas (again, you can use relative paths).

TIP

You can enter relative paths in this box.
That is, if you always want this particular project to search a folder one up
from its current location, you can enter
`..\` into the search path box.

Global Search Paths

You set up global search paths in a totally different location. Instead of going to the Project
Settings dialog box, select Options from the Tools drop-down menu. Click the Directories tab,
and your dialog box will look like the one in Figure B.12.

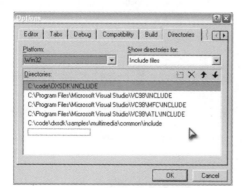

Figure B.12

*The Directories tab of
the Options dialog box.*

You can alter the global
search path by adding or
deleting entries from the
list box, or by clicking
the up and down arrows
at the top of the list,
which move the current
selection up or down the
list. Change the search
path by selecting a different entry from the
combo box labeled Show
Directories For.

CAUTION

It's very important that you add the `include` and `library`
paths for the DirectX API. Also, it's vital that these directories take precedence over the other `include` and `library`
files (that is, they should be at the very top of the list). The
reason is that DevStudio ships with `header` and `library` files
for an older version of DirectX. If you try to compile
DirectX 8 applications without adding the DirectX 8 `header`
and `library` paths, everything will appear to be normal, but
you'll run into all sorts of weird compiler errors that appear
to be errors in the DirectX code itself. Watch out for this.

Search Paths for the Sample Programs

If you're getting errors compiling the sample programs of this book, you should check to make sure that you've added the Common Code directory to your code search path. I'd recommend adding this to each individual project, rather than adding it to the global code search path, but it's ultimately up to you.

LINKING IN THE DIRECTX LIBRARIES

Now that you know all about project options and search paths, it's time to integrate DirectX into your project.

The way you do this is by adding some libraries to your linker settings. Table B.1 shows the DirectX libraries that you usually need.

Microsoft provides other DirectX libraries, but the ones listed in Table B.1 are the ones you'll use most often. For most of the sample programs in this book, you need to link with dinput8.lib, d3dx8dt.lib, d3d8.lib, d3dxof.lib, winmm.lib, and dxguid.lib.

BUILDING AND RUNNING PROGRAMS

Finally! You've set up all your options and are now ready to build and run your programs.

The easiest way to do this is to select Build <yourproject> from the Build drop-down menu (don't worry, you'll learn the hot key for Build, F7, very quickly).

As DevStudio builds, it outputs warnings and errors to your output window at the bottom of your screen (if this window isn't visible, select Output from the View menu to make it appear). You can double-click on any error or warning line, and DevStudio will take you to the appropriate source code file and line number.

Once you get your program built without any errors, you can choose to run it two different ways. First, you can launch it from DevStudio by selecting Execute <projname> from the Build drop-down menu. This is the equivalent to double-clicking the EXE from within Explorer. Your program launches as a completely separate process, and it doesn't get wired up to the DevStudio debugger.

The second way to launch the program is by selecting Go from the Start Debug submenu, contained inside the Build drop-down menu. This is the most common way to run the program, so remember the hot key (F5). If you run your program this way, you hook it up to the DevStudio debugger so that you can break into it at any time.

Table B.1 DirectX Libraries

Library Name	Description
D3D8.lib	This library contains the source code to interface with the Direct3D component of DirectX. If you're doing Direct3D programming, you need to link with this.
D3DX8.lib	This library contains the D3DX helper functions. You need to link with this if you use any D3DX items.
DDraw.lib	This library contains the DirectDraw interfaces. You won't usually need this for 3D stuff, but if your code is written for older versions of DirectX, and uses DirectDraw, you'll need to link with this.
DInput8.lib	This library contains the source code to interface with the DirectInput component of DirectX. If you're using DirectInput, you need to link with this.
Dsound.lib	This library contains the source code to interface with the DirectSound component of DirectX. If you're using DirectSound, you need to link with this.
Dxerr8.lib	This library contains source code to help you use and translate DirectX error codes (for example, the function DXGetErrorString8).
D3dxof.lib	This library contains routines used to load and save X files. If you're using anything from the dxfile.h header, you need to link with this.
D3dx8dt.lib	This library contains additional D3DX routines. If you're using any D3DX functions, you probably need to link with this.
Dxguid.lib	This library contains the GUIDs (globally unique identifiers) for the DirectX components. If you're using any part of DirectX, you need to link with this.

DEBUGGING

When it comes to integrated debugging, DevStudio really shines. This section will explain how to accomplish the most basic debugging tasks, once you've selected Go from the Start Debug menu. For a complete feature breakdown, refer to the DevStudio online help.

Breakpoints

The easiest way to set a breakpoint is to simply right-click the line of the source code file at which you'd like to break. Select Insert/Remove Breakpoint from the context menu that appears. Lines that contain a breakpoint have a little red circle in the margin.

You can quickly delete all of your breakpoints by selecting Breakpoints from the Edit drop-down menu, and clicking the Remove All button on the dialog that appears. You can also set up conditional or data-driven breakpoints from within this dialog box.

Stepping through Code

There are a few main ways you can step through code:

- **Step Over**. This is the most common way to step. Stepping over means that you execute the line you're on, and then pause again. You'll quickly learn the hotkey for Step Over (F10).
- **Step Into**. This is slightly different from step over. If the current line contains a call to a function, you can use step into to follow the code down into that function (whereas step over just completes the entire function call in one step).
- **Step Out**. Use this command to get out of function calls. Step out runs until you return from the function that you're in. Use it to quickly get out of function calls once you've determined that the bug you're looking for isn't in the function you stepped into.
- **Run To Cursor**. Use this command to skip over large segments of code. When you select this command, the debugger will execute the code until it arrives at the line the cursor is at. It will then stop. In a way, this is like a shortcut for setting a breakpoint, running, and then removing that breakpoint immediately after you hit it.

Watches

The DevStudio integrated debugger enables you to watch the values of variables change as your program executes. There are two main windows in DevStudio that provide access to most of the Watch functionality. You'll find these two windows in the bottom section of your screen when you're running a program in Debug mode (see Figure B.13).

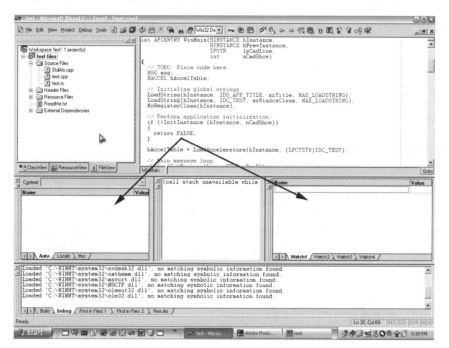

Figure B.13

The watch windows that appear when running a program in the debugger.

One watch window enables you to enter any variable names you like. Click on an empty list entry and type the variable name you're interested in, and DevStudio will show you its value. As you step through your program, DevStudio will update this value. It will turn red when it changes.

The second watch window automatically gives you a view of the variables you're probably most interested in. This includes variables used by the line of code that's currently executing, as well as this pointers and function return values.

TIP

You can also use the memory viewer to view the contents of raw memory locations. This is most useful when you need to look at a huge chunk of data; because DevStudio often clips huge strings in the watch window, to see the entire string, you'll need to manually copy its address into the memory viewer. You access the memory viewer by selecting Memory from the Debug Windows submenu contained in the View drop-down menu.

Debug Output

One of the most common ways to debug software is to print out diagnostic messages that let you know what your program is doing when it's impossible (or just really irritating) to break into a debugger and start stepping through the code. Microsoft provides support for these diagnostic messages through a Win32 API function called OutputDebugString. This function takes a single parameter—a string to send to the debugger. Any messages you push out using OutputDebugString end up inside your debug output, in your IDE. This allows you to keep tabs on your program without having to trace through code.

Accessing Help

I've saved the most important discussion for last! DevStudio help is something that all programmers use very frequently. This is partly because DevStudio itself is huge, and it takes a long time to get familiar with all of its features.

Thankfully, there are no office assistants in DevStudio. To get help, select Index from the Help pull-down menu. Also, DevStudio has a comprehensive context-sensitive help system, so keep an eye out for those little question mark buttons in the corners of dialog boxes and tool windows. Clicking on one of those will often take you exactly where you need to go.

DevStudio Wrap-Up

This appendix was a crash course. I didn't cover everything, but I covered the key points you need to know to get the most out of this book and DevStudio in general.

The best way to learn DevStudio is simply to use it. The IDE is the lifeblood of a programmer, and you'll quickly pick up the shortcuts and the tricks by simply using it frequently. Have fun!

APPENDIX C

WHAT'S ON THE CD?

ttached to the back cover of this book you'll find a plastic disc containing a spiral arrangement of approximately 650,000,000 bytes of data, commonly referred to as a CD. Here's what that CD contains.

Bitmap Font Builder

This is a handy utility for creating bitmap fonts for use in your DirectX or OpenGL applications.

DirectX 8.1 SDK

Since the name of this book is *Special Effects Game Programming with DirectX*, I thought it might be nice to include a copy of the actual DirectX SDK. Contained on the CD is the full release of the DirectX 8.1 SDK.

One of the best ways to round out your understanding of DirectX is by looking at the sample programs and associated source code that Microsoft provides as part of this SDK. In particular, look at the Direct3D demo programs—they can teach you a lot about 3D game programming.

Also included in the SDK is the DirectX online help. If you haven't used the DirectX API Help yet, you'll quickly learn that it is one of your best friends when it comes to developing 3D graphics. Don't just use the index—read closely the books contained under the Contents tab as well because they contain valuable information on the architecture of features as a whole (as well as specific information about each component).

FreeImage

The FreeImage library enables you to read and write a variety of different image file formats. Formats supported include BMP, ICO, JPEG, KOALA, LBM, MNG, PCD, PCX, PNG, PNM, RAS, TARGA, and TIFF. The library also contains some image conversion functions.

nVidia DX8 SDK

Coupled closely to the Microsoft SDK is another software development kit, made by nVidia, called the nVidia SDK. This SDK is also on your CD.

The nVidia SDK is most valuable when it comes to vertex and pixel shader development. nVidia's GeForce 3 graphics card was one of the first to support vertex and pixel shaders in hardware, so it's only natural that nVidia would want to show off its hardware by providing several good examples of how to use vertex and pixel shaders to create effects. Check out the nVidia Effects Browser, and some of the demos. That chameleon one is especially sweet!

Also, be sure to spend some time with the nVidia vertex and pixel shader assembler, NVASM. NVASM is a great tool which enhances the vertex and pixel shader language, providing support for #include and #define directives. These directives make your life as a graphics programmer much easier. For example, instead of using the actual constant registers in your vertex and pixel shader code, you can create #defines for each register index, and store those in an include file that both your C++ and your shader programs use.

PAINT SHOP PRO

Paint Shop Pro is a trial version of one of the best tools for image creation, editing, and retouching. Paint Shop Pro is a powerful paint program that can easily provide you the essential tools you need to create textures and backdrops. For most of us coders, the hardest part will be learning how to draw.

POV-RAY RAYTRACER

I used the POV-Ray renderer in conjunction with a lens flare header (below), to create the lens flare shapes for Chapter 22. The POV-Ray renderer is a powerful raytracer with a cornucopia of nifty features.

GALAXY AND LENS FLARE POV-RAY HEADER FILES

These two header files for POV-Ray enable easy creation of galaxies and lens flares. Both were written by Chris Colefax.

UNIVERSE IMAGE CREATOR, BY DIARD SOFTWARE

Universe is a cool program that enables you to create deep-space scenes by dragging and dropping various space elements (gas clouds, star clusters). I used the Universe program to create the cool-looking deep space skybox seen in some of the 3D sample programs.

Universe comes in two flavors—a stand-alone app, and a Photoshop plug-in. The shareware versions of both are on your CD.

PYROMANIA SAMPLES

Also on your CD are some selected samples from the Pyromania video clip-art library. Pyromania is a collection of video clips of explosions and all sorts of other nifty fire effects. I used one Pyromania video as the basis of the explosion animation in Chapter 20.

ZLIB

ZLib is a freeware library that enables you to work with ZIP files. The ability to uncompress a ZIP file from within your own code is invaluable for creating professional games.

THE LAUNCHER APPLICATION AND OTHER MISCELLANY

Last but not least, I've assembled a small application that will guide you through viewing the sample programs, copying the source code, and installing the other CD goodies. Through the magic of AutoRun, this launcher should appear automatically when you insert the CD. If it does not, you can run it manually by double-clicking on the CDLauncher.exe file inside the Launcher folder.

Also, be sure to check the readme.html file on your CD for last-minute information about the book.

INDEX

3D geometry pipeline
    clipping, 257
    projection transformation, 257
    viewport scaling, 257
    view transformation, 255–256
    world transformation, 254–255
8-bit quality, sound waves, 135
32-bit value
    action maps, 119
    DirectX enumeration functions, 108

A

-A argument, Conv3ds, 238
action maps
    Asteroids clone example code, 120
    ConfigureDevices method, 125
    devices, enumerating, 123–125
    game controls, default, setting up, 121–122
    genre, specifying, 120–121
    overview, 118
    ProcessInput method, 119
    SetActionMap method, 125
    setting up, 119–120
Adapter parameter, CreateDevice method, 272
AddFrame method, 686–687
addressing modes (texture)
    border color, 342–343
    clamp, 341
    mirror, 340
    wrap, 340
alpha blending
    fade effects, 561–564
    warping effects, 517
ambient lighting, 313
an register, 399
anisotropic texture filtering mode, 339–340

architecture
    DirectAudio, 136–137
    DirectGraphics, 268–269
    DirectInput, 109–110
    DirectPlay, 152–154
attenuation property
    lighting and, 316–317
    properties, list of, 317
audio path
    defined, 136
    flags specifying features of, 139
audio scripts. *See also* sound
    loading and initializing, 150
    overview, 149–150
    routines, calling, 150
    variables, setting, 150

B

BeginScene method, 297
BeginWithDelay function, 688
BehaviorFlags parameter, 272
billboarding, 693–694
BitBlt function, 60–61
bitmaps
    CGDIBitmap class, 62–63
    creating, 59
    DC
        creating, 59
        rendering to bitmaps, 60
    deleting, 61–62
    drawing, 60–61
    loading, 58
    overview, 56–57
blurring effects, 542
    class layout, 547–554
    edge detection, 546

maximizing, 545
optimizing, 556
sharpening, 545–546
uses for, 555
weight values, 543
bone effects, 393
border color texture addressing mode, 342–343
breakpoints (DevStudio), 888
brushes
CreateSolidBrush function, 55–56
creation functions, list of, 55
buffered data
DIDEVICEOBJECTDATA structure members, 118
GetDeviceData method, 116–117
SetProperty method, 113
buffers
index, 234–235
vertex, 233–234
BuildActionMap method, 123–124
bump mapping, 330

C

C++
dynamic memory allocation, 828–831
exception handling, 839
basics of, 841–842
catching different types, 842–844
do's and don'ts of, 846–847
nested try blocks, 844–846
inline functions, 825–826
namespaces, 826–828
overview, 824
polymorphism and pure virtual functions, 831
aggregation *vs.* inheritance, 832–833
pure virtuals, 835–837
virtual destructors, 837–839
virtual functions, 833–835
RTTI (run-time type identification), 851–853
style casting, 848–851
templates, 853
classes, 856–859
functions, 854–856
callback function, 5

cameras
field of view, 249
orientation, specifying, 251–252
overview, 246
position, specifying, 251–252
projection modes, 250–252
view frustum, 249
cartoon shading
overview, 802
pen strokes, adding, 809–810
regular lighting, 802–803
sample programs, 819
smooth texture lighting, 803–804
texture stage states, 808
adding edge texture to, 811–812
vertex shader
adding edge support to, 811
constants, setting, 806
loading, 805
cbObjectData parameter, 117
cbSize member, 12
cBufferDesc parameter, 167
c_cfDIJoystick variable, 111
CComPtr implementation, 103
cDeviceInfo parameter, 162
c_dfDIKeyboard variable, 111
c_dfDIMouse variable, 111
CD-quality, sound waves, 135
CGDIBitmap class, 62–63
CheckAudioSetup method, 175
check boxes, dialog box controls, 94
CheckDeviceFormat method, 494
ChooseFont function, 69–70
structure members, 71–72
Chorus (DirectX Media Object), 147
CImageManipulator class, 548–550
CImageManipulatorKernel, 550–555
clamp texture addressing mode, 341
class ID. *See* CLSID
clearing depth buffers, 263
Clear method, 263
clipping, 37
3D geometry pipeline and, 257
Close method, 168

cloud effects
    blending factors, 536
    color clouds, 536–537
    colors, squaring, 528
    noise layers
        combining, 533–535
        filtering, 528
        smoothing, 532–533
    optimizing, 538–539
    overview, 522–523
    Perlin noise technique, 523
        amplification, 526
        frequency, 526
        using 3D card to generate, 524–525
    squaring, 535
    texture
        creating, 529–530
        subtracting, 528–529
CLSID (class ID), using to get interfaces, 106
CoCreateInstance function, 106–107
CoInitializeEx function, 104–105
color saturation, texture and, 382–383
COM, DirectX
    CoInitializeEx function, 104–105
    CoUninitialize function, 105
    HRESULT return values, checking, 105–106
CombineRgn function, 77
combo boxes, dialog box controls, 95
compression
    DirectX Media Object, 147
    lossy, 136
concatenation, 219–220
conditional force effect type, 127
ConfigureDevices method, 125
ConstantCount parameter, 408
constant force effect type, 127
converting 3D Studio model to X files, 237–238
cooling arrays, fire effects, 448–449
coordinate systems, 191–195
CoUninitialize function, 105
CParticle class, 593–594
CParticleEmitter class, 594–596
CParticleEvent Sequence member, 703
crColor parameter, 50
Create3DsoundBuffer method, 175
CreateBrushIndirect function, 55

CreateCompatibleBitmap function, 59
CreateCompatibleDC function, 59
CreateDevice method
    IDirectInput8Create function, 110
    parameters, list of, 272
CreateDialog function, 92
CreateDIBPatternBrushPt function, 55
CreateEffect method, 126, 129
CreateFont function, 65–69
CreateHatchBrush function, 55
CreateIndexBuffer method, 235
CreatePatternBrush function, 55
CreatePen function, 50
CreatePenIndirect function, 52–53
CreateSolidBrush function, 55
CreateTexture method
    IDirect3DTexture8 interface, 107
    parameters, list of, 353
CreateVertexBuffer method, 291
CreateWindowEx function, 17–19
creating
    bitmaps, 59
    matrix stack, 243
    pixel shaders, 420
    texture
        CreateTexture method, 352–355
        D3DXCreateTexture method, 355
        from images using D3DX, 355–358
    vertex buffers, 290
    vertex shaders, 406–407
CRecyclingArray class, 596–601
cross product, vectors and, 204–205
crunch transitions, 573–574
cubic environment mapping, 381
custom and device effect type, 127

D

D3DX
    matrix functions, 220–222
    vector functions, 206–207
D3DXCreateTexture method, fire effects, 431
D3DXLoadMeshFromX method, 237
DC (device context)
    getting, 48
    overview, 47–48
    releasing, 48–49

debugging (DevStudio), 888
DeleteDC function, 62
DeleteObject function, 61–62
deleting bitmaps, 61–62
depth buffers
    clearing, 263
    comparison function, changing, 263
    disabling, 262
    overview, 258–259
    rendering objects using, 261–262
    W-buffers, 260–261
    Z-buffers, 260–261
detail mapping, 382
device contexts. *See* DC
devices
    acquire/unacquire mechanism, 110–111
    ConfigureDevices method, 125
    EnumDeviceBySemantics method, 123–125
    joysticks, DIJOYSTATE structure, 115
    keyboard, GetDeviceState method, 114
    mouse, GetDeviceState method, 114
    SetDataFormat method, 110
    setting up, 110
    switching between, 283–284
DeviceType parameter, 272
DevStudio
    breakpoints, 888
    compiler options, setting, 880–882
    debugging, 888
    DirectX libraries, linking to, 886
    help, accessing, 890
    optimization level, setting, 883
    RTTI, turning on, 883
    search paths, 883
        global, 885
        per-project, 884–885
    source code files, adding, 879
    warning levels, setting, 882–883
    workspace, creating, 876–878
DIACTION structure, 121–122
dialog boxes, 87–88
    controls, 93–95
    modal, 90–91
    modeless, 91–93
    template, creating in Resource Editor, 89–90

DialogProc function, 90
DIDATAFORMAT function, global variables for, 111
DIDEVICEOBJECTDATA structure members, 118
DIEFFECT structure, 129–130
diffuse color property, lighting and, 316, 320–321
DIJOYSTATE structure, 115–116
DirectAudio
    architecture, 136–137
    audio path, 136
    audio scripts
        loading and initializing, 150
        overview, 149–150
        routines, calling, 150
        variables, setting, 150
    audio types, list of, 140
    defined, 101
    DMOs (DirectX Media Objects), 146
    files, loading, 141–144
    overview, 132
    primary buffers, 136
    sample quality, 135
    secondary buffers, 136
    segments
        downloading, 144
        playing, 144–146
    SetSearchDirectory method, 140–141
    setting up, 136–137
    sound waves
        CD-quality, 135
        lossy compression, 136
        measuring shape of, 132–133
        sampling rate, 134
DirectGraphics
    architecture, 268–269
    back buffer, 279
    defined, 101
    devices
        creating, 270–271
        switching between, 283–284
    double buffering, 279
    fading in, 304–305
    fading out, 305
    front buffer, 277
    gamma ramps, 302–303
        getting, 306
        setting, 307

Hal device type, 269
lost devices, 281–283
pluggable software device type, 270
Reference device type, 269
refresh rates, 279
triple buffering, 280
vertex formats
describing, 285–287
flexible, texture coordinates in, 288–289
overview, 284
sample, 289–290
transformed, 287–288
untransformed, 287–288
vertical retrace, 280
video mode, finding, 280–281
DirectInput, 108
action maps
BuildActionMap method, 123–124
ConfigureDevices method, 125
EnumDeviceBySemantics method, 123–125
game controls, default, setting up, 121–122
genre, specifying, 120–121
overview, 118
SetActionMap method, 125
setting up, 119–120
architecture, 109–110
buffered data
DIDEVICEOBJECTDATA structure members, 118
GetDeviceData method, 116–117
SetProperty method, 113
defined, 101
devices, setting up, 110
force feedback
CreateEffect method, 126–128
diagram of, 128
DIEFFECT structure, 129–130
effect types, list of, 127
EnumEffects function, 126
EnumEffectsInFile method, 130
immediate data, 112
versus buffered data, 112–113
joystick data, reading, 115
keyboard data, reading, 114
mouse data, reading, 114
OOP (object-oriented programming), 131
DirectInput8Create function, 109

directional lights, 320
directional wipes, 566–568
DirectInput devices, setting up, 110
direct lighting, 313
DirectMusic segment file type, 140
DirectPlay
advantages of, 152
callback function, setting up, 155–156
client/server architecture, 152–154
data
receiving, 168
sending, 166–167
defined, 101
games
connecting to, 163–166
hosting, 159–162
lobby launching, 171
messages, list of, 169–171
multiple threads and callbacks, 156–158
overview, 151–152
peer-to-peer architecture, 152–154
service providers, selecting, 158–159
voice features, 172
DirectPlayMessgeHandler method, 155–156
DirectShow
architecture, 176–177
defined, 101
filter graph manager, 176–177
MP3s, playing, 179
video, playing, 178–179
DirectX
COM
CoInitializeEx function, 104–105
CoUninitialize function, 105
HRESULT return values, 105–106
cross-platform equivalence, 101
DirectAudio
architecture, 136–137
audio path, 136
audio scripts, 149–151
audio types, list of, 139–140
defined, 101
DMOs (DirectX Media Objects), 146
files, loading, 141–144
overview, 132
primary buffers, 136
secondary buffers, 136

segments, downloading, 144
segments, playing, 144–146
SetSearchDirectory method, 140–141
setting up, 136–137
sound waves, 132–136
DirectGraphics, 101
DirectInput
architecture, 109–110
buffered data, 113, 116–117
defined, 101
devices, acquire/unacquire mechanism,
110–111
devices, settings up, 110
force feedback, 126–131
immediate data, 112–115
OOP (object-oriented programming), 131
overview, 108
DirectPlay
action mapping, 118–125
advantages of, 152
callback function, setting up, 155–156
client/server architecture, 152–154
data, receiving, 168
data, sending, 166–167
defined, 101
games, connecting to, 163–166
games, hosting, 159–162
lobby launching, 171
messages, 169–171
multiple threads and callbacks, 156–158
overview, 151–152
peer-to-peer architecture, 152–154
service providers, selecting, 158–159
voice features, 172–175
DirectShow
architecture, 176–177
defined, 101
filter graph manager, 176–177
MP3s, playing, 179
video, playing, 177–179
enumeration, 107–108
interfaces, 102–103
IUnknown* parameter, 104
releasing, 103–104
using CLSIDs to get, 106
overview, 100

DirectX Media Objects. *See* DMOs
disabling depth buffers, 262
DispatchMessage function, 31–32
distortion (DirectX Media Object), 147
DMOs (DirectX Media Objects), 146–148
DMUS_OBJECTDESC structure members, 142–143
dot products, vectors and, 201–203
double buffering, 279
Download method, 144
dpnid parameter, 167
dpnidSend parameter, 169
drawing bitmaps, 60–61, 64
DrawPrimitive method, 300
DrawText function, 74, 76–77
dwClsContext parameter, 107
dwCoInit parameter, 105
dwData member (DIDEVICEOBJECT DATA structure), 118
dwDefaultPathType, 137
dwEnumCount parameter, 165
dwExStyle parameter, 18
dwFlags parameter
DIACTION structure, 122
EnumHost function, 165
EnumServiceProvider function, 160
GetDeviceData method, 117
Host method, 162
InitAudio method, 139
PlaySegmentEx method, 145
SentTo method, 167
Start method, 131
dwHow member, 122
dwIterations parameter, 131
dwMessageType parameter, 155
dwObjID member, 122
dwOfs member (DIDEVICEOBJECT DATA
structure), 118
dwPChannelCount parameter, 139
dwRetryInterval parameter, 165
dwSemantic, 122
dwSize member
DMUS_OBJECTDESC structure, 142
DPNMSG_RECEIVE structure, 169
dwStyle parameter, 18
dwTimeOut parameter
EnumHost function, 165
SendTo method, 167

dwTimeStamp member (DIDEVICEOBJECTDATA structure), 118
dynamic memory allocation (C++), 828–831

E

echo (DirectX Media Object), 147
edit boxes, dialog box controls, 94
effect scripts
    defined, 383
    files, creating, 385–386
    PASS blocks, 387
    process of, 382, 384
    variable declarations, 386
emissive color, lighting and, 321
EndScene method, 301
EnumDeviceBySemantics method, 123–125
EnumEffects function, 126
EnumEffectsInFile method, 130
enumeration
    DirectX, 107–108
    EnumDeviceBySemantics method, 123–125
EnumHosts function, 163–165
EnumObjects method, 110
EnumServiceProvider method, 160
environmental reverberation (DirectX Media Object), 147
environment mapping, 330
    fire effects, 450–451
    texture and, 379
        cubic mapping, 381
        spherical mapping, 380
    water effects and, 792
error checking, 77
    FormatMessage function, 80
    GetLastError function, 78, 80
    MessageBox function, 80–82
event-driven programming, 4–6
events, 636
    EventTimer property, 648–649
    factory, using to create, 664–665
    fading, 647
    final keyword, 647–648
    parsing time element of, 664
    Render mechanism, 670
    sequences, 637–645
    storing, 665
    Update function, 666–670

explosion
    animation classes, 685–687
    billboarding, 693–694
    clusters, 696–698
    CTimer class, problems with, 691–692
    frame classes, 685–687
    frames, displaying, 690–691
    loop command, 698–699
        implementing, 703–704
        interpreting inside particle script, 700–703
    particle system, integrating, 704–706
    rendering, 694–695
    sample programs, 713
    shockwave, adding, 706
        fading, 712–713
        rendering, 711–712
        texture, creating, 707
    sprites, 682
    start and stop methods, 699
    textures, 683–684
    timer class, creating, 687–688
    vertices and texture coordinates, setting up, 707–711

F

fade effects
    alpha blending, 561–564
    cross fades, 564–566
fading in, 304–305
fading out, 305
FAILED macros, 105
Falloff property, 319
fClear parameter, 141
fdItalic parameter, 67
fdQuality parameter, 68
fdwCharSet parameter, 67
fdwClipPrecision parameter, 67
fdwOutputPrecision parameter, 67
fdwPitchAndFamily parameter, 68
fdwStrikeOut parameter, 67
fdwUnderline parameter, 67
fErase member, 38
filtering modes (texture), 335
    anisotropic, 339–340
    linear, 337
    mipmap, 338–339
    nearest-point sampling, 336

fire effects, 428–430
  color palette, creating, 431, 449–450
    image files, grabbing a palette out of, 434
    palette files, 432–435
  cooling arrays, 448–449
  environment mapping, 450–451
  fuel, 449
  multitexturing, 451
  orthogonal projections, 442–444
  paletted textures, 452
  perspective projection, 441–442
  processing code, 435–436
  texel/pixel alignment, 445–447
  texture
    creating, 431
    filling, 437–440
    locking, 437
    unlocking, 440
Flags parameter
  Lock method, 293
  LockRect method, 438
  SetGammaRamp method, 308
flange (DirectX Media Object), 147
flat shading mode, 314
fnWeight parameter, 67
fonts
  ChooseFont function, 69–70
    structure members, 71–72
  CreateFont function, 65
    parameters, list of, 66–69
  DrawText function, 76–77
  TextOut function, 74–76
Force Editor, 129–130
force feedback
  CreateEffect method, 126–128
  DIEFFECT structure, 129–130
  effect types, list of, 127
  EnumEffects function, 126
  EnumEffectsInFile method, 130
  types, diagram of, 128
FormatMessage function, 80
Format parameter, 353
ftDate (DMUS_OBJECTDESC structure), 143
FVF method, 291

G

gamma ramps, 302–303
  getting, 306
  setting, 307
gargle (DirectX Media Object), 147
GetAdapterIdentifier method, 281
GetDefaultAudioPath method, 148
GetDeviceData method
  buffered data, reading, 116
  parameters, list of, 117
GetLastError function, 78
GetLight method, 323
GetMessage function, 30–31
GetObjectInPath method, 148
GetObject method, 141
GetTop method, 244
glow mapping, 382
Gouraud shading mode, 314
graphics. *See* DirectGraphics
guidClass (DMUS_OBJECTDESC structure), 142
guidInstance member, 122
guidObject member (DMUS_OBJECTDESC structure), 142
gun effects
  bullets, 736–738
  CanFire method, 729
  CMachine::Render, 727–729
  gun base class, 722–723
  laser, 741
    CLaserGun class, 742–743
    drawing, 744–746
    firing, 743
    particle system, integrating, 746
  machine guns, 730
    firing, 731–733
    muzzle flash, drawing, 733–734
    muzzle flash sprite, loading, 731
    recoil, 734–735
  plasma cannon, 735
    bullets, CanFire method, 740
    bullets, firing, 739–740
    bullets, rendering, 738
    bullets, updating, 738
  sample programs, 747
  weapons, switching, 723–726

H

Hal device, 269
hbrBackground parameter, 14
hBufferHandle parameter, 169
hCursor parameter, 13
hdc parameter, 38
    ChooseFont function, 71
    CreateCompatibleBitmap function, 59
hDestWindowOverride parameter, 301
Height parameter
    CreateTexture method, 353
    D3DVIEWPORT8 structure, 248
help, accessing (DevStudio), 890
hFocusWindow parameter, 272
hIcon parameter, 13
hIconSm parameter, 15, 85
hierarchical models, 240–242
hInstance parameter
    ChooseFont function, 72
    CreateWindowEx function, 19
    DialogProc function, 91
    Winmain() function, 8
    WNDCLASSEX, 13
hMenu parameter, 19
Host method parameters, list of, 162
hPrevInstance parameter, Winmain() function, 8
Hungarian notation, 21–22
hwndOwner parameter, 71
hWnd parameter
    InitAudio method, 138
    MessageBox function, 81
    PeekMessage function, 29
    WindowProc function, 34
hWndParent parameter, 19

I

i64StartTime parameter, 145
icons
    hIconSm parameter, 85
    LoadIcon function, 86
identity matrix, 218–219
IDirect3DDevice8 interface
    BeginScene method, 297
    Clear method, 263, 297

    CreateIndexBuffer method, 235
    LightEnable method, 325
    Present method, 301
    SetStreamSource method, 298–299
    SetVertexShader method, 300, 392
    SetViewport method, 247
IDirectInput8 function
    ConfigureDevices method, 125
    CreateDevice method, 110
    CreateEffect method, 126–128
    EnumDeviceBySemantics method, 123–125
    EnumEffectsInFile method, 130
    EnumEffects member, 126
    EnumObjects method, 110
    SetDataFormat method, 110
    Start method, 130–131
IDirectMusicAudioPath8 interface, 148
IDirectMusicLoader8 interface
    GetObject method, 141
    LoadObjectFromFile method, 150
    SetSearchDirectory method, 140–141
IDirectMusicPerformance8 interface
    GetDefaultAudioPath method, 148
    InitAudio method, 137
IDirectMusicScript8 interface, 150
IDirectPlay8Peer interface, 163
IDirectSoundBuffer8 interface, 148
IID (interface ID), 106
image feedback effects, 488–491
    code for, writing, 492
    feedback transformation, 503
    textures
        creating, 493–494
        rendering to, 494–498
    uses of, 503
immediate data
    versus buffered data, 112–113
    reading, 113
        joystick data, 115
        keyboard data, 114
        mouse data, 114
index buffers, 234–235
Index parameter, 323
InitAudio method, 137–139
inline functions (C++), 825–826

instructions
    pixel shaders, 417–418
    vertex shader, list of, 401–405
interface ID. *See* IID
interfaces
    DirectX and, 102–103
    Hungarian notation, 103
    IUnknown* parameter, 104
    releasing, 103–104
    using CLSIDs to get, 106
iPointSize parameter, 71
IUnknown* parameter, interfaces and, 104

J

joysticks
    c_dfDIJoystick variable, 111
    DIJOYSTATE structure, 115

K

keyboards
    c_dfDIKeyboard variable, 111
    GetDeviceState method, 114
    mapping constants, 122

L

lCustData parameter, 72
left-handed systems, 186–187
Length parameter, 291
lens flares
    CLensFlare class, 755–758
    CLensFlareSpot class, 755–758
    drawing, 768–770
    flare spots, 751–752
    intensity of, calculating, 759–760
    overview, 750–751
    ray direction, calculating, 770–771
    ray/triangle intersection text, 771–773
    rendering in 3D, 765–768
    sample programs, 774
    triangle
        positions, calculating, 761–763
        rendering, 763–764
    without sun, 753–754

Levels parameter
    CreateTexture method, 353
    GetSurfaceLevel method, 496
    LockRect method, 438
LightEnable method, 325
lighting
    ambient, 313
    attenuation property, 316–317
    default light properties, list of, 326
    diffuse color, 316, 320–321
    direct, 313
    emissive color, 321
    flat shading mode, 314
    GetLight method, 323
    Gouraud shading mode, 314
    light direction, 317
    LightEnable method, 325
    light types
        directional, 320
        point lights, 318
        spotlights, 318–320
    positioning of, 316
    power property, 321–322
    range of, 316
    ray tracing, 312–313
    SetLight method, 322–323
    specular color, 316, 321–322
light mapping, texture and, 376–378
lightning bug effects, 677
linear texture filtering mode, 337
list boxes, dialog box controls, 95
LoadIcon function, 86
LoadIdentitiy method, 244
LoadImage function, 58
loading
    bitmaps, 58
    models from X files, 236
LoadMatrix method, 244
LoadObjectFromFile method, 150
lobby launching, 171
Lock method parameters, list of, 293
LockRect method, fire effects, 437
lossy compression, 136
lost devices, 281–283
lParam parameter, 34
lpCaption parameter, 81

lpClassName parameter, 18
lpCmdLine parameter, 8
lpeff parameter, 129
lpfnHook parameter, 72
lpfnWndProc member, 12
lpLogFont parameter, 71
lpMsg parameter, 29
lpParam parameter, 19
lpszClassName parameter, 15
lpszFace parameter, 69
lpszMenuName parameter, 15
lpszStyle parameter, 72
lpTemplateName parameter, 72
lpText parameter, 81
lpWindowName parameter, 18
lStructureSize parameter, 71

M

macros
    FAILED, 105
    SAFE_RELEASE, 104
    SUCCEEDED, 105
magic effects, 673–677
-m argument, Conv3ds, 238
math, 179
    3D primitives, 187–188
    3D transformations
        overview, 188
        rotation, 190–191
        scaling, 189–190
        translation, 188–190
    coordinate systems, 191–195
    left-handed systems, 186–187
    matrices
        concatenation, 219–220
        D3DX matrix functions, 220–222
        function of, 209
        identity matrix, 218–219
        multiplication, 209–213
        overview, 208
        rotation formulas, 216–218
        scaling transformation example, 214–215
        transforming points using, 214
        translation example, 215–216
        vectors and, 213

quaternions
    conjugate of, 224
    inverse of, 225
    multiplication, 225
    norm of, 224
    overview, 222–224
    unit, 225
right-handed systems, 186–187
vectors
    adding, 198
    cross product of two, 204–205
    D3DX functions, 205–207
    defined, 195
    direction, determining, 196
    dot product of two, 201–203
    magnitude, determining, 196
    normalizing, 199–201
    scalar multiplication of, 199
    subtracting, 198
matrices
    concatenation, 219–220
    D3DX functions, 220–222
    function of, 209
    identity matrix, 218–219
    matrix stack, creating, 243
    multiplication, 209
        two 2x2, 210–211
        two 3x3, 212–213
    overview, 208
    rotation formulas, 216–218
    scaling transformation example, 214–215
    transforming points using, 214
    translation example, 215–216
    vectors and, 213
MaxZ parameter, 248
melting effects, 569–571
memory, primary buffer, 136
MessageBox function, 80
message pump
    defined, 25
    flowchart, 26
MIDI file type, 139
MinZ parameter, 248
mipmap texture filtering mode, 338–339
mirror texture addressing mode, 340
modal dialog boxes, 90–91

modeless dialog boxes, 91–93
models
    converting 3D Studio to X files, 237–238
    hierarchical, 240–242
    index buffers, 234–235
    loading from X files, 236
    overview, 230–231
    triangle fans, 232
    triangle lists, 231
    triangle strips, 232
    vertex buffers, 233–234
mouse
    c_dfDIMouse variable, 111
    DIMOUSESTATE structure, 114
    GetDeviceState method, 114
    WM_SETCURSOR message, 87
MP3s, playing, 179
multiple texturing, 330, 366–367
multiplication
    matrices, 209
        two 2x2, 210–211
        two 3x3, 212–213
    quaternions, 225
multitexturing, fire effects, 451
MultMatrixLocal method, 244
MultMatrix method, 244
muscle effects, 393

N

namespaces (C++), 826–828
nCmdShow parameter, 8
nearest-point sampling texture mode, 336
nEscapement parameter, 66
nFontType parameter, 72
nHeight parameter
    CreateFont function, 66
    CreateWindowEx function, 19
nOrientation parameter, 66
normalizing vectors, 199–201
nSizeMax parameter, 72
nSizeMin parameter, 72
nWidth parameter
    CreateFont function, 66
    CreatePen function, 50
    CreateWindowEx function, 19

O

object-oriented programming. *See* OOP
oDn register, 400
OffsetToLock parameter, 293
OOP (object-oriented programming), 131
orthogonal projection, 251
    fire effects and, 442–444

P

pApplicationDesc parameter, 164
parametric equalizer (DirectX Media Object), 147
particle system
    black holes, 678
    complexity of, 589–590
    CParticle class, 593–594
    CParticleEmitter class, 594–596
    CRecyclingArray class, 596–601
    events, 636
        EventTimer property, 648–649
        factory, using to create, 664–665
        fading, 647
        final keyword, 647–648
        parsing time element of, 664
        Render mechanism, 670
        sequences, 637–645
        storing, 665
        Update function, 666–670
    explosions and, 704–706
    flicker values, 678
    lightning bugs, 677
    magic effects, 673–677
    message processing, 622
    overview, 586–588
    particle properties, 591, 616
        map, creating, 617–618
        map, searching, 618–619
    particles
        animating, 611–613
        creating new, 613–614
        moving, 611–613
    rendering, 604
        render states, setting, 605–607
        vertex buffer, locking, 608
        vertex buffer, pumping particles into,
            608–609

vertex buffer, pushing out to graphics card, 609–610

vertex buffer, setting active, 608

setting up, 602–603

snow effects, 671–672

system properties, 591–593

wiggle values, 678

PASS blocks, 387

pAsyncHandle parameter, 165

pAudioPath parameter, 145

pBufferDesc parameter, 167

pcbEnumData parameter, 160

pConstantData parameter, 408

pcReturned parameter, 160

pDesc parameter, 142

pDestRect parameter, 301

pDirtyRegion parameter, 301

pdnAppDesc parameter, 162

pdpaddrDeviceInfo parameter, 164

pdpaddrHost parameter, 164

pdpSecurity parameter, 162

pdwInOut parameter, 117

PeekMessage function, 28–29

peer-to-peer DirectPlay topology, 172

pens, 49

color RGB values, 52

CreatePen function, 50

CreatePenIndirect function, 52–53

style flags, list of, 51

periodic force effect type, 127

perspective projection, 250

fire effects and, 441–442

pFilename parameter, 237

pFrom parameter, 145

pguidApplication parameter, 160

pguidServiceProvider parameter, 160

phAsyncHandle parameter, 167

Phi property, spotlights, 319

pixel shaders

black-and-white shaders, 817–818

creating, 420

image processing using, framework, 814

instructions, 417–418

modifiers, 419–420

registers, 414–416

simple example of, 420–421

uses of, 414

PlaySegmentEx method, 144–145, 156

Plight parameter, 323

pLockedRect parameter, 438

pluggable software devices, 270

pMatrix parameter, 296

pMsgBuffer parameter, 155

pNewZStencil parameter, 495

point lights, 318

Pool parameter

CreateTexture method, 353

CreateVertexBuffer method, 291

Pop method, 244

PostQuitMessage function, 36

pParams parameter, 139

ppbData parameter, 293

ppdeff parameter, 129

ppDirectMusic parameter, 138

ppDirectSound parameter, 138

pPresentationParameters parameter, 272

ppReturnDeviceInterface parameter, 272

ppSegmentState parameter, 145

ppSurfaceLevel parameter, 496

ppTexture parameter, 353

ppVertexBuffer parameter, 291

ppv parameter

CoCreateInstance function, 107

GetObject method, 142

pRamp parameter, 308

pReceiveData parameter, 169

pRect parameter, 438

pRenderTarget parameter, 495

Present method parameters, list of, 301

prgpDeviceInfo parameter, 162

primary buffers, 136

primitives, 3D primitives, 187–188

ProcessInput method, 119

programming, event-driven, 4–6

projection modes, 250–251

projection transformation, 257

pSInfoBuffer parameter, 160

pSource parameter, 145

pSourceRect parameter, 301

pStream parameter

DMUS_OBJECTDESC structure, 143

SetStreamSource method, 300

pTexture parameter, 361

pTransition parameter, 145

pUnkOuter parameter, 107, 129
push buttons, dialog box controls, 94
Push method, 244
push-to-talk transmission control, 174
pvAsyncContext parameter, 167
pvPlayerContext parameter
    DPNMSG_RECEIVE structure, 169
    Host method, 162
pvReserved parameter, 105
pvUserContext parameter
    DirectPlayMessageHandler method, 155
    EnumHost function, 165
pvUserEnumData parameter, 164
pvUserEnumDataSize parameter, 164
pwszPath parameter, 141
pwzSegmentName parameter, 145

Q

quaternions
    conjugate of, 224
    inverse of, 225
    multiplication, 225
    norm of, 224
    overview, 222–224
    unit, 225

R

radians, 192
radio buttons, dialog box controls, 94
rain effects, 482
ramp force effect type, 127
ray tracing, 312–313
    water effects
        bending light, 462–464
        bending lights, 460–462
        light rays, determining where, 467
        surface normal and light ray, calculating
            angle between, 464–467
rclsid parameter, 107
rcPaint member, 38
Reference devices, 269
reflection, water and, 779
refraction, water effects, 779
refresh rates, 279

RegisterClassEx function, 10–11
Register parameter, 408
registers
    pixel shaders, 414–416
    vertex shaders, 399–401
RenderFile method, 178
rendering
    explosion, 694–695
    lens flares in 3D, 765–768
    objects using depth buffers, 261–262
    particle system, 604
        render states, setting, 605–607
        vertex buffer, locking, 608
        vertex buffer, pumping particles into,
            608–609
        vertex buffer, pushing out to graphics card,
            609–610
        vertex buffer, setting active, 608
    using vertex shaders, 407
    water effects, 481, 797–798
resource IDs, 83–84
RestoreDeviceObjects method, 705
rgbButtons member (DIJOYSTATE structure), 116
rgbColors parameter, 72
RGB values, 52
rgdod parameter, 117
rglSlider member (DIJOYSTATE structure), 116
rguidClass parameter, 141
rguid parameter, 129
right-handed systems, 186–187
riid parameter
    CoCreateInstance function, 107
    GetObject method, 142
rn register, 400
RotateAxisLocal method, 244
RotateAxis method, 244
RotateYawPitchRollLocal method, 245
RotateYawPitchRoll method, 245
rotation, 188
    formulas, 190–191
    matrix formulas, 216–218
RTTI (run-time type identification), 851–853
    turning on, 883

S

SAFE_RELEASE macro, 104
sampling rate, sound waves, 134
-s argument, Conv3ds, 238
scalar multiplication of vectors, 199
ScaleLocal method, 245
Scale method, 245
scaling, 189–190
    transformation example, 214–215
secondary buffers, 136
segments
    downloading, 144
    playing, 144–146
SendTo method, 166–167
SetActionMap method, 125
SetDataFormat method, 110
SetGammaRamp method parameters, list of, 308
SetLight method, 322–323
SetProperty method, 113
SetSearchDirectory method, 140–141
SetStreamSource method, 298–299
SetTexture method, 361
SetTextureStageSet method, 351
SetTransform method, 296
SetVertexShaderConstant method, 408
SetVertexShader method, 300, 392
SetViewport method, 247
shaders
    overview, 390–391
    pixel
        black-and-white shaders, 817–818
        creating, 420
        image processing using, 814
        instructions, 417–418
        modifiers, 419–420
        registers, 414–416
        simple example of, 420–421
        uses of, 414
    vertex
        bone effects, 393
        complex example of, 411–413
        constant registers, 408
        creating, 406–407
        inputs, specifying, 394–398
        instruction modifiers, 406
        instructions, list of, 401–405

muscle effects, 393
        overview, 391–393
        registers, 399–401
        rendering using, 407
        simple example of, 409–411
        VertexShaderVersion method, 394
        wave effects, 393
shading modes, 314
shapes, GDI drawing functions, 57
ShowWindow function, 23
shrinking, 576
SizeToLock parameter, 293
skyboxes, 714
    code for, 715–719
    images, creating, 715
smart pointers, 103
smashing, 576
smoke effects. See particle system
snow effects, 671–672
sound. See also audio scripts
    DMOs (DirectX Media Objects), list of, 147–148
    effects
        activating, 146–148
        removing, 148
sound waves
    CD-quality, 135
    lossy compression, 136
    measuring shape of, 132–133
    sample quality, 135
    sampling rate, 134
specular color, lighting and, 316, 321–322
spherical environment mapping, 380
spinning, 576
split wipes, 568
spotlights, 318–320
Stage parameter, 361
Standard Temple Library. See STL
Start method, 130–131
State parameter, 296
STL (Standard Template Library)
    maps
        creating, 870
        items, adding, 870–871
        items, deleting, 872
        items, finding, 871–872
        multimaps, 872–873
        overview, 867–869

overview, 860
sample programs, 874
strings, 859–861
vectors
    creating, 862
    items, adding, 862–863
    items, deleting, 865
    items, editing, 863–864
    items, getting, 863–864
StreamNumber parameter, 300
StretchBlt function, 60–61
Stride parameter, 300
Style member, 12
subtracting vectors, 198
SUCCEEDED macros, 105

T

-T argument, Conv3ds, 238
templates (C++)
    classes, 856–859
    functions, 854–856
TextOut function, 74–76
texture
    addressing mode
        border color, 342–343
        clamp, 341
        mirror, 340
        wrap, 340
    bump mapping, 330
    color saturation, 382–383
    creating
        CreateTexture method, 352–355
        D3DXCreateTexture method, 355
        from images using D3DX, 355–358
    detail mapping, 382
    DevCaps flags, 350
    environment mapping, 330, 379
        cubic, 381
        spherical, 380
    filtering modes, 335
        anisotropic, 339–340
        linear filtering, 337
        mipmap, 338–339
        nearest-point sampling, 336
    glow mapping, 382
    light mapping, 376–378

multiple texturing, 330, 366–367
selecting, 361–362
SetTextureStageSet method, 351
terminology, 367
TextureAddressCaps flags, 349
TextureCaps flags, 348
TextureFilterCaps flags, 349
texture management, 331
texture stages
    complex example of, 371–372
    input arguments, 369
    operators, list of, 369–370
    overview, 369
    programming, 373–376
    simple example of, 370
transparent, 344
    through alpha blending, 345
    through alpha testing, 345–346
vertex, tying to, 332–334
volumetric textures, 330
when to use, 331–332
wrapping, 334–335
Theta property, spotlights, 319
threads, 157–158
tile transitions, 575–576
    delay patterns for, 577–578
    uses for, 576
transformations
    overview, 188
    projection, 257
    rotation, 188, 190–191
    scaling, 189–190
    translation, 188–190
    view, 255–256
    world, 254–255
transformed vertex formats, 287–288
transitions, 560
    class hierarchy for, 579–580
    crunches, 573–574
    fade effects
        alpha blending, 561–564
        cross fades, 564–566
    melting effects, 569–571
    tiles, 575–576
        delay patterns for, 577–578
        uses for, 576

warp fading, 574–575

wipes

directional, 566–568

split, 568

window blinds, 569

TranslateLocal method, 245

TranslateMessage function, 31

Translate method, 245

translation, 188–190

matrix multiplication, 215–216

transparent texture, 344

through alpha blending, 345

through alpha testing, 345–346

triangle fans, 232

triangle lists, 231

triangle strips, 232

triple buffering, 280

U

uAppData member

DIACTION structure, 122

DIDEVICEOBJECTDATA structure, 118

uMsg parameter, 34

unit quaternions, 225

Unlock method, 294–295

UnLockRect method, fire effects, 440

Update function, events and, 666–670

Usage parameter

CreateTexture method, 353

CreateVertexBuffer method, 291

uType parameter, 81

V

vectors

adding, 198

cross product of two, 204–205

D3DX functions, 205–207

defined, 195

direction, determining, 196

dot product of two, 201–203

magnitude, determining, 196

normalizing, 199–201

scalar multiplication of, 199

subtracting, 198

vertex buffers, 233–234

creating, 290

lock parameters, 293

Unlock method, 294–295

vertex formats

describing, 285–287

flexible, texture coordinates in, 288–289

overview, 284

sample, 289–290

transformed, 287–288

untransformed, 287–288

vertex shaders

bone effects, 393

cartoon shading

adding edge support to, 811

constants, setting, 806

loading, 805

complex example of, 411–413

constant registers, 408

creating, 406–407

inputs, specifying, 394–398

instruction modifiers, 406

instructions, list of, 401–405

muscle effects, 393

overview, 391–393

registers, 399–401

rendering using, 407

simple example of, 409–411

VertexShaderVersion method, 394

wave effects, 393

vertical retrace, 280

video modes, finding, 280–281

view frustum, 249

viewports

overview, 246

setting, 247

view transformation, 255–256

vn register, 400

voice features

audio device, testing, 175

Create3DsoundBuffer method, 175

forwarding server topology, 172

mixing server topology, 172

peer-to-peer topology, 172

push-to-talk transmission control, 174

voice activation transmission control, 174

volumetric textures, 330
vVersion (DMUS_OBJECTDESC structure), 143

W

warping effects
    alpha blending, 517
    code, writing, 508–509
    cumulative, 517
    grid density, 516–517
    overview, 506–507
    perturbation amount, 517
    uses for, 518
    vertex grid, setting up, 511
        index buffer, filling, 515–516
        vertex buffer, filling, 512–514
    warp fading, 574–575
water effects, 456, 778
    animating, 473–474
    arrays, 457–459
        processing code, 472–473
        reducing size of, 484
    blending function, 480–481
    boat wakes, 483
    currents, 479
    depth of, 479–480
    displacement, calculating, 788
    environment map, creating, 792
    height values
        applying to vertex grid, 786–787
        calculating, 784–785
    normals, calculating, 788–791
    rain, 482
    ray tracing
        bending light, 460–464
        light rays, determining where, 467
        surface normal and light ray, calculating angle between, 464–467
    reflection, 779
    refraction, 779
    rendering, 481, 797–798
    rendering method
        core, 794
        cube map, 794–797
        screen, 793–794

sample programs, 799
source texture, rendering onto destination, 474–477
textures, creating, 471
water plane, setting up, 781–783
waves
    boat wakes, 483
    dampening factor, 478–479
    generating, 468–469
    parallel, 482–483
    speed, 477–478
    strength of, 479
wave effects, 393
    dampening factor, 478–479
    generating, 468–469
    parallel, 482–483
    speed of, 477–478
    strength of, 479
waves reverberation (DirectX Media Object), 147
WAV files, 140
w-buffers, 260–261
Width parameter
    CreateTexture method, 353
    D3DVIEWPORT8 structure, 248
WindowProc function, 34
Windows GDI functions, 44–46
Windows Messages
    WM_KEYDOWN, 27
    WM_MOUSEDOWN, 27
Winmain(), 7–8
wipes
    directional, 566–568
    split, 568
    window blinds, 569
WM_CHAR message, 40
WM_CLOSE message, 35
WM_KEYDOWN, 27
WM_MOUSEDOWN, 27
WM_PAINT message, 36–38
WM_SETCURSOR message, 87
wMsgFilterMax parameter, 29
wMsgFilterMin parameter, 29
WNDCLASSEX structure members, list of, 12–15
world transformation, 254–255
wParam parameter, 34

wrap texture addressing mode, 340
wRemoveMsg parameter, 29
wszName member (DMUS_OBJECTDESC
        structure), 143

X

x-axis
    joysticks, 116
    rotation formula, 190
x parameter
    CreateWindowEx function, 18
    D3DVIEWPORT8 structure, 248

Y

y-axis
    joysticks, 116
    rotation formula, 190
y parameter
    Create WindowEx function, 18
    D3DVIEWPORT8 structure, 248

Z

z-axis
    joysticks, 116
    rotation formula, 190
z-buffers, 260–261

nVSDK

developer.nvidia.com

License Agreement/Notice of Limited Warranty

By opening the sealed disc container in this book, you agree to the following terms and conditions. If, upon reading the following license agreement and notice of limited warranty, you cannot agree to the terms and conditions set forth, return the unused book with unopened disc to the place where you purchased it for a refund.

License:

The enclosed software is copyrighted by the copyright holder(s) indicated on the software disc. You are licensed to copy the software onto a single computer for use by a single user and to a backup disc. You may not reproduce, make copies, or distribute copies or rent or lease the software in whole or in part, except with written permission of the copyright holder(s). You may transfer the enclosed disc only together with this license, and only if you destroy all other copies of the software and the transferee agrees to the terms of the license. You may not decompile, reverse assemble, or reverse engineer the software.

Notice of Limited Warranty:

The enclosed disc is warranted by Premier Press, Inc. to be free of physical defects in materials and workmanship for a period of sixty (60) days from end user's purchase of the book/disc combination. During the sixty-day term of the limited warranty, Premier Press will provide a replacement disc upon the return of a defective disc.

Limited Liability:

THE SOLE REMEDY FOR BREACH OF THIS LIMITED WARRANTY SHALL CONSIST ENTIRELY OF REPLACEMENT OF THE DEFECTIVE DISC. IN NO EVENT SHALL PREMIER PRESS OR THE AUTHORS BE LIABLE FOR ANY OTHER DAMAGES, INCLUDING LOSS OR CORRUPTION OF DATA, CHANGES IN THE FUNCTIONAL CHARACTERISTICS OF THE HARDWARE OR OPERAT-ING SYSTEM, DELETERIOUS INTERACTION WITH OTHER SOFTWARE, OR ANY OTHER SPE-CIAL, INCIDENTAL, OR CONSEQUENTIAL DAMAGES THAT MAY ARISE, EVEN IF PREMIER AND/OR THE AUTHORS HAVE PREVIOUSLY BEEN NOTIFIED THAT THE POSSIBILITY OF SUCH DAMAGES EXISTS.

Disclaimer of Warranties:

PREMIER AND THE AUTHORS SPECIFICALLY DISCLAIM ANY AND ALL OTHER WARRANTIES, EITHER EXPRESS OR IMPLIED, INCLUDING WARRANTIES OF MERCHANTABILITY, SUITABILI-TY TO A PARTICULAR TASK OR PURPOSE, OR FREEDOM FROM ERRORS. SOME STATES DO NOT ALLOW FOR EXCLUSION OF IMPLIED WARRANTIES OR LIMITATION OF INCIDENTAL OR CONSEQUENTIAL DAMAGES, SO THESE LIMITATIONS MIGHT NOT APPLY TO YOU.

Other:

This Agreement is governed by the laws of the State of Indiana without regard to choice of law princi-ples. The United Convention of Contracts for the International Sale of Goods is specifically dis-claimed. This Agreement constitutes the entire agreement between you and Premier Press regarding use of the software.